Computability and Complexity

Foundations of Computing
Michael Garey and Albert Meyer, editors

Complexity Issues in VLSI: Optimal Layouts for the Shuffle-Exchange Graph and Other Networks, Frank Thomson Leighton, 1983

Equational Logic as a Programming Language, Michael J. O'Donnell, 1985

General Theory of Deductive Systems and Its Applications, S. Yu Maslov, 1987

Resource Allocation Problems: Algorithmic Approaches, Toshihide Ibaraki and Naoki Katoh, 1988

Algebraic Theory of Processes, Matthew Hennessy, 1988

PX: A Computational Logic, Susumu Hayashi and Hiroshi Nakano, 1989

The Stable Marriage Problem: Structure and Algorithms, Dan Gusfield and Robert Irving, 1989

Realistic Compiler Generation, Peter Lee, 1989

Single-Layer Wire Routing and Compaction, F. Miller Maley, 1990

Basic Category Theory for Computer Scientists, Benjamin C. Pierce, 1991

Categories, Types, and Structures: An Introduction to Category Theory for the Working Computer Scientist, Andrea Asperti and Giuseppe Longo, 1991

Semantics of Programming Languages: Structures and Techniques, Carl A. Gunter, 1992

The Formal Semantics of Programming Languages: An Introduction, Glynn Winskel, 1993

Hilbert's Tenth Problem, Yuri V. Matiyasevich, 1993

Exploring Interior-Point Linear Programming: Algorithms and Software, Ami Arbel, 1993

Theoretical Aspects of Object-Oriented Programming: Types, Semantics, and Language Design, edited by Carl A. Gunter and John C. Mitchell, 1994

From Logic to Logic Programming, Kees Doets, 1994

The Structure of Typed Programming Languages, David A. Schmidt, 1994

Logic and Information Flow, edited by Jan van Eijck and Albert Visser, 1994

Circuit Complexity and Neural Networks, Ian Parberry, 1994

Control Flow Semantics, Jaco de Bakker and Erik de Vink, 1996

Algebraic Semantics of Imperative Programs, Joseph A. Goguen and Grant Malcolm, 1996

Algorithmic Number Theory, Volume I: Efficient Algorithms, Eric Bach and Jeffrey Shallit, 1996

Foundations for Programming Languages, John C. Mitchell, 1996

Computability and Complexity: From a Programming Perspective, Neil D. Jones, 1997

Computability and Complexity
From a Programming Perspective

Neil D. Jones

The MIT Press
Cambridge, Massachusetts
London, England

This book was set in Palatino by the author and was printed and bound in the United States of America.

Library of Congress Cataloging-in-Publication Data

Jones, Neil D.
  Computability and complexity: from a programming perspective / Neil D. Jones.
    p.   cm.—(Foundations of computing)
  Includes bibliographical references and index.
  ISBN 0-262-10064-9 (hc: alk. paper).
  1. Electronic digital computers—programming. 2. Computational complexity. I. Title. II. Series.
QA76.6.J6658   1997
005.13′1—dc21   96-44043
                                                                              CIP

Contents

Series Foreword   vii

Preface   ix

I Toward the Theory

1 Introduction   3

2 The WHILE Language   27

3 Programs as Data Objects   47

II Introduction to Computability

4 Self-interpretation: Universal Programs for WHILE and I   69

5 Elements of Computability Theory   75

6 Metaprogramming, Self-application, and Compiler Generation   89

7 Other Sequential Models of Computation   111

8 Robustness of Computability   127

9 Computability by Functional Languages (partly by T. Æ. Mogensen)   137

10 Some Natural Unsolvable Problems   151

III Other Aspects of Computability Theory

11 Hilbert's Tenth Problem (by M. H. Sørensen)   167

12 Inference Systems and Gödel's Incompleteness Theorem   187

13 Computability Theory Based on Numbers   205

14 More Abstract Approaches to Computability   215

IV   Introduction to Complexity

15 Overview of Complexity Theory   239

16 Measuring Time Usage   249

17 Time Usage of Tree-manipulating Programs   261

18 Robustness of Time-bounded Computation   271

19 Linear and Other Time Hierarchies for WHILE Programs   285

20 The Existence of Optimal Algorithms (by A. M. Ben-Amram)   297

21 Space-bounded Computations   315

22 Nondeterministic Computations   331

23 A Structure for Classifying the Complexity of Various Problems   335

24 Characterizations of LOGSPACE and PTIME by GOTO Programs   349

V   Complete Problems

25 Completeness and Reduction of One Problem to Another   365

26 Complete Problems for PTIME   383

27 Complete Problems for NPTIME   397

28 Complete Problems for PSPACE   407

VI   Appendix

A Mathematical Terminology and Concepts   419

Bibliography   447

List of Notations   457

Index   459

Series Foreword

Theoretical computer science has now undergone several decades of development. The "classical" topics of automata theory, formal languages, and computational complexity have become firmly established, and their importance to other theoretical work and to practice is widely recognized. Stimulated by technological advances, theoreticians have been rapidly expanding the areas under study, and the time delay between theoretical progress and its practical impact has been decreasing dramatically. Much publicity has been given recently to breakthroughs in cryptography and linear programming, and steady progress is being made on programming language semantics, computational geometry, and efficient data structures. Newer, more speculative, areas of study include relational databases, VLSI theory, and parallel and distributed computation. As this list of topics continues expanding, it is becoming more and more difficult to stay abreast of the progress that is being made and increasingly important that the most significant work be distilled and communicated in a manner that will facilitate further research and application of this work. By publishing comprehensive books and specialized monographs on the theoretical aspects of computer science, the series on Foundations of Computing provides a forum in which important research topics can be presented in their entirety and placed in perspective for researchers, students, and practitioners alike.

Michael R. Garey
Albert R. Meyer

Preface

This book is a general introduction to computability and complexity theory. It should be of interest to beginning programming language researchers who are interested in computability and complexity theory, or vice versa.

The view from Olympus

Unlike most fields within computer science, computability and complexity theory deals with analysis as much as with synthesis and with some concepts of an apparently absolute nature. Work in logic and recursive function theory spanning nearly the whole century has quite precisely delineated the concepts and nature of effective procedures, and decidable and semi-decidable problems, and has established them to be essentially invariant with respect to the computational device or logical theory used.

Surprisingly, a few similarly invariant concepts have also arisen with respect to computations within bounded resources: polynomial time (as a function of a decision problem's input size), polynomial storage, computation with or without nondeterminism: the ability to "guess," and computation with "read-only" data access.

Computability and complexity theory is, and should be, of central concern for practitioners as well as theorists. For example, "lower complexity bounds" play a role analogous to channel capacity in engineering: No matter how clever a coding (in either sense of the word) is used, the bound cannot be overcome.

Unfortunately, the field is well-known for impenetrability of fundamental definitions, proofs of theorems, and even statements of theorems and definitions of problems. My thesis is that this owes to some extent to the history of the field, and that a shift away from the Turing machine- and Gödel number-oriented classical approaches toward a greater use of concepts familiar from programming languages will render classical computability and complexity results more accessible to the average computer scientist, and can make its very strong theorems more visible and applicable to practical problems.

This book covers classical models of computation and central results in computability and complexity theory. However, it aims to differ from traditional texts in two respects:

1. To be significantly more accessible, without sacrificing precision. This is achieved by presenting the theory of computability and complexity using programming

techniques and motivated by programming language theory.[1]

2. To relieve some tensions long felt between certain results in complexity theory and daily programming practice. A better fit is achieved by using a novel model of computation, differing from traditional ones in certain crucial respects.

Further, many of the sometimes baroque constructions of the classical theory become markedly simpler in a programming context, and sometimes even lead to stronger theorems. A side effect is that many constructions that are normally only sketched in a loose way can be done more precisely and convincingly.

The perspective of the book

For those already familiar with computability and complexity theory, the two points above can be somewhat elaborated.

As for the first point, I introduce a simple programming language called WHILE, in essence a small subset of Pascal or LISP. The WHILE language seems to have just the right mix of expressive power and simplicity. *Expressive power* is important when dealing with programs as data objects. The data structures of WHILE are particularly well suited to this, since they avoid the need for nearly all the technically messy tasks of assigning *Gödel numbers* to encode program texts and fragments (used in most if not all earlier texts), and of devising code to build and decompose Gödel numbers. *Simplicity* is also essential to prove theorems about programs and their behavior. This rules out the use of larger, more powerful languages, since proofs about them would be too complex to be easily understood.

More generally, I maintain that each of the fields of computability and complexity theory, and programming languages and semantics has much to offer the other. In the one direction, computability and complexity theory has a breadth, depth, and generality not often seen in programming languages, and a tradition for posing precisely defined and widely known *open problems* of community-wide interest. Also, questions concerning the *intrinsic* impossibility or infeasibility of programs solving certain problems regarding programs should interest programming language researchers. For instance, many problems that turn up in the field of analysis and transformation of programs turn out to be undecidable or of intractably high complexity.

---

[1]Dana Scott was an early proponent of programming approach to automata [153], but it has not yet been widely used.

In the other direction, the programming language community has a firm grasp of algorithm design, presentation and implementation, and several well-developed frameworks for making precise semantic concepts over a wide range of programming language concepts, e.g., functional, logic, and imperative programming, control operators, communication and concurrency, and object-orientation. Moreover programming languages constitute computation models some of which are more realistic in certain crucial aspects than traditional models.

A concrete connection between computability and programming languages: the dry-as-dust "s-m-n theorem" has been known in computability since the 1930s, but seemed only a technical curiosity useful in certain proofs. Nonetheless, and to the surprise of many people, the s-m-n theorem has proven its worth under the alias *partial evaluation* or *program specialization* in practice over the past 10 years: when implemented efficiently, it can be used for realistic *compiling*, and when self-applied it can be used to *generate program generators* as well.

Another cornerstone of computability, the "universal machine," is nothing but a *self-interpreter* in programming languages. Further, the "simulations" seen in introductory computability and complexity texts are mostly achieved by informal compilers or, sometimes, interpreters.

As for the second point above, a tension has long been felt between computability and complexity theory, and "real computing." This is at least in part because one of the first results proven in complexity is the *Turing machine speedup theorem*, which asserts a counterintuitive (but true) fact: that *any* Turing machine program running in superlinear time can be replaced by another running twice as fast in the limit.[2] The existence of *efficient* self-interpreters in programming language theory leads to the opposite result: a *hierarchy* theorem showing, for a more realistic computing model than the Turing machine, that *constant time factors do matter*. More precisely, given time bound $f(n)$, where n measures the size of a problem input, there are problems solvable in time $249f(n)$ which cannot be solved in time $f(n)$. Thus multiplying the available computing time by a constant *properly increases* the class of problems that can be solved.

This and other examples using programming language concepts lead (at least for computer scientists) to more understandable statements of theorems and proofs in computability and complexity, and to stronger results. Further new results include "intrinsic" characterizations of the well-known problem classes LOGSPACE and PTIME on the

---

[2]The tension arises because the "trick" used for the Turing machine construction turns out to be useless when attempting to speed up real computer programs.

basis of program syntax alone, without any externally imposed space or time bounds.

Finally, a number of old computability and complexity questions take on new life and natural new questions arise. An important class of new questions (not yet fully resolved) is: what is the effect of the *programming styles* we employ, i.e., functional style, imperative style, etc., on the *efficiency* of the programs we write?

How to read this book

If used as an introduction to computability (recursive function) theory, parts I–III are relevant. If used as an introduction to complexity theory, the relevant parts are I, IV, and V, and chapters 6 through 8. The book contains approximately two semesters' worth of material which one can "mix and match" to form several courses, for instance:

Introduction to computability (1 semester): chapters 1 through 8, chapter 10, perhaps just skimming chapter 6; and as much of chapters 9, and 11 through 14, as time and interest allow.

Introduction to complexity (1 semester): Quickly through chapters 1, 2, 3, 4, 7, 8; then chapters 15 through 19, chapters 21 through 23, and 25 through 27; and as much of the remainder as time and interest allow.

Computability and complexity (2 semesters): the whole book.

Exercises. Numerous exercises are included, some theoretical and some more oriented toward programming. An asterisk * marks ones that are either difficult or long (or both).

Correction of errors and misprints. Reports of errors and misprints may be sent to the author by e-mail, at neil@diku.dk. A current list may be found on the World Wide Web at http://www.diku.dk/users/neil/.

Overall comments. Practically minded students may find chapter 6 of particular interest, since it describes application of the s-m-n theorem, widely called *partial evaluation*, to compiling and compiler generation. Theoretically or philosophically minded students may find chapter 12 of particular interest because of its connections with *Gödel's theorem*. Chapter 20 clarifies the question of the existence of "best" or optimal programs: Levin's theorem proves that search problems whose solutions can be efficiently checked possess near-optimal algorithms. In contrast, Blum's speedup theorem shows that there exist problems which possess, in a very strong sense, no optimal algorithm at all.

Goals, and chapters that can be touched lightly on first reading. The book's overall computability goals are first: to argue that the class of all computably solvable problems is well-defined and independent of the computing devices used to define it, and second: carefully to explore the boundary zone between computability and uncomputability. Its complexity goals are analogous, given naturally defined classes of problems solvable within time or memory resource bounds.

The *Church-Turing thesis* states that all natural computation models are of equivalent power. Powerful evidence for it is the fact that any two among a substantial class of computation models can simulate each other. Unfortunately, proving this fact is unavoidably complex since the various computation models must be precisely defined, and constructions given to show how an arbitrary program in one model can be simulated by programs in each of the other models.

Chapters 7 and 8 do just this: they argue for the Church-Turing thesis without considering the time or memory required to do the simulations. Chapters 16, 17 and 18 go farther, showing that polynomial time-bounded or space-bounded computability are similarly robust concepts.

Once the Church-Turing thesis has been convincingly demonstrated, a more casual attitude is quite often taken: algorithms are just sketched, using whichever model is most convenient for the task at hand. The reader may wish to anticipate this, and at first encounter only to skim chapters 7, 8, 16, 17 and 18.

Prerequisites

The reader is expected to be at the beginning graduate level having studied some theory, or a student at the senior undergraduate level with good mathematical maturity. Specifically, the book uses sets, functions, graphs, induction, and recursive definitions freely. These concepts are all explained in an appendix, but the appendix may be too terse to serve as a first introduction to these notions. Familiarity with some programming language is a necessity; just which language is much less relevant.

Novel aspects, in a nutshell

Classical computability results in this book include unsolvability of the halting problem and several other natural problems, including context-free ambiguity and Hilbert's Tenth Problem; Rice's result that *all* nontrivial extensional program properties are undecidable; characterizations of the recursive functions, and recursive and recursively enumerable sets; Kleene's s-m-n, second recursion, and normal form theorems; recursion by fixpoints; Rogers' isomorphism theorem; and Gödel's incompleteness theorem.

Classical complexity results include study of the hierarchy of classes of problems: LOGSPACE, NLOGSPACE, PTIME, NPTIME, PSPACE; the robustness of PTIME, PSPACE and LOGSPACE; complete problems for all these classes except the smallest; the speedup and gap theorems from Blum's machine-independent complexity theory.

In contrast with traditional textbooks on computability and complexity, this treatment also features:

1. A language of WHILE programs with LISP-like data. Advantages: programming convenience and readability in constructions involving programs as data; and freedom from storage management problems.

2. Stronger connections with familiar computer science concepts: compilation (simulation), interpretation (universal programs), program specialization (the s-m-n theorem), existence or nonexistence of optimal programs.

3. Relation of self-application to compiler bootsrapping.

4. Program specialization in the form of partial evaluation to speed programs up, or to compile and to generate compilers by specialising interpreters.

5. Speedups from self-application of program specializers.

6. Simpler constructions for "robustness" of fundamental concepts, also including functional languages and the lambda calculus.

7. An construction to prove Kleene's second recursion theorem that gives more efficient programs than those yielded by the classical proof.

8. Proof that "constant time factors *do* matter" for a computation model more realistic than the Turing machine, by an unusually simple and understandable diagonalization proof.

9. A new and much more comprehensible proof of Levin's important result on the existence of optimal algorithms;

10. Intrinsic characterizations of the problem classes LOGSPACE and PTIME by restricted WHILE programs.

11. The use of programs manipulating boolean values to identify "complete" or hardest problems for the complexity classes mentioned above.

Items 7 through 11 above appear here for the first time in book form.

What is not considered

There are numerous things in the enormous realm of complexity and computability theory that I have chosen not to include at all in the present text. A list of some of the most obvious omissions:

- *Parallelism.* In the present text all computation models are *sequential* in the sense that only one operation can be executed at a time. Many models of parallel computation have been suggested in the literature; overviews by Karp and Valiant may be found in [91, 163].

- *Approximate solutions.* Another approach to solving problems whose algorithms have prohibitively long running times, is to devise a quicker algorithm which does not always give the correct answer, but only an approximate solution. Examples include numerous algorithms testing properties of graphs, e.g. by Johnson and Kann [69, 89].

- *Stochastic algorithms.* Some problems seem only to be solvable by programs that have prohibitively long running times. In some cases, it is possible to derive an algorithm using random numbers which runs faster, but which only returns a correct result with a certain probability more than 0.5, but less than 1. Often the probability of correctness can be increased to $1 - \varepsilon$ for any $1 > \varepsilon > 0$ by repeatedly running the program. Such algorithms are called *stochastic* or *probabilistic*. Examples include testing whether a given number is a prime, e.g., by Rabin [140].

- *Nonuniform complexity, circuits, cell probe models.* Lower bounds on computation time or space are often extremely difficult to obtain. Sometimes these can be obtained more easily by abstracting away from the algorithm altogether, and just concentrating on a problem's combinatorial aspects. In terms of computational models, this amounts to allowing different computational methods (e.g. different circuits) for different sizes of inputs. Progress has been made in this direction, e.g., by Håstad [63] and by Miltersen [123].

- *Computing with real numbers.* In the present text all computation models are concerned with countable data structures, but models of computation with *real* numbers also exist, e.g., by Blum, Shub and Smale [12].

- *Communicating systems.* The view of computation as a continuing and nonterminating exchange of information among a set of active agents has been developed by Milner and others [121], but is beyond the scope of this book.

Acknowledgments

Many have helped with the preparation of the manuscript. Three in particular have made outstanding contributions to its content, style, and editorial and pedagogical matters: Morten Heine Sørensen, Amir Ben-Amram, and Arne John Glenstrup. DIKU (the Computer Science Department at the University of Copenhagen) helped significantly with many practical matters involving secretarial help, computing, and printing facilities. The idea of using list structures with only one atom is due to Klaus Grue [54].

From outside DIKU I have received much encouragement from Henk Barendregt, Jim Royer, and Yuri Gurevich. Invaluable feedback was given by the students attending the courses at which earlier versions of the manuscript were used, and many have helped by reading various parts, including Nils Andersen, Kristian Nielsen, and Jakob Rehof from DIKU, Antanas Zilinskas from Vilnius, and anonymous referees from the MIT Press and Addison-Wesley Publishing Co. Chapter 11 and the Appendix were written by Morten Heine Sørensen, chapter 20 was written by Amir Ben-Amram, and sections 9.3 and 9.4 were written by Torben Æ. Mogensen.

Computability and Complexity

Part I

Toward the Theory

1   Introduction

This book is about *computability theory* and *complexity theory*. In this first chapter we try to convey what the scope and techniques of computability and complexity theory are. We are deliberately informal in this chapter; in some cases we will even introduce a definition or a proposition which is not rigorous, relying on certain intuitive notions. In these cases, the definition or proposition is marked with the symbol "◇." In the subsequent chapters all such definitions and propositions are reintroduced in a rigorous manner before they occur in any development.

Section 1.1 explains the scope and goals of computability theory. Sections 1.2–1.3 concern questions that arise in that connection, and Section 1.4 gives examples of techniques and results of computability theory. Section 1.5 describes the scope and goals of complexity theory. Section 1.6 reviews the historical origins of the two research fields. Section 1.6 contains exercises; in general the reader is encouraged to try all the exercises. Section 1.6 gives more references to background material.

A small synopsis like this appears in the beginning of every chapter, but from now on we will not mention the two sections containing exercises and references.

1.1   The scope and goals of computability theory

Computability theory asks questions such as: do there exist *problems* unsolvable by any *effective procedure* — unsolvable by any program in any conceivable programming language on any computer?

Our programming intuitions may indicate a *no* answer, based on the experience that once a problem is made precise in the form of a specification, it is a more or less routine task to write a program to satisfy the specification. Indeed, a related intuition predominated the work of Hilbert on the foundations of mathematics, as explained in section 1.6: they conjectured that all of mathematics could be axiomatized. However, we shall see that both of these intuitions are disastrously wrong. There *are* certain problems that cannot be solved by effective procedures.

To prove this, we must make precise what is meant by an *effective procedure* and what is meant by a *problem*. It is not *a priori* obvious that any single formalization of effective procedure could be adequate; it might seem that any specific choice would be too narrow because it would exclude computing devices with special capabilities. Thus, different formalizations might lead to different theories of computability. However, one of the great insights of computability theory was the gradual realization in the 1930's that any reasonable choice of formalization of the notion of effective procedure leads, in a certain sense, to the same theory. This has been called the *Church-Turing thesis*, since Alonzo Church and Alan M. Turing first formulated and substantiated versions of this insight. Explaining why different formalizations lead to the same theory is itself one of the topics of computability theory; we thus devote considerable effort to the matter.

Granted precise definitions of the notions of problem and effective procedure, computability theory is concerned with the boundary between computability and uncomputability, and addresses questions such as:

- Can every precisely stated problem be solved by some effective procedure?
- What is the class of problems that can be solved by effective procedures and its basic properties?
- What is the relationship between various problems that cannot be solved by effective procedures?

If a problem can be solved by an effective procedure we shall say that is *effectively solvable*, or sometimes just *solvable*. The result that a certain computational problem is *unsolvable* is not a purely negative fact; for instance, it conveys the important knowledge that searching for an effective procedure to solve the problem is futile. This may indicate that one should try to find an approximate, solvable, solution to the problem at hand instead of trying to solve the exact, but unsolvable, problem.

In the next two sections we discuss formalization of the notions of effective procedure and problem. After this, we present, informally, some of the elementary results of computability theory, including two precisely stated problems which are unsolvable.

1.2   What is an effective procedure?

There are various strategies one can employ in formalizing the notion of effective procedure. Of course, we are free to define notions as we please, but the definitions should capture the intuitive notion of effective procedure; for example, it should not be the case that some problem is unsolvable according to our theory, but nevertheless can be solved on a real-world computer.

Therefore it will be useful to try and analyze the notion of effective procedure and devise a formalization so that every intuitively effective procedure can be carried out in the formalism, and such that all the formalism's computations are effective.

1.2.1 Alan Turing's analysis of computation

Alan Turing's analysis attempting to formalize *the class of all effective procedures* was carried out in 1936 [162], resulting in the notion of a *Turing machine*. Its importance is that it was the first really general analysis to understand how it is that computation takes place, and that it led to a convincing and widely accepted abstraction of the concept of effective procedure.

It is worth noting that Turing's analysis was done before any computers more powerful than desk calculators had been invented. His insights led, more or less directly, to John von Neumann's invention in the 1940's of the stored program digital computer, a machine with essentially the same underlying architecture as today's computers.

We give the floor to Turing. Note that by a "computer" Turing means a human who is solving a computational problem in a mechanical way, not a machine.

> Computing is normally done by writing certain symbols on paper. We may suppose this paper is divided into squares like a child's arithmetic book. In elementary arithmetic the two-dimensional character of the paper is sometimes used. But such a use is always avoidable, and I think that it will be agreed that the two-dimensional character of paper is no essential of computation. I assume then that the computation is carried out on one-dimensional paper, i.e., on a tape divided into squares. I shall also suppose that the number of symbols which may be printed is finite. If we were to allow an infinity of symbols, then there would be symbols differing to an arbitrarily small extent[1]. The effect of this restriction of the number of symbols is not very serious. It is always possible to use sequences of symbols in the place of single symbols. Thus an Arabic numeral such as 17 or 999999999999999 is normally treated as a single symbol. Similarly in any European language words are treated as single symbols (Chinese, however, attempts to have an enumerable infinity of symbols). The differences from our point of view between the single and compound symbols is that the compound symbols, if they are too lengthy, cannot be observed at one glance. This is in accordance with experience. We cannot tell at a glance whether 9999999999999999 and 999999999999999 are the same.

---

[1]If we regard a symbol as literally printed on a square we may suppose that the square is $0 \leq x \leq 1$, $0 \leq y \leq 1$. The symbol is defined as a set of points in this square, viz. the set occupied by printer's ink. If these sets are restricted to be measurable, we can define the "distance" between two symbols as the cost of transforming one symbol into the other if the cost of moving a unit area of printer's ink unit distance istoward unity, and there is an infinite supply of ink at $x = 2, y = 0$. With this topology the symbols form a conditionally compact space. [Turing's note].

The behaviour of the computer at any moment is determined by the symbols which he is observing, and his "state of mind" at that moment. We may suppose that there is a bound B to the number of symbols or squares which the computer can observe at one moment. If he wishes to observe more, he must use successive observations. We will also suppose that the number of states of mind which need be taken into account is finite. The reasons for this are of the same character as those which restrict the number of symbols. If we admitted an infinity of states of mind, some of them will be "arbitrarily close" and will be confused. Again, the restriction is not one which seriously affects computation, since the use of more complicated states of mind can be avoided by writing more symbols on the tape.

Let us imagine the operations performed by the computer to be split up into "simple operations" which are so elementary that it is not easy to imagine them further divided. Every such operation consists of some change of the physical system consisting of the computer and his tape. We know the state of the system if we know the sequence of symbols on the tape, which of these are observed by the computer (possible with a special order), and the state of mind of the computer. We may suppose that in a simple operation not more than one symbol is altered. Any other changes can be split up into simple changes of this kind. The situation in regard to the squares whose symbols may be altered in this way is the same as in regard to the observed squares. We may, therefore, without loss of generality, assume that the squares whose symbols are changed are always "observed" squares.

Besides these changes of symbols, the simple operations must include changes of distribution of observed squares. The new observed squares must be immediately recognizable by the computer. I think it is reasonable to suppose that they can only be squares whose distance from the closest of the immediately previously observed squares does not exceed a certain fixed amount. Let us say that each of the new observed squares is within L squares of an immediately previously observed square.

In connection with "immediate recognizability," it may be thought that there are other kinds of squares which are immediately recognizable. In particular, squares marked by special symbols might be taken as immediately recognizable. Now if these squares are marked only by single symbols there can be only a finite number of them, and we should not upset our theory by adjoining these marked squares to the observed squares. If, on the other hand, they are marked by a sequence of symbols, we cannot regard the process of recognition as a simple process. This is a fundamental point and should be illustrated. In most mathematical papers the equations and theorems are numbered. Normally the numbers do not go beyond (say) 1000. It is, therefore, possible to recognize a theorem at a glance by its number. But if the paper was very long, we might reach Theorem 157767733443477; then, further on in the paper, we might find "... hence (applying Theorem 157767733443477) we have ..." In order to make sure which was the relevant theorem we should have to compare the two numbers figure by figure, possible ticking the figures off in pencil to make sure of their not being counted twice. If in spite of this it is still thought that there are other "immediately recognizable" squares, it does not upset my contention so long as these squares can be found by some process of which my type of machine is capable.

The simple operations must therefore include:

(a) Changes of the symbol on one of the observed squares.

(b) Changes of one of the squares observed to another square within L squares of one of the previously observed squares.

It may be that some of these changes necessarily involve a change of state of mind. The most general single operation must therefore be taken to be one of the following:

(A) A possible change (a) of symbol together with a possible change of state of mind.

(B) A possible change (b) of observed squares, together with a possible change of state of mind.

The operation actually performed is determined, as has been suggested [above] by the state of mind of the computer and the observed symbols. In particular, they determine the state of mind of the computer after the operation.

We may now construct a machine to do the work of this computer. To each state of mind of the computer corresponds an "m-configuration" of the machine. The machine scans B squares corresponding to the B squares observed by the computer. In any move the machine can change a symbol on a scanned square or can change any one of the scanned squares to another square distant not more than L squares from one of the other scanned squares. The move which is done, and the succeeding configuration, are determined by the scanned symbol and the m-configuration. The machines just described do not differ very essentially from computing machines as defined (previously) and corresponding to any machine of this type a computing machine can be constructed to compute the same sequence, that is to say the sequence computed by the computer.

1.2.2   The Church-Turing thesis

The machines mentioned in Turing's analysis are called *Turing machines*. The wide-ranging identification of the intuitive notion of effective procedure with the mathematical concept of Turing machine (and related identifications) has become well-known as the *Church-Turing thesis*, named after Church and Turing, two pioneers of computability [162, 21, 22].

The thesis is not amenable to mathematical proof since it identifies an intuitive notion with a mathematical concept; however we shall provide various kinds of evidence supporting it. In one direction this is easy: the Turing machine (as well as other computational models we will introduce) is sufficiently simple that its computations are certainly effective in any reasonable sense. In the other direction, Turing's analysis is a rather convincing argument for the Turing machine's generality.

There are many other notions of effective procedure than Turing machines, e.g.,

- *Recursive functions* as defined by Kleene [93]
- The *lambda calculus* approach to function definitions due to Church [21, 22].
- *Random access machines* [155]
- *Markov algorithms* [110]

Despite considerable differences in formalism, some common characteristics of these notions are [147]:

1. An effective procedure is given by means of a set of instructions of finite size. There are only finitely many different instructions.

2. The computation is carried out in a discrete stepwise fashion, without the use of continuous methods or analogue devices.

3. The computation is carried out deterministically, without resort to random methods or devices, e.g., dice.

4. There is no *a priori* fixed bound on the amount of "memory" storage space or time available, although a terminating computation must not rely on an infinite amount of space or time.

5. Each computational step involves only a finite amount of data.

All of the above notions of effective procedure have turned out to be equivalent. In view of this, the Church-Turing thesis is sometimes expressed in the following form:

1. All reasonable formalizations of the intuitive notion of effective computability are equivalent;
2. Turing machine computability is a reasonable formalization of effective computability.

In support of this, later chapters will consider a number of formalizations and prove them equivalent. For the remainder of this chapter the notion of an effective procedure, or *algorithm*, will remain intuitive.

1.2.3   Are algorithms hardware or software?

Discussions of the question whether algorithms are hardware of software resemble those of whether the chicken or the egg came first, but are nonetheless worthwhile since much literature on computability, and especially on complexity theory, is implicitly biased toward one or the other viewpoint. For example, the phrase "Turing machine" carries overtones of hardware, and the "states of mind" of Turing's argument seem to correspond to machine states.

The hardware viewpoint states that an algorithm is a piece of machinery to realize the desired computations. The "set of instructions" is a specification of its architecture. At any one point in time a total machine state comprises the instruction it is currently executing and its memory state. Larger algorithms correspond to larger pieces of hardware.

The problem of not limiting the amount of storage can be handled several ways:

- Assume given an infinite separate storage unit, e.g., Turing's "tape";
- Assume an idealized hardware which is indefinitely expandable, though always finite at any one point in time; or
- Work with an infinite family of finite machines $M_1, M_2, \ldots$, so larger input data is processed by larger machines.

The last way corresponds to what is often called *circuit complexity*. One usually requires the sequence $M_1, M_2, \ldots$ to be *uniform*, so progressively larger data are not processed by completely disparate machines.

The software viewpoint states that the algorithm is a set or sequence of instructions. For instance an algorithm can simply be a program in one's favorite programming language. The "computing agent" then interprets the algorithm; it can be a piece of hardware, or it can be software: an interpreter program written in a lower-level programming language. Operationally, an interpreter maintains a pointer to the current instruction within the algorithm's instruction set, together with a representation of that algorithm's current storage state. Larger algorithms correspond to larger interpreted programs, but the interpreter itself remains fixed, either as a machine or as a program.

The first fully automatic computer was von Neumann's "stored program" machine. It consisted of a piece of hardware, the central processing unit (CPU), specifically designed to interpret the program stored in its memory; and this memory was physically decoupled from the CPU. Thus the software viewpoint was present from hardware's first days and characterizes most of today's computers. Nonetheless the distinction is becoming yet less clear because today's "chip" technology allows relatively easy construction of special-purpose digital hardware for rather complex problems, something which was impractical only a few years ago. Further, even though Turing's machine is described in hardware terms, it was Alan Turing himself who proved the existence of a "universal machine": a single Turing machine capable of simulating any arbitrary Turing machine, when given its input data and an encoding of its instruction set.

This book mostly takes the viewpoint of algorithm as software, though the "random access machine" model will come closer to hardware.

1.3   What is a problem?

By a problem we have in mind some uniform, in general unbounded, class of questions each of which can be given a definite, finite answer. Thus we consider two concrete instances of the abstract notion of solving a problem: *computing a function* and *deciding membership in a set*.

1.3.1   Effectively computable functions

In this book, a total function is written $f : A \rightarrow B$. A partial function is written $g : A \rightarrow B_\perp$. For $a \in A$, if $g(a)$ is defined or *convergent* we write $g(a)\!\downarrow$, and if $g(a)$ is undefined or *divergent* we write $g(a)\!\uparrow$ or $g(a) = \perp$. If both $f(a)$ and $g(a)$ are undefined we also allow the notation $f(a) = g(a)$. Total and partial functions are explained in greater detail in Subsections A.3.1–A.3.4 in Appendix A. We use the symbol $\simeq$ to denote equivalence of partial functions, see Subsection A.3.5.

Definition 1.3.1 $^\diamond$ Let D, E be sets. A partial mathematical function $f : D \to E_\perp$ is *effectively computable* if there is an effective procedure such that for any $x \in D$:

1. The procedure eventually halts, yielding $f(x) \in E$, if $f(x)$ is defined;
2. The procedure never halts if $f(x)$ is undefined.   □

The function $f : \mathbb{N} \times \mathbb{N} \to \mathbb{N}$ where $f(x, y) = x + y$ is effectively computable by the effective procedure, known from elementary school, for digit-by-digit addition, assuming x, y, and $x + y$ are expressed in decimal notation. As another example, the function $gcd : \mathbb{N} \times \mathbb{N} \to \mathbb{N}$ which maps two natural numbers into their greatest common divisor can be computed by Euclid's algorithm.

The effective procedure for computing f must give the correct answer to each question which is within its set of applicability D. In particular, if f is total, the effective procedure must halt for all arguments in D. Its behavior when applied to questions outside this set is not of interest; it may fail to terminate, or may terminate in a nonstandard way. For instance, Euclid's algorithm can fail to terminate when applied to negative numbers.

1.3.2   On data representation

It might seem that the definition of an effectively computable function depends on the notation used to represent the arguments. For instance, the addition procedure above uses the decimal representation of natural numbers.

However, this makes no difference as long as there is an effective procedure that translates from one notation to another and back. Suppose we have an effective procedure p which will compute f if the argument is expressed in notation B. The following effective procedure will then compute f in notation A:

1. Given x in notation A, translate it into notation B, yielding y.
2. Apply procedure p to y, giving $z = f(y)$, in notation B.
3. Translate z back into notation A, giving the result.

In the remainder of this chapter we shall be informal about data representations.

1.3.3   Algorithms versus functions

We stress the important distinction between an algorithm and the mathematical function it computes. A mathematical function is a *set*. For instance, the unary number-theoretic function which returns its argument doubled is:

$$\{(1,2),(2,4),(3,6),\ldots\}$$

For convenience one always writes this function thus: $f(n) = 2n$. So, a function associates a result with each input, but does not say anything about *how* the result can be computed[1].

On the other hand, an algorithm is a *text*, giving instructions on how to proceed from inputs to result. We can write algorithms which, when fed a representation of a number as input, will compute the representation of another number as output, and the connection between input and output can be described by a mathematical function. For instance, an algorithm p may, from the representation of n, compute the representation of $2n$. In this case we say that p *computes* the function $f(n) = 2n$, and we write $[\![p]\!] = f$. We pronounce $[\![p]\!]$ "the meaning of p."

Given a formalization of effective procedure, that is, given a programming language L, we may ask: what mathematical functions can be computed by algorithms in the language? We say that the programming language *defines* the class of all such mathematical functions:

$$\{[\![p]\!] \mid p \text{ is an L-program }\}$$

The relationship between algorithms and functions is a bit subtle. Consider, for instance, the function $f : \mathbb{N} \to \mathbb{N}$, defined by:

$$f(n) = \begin{cases} 0 & \text{if Goldbach's conjecture is true} \\ 1 & \text{otherwise} \end{cases}$$

(Goldbach's conjecture states that every even number greater than 2 is the sum of two prime numbers. Whether the conjecture is true, is not known [147]). There is an algorithm computing f; either it is the algorithm which always return the representation of 0, or it is the algorithm which always returns the representation of 1 — *but we do not know which of the two yet it is.*

---

[1]If the reader is not comfortable with the notion of a function simply being a certain set, Subsection A.3.1 may be consulted.

Thus there are functions for which it is has been proved that an algorithm exists, and yet no concrete algorithm computing the function is known[2]. There are also examples of functions where it is not yet known whether corresponding algorithms exist at all, and there are functions for which it is known that there definitely do not exist any algorithms that compute them. We shall soon see an example of the last kind of function.

1.3.4 Effectively decidable and enumerable sets

How can we apply the idea of an effective procedure to the problem of definition of sets? For example the set of prime numbers seems intuitively effective, in that given an arbitrary number we can decide whether or not it is a prime.

Definition 1.3.2 $^\diamond$ Given a set D, and a subset $S \subseteq D$. S is *effectively decidable* iff there is an effective procedure which, when given an object $x \in D$, will eventually answer "yes" if $x \in S$, and will eventually answer "no" if $x \notin S$. $\qquad\square$

Note that the procedure eventually halts for any input x.

The problem of deciding some set S can sometimes equally naturally be phrased as the problem of computing a certain function, and vice versa, as we shall see later on. An alternative notion is to call a set effective if its elements can be listed in an effective way.

Definition 1.3.3 $^\diamond$ Given a set D, and a subset $S \subseteq D$. S is *effectively enumerable* iff there is an effective procedure which, when given an object $x \in D$, will eventually answer "yes" if $x \in S$, and will answer "no" or never terminate if $x \notin S$. $\qquad\square$

The collection of all subsets of any infinite set (for example $\mathbb{N}$) is not countable (Exercise 1.3). This can be proven by diagonalization as introduced in the next section.

On the other hand, the collections of all effectively decidable (or effectively enumerable) subsets of $\mathbb{N}$ are each countable, since for each nonempty set there exists a program computing a function that decides it (enumerates it), and there is only one empty set.

We will see that there exist effectively enumerable sets which are not effectively decidable. This, too, can be proven by diagonalization; a formal version will be seen later, as Corollary 5.6.2.

---

[2]This can only happen if the proof is by classical logic; in intuitionistic logic proofs of existence are always constructive.

1.4   A taste of computability theory

In this section we review some of the basic results and techniques of computability in an informal manner.

1.4.1   Countable sets and enumeration functions

A set S is *countable* if S is empty or there is a sequence $s_0, s_1, \ldots$ containing all and only all the elements of S, i.e., for all $s \in S$ there is an i such that $s = s_i$. This sequence is called an *enumeration* of S.

The sequence $s_0, s_1, \ldots$ is actually a function[3] $f : \mathbb{N} \to S$ defined by $f(i) = s_i$. Thus a set is countable if and only if it is empty, or there is a surjective[4] total function from $\mathbb{N}$ to S. Such a function is said to *enumerate S*.

Note that the sequence above is allowed to have repetitions. This amounts to saying that f is allowed to be non-injective. Examples include:

1. The set $\mathbb{N}$ is countable; an obvious sequence mentioning all elements is $0, 1, 2, \ldots$. In other words, the required surjective function is the function $f : \mathbb{N} \to \mathbb{N}, f(i) = i$.

2. The set of all integers is countable; a sequence is: $0, 1, -1, 2, -2, 3, \ldots$.

3. $\mathbb{N} \times \mathbb{N}$ is countable; a sequence is: $(0,0), (0,1), (1,0), (0,2), (1,1), (2,0), (0,3), (1,2), (2,1), (3,0), \ldots$.

The preceding terminology in particular applies to sets of functions, partial or total. Let A and B be sets and let S be a non-empty set of partial functions from A into B, i.e., $S \subseteq A \to B_{\perp}$. Then S is countable iff there is a sequence $f_0, f_1, \ldots$ so that $g \in S$ if and only if $g \simeq f_i$ for some i.

1.4.2   The diagonal method and uncountable sets

Proposition 1.4.1 The set of all total functions $f : \mathbb{N} \to \mathbb{N}$ is uncountable.   □

Proof. We use Cantor's well-known *diagonal argument*. Suppose the set of all functions $f : \mathbb{N} \to \mathbb{N}$ were countable. Then there would be an enumeration $f_0, f_1, f_2, \ldots$ such that for any total function $f : \mathbb{N} \to \mathbb{N}$, there is an i such that $f_i = f$, i.e., $f_i(x) = f(x)$ for all $x \in \mathbb{N}$. Consider the function g defined by:

---

[3]More details appear in Subsection A.3.2.
[4]Surjective and injective functions are explained in Subsection A.3.9.

$$g(x) = f_x(x) + 1$$

This is certainly a total function from $\mathbb{N}$ to $\mathbb{N}$. Therefore g must be f_i for some i. But this is impossible, as it implies, in particular, that

$$f_i(i) = g(i) = f_i(i) + 1 \tag{1.1}$$

and so $0 = 1$ which is impossible.[5] □

The proof technique above, called *diagonalization*, has many applications in computability and complexity theory. To understand the name of the technique, imagine the values of countably many functions $f_0, f_1, f_2, \ldots$ listed in an "infinite table" for the arguments $0, 1, 2, \ldots$:

n	$f_0(n)$	$f_1(n)$	$f_2(n)$	$\cdots$
0	$f_0(0)$	$f_1(0)$	$f_2(0)$	$\cdots$
1	$f_0(1)$	$f_1(1)$	$f_2(1)$	$\cdots$
2	$f_0(2)$	$f_1(2)$	$f_2(2)$	$\cdots$
$\vdots$	$\vdots$	$\vdots$	$\vdots$	$\ddots$

For instance, the first column defines f_0. Given a countable set of total functions from $\mathbb{N}$ to $\mathbb{N}$, the diagonal method constructs a new function which differs from the ith function on the argument i in the diagonal. Thus from any enumeration of total functions from $\mathbb{N}$ to $\mathbb{N}$, at least one total function from $\mathbb{N}$ to $\mathbb{N}$ must be absent.

Note that diagonalization does not directly imply the uncountability of the set of *partial* functions from $\mathbb{N}$ to $\mathbb{N}$, since the analog of (1.1) for partial functions is *not* a contradiction in case $f_i(i)$ is undefined.

Corollary 1.4.2 The following sets are also uncountable:

1. All partial functions $f : \mathbb{N} \to \mathbb{N}_\perp$.
2. All total functions $f : \mathbb{N} \to \{0, 1\}$.
3. All total functions $f : A \to B$ where A is infinite and B has at least two elements. □

Proof. See the Exercises. □

---

[5]Remark the similarity between this argument and Russell's Paradox: The class $\mathcal{U} = \{A \mid A \text{ is a set and } A \notin A\}$ is not a set. The reasoning is that if $\mathcal{U}$ were a set, we would have $\mathcal{U} \in \mathcal{U}$ iff $\mathcal{U} \notin \mathcal{U}$.

1.4.3 Existence of effectively uncomputable functions

Proposition 1.4.3 $^\diamond$ The set of all effectively computable partial functions from $\mathbb{N}$ to $\mathbb{N}$ is countable. □

Proof. By the Church-Turing Thesis each effectively computable function is computed by some Turing machine. A Turing machine can be represented as a finite string of symbols over an alphabet consisting of English letters and mathematical and punctuation symbols. The set of all finite strings over any finite alphabet is countable, so the set of all Turing machines is countable; hence the set of all effectively computable functions must be countable as well. □

Corollary 1.4.4 $^\diamond$ The set of all effectively computable total functions from $\mathbb{N}$ to $\mathbb{N}$ is countable. □

Proof. A subset of a countable set is countable. □

Corollary 1.4.5 $^\diamond$

1. There exists an effectively uncomputable total function from $\mathbb{N}$ to $\mathbb{N}$.
2. There exists an effectively uncomputable partial function from $\mathbb{N}$ to $\mathbb{N}$. □

Proof. By Corollary 1.4.2 there are uncountably many total and partial functions, but by Proposition 1.4.3 and Corollary 1.4.4 only countably many of these are effectively computable. If S is a countable subset of an uncountable set T then $T \setminus S \neq \emptyset$. □

It follows from this that the set of computable functions is small indeed, and that there are uncountably many uncomputable functions.

As a concrete example of an unsolvable problem we shall see later that it is impossible effectively to decide, given an arbitrary effective procedure p and input d, whether or not the computation resulting from applying p to d halts. The next subsection gives another example.

1.4.4 The Busy Beaver problem: an explicit uncomputable function

The argument in the preceding subsection shows the *existence* of uncomputable functions but not in a constructive way. The *busy beaver* function below, due to Rado [141] and related to the Richard paradox [144], is mathematically well-defined, but, based on certain reasonable assumptions about the language used to express computation, we will show that there is no algorithm which computes it.

Assumptions: Any program p denotes a partial mathematical function $[\![p]\!]: N \to N_\perp$, as sketched in subsection 1.3.3. Any program p has a *length* $|p| \in N$: the number of symbols required to write p. For any n, there are only finitely many programs with length not exceeding n.

We use programs in a small subset of Pascal [68, 166] with the following syntax. Programs have the form `read X; C; write Y`, where X, Y are variables. A command C can be an assignment `X:=E` where E is an expression built from operators `+`, `*`, etc., and variables and numbers in decimal representation. (Similar constructions can be carried through with unary and other representations.) Commands of the forms `C;C` and `while X>0 do begin C end` have the usual meanings.

Observation: $|p| \geq 19$ for any program p = `read X;C;write Y`.

Proposition 1.4.6 The total function

$$BB(n) = max\{\ [\![p]\!](0) \mid p \text{ is a program with } |p| \leq n, \text{ and } [\![p]\!](0)\!\downarrow\}$$

is computed by no program.[6] □

Proof. Suppose for the sake of contradiction that some program q computes BB:

$$\texttt{read X; C; write Y}$$

The proof uses a form of diagonalization. We present the idea in three small steps.

Step 1. The idea in deriving a contradiction is to find a number K and a program r such that $|r| \leq K$ and $[\![r]\!](0) = [\![q]\!](K) + 1$. This implies

$$
\begin{aligned}
[\![q]\!](K) &= BB(K) &&\text{Since q computes } BB. \\
&\geq [\![r]\!](0) &&\text{Since } |r| \leq K \text{ and } [\![r]\!](0)\!\downarrow \\
&= [\![q]\!](K) + 1 &&\text{By definition of r}
\end{aligned}
$$

which is a contradiction.

Step 2. How to determine r and K? Well, since we are to compute $[\![q]\!](K) + 1$, it seems sensible to use q in the construction of r. Since $|r|$ must be less than K this forces K to be at least $|q|$. As a first try, let $K = |q|$ and and r be the following program computing $[\![q]\!](K) + 1$:

---

[6]Where we define $max\ \emptyset = 0$.

```
read X;
   X:=c;
   C;
   Y:=Y+1;
write Y
```

where c is a numerical constant representing the number $|q|$. This program does not quite meet the requirements of Step 1, since q is part of it and so $|r| > K = |q|$. In other words, the size of program r is too large compared to the input to the command C.

Step 3. As a second try, we increase the input to command C, i.e., the value of X, without increasing the size of program r by the same amount. Let $K = 3|q|$ and let r be the program above slightly modified, where c is again the decimal representation of number $|q|$:

```
read X;
   X:=3*c;
   C;
   Y:=Y+1;
write Y
```

Clearly program r consists of the symbols to write q (i.e., read X;C;write Y), plus the symbols required to write the constant c, plus (count for yourself) 13 additional symbols.

Since c is the decimal representation of the number $|q|$, it follows that $|c| \leq |q|$. Further, any program is at least 19 symbols long, so it follows that

$$\begin{aligned} |r| &= 13 + |c| + |q| & \text{By construction of } r \\ &\leq |q| + |q| + |q| & \text{Since } 19 \leq |q| \text{ and } |c| \leq |q| \\ &= 3|q| = K \end{aligned}$$

Hence, with $K = 3|q|$, we have $|r| \leq K$ and $[\![r]\!](0) = [\![q]\!](K) + 1$, as required for the argument seen earlier. (The constant 3 can be replaced by any larger value.)   □

1.4.5   Unsolvability of the halting problem

It is not hard to write programs in the small subset of Pascal of the previous section which do not halt, e.g.,

```
read X; X:=1; while X > 0 do begin X:=X end; write X
```

The following shows that it is impossible effectively to decide, given an arbitrary program p and input n, whether or not p applied to n halts, i.e., whether or not $[\![p]\!](n)\!\downarrow$.

Corollary 1.4.7 $^\diamond$ The total function

$$halt(\mathrm{p}, n) = \left\{ \begin{array}{ll} 1 & \text{if } [\![\mathrm{p}]\!](n)\!\downarrow \\ 0 & \text{otherwise} \end{array} \right.$$

is computed by no effective procedure.   □

Proof. Suppose, for the sake of contradiction, that such a procedure does exist. Then *BB* can also be computed by the following procedure:

1. Read *n*.
2. Set *max* = 0.
3. Construct $\{\mathrm{p}_1, \ldots \mathrm{p}_k\} = \{\mathrm{p} \mid \mathrm{p}$ is a program and $|\mathrm{p}| \leq n\}$.
4. For $i = 1, 2, \ldots, k$ do: if $[\![\mathrm{p}]\!]_i(n)\!\downarrow$ and $max < [\![\mathrm{p}_i]\!](0)$, then reassign $max := [\![\mathrm{p}_i]\!](0)$.
5. Write *max*.

Step 3 is effective since there are only finitely many programs of any given size, and step 4 is effective by assumption. By the Church-Turing thesis one can turn this procedure into a program in our subset of Pascal. The conclusion that *BB* is computable by a program in this language is in contradiction with Proposition 1.4.6, so the (unjustified) assumption that q exists must be false.   □

1.4.6   Consequences of unsolvability of the halting problem

We have just argued informally that the halting problem for programs in our Pascal subset is not decidable by any program of the same sort. This is analogous to the classical impossibility proofs, for example that the circle cannot be squared using tools consisting of an unmarked ruler and a compass. Such classical impossibility proofs, however, merely point out the need for stronger tools, for instance a marked ruler, to solve the named problems.

Our "busy beaver" argument similarly asserts that one particular problem, the halting problem, cannot be solved be means of any of a class of tools: programs in our Pascal subset. But here a major difference arises because of the Church-Turing thesis. This gives the undecidability of the halting problem much more weight since it implies that the halting problem is *not decidable by any intuitively effective computing device* whatsoever.

1.5   The scope and goals of complexity theory

Recall that computability theory is concerned with questions such as whether a problem is solvable at all, assuming one is given unlimited amounts of space and time. In contrast, *complexity theory* is concerned with questions such as whether a problem can be solved within certain limited computing resources, typically space or time. Whereas computability theory is concerned with unsolvable problems and the boundary between solvable and unsolvable problems, complexity theory analyzes the set of solvable problems.

To address such questions, one must have a precise definition of space and time costs. Granted that, complexity theory asks questions such as:

- Which problems can be solved within a certain limit of time or space, and which cannot?
- Are there resource limits within which a known combinatorial problem definitely cannot be solved?
- Are there problems which inherently need more resources than others?
- What characteristics of problems cause the need for certain amounts of resources?
- What is the class of problems solvable within certain resource limits, and what are the basic properties of this class?
- Given a problem, what is the complexity of its best algorithm?
- Do best algorithms always exist?
- Does adding more resources allow one to solve more problems?

1.5.1   Polynomial time

Similarly to the situation in computability theory, one might fear that one single definition of resource accounting would not suffice, and in fact different models exist giving rise to different theories of complexity. Specifically, the class of problems solvable within certain sharp limits may vary from model to model.

However, we will see that many computation models define precisely the same class PTIMEof problems decidable within time bounded by some polynomial function of the length of the input. Many researchers identify the class of *computationally tractable* problems with those that lie in PTIME, thereby suggesting what could well be called *Cook's thesis*, after Stephen C. Cook, a pathbreaking researcher in computational complexity:

1. All reasonable formalizations of the intuitive notion of tractable computability are equivalent (they can simulate each other within a polynomially bounded overhead in time);

2. Polynomial-time Turing machine computability is a reasonable formalization of tractable computability.

Note the close similarity with the Church-Turing thesis: "Turing machine computability" has been replaced by "polynomial time Turing machine computability," and "effectively computable" by "tractable computability." A stronger form of the first part is sometimes called the *Invariance Thesis* [14].

Cook's thesis is a useful working assumption but should not be taken as being as solidly founded as the Church-Turing thesis, which concerns computability in a world of unlimited resources. Reasons for a certain skepticism about Cook's thesis include the facts that an algorithm running in time $|x|^{100}$, where $|x|$ is the length of the input to the algorithm, can hardly be regarded as computationally tractable; and that there are algorithms (for instance as used in factorizing large integers) that run in a superpolynomial time bound such as $|x|^{\log \log |x|}$, but with constant factors that are small enough for practical use.

1.5.2 Complexity hierarchies and complete problems

Ideally, one would like to be able to be able to make statements such as "the XXX problem can be solved in time $O(n^3)$ (as a function of its input size); and it cannot be solved in time $O(n^{3-\varepsilon})$ for any $\varepsilon > 0$." Alas, such definitive statements can only rarely be proven. There are a few problems whose exact complexity can be identified, but very few.

Because of this, a major goal of complexity theory is *classification of problems by difficulty*. This naturally leads to a division of all problems into hierarchies of *problem classes*. Standard classes of problems include: LOGSPACE, NLOGSPACE, PTIME, NPTIME, PSPACE. Each class is characterized by certain *computational resource bounds*. For example, problems in LOGSPACE can be solved with very little storage; those in PTIME can be solved with unlimited storage, but only by algorithms running in polynomial time; and those in NPTIME can be solved by polynomial time algorithms with an extra feature: they are allowed to "guess" from time to time during their computations.

Various combinations of these resources lead to a widely encompassing "backbone" hierarchy:

$$\text{LOGSPACE} \subseteq \text{NLOGSPACE} \subseteq \text{PTIME} \subseteq \text{NPTIME} \subseteq \text{PSPACE} = \text{NPSPACE} \subset \text{REC} \subset \text{RE}$$

Surprisingly, it is not known whether *any one* of the inclusions above is proper: for example, the question PTIME = NPTIME?, often expressed as P = NP?, has been open for decades.

Nonetheless, this hierarchy has proven itself useful for classifying problems. A great many problems have been precisely localised in this hierarchy. A typical example is SAT, the problem of deciding whether a Boolean expression can be made true by assigning truth values to the variables appearing in it. This problem is *complete for* NPTIME, meaning the following. First, SAT is in NPTIME: There is a nondeterministic algorithm that solves it and runs in polynomial time. Second, it is "hardest" among all problems in NPTIME: *If* it were the case that SAT could be solved by a PTIME algorithm, then *every* problem in NPTIME would have a deterministic polynomial time solution, and PTIME = NPTIME would be true. This means that two stages of the hierarchy would "collapse."

The last four chapters of this book concern complete problems for the various complexity classes.

1.6 Historical background

At the Paris Conference in 1900 D. Hilbert gave a lecture which was to have profound consequences for the development of Mathematics, particularly Mathematical Logic, and the not yet existing field of Computer Science. Hilbert's ambitions were high and his belief in the power of mathematical methods was strong, as indicated by the following quote from his lecture:

> Occasionally it happens that we seek the solution under insufficient hypotheses or in an incorrect sense, and for this reason do not succeed. The problem then arises: to show the impossibility of the solution under the given hypotheses, or in the sense contemplated. Such proofs of impossibility were effected by the ancients, for instance when they showed the ratio of the hypotenuse to the side of an isosceles triangle is irrational. In later mathematics, the question as to the impossibility of certain solutions plays a preeminent part, and we perceive in this way that old and difficult problems, such as the proof of the axiom of parallels, the squaring of the circle, or the solution of equations of the fifth degree by radicals have finally found fully satisfactory and rigorous solutions, although in another sense than originally intended. It is probably this important fact along with other philosophical reasons that gives rise to the conviction (which every mathematician shares, but which no

one has as yet supported by a proof) *that every definite mathematical problem must necessarily be susceptible to an exact settlement, either in the form of an exact answer, or by proof of the impossibility of its solution and therewith the necessary failure of all attempts*[7].

At the conference Hilbert presented 23 unsolved mathematical problems. One of these, the *Entscheidungsproblem* (decision problem), was described as follows:[8]

> The Entscheidungsproblem is solved if one knows a procedure which will permit one to decide, using a finite number of operations, on the validity, respectively the satisfiability of a given logical expression.

This problem was part of *Hilbert's program* which included an endeavour to formalize number theory in a first-order deductive system. It was hoped that the provable theorems of the system would be precisely the true number-theoretic propositions, and that one could devise a procedure to decide whether or not a given proposition were a theorem of the system.

A negative answer to the Entscheidungsproblem, i.e., a proof that no such procedure exists, must necessarily be grounded in a precise definition of the notion of *procedure*. However, Hilbert and his school believed that such a universal decision procedure existed, and so had no reason to formalize the notion of a procedure in general terms.

In 1931 Gödel showed his celebrated *Incompleteness Theorem* [51] stating, roughly, that for any consistent, sufficiently strong formalization of number theory, there are true propositions which cannot be proved in that formalization. To the experts this result made it seem highly unlikely that the Entscheidungsproblem could have a positive solution.

In 1936 it was shown independently by Church [21, 22] and Turing [162] that the Entscheidungsproblem does not have a positive solution. Further, and just as important in the long run, each author gave a formalization of the notion of procedure (via λ-expressions and Turing machines, respectively), and derived the unsolvability of the Entscheidungsproblem from unsolvability of the Halting problem, which they both showed for their respective formalisms. Similar work on other formalizations, also in 1936, was done by Kleene [93] and Post [133]. Gandy [48] describes this astonishing "confluence of ideas in 1936."

---

[7]Our italics; not present in the original.
[8]In a formulation from 1928; the English translation from German is adopted from [48].

It is a remarkable fact that the different formalisms all define the same class of number-theoretic functions, the so-called *partial recursive functions*, and equivalences between various formalisms were soon proved by Kleene, Turing, and others. In fact, one can write *compilers* that turn a program in one formalism into a program in one of the other formalisms that computes the same function, supporting what we have previously called the Church-Turing thesis. It should be noted that this correspondence between the *algorithms* in the various formalisms is a stronger result than the fact that the various formalisms define the same class of *functions*.

The initial work in complexity theory in the late 1920's and early 1930's was concerned with subclasses of the effectively computable functions, e.g., the primitive recursive functions studied by Hilbert [65], Ackermann [1], and others. Subclasses of primitive recursive functions were studied by Kalmar [87] and Grzegorczyk [55]. More programing language oriented versions of these classes were later introduced by Meyer and Ritchie [119].

With the appearance of actual physical computers in the 1950's, an increasing interest emerged in the resource requirements for algorithms solving various problems, and the field of complexity as it is known today, began around 1960. One of the first to consider the question as to how difficult it is to compute some function was Rabin [137, 138]. Later, Blum [13] introduced a general theory of complexity independent of any specific model of computation.

The first systematic investigation of time and space hierachies is due to Hartmanis, Lewis, and Stearns [62, 61, 104] in the 1960's, who coined the term "computational complexity" for what we call complexity theory in this book.

Important results concerning the classes of problems solvable in polynomial time and non-deterministic polynomial time were established by Cook [25] and Karp [90] who were among the first to realize the importance of these concepts.

Exercises

1.1 Does Turing argue that the tape symbol alphabet size should be uniformly bounded, or that each machine may have its own number of characters?   □

1.2 The Turing machine has a bounded tape symbol alphabet size, but an unboundedly large set of states. Could one reasonably argue that the set of states should be uniformly bounded as well? What would be the effect of bounding both of these on the number of problems solvable by Turing machines?   □

1.3 Prove that $\mathcal{P}(\mathbb{N})$, the set of all subsets of $\mathbb{N}$, is uncountable, using the diagonal method. *Hint:* if all of $\mathcal{P}(\mathbb{N})$ could be listed $S_1, S_2, \ldots$, then one can find a new subset of $\mathbb{N}$ not in this list. □

1.4 Prove that the set of all total functions $\mathbb{N} \to \{0,1\}$ is not countable. □

1.5 Let A and B be sets and let S be a non-empty set of partial functions from A into B, i.e., $S \subseteq A \to B_\perp$. Show that the following conditions are equivalent.

1. S is countable.
2. There is a sequence $f_0, f_1, \ldots$ so that $g \in S$ if and only if $g \simeq f_i$ for some i.
3. There is a surjective function $u : \mathbb{N} \to S$.
4. There is a function $u : \mathbb{N} \to (A \to B_\perp)$ such that $g \in S$ if and only if $g \simeq u(i)$ for some i.
5. There is a partial function $u : (\mathbb{N} \times A) \to B_\perp$ such that $g \in S$ if and only if there is an $i \in \mathbb{N}$ such that $g(a) \simeq u(i,a)$ for all a in A.

The reader should note that the f's, g's, etc. above are *functions*, and that these are not necessarily computed by any *algorithms*. □

1.6 Consider a language like the subset of Pascal in Subsection 1.4.4, but with the following modification. Instead of commands of form

```
while X>0 do begin C end
```

there are only commands of form

```
for X := 1 to n do begin C end
```

where n is a numerical constant, with the usual meaning. (It terminates immediately if n < 1.) Variable X may not be re-assigned within command C.

Use a construction similar to the one in Subsection 1.4.4 to show that there is a function which is not computable in this language. Is the function effectively computable at all? □

1.7 * Change the language of the previous exercise by expanding the iteration statement's syntax to

```
for X := E1 to E2 do begin C end
```

where E1 and E2 are numerical expressions. (X may still not be assigned within command C.) Consider two alternative ways to interpret this statemnt (using a "goto" syntax):

Semantics 1: equivalent to the following, where `Tem` is a new variable.

```
    X := E1; Tem := E2;
1: if X > Tem then goto 2
    C
    X := X + 1
    goto 1
2:
```

Semantics 2: equivalent to the following.

```
    X := E1;
1: if X > E2 then goto 2
    C
    X := X + 1
    goto 1
2:
```

Show that every program terminates under semantics 1, but that some may loop under semantics 2. □

References

For more on the historical development of computability theory, in particular fuller discussions of the Church-Turing Thesis, see Gandy's paper [48] or Kleene's classical book [95]. A number of early papers on computability are reprinted in Davis' book [32] with comments. This includes an English translation of Gödel's paper. Presentations of Gödel's results for non-specialists appear in the books by Nagel and Newman [127] and Hofstaedter [66].

More information about the scope and historical development of complexity theory may be found in the surveys [14, 16, 27, 60, 139]. Broadly encompassing surveys of complete problems may be found in the books by Garey and Johnson, and by Greenlaw, Hoover, and Ruzzo [49, 53].

2 The WHILE Language

The notions of the introductory chapter, e.g., "effectively computable," were imprecise, because they relied on an intuitive understanding of the notion "effective procedure." We now present a model of computation, or programming language, called WHILE, which is used throughout the book. In subsequent chapters we define the intuitive notions of the preceding chapter precisely, by identifying "effective procedure" with "WHILE program."

It may seem that we avoid the vagueness of intuitive argumentation by going to the opposite extreme of choosing *one* model of computation which is too simple to model realistic computing. Later chapters will argue that this is not the case, by proving the equivalence of WHILE with a variety of other computation models.

The WHILE language has just the right mix of expressive power and simplicity. *Expressive power* is important because we will be presenting many algorithms, some rather complex, that deal with *programs as data objects*. The data structures of WHILE are particularly well suited to this, and are far more convenient than the natural numbers used in most theory of computation texts. *Simplicity* is essential since we will be proving many theorems about programs and their behaviour. This rules out the use of larger, more powerful languages, since proofs about them would simply be too complex to be easily understood.

Section 2.1 describes the WHILE syntax and informally describes the semantics of programs. Section 2.2 precisely describes the semantics. Section 2.3 describes a shorthand notation used in the rest of the book. This last section can be skipped and consulted on a "by need" basis later. Section 2.4 shows that equality tests may without loss of generality be restricted to atomic values, each taking constant time. This will be relevant later, when discussing time-bounded computations.

2.1 Syntax of WHILE data and programs

The syntax of WHILE data structures and programs is described in Subsections 2.1.1–2.1.2. Subsection 2.1.3 informally explains the semantics of WHILE-programs by means of an elaborate example. Subsection 2.1.4 concerns conditionals and truth values in WHILE, and Subsections 2.1.5-2.1.6 show how to compute with numbers and lists in WHILE. Finally, Subsection 2.1.7 describes a useful macro notation.

2.1.1   Trees over a finite set

Recall the *idealized* subset of Pascal that we used in Subsection 1.4.4 in which one can compute with numbers.[1] It has commands to assign an arbitrary number to a variable, and to increment and decrement a variable by one.

The language WHILE is very similar but with one very important difference: instead of computing with *numbers*, the language computes with certain *trees* over a finite set. For instance, a and (a.c) as well as (a.(b.c)) are trees over the set {a,b,c}. The objects a,b,c are called *atoms (definition)* because, unlike for instance (a.c), they cannot be divided further into subparts. The reason we call these objects "trees" is that they can be represented in a graphical form as trees with atoms as leaf labels, see Figure 2.1.

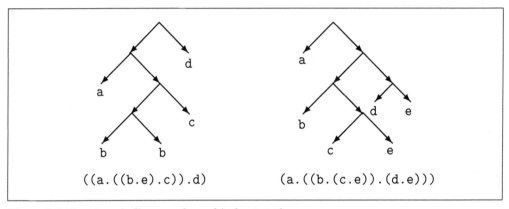

$$((a.((b.e).c)).d) \qquad (a.((b.(c.e)).(d.e)))$$

Figure 2.1: Two trees in linear and graphical notation.

Formally we define the set of trees $\mathbb{D}_A$ over the set A as follows.

Definition 2.1.1 Given a finite set A (the *atoms*), $\mathbb{D}_A$ is defined by:

1. Any element of A is an element of $\mathbb{D}_A$;
2. Whenever d_1 and d_2 are elements of $\mathbb{D}_A$, then so is $(d_1.d_2)$; and
3. $\mathbb{D}_A$ is the smallest set satisfying the previous two points.

We will often use a designated element of A, named "nil."   □

When the set A is clear from the context, $\mathbb{D}_A$ will be written $\mathbb{D}$. Values in $\mathbb{D}_A$ are written d, d_1, etc. Objects in $\mathbb{D}_A$ that are named a, a_1, a_2, etc., always denote elements of A.

---

[1]The reason we call it "idealized" is that it has representations of *all* natural numbers $0, 1, 2, \ldots$, and not just, say, 0 to 65535.

Definition 2.1.2 The function $|\bullet| : \mathbb{D} \to \mathbb{N}$ defined by:

$$|d| = \begin{cases} 1 & \text{if } d \in A \\ 1 + |d_1| + |d_2| & \text{if } d = (d_1.d_2) \end{cases}$$

denotes the *size* of a $d \in \mathbb{D}$.   □

In Figure 2.1, the leftmost value has size 9, and the rightmost value has size 11.

2.1.2   Syntax of WHILE programs

The operation in WHILE, analogous to the increment operation on numbers in the idealized subset of Pascal in Subsection 1.4.4, is the operation that combines two trees d_1 and
d_2 into one $(d_1 . d_2)$. This operation is called *cons*. The operations in WHILE, analogous
to the decrement operation on numbers, are the two operations that decompose a tree
$(d_1 . d_2)$ into the subtrees d_1 and d_2. These are called *head* and *tail*, respectively. There
is also an operation to test equality of elements of $\mathbb{D}$.

Definition 2.1.3 Let A be a finite set of atoms, and $\mathtt{Vars} = \{V_0, V_1, \ldots\}$ a countable set
of variables. We use the conventions $d, e, f, \ldots \in \mathbb{D}_A$ and $X, Y, Z, \ldots \in \mathtt{Vars}$. Then the
syntax of $\mathtt{WHILE}_A$ is given by the following grammar:

```
Expressions  ∋  E, F  ::=  X
                       |   d
                       |   cons E F
                       |   hd E
                       |   tl E
                       |   =? E F
Commands     ∋  C, D  ::=  X := E
                       |   C; D
                       |   while E do C
Programs     ∋  P     ::=  read X; C; write Y
```

Here X and Y are the not necessarily distinct *input* and *output variables*. We omit the A
from $\mathtt{WHILE}_A$ when clear from the context.   □

We use indentation to indicate the scope of while and other commands. For instance,
consider the two commands:

```
while E do        while E do
  C;                C;
D;                D;
```

The leftmost command repeatedly executes C as long as e is true and executes D once when e has become false (what it means that an expression is true or false will be clear later on). The rightmost command repeatedly executes first C and then D, as long as e is true.

We also use braces to indicate scope, so the two above commands might have been written {while E do C }; D and while E do {C;D}. Similarly we use parentheses to explicate scope in expressions, such as cons (hd (tl X)) Y.

Note that a program always expects exactly *one* input. A program of, say, two inputs can be expressed as a function which expects one input of form (d.e):[2]

```
read X;        (* X is (d.e) *)
  Y := hd X;   (* Y is d     *)
  Z := tl X;   (* Z is e     *)
  C;
write Y;
```

2.1.3   Informal semantics

We now explain the semantics of a simple program to *reverse* a list, which illustrates most aspects of WHILE.

Example 2.1.4 Consider the following program, reverse:

```
read X;
  Y := nil;
  while X do
    Y := cons (hd X) Y;
    X := tl X;
write Y
```

The program consists of a *read* command, a *body*, and a *write* command. The idea is that some *input* d $\in \mathbb{D}$ is assigned to the variable X, and then the body is *executed*. At any point during execution every variable is bound to an element of $\mathbb{D}$; the collection of all such bindings at one point is a *store*. Initially X is bound to the input d $\in \mathbb{D}$, and all

---

[2]Comments are written in the form (* ... *), as in Pascal.

other variables in the program are bound to `nil`. If execution of the body terminates, the value $e \in \mathbb{D}$ bound to Y is the *output*.

For `reverse`, if X is initially bound to input

$$(d_0 . (d_1 . (\cdots . (d_{n-1} . (d_n . \texttt{nil})) \cdots)))$$

then Y is bound to

$$(d_n . (d_{n-1} . (\cdots . (d_1 . (d_0 . \texttt{nil})) \cdots)))$$

when execution reaches the final write command, and this later element of $\mathbb{D}$ is then the output.

To bind a variable, say Y, to some $f \in \mathbb{D}$ one uses the assignment Y:=f. So the second line assigns `nil` to Y.[3]

More generally every expression E *evaluates* to some $e \in \mathbb{D}$, and Z := E assigns this e to Z. Specifically, E evaluates to e. As another example cons E F evaluates to (e.f) if E evaluates to e and F evaluates to f. Further, hd E and tl E evaluate to e and f, respectively, if E evaluates to (e.f). Finally, a variable Z evaluates to the value it is currently bound to.

The expression =? E F evaluates to `true`, if E and F evaluate to the same value, and to `false` otherwise. Thus =? (nil.nil) (nil.nil) evaluates to `true`, and =? (nil.nil) nil evaluates to `false`.

Turning to our program, the next thing that happens is that the while command beginning in the third line is executed. The meaning of the command while E do C is as follows. If E evaluates to `nil` proceed to the command following while E do C. In the example this is the command write Y. However, if E evaluates to something other than `nil` execute C, and test again whether E evaluates to `nil`. The outcome of this test may be different from the first since the variables occurring in E may have been assigned new values by the command C. If E evaluates to `nil`, go to the next command, and otherwise execute C and test E again, etc.

So in the example program, the commands Y := cons (hd X) Y; X := tl X are executed in sequence as long as X is not bound to `nil`. Before the first of these two commands X is bound to (e.d) (otherwise execution would have proceeded to

---

[3]Since all variables are initially bound to `nil` this command is superfluous. However it often happens that one assigns some $f \in \mathbb{D}$ to a variable without ever making use of the initial value `nil`. Therefore, if one *does* want to make use of the initial value `nil`, it is good programming practice to enter an explicit assignment Y := nil in the program.

the write command) and Y is bound to some f. After the first command Y is bound to (e.f), and after the second command X is bound to d.

If we think of the value $(d_0.(d_1.(\cdots(d_{n-1}.(d_n.\text{nil}))\cdots)))$ as a *list* d_0, d_1,..., d_{n-1}, d_n, then the program reverses lists; more about lists in Subsection 2.1.5.   □

2.1.4   Truth values and if-then-else

As is apparent from the preceding example, whenever evaluating expressions in tests one should think of nil as "false" and any other element of $\mathbb{D}$ as "true." This intuition is so predominant that we explicate it in a definition:

Definition 2.1.5 We use the following abbreviations:

```
false  =  nil
true   =  (nil.nil)
```

Conditional commands and boolean expressions.   We now see that conditional commands can be expressed by while-commands alone.

Example 2.1.6 The following compound command executes C if and only if E evaluates to true. Variable Z must be chosen different from existing variables.

```
Z := E;              (*  if E then C *)
while Z do { Z := false; C };
```

The next statement will execute C1 if E evaluates to true and otherwise C2.

```
Z := E;              (*  if E then C1 else C2 *)
W := true;
while Z do { Z := false; W := false; C1 };
while W do { W := false; C2 };
```

□

The same idea may be applied to expressions, rather than just commands, thus expressing conjunction E and F, disjunction E or F, or negation not E, etc..

Testing for atomicity.   Aabbreviation "cons? X" stands for

```
=? X cons (hd X) (tl X)
```

The value of cons? X is true if the value of X is a pair (d.e), else its value is false. Its negation will be written "atom? X" and yields true if and only if X's value is atomic. atom?cons?

2.1.5 Lists

As one can see from the example in subsection 2.1.3, elements of $\mathbb{D}$ sometimes have deeply nested parentheses that are hard to read; one has to resort to counting to parse an element like ((a.(b.nil)).((d.(e.nil)).nil).

Often the nesting has a certain structure, because we often express a *list* of elements $d_0, d_1, \ldots, d_{n-1}, d_n$ as the tree $(d_0.(d_1.(\cdots.(d_{n-1}.(d_n.nil))\cdots)))$. For instance (a.(b.nil)) represents the list consisting of elements a, b. Therefore it would be particularly convenient to have a short notation for this form. Hence the idea is to use the notation $(d_0 \cdots d_n)$ for the tree $(d_0.(d_1.(\cdots.(d_{n-1}.(d_n.nil))\cdots)))$. Then the tree (a.(b.nil)) can be written (a b) in short notation and, as another example, the tree ((a.(b.nil)).((d.(e.nil)).nil) can be written ((a b) (d e)).

This is introduced in the following definition.

Definition 2.1.7 The *list representation* $\underline{d}$ of $d \in \mathbb{D}_A$ is the string of symbols from alphabet $A \cup \{(,.,)\}$ defined recursively as follows:

$$\underline{d} = \begin{cases} d & \text{if } d \in A \\ (\underline{d_1} \cdots \underline{d_n}.a) & \text{if } d = (d_1.(d_2.(\cdots(d_n.a)\cdots))) \text{ where } a \in A \backslash \{nil\} \\ (\underline{d_1} \cdots \underline{d_n}) & \text{if } d = (d_1.(d_2.(\cdots(d_n.nil)\cdots))) \end{cases}$$

We call $(d_1 \cdots d_n)$ a *list* of $l(d) = n$; nil is the empty list of length 0. □

Notice that every element of $\mathbb{D}$ has at exactly one list representation. Henceforth we will omit the underlines and write all values in the list form. Figure 2.2 gives some examples of elements in $\mathbb{D}$ and their list representations.

The first example in the preceding subsection can now be expressed as saying that the program reverses lists: if X was initially bound to input $(d_0 \cdots d_n)$ then Y is bound to $(d_n \cdots d_0)$ when execution reaches the final write command.

2.1.6 Numbers

WHILE$_A$ has a finite number of atoms, so how can we compute with numbers? Letting each element of A represent a number clearly will not do, since A is finite. The idea,

Value d in $\mathbb{D}$	Representation	$\|d\|$	$l(d)$
nil	nil	1	0
(a.(b.nil))	(a b)	5	2
(a.((b.(c.nil)).(d.nil))))	(a (b c) d)	11	3
((1.2).(3.4))	((1.2).(3.4))	7	?
((a.((b.nil).c)).nil)	((a ((b).c)))	9	?

Figure 2.2: Some trees and their list representation

then, is to represent the number n by a list of length n.

Definition 2.1.8 Define $\underline{n} = \texttt{nil}^n$, where

$$
\begin{aligned}
\texttt{nil}^0 &= \texttt{nil} \\
\texttt{nil}^{n+1} &= (\texttt{nil.nil}^n)
\end{aligned}
$$

and let $\mathcal{N} = \{\underline{n} \mid n \in \mathbb{N}\}$. The elements of $\mathcal{N}$ are called *numerals.*   □

As a matter of convenience, we will omit underlines and simply write $0,1,2,$ $\ldots$ instead of $\underline{0},\underline{1},\underline{2},\ldots$ or $\texttt{nil}^0$, $\texttt{nil}^1$, $\texttt{nil}^2,\cdots$. With the representation in this definition, while E do C means: as long as E does not evaluate to 0, execute C. As two very simple examples, the *successor* and *predecessor* functions are computed by:

```
read X; (* succ *)         read X;  (* pred *)
   Y := cons nil X;           Y:=tl X;
write Y;                   write Y;
```

Here is a program for adding two numbers (note that XY is a single variable, whose value is a pair):

```
read XY; (* add X Y *)
   X := hd XY;
   Y := tl XY;
   while X do
      Y := cons nil Y;
      X := tl X;
write Y;
```

More programs computing with numbers are examined in the Exercises.

2.1.7   Syntactic sugar: some useful macro notations

We introduce some programming shorthand devices to increase human readability of program texts. The first is nearly trivial: let SKIP be a command with no effect, say X:=X.

Two notations for building lists.   The expression list $E_1 \cdots E_n$ will be used as short-hand for cons E_1 (cons E_2 $\cdots$ (cons E_{n-1} (cons E_n nil)) $\cdots$) for any $n \in \mathbb{N}$. Its value is $(d_1\ d_2 \cdots\ d_{n-1}\ d_n)$ if the value of each list E_i is d_i.

The expression cons* $E_1 \cdots E_n$ will be used as shorthand for cons E_1 (cons $E_2 \cdots$ (cons E_{n-1} $E_n) \cdots$) for any $n \in \mathbb{N}$. (This differs slightly in that nil is not added at the end, which makes it more useful than list for extending an already-existing list.) Its value is $(d_1\ d_2 \cdots\ d_{n-1}\ d_n\ e_1\ e_2 \cdots\ e_m)$ if the value of each list E_i is d_i for $1 \leq i < n$ and the value of list E_n is $(e_1\ e_2 \cdots\ e_m)$

Inline procedure expansion.   Note in the example for adding two numbers that the program incremented and decremented X and Y, respectively, explicitly by means of cons and tl expressions. A more abstract formulation of add, hiding the specific way numbers are implemented, is:

```
read XY; (* add X Y *)
  X := hd XY;
  Y := tl XY;
  while X do
    Y := succ Y;
    X := pred X;
write Y;
```

where we allow the add program to use the succ and pred programs. Strictly speaking we have not yet explained how this can be allowed. That is done in this subsection.

Given a program p we will allow a program q to use the command B := p A. The meaning is as follows. Suppose that the input and output variable in p are X and Y, respectively. Now make a copy pp of p where X and Y are replaced by A and B, respectively, and where all variables are renamed so that no variable of pp other than A and B occurs in q. Then replace in q the command B := p A by the body of pp.

Example 2.1.9 Consider the following program, append, which for input (d.e) with d = $(d_1 \cdots d_n)$ and e = $(e_1 \cdots e_m)$ computes $(d_1 \cdots d_n\ e_1 \cdots e_m)$.

```
read X;            (* X is (d.e) *)
  A := hd X;       (* A is d *)
  Y := tl X;       (* Y is e *)
  B := reverse A;  (* B is d reversed *)
  while B do
    Y := cons (hd B) Y;
    B := tl B;
write Y            (* Y is A with B appended *)
```

Written out explicitly the program is:

```
read X;            (* X is (d.e) *)
  A := hd X;       (* A is d *)
  Y := tl X;       (* Y is e *)
  B := nil;        (* B becomes d reversed *)
  while A do
    B := cons (hd A) B;
    A := tl A;
  while B do
    Y := cons (hd B) Y;
    B := tl B;
write Y            (* Y is A with B appended *)
```

$\square$

We will also allow names to stand for sequences of commands. Thus from now on, programs may make free use of conditionals.

2.2   Semantics of WHILE programs

Recall from the introductory chapter the important distinction between algorithms and the mathematical functions they compute. In this section we show how any program in WHILE can be used to define a partial function from $\mathbb{D}$ to $\mathbb{D}$. The interpretation is nothing more than a precise statement of the informal semantics mentioned in Subsection 2.1.3.

Subsection 2.2.1 formalizes the notion of a *store* that was mentioned in Example 2.1.4. Subsections 2.2.2–2.2.3 then formalize the notions of *evaluation* of an expression and *execution* of a command, also mentioned in Example 2.1.4. Finally, Subsection 2.2.4 puts together the pieces.

2.2.1   Stores

The notation $[x_1 \mapsto d_1, \ldots, x_n \mapsto d_n]$ denotes the function f such that $f(x_i) = d_i$. The notation $f[x \mapsto d]$ denotes the function g such that $g(x) = d$, and $g(y) = f(y)$ for $y \neq x$. See Subsection A.3.6 in the Appendix for more information.

Definition 2.2.1 Given a program p=read X; C; write Y.

1. Vars(p) denotes the set of all variables occurring in p.

2. A *store* σ for p is a function from Vars(p) to elements of $\mathbb{D}$. The set of all stores for p, i.e., the set Vars(p) $\to \mathbb{D}$, is called Store^p.

3. The *initial store* $\sigma_0^p(\text{d}) \in$ Store^p for input d $\in \mathbb{D}$ is:

$$[\text{X} \mapsto \text{d}, \text{Z}_1 \mapsto \text{nil} \ldots, \text{Z}_m \mapsto \text{nil}]$$

where Vars(p) $= \{\text{X}, \text{Z}_1, \ldots, \text{Z}_m\}$. Note that if Y and X are different, Y is among the Z_i.
□

2.2.2   Evaluation of expressions

Given a store σ containing the values of the variables in an expression E, the function $\mathcal{E}$ maps E and σ into the value $\mathcal{E}[\![\text{E}]\!]\sigma = \text{d}$ in $\mathbb{D}$ that E denotes. For example $\mathcal{E}[\![\text{cons X Y}]\!]\sigma = ((\text{nil}.\text{nil}).\text{nil})$ if $\sigma = [\text{X} \mapsto (\text{nil}.\text{nil}), \text{Y} \mapsto \text{nil}]$.

Definition 2.2.2 The function $\mathcal{E} : \text{Expression} \to (\text{Store}^p \to \mathbb{D})$ is defined by:

$$
\begin{aligned}
\mathcal{E}[\![\text{X}]\!]\sigma &= \sigma(\text{X}) \\
\mathcal{E}[\![\text{d}]\!]\sigma &= \text{d} \\
\mathcal{E}[\![\text{cons E F}]\!]\sigma &= (\mathcal{E}[\![\text{E}]\!]\sigma \, . \, \mathcal{E}[\![\text{F}]\!]\sigma) \\
\mathcal{E}[\![\text{hd E}]\!]\sigma &= \begin{cases} \text{e} & \text{if } \mathcal{E}[\![\text{E}]\!]\sigma = (\text{e}.\text{f}) \\ \text{nil} & \text{otherwise} \end{cases} \\
\mathcal{E}[\![\text{tl E}]\!]\sigma &= \begin{cases} \text{f} & \text{if } \mathcal{E}[\![\text{E}]\!]\sigma = (\text{e}.\text{f}) \\ \text{nil} & \text{otherwise} \end{cases} \\
\mathcal{E}[\![\text{=? E F}]\!]\sigma &= \begin{cases} \text{true} & \text{if } \mathcal{E}[\![\text{E}]\!]\sigma = \mathcal{E}[\![\text{F}]\!]\sigma \\ \text{false} & \text{otherwise} \end{cases}
\end{aligned}
$$

2.2.3   Execution of commands

Given a store σ, the relation $C \vdash \sigma \to \sigma'$ expresses the fact that the new store is σ' after executing the command C in the store σ. (If command C does not terminate in the given store σ, then there will be no σ' such that $C \vdash \sigma \to \sigma'$.) For instance,

$$X:=\text{cons } X \text{ } Y \vdash [X \mapsto \text{nil}, Y \mapsto \text{nil}] \to [X \mapsto (\text{nil}.\text{nil}), Y \mapsto \text{nil}]$$

Definition 2.2.3 Define the relation $\bullet \vdash \bullet \to \bullet \subseteq \text{Command} \times \text{Store}^P \times \text{Store}^P$ to be the smallest relation satisfying:

$$\begin{array}{ll}
X:=E \vdash \sigma \to \sigma[X \mapsto d] & \text{if } \mathcal{E}[\![E]\!]\sigma = d \\
C;D \vdash \sigma \to \sigma'' & \text{if } C \vdash \sigma \to \sigma' \text{ and } D \vdash \sigma' \to \sigma'' \\
\text{while } E \text{ do } C \vdash \sigma \to \sigma'' & \text{if } \mathcal{E}[\![E]\!]\sigma \neq \text{nil}, C \vdash \sigma \to \sigma', \text{while } E \text{ do } C \vdash \sigma' \to \sigma'' \\
\text{while } E \text{ do } C \vdash \sigma \to \sigma & \text{if } \mathcal{E}[\![E]\!]\sigma = \text{nil}
\end{array}$$

$\square$

2.2.4   Semantics of WHILE programs

The function $[\![\bullet]\!]$ maps a program p and input value d into a value $[\![p]\!](d) = e$ in $\mathbb{D}$ if the program terminates. (If the program does not terminate there will be no $e \in \mathbb{D}$ with $[\![p]\!](d) = e$.) This is done by executing C in the initial store $\sigma_0^P(d)$ and writing the value $\sigma'(Y)$ bound to Y in the new store σ' resulting from execution of C.

Definition 2.2.4 The semantics of WHILE programs is the function

$$[\![\bullet]\!]^{\text{WHILE}} : \text{Program} \to (\mathbb{D} \to \mathbb{D}_\perp)$$

defined for $p = \text{read } X; \text{ } C; \text{ write } Y$ by:

$$[\![p]\!]^{\text{WHILE}}(d) = e \text{ if } C \vdash \sigma_0^P(d) \to \sigma \text{ and } \sigma(Y) = e$$

We write $[\![p]\!]$ instead of $[\![p]\!]^{\text{WHILE}}$ when no confusion is likely to arise. If there is no e such that $[\![p]\!](d) = e$, then p *loops* on d;[4] otherwise p *terminates* on d. We also say that p *computes* $[\![p]\!]$. $\square$

Given the precise semantics of programs one can prove rigorously such properties as $[\![\text{reverse}]\!](d_1 \cdots d_n) = (d_n \cdots d_1)$, see the exercises.

---

[4]In this case, we write $[\![p]\!](d) = \perp$, as usual for partial functions.

2.2.5   Calculating semantic values

Given a program p and an input d on which p does not loop, how can we find the corresponding output [[p]](d)? According to Definition 2.2.4 we have to find a store σ such that $C \vdash \sigma_0^p(d) \to \sigma$, and then look up Y's value in σ.

How do we solve the problem, given some C and store σ_0, of finding a σ such that $C \vdash \sigma_0 \to \sigma$? This can be done by applying the rules in Definition 2.2.3 as follows.

- If C has form C;D we first solve the problem of finding a σ' such that $C \vdash \sigma_0 \to \sigma'$, and then the problem of finding a σ'' such that $D \vdash \sigma' \to \sigma''$, and then we can use $\sigma = \sigma''$.

- If C has form X := E we calculate $\mathcal{E}[[E]]\sigma_0 = d$ and then σ is the same as σ_0 except that $X \mapsto d$.

- if C has form while E do C we calculate $\mathcal{E}[[E]]\sigma_0 = d$. If d is nil then σ is σ_0. Otherwise, first solve the problem of finding a σ' such that $C \vdash \sigma_0 \to \sigma'$, and then the problem of finding a σ'' such that while E do $C \vdash \sigma' \to \sigma''$, and then we can use $\sigma = \sigma''$.

2.3   Case commands

In this section we describe a shorthand notation, namely the *case command*. The shorthand is very useful later on, but also a bit complicated to explain in all details. Therefore, the section can be omitted on a first reading, and consulted later, when necessary.

2.3.1   An example of case commands

Case commands are very useful for writing programs that examine the structure of their input extensively.

Recall that in Pascal one can write something like

```
case X of
  1:  Y := X+1;        (* here X is 1 and Y becomes 2 *)
  2:  Y := 5;          (* here X is 2 and Y becomes 5 *)
```

The case commands in our setting are similar but more sophisticated, somewhat resembling those of ML [131, 122], but also having assignments as side-effects.

Example 2.3.1 The following (contrived) program reads a $d \in \mathbb{D}$. If $d = (d_1 . d_2)$ then the output is d_1, and otherwise the output is the atom a.

```
read X;
  case X of
    (V.W) ⇒   Y := V; (* here X is (d.e),    and Y becomes d *)
        Z ⇒   Y := a; (* here X is an atom, and Y becomes a *)
  write Y;
```

The meaning of the case construction is as follows. First X is evaluated to a value $d \in \mathbb{D}$. It is then tested whether d *matches* the *pattern* (V.W), i.e., whether $d = (d_1 . d_2)$ for some d_1, d_2. If so, d_1 and d_2 are *assigned* to V and W, respectively, and then Y := V is executed.

If the value did not match the pattern (V.W) then no assignment takes place, and it is tested whether it matches the next pattern Z. Any value matches a variable, so the value is assigned to Z and Y := a is executed.   □

As a more natural example, here is the reverse program expressed by means of a case command:

Example 2.3.2

```
read X;
  Y  := nil; GO := true;
  while GO do
    case X of
        nil ⇒   GO := false;
      (H.X) ⇒   Y  := cons H Y;
  write Y;
```

A destructive side-effect of matching.   The use of hd and tl has been replaced by the pattern matching in the case command. Notice in particular that the match against (H.X) *overwrites the previous value of X*, thus achieving the effect of X := tl X.

2.3.2   Syntax and semantics of case commands

The general syntax of case commands is:

```
case E of
    P1   ⇒   C1;
         ⋮
    Pn   ⇒   Cn;
```

where a pattern has the following form (where no variable is allowed to occur twice):

```
P   ::=   d            where d ∈ 𝔻 is any value
      |   Z            where Z is a variable
      |   (P1.P2)
```

The overall case command can be expressed as follows:

```
X:= E
if match(X,P1)   then   {assign(X,P1); C1;}   else
if match(X,P2)   then   {assign(X,P2); C2;}   else
                            ⋮
if match(X,Pn)   then   {assign(X,P1); Cn;}
```

where $match(X,P)$ is an expression that evaluates to true iff the value bound to X matches the pattern P, and $assign(X,P)$ is a sequence of assignments according to the matching of the value bound to X with P.

First we define exactly what it means that a value matches a pattern and what the corresponding assignments are, and then we show how to write code that realizes these definitions.

An $e \in \mathbb{D}$ matches a pattern P if

1. $e=(e_1.e_2)$ and $P=(P_1.P_2)$ where e_1 and e_2 match P_1 and P_2, respectively.
2. $P = Z$ for some variable Z.
3. $e=d$ and $P=d$ for some value d.

If $e \in \mathbb{D}$ matches P the following assignments arise as side effects.

1. Matching $e = (e_1.e_2)$ with $P=(P_1.P_2)$ gives rise to the sequence of assignments C1;C2, where C1 is the assigments arising from the matching of e_1 with P_1 and C2 is the assigments arising from the matching of e_2 with P_2.
2. Matching e with P=Z for some variable Z gives rise to Z := e.
3. Matching e=d with P=d for some value d gives rise to no assignments.

The expression *match*(E,P) defined below is such that for any σ, $\mathcal{E}[\![E]\!]\sigma$ matches P if and only if $\mathcal{E}[\![match(E,P)]\!]\sigma = \texttt{true}$.

$$
\begin{aligned}
match(\texttt{E, (P.Q))} \quad &= \quad \texttt{and} \quad \texttt{(cons? E)} \\
&\qquad\qquad \texttt{(and } match(\texttt{hd E, P})\ match(\texttt{tl E,Q))} \\
match(\texttt{E,Y}) \quad &=, \quad \texttt{true} \\
match(\texttt{E,d}) \quad &= \quad \texttt{=? E d}
\end{aligned}
$$

where `cons? E` evalutes to `true` iff E evaluates to an element of form `(d.e)` (this is easy to program). For instance,

$$match(\texttt{X, (d.Y))} = \texttt{and (cons? X) (and (=? (hd X) d) true)}$$

which evaluates to `true` iff X is bound to a an element of form `(d.f)` for some f.

We define *assign*(E,P) to be the sequence of assigments caused by matching the value of E with P.

$$
\begin{aligned}
assign(\texttt{E,Y}) \quad &= \quad \texttt{Y := E;} \\
assign(\texttt{E,d}) \quad &= \quad \texttt{SKIP;} \\
assign(\texttt{E,(P.Q))} \quad &= \quad \texttt{assign(hd E, P); assign(tl E,Q)}
\end{aligned}
$$

For instance,

$$assign(\texttt{X, (d.Y))} = \texttt{SKIP; Y:=tl X}$$

Hence, altogether

```
case E of
   (d.Y)  ⇒  C1;
   Z      ⇒  C2;
```

becomes

```
        X:= E
        if  (and (cons? X) (and (=? (hd X) d) true))
            then {SKIP; Y:=tl X; C1;} else
        if  true
            then {Z:=X; C2}
```

2.3.3   Case commands testing several expressions

We will also allow case commands that test several expressions:

```
case E, F of
    P₁, Q₁  ⇒  C₁;
              ⋮
    Pₙ, Qₙ  ⇒  Cₙ;
```

where in each clause both matchings must succeed for the corresponding command to be executed. This can be expressed by:

```
case (cons E F) of
    (P1.Q1)   ⇒    C1;
              ⋮
    (Pn.Qn)   ⇒    Cn;
```

2.4 Equality versus atomic equality

One could argue, as in Turing's analysis of section 1.2.1, against our use of the tree comparison operator =? on the grounds that it is not "atomic" enough. This can be countered by showing how to express general equality in terms of a test `atom=?`, which returns `true` if both arguments have the same *atom* as value, and `false` otherwise.

Case commands allow this to be done in a straightforward way. The following program assumes given input as a pair (d.e), and tests them for equality using only `atom=?`:

```
read X;
  D  := hd X;  E := tl X;
  GO := true;
  while GO do
    case D, E of
      ((D1.D2).D3),((E1.E2).E3) ⇒  D:=cons D1 (cons D2 D3);
                                    E:=cons E1 (cons E2 E3);
      ((D1.D2).D3),(   W   .E3) ⇒  Y:= false; GO:=false;
      (   V  .D3).((E1.E2).E3) ⇒  Y:= false; GO:=false;
      (   A  .D3),(   B   .E3) ⇒  if (atom=? A B)
                                    then D:=D3; E:=E3
                                    else Y:= false; GO:=false;
              A       ,     B    ⇒  Y:= atom=? A B; GO := false;
  write Y;
```

A few words on the correctness of this program are in order. First of all, termination is ensured by the fact that a certain number gets smaller every time the body of the while loop is executed; this is addressed in an exercise.

Assume that the values d and e have been assigned to program variables D and E. In the first clause of the case expression d and e have form $((d_1.d_2).d_3)$ and $((e_1.e_2).e_3)$. Then D and E are re-assigned values $(d_1.(d_2.d_3))$ and $(e_1.(e_2.e_3))$, and the loop is repeated. It is clear that the new values for D and E are equal iff the original ones were equal.

In the second clause e has form $(a.e_3)$ where a is an atom since the match in the first clause failed. Then the two values cannot be equal. Similarly for the third clause.

If execution enters the fourth clause d and e have form $(a.d_3)$ and $(b.e_3)$ where a and b are atoms. For d and e to be equal, a and b must be the same atom, and d and e must be equal.

In the fifth clause both values are atoms.

Exercises

2.1 Write a WHILE program that takes an input d and returns the list of atoms in d from left to right. For instance, with d=((a.b).(a.(c.d)) the program should yield (a b a c d) (i.e., (a.(b.(a.(c.(d.nil))))))).   □

2.2 Write a WHILE program that expects an input of the form $(a_1 \cdots a_n)$ (a list of atoms), and removes adjacent identical atoms. For instance, if the input is (a a a b b c a), the program should yield (a b c a).   □

2.3 Let $\sigma = \{X \mapsto (\text{nil.nil})\}$, C be while X do X:=X, and show that there is no σ' such that $C \vdash \sigma \to \sigma'$.   □

2.4 Given d = (a b c), and let p = read X; C; write Y be the reverse program from Subsection 2.1.3. Find a σ such that $C \vdash \sigma_0^p \to \sigma$. Explain in detail how σ is computed.   □

2.5 Prove that $[\![\text{reverse}]\!](d_1 \cdots d_n) = (d_n \cdots d_1)$. *Hint*: Proceed by induction on n.[5]   □

2.6 * Prove that the general program for testing equality in section 2.4 runs in time bounded by $k \cdot \min(|d|, e|)$, where d, e are the inputs and k is some constant. Estimate the value of this constant.

---
[5]See Subsection A.6 for a presentation of induction.

Hint: consider the weight $w : \mathbb{D} \to \mathbb{N}$ defined by:

$$w(\text{a}) \quad = \quad 1$$
$$w(\text{d}_1.\text{d}_2) \quad = \quad 2|\text{d}_1| + |\text{d}_2|$$

Show that $w(\text{d}) \leq 2|\text{d}|$ for all $\text{d} \in \mathbb{D}$, and show that the running time of the program is bounded by $l \cdot \min\{w(\text{d}), w(\text{e})\}$ for some constant l.   □

2.7 Prove that the size $|\text{d}|$ of a value $\text{d} \in \mathbb{D}$ can be computed in time $O(|\text{d}|)$. Hint: modify the program for testing equality in section 2.4, so it compares d against itself, and increases a counter nil^n each time a new " . " is found in d.   □

References

The data structure of WHILE is very similar to those of Scheme and LISP. The book by Kent Dybvig [39] is a good introduction to Scheme. The semantics of the WHILE language is in essence a natural semantics as one would find it in an introductory text on programming language semantics, e.g., the books by Schmidt [150] or by Nielson and Nielson [128].

Some other textbooks on computability and complexity use a language very similar to WHILE, but in most cases the data structure used is numbers, rather than trees [92, 156]. The author has used structured data as well as structured programs for teaching for several years at Copenhagen. The idea of restricting trees to the single atom nil was due to Klaus Grue [54]. The same WHILE language was used in article [80], which contains several results and definitions appearing later in this book.

3 Programs as Data Objects

In this chapter we are concerned with programs that take other programs as data. This requires that programs be part of the data domain; we show how to achieve this in section 3.2. We then study three kinds of programs that have other programs as input in sections 3.3–3.6: compilers, interpreters, and specializers. The chapter concludes with several simple examples of compilation in section 3.7.

A *compiler* is a program transformer which takes a program and translates it into an equivalent program, possibly in another language. An *interpreter* takes a program and its input data, and returns the result of applying the program to that input. A *program specializer*, like a compiler, is a program transformer but with two inputs. The first input is a program p that expects two inputs X,Y. The other input to the program specializer is a value s for X. The effect of the specializer is to construct a new program p_s which expects one input Y. The result of running p_s on input d, is to be the same as that of running p on inputs s and d.

The reason we emphasize these program types is that many proofs in computability theory involve constructing an interpreter a compiler, or a specializer.

First we define what constitutes a programming language in section 3.1.

3.1 Programming languages and simulation

Definition 3.1.1 A *programming language* L consists of

1. Two sets, L−*programs* and L−*data*;
2. A function $[\![\bullet]\!]^L : L-programs \rightarrow (L-data \rightarrow L-data_\perp)$

Here $[\![\bullet]\!]^L$ is L's *semantic function*, which associates with every L-program $p \in$ L−*programs* a corresponding partial function $[\![p]\!]^L : L-data \rightarrow L-data_\perp$. $\qquad\square$

We have already seen one example of a programmming language according to this definition, viz. the language WHILE, which had L−*data* = $\mathbb{D}$ and L−*programs* as in Definition 2.1.3. We shall see several programming languages in later chapters. As was the case for WHILE, we will drop L from the notation $[\![\bullet]\!]^L$ whenever L is clear from the context.

Imagine one has a computer with machine language L. How is it possible to run programs written in another language M?

We will answer this question in two steps. First, we say what it means that language L is able to simulate an arbitrary M program. (In effect, this says L is at least as *expressive* as M.) Second, we will show *how* L can simulate M, in two different ways: compilation and interpretation.

Definition 3.1.2 Suppose L-*data* = M-*data*. Language L *can simulate* language M if for every p ∈ L-*programs* there is an m-program q such that for all d ∈ L-*data* we have

$$[\![p]\!]^L(d) = [\![q]\!]^M(d)$$

Equivalently: L can simulate M iff there is a total function $f : $ L-*programs* → M-*programs* such that $[\![p]\!]^L = [\![f(p)]\!]^M$ for all L-*programs* p.

Language L *is equivalent to* language M, written L ≡ M, if language L and language M can simulate each other.   □

This definition expresses the facts that L and M can compute the same functions; but it does not assert the existence of any *constructive* way to obtain an M-program equivalent to a given L-program. The remainder of this chapter concerns how simulation may be done computably, by either translation (applying a compiling function) or by interpretation. First, however, we will need a way to regard programs as data objects.

3.2   A concrete syntax for WHILE programs

We have earlier given a syntax for WHILE-*programs* and WHILE-*data*. Suppose we want to give a WHILE program as input to another WHILE program. Presently this is not possible simply because elements of WHILE-*programs* are not objects in WHILE-*data*. Therefore we now give a *concrete syntax* for WHILE programs.

Definition 3.2.1 Let $A = \{a_1, \ldots, a_n\}$ be a finite set of atoms with $n \geq 10$, and let the names ":=," ";," "while," "var," "quote," "cons," "hd," "tl," "=?," "nil" denote 10 distinct elements of A. The concrete syntax p̱ of WHILE$_A$ program p is defined by the map shown in Figure 3.1[1]:

$$\underline{\bullet} : \text{WHILE}-programs \rightarrow \text{WHILE}-data$$

---

[1]Recall that Vars = $\{V_1, V_2, \ldots\}$. While we often use X and Y to denote arbitrary elements of Vars, it is convenient in the definition of ● to know the index of the variable to be coded. We assume that no program contains a variable with higher index than its output variable.

where we use the list and number notation of Subsections 2.1.5–2.1.6.   □

$$
\begin{array}{lcl}
\underline{\texttt{read V}_i\texttt{; C; write V}_j} & = & \texttt{((var i) }\underline{\texttt{C}}\texttt{ (var j))} \\
\\
\underline{\texttt{C;D}} & = & \texttt{(; }\underline{\texttt{C}}\texttt{ }\underline{\texttt{D}}\texttt{)} \\
\underline{\texttt{while E do C}} & = & \texttt{(while }\underline{\texttt{E}}\texttt{ }\underline{\texttt{C}}\texttt{)} \\
\underline{\texttt{V}_i\texttt{:=E}} & = & \texttt{(:= (var i) }\underline{\texttt{E}}\texttt{)} \\
\\
\underline{\texttt{V}_i} & = & \texttt{(var i)} \\
\underline{\texttt{d}} & = & \texttt{(quote d)} \\
\underline{\texttt{cons E F}} & = & \texttt{(cons }\underline{\texttt{E}}\texttt{ }\underline{\texttt{F}}\texttt{)} \\
\underline{\texttt{hd E}} & = & \texttt{(hd }\underline{\texttt{E}}\texttt{)} \\
\underline{\texttt{tl E}} & = & \texttt{(tl }\underline{\texttt{E}}\texttt{)} \\
\underline{\texttt{=? E F}} & = & \texttt{(=? }\underline{\texttt{E}}\texttt{ }\underline{\texttt{F}}\texttt{)}
\end{array}
$$

Figure 3.1: Mapping WHILE programs to their concrete syntax.

For example, if X and Y are the variables V_1 and V_2, respectively, then the program written as

```
read X;
  Y := nil;
  while X do
      Y := cons (hd X) Y;
      X := tl X
  write Y;
```

would be translated to the value in $\mathbb{D}$:

```
(
  (var 1)
  (; (:= ((var 2) (quote nil)))
     (while (var 1)
        (; (:= (var 2) (cons (hd (var 1)) (var 2)))
           (:= (var 1) (tl (var 1)))))))
  (var 2)
)
```

For readability we will continue to use the original syntax when writing programs, but it should be understood that whenever a program p is input to another, it is the corresponding concrete syntax program p̲ that we have in mind.

Analogous ideas can be used for other languages L as well, though encoding programs as data is harder if L-*data* is, as in many texts, the set of natural numbers.

3.3   Compilation

Suppose we are given three programming languages:

- A *source language* S,
- A *target language* T, and
- An *implementation language* L.

A compiler comp $\in$ L-*programs* from S to T has one input: a *source program* p $\in$ S-*programs* to be compiled. Running the compiler with input p (on an L-machine) must produce another program target, such that running target on a T-machine has the same effect as running p on an S-machine.

This is easiest to describe (and do) if the source and target languages have the same data representations S-*data* = T-*data*, as one can simply demand that $[\![\text{source}]\!]^S(\text{d}) = [\![\text{target}]\!]^T(\text{d})$ for all inputs d.

3.3.1   Compiling without change of data representation

Definition 3.3.1 Suppose

- S$-data$ = T$-data$ = L$-data$;
- S$-programs \cup$ T$-programs \subseteq$ L$-data$.[2]

Then:

1. A total function $f : L-data \to L-data$ is a *compiling function* from S to T iff for all p $\in$ S-*programs*: $f(\text{p}) \in$ T-*programs*, and $[\![\text{p}]\!]^S \simeq [\![f(\text{p})]\!]^T$.
2. An L-program comp is a *compiler* from S to T if $[\![\text{comp}]\!]^L$ is a compiling function. □

Note that we carefully distinguish between a compiling function, and a compiler, i.e., a compiling program. Spelled out, a compiling function f satisfies for all p $\in$ S$-programs$ and all d $\in$ S$-data$:

$$[\![\text{p}]\!]^S(\text{d}) = [\![f(\text{p})]\!]^T(\text{d})$$

---

[2]In other words: languages S and T have concrete syntax where programs are L-data elements.

If language T *can simulate* language S, then by definition there exists a total compiling function from S to T. On the other hand, a *compiler* comp is an L-program whose meaning is a compiling function, and so necessarily computable; it satisfies for every p ∈ S—*programs* and every d ∈ S—*data* = T—*data*,

$$[\![p]\!]^S(d) = [\![[\![comp]\!]^L(p)]\!]^T(d)$$

(where both sides may be undefined, see Subsection A.3.3).

3.3.2　TI-diagrams

We use the symbol

$$= \{ \text{comp} \mid \forall p \in S\text{—}programs, \forall d \in S\text{—}data.$$
$$[\![p]\!]^S(d) = [\![[\![comp]\!]^L(p)]\!]^T(d)\}$$

to denote the set of compilers from S to T written in L. Suppose we are given a collection of S-*programs*, nature unspecified. This set can be denoted by

to denote the set of compilers from S to T written in L. Suppose we are given a collection of S-*programs*, nature unspecified. This set can be denoted by

If we also have a compiler comp from source language S to target language T, written in L, then we can perform translations, as described by the diagram:

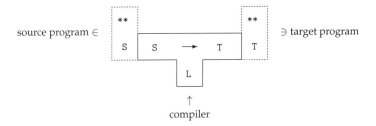

In this book compilation will most often be described by informal constructions, and if such diagrams are used, we will replace implementation language L above by H, indicating "human." In fact, all of our programming language translations could be automated

in principle, but going to that level of detail would be more appropriate to a programming language course than to a theory course.

On the other hand interpreters, under the name *universal programs*, will be treated more formally. They play a central role in theorems of both complexity and computability theory. Since their structure and running times are so important, several interpreters will be given in considerable detail by programs.

3.3.3   Compiling with change of data representation

In order to compare computation by machines with different sorts of input/output data we define one way that a (possibly partial) function on one data set can be represented by a function on another set. This is a natural generalization of the concept of "commuting diagram" to the case where some arrows denote partial functions.

Definition 3.3.2 Given sets A, B, a *coding* from A to B is a one-to-one total function $c : A \to B$. A partial function $g : B \to B_\perp$ *implements* partial function $f : A \to A_\perp$ relative to coding c if for all $a \in A$

1. $f(a) \neq \perp$ implies $g(c(a)) = c(f(a))$
2. $f(a) = \perp$ implies $g(c(a)) = \perp$ □

Intuitively: in the following diagram, whenever an instance $f : a \mapsto f(a)$ of its topmost arrow is defined, there exists a corresponding defined instance $g : c(a) \mapsto c(f(a))$ of the bottom arrow. Further, any undefined instance $f : a \mapsto \perp$ of its topmost arrow corresponds to an undefined instance $g : c(a) \mapsto \perp$ of the bottom arrow. The behaviour of g on values outside the range of c is irrelevant to the definition.

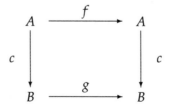

Definition 3.3.3 Suppose

- given a coding $c :$ S-*data* $\to$ T-*data*;
- S$-programs \cup$ T$-programs \subseteq$ L$-data$.

1. $f : L\text{-}data \to L\text{-}data$ is a *compiling function relative to coding c* if for every $p \in$ S-*programs*, $[\![f(p)]\!]^T$ implements $f(p) \in T\text{-}programs\ [\![p]\!]^S$ relative to c.

2. An L-program comp is a *compiler* from S to T *with respect to coding c* if $[\![comp]\!]^L$ is a compiling function relative to c. □

The first part of this definition amounts to the generalized commutativity of the following diagram.

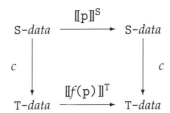

3.4   Interpretation

Suppose we are given two programming languages:

- An *implementation language* L, and
- A *source language* S.

An interpreter int $\in$ L-*programs* for S-*programs* takes an input (p.d), where $p \in$ S-*programs* is a program and $d \in$ S-*data* its input data. Running the interpreter with input (p.d) on an L-machine must produce the same result as running p with input d on an S-machine. Typically the time to run p interpretively is significantly larger than to run it directly; we will return to this topic later.

A language S such that S-*programs* $\subseteq$ S-*data* will henceforth be said to have *concrete syntax*. Also, if in language S it holds that S-*data* $\times$ S-*data* $\subseteq$ S-*data*, then we shall say that S has *pairing*.

3.4.1   Interpretation without change of data representation

Definition 3.4.1 Assume that language S has concrete syntax and pairing, and that L-*data* = S-*data*. Then:

1. A partial function $i : L-data \rightarrow L-data_\perp$ is an *interpreting function* of S if for all $p \in S-programs$ and $d \in S-data$:

$$[\![p]\!]^S(d) = i(p.d)$$

2. L-program int is an *interpreter* of S in L if $[\![int]\!]^L$ is an interpreting function of S.

□

We use the symbol

$$\boxed{\begin{array}{c} S \\ L \end{array}} = \{\, \text{int} \mid \forall p, d.\ [\![p]\!]^S(d) = [\![\text{int}]\!]^L(p.d)\,\}$$

to denote the set of all interpreters for S written in L.

3.4.2   An interpretion example: straightline Boolean programs

In this example a source program is a linear sequence of commands built from true and Boolean variables $X_0, \dots, X_n$ using boolean operations "and" and "not." Informal syntax is defined by the following grammar:

```
Program   ::=   read X₀; I₁ I₂··· Iₘ; write X₀
I         ::=   Xᵢ := true | Xᵢ := Xⱼ and Xₖ | Xᵢ := not Xⱼ
```

Expressed in concrete syntax, a program can be written as an element of $\mathbb{D}_A$ (where :=true, :=and, :=not are atoms in A) with the following grammar. We use the number notation nil^i for $i \in \mathbb{N}$ from Definition 2.1.8).

```
Program   ::=   (I₁; I₂;···; Iₘ)
I         ::=   (:=true X) | (:=and X Y Z) | (:=not X Y)
X, Y, Z   ::=   nil⁰ | nil¹ | nil² | ...
```

The interpreter body

```
read PD;                   (* Input = program and value of X0    *)
P := hd PD; D := tl PD;    (* Extract program and data from PD    *)
Store := update 0 D nil;   (* Initialize store: X0 equals D       *)

while P do
  { case hd P of           (* First instruction of remainder of P *)

    (:=true X)         ⇒ Store := update X true Store;

    (:=and X Y Z)      ⇒ V := (lookup Y Store) and (lookup Z Store);
                          Store :=  update X V Store;

    (:=not X Y)        ⇒ V := not (lookup Y Store);
                          Store :=  update X V Store;

    P := tl P };           (* Remove first instruction            *)

V := lookup 0 Store;
write V
```

Explanation: The store $\sigma = [X_0 \mapsto d_0, \cdots, X_n \mapsto d_n]$ will be represented as a list $(d_0 \ d_1 \cdots d_n)$. Two auxiliary functions are detailed in the next section: lookup, which finds the value d_i, if given the store and i as arguments; and update, which assigns a new value to variable X_i.

The interpreter first initializes the store by binding the input value d to variable X_0 using update. It then repeatedly dispatches on the form of the first instruction in the remainder P of the program, and performs lookups or updates to implement the language's three command forms. After the case command, P is reassigned to what follows after the current instruction; so P decreases until empty.

Once the last command is executed, the value of X_0 is looked up in the final store and written out.

Auxiliary functions for storing and fetching

Suppose $(d_0 \ldots d_n)$ is a list of length $n + 1$, and j denotes a numeral j between 0 and n. How do we perform the assignment X:=d_j? This is done by the following sequence of commands, where the GOTO variable J contains the numeral j, and Store contains the list $(d_0 \ldots d_n)$. Note that after execution of the commands, Store and J have their original values.

```
T := Store;        (* X := lookup J Store *)
K := J;
while K do         (* Remove the first i elements from a copy of Store *)
  K := pred K;
  T := tl T;
X := hd T;
```

Conversely, given a list $(d_0 \ldots d_n)$, a value d, and a number j, how do we compute the list $(d_0 \ldots d_{j-1} \, d \, d_{j+1} \ldots d_n)$? This can be done by the following program, which assumes that the list is in `Store`, the number is in J, and the value d is in V.

```
T := nil;                   (* Store := update J V Store       *)
K := J;
while K do                  (* Net effect is to set            *)
  T := cons (hd Store) T;   (* T     = (dj-1 ... d0) and        *)
  Store := tl Store;        (* Store = (dj dj+1 ... dn)         *)
  K := tl K;
Store := cons V (tl Store); (* Store = (d dj+1 ... dn)          *)
while T do                  (* Repace d0 d1 ... dj-1 on Store *)
  Store := cons (hd T) Store;
  T := tl T;
```

3.5 Ways to combine compiler and interpreter diagrams

Diagrams such as the preceding one, and more complex ones with several interpreter blocks, compiler blocks, or other blocks put together, can be thought of as describing one or more "computer runs." For example, suppose a Lisp system is processed interpretively by an interpreter written in Sun RISC machine code (call this M). The machine code itself is processed by the central processor (call this C) so two levels of interpretation are involved, as described by Figure 3.2.

Assume that certain languages are *directly executable*; typically a machine language T, or an implementation language L for which one already has a compiler or interpreter available. Then a *composite diagram* composed of several TI-diagrams is defined to be directly executable if and only if every "bottom-most" diagram in it is implemented in an executable language.

In order to be meaningful a diagram must be "well-formed," that is satisfy some natural constraints:

1. All languages appearing bottom-most in the diagram must be executable (either

Figure 3.2: Diagram of program execution with two interpretation levels.

because they are machine languages, or because implementations are known to exist even though not shown in the diagram).

2. Let us define language L to *match* language M, written L ⊑ M, to mean that any L-program is also an M-program, and has the same semantics. A special case: L ⊑ L, that is, any language matches itself.

3. The second constraint is that in any subdiagram of either of the following two forms:

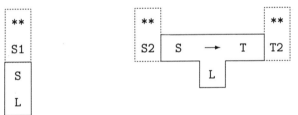

must satisfy:

$$S1 \sqsubseteq S, S2 \sqsubseteq S \text{ and } T \sqsubseteq T2$$

3.6   Specialization

Suppose again that we are given three programming languages:

- A *source language* S,
- A *target language* T, and

- An *implementation language* L.

A *program specializer* is given an S-program p together with part of its input data, s. Its effect is to construct a T-program p_s which, when given p's remaining input d, will yield the same result that p would have produced given both inputs. We leave open the possibility that S and T are different languages, although we will require S-*data*=T-*data*, i.e., we only consider specialization without change in data representation.

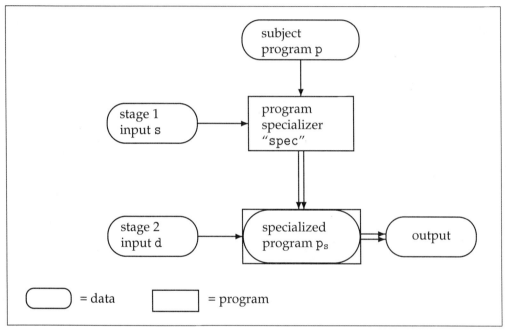

Figure 3.3: A program specializer.

Thus we may think of specialization as a *staging transformation*. Program p's computation is not performed all at once on (s.d), but rather in two stages. The first stage is a program transformation which, given p and s, yields as output a specialized program p_s. In the second stage, program p_s is run with the single input d—see Figure 3.3.[3] The specialized program p_s is correct if, when run with any value d for p's remaining input

---

[3]Notation: data values are in ovals, and programs are in boxes. The specialized program p_s is first considered as data and then considered as code, whence it is enclosed in both. Further, single arrows indicate program input data, and double arrows indicate outputs. Thus spec has two inputs while p_s has only one; and p_s is the output of spec.

data, it yields the same result that p would have produced when given both s and the remaining input data d.

Definition 3.6.1 Assume that S has pairing, that S and T have concrete syntax, and that $S-data = L-data = T-data$. Then:

1. A total function $f : L-data \rightarrow L-data$ is a *specializing function* from S to T iff for all $p \in S-programs$ and $d \in S-data$ $f(\texttt{p.d}) \in T-programs$ and

$$[\![\texttt{p}]\!]^{S}(\texttt{s.d}) = [\![f(\texttt{p.s})]\!]^{T}(\texttt{d})$$

2. L-program spec is a *specializer* from S to T if $[\![\texttt{spec}]\!]^{L}$ is a specializing function. Specifically,

$$[\![\texttt{p}]\!]^{S}(\texttt{s.d}) = [\![[\![\texttt{spec}]\!]^{L}(\texttt{p.s})]\!]^{T}(\texttt{d})$$

$\Box$

Theorem 3.6.2 Language L can simulate language M if either there exists a compiler from L to M, or if M has a specializer, and there exists an interpreter for L written in M.

Proof. This is immediate if there is an L-to-M compiler comp written in T, since function $[\![\texttt{comp}]\!]^{T}$ satisfies Definition 3.1.2. Further, if L can be interpreted by M, there exists an L-to-M compiler by Exercise 3.1. $\Box$

3.7 Some simple examples of compilation

In this section we consider some fragments of WHILE and show by means of translations that the fragments are as expressive, in a certain sense, as the whole language.

The first section describes a restriction on the size of expressions. The second section describes a restriction on the number of variables a program may use, and the third section restricts the set $\mathbb{D}_A$ to trees built from the single atom nil.

3.7.1   Restriction to one operator

Definition 3.7.1 Restrict the syntax of WHILE programs as follows arriving at WHILE^{1op}.

```
E  ::=  X              C  ::=  X := E
     |  d                   |  C1 ; C2
     |  cons X Y            |  while X do C
     |  hd X         P  ::=  read X; C; write Y
     |  tl X
     |  =? X Y
```

Note that in assignments the expression may contain at most one operator, and in while loops the tested expression must contain no operators at all. The semantics and running times is the same as for WHILE programs.

Any WHILE program p can be translated into a WHILE^{1op} program with the same semantics. The problem is to break complex expressions and while tests into simple ones. This can be done systematically introducing new variables and assignment statements.

Example 3.7.2 The program

```
read XY;
   X := hd XY;
   Y := tl XY;
   while (hd X) do
      Y := cons (hd X) (cons (tl Y) (hd Y));
      X := tl X ;
   write Y
```

can be translated into:

```
read XY;
   X := hd XY;
   Y := tl XY;
   Z := hd X;
   while Z do
      A := hd X;
      B := tl Y;
      C := hd Y;
      D := cons B C;
      Y := cons A D;
      X := tl X;
      Z := hd X;
   write Y
```

We state the general translation using the informal syntax, but it could clearly be expressed via the concrete syntax introduced earlier.

Definition 3.7.3 Given a program p, construct the transformed program p̲ by applying the rules given in Figure 3.4 recursively. Variables Y, Y1, Y2 are fresh variables, chosen anew every time a rule containing them is used.

```
read X; C; write Y  =  read X; C; write Y


C1 ; C2             =  C1; C2
while E do C         =  Y:=E; {while Z do C; Y:=E}


Z:=Y                =  Z:=Y
Z:=d                =  Z:=d
Z:=cons E1 E2        =  Y1:=E1; Y2:=E2; Z:=cons Y1 Y2
Z:=hd E             =  Y:=E; Z:=hd Y
Z:=tl E             =  Y:=E; Z:=tl Y
Z:= (=? E1 E2)       =  Y1:=E1; Y2:=E2; Z:= (=? Y1 Y2)
```

Figure 3.4: Transformation rules.

Proposition 3.7.4 _ is a compiling function from WHILE to WHILE^{1op}.

Proof. See the Exercises.

3.7.2   Restriction to one variable

WHILE^{1var} is the same language as WHILE except that the language only contains one variable X, which is also used for both input and output. Any WHILE program can be translated into a WHILE^{1var} program with the same semantics.

Example 3.7.5 Recall the following program to reverse a list:

```
read X;
  Y := nil;
  while X do
    Y := cons (hd X) Y;
    X := tl X;
write Y
```

The program has two variables. To convert it into an equivalent 1-variable program "pack" the two into one A=(cons X Y). Whenever we need X in some expression we take (hd A), and whenever we need Y we take (tl A). Whenever we wish to assign E to X we assign cons E (tl A) to A, and whenever we wish to assign E to Y we assign cons (hd A) E to A. We thus arrive at the following program.

```
read A;
  A := cons A nil;          (* now A = cons X Y *)
  while (hd A) do
    A := cons (hd A) (cons (hd (hd A)) (tl A));
    A := cons (tl (hd A)) (tl A);
  A:= hd A;                 (* write X *)
write A
```

For the general translation we will pack the variables X1, ..., Xn together by cons'ing to form a list (X1 ⋯ Xn). More efficient translated programs could be obtained by packing into balanced trees instead of lists.

Definition 3.7.6 Define $tl^0E = E$ and $tl^{i+1}E = tl^i(tl\ E)$. Given a program p with input variables X1,..., Xn apply the transformation $\underline{p}$ defined in Figure 3.5.

```
read X1; C; write X2  =  read A; A := cons A nil; C;
                         A := hd (tl X); write A


C1 ; C2               =  C1 ; C2
while E do C           =  while E do C
Xi := E               =  A := cons T₁(...(cons Tₙnil)...)
                         where Tᵢ = E and Tⱼ = Xj, j ≠ i.


Xi                    =  hd (tl^{i-1}A)
d                     =  d
cons E1 E2            =  cons E1 E2
hd E                  =  hd E
tl E                  =  tl E
=? E1 E2              =  =? E1 E2
```

Figure 3.5: Transformation rules.

Proposition 3.7.7 _ is a compiling function from WHILE to WHILE^{1var}.

3.7.3 Restriction to one atom

WHILE^{1atom} is the same language as WHILE except that the set $\mathbb{D}$ contains only the atom nil. Any WHILE program can be translated into a WHILE^{1atom} program with essentially the same semantics, but operating on encoded data.

For this we need to encode, as elements in $\mathbb{D}_{\{nil\}}$, arbitrary values from the set $\mathbb{D}_{\{nil,a_2...a_m\}}$, where m is a fixed number and $nil = a_1$. More precisely, we seek a simple injective mapping from $\mathbb{D}_{\{nil,a_2...a_m\}}$ to $\mathbb{D}_{\{nil\}}$. This can be done as follows. Recall that $nil^0 = nil$ and $nil^{i+1} = (nil.nil^i)$. Then define the coding:

$$
\begin{aligned}
c(a_i) &= nil^{i-1} && \text{For } i = 1,\dots,m \\
c(d_1.d_2) &= ((nil.nil).(c(d_1).c(d_2)))
\end{aligned}
$$

Atom nil is mapped to nil. The remaining elements $d \in \mathbb{D}$ are mapped to pairs (s.v), where s codes the structure of d, and v codes the value of d. Specifically, for atoms s is nil and for pairs s is (nil.nil). For atom a_i, v is the list nil^{i-1} of $i-1$ nil's. For pairs, v is the pair of the codings. Clearly, this encoding is injective, and $|c(d)| \leq k \cdot |d|$ for any $d \in \mathbb{D}$, where $k = \max\{2m-1,5\}$,

To obtain a general translation of programs from WHILE to programs of WHILE^{1atom} (such that the translated programs simulate the semantics of the original programs) we need to devise operations on $\mathbb{D}_A$ simulating operations hd, tl, cons, =? on $\mathbb{D}_A$.

It is easy to give programs hdrep, tlrep, consrep of hd, tl such that

$$
\begin{aligned}
[\![hdrep]\!](c((d1.d2))) &= c(d1) \\
[\![hdrep]\!](nil) &= nil \\
[\![tlrep]\!](c((d1.d2))) &= c(d2) \\
[\![tlrep]\!](nil) &= nil \\
[\![consrep]\!](c(d1).c(d2)) &= c(d1.d2)
\end{aligned}
$$

which run in constant time (see the Exercises.)

For an operation atom=?rep simulating atom=? one first checks whether the two arguments are both representations of atoms; this can be done in constant time. Then one uses the program =? from section 2.4. Since encoded atoms are bounded in size by a certain number depending on the number of atoms in A and since =? runs in time proportional to the smaller of its two arguments, the time to execute atom=?rep E1 E2 is constant for a given alphabet A.

We can now define a general translation on programs as follows:

Definition 3.7.8 Given a program p with input variables X1,..., Xn apply the transformation p̲ defined in Figure 3.6.

```
read X; C; write Y  =  read X; C; write Y

C1 ; C2             =  C1 ; C2
while E do C         =  while E do C
Xi:=E               =  Xi:=E


Xi                   =  Xi
d                    =  e  where e = c(d)
cons E1 E2           =  cons (nil.nil) (cons E1 E2)
hd E                 =  hdrep E
tl E                 =  tlrep E
atom=? E1 E2         =  atom=?rep E1 E2
```

Figure 3.6: Transformation rules.

Proposition 3.7.9 _ is a compiling function from WHILE to WHILE^{1atom} relative to the coding c.

Proof. See the Exercises.

Exercises

3.1 Show how one can compile from S–*programs* to T–*programs*, if given an S-interpreter written in L and a L-specializer. State appropriate assumptions concerning the relationships between various input and output domains.   □

3.2 Prove Proposition 3.7.4.   □

3.3 Prove Proposition 3.7.7.   □

3.4 Prove Proposition 3.7.9.   □

3.5

1. Program `hdrep`, `tlrep`, `consrep` mentioned in section 3.7.3, for $m = 2$.

2. Try to rewrite your programs so that they use a single variable both for input, for output, and internally in the program. For `consrep` assume that the two inputs d_1 and d_2 are fed to the program in the form $(d_1 . d_2)$. □

3.6 Can one compile an arbitrary `WHILE` program into an equivalent with only one variable *and* one operator per command, i.e., can one combine the results of Propositions 3.7.4 and 3.7.7?

A partial answer: explain what happens when these two compilations are combined. A full answer: establish that such a compilation is possible (by a construction) or impossible (by a proof). □

References

The practical and theoretical study of compilers and interpreters constitutes a branch of Computer Science. An introduction to interpreters can be found in [88]. A good introduction to compiler technology can be found in [3]. The compiler and interpreter diagrams are due to Bratman [17]. As mentioned, interpretation, compilation, and specialization all play important roles in computability and complexity theory, and we will say more about all three types of programs in due course.

The practical study of specializers is yet another branch of Computer Science, also called *partial evaluation*, see e.g. the textbook [84] or survey article [82].

Part II

Introduction to Computability

4 Self-interpretation: Universal Programs for WHILE and I

Our first example of a universal program is an interpreter for WHILE written in WHILE, developed in section 4.1. We then develop a universal program for a small subset called I, in which programs have only one variable and one atom, in section 4.2. Both of these self-interpreters will be used extensively in the remainder of the book.

4.1 A universal program for the WHILE language

We first develop an interpreter in WHILE for WHILE programs that use only a single variable, and then modify this interpreter so as to interpret the full WHILE language.

In this section we assume that the set $\mathbb{D}_A$ is such that A in addition to the 10 elements "nil," "quote," "var," "tl," "hd," "cons," ":=," ";," "while," "=?" mentioned in Definition 3.2.1, also contains 6 members denoted by the names "dohd," "dotl," "docons," "doasgn," "dowh," "do=?."

4.1.1 Interpretation of a subset of WHILE in WHILE

Proposition 4.1.1 There exists a WHILE program u1var such that $[\![\text{u1var}]\!](\text{p.d}) = [\![\text{p}]\!](\text{d})$ for all $\text{p} \in$ WHILE-programs with exactly one variable and all $\text{d} \in$ WHILE-*data*.

$\square$

Proof. The overall structure of the program is given in the following program fragment where STEP is the sequence of commands in Figure 4.1 (explained below). Exercise 4.1 is to prove correctness of the algorithm.

```
read PD;              (* Input (p.d)                        *)
 P   := hd PD;        (* P = ((var 1) c (var 1))            *)
 C   := hd (tl P)     (* C = c           program code is c  *)
 Cd := cons C nil;    (* Cd = (c.nil), Code to execute is c *)
 St := nil;           (* St = nil,     Stack empty          *)
 Vl := tl PD;         (* Vl = d        Initial value of var.*)
 while Cd do STEP;    (* do while there is code to execute  *)
 write Vl;
```

Input is a program in the abstract syntax of Definition 3.2.1. (Input and output are through the first and only variable, hence the (var 1)). The program uses three variables: Cd, St, Vl. The first is the *code stack* holding the code to be executed. Intially this is the whole program. The second is the *value stack* holding intermediate results. Finally, the third variable is the *store* holding the current value of the single program variable. Initially this is d, the input to program p.

The effect of the sequence of commands STEP, programmed using the case-expression shorthand notation, is to test what the next instruction in Cd is and update variables Cd, St, Vl accordingly. Recall the SKIP and cons* notations from section 2.1.7.

```
    case Cd, St of

((quote D).Cd),                St    ⇒  St:= cons D St;
((var 1).Cd),                  St    ⇒  St:= cons Vl St;
((hd E).Cd),                   St    ⇒  Cd:= cons* E dohd Cd;
(dohd.Cd),                  (T.St)   ⇒  St:= cons (hd T) St;
((tl E).Cd),                   St    ⇒  Cd:= cons* E dotl Cd;
(dotl.Cd),                  (T.St)   ⇒  St:= cons (tl T) St;
((cons E1 E2).Cd),             St    ⇒  Cd:= cons* E1 E2 docons Cd;
(docons.Cd),             (U.(T.St))  ⇒  St:= cons (cons U T) St;
((=? E1 E2).Cd),               St    ⇒  Cd:= cons* E1 E2 do=? Cd;
(do=?.Cd),               (U.(T.St))  ⇒  St:= cons (=? U T) St;
((; C1 C2).Cd),                St    ⇒  Cd:= cons* C1 C2 Cd;
((:= (var 1) E).Cd),           St    ⇒  Cd:= cons* E doasgn Cd;
(doasgn.Cd),                (W.St)   ⇒  Vl:= W;
((while E C).Cd),              St    ⇒  Cd:=cons* E dowh (while E C) Cd;
(dowh.((while E C).Cd)),(nil.St) ⇒  SKIP;
(dowh.((while E C).Cd)),    (D.St)   ⇒  Cd:= cons* C (while E C) Cd;
   nil,                        St    ⇒  SKIP;
```

Figure 4.1: The STEP Macro.

Expression evaluation is based on the following *invariant*. Suppose that, at some point, p evaluates expression E in store $[X \mapsto d]$ to e, i.e., $\mathcal{E}[\![E]\!][X \mapsto d] = e$. Then initially the values of Cd, St, Vl in ulvar will be (E.CC), S, d, i.e., E will be on top of the code stack. Then after a number of iterations of STEP, the new values will be CC, (e.S), d, i.e., the code for E will be popped from the code stack, and the value of E will be pushed to the value stack. The store remains unchanged.

For example if the three values are ((hd E).C), S, and d, then after one iteration of STEP the values are (E.(dohd.C)), S, d. This signifies that first the expression E is to be evaluated, and then afterwards the hd must be taken. By the invariant, after a number of iterations of STEP the values are (dohd.C), (e.S), and d where e is the value of E in the given store. Supposing e = (e1.e2), after one more iteration the values are C, (e1.S), d. So the overall effect, starting from the original values ((hd E).C), S, d has been to calculate the value of hd E and push it to the value stack while popping the expression from the code stack.

Command execution is based on the following similar invariant. Suppose that, at some point, p executes command C in store $[X \mapsto d]$ arriving at a new store $[X \mapsto e]$, i.e., $C \vdash [X \mapsto d] \rightarrow [X \mapsto e]$. Assume the values of Cd, St, Vl are (C.CC), S, d, i.e., C is on top of the code stack. Then after a number of iterations of STEP, the new values will be CC, S, e, i.e., the code for C will be popped from the code stack, and the new value for X will have been saved in the store. □

It is not hard to see that the evaluation of any expression terminates in a fixed number of steps; the only source of possible nontermination is in the rules implementing the while command. This is addressed in Exercise 4.2.

4.1.2 Interpretation of the full WHILE language

We now show how the interpreter u1var for single-variable programs can be extended to accomodate programs using several variables. For this it is useful to have available certain techniques which we first develop. The construction is straightforward and uses the lookup and update functions from section 3.4.2.

Theorem 4.1.2 There exists a WHILE program u such that for all $p \in$ WHILE-*programs* and all $d \in$ WHILE-*data*$[\![p]\!](d) = [\![u]\!](p.d)$. □

Proof. The overall structure of the program is given in the program fragment of Figure 4.2, where STEP is similar to the earlier command sequence.

In contrast to Vl in the preceding version, Vl is now a list of k variables. Initially all these are bound to nil, except the input variable V_i which is bound to the input d. The output is now the value of variable V_j at the end of execution. The new version of STEP is identical to the preceding one, except for the cases:

```
read PD;                            (* Input (p.d)                  *)
 Pgm := hd PD;                      (* p = ((var i) c (var j))      *)
 D   := tl PD;                      (* D = d  (input value)         *)
 I   := hd (tl (hd Pgm))            (* I = i  (input variable)      *)
 J   := hd (tl (hd (tl (tl Pgm)))); (* J = j  (output variable)     *)
 C   := hd (tl Pgm))                (* C = c, program code          *)
 Vl  := update I D nil    (* (var i) initially d, others nil        *)
 Cd  := cons C nil;       (* Cd = (c.nil), Code to execute is c     *)
 St  := nil;              (* St = nil, computation Stack empty      *)
 while Cd do STEP;        (* do while there is code to execute      *)
 Out := lookup J Vl       (* Output is the value of (var j)         *)
 write Out;
```

Figure 4.2: Universal program u.

```
((var J).Cd),           St   ⇒   X := lookup J Vl; St:=cons X St;
((:= (var K) E).Cd),    St   ⇒   Cd := cons* E doasgn K Cd;
(doasgn.(K.Cd)),        (T.St) ⇒ Vl := update K T Vl;              □
```

The program u is called a *self-interpreter* in programming language theory, because it interprets the same language as it is written in. In computability theory u is called a *universal program*, since it is capable of simulating any arbitrary program p.

4.2   A universal program for the I language: one atom and one variable

Definition 4.2.1 The syntax of I is given by grammar of Figure 4.3, where $d \in \mathbb{D}$. Program semantics is as in section 2.2.   □

Recall the interpreter u1var for one-variable WHILE programs constructed in section 4.1.1. We obtain a universal program for I by applying methods from section 3.7 to u1var.

Program u1var is not a self-interpreter for I, since it itself uses more than one variable (such as Cd and St) and more than one atom. We now describe how a 1-variable, 1-atom universal program can be built, using the example compilations from section 3.7.

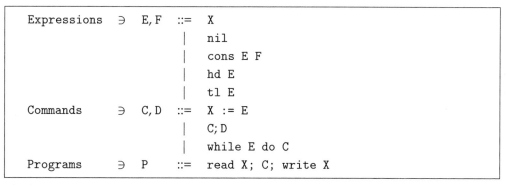

Figure 4.3: Syntax of the I language.

First, to avoid the problem that ulvar uses more than one atom, we code its non-nil atoms using only nil.

The atoms used, all visible in the STEP macro of Figure 4.1, are the following: quote, var, ..., while, needed to express the concrete syntax of WHILE-programs, together with several auxiliaries: dohd, dotl, ..., dowh used internally by the interpreter.

Definition 4.2.2 Suppose given is an arbitrary I-program p, whose concrete syntax regarded as a WHILE-program as in Definition 3.2.1 is p^{WHILE}. The *concrete syntax of* p *regarded as an I-program* is, by definition, $p^I = c(p^{WHILE})$, where c is the one-to-one encoding of $\mathbb{D}_A$ into $\mathbb{D}$ given in section 3.7.3.

Lemma 4.2.3 There exists a WHILE program ilatom which is an interpreter for I. Program ilatom uses only the atom nil, and the concrete syntax of Definition 4.2.2.

Proof. Construct ilatom from ulvar by the following modification: Replace any atom *at* among quote, ..., while, ..., dohd, ..., dowh appearing in the STEP macro by $c(at)$. Let ilatom be identical to ulvar, but with the modified STEP macro.

The net effect of ilatom on p^I and program input data $d \in \mathbb{D} = \mathbb{D}_{\{nil\}}$ will be the same (aside from encoding) as that of ulvar on p^{WHILE} and input $d \in \mathbb{D}$. *Remark*: each operation hdrep, tlrep, or consrep (from section 3.7.3) needed in the expansion of STEP into actual WHILE code can be realized by a constant number of operations. □

Finally, we construct from ilatom a true self-interpreter i for I. This is easily done, since the "packing" technique of Proposition 3.7.7, translates program ilatom into an equivalent one-variable program i with $[\![i]\!]^I = [\![i]\!]^{WHILE} = [\![\texttt{i1atom}]\!]^{WHILE}$. We have thus proven

Theorem 4.2.4 There exists a self-interpreter i for I using the concrete syntax of Definition 4.2.2.

Exercises

4.1 * Prove that for all $p \in$ WHILE-*programs* and all $d \in \mathbb{D}$, $[\![p]\!](d) = [\![\texttt{i1var}]\!](p.d)$. This can be done by induction on the lengths of computations of program execution and execution of the interpreter.   □

4.2 Show that for any WHILE-program p without any WHILE commands and for all $d \in \mathbb{D}$, it holds that $[\![\texttt{i1var}]\!](p.d)\!\downarrow$. This can be done by induction on the length of p.   □

4.3 Extend the WHILE language with a construction `repeat C until E`, with a Pascal-like semantics. Explain the emantics informally, e.g., when is E evaluated? Extend `u1var` so as to interpret this new construction (still for programs with one variable).   □

References

A universal program first appeared in Turing's paper [162], and in practically every book on computability published since then. The universal program for I much resembles the one sketched in [80].

5 Elements of Computability Theory

Chapter 2 set up our model WHILE of computation, chapter 3 gave a way to pass WHILE programs as input to other WHILE programs, and chapter 4 showed the existence of universal programs. We are now in a position to state and prove some of the fundamental results of computability theory, including those that were informally proven in chapter 1.

Section 5.1 defines the notions of computable function and decidable set, and the two related notions of semi-decidable and enumerable sets. Section 5.2 presents a specializer for WHILE programs. Section 5.3 proves that the halting problem is undecidable. Section 5.4 proves that all properties of WHILE programs that depend only on the program's input-output behaviour are undecidable. Section 5.5 proves some properties of decidable and semi-decidable sets, and section 5.6 shows that the halting problem is semi-decidable. Section 5.7 proves some properties of enumerable and semi-decidable sets.

5.1 Computability, decidability, enumerability

As mentioned earlier, a function is henceforth called computable if it is computed by some WHILE program:

Definition 5.1.1 A partial function $f : \mathbb{D} \to \mathbb{D}_\perp$ is WHILE *computable* iff there is a WHILE program p such that $f \simeq [\![p]\!]$, i.e., for all $d, e \in \mathbb{D}$:

1. If $f(d) = \perp$ then $[\![p]\!](d) = \perp$.
2. If $f(d) = e$ then $[\![p]\!](d) = e$. □

A set A will be called decidable if the membership question for A can be answered by a program that *always terminates*. If the program possibly loops on elements outside A, the set will be called semi-decidable.

We will show semi-decidability equivalent to *enumerability*, where a set A is called enumerable if there is some program that lists *all and only* the elements of A in some order. This allows repetitions, and does not necessarily list A's elements in any specific order, for instance the order need not be increasing or without repetitions.

Definition 5.1.2

1. A set $A \subseteq \mathbb{D}$ is WHILE *decidable* iff there is a WHILE program p such that $[\![p]\!](d)\!\downarrow$ for all $d \in \mathbb{D}$, and moreover $d \in A$ iff $[\![p]\!](d) = \texttt{true}$.

2. A set $A \subseteq \mathbb{D}$ is WHILE *semi-decidable* iff there is a WHILE-program p such that for all $d \in \mathbb{D}$: $d \in A$ iff $[\![p]\!](d) = \texttt{true}$.

3. A set $A \subseteq \mathbb{D}$ is WHILE *enumerable* iff $A = \emptyset$ or there is a WHILE program p such that for all $d \in \mathbb{D}$: $[\![p]\!](d)\!\downarrow$, and $A = \{[\![p]\!](d) \mid d \in \mathbb{D}\}$. □

5.2 Kleene's s-m-n theorem

Recall from chapter 3 the notion of a specializer. We now prove that there exists a program specializer from WHILE to WHILE written in WHILE.

Theorem 5.2.1 There is a WHILE program spec such that for all $p \in$ WHILE−*programs* and $s \in$ WHILE−*data*, $[\![\texttt{spec}]\!](\texttt{p.s}) \in$ WHILE−*programs*, and for all $s \in$ WHILE−*data*

$$[\![[\![\texttt{spec}]\!](\texttt{p.s})]\!](d) = [\![p]\!](\texttt{s.d})$$

Proof. Given a program p:

    read X; C; write Y

Given input s, consider the following program p_s

    read X; X := cons s X; C; write Y

It clearly holds that $[\![p]\!](\texttt{s.d}) = [\![p_s]\!](d)$. It therefore suffices to write a program that transforms the pair $(\texttt{p.s})$ into p_s, when both p_s and p are expressed in concrete syntax. The program p is expressed in concrete syntax as

    ((var i) C̲ (var j))

and p_s in concrete syntax would be:

    ((var i) (; (:= (var i) (cons (quote s) (var i))) C̲) (var j))

where C̲ is the concrete syntax of C. This is done by using the following program, spec, which uses the list notation of section 2.1.7. Note that the cons, := and ; in Consexp :=..., NewC:=..., and AssignX:=... are atoms.

```
read PS;                     (* PS is (((var i) C (var j)).s) *)
   P        := hd PS;         (* P is ((var i) C (var j))      *)
   S        := tl PS;         (* S is s                        *)
   Vari     := hd P;          (* Vari is (var i)               *)
   C        := hd (tl P)      (* C is C                        *)
   Varj     := hd (tl (tl P)); (* Varj is (var j)              *)

   QuoteS  := list quote S;
   ConsExp := list cons QuoteS Vari;
   AssignX := list := Vari ConsExp;
   NewC    := list ; AssignX C ;
   NewP    := list Vari  NewC Varj;
write NewP;
```

□

The same idea can be generalized to specialize programs accepting $m + n$ arguments to their first m arguments. This is known in recursive function theory as Kleene's *s-m-n theorem*, and plays an important role there.

The specializer above is quite trivial, as it just "freezes" the value of X by adding a new assignment. It seems likely that spec could sometimes exploit its knowledge of p's first input more extensively, by performing at specialization time all of p's computations that depend only on s. This can indeed be done, and is known in the programming languages community as *partial evaluation*. We return to this topic in the next part of this book.

5.3 Unsolvability of the halting problem

We now prove in a precise setting that the halting problem is unsolvable. As a consequence, many other problems are unsolvable. This includes many natural problems, as we shall see in chapter 10.

Theorem 5.3.1 The total function

$$halt(\text{p.d}) = \begin{cases} \texttt{true} & \text{if } [\![\text{p}]\!](\text{d}){\downarrow} \\ \texttt{false} & \text{otherwise} \end{cases}$$

is not computed by any WHILE-program. □

Proof. Suppose *halt* were computed by a WHILE-program q, i.e.,

$$[\![\text{q}]\!](\text{p.d}) = \begin{cases} \texttt{true} & \text{if } [\![\text{p}]\!](\text{d}){\downarrow} \\ \texttt{false} & \text{otherwise} \end{cases}$$

This must have form:

```
read X; C; write Y
```

Consider the following program r, built from q:

```
read X;
   X := cons X X;        (* Does program X stop on input X? *)
   C;                    (* Apply program q to answer this  *)
   if Y then
      while Y do Y := Y  (* Loop if X stops on input X      *)
   write Y               (* Terminate if it does not stop   *)
```

Consider the input $X = r$ (in concrete syntax). Now either $[\![r]\!](r) \neq \perp$ or $[\![r]\!](r) = \perp$ must be true.

If $[\![r]\!](r) \neq \perp$, then control in r's computation on input r must reach the else branch above (else r would loop on r). But then $Y = \mathtt{false}$ holds after command C, so $[\![r]\!](r) = \perp$ by the assumption that q computes *halt*. This is contradictory.

The only other possibility is that $[\![r]\!](r) = \perp$. But then r must reach the then branch above (else r would halt on r), so $Y \neq \mathtt{false}$ holds after command C. This implies $[\![r]\!](r) \neq \perp$ by the assumption that q computes *halt*, another contradiction.

All possibilities lead to a contradiction. The only unjustified assumption above was the existence of a program q that computes *halt*, so this must be false.[1]   □

The halting problem above is formulated as the problem of computing the function *halt*; as such it is uncomputable. One can also formulate the same problem as one of deciding membership of the subset of $\mathbb{D}$:

$$HALT = \{(\mathtt{p.d}) \mid \mathtt{p} \in \mathtt{WHILE}\text{-}programs, \mathtt{d} \in \mathtt{WHILE}\text{-}data, \text{and } [\![\mathtt{p}]\!](\mathtt{d}){\downarrow}\}$$

It is easy to see that this set is undecidable. If it were decidable, it would follow easily that *halt* were computable. Similarly, if *halt* were computable, it would follow immediately that *HALT* were decidable.

5.4   Rice's theorem

Rice's theorem shows that the unsolvability of the halting problem is far from a unique phenomenon; in fact, *all nontrivial extensional program properties are undecidable.*

---

[1] This argument is closely related to the paradoxes of mathematical logic. An informal but essentially similar example: "The barber shaves just those who do not shave themselves. Who shaves the barber?"

Definition 5.4.1

1. A *program property* A is a subset of WHILE-*programs*.

2. A program property A is *non-trivial* if $\{\} \neq A \neq$ WHILE-*programs*.

3. A program property A is *extensional* if for all p,q $\in$ WHILE-*programs* such that $[\![p]\!] \simeq [\![q]\!]$ it holds that $p \in A$ iff $q \in A$.   □

In other words, a program property is specified by a division of the world of all programs into two parts: those which have the property, and those which do not. A nontrivial program property is one that is satisfied by at least one, but not all, programs. An extensional program property depends exclusively on the program's input-output behaviour, and so is independent of its appearance, size, running time or other so-called *intensional* characteristics.

An example property of program p is the following: is $[\![p]\!](\text{nil}) = \text{nil}$? This is extensional, since $[\![p]\!] = [\![q]\!]$ implies that $[\![p]\!](\text{nil}) = \text{nil}$ if and only if $[\![q]\!](\text{nil}) = \text{nil}$. On the other hand, the following program property is *nonextensional*: is the number of variables in p more than 100? This is clear, since one can have two different programs p, q that compute the same input-output function $[\![p]\!] = [\![q]\!] : \mathbb{D} \to \mathbb{D}_\perp$, but such that one has more than 100 variables and the other does not.

Theorem 5.4.2 *If A is an extensional and nontrivial program property, then A is undecidable.*   □

Proof. Assume A is both decidable and nontrivial. We will show that this implies that the halting problem is decidable, which it is not. Let b be a program computing the totally undefined function: $[\![b]\!](d) = \perp$ for all d $\in \mathbb{D}$, e.g.,

$$\text{read X; while true do X := X; write Y}$$

Assume to begin with that A contains b. By extensionality, A must also contain all other programs computing the totally undefined function. By nontriviality of A there must be a program c in WHILE-*programs* which is not in A.

We now show how the halting problem (is $[\![p]\!](e) = \perp$?) could be solved if one had a decision procedure for A. Suppose we are given a program of form:

$$\text{p} \;=\; \text{read Y; C; write Result}$$

in WHILE-*programs*, and a value e $\in \mathbb{D}$ of its input, and we want to decide whether $[\![p]\!](e) = \perp$. Without loss of generality, programs p and c have no variables in common (else one can simply rename those in p). Construct the following program q (using the macro notation of Subsection 2.1.7):

```
read X;              (* Read X                               *)
  Resultp := p e;    (* First, run program p on the constant e *)
  Resultc := c X;    (* Then run program c on input X          *)
write Resultc
```

Clearly if $[\![p]\!](e)\uparrow$, then $[\![q]\!](d)\uparrow$ for all $d \in \mathbb{D}$. On the other hand, if $[\![p]\!](e)\downarrow$, then $[\![q]\!](d) = [\![c]\!](d)$ for all $d \in \mathbb{D}$. Thus

$$[\![q]\!] = \begin{cases} [\![b]\!] & \text{if } [\![p]\!](e) = \bot \\ [\![c]\!] & \text{if } [\![p]\!](e) \neq \bot \end{cases}$$

If p does not halt on e then $[\![q]\!] = [\![b]\!]$, so extensionality and the fact that $b \in A$ implies that $q \in A$. If p does halt on e then $[\![q]\!] = [\![c]\!]$, and again by extensionality, $c \notin A$ implies $q \notin A$. Thus p halts on e if and only if $q \notin A$, so decidability of A implies decidability of the halting problem.

The argument above applies to the case $b \in A$. If $b \notin A$ then exactly the same argument can be applied to $\overline{A} = \text{WHILE-}programs \backslash A$. Both cases imply the decidability of the halting problem, so the assumption that A is decidable must be false. $\qquad \square$

In conclusion, all nontrivial questions about programs' input-output behaviour are undecidable. For example

- Does $[\![p]\!](\texttt{nil})$ converge?
- Is the set $\{d \mid [\![p]\!](d)\}$ converges finite? Infinite?
- Is $[\![p]\!]$ a total function?

and *many* others.

5.5   Decidable versus semi-decidable sets

In this section we present some results about WHILE decidable and semi-decidable sets. In one of these results we encounter the first application of our interpreter u.

Theorem 5.5.1

1. Any finite set $A \subseteq \mathbb{D}$ is decidable.

2. If $A \subseteq \mathbb{D}$ is decidable then so is $\mathbb{D} \setminus A$.

3. Any decidable set is semi-decidable.

4. $A \subseteq \mathbb{D}$ is decidable if and only if both A and $\mathbb{D} \setminus A$ are semi-decidable. □

Proof.

1. If $A = \{\texttt{d1}, \ldots, \texttt{dn}\} \subseteq \mathbb{D}$, then it can be decided by program

```
read X;
  if (=? X d1) then X := true else
  if (=? X d2) then X := true else
              ⋮
  if (=? X dn) then X := true else
              X := false;
```

2. Let $\texttt{p} = \texttt{read X; C; write R}$ decide A. Then $\mathbb{D} \setminus A$ is decided by

```
read X;
  C;
  R := not R;
write R;
```

3. Obvious from Definition 5.1.2.

4. "Only if" follows from 3 and 2. For "if," we use a technique called *dovetailing*. The idea is to simulate two computations at once by interleaving their steps, one at a time[2]. Suppose now that A is semi-decided by program p:

$$\texttt{read X1; C1; write R1}$$

and that $\mathbb{D} \setminus A$ is semi-decided by program q:

$$\texttt{read X2; C2; write R2}$$

where we can assume that C1 and C2 have no variables in common.

Given $\texttt{d} \in \mathbb{D}$, if $\texttt{d} \in A$ then $[\![\texttt{p}]\!](\texttt{d}) = \texttt{true}$, and if $\texttt{d} \in \mathbb{D} \setminus A$ then $[\![\texttt{q}]\!](\texttt{d}) = \texttt{true}$. Consequently one can decide membership in A by running p and q alternately, one step at a time, until one or the other terminates with output $\texttt{true}$.

This is easily done using the universal program for WHILE; the details are left to the reader in an exercise. □

---

[2]Dovetailing of unboundedly many computations at once will be used in Exercise 13.5 and in chapter 20.

Theorem 5.5.2

1. If A, B are decidable then $A \cup B$ and $A \cap B$ are both decidable.
2. If A, B are semi-decidable then $A \cup B$ and $A \cap B$ are both semi-decidable.   □

5.6   The halting problem is semi-decidable

Theorem 5.3.1 established that the halting problem is undecidable. Now we show that it is semi-decidable.

Theorem 5.6.1 The halting problem for WHILE-programs is semi-decidable.   □

Proof. This is provable by means of the universal program u for WHILE:

```
read PD;
  V1:= u PD;
write 'true;
```

where we have used the macro notation V1:=u PD. Given input (p.d), the sequence of commands for V1:=u PD will terminate if and only if program p terminates on input d. Thus the program above writes true if and only if its input lies in *HALT*.   □

Corollary 5.6.2 $\mathbb{D} \setminus HALT$ is neither decidable nor semi-decidable.   □

Proof. Immediate from Theorem 5.5.1.   □

5.7   Enumerability related to semi-decidability

It is not hard (though not as easy as for $\mathbb{N}$) to show that the elements of $\mathbb{D}$ can be enumerated in sequence, one at a time:

Lemma 5.7.1

1. There is an enumeration $d_0, d_1, \ldots$ of all elements of $\mathbb{D}$ such that $d_0 = $ nil, and no elements are repeated;
2. There are commands start and next such that for any $i \geq 0$, the value of variable New after executing ⟦start; next; ...; next⟧ (with i occurrences of next) is d_i.

```
Program start:

     L := ();
     N := (nil);
     New := hd N;

Program next:

     N := tl N;
     Old := L;
     Tmp := cons (cons New New) nil;
     while Old do
       Tmp := cons (cons New (hd Old)) Tmp;
       Tmp := cons (cons (hd Old) New) Tmp;
       Old := tl Old;
     N := append N Tmp;
     L := cons New L;
     New := hd N;
```

Figure 5.1: Enumerating $\mathbb{D}$.

Proof. Figure 5.1 shows WHILE codes for start, next. Explanation: they actually follow the defining equation $\mathbb{D} = \{\texttt{nil}\} \cup \mathbb{D} \times \mathbb{D}$, using the fact that if $X \subseteq \mathbb{D}$ and $\texttt{d} \notin X$, then

$$(X \cup \{\texttt{d}\}) \times (X \cup \{\texttt{d}\}) = \begin{array}{l} X \times X \cup \{(\texttt{d.d})\} \cup \\ \{(\texttt{d.x}) \mid \texttt{x} \in X\} \cup \{(\texttt{x.d}) \mid \texttt{x} \in X\} \end{array}$$

The trees created are placed on the list N. They are moved to the list L once they have served their purpose in creating bigger trees, and New will always be the first element of N. Thus initially, N contains the single tree nil and L is empty. Every time next is performed, one tree New is removed from the list N and paired with all the trees that are already in L as well as with itself. The trees thus created are added to N, and New itself is added to L. The following claims are easy to verify:

(1) Every iteration adds a single element to L.

(2) Every element of $\mathbb{D}$ is eventually put on L. □

5.7.1 Enumerability characterized by semi-decidability

Theorem 5.7.2 The following statements about a set $A \subseteq \mathbb{D}$ are equivalent:

1. A is WHILE enumerable.

2. A is WHILE semi-decidable.

3. A is the range of a WHILE computable partial function, so for some p:

$$A = \{[\![p]\!](d) \mid d \in \mathbb{D} \text{ and } [\![p]\!](d) \neq \bot\}$$

4. A is the domain of a WHILE computable partial function, so for some p:

$$A = \{d \in \mathbb{D} \mid [\![p]\!](d) \neq \bot\}$$

□

Proof. We show that 1 implies 2, 2 implies 3, 3 implies 1, and 2 is equivalent to 4.

1 ⇒ 2. If $A = \emptyset$ then 2 holds trivially, so assume there is a WHILE program p such that for all $d \in \mathbb{D}$: $[\![p]\!](d)\!\downarrow$, and $A = \{[\![p]\!](d) \mid d \in \mathbb{D}\}$. Let p = read Xp; Cp; write Rp, and let $d_0, d_1, \ldots$ be as in the enumeration of Lemma 5.7.1.

The following program, given input d, computes $[\![p]\!](d_0), [\![p]\!](d_1), \ldots$, and compares d to each in turn. If $d = d_i$ for some i, then p terminates after writing true. If $d \neq d_i$ for all i then p will loop infinitely, as needed for 2.

```
read D;
  start;
  GO := true
  while GO do
    Y := p New;
    if (=? Y D) then GO:=false;
    next;
  write true
```

2 ⇒ 3. Assume that A is semi-decided by program p of form read I; C; write R, and construct the program q:

```
read I;
  Save := I;
  C;
  if R then SKIP else while true do SKIP;
  write Save
```

Clearly $[\![p]\!](d)\!\downarrow$ and $[\![p]\!](d) = $ true together imply $[\![q]\!](d) = d$. On the other hand, if either $[\![p]\!](d)\!\uparrow$ or $[\![p]\!](d) \neq$ true, then $[\![q]\!](d)\!\uparrow$. Thus $d \in A$ iff $[\![q]\!](d) = d$, so $A = \{[\![q]\!](e) \mid e \in \mathbb{D} \text{ and } [\![q]\!](e)\!\downarrow\}$.

3 ⇒ 1. If $A = \emptyset$ then 3 holds trivially, so assume A contains at least one member d0, and that A is the range of partial function $[\![p]\!]$, where p=((var i) C (var j)), i.e., $A = rng([\![p]\!])$. Define f such that $f(a) = d0$ for every atom a, and

$$f(\texttt{e.d}) = \begin{cases} [\![p]\!](\texttt{d}) & \text{if p stops when applied to d within } |e| \text{ steps} \\ \texttt{d0} & \text{otherwise} \end{cases}$$

f is obviously total. *Claim:* $A = rng(f)$. Proof of $\subseteq$: if $a \in A = rng([\![p]\!])$ then $a = [\![p]\!](\texttt{d})$ for some $d \in \mathbb{D}$. Thus p, when applied to d, terminates within some number of steps, call it m. Then clearly

$$f(1^m.\texttt{d}) = [\![p]\!](\texttt{d}) = \texttt{a}$$

so $a \in rng(f)$. Proof of $\supseteq$: Values in the range of A are either of form $[\![p]\!](\texttt{d})$ and so in the range of $[\![p]\!]$ and so in A, or are d0 which is also in A.

Finally, the following program q, using the STEP macro from the universal program u, computes f:

```
read TD;                (* Input (t.d)                         *)
    D  := tl PD;        (* D = d                               *)
    Vl := update i D j  (* (var i) initially d, all others nil *)
    Cd := cons C nil;   (* Cd = (C.nil), Code to execute is C  *)
    St := nil;          (* St = nil,      Stack empty          *)
    Time := hd TD       (* Time = t,      Time bound is t      *)
    while Cd do         (* Run p for up to t steps on d        *)
       STEP; Time := tl Time;
       if (=? Time nil) then Cd := nil;  (* Abort if time out  *)

    if Time             (* Output d0 if time ran out, else J   *)
       then Out := lookup J Vl else Out := d0;
    write Out;
```

2 ⇔ 4. A program p which semi-decides A can be modified to loop infinitely unless its output is true, hence 2 implies 4. If p is as in 4, replacing its write command by write true gives a program to semi-decide A.   □

5.7.2 Recursive and recursively enumerable sets

The preceding theorem justifies the following definition of two of the central concepts of computability theory. Even though at this point only WHILE (and I languages have need considered, we will see as a result of the "robustness" results of chapter 8 that the concepts are invariant with respect to which computing formalism is used.

Definition 5.7.3 A set A is *recursive* iff there is a terminating program $[\![p]\!]$ that decides the problem $x \in A$?. A set A is *recursively enumerable* (or just *r.e.*, for short) iff there is a program $[\![p]\!]$ that semi-decides the problem $x \in A$?.

Exercises

5.1 Consider a language WHILE-forloop which is just like WHILE, except that instead of the while command, WHILE-forloop has a command

```
for X := alltails(E) do C
```

Its informal semantics: First, E is evaluated to yield a value d. If d = (d1.d2), then X is first bound to d, and command C is executed once. The same procedure is now repeated with X being bound to d2. In this way command C is executed repeatedly, until X is bound to an atom (which must eventually happen). At that time the for command terminates and control goes to the next command.

1. Define the semantics of WHILE-forloop by rules similar to those for the WHILE-semantics.
2. Show how WHILE-forloop programs can be translated into equivalent while-programs.
3. Prove that your construction in (2) is correct using the semantics for WHILE and your semantics from (1) for WHILE-forloop.
4. Is the halting problem decidable for WHILE-forloop-programs?
5. Can all computable functions be computed by WHILE-forloop-programs?   □

5.2 Show that there exists a total function which is WHILE-computable, but uncomputable by any WHILE-forloop-program. Hint: consider $f(\text{p.d}) = \text{true}$ if $[\![p]\!](\text{d}) = \text{true}$, and false otherwise.   □

5.3 Prove that it is undecidable whether a given program computes a total function.   □

5.4 Prove that it is undecidable whether two programs compute the same function. *Hint:* show that it is undecidable whether a program computes the identity function, and derive the more general result from this.   □

5.5 Use Rice's theorem to prove that *unnecessary code elimination* is undecidable: given a program p

```
read X; C1; while E do C; C2; write Y
```

with an identified while command, it is undecidable whether test E will be false every time control reaches the command. □

5.6 Prove Theorem 5.5.1 part 4. Hint: you will need two copies of the universal program. □

5.7 * Prove Theorem 5.5.2. Hint: the results for decidable A, B are straightforward, as is semi-decidability of $A \cap B$. For semi-decidability of $A \cup B$, use Theorem 5.7.2, or the "dovetailing" technique of Theorem 5.5.1, Part 4. □

5.8 List the first 10 elements of $\mathbb{D}$ as given in Lemma 5.7.1. □

5.9 Use induction to prove the two claims made about the enumeration of $\mathbb{D}$ in the proof of Lemma 5.7.1. □

5.10 * The pairs in list Tmp (Lemma 5.7.1) are added to the end of list N by append. Show that the simpler alternative of adding them to the start of N does not work. What goes wrong in the proof of the previous Exercise 5.9 if this change is made? □

5.11 Devise alternative start and next commands that take only $O(n)$ time when next is called, where n is the length of list L. Hint: find a faster way to achieve the effect of append. More variables may be used, if convenient. □

5.12 * Devise alternative start and next commands that take only constant time when next is called. Hint: at each next call the only essential action is that a new element is added to L. Find a way to defer the addition of elements to N until needed. One method can be found in [20]. □

5.13 Show that if an infinite set is WHILE enumerable, then it is WHILE enumerable without repetitions (i.e., the range of a one-to-one effective total function). □

5.14 Show that a set $A \neq \emptyset$ can be WHILE enumerated in increasing order if and only if it is decidable. □

5.15 Show that a set $A \neq \emptyset$ is decidable if it is

- the range of a WHILE computable total monotonic function; or
- the range of a while computable total function greater than the identity. □

5.16 * Show that any infinite WHILE enumerable set must contain an infinite WHILE decidable subset. *Hint:* use the result of Exercise 5.14. □

References

Most of the results proved in this chapter appear in classical papers by the pioneers in computability theory. The *s-m-n* theorem was proved by Kleene in the paper [93], and also appears in his book [95]. The halting problem was studied first by Kleene [93], Turing [162], and Church [21, 22]. Rice [143] developed a general technique to prove undecidability of sets. A universal program first appeared in Turing's paper [162]. Properties of recursively decidable and enumerable sets, and their relationship, were studied by Kleene [94] and Post [134, 135].

6 Metaprogramming, Self-application, and Compiler Generation

In this chapter we investigate some aspects of computability pertaining to *running times*, i.e., the number of steps that computations take. Two aspects are given special attention: *execution of metaprograms*, i.e., compilers, interpreters, and specializers, and *self-application*, e.g., application of a program to itself, and in particular a specializer.

The main purpose of this chapter is not to prove new results in computability theory (although the Futamura projections may be new to some theorists.) Rather, our main aim is to link the perhaps dry framework and results of this book's material through chapter 5 to daily computing practice.

This involves relating the time usage of compilation and interpretation; the deleterious effects of multiple levels of interpretation; the use of "bootstrapping" (a form of self-application) in compiling practice to gain flexibility and speed. Last but not least, the Futamura projections show how, using a specializer and an interpreter, one may *compile*, *generate compilers*, and even *generate a compiler generator*, again by self-application. Interestingly, the Futamura projections work well in practice as well as in theory, though their practical application is not the subject of this book (see [84].)

Section 6.1 first introduces running times into the notion of a programming language arriving at a *timed* programming language. Section 6.2 is concerned with with interpretation. Section 6.3 describes self-application of compilers, and section 6.4 introduces *partial evaluation*, the well-developed practice of using program specialization for automatic program optimization. Section 6.5 shows how it can be applied to compiling and compiler generation, and discusses some efficiency issues, showing that self-application can actually lead to speedups rather than slowdowns.

The final two sections (which readers focused more on theoretical issues may wish to skip) include 6.6 on pragmatically desirable properties of a specializer for practical applications; and section 6.7, which sketches an offline algorithm for partial evaluation.

6.1 Timed programming languages

Definition 6.1.1 A *timed programming language* L consists of

1. Two sets, L−*programs* and L−*data*;

2. A function $[\![\bullet]\!]^L : L-programs \rightarrow (L-data \rightarrow L-data_\perp)$; and

3. A function $time^L : L-programs \rightarrow (L-data \rightarrow \mathbb{N}_\perp)$ such that for any $p \in L-programs$ and $d \in L-data$, $[\![p]\!]^L(d) = \perp$ iff $time^L_p(d) = \perp$.

The function in 2 is L's *semantic function*, which associates with every $p \in L-programs$ a corresponding partial input-output function from L-*data* to L-*data*. The function in 3 is L's *running time function* which associates with every program and input the number of steps that computation of the program applied to the input takes.   □

Much more will be said about program running times in the Complexity Theory parts of this book. In this chapter we discuss time aspects of interpretation, specialization etc. only informally, relying on the reader's experience and intuition.

6.2   Interpretation overhead

In the first subsection we discuss overhead in practice, i.e., for existing interpreters, and the second subsection is concerned with self-application of interpreters. It will be seen that interpretation overhead can be substantial, and must be multiplied when one interpreter is used to interpret another one.

Section 6.4 will show how this overhead can be removed (automatically), provided one has an efficient program specializer.

6.2.1   Interpretation overhead in practice

In the present and the next subsection, we are concerned with interpreters in practice, and therefore address the question: how slow can an interpreter get, i.e., what are the *lower* bounds for the running time of practical interpreters. Suppose one has an S-interpreter int written in language L, i.e.,

$$
\texttt{int} \in \boxed{\begin{array}{c} S \\ \hline L \end{array}}
$$

In practice, assuming one has both an L-machine and an S-machine at one's disposal, interpretation often turns out to be rather slower than direct execution of S-programs. If an S-machine is not available, a compiler from S to L is often to be preferred because the running time of programs compiled into L (or a lower-level language) is faster than that of interpretively executed S-programs.

In practice, a typical interpreter `int`'s running time on inputs p and d usually satisfies a relation

$$\alpha_p \cdot time_p^S(d) \leq time_{int}^L(p \cdot d)$$

for all d. Here α_p is a "constant" independent of d, but it may depend on the source program p. Often $\alpha_p = c + f(p)$, where constant c represents the time taken for "dispatch on syntax" and $f(p)$ represents the time for variable access. In experiments c is often around 10 for simple interpreters run on small source programs, and larger for more sophisticated interpreters. Clever use of data structures such as hash tables, binary trees, etc. can make α_p grow slowly as a function of p's size.

6.2.2 Compiling (usually) gives faster execution than interpretation

If the purpose is to execute S-programs, then it is nearly always better to compile than to interpret. One extreme: if S = L, then the identity is a correct compiling function and, letting q = [[comp]](p) = p, one has $time_p^S(d) = time_q^L(d)$: considerably faster than the above due to the absence of α_p. Less trivially, even when S ≠ L, execution of a compiled S-program is nearly always considerably faster than running the same program interpretively.

6.2.3 Layers of interpretation

Suppose a Lisp system (called L2) is processed interpretively by an interpreter written in Sun RISC machine code (call this L1). The machine code itself is processed by the central processor (call this L0) so two levels of interpretation are involved, as described in the interpreter diagram in Figure 6.1.

The major problem with implementing languages interpretively is that the running time of the interpreted program is be multiplied by the overhead occurring in the interpreter's basic cycle. This cost, of one level of interpretation, may well be an acceptable price to pay in order to have a powerful, expressive language (this was the case with Lisp since its beginnings). On the other hand, if one uses several layers of interpreters, each new level of interpretation multiplies the time by a significant constant factor, so the total interpretive overhead may be excessive (also seen in practice). Compilation is clearly preferable to using several interpreters, each interpreting the next.

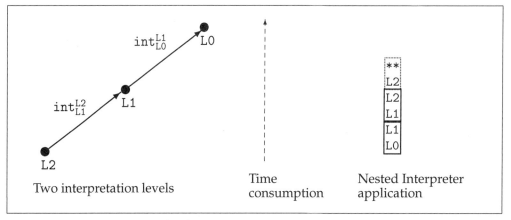

Figure 6.1: Interpretation overhead.

Indeed, suppose now that we are given

- An interpreter int_0^1 written in L0 that implements language L1; and
- An interpreter int_1^2 written in L1 that implements language L2.

where L0, L1, and L2 all have pairing and concrete syntax, and all have the same data language. By definition of an interpreter,

$$[\![\text{p2}]\!]^{\text{L2}}(\text{d}) \ = \ [\![\text{int}_1^2]\!]^{\text{L1}}(\text{p2.d}) \ = \ [\![\text{int}_0^1]\!]^{\text{L0}}(\text{int}_1^2.(\text{p2.d}))$$

One can expect that, for appropriate constants α_{01}, α_{12} and any L1-program p1, L2-program p2 and data d,

$$\alpha_{01} \cdot time_{\text{p1}}^{\text{L1}}(\text{d}) \leq time_{\text{int}_0^1}^{\text{L0}}(\text{p1.d}) \quad \text{and}$$

$$\alpha_{12} \cdot time_{\text{p2}}^{\text{L2}}(\text{d}) \leq time_{\text{int}_1^2}^{\text{L1}}(\text{p2.d})$$

where α_{01}, α_{12} are constants representing the overhead of the two interpreters (often sizable, as mentiond in the previous section).

Consequently replacing p1 in the first by int_1^2 and d by p2.d, and multiplying the second inequality by α_{01} we obtain:

$$\alpha_{01} \cdot time^{L1}_{int_1^2}(\text{p2.d}) \leq time^{L0}_{int_0^1}(int_1^2.(\text{p2.d}))$$

$$\alpha_{01} \cdot \alpha_{12} \cdot time^{L2}_{\text{p2}}(\text{d}) \leq \alpha_{01} \cdot time^{L1}_{int_1^2}(\text{p2.d})$$

Thus $\alpha_{01} \cdot \alpha_{12} \cdot time^{L2}_{\text{p2}}(\text{d}) \leq time^{L0}_{int_0^1}(int_1^2.(\text{p2.d}))$, confirming the multiplication of interpretive overheads.

6.3   Compiler bootstrapping: an example of self-application

The term "bootstrapping" comes from the phrase "to pull oneself up by one's bootstraps" and refers to the use of compilers to compile themselves. The technique is widely used in practice, including industrial applications. Examples are numerous. We choose a common one, that of extending an existing compiler for language S to accept a larger language S', based on the following assumptions:

1. The new language S' is a *conservative extension* of S. By definition this means that every S-program p is also an S'-program (so S-programs $\subseteq$ S'-programs), and has the same semantics in both languages (so $[\![p]\!]^S = [\![p]\!]^{S'}$).

2. We have a compiler h $\in$ S-programs, from source language S to target language T available in source form. By definition of compiler, $[\![p]\!]^S = [\![[\![h]\!]^S(p)]\!]^T$ for any S-program p.

3. Further, we assume that we have an equivalent program t $\in$ T-programs available in target form, so $[\![h]\!]^S = [\![t]\!]^T$.

high-level compiler h $\in$ [S $\longrightarrow$ T / S]   low-level compiler t $\in$ [S $\longrightarrow$ T / T]

Now h and t can be used to create a compiler from S' to T as follows:

1. Rewrite the existing compiler h, extending it to make a compiler h' $\in$ S-programs for S', using *only features already available in* S:

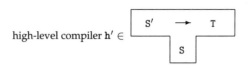

high-level compiler $h' \in$

This must be equivalent to h on the old source language S, so for all S-programs[1]
$p \; [\![\,[\![h]\!]^S \, (p) \,]\!]^T = [\![\,[\![h']\!]^S \, (p) \,]\!]^T.$

2. Now apply t to h' to obtain an S' compiler $t1'$ in target language form:

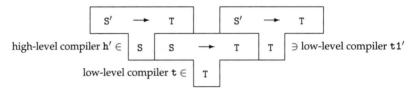

high-level compiler $h' \in$ low-level compiler $t1'$

low-level compiler $t \in$

Now we have obtained the desired extended compiler $t1' = [\![t]\!]^T \, (h')$. It is easy to see
that it is a target program equivalent to h', since:

$$
\begin{aligned}
[\![t1']\!]^T &= [\![\,[\![t]\!]^T \, (h') \,]\!]^T && \text{(substitution of equals)} \\
&= [\![\,[\![h]\!]^S \, (h') \,]\!]^T && \text{Since } t \text{ and } h \text{ are equivalent} \\
&= [\![h']\!]^S && h \text{ compiles source program } h' \text{ from } S \text{ to } T.
\end{aligned}
$$

What happens if we continue this game?

1. Use $t1'$ to obtain an S' compiler $t2'$ in target language form:

high-level compiler $h' \in$ low-level compiler $t2'$

low-level compiler $t1' \in$

2. Use $t2'$ to obtain an S' compiler $t3'$ in target language form:

high-level compiler $h' \in$ low-level compiler $t3'$

low-level compiler $t2' \in$

---

[1]Note that this does not require h and h' to produce the same target code, just target code which will have
identical effects when run.

These runs can be written more concisely as follows:

$$
\begin{aligned}
\text{t1}' &= [\![t]\!]^T\,(\text{h}') \\
\text{t2}' &= [\![\text{t1}']\!]^T\,(\text{h}') \\
\text{t3}' &= [\![\text{t2}']\!]^T\,(\text{h}')
\end{aligned}
$$

Now t1′ and t2′ (and t3′) are *semantically equivalent* since they are all obtained by correct compilers from the same source program, h′:

$$
\begin{aligned}
[\![\text{t1}']\!]^T &= [\![\,[\![t]\!]^T\,(\text{h}')\,]\!]^T & \text{by definition of t1}' \\
&= [\![\,[\![\text{h}]\!]^S\,(\text{h}')\,]\!]^T & \text{Since t and h are equivalent} \\
&= [\![\,[\![\text{h}']\!]^S\,(\text{h}')\,]\!]^T & \text{since h}' \text{ is a conservative extension of h} \\
&= [\![\,[\![\,[\![t]\!]^T\,(\text{h}')\,]\!]^T\,(\text{h}')\,]\!]^T & \text{since t is a compiler from S to T} \\
&= [\![\,[\![\text{t1}']\!]^T\,(\text{h}')\,]\!]^T & \text{by definition of t1}' \\
&= [\![\text{t2}']\!]^T & \text{by definition of t2}'
\end{aligned}
$$

Note that t1′ and t2′ may not be *textually* identical, since they were produced by two different compilers, t and t1′, and it is quite possible that the extended language S′ may require different target code than S.

However, one easily sees that t2′ and t3′ *are* textually identical since the compilers used to compile them are semantically equivalent:

$$
\begin{aligned}
\text{t2}' &= [\![\text{t1}']\!]^T\,(\text{h}') & \text{by definition of t2}' \\
&= [\![\text{t2}']\!]^T\,(\text{h}') & \text{Since t1}' \text{ and t2}' \text{ are equivalent: } [\![\text{t1}']\!]^T = [\![\text{t2}']\!]^T \\
&= \text{t3}' & \text{by definition of t3}'
\end{aligned}
$$

The difference between being semantical and syntactical identity of the produced compilers stems from the relationship between the compilers we start out with: t and h are equivalent in the sense that given the same input program they produce syntactically the same output program. However h and h′ are equivalent on S programs only in the sense that given the same program, the two output programs they produce are *semantically* equivalent (natural: when one revises a compiler, the old target code may need to be modified).

Note that bootstrapping involves self-application in the sense that (compiled versions of) h′ are used to compile h′ itself. Note also that self-application is useful in that it eases the tasks of transferring a compiler from one language to another, of extending a compiler, or of producing otherwise modified versions.

6.4   Partial evaluation: efficient program specialization

The goal of partial evaluation is to specialize *general* programs so as to generate *efficient* ones from them by completely automatic methods. On the whole, the general program will be more generic, and perhaps simpler but less efficient, than the specialized versions a partial evaluator produces. A telling catch phrase is *binding-time engineering* — making computation faster by changing the times at which subcomputations are done (see Figure 3.3).

The program specializer of section 5.2 is very simple, and the programs it ouputs are slightly slower than the ones from which they were derived. On the other hand, program specialization can be done much less trivivally, so as to yield *efficient* specialized programs. This is known as *partial evaluation*, a field at the borderline between in programming language theory and practice.

Consider, for instance, the following program, which reads a pair of numerals and returns the product. Data is assumed in "base 1" notation, addition is done by repeatedly adding 1 (succ below), and multiplication by repeated addition.

```
read XY;          (*  Input is a pair  XY = (x.y)        *)
   X := hd XY;     (*  Unary notation: X = nil^x          *)
   Y := tl XY;
   P := 0;         (*  P will be the product              *)
   while Y do      (*  Add X to P for Y times             *)
      Y := pred Y;
      T := X;
      while T do   (*  Add 1 to P for X times             *)
         T := pred T;
         P := succ P;
   write P;
```

Suppose that we want to specialize this program so that X is $3 = nil^3$. Then we could get the following program:

```
read Y;
   P := 0;
   while Y do
      Y := pred Y;
      P := succ P;
      P := succ P;
      P := succ P;
   write P;
```

Rather than calling the first program with arguments of form (3.d) it is clearly better to use the second, more efficient program. A typical partial evaluator, i.e., specializer, will be capable of transforming the former into the latter.

6.4.1 A slightly more complex example: Ackermann's function

Consider Ackermann's function, with program:

```
a(m,n) = if m =? 0 then n+1 else
           if n =? 0 then a(m-1,1)
           else a(m-1,a(m,n-1))
```

Computing `a(2,n)` involves recursive evaluations of `a(m,n)` for m = 0, 1 and 2, and various values of n. A partial evaluator can evaluate expressions m=?0 and m-1, and function calls of form `a(m-1,...)` can be unfolded. We can now specialize function a to the values of m, yielding a less general program that is about twice as fast:

```
a2(n) = if n =? 0 then 3 else a1(a2(n-1))
a1(n) = if n =? 0 then 2 else a1(n-1)+1
```

6.5 Compiling and compiler generation by specialization

This section shows the sometimes surprising capabilities of partial evaluation for generating program generators. We will see that it is possible to use program specialization to compile, if given an interpreter and a source program in the interpreted language; to convert an interpreter into a compiler:

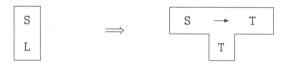

by specializing the specializer itself; and even to generate a compiler generator. This is interesting for several practical reasons:

- Interpreters are usually smaller, easier to understand, and easier to debug than compilers.
- An interpreter is a (low-level form of) operational semantics, and so can serve as a definition of a programming language, assuming the semantics of L is solidly understood.

- The question of compiler correctness is completely avoided, since the compiler will always be faithful to the interpreter from which it was generated.

The results are called the *Futamura projections* since they were discovered by Yoshihiko Futamura in 1971 [46]. We consider for simplicity only specialization without change in data representation. That is, we assume that all the languages below have concrete syntax and pairing, and that all the data languages are the same. Suppose we are given

- a specializer `spec` from L to T written in an implementation language `Imp`.
- an interpreter `int` for S-programs which is written in language L; and
- an arbitrary S-program `source`.

6.5.1   The first Futamura projection

The following shows that given an L to T-specializer, an S interpreter written in L, and an S-program `source`, one can get a T program `target` equivalent to `source`. Concretely:

$$\texttt{target} = [\![\texttt{spec}]\!]^{\texttt{Imp}}(\texttt{int.source})$$

is a T-program equivalent to S-program `source`, i.e., that one can compile by partial evaluation. (This is a solution of Exercise 3.1.)

This equation is often called the *first Futamura projection* [46], and can be verified as follows, where `in` and `out` are the input and output data of `source`.

$$
\begin{aligned}
\texttt{out} &= [\![\texttt{source}]\!]^{\texttt{S}}(\texttt{in}) & &\text{Assumption}\\
&= [\![\texttt{int}]\!]^{\texttt{L}}(\texttt{source.in}) & &\text{Definition 3.4.1 of an interpreter}\\
&= [\![[\![\texttt{spec}]\!]^{\texttt{Imp}}(\texttt{int.source})]\!]^{\texttt{T}}(\texttt{in}) & &\text{Definition 3.6.1 of a specializer}\\
&= [\![\texttt{target}]\!]^{\texttt{T}}(\texttt{in}) & &\text{Definition of \texttt{target}}
\end{aligned}
$$

In other words, one can *compile* a new language S to the output language of the specializer, provided that an interpreter for S is given in the input language of the specializer. Assuming the partial evaluator is correct, this always yields target programs that are correct with respect to the interpreter. This approach has proven its value in practice. See [10, 85, 84] for some concrete speedup factors (often between 3 and 10 times faster).

A common special case used by the Lisp and Prolog communities is that $\texttt{Imp} = \texttt{T} = \texttt{L}$, so one can compile from a new language S to L by writing an S-interpreter in L.

Speedups from specialization   As mentioned before, compiled programs nearly always run faster than interpreted ones, and the same holds for programs output by the first Futamura projection. To give a more complete picture, though, we need to discuss two sets of running times:

1. Interpretation versus execution:

$$time_{\tt int}({\tt p}.{\tt d}) \text{ versus } time_{\tt int_p}({\tt d})$$

2. Interpretation plus specialization versus execution:

$$time_{\tt int}({\tt p}.{\tt d}) + time_{\tt spec}({\tt int}.{\tt p}) \text{ versus } time_{\tt int_p}({\tt d})$$

If program `int` is to be specialized just once, then comparison 2 is the most fair, since it accounts for what amounts to a form of "compile time." If, however, the specialized program `int`$_{\tt p}$ is to be run often (e.g., as in typical compilation situations), then comparison 2 is more fair since the savings gained by running `int`$_{\tt p}$ instead of `int` will, in the long term, outweigh specialization time, even if `int`$_{\tt p}$ is only a small amount faster than `int`.

6.5.2   Compiler generation by the second Futamura projection

The second equation shows that one can *generate an S to T compiler* written in T, provided that an S-interpreter in L is given and `Imp` = L: the specializer is written in its own input language. Concretely, we see that

$$\texttt{compiler} = [\![\texttt{spec}]\!]^{\tt L}(\texttt{spec}.\texttt{int})$$

is a stand-alone compiler: an L-program which, when applied to a single input `source`, yields `target`. It is thus a compiler from S to L, written in L. Verification is straightforward as follows:

$$
\begin{aligned}
\texttt{target} \quad &= \quad [\![\texttt{spec}]\!]^{\tt L}(\texttt{int}.\texttt{source}) &&\text{First Futamura projection} \\
&= \quad [\![[\![\texttt{spec}]\!]^{\tt L}(\texttt{spec}.\texttt{int})]\!]^{\tt T}(\texttt{source}) &&\text{Definition 3.6.1 of a specializer} \\
&= \quad [\![\texttt{compiler}]\!]^{\tt T}(\texttt{source}) &&\text{Definition of } \texttt{comp}
\end{aligned}
$$

Equation $\texttt{compiler} = [\![\texttt{spec}]\!]^{\tt L}(\texttt{int}.\texttt{source})$ is called the second Futamura projection. The compiler generates specialized versions of interpreter `int`. Operationally, constructing a compiler this way is hard to understand because it involves self-application — using `spec` to specialize itself. But it gives good results in practice, and faster compilation than by the first Futamura projection.

6.5.3   Compiler generator generation by the third Futamura projection

Finally, we show (again assuming $\mathtt{Imp} = L$) that

$$\mathtt{cogen} = [\![\mathtt{spec}]\!]^L(\mathtt{spec}.\mathtt{spec})$$

is a *compiler generator*: a program that transforms interpreters into compilers. Verification is again straightforward:

$$
\begin{aligned}
\mathtt{compiler} \quad &= \quad [\![\mathtt{spec}]\!]^L(\mathtt{spec}.\mathtt{int}) && \text{Second Futamura projection} \\
&= \quad [\![[\![\mathtt{spec}]\!]^L(\mathtt{spec}.\mathtt{spec})]\!]^T(\mathtt{int}) && \text{Definition 3.6.1 of a specializer} \\
&= \quad [\![\mathtt{cogen}]\!]^T(\mathtt{int}) && \text{Definition of } \mathtt{compiler}
\end{aligned}
$$

The compilers so produced are versions of $\mathtt{spec}$ itself, specialized to various interpreters. This projection is even harder to understand intuitively than the second, but also gives good results in practice.

The following more general equation, also easily verified from Definition 3.6.1, sums up the essential property of $\mathtt{cogen}$ (we omit language L for simplicity):

$$[\![\mathtt{p}]\!]\,(\mathtt{s}.\mathtt{d}) \;=\; [\![[\![\mathtt{spec}]\!]\,(\mathtt{p}.\mathtt{s})\,]\!]\,\mathtt{d} \;=\; \ldots \;=\; [\![[\![[\![\mathtt{cogen}]\!]\,\mathtt{p}\,]\!]\,\mathtt{s}\,]\!]\,\mathtt{d}$$

Further, $\mathtt{cogen}$ can produce itself as output (Exercise 6.9.)

While the verifications above by equational reasoning are straightforward, it is far from clear what their pragmatic consequences are. Answers to these questions form the bulk of the book [84].

6.5.4   Speedups from self-application

A variety of partial evaluators generating efficient specialized programs have been constructed. Easy equational reasoning from the definitions of specializer, interpreter, and compiler reveals that program execution, compilation, compiler generation, and compiler generator generation can each be done in two different ways:

$$
\begin{aligned}
\mathtt{out} \quad &= \quad [\![\mathtt{int}]\!](\mathtt{source}.\mathtt{input}) &&= \quad [\![\mathtt{target}]\!](\mathtt{in}) \\
\mathtt{target} \quad &= \quad [\![\mathtt{spec}]\!](\mathtt{int}.\mathtt{source}) &&= \quad [\![\mathtt{compiler}]\!](\mathtt{source}) \\
\mathtt{compiler} \quad &= \quad [\![\mathtt{spec}]\!](\mathtt{spec}.\mathtt{int}) &&= \quad [\![\mathtt{cogen}]\!](\mathtt{int}) \\
\mathtt{cogen} \quad &= \quad [\![\mathtt{spec}]\!](\mathtt{spec}.\mathtt{spec}) &&= \quad [\![\mathtt{cogen}]\!](\mathtt{spec})
\end{aligned}
$$

The exact timings vary according to the design of spec and int, and with the implementation language L. We have often observed in practical computer experiments [85, 84] that each equation's *rightmost run is about 10 times faster than the leftmost*. Moral: self-application can generate programs that run faster!

6.5.5 Metaprogramming without order-of-magnitude loss of efficiency

The right side of Figure 6.2 illustrates graphically that partial evaluation can substantially reduce the cost of the multiple levels of interpretation mentioned in section 6.2.3.

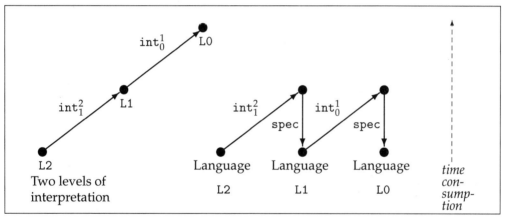

Figure 6.2: Overhead introduction and elimination.

A literal interpretation of Figure 6.2 would involve writing two partial evaluators, one for L1 and one for L0. Fortunately there is an alternative approach using only *one* partial evaluator, for L0. For concreteness let p2 be an L2-program, and let in, out be representative input and output data. Then

$$\mathtt{out} = [\![\mathtt{int}_0^1]\!]^{L0}(\mathtt{int}_1^2.(\mathtt{p2.in}))$$

One may construct an interpreter for L2 written in L0 as follows:

$$\mathtt{int}_0^2 := [\![\mathtt{spec}]\!]^{L0}(\mathtt{int}_0^1.\mathtt{int}_1^2) \quad \text{satisfying}$$
$$\mathtt{out} = [\![\mathtt{int}_0^2]\!]^{L0}(\mathtt{p2.in})$$

By partial evaluation of int_0^2, any L2-programs can be compiled to an equivalent L0-program. Better still, one may construct a compiler from L2 into L0 by

$$\text{comp}_0^2 := [\![\text{cogen}]\!]^{L0}(\text{int}_0^2)$$

The net effect is that metaprogramming may be used without order–of–magnitude loss of efficiency. The development above, though conceptually complex, has actually been realized in practice by partial evaluation, and yields substantial efficiency gains.

6.6   Desirable properties of a specializer

Totality

It is clearly desirable that specialization function $[\![\text{spec}]\!]$ is total, so *every* program p and partial input s leads to a defined output $\text{p}_\text{s} = [\![\text{spec}]\!](\text{p}.\text{s})$.

Computational completeness

The significant speedups seen in the examples above naturally lead to another demand: that given program p and partial data s, *all* of p's computations that depend only on its partial input s will be performed.

Unfortunately this is in conflict with the desire that $[\![\text{spec}]\!]$ be total. Suppose, for example, that program p's computations are independent of its second input d, and that $[\![\text{p}]\!]$ is a partial function. Then computational completeness would require $[\![\text{spec}]\!](\text{p}.\text{s})$ to do *all* of p'a computation on s, so it would also fail to terminate whenever $[\![\text{p}]\!](\text{s}.\text{d}) = \bot$. This is a problem, since nobody likes compilers or other program transformers that sometimes loop infinitely!

A typical example which is difficult to specialize nontrivially without having the specializer fail to terminate is indicated by the program fragment

```
if    complex-but-always-true-condition-with-unavailable-input-d
then  X := nil
else  while true do S := cons S S;
```

One cannot reasonably expect the specializer to determine whether the condition will always be true. A specializer aiming at computational completeness and so less trivial than that of section 5.2 will likely attempt to specialize both branches of the while loop, leading to nontermination at specialization time.

A tempting way out is to allow p_s to be less completely specialized in the case that $[\![p]\!](s.d) = \bot$, e.g., to produce a trivial specialization as in section 5.2. This is, however, impossible in full generality, as it would require solving the halting problem.

Some practical specializers make use of run-time nontermination checks that monitor the static computations as they are being performed, and force a less thorough specialization whenever there seems to be a risk of nontermination. Such strategies, if capable of detecting all nontermination, must necessarily be overly conservative in some cases; for if perfect, they would have solved the halting problem.

Optimality

It is desirable that the specializer be "optimal" when used for compiling, meaning that `spec` removes *all interpretational overhead*. This can be made somewhat more precise, given a self-interpreter `sint`:

$$\text{sint} \in \begin{array}{|c|} \hline L \\ \hline L \\ \hline \end{array}$$

By definition of interpreter and specialization (or by the first Futamura projection), for every $d \in \mathbb{D}$

$$[\![p]\!](d) = [\![\text{sint}_p]\!](d)$$

where $\text{sint}_p = [\![\text{spec}]\!](\text{sint}.p)$. Thus program sint_p is semantically equivalent to p. One could reasonably say that the specializer has *removed all interpretational overhead* in case sint_p is at least as efficient as p. We elevate this into a definition:

Definition 6.6.1 Program specializer `spec` is *optimal* for a self-interpreter `sint` in case for every program p and data d, if $\text{sint}_p = [\![\text{spec}]\!](\text{sint}.p)$ then

$$time_{\text{sint}_p}(d) \leq time_p(d)$$

This definition of "optimality" has proven itself very useful in constructing practical evaluators [84]. For several of these, the specialized program sint_p is *identical up to variable renaming* to the source program p. Further, achieving optimality in this sense has shown itself to be an excellent stepping stone toward achieving successful and satisfactory compiler generation by self-application.

An open problem. Unfortunately there is a fly in the ointment. The condition just proposed is a definition *relative to one particular self-interpreter* sint. It could therefore be "cheated," by letting spec have the following structure:

```
read  Program, S;
  if  Program = sint
  then  Result := S
  else  Result := the trivial specialization of Program to S;
write Result
```

On the other hand, it would be too much to demand that spec yield optimal specializations of *all possible* self-interpreters. Conclusion: the concept of "optimality" is pragmatically a good one, but one which mathematically speaking is unsatisfactory. This problem has not been resolved at the time of writing, and so could be a research topic for a reader of this book.

6.7   How specialization can be done

Suppose program p expects input (s.d) and we know what s but not d will be. Intuitively, specialization is done by performing those of p's calculations that depend only on s, and by generating code for those calculations that depend on the as yet unavailable input d. A partial evaluator thus performs a mixture of execution and code generation actions — the reason Ershov called the process "mixed computation" [43], hence the generically used name mix for a partial evaluator (called spec in chapter 3). Its output is often called the *residual program*, the term indicating that it is comprised of operations that could not be performed during specialization.

For a simple but illustrative example, we will show how Ackermann's function (seen earlier in section 6.4.1) can automatically be specialized to various values of its first parameter. Ackermann's function is useless for practical computation, but an excellent vehicle to illustrate the main partial evaluation techniques quite simply. An example is seen in Figure 6.3. (The underlines should be ignored for now.) Note that the specialized program uses *less than half as many* arithmetic operations as the original.

Computing a(2,n) involves recursive evaluations of a(m,n) for m = 0, 1 and 2, and various values of n. The partial evaluator can evaluate expressions m=0 and m−1 for the needed values of m, and function calls of form a(m−1,...) can be unfolded (i.e., replaced by the right side of the recursive definition above, after the appropriate substitutions).

A two input program $p =$

```
a(m,n) = if m = 0 then n+1 else

        if n = 0 then a(m-1,1) else

    a(m-1,a(m,n-1))
```

Program p, specialized to static input m = 2:

$p_2 =$

```
a2(n) = if n=0 then a1(1) else a1(a2(n-1))
a1(n) = if n=0 then a0(1) else a0(a1(n-1))
a0(n) = n+1
```

Figure 6.3: Specialization of a Program for Ackermann's Function.

More generally, three main partial evaluation techniques are well known from program transformation: *symbolic computation, unfolding function calls,* and *program point specialization*. Program point specialization was used in the Ackermann example to create specialized versions a0, a1, a2 of the function a.

On-line and Off-line Specialization.   Figure 6.3 illustrates *off-line* specialization, an approach that makes use of program *annotations*, indicated there by underlines. The alternative is called *on-line* specialization: computing program parts as early as possible, taking decisions "on the fly" using only (and all) available information.

These methods sometimes work better than off-line methods. Program p_2 in Figure 6.3 is a clear improvement over the unspecialized program, but can obviously be improved even more; a few online reductions will give:

```
a2(n) = if n=0 then 3 else a1(a2(n-1))
a1(n) = if n=0 then 2 else a1(n-1)+1
```

In particular, on-line methods often work well on structured data that is partially static and partially dynamic. On the other hand they introduce new problems and the need for new techniques concerning termination of specializers. For a deeper discussion of the merits of each approach, see [84].

6.7.1   Annotated programs and a sketch of an off-line partial evaluator

The interpretation of the underlines in Figure 6.3 is extremely simple:

1. *Evaluate* all non-underlined expressions;

2. *generate residual code* for all underlined expressions;

3. *unfold at specialization time* all non-underlined function calls; and

4. *generate residual function calls* for all underlined function calls.

Sketch of an off-line partial evaluator.   We assume given:

1. A first-order functional program p of form

   ```
   f1(s,d)   = expression1  (* resp. static & dynamic inputs *)
   g(u,v,...) = expression2
   ...
   h(r,s,...) = expressionm
   ```

2. **Annotations** that mark every function parameter, operation, test, and function call as either *eliminable*: to be performed/computed/unfolded during specialization, or *residual*: generate program text to appear in the specialized program.

In particular the parameters of any definition of a function f can be partitioned into those which are *static* and the rest, which are *dynamic*. For instance m is static and n is dynamic in the Ackermann example.

The specialized program will have the same form as the original, but it will consist of definitions of *specialized functions* $g_{statvalues}$ (program points), each corresponding to a pair (g, statvalues) where g is defined in the original program and statvalues is a tuple consisting of some values for all the static parameters of g. The prameters of function $g_{statvalues}$ in the specialized will be the remaining, dynamic, parameters of g.

A specialization algorithm

Assumptions:

1. The input program p is as above, with defining function given by f1(s,d) = expression1, and static s and dynamic d.

2. Every part of p is annotated as eliminable (no underlines) or residual (underlined).

3. The value of s is given.

In the following, variables `Seenbefore` and `Pending` both range over sets of specialized functions $g_{statvalues}$. Variable `Target` will always be a list of (residual) function definitions.

1. Read `Program` and S. (Program p and static input value s.)
2. `Pending` := {$f1_S$}; `Seenbefore` := {};
3. While `Pending` is nonempty do the following:
4. Choose and remove a pair $g_{statvalues}$ from `Pending`, and add it so `Seenbefore` if not already there.
5. Find g's definition `g(x1,x2,...)` = `g-expression`.
6. • Let `D1,...,Dm` be its subset of dynamic parameters.
    • Let $s_1,...,s_n$ = `statvalues` be its list of current static parameter values.
7. Generate and append to `Target` the definition

    $g_{statvalues}$`(D1,...,Dm)` = *Reduce*(E);

    where E is the result of substituting s_i in place of each static g-parameter `xi` occurring in `g-expression`, and *Reduce* simplifies the result E.

Given the list `statvalues` of values of all of g's static parameters, reduction of an expression E to its residual equivalent RE = *Reduce*(E) is defined as follows:

1. If E is constant or a dynamic parameter of g, then RE = E.
2. If E is a static parameter of g then then RE = its value, extracted from the list `statvalues`.
3. If E is not underlined and of form `operator(E1,...,En)` then compute the values $v_1,...,v_n$ of *Reduce*(E1),...,*Reduce*(En). (These must be totally computable from g's static parameter values, else the annotation is in error.) Then set

    RE = the value of `operator` applied to $v_1,...,v_n$.

4. If E is $\underline{operator}$(E1,...,En) then compute E1' = *Reduce*(E1), ..., En' = *Reduce*(En).

    RE = the expression "`operator(E1',...,En')`."

5. If E is not underlined and of form `if E0 then E1 else E2` then compute *Reduce*(E0). This must be constant, else the annotation is in error. If *Reduce*(E0) equals `true`, then RE = *Reduce*(E1), otherwise RE = *Reduce*(E2).

6. If E is `if E0 then E1 else E2` and each Ei' equals *Reduce*(Ei), then

    RE = the expression "if E0' then E1' else E2'"

7. Suppose E is `f(E1, E2,...,En)` and `Program` contains definition

    ```
    f(x1 ... xn) = f-expression
    ```

    Since E is not underlined, the call is to be unfolded. Then RE = *Reduce*(E'), where E' is the result of substituting *Reduce*(Ei) in place of each static `f`-parameter `xi` occurring in `f-expression`.

8. If E is `f(E1, E2,...,En)`, then

    (a) Compute the tuple `statvalues'` of the static parameters of `f`, by calling *Reduce* on each. This will be a tuple of constant values (if not, the annotation is incorrect.)

    (b) Compute the tuple `Dynvalues` of the dynamic parameters of `f`, by calling *Reduce*; this will be a list of expressions.

    (c) Then RE = the call "$f_{statvalues'}$(Dynvalues)."

    (d) A side-effect: if $f_{statvalues'}$ is neither in `Seenbefore` nor in `Pending`, then add it to `Pending`.

6.7.2 Congruence, binding-time analysis, and finiteness

Where do the annotations used by the algorithm above come from? Their primal source is knowledge of which inputs will be known when the program is specialized, for example m but not n in the Ackermann example. There are two further requirements for the algorithm above to succeed.

First, the internal parts of the program must be properly annotated (witness comments such as "if ... the annotation is incorrect"). The point is that if any parameter or operation has been marked as eliminable, then one needs a guarantee that it actually will be so when specialization is carried out, for *any possible static program inputs*. For example, an `if` marked as eliminable must have a test part that always evaluates to a constant. This requirement (properly formalized) is called the *congruence* condition in [84].

The second condition is *termination*: regardless of what the values of the static inputs are, the specializer should neither attempt to produce infinitely many residual functions, nor an infinitely large residual expression.

It is the task of *binding-time analysis* to ensure that these conditions are satisfied. Given an unmarked program together with a division of its inputs into static (will be known when specialization begins) and dynamic, the binding-time analyzer proceeds to annotate the whole program. Several techniques for this are described in [84]. The problem is complex for the following reason:

1. A specializer must account for all possible runtime actions, but only knows the value of static data. It thus accounts for consequences one step into the future.

2. A binding-time analyzer must account for all possible runtime actions, but only knows *which input values will be static*, but not what their values are. It thus accounts for computational consequences two steps into the future.

The current state of the art is that congruence is definitely achieved, whereas binding-time analyses that guarantee termination are only beginning to be constructed.

Exercises

6.1 Section 6.3 assumed one already had compilers for language S available in both source form h and target form h. In practice, however, writing target code is both involved and error-prone, so it would be strongly preferable only to write h, and the by some form of bootstrapping obtain t satisfying $[\![h]\!]^S = [\![t]\!]^T$.

Explain how this can be done, assuming one only has a compiler for language S available in source form h. Start by writing an interpreter int for S in some existing and convenient executable language L.   □

6.2 Find another way to accomplish the same purpose.   □

6.3 Another practical problem amenable to bootsrapping is that of *cross-compiling*: given a compiler h from S to T written in S, and an executable target version t in an available target language T, the problem is to obtain an executable target version t1 in a new target language T1.

Explain how this can be done. One way is, as a first step, to modify the "code generation" parts of h to obtain compiler h1 from S to T1.   □

6.4 Find another way to accomplish the same purpose. □

6.5 Explain informally the results claimed in section 6.5.4, e.g., why compilation by target = $[\![\text{compiler}]\!]^T(\text{source})$ should be faster than compilation by target = $[\![\text{spec}]\!]^L(\text{int.source})$. □

6.6 Prove that $[\![\text{p}]\!]$ (s.d) = $[\![[\![[\![\text{cogen}]\!]$ (p) $]\!]$ (s) $]\!]$ (d) □

6.7 * Apply the algorithm sketched in section 6.7.1 to the program of Figure 6.3 with static input m = 2. □

6.8 Find an appropriate set of annotations (underlines) for the multiplication program specialized In section 6.4. □

6.9 Prove that cogen = $[\![\text{cogen}]\!]$ (spec). □

References

As mentioned earlier, the possibility, in principle, of partial evaluation is contained in Kleene's *s-m-n* Theorem [95] from the 1930s. The idea to use partial evaluation as a *programming tool* can be traced back to work beginning in the late 1960's by Lombardi and Raphael [107, 106], Dixon [37], Chang and Lee [19], and Sandewall's group [8],

Futamura showed the surprising equations which are nowadays called the Futamura projections in a paper from 1971 [46]. Essentially the same discoveries were made independently in the 1970's by A.P. Ershov [41, 42, 43] and V.F. Turchin [160, 161]. Glück and others have described other ways of combining interpreters, compilers, and specializers, see e.g., [50]. The first implementation of a self-applicable partial evaluator was done at Copenhagen in 1984 [85]. Much of the material in this chapter stems from [84].

In the 1980's and 1990's partial evaluation became a research field of its own, with the first conference in 1988 [11]. For more historical information and references, see [47, 44, 84, 81].

7   Other Sequential Models of Computation

We now define some new machine models that differ more or less radically in their architectures from WHILE. section 7.1 describes some comon features of these models, and sections 7.2–7.5 presents the details of each. New models include:

- GOTO, a model similar to WHILE but with jumps instead of structured loops;
- TM, the *Turing machines* originating in Turing's 1936 paper;
- RAM, the *random access machines*, a model of computer machine languages.
- CM, the *counter machines*, a simple model useful for undecidability proofs.

Remark to the reader.   This chapter and chapter 8 introduce a series of new computational models based, loosely speaking, on new architectures; and chapter 9 introduces two models based on languages: one for first-order data, and the other, the lambda calculus, allowing arbitrary functions as values.

The net effect and goal of these three chapters is to provide evidence for the Church-Turing thesis: that *all computation models are equivalent*. The means by which the goal is achieved involve defining the several new machine types (input-output data sets, computational states, computations, etc.); defining codings between their various data types; and showing how machines or programs of the one sort can simulate ones of the other sorts. Some of these constructions will be revisited later when arguing for the robustness of, for example, polynomially time-bounded computations.

Some readers, already convinced of this, may wish to skip forward to chapter 10, on natural undecidable problems. For their sake we point out two facts used several places later in the book:

- Counter machines, with just two counters and instructions to increment or decrement either by 1, or test either for zero, are a *universal computing model*: any computable function can, modulo some data encoding, be computed by some two-counter program. (Theorem 8.7.2.)
- Further, the GOTO language, whose programs are essentially "flow chart" equivalents to WHILE programs, are also a universal computing model. Some future constructions will be based on this representation.

7.1   Common characteristics of GOTO, TM, RAM, CM

7.1.1   Data structures: one atom nil, two symbols 0, 1

For simplicity we use $A = \{\texttt{nil}\}$ in the models where L–*data* $= \mathbb{D}_A$. By Proposition
3.7.9, this does not involve any loss of generality since any set $\mathbb{D}$ where A is a finite set
of atoms can be encoded in the set $\mathbb{D}_{\{\texttt{nil}\}}$. Thus, below $\mathbb{D}$ stands for $\mathbb{D}_{\{\texttt{nil}\}}$.

Further, we assume without loss of generality that TM-*data* $= \{0,1\}^*$, since a Turing
machine with a larger tape alphabet can be simulated with at most linear loss of time,
by one that works on symbols encoded as strings in $\{0,1\}^*$ by encoding each symbol in
an k-symbol alphabet as a block of $\lceil \log k \rceil$ bits.

Our presentation of Turing machines is nonstandard because of its programmed control, and a fixed tape alphabet. A later section on the "speedup theorem" will use the
classical model, defined in section 7.6.

7.1.2   Control structures

Each of the computational models GOTO, TM, RAM, and CM has an imperative control
structure, naturally expressible by a program which is a finite sequence of instructions:
$\texttt{p} = \texttt{I}_1 \; \texttt{I}_2 \; \ldots \; \texttt{I}_m$. Sometimes this will be written with explicit labels: $\texttt{p} = \; \texttt{1}:$
$\texttt{I}_1 \; \texttt{2}: \; \texttt{I}_2 \; \ldots \; \texttt{m}: \; \texttt{I}_m \; \texttt{m+1}: \;$. The exact form of each instruction $\texttt{I}_\ell$ will be different
for the various machine types. At any point in its computation, the program will be in
a *state* of form

$$s = (\ell, \sigma) \text{ where } \quad \ell \in \{1, 2, \ldots, m, m+1\} \text{ is a program label and}$$
$$\sigma \text{ is a } \textit{store} \text{ whose form will vary from model to model}$$

A *terminal state* has label $\ell = m + 1$, indicating that the computation has terminated. To
describe computations we use the common judgment forms:

Judgment form:	Read as:
$[\![\texttt{p}]\!](\texttt{x}) = \texttt{y}$	y is the output from running program p on input x
$\texttt{p} \vdash s \rightarrow s'$	A control transition from state s to state s' in one step
$\texttt{p} \vdash s \rightarrow^* s'$	Control transition in 0, 1, or more steps

Sequences of control transitions or *computations* are defined in terms of one-step transitions as follows, for any stores s, s', s'':

$$p \vdash s \rightarrow^* s$$
$$p \vdash s \rightarrow^* s' \quad \text{if } p \vdash s \rightarrow s'' \text{ and } p \vdash s'' \rightarrow^* s'$$

In any one run, the store will be initialized according to the program input, and the program's computed result will be read out from the final store. Details differ from machine to machine, so we assume given functions of the following types, to be specified later for each model:

$$\begin{array}{lll} Readin: & \text{L-}data & \rightarrow & \text{L-}store \\ Readout: & \text{L-}store & \rightarrow & \text{L-}data \end{array}$$

Finally, we can define the effect of running program p on input x by: $[\![p]\!](x) = y$ if

1. $\sigma_0 = Readin(x)$
2. $p \vdash (1, \sigma_0) \rightarrow^* (m+1, \sigma)$, and
3. $y = Readout(\sigma)$

7.2   A flowchart language GOTO

Definition 7.2.1 First, GOTO-*data* = $\mathbb{D}$ as in Definition 9.1.1. Let Vars be a countable set of variables. We use the conventions $d, e \in \mathbb{D}$ and $X, Y, Z \in$ Vars. Then GOTO-*prog* = the set of imperative programs as in section 7.1, where informal syntax of a GOTO instruction is given by the following grammar:

```
I  ::=  X := nil | X := Y | X := hd Y | X := tl Y
   |    X := cons Y Z | if X goto ℓ else ℓ'
```

Labels ℓ in if statements must be between 1 and $m+1$.

The test =? has been omitted since, by section 2.4, general equality can be expressed using atomic equality; and there is only one atom nil, which can be tested for using the if instruction.   □

Note that every expression has at most one operator, and tests must use variables rather than expressions. The intuitive semantics of GOTO-programs is as follows. Execution begins with instruction I_1. Assignments are executed as in WHILE. A statement if X goto ℓ else ℓ' is executed in the obvious way: if the value of X is not nil then execution proceeds with instruction I_ℓ, and otherwise instruction instruction I'_ℓ is executed.

Here is a version of the reverse program in GOTO, where instructions goto ℓ and if X goto ℓ abbreviate the obvious special cases of if X goto ℓ else ℓ'. The input will be read into X and the output will be written from X.

```
I1: Y := nil;
I2: if X goto 4;
I3: goto 8;
I4: Z := hd X;
I5: Y := cons Z Y;
I6: X := tl X;
I7: goto 2;
I8: X:= Y
```

Note how the combination of if and goto simulates the effect of while.

Definition 7.2.2 Consider a program $p = I_1 \; \ldots \; I_m$ and let $\texttt{Vars(p)} = \{\texttt{X,Z1}\ldots,\texttt{Zn}\}$ be the set of all variables in p.

1. A *store* for p is a function from $\texttt{Vars(p)}$ to $\mathbb{D}$. A *state* for p is a pair (ℓ,σ) where $1 \leq \ell \leq m+1$ and σ is a store for p.

2. *Readin*$(\texttt{d}) = [\texttt{X} \mapsto \texttt{d}, \texttt{Z1} \mapsto \texttt{nil}, \ldots \texttt{Zn} \mapsto \texttt{nil}]$.

3. *Readout*$(\sigma) = \sigma(\texttt{X})$.

4. The one-step transition rules for GOTO appear in Figure 7.1.   □

(ℓ,σ)	$\rightarrow$	$(\ell+1,\sigma[\texttt{X} \mapsto \texttt{nil}])$	If $I\ell = \texttt{X:=nil}$
(ℓ,σ)	$\rightarrow$	$(\ell+1,\sigma[\texttt{X} \mapsto \sigma(\texttt{Y})])$	If $I\ell = \texttt{X:=Y}$
(ℓ,σ)	$\rightarrow$	$(\ell+1,\sigma[\texttt{X} \mapsto \texttt{d}])$	If $I\ell = \texttt{X:=hd Y}$ and $\sigma(\texttt{Y}) = (\texttt{d.e})$
(ℓ,σ)	$\rightarrow$	$(\ell+1,\sigma[\texttt{X} \mapsto \texttt{nil}])$	If $I\ell = \texttt{X:=hd Y}$ and $\sigma(\texttt{Y}) = \texttt{nil}$
(ℓ,σ)	$\rightarrow$	$(\ell+1,\sigma[\texttt{X} \mapsto \texttt{e}])$	If $I\ell = \texttt{X:=tl Y}$ and $\sigma(\texttt{Y}) = (\texttt{d.e})$
(ℓ,σ)	$\rightarrow$	$(\ell+1,\sigma[\texttt{X} \mapsto \texttt{nil}])$	If $I\ell = \texttt{X:=tl Y}$ and $\sigma(\texttt{Y}) = \texttt{nil}$
(ℓ,σ)	$\rightarrow$	$(\ell+1,\sigma[\texttt{X} \mapsto (\texttt{d.e})])$	If $I\ell = \texttt{X:=cons Y Z}$ and $\sigma(\texttt{Y}) = \texttt{d},\sigma(\texttt{Z}) = \texttt{e}$
(ℓ,σ)	$\rightarrow$	(ℓ',σ)	If $I\ell = \texttt{if X goto}\,\ell'$ else ℓ'' and $\sigma(\texttt{X}) \neq \texttt{nil}$
(ℓ,σ)	$\rightarrow$	(ℓ'',σ)	If $I\ell = \texttt{if X goto}\,\ell'$ else ℓ'' and $\sigma(\texttt{X}) = \texttt{nil}$

Figure 7.1: One-step transition rules for GOTO-programs.

7.3 The Turing machine TM

This model is a direct formalization of Turing's analysis of computational processes, using a sequence of instructions for control.

First, TM-*data* = $\{0,1\}^*$, so an input is a bit string. A Turing machine has one or more tapes. Each tape is a two-way infinite sequence of *squares*, where a square contains a symbol from a finite *tape alphabet* A including the "blank symbol" B. During a computation the square's contents may be tested or overwritten. At any time during a computation there will only be finitely many nonblank symbols on any tape.

In the literature the tape alphabet can sometimes be arbitrarily large, but we use $\{0,1,B\}$ for simplicity and because it only makes small constant changes in running times: the same reasons for restricting the GOTO language to one atom.

In a computational total state at some moment, each of the machine's *read/write heads* is scanning one "current" square on each tape, and it is about to perform one of its program instructions. This directs the machine to do one of the following for one of the tapes: *write* a new symbol on the tape, replacing the previous scanned tape square's contents; *move* its read/write head one square to the left or to the right; or *compare* the contents of its scanned square against a fixed symbol and then transfer control to one instruction if it matches, and to another instruction if not.

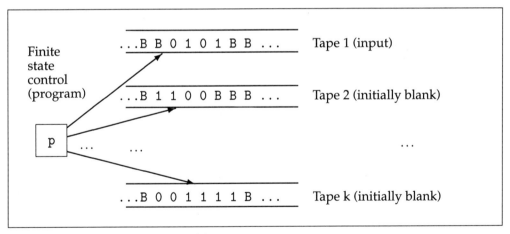

Figure 7.2: A multitape Turing machine.

The following grammar describes TM-*prog* by giving the syntax of both instructions and data. Subscript $j, 1 \leq j \leq k$, indicates which tape is involved. For one-tape Turing machines the subscript will be omitted.

$$
\begin{array}{llll}
\text{I}: & \text{Instruction} & ::= & \text{right}_j \mid \text{left}_j \mid \text{write}_j \text{ S} \mid \text{if}_j \text{ S goto } \ell \text{ else } \ell' \\
\text{S,S}': & \text{Symbol} & ::= & 0 \mid 1 \mid \text{B} \\
\text{L,R}: & \text{String} & ::= & \text{S String} \mid \varepsilon \quad (\varepsilon \text{ is the empty string}) \\
\sigma: & \text{Tapes} & ::= & \text{Tape}^k \\
& \text{Tape} & ::= & \text{L } \underline{\text{S}} \text{ R}
\end{array}
$$

A store σ is conceptually a k-tuple of two-way infinite tapes. The tapes must be represented finitely in order to define the transition rules. One way is to include all nonblank symbols, so a full tape is obtained by appending infinitely many blanks to each end of a finite tape representation. A full storage state consists of a store in which the scanned symbol will be underlined. Thus we define

$$
\text{TM-}store = \{ (\text{L}_1 \underline{\text{S}}_1 \text{R}_1, \dots, \text{L}_k \underline{\text{S}}_k \text{R}_k) \mid \text{L}_i, \text{S}_i, \text{R}_i \text{ as above} \}
$$

Here the underlines mark the scanned symbols S_i, and L_i and R_i are (perhaps empty) strings of symbols.

Inputs and outputs are strings in TM-*data* = $\{0,1\}^*$, are found on the first tape, and consist of all symbols to the right of the scanned symbol, extending up to but not including the first blank. The store initialization and result readout functions are defined as follows:

$$
\begin{array}{lll}
Readin(\text{x}) & = (\underline{\text{B}}\text{x}, \underline{\text{B}}, \dots, \underline{\text{B}}) & \text{Start just left of input} \\
Readout(\text{L}_1 \underline{\text{S}}_1 \text{R}_1, \text{L}_2\underline{\text{S}}_2\text{R}_2, \dots, \text{L}_k\underline{\text{S}}_k\text{R}_k) & = Pfx(\text{R}_1) & \text{Tape 1, right to first B}
\end{array}
$$

where

$$
Pfx(\text{R}) = \begin{cases} \varepsilon & \text{if R} = \varepsilon \text{ or if R begins with B} \\ \text{S } Pfx(\text{R}') & \text{if R} = \text{S R}' \text{ and S} = 0 \text{ or } 1 \end{cases}
$$

Finally, one-tape Turing machine one-step transition rules are defined as in Figure 7.3, where I_ℓ is the instruction about to be executed. Extension to multiple tapes is straightforward but notationally tedious, and so is omitted.

7.4 The counter machine CM

A counter machine program has as storage a finite number of *counters* (also called *registers* or *cells*) X0, X1, X2,..., each holding a natural number. Thus CM-*data* = $\mathbb{N}$.

$$
\begin{array}{lll}
\mathtt{p} \vdash (\ell, \mathrm{L\underline{S}S'R}) \to (\ell+1, \mathrm{LS\underline{S}'R}) & \text{If } \mathrm{I}_\ell = \mathtt{right} \\
\mathtt{p} \vdash (\ell, \mathrm{L\underline{S}}) \quad \to (\ell+1, \mathrm{LS\underline{B}}) & \text{If } \mathrm{I}_\ell = \mathtt{right} \\
\mathtt{p} \vdash (\ell, \mathrm{LS'\underline{S}R}) \to (\ell+1, \mathrm{LS'\underline{S}R}) & \text{If } \mathrm{I}_\ell = \mathtt{left} \\
\mathtt{p} \vdash (\ell, \mathrm{\underline{S}R}) \quad \to (\ell+1, \mathrm{\underline{B}SR}) & \text{If } \mathrm{I}_\ell = \mathtt{left} \\
\mathtt{p} \vdash (\ell, \mathrm{L\underline{S}R}) \quad \to (\ell+1, \mathrm{L\underline{S}'R}) & \text{If } \mathrm{I}_\ell = \mathtt{write \ S'} \\
\mathtt{p} \vdash (\ell, \mathrm{L\underline{S}R}) \quad \to (\ell', \mathrm{L\underline{S}R}) & \text{If } \mathrm{I}_\ell = \mathtt{"if \ S \ goto} \ \ell''' \mathtt{"} \\
\mathtt{p} \vdash (\ell, \mathrm{L\underline{S}R}) \quad \to (\ell', \mathrm{L\underline{S}R}) & \text{If } \mathrm{I}_\ell = \mathtt{"if \ S' \ goto} \ \ell' \ \mathtt{else} \ \ell''' \mathtt{"} \text{ and } \mathrm{S} \neq \mathrm{S}' \\
\end{array}
$$

Figure 7.3: Turing machine one-step transition rules.

Program instructions allow testing a counter for zero, or incrementing or decrementing a counter's contents by 1 (where $0 \mathbin{\dot-} 1 = 0$ by definition, else $x \mathbin{\dot-} 1 = x-1$). All counter contents are initially zero except for the input. The following grammar describes the CM instruction syntax and so defines CM-*prog*.

$$
\mathtt{I} \quad ::= \quad \mathtt{Xi := Xi + 1 \mid Xi := Xi \mathbin{\dot-} 1 \mid if \ Xi=0 \ goto} \ \ell \ \mathtt{else} \ \ell'
$$

(Sometimes the dot will be omitted.) Additional computable instructions could be added, e.g., $\mathtt{Xi := 0}$, $\mathtt{Xi := Xj}$, $\mathtt{if \ Xi = 0 \ goto} \ \ell$, or $\mathtt{goto} \ \ell$. Such extensions are, however, unnecessary in principle since they are special cases of or can be simulated using the instruction set above.

A store σ is a function in

$$
\text{CM-}store = \{\ \sigma \mid \sigma : \mathbb{N} \to \mathbb{N}\}
$$

where $\sigma(i)$ is the current contents of counter $\mathtt{Xi}$ for any $i \in \mathbb{N}$. The store initialization and result readout functions are defined as follows:

$$
\begin{array}{lll}
Readin(\mathtt{x}) & = & [0 \mapsto x, 1 \mapsto 0, 2 \mapsto 0, \ldots] \quad \text{Input in counter 0} \\
Readout(\sigma) & = & \sigma(0) \qquad\qquad\qquad\qquad\quad \text{Output from counter 0}
\end{array}
$$

Any one program can only reference a fixed set of counters. Thus for any store σ used to execute it, $\sigma(i) = 0$ will hold for all but a fixed finite set of indices. Finally, the counter machine one-step transition rules are defined as in Figure 7.4.

$$p \vdash (\ell, \sigma) \rightarrow (\ell+1, \sigma[i \mapsto j+1])$$ If $\mathtt{I}_\ell$ = "Xi := Xi + 1" and $\sigma(i) = j$
$$p \vdash (\ell, \sigma) \rightarrow (\ell+1, \sigma[i \mapsto j-1])$$ If $\mathtt{I}_\ell$ = "Xi := Xi ∸ 1" and $\sigma(i) = j \neq 0$
$$p \vdash (\ell, \sigma) \rightarrow (\ell+1, \sigma[i \mapsto 0])$$ If $\mathtt{I}_\ell$ = "Xi := Xi ∸ 1" and $\sigma(i) = 0'$
$$p \vdash (\ell, \sigma) \rightarrow (\ell', \sigma)$$ If $\mathtt{I}_\ell$ = "if Xi=0 goto ℓ' else ℓ'''" $\land \sigma(i) = 0$
$$p \vdash (\ell, \sigma) \rightarrow (\ell'', \sigma)$$ If $\mathtt{I}_\ell$ = "if Xi=0 goto ℓ' else ℓ'''" $\land \sigma(i) \neq 0$

Figure 7.4: Counter machine one-step transition rules.

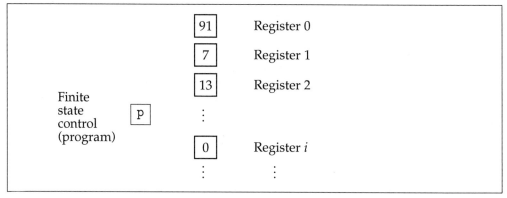

Figure 7.5: Picture of a random access machine.

7.5   The random access machine RAM

This machine is an extension of the counter machine which more closely resembles current machine languages. It has a number of storage registers containing natural numbers (zero if uninitialized), and a much richer instruction set than the counter machine. The exact range of instructions allowed differ from one application to another, but nearly always include

1. Copying one register into another.
2. Indirect addressing or indexing, allowing a register whose number has been computed to be fetched from or stored into.
3. Elementary operations on one or more registers, for example adding or subtracting 1, and comparison with zero.
4. Other operations on one or more registers, for example addition, subtraction, multiplication, division, shifiting, or bitwise Boolean operations (where register con-

tents are regarded as binary numbers, i.e., bit sequences).

The *successor random access machine*, SRAM, has only instruction types 1, 2, 3 above. General RAM operations vary within the literature. Although rather realistic in some aspects, the SRAM is, nonetheless, an idealized model with respect to actual machine codes. The reason is that there is no built-in limit to word size or memory address space: it has a potentially infinite number of storage registers, and each may contain an arbitrarily large natural number. Even though any one program can only address a constant number of storage registers directly, indirect addressing allows unboundedly many other registers to be accessed.

The following grammar describes the SRAM instruction syntax.

$$I \quad ::= \quad \texttt{Xi := Xi + 1} \mid \texttt{Xi := Xi} \doteq \texttt{1} \mid \texttt{if Xi=0 goto } \ell \texttt{ else } \ell'$$
$$\mid \quad \texttt{Xi := Xj} \mid \texttt{Xi := <Xj>} \mid \texttt{<Xi> := Xj}$$

While this machine resembles the counter machine, it is more powerful in that it allows programs to fetch values from and store them into *cells with computed addresses*. The intuitive meaning of `Xi := <Xj>` is an *indirect fetch*: register `Xj`'s contents is some number n; and that the contents of register `Xn` are to be copied into register `Xi`. Similarly, the effect of `<Xi> := Xj` is an *indirect store*: register `Xi`'s contents is some number m; and the contents of register `Xj` are to be copied into register `Xm`.

This version is nearly minimal, but will suffice for our purposes. More general RAM models seen in the literature often have larger instruction sets including addition, multiplication, or even all functions computed by finite-state automata with output, operating on their argments' binary representations. We will argue that such extensions do not increase the class of computable functions. They can, however, affect the class of polynomial-time solvable problems, as the more powerful instructions can allow constructing extremely large values within unrealistically small time bounds.

The RAM storage has the form

$$\textrm{SRAM-}store = \{\ \sigma \mid \sigma : \mathbb{N} \to \mathbb{N}\}$$

where $\sigma(j)$ is the current contents of register `Xj`. Further,

$$
\begin{array}{lll}
Readin(\mathrm{x}) & = & [0 \mapsto x, 1 \mapsto 0, \ldots] \quad \text{Input in register X0} \\
Readout(\sigma) & = & \sigma(0) \quad\quad\quad\quad\quad\quad \text{From register X0}
\end{array}
$$

Even though one program can directly reference only a fixed set of registers, the indirect operations allow access to registers not appearing in the program text (perhaps unboundedly many). On the other hand, the store is initialized to zero except for its input register, so at any point during a computation only finitely many registers can contain nonzero values. Consequently the machine state can be represented finitely (in fact we will see that a Turing machine can simulate a SRAM).

The SRAM one-step transition rules are defined as in Figure 7.6.

$$
\begin{array}{lll}
\mathtt{p} \vdash (\ell, \sigma) & \rightarrow & (\ell + 1, \sigma[i \mapsto \sigma(i) + 1]) \quad \text{If } \mathtt{I}_\ell = \text{"Xi := Xi+1"} \\
\mathtt{p} \vdash (\ell, \sigma) & \rightarrow & (\ell + 1, \sigma[i \mapsto \sigma(i) - 1]) \quad \text{If } \mathtt{I}_\ell = \text{"Xi := Xi} \dot{-} \text{ 1" and } \sigma(i) \neq 0 \\
\mathtt{p} \vdash (\ell, \sigma) & \rightarrow & (\ell + 1, \sigma[i \mapsto 0]) \quad \text{If } \mathtt{I}_\ell = \text{"Xi := Xi} \dot{-} \text{ 1" and } \sigma(i) = 0 \\
\mathtt{p} \vdash (\ell, \sigma) & \rightarrow & (\ell + 1, \sigma[i \mapsto 0]) \quad \text{If } \mathtt{I}_\ell = \text{"Xi := 0"} \\
\mathtt{p} \vdash (\ell, \sigma) & \rightarrow & (\ell', \sigma) \quad \text{If } \mathtt{I}_\ell = \text{"if Xi=0 goto } \ell' \text{ else } \ell'''" \\
& & \qquad\qquad \text{and } \sigma(i) = 0 \\
\mathtt{p} \vdash (\ell, \sigma) & \rightarrow & (\ell'', \sigma) \quad \text{If } \mathtt{I}_\ell = \text{"if Xi=0 goto } \ell' \text{ else } \ell'''" \\
& & \qquad\qquad \text{and } \sigma(i) \neq 0 \\
\mathtt{p} \vdash (\ell, \sigma) & \rightarrow & (\ell + 1, \sigma[i \mapsto \sigma(j)]) \quad \text{If } \mathtt{I}_\ell = \text{"Xi := Xj"} \\
\mathtt{p} \vdash (\ell, \sigma) & \rightarrow & (\ell + 1, \sigma[i \mapsto \sigma(\sigma(j))]) \quad \text{If } \mathtt{I}_\ell = \text{"Xi := <Xj>"} \\
\mathtt{p} \vdash (\ell, \sigma) & \rightarrow & (\ell + 1, \sigma[\sigma(i) \mapsto \sigma(j)]) \quad \text{If } \mathtt{I}_\ell = \text{"<Xi>:= Xj"}
\end{array}
$$

Figure 7.6: Successor random access machine one-step transition rules.

7.6   Classical Turing machines

We will later on prove certain results for which it matters whether one chooses the formulation of Turing machines above, or the classical formulation usually adopted in the literature. Therefore we now briefly review the classical definition.

Definition 7.6.1 A k-tape classical Turing machine is a quintuple

$$(\Sigma, Q, \ell_{init}, \ell_{fin}, T)$$

where

1. Σ is a finite alphabet containing a distinguished symbol B;
2. Q is a finite set of states, including ℓ_{init}, ℓ_{fin}; and
3. T is a set of tuples of form

$$(\ell, (\mathtt{a}_1, \mathtt{b}_1, M_1), \ldots, (\mathtt{a}_k, \mathtt{b}_k, M_k), \ell')$$

where

(a) $a_1, \ldots, a_k, b_1, \ldots, b_k \in \Sigma$;

(b) $M_1, \ldots, M_k \in \{\leftarrow, \downarrow, \rightarrow\}$; and

(c) $\ell, \ell' \in Q$ and $\ell \neq \ell_{fin}$.

The Turing machine is *deterministic* if for every ℓ and $a_1, \ldots, a_k$ there exists at most one $b_1, \ldots, b_k$, $M_1, \ldots, M_k$, and ℓ' such that $(\ell, (a_1, b_1, M_1), \ldots, (a_k, b_k, M_k), \ell') \in T$.   □

It is perhaps easiest to understand the definition by comparison with the previous definition of Turing machines. Whereas the previous definition insisted that every Turing machine use the same tape alphabet $\{0, 1, B\}$, the present definition allows each machine to have its own tape alphabet Σ. Moreover, whereas the previous Turing machine was controlled by a sequence of labeled commands, we now have instead a set of states Q, and a set of transitions T between these states. Roughly, every state $\ell \in Q$ corresponds to a label in the earlier definition, and every transition $t \in T$ corresponds to a command.

Consider, for instance, a 1-tape Turing machine with transition

$$(\ell, (a, b, M), \ell')$$

Such transitions will also simply be written

$$(\ell, a, b, M, \ell')$$

The meaning of the transition is: in state ℓ, if the scanned square contains a, overwrite a with b, perform an action as specified by M, and goto state ℓ', where the different values of M are interpreted as follows:

$\leftarrow$:   move the read/write head one square to the left
$\downarrow$:   do not move the read/write head
$\rightarrow$:   move the read/write head one square to the right

All this is counted as taking 1 step.

A tuple

$$(\ell, (a_1, b_1, M_1), \ldots, (a_k, b_k, M_k), \ell')$$

specifies the analogous k-tape Turing machine state transition: in state ℓ, if the scanned symbol on tape i is a_i, for all $i \in \{1, \ldots k\}$, then b_i is to be written in place of a_i for all $i \in \{1, \ldots k\}$, the read/write head on tape i is moved according to M_i, for all $i \in \{1, \ldots k\}$, and the new state becomes ℓ'. All this is also counted as taking 1 step. Note that all the a_i are replaced by the b_i if this tuple applies; else none of them are replaced.

In order to formalize computations we make use of *configurations*. For a 1-tape Turing machine a configuration is a pair $(\ell, (L, \sigma, R))$, where ℓ is the current state, σ is the current scanned symbol, and L and R are the contents of the tape to the left and right of σ, respectively. Transitions modify the configurations as sketched above. A computation always begins in state ℓ_{init} with a blank as the scanned symbol, blank tape to the left, and the input to the right. Computations end in ℓ_{fin} (if they end at all) with the output to the right of the scanned symbol up to the first blank. There are no transitions from ℓ_{fin}.

The tape to the left and right of the scanned symbol are at all times finite. In the situation where one moves, say, to the right and the tape to the right is empty, we simply add a blank.

This is all made precise in the following definition.

Definition 7.6.2 Given a k-tape Turing machine $M = (\Sigma, Q, \ell_{init}, \ell_{fin}, T)$.

1. A *configuration* of M is an element of $Q \times (\Sigma^* \times \Sigma \times \Sigma^*)^k$.

2. One configuration C *leads to* another C', notation $C \rightsquigarrow C'$, if

$$
\begin{aligned}
C &= (\ell, (L_1, \sigma_1, R_1), \ldots, (L_n, \sigma_n, R_n)) \\
C' &= (\ell', (L_1', \sigma_1', R_1'), \ldots, (L_n', \sigma_n', R_n'))
\end{aligned}
$$

and there is a transition $(\ell, (a_1, b_1, M_1), \ldots, (a_k, b_k, M_k), \ell') \in T$ such that for all $i = 1, \ldots, k$ both $\sigma_i = a_i$, and:

(a) if $M_i = \leftarrow$ then

    i. if $L_i = \varepsilon$ then $L_i' = \varepsilon$, $\sigma_i' = B$, and $R_i' = b_i R_i$;

    ii. if $L_i = \gamma\sigma$ then $L_i' = \gamma$, $\sigma_i' = \sigma$, and $R_i' = b_i R_i$.

(b) if $M_i = \downarrow$ then $L_i' = L_i$, $\sigma_i' = b_i$, and $R_i' = R_i$

(c) if $M_i = \rightarrow$ then

    i. if $R_i = \varepsilon$ then $R_i' = \varepsilon$, $\sigma_i' = B$, and $L_i' = b_i L_i$;

    ii. if $R_i = \sigma\gamma$ then $R_i' = \gamma$, $\sigma_i' = \sigma$, and $L_i' = b_i L_i$.

3. C leads to C' in m steps, notation $C \rightsquigarrow^m C'$, if there is a sequence of configurations $C_1, \ldots, C_n$ such that $C = C_1$ and $C' = C_n$.

4. For $x, y \in (\Sigma \backslash \{B\})^*$ we write $M(x) = y$, if for some m

$$
\begin{aligned}
&(\ell_{init}, (\varepsilon, B, x), (\varepsilon, B, \varepsilon), \ldots, (\varepsilon, B, \varepsilon)) \quad \rightsquigarrow^m \\
&(\ell_{fin}, (L_1, \sigma_1, yR_1), (L_2, \sigma_2, R_2), \ldots, (L_k, \sigma_k, R_k))
\end{aligned}
$$

where R_1 is either ε or begins with B.

5. *M decides* a set $L \subseteq \Sigma$, if

$$M(x) = \begin{cases} 1 & \text{for every } x \in \Sigma \\ 0 & \text{for every } x \in \Sigma \backslash L \end{cases}$$

$\square$

Example 7.6.3 Here is a 1-tape Turing machine M that takes a number in the unary number system as input, and returns its successor as output, i.e., $M(x) = x1$ for all unary numbers x.

1. $\Sigma = \{0, 1, B\}$;
2. $Q = \{\ell_1, \ell_2, \ell_3, \ell_4\}$;
3. $\ell_{init} = \ell_1$;
4. $\ell_{fin} = \ell_4$;
5. $T = \{(\ell_1, B, B, \rightarrow, \ell_2), (\ell_2, 1, 1, \rightarrow, \ell_2), (\ell_2, B, 1, \leftarrow, \ell_3), (\ell_3, 1, 1, \leftarrow, \ell_3), (\ell_3, B, B, \downarrow, \ell_4)\}$

The machine is started with scanned symbol B, blank tape to the left, and the input $1 \cdots 1$ to the right. Therefore it begins (first transition) by moving one step to the right. Then (second transition) it moves one step to the right as long as it sees 1's. When it reaches a blank after the 1's, it replaces the blank by an extra 1 (third transition). It then moves to the left to get back to the initial blank (fourth transition), and when it arrives, it terminates (fifth transition).

Here is a more clever machine computing the same function:

1. $\Sigma = \{0, 1, B\}$;
2. $Q = \{\ell_1, \ell_2\}$;
3. $\ell_{init} = \ell_1$;
4. $\ell_{fin} = \ell_2$;
5. $T = \{(\ell_1, B, 1, \leftarrow, \ell_2)\}$.

$\square$

Note that every transition must write something to the scanned square. In order to simply move the read/write head one must write the same symbol to the scanned square as is already present. For instance,

$$(\ell_1, B, B, \rightarrow, \ell_2)$$

is the first transition in the example above which moves the read/head one square to the right. It is convenient to let *nop* be an abbreviation for the triple $(B, B, \downarrow)$. In case we know the scanned square is a blank, this operation neither moves the read/write head nor writes anything to the tape—it performs a "no-operation."

Exercises

7.1 Show that a program with several one-dimensional arrays can be simulated in a RAM. □

7.2 Show that it is not necessary to assume that every RAM memory cell is initialized to 0. Show how, given a RAM program p as defined above, to construct a RAM program q which has the same input-output behavior as p, regardless of the initial state of its memory. □

7.3

1. Show that function $x + 1$ is computable by a Turing machine, if given as input the binary representation of x.
2. Show that a Turing machine can, given input of form xBy where $y, x \in \{0,1\}^*$, decide whether $x = y$. An alphabet larger than $\{0,1,B\}$ may be assumed, if convenient. □

7.4 Show how to simulate instructions `Xi := 0`, `Xi := Xj`, `goto` ℓ, and `if Xi` $\neq 0$ `goto` ℓ `else` ℓ' on a counter machine as defined above. □

7.5 Show that a counter machine can compute functions $x + y, 2 \cdot x, x/2$. □

7.6 * This exercise and the next concern the construction of a self-interpreter for SRAM programs. Part 1: devise an appropriate way to represent the instruction sequence comprising an SRAM program as SRAM data in memory. (Hint: you may wish to use more than memory cell to contain one instruction.) □

7.7 * Part 2: Sketch the operation of the self-interpreter for SRAM programs. This can store the program to be interpreted in odd memory locations, and can represent memory cell *loc* of the program being interpreted by the interpreter's memory cell $2 \cdot loc$. □

7.8 Prove that the function $f(x) =$ the largest u such that $x = 3^u \cdot y$ for some y is CM-computable. □

References

The data structure of `GOTO` is very similar to that of first-order LISP or Scheme, and its control structure is very similar to early imperative languages, e.g., BASIC. Counter and random access machines were first studied by Shepherdson and Sturgis [155], and are now very popular in complexity theory, for instance in the book by Aho, Hopcroft and Ullman [2].

The SRAM and equivalent *storage modification machines* were studied by Scönhage [152]. Turing machines were introduced in [162] and are widely studied in computability and complexity theory. The book by Papadimitriou [130] gives a large-scale introduction to complexity theory and computation models. and [165] covers an even broader range.

8 Robustness of Computability

In this chapter we undertake the task of justifying the Church-Turing thesis, by proving that all the different models introduced in the preceding chapter are equivalent[1] to the WHILE model introduced earlier. The result is that computability, without limitations on resource bounds, is equivalent for all of: WHILE, I, GOTO, CM, 2CM, RAM, and TM. This implies that many results about WHILE carry over to the other models directly. For instance, the halting problem is undecidable for all of the above languages.

Section 8.1 presents an overview of the equivalence proof. Sections 8.5-8.2 then prove the various equivalences by means of compilation and interpretation.

8.1 Overview

Figure 8.1 gives an overview of the translations and interpretations in this chapter (plus two involving functional language F, to be given in the next chapter). The labels in the diagram sum up the techniques that are used. The proofs of equivalence come in three variations:

1. Show for a language pair X, Y how to compile an arbitrary X-program p into an equivalent Y-program q (possibly with change in data representation, as in Definition 3.3.3).
2. Show for a language pair X, Y how to write an interpreter for X in Y.
3. The remaining arcs, labeled with ⊂, are trivial. For instance, every 2CM-program is a CM-program with exactly the same computational meaning.

Figure 8.2 shows the form of data and store in each of the computation models. Compilation from WHILE to I was dealt with in section 3.7.3; this involves coding multi-atom trees into ones with only nil.

8.2 From GOTO to WHILE and back

Proposition 8.2.1 There is a compiling function from WHILE to GOTO.

Proof. By standard techniques; see the Exercises. □

---

[1] Effectively so: There are computable compiling functions between any two.

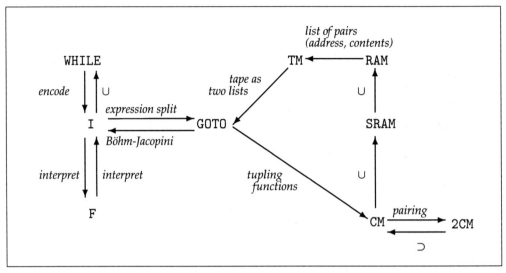

Figure 8.1: Equivalences among computational models.

Language L	L-*data*	L-*store*	Input	Output
TM	$\{0,1\}^*$	$\sigma = L \underline{S} R$	$\underline{B} R$	R
GOTO	$\mathbb{D}$	$\sigma : \mathbb{N} \to \mathbb{D}$	$\sigma(0)$	$\sigma(0)$
WHILE and I	$\mathbb{D}$	$\sigma : \mathbb{N} \to \mathbb{D}$	$\sigma(0)$	$\sigma(0)$
CM	$\mathbb{N}$	$\sigma : \mathbb{N} \to \mathbb{N}$	$\sigma(0)$	$\sigma(0)$
RAM	$\mathbb{N}$	$\sigma : \mathbb{N} \to \mathbb{N}$	$\sigma(0)$	$\sigma(0)$

Figure 8.2: Forms of data and stores

The converse of the above proposition also holds. The classic *Böhm-Jacopini construction* in effect shows that every program can be written in the form of one while loop (and no goto's) by adding an extra "instruction counter" variable. For instance, the GOTO version of the `reverse` program can be converted back into the WHILE program shown in Figure 8.3, where we use numerals from Subsection 2.1.6.

Proposition 8.2.2 There is a compiling function from GOTO to WHILE.

Proof. See the Exercises.   □

There is a controversy, sometimes experienced in undergraduate programming courses, as to whether the use of goto-statements in Pascal is acceptable. It is often claimed that

```
    read X;
      C := 1;
      while C do
        if (=? C 1) then { Y := nil; C := 2 };
        if (=? C 2) then { if X then C := 4 else C := 3};
        if (=? C 3) then { C := 8 };
        if (=? C 4) then { Z := hd X; C := 5 };
        if (=? C 5) then { Y := cons Z Y; C := 6 };
        if (=? C 6) then { X := tl X; C := 7 };
        if (=? C 7) then { C := 2 };
        if (=? C 8) then { X := Y; C := 0 };
    write X
```

Figure 8.3: The result of using the Böhm-Jacopini construction on `reverse`.

GOTO programs are unstructured whereas WHILE programs are well-structured. The preceding example shows that WHILE programs can be exactly as unstructured as GOTO programs. In practice, however, using WHILE programs often yields better-structured programs.

The preceding theorem is related to Kleene's Normal Form Theorem (13.4.3) for recursive functions in that it shows that any WHILE program can be written on the form

```
    read X;
      Y := 1;
      while Y do C;
    write X
```

where C does not contain any while loops (except those required by the macro facility to program if-statements).

8.3   Compilations with change of data

The various remaining machine types have different forms of input-output data, which necessitates transforming back and forth between different data domains. Figures 8.4, 8.5 show the encodings that we will use to represent one machine type's data for simulation by another machine type. (The notation $< \_,\_ >$ used for c_{pr} will be defined shortly.)

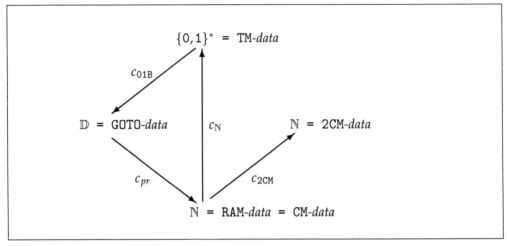

Figure 8.4: Data encodings between machine models.

8.3.1   Common characteristics of the simulations

All the simulations proceed by step-by-step simulation of program instructions. The process of establishing that one can correctly embed computations by model L into those of M can be summed up as follows, following the pattern of Definition 3.3.3:

1. Define a one-to-one data encoding $c : \text{L-}data \to \text{M-}data$.

2. Define a representation of any store $\sigma \in \text{L-}store$ by a store $\bar{\sigma} \in \text{M-}store$.

3. Define the construction of an M-program $\bar{p} = \bar{I}_0 ; \bar{I}_1 ; \bar{I}_2 ; \ldots \bar{I}_k ; \bar{I}_{k+1}$ from an L-program $p = I_1 ; I_2 ; \ldots ; I_k$.
   Here $\bar{I}_0$ and and $\bar{I}_{k+1}$ (if present) are respectively "set-up" code needed to prepare the simulation, and "clean-up" code to deliver the result in the needed final format.

4. Prove that $\bar{p}$ correctly simulates the actions of p.

We will mostly gloss over the correctness problem except where the construction is non-trivial, hoping the reader will find the other constructions sufficiently straightforward not to need formal proof.

Coding function c		Definition of c
c_{01B}	: $\{0,1,B\}^* \to \mathbb{D}$	$c_{01B}(a_1 a_2 \ldots a_k) = (a_1^\dagger a_2^\dagger \cdots a_k^\dagger)$ (in list notation)
		where $B^\dagger = \texttt{nil}, 0^\dagger = (\texttt{nil.nil}), 1^\dagger = (\texttt{nil.(nil.nil)})$
c_{pr}	: $\mathbb{D} \to \mathbb{N}$	$c_{pr}(\texttt{nil}) = 0$ and $c_{pr}(\texttt{d1.d2}) = 1 + 2^{c_{pr}(\texttt{d1})} \cdot 3^{c_{pr}(\texttt{d2})}$
$c_{\mathbb{N}}$	: $\mathbb{N} \to \{0,1\}^*$	$c_{\mathbb{N}}(v) = c_{\mathbb{N}}(v)$ as defined in section 8.3.2.
c_{2CM}	: $\mathbb{N} \to \mathbb{N}$	$c_{2CM}(v) = 2^v$

Figure 8.5: Coding functions.

8.3.2   Coding numbers as bit strings — isomorphically

The shortest binary representation of a natural number $n \in \mathbb{N}$ gives a one-to-one function $bin : \mathbb{N} \to \{0,1\}^*$. It is not onto and so not an isomorphism, though, since any number of leading zeroes can be prefixed onto a bit string without affecting its value. An isomorphism $c_{\mathbb{N}} : \mathbb{N} \to \{0,1\}^*$ can be defined by a slight variation (Exercise 8.1):

$$c_{\mathbb{N}}(v) \quad = \quad \varepsilon \quad \text{if } v = 0, \text{ else}$$
$$c_{\mathbb{N}}(v) \quad = \quad d \quad \text{where string } 1d \text{ is the shortest binary representation of } v+1$$

which maps $0,1,2,3,4,5,6,7,\ldots$ into ε, 0, 1, 00, 01, 10, 11, 000, $\ldots$

8.4   Compiling RAM to TM

We begin with the most complex compilation, from the most complex machine type (the RAM) to the a quite simple one (the Turing machine).

First, to simplify the construction we reduce RAM instructions to what might be called a RISC or "reduced instruction set" version using register X0 as an accumulator, and with instruction forms:

```
I   ::=   X0 := X0 + 1 | X0 := X0 ÷ 1 | if X0 = 0 goto ℓ
     |    X0 := Xi | Xi := X0 | X0 := <Xi> | <X0>:= Xi
     |    Other operations: X0 := X0 Operation Xi
```

Clearly any RAM program can be converted to an equivalent reduced form program, slowing down its running time by at most a small constant factor.

The Turing machine simulating a RISC RAM program p will have 4 tapes as in the following table, using the encoding $c_N : N \to \{0, 1, B\}^*$ as defined in Figure 8.5. With each tape form we have marked, by underlining, the "standard scan position." This is the position the scan heads are to occupy between simulation of any two RAM instructions.

The first two tapes represent the locations and values of nonzero entries in the RAM store $\sigma = [a_0 \mapsto c_0, \ldots, a_k \mapsto c_k]$. The third tape is the accumulator X0, the fourth is an auxiliary "scratch" tape for various purposes.

Note that "standard scan position" can easily be located: since all number encodings have at least one bit, it will always be the rightmost B in the first BB to the left of any tape's nonblank contents.

Tape number	Tape name	Tape form, standard scan position
1	Addresses	$\ldots \text{BB}\underline{\bar{a}}_0\text{B}\bar{a}_1 \ldots \text{B}\bar{a}_k\text{BB} \ldots$
2	Contents	$\ldots \text{BB}\underline{\bar{c}}_0\text{B}\bar{c}_1 \ldots \text{B}\bar{c}_k\text{BB} \ldots$
3	Accumulator X0	$\ldots \underline{\text{B}} \ \text{---} \ \text{B} \ldots$
4	Scratch	$\ldots \underline{\text{B}} \ \text{---} \ \text{B} \ldots$

Initialization code: the RAM program input $\bar{i}$ is on tape 1. This is first copied to tape 2 and 0 is placed on tape 1, signifying that cell 0 contains value $\bar{i}$. After this, both heads are moved one position left to assume standard position. *Termination code*: the first value $\bar{c}_0$ on tape 2 is copied onto tape 1, and all other information is erased.

The simulation is described by three examples; the reader can fill in the rest.

1. X0 := X0 + 1:

   Find the right end of the (nonblank portion of the) Accumulator tape 3. Repeatedly replace 1 by 0 on it, and shift left one position, as long as possible. When a 0 or B is found, change it to 1 and move one left to stop in standard position..

2. X23 := X0:

   Scan right on tapes 1 and 2, one B block at a time, until the end of tape 1 is reached or tape 1 contains a block B10111B. (Note: 10111 is 23 in binary notation.)

   If the end of tape 1 was reached, location 23 has not been seen before. Add it, by writing 10111 at the end of tape 1, and copy tape 3 (the value of X0) onto tape 2; and return to standard position.

If, however, B10111B was found on tape 1, then $\bar{c}_{23}$ is scanned on tape 2. In this case it must be overwritten, done as follows:

- copy $\bar{c}_{24}...B\bar{c}_k B$ onto scratch tape 4;

- copy tape 3 (the value of X0) in place of $\bar{c}_{23}$ on tape 2;

- write B and copy tape 4 onto tape 2, thus reinstating the remainder $\bar{c}_{24}...B\bar{c}_k B$ after the new $\bar{c}_{23}$; and finally

- return to standard position.

3. X0 := <X23>:

   Starting at the left ends of tapes 1 and 2, scan right on both, one B block at a time, until the end of tape 1 is reached or tape 1 contains a block with B10111B.
   If the end is reached do nothing, as $c_{23} = 0$ and tape 3 already contains c_0.
   If B10111B was found on tape 1, then $\bar{c}_{23}$ is scanned on tape 2. Copy $\bar{c}_{23}$ onto tape 4. As above, search tapes 1 and 2 in parallel until location $B\bar{c}_{23}B$ is found on tape 1, or tape 1's end is found. If the end was reached, write 0 on tape 3, since $c_{c_{23}} = c_0$. Otherwise copy the tape 2 block corresponding to tape 1 onto tape 3, as the tape 2 block contains $c_{(c_{23})}$, and return to standard position.

Finally, "other operations" X0 := X0 Operation Xi can be simulated as long as they denote Turing-computable functions on natural numbers. This holds for all operations in the various RAM models which have been proposed.

8.5 Compiling TM to GOTO

For simplicity of notation we describe how to compile one-tape Turing machine programs into equivalent GOTO programs; the extension to multiple tapes is obvious and simple. We follow the "common pattern." The encoding of Turing machine tapes as GOTO values uses the encoding c_{01B} defined in Figure 8.5.

A Turing machine store $\sigma = L \underline{S} R$ will be represented by three GOTO variables Lf, C, Rt, whose values are related to the tape parts by $C = S^\dagger$ (notation defined in Figure 8.5), $Rt = c_{01B}(R)$, and $Lf = c_{01B}\tilde{L}$, where $\tilde{L}$ is L written backwards, last symbol first. A Turing machine program $p = I_1 ; I_2 ; \ldots I_k$ is compiled into a simulating GOTO-program $\bar{p} = \bar{I}_1 ; \bar{I}_2 ; \ldots \bar{I}_k$, where each $\bar{I}_i$ is the sequence of GOTO commands defined next (with some syntactic sugar for readability).

TM command	GOTO code must achieve
right	if (=? Rt nil) then Rt := (nil . nil); Lf := cons C Lf; C := hd Rt; Rt := tl Rt;
left	if (=? Lf nil) then Lf := (nil . nil); Rt := cons C Rt; C := hd Lf; Lf := tl Lf;
write S	C := d where d = S†
if S goto ℓ	if C = d then goto ℓ where d = S†

The initial GOTO store for Turing Machine input $\underline{B}R$ is

$$[\text{Rt} \mapsto c_{01B}(\text{R}), \text{C} \mapsto \text{nil}, \text{Lf} \mapsto \text{nil}]$$

It is straightforward to prove that $\bar{\text{p}}$ correctly simulates the actions of p.

8.6 Compiling GOTO to CM

CM program values are natural numbers, so we represent tree structures in $\mathbb{D}$ by numbers, using c_{pr} as defined in Figure 8.5. For every GOTO variable with value x, there will be a corresponding CM variable with value $c_{pr}(x)$. Consequently every CM variable will have value 0 or $2^u \cdot 3^v$ for some u, v; and both u and v will have the same property (recursively).

A GOTO program $\text{p} = \text{I}_1; \text{I}_2; \ldots \text{I}_k$ is compiled into a simulating CM-program $\bar{\text{p}} = \bar{\text{I}}_1; \bar{\text{I}}_2; \ldots \bar{\text{I}}_k$, where each $\bar{\text{I}}_i$ is the sequence of extended CM commands defined next (with some syntactic sugar for readability).

GOTO command	Extended CM code
Xi := nil	Xi := 0
Xi := cons Xj Xk	Xi := $2^{\text{Xj}} \cdot 3^{\text{Xk}}$
Xi := hd Xj	Xi := u where Xi$= 2^u \cdot 3^v$
Xi := tl Xj	Xi := v where Xi$= 2^u \cdot 3^v$
if Xi = a goto ℓ	if Xi $= c_{pr}(\text{a})$ then goto ℓ

It is straightforward to prove that $\bar{\text{p}}$ correctly simulates the actions of p. The only remaining task is to show that these extended CM-commands are in fact CM-computable.

Definition 8.6.1 Function $f : \mathbb{N}^k \to \mathbb{N}_\perp$ is *CM-computable* iff there is a CM-program q with counters X1,...,Xk such that if $\sigma_0 = [1 \mapsto x_1, \ldots, k \mapsto x_k,$ all other $i \mapsto 0]$ and $y, x_1, \ldots, x_n \in \mathbb{N}$, then

$$f(x_1, \ldots, x_n) = y \text{ iff } q \vdash \sigma_0 \to^* [0 \mapsto y, \ldots]$$

Lemma 8.6.2 The following functions are all CM-computable, where c is any constant:
$a(x) = x + c$, $g(x, y) = x + y$, $h(x, y) = x \cdot y$, $e(x) = c^x$, and
$m(x) = \max\{y \mid \exists z . x = c^y \cdot z\}$.

Proof. The c-instruction sequence X1:=X1+1; ... ; X1:=X1+1 computes function $a(x) = x + c$. Functions $g(x, y) = x + y$, $h(x, y) = x \cdot y$, and $e(x) = c^x$ are computable by the three programs:

```
X0 := X1; while X2 ≠ 0 do { X0 := X0+1; X2 := X2-1 }

X3 := X1; X0 := 0;
while X2 ≠ 0 do { X0 := X0 + X3; X2 := X2-1 }

X3 := X1; X0 := 1;
while X2 ≠ 0 do { X0 := X0 · X3; X2 := X2-1 }
```

This nearly completes the proof that the functions used in the compilation are CM-computable, except for $m(x)$. This is left as Exercise 8.2.   □

8.7   Compiling CM to 2CM

Lemma 8.7.1 Suppose CM program p has one input and contains k variables X1,...,Xk where $k \geq 3$. Then there is an CM program q with only two variables Y, Z such that $[\![p]\!]$ can be incorporated into $[\![q]\!]$ by encoding $c_{2CM}(x) = 2^x$.   □

Proof. Each command I_ℓ of p will be replaced by a sequence of commands $\overline{I}_\ell$ in q. Variables X1,...,Xk are represented in q by two variables Y, Z. Letting h be the k-th prime number, the following *simulation invariant property* will be maintained:

If variables X1, X2,...Xk have values $x_1, x_2, \ldots, x_k$ (respectively) before execution of any p-instruction I_ℓ, then

$$\text{Value\_of}(Y) = 2^{x_1} \cdot 3^{x_2} \cdot \ldots \cdot h^{x_k}$$

will hold before execution of the corresponding q-instruction sequence $\overline{I}_\ell$.

Explanation of the simulation method: variable Z is used as an auxiliary. Assuming the simulation invariant to hold, operations X2:= X2 + 1, X2 := X2 - 1, and X2=0? (for instance) can be realized by replacing y by $3 \cdot y$, or $y \div 3$, or deciding whether y is divisible by 3. It is easy to see that these can be done with two counters; for example $y \div 3$ can be computed by

```
while Y>0 do { Y:=Y-1; Z:=Z+1 }
while Z ≥ 4 do {Y := Y+1; Z := Z-3 }
```

where the test Z ≥ 4 and the operation Z := Z-3 are easily programmed. Operations on the other Xi are similarly realized, completing the construction. Initially p has its input x as value of X1, and every other variable has value 0. By the invariant this corresponds to initial q value $y = 2^x \cdot 3^0 \cdot 5^0 \cdot \ldots = 2^x$ of Y. Thus q is a 2-counter program which, given input $y = 2^x$, terminates with $y = 2^{f(x)} \cdot 3^0 \cdot 5^0 \cdot \ldots = 2^{f(x)}$, as required.   □

Theorem 8.7.2 Any CM-computable function $f(x)$ can be incorporated into a 2CM-computable function.   □

Corollary 8.7.3 The halting problem *HALT-2CM* for 2CM programs is undecidable.   □

Exercises

8.1 Show that the function $c_N : \mathbb{N} \to \{0,1\}^*$ of section 8.3.2 is both one-to-one and onto, and so an isomorphism.   □

8.2 Show that the function: $m(x) = \max\{y \mid \exists z. x = c^y \cdot z\}$ can be computed by a counter machine program, for any fixed c.   □

8.3 Give a compiling function from WHILE programs to GOTO programs. Illustrate on a small example.   □

8.4 Give a compiling function from GOTO programs to WHILE programs. Illustrate on a small example.   □

8.5 Prove Corollary 8.7.3.   □

References

Other kinds of support of the Church-Turing thesis include works by Gandy [48], Kleene [95], Minsky [124], Rogers [147], and Shepherdsen and Sturgis [155].

9 Computability by Functional Languages

(partly by T. Æ. Mogensen)

9.1 A first-order functional language

The language WHILE is *imperative*. This means that WHILE programs have a global *store* that they *update* by means of assignments. In contrast to this, *functional* languages do not have a store. Instead they pass values to other functions in *calls* and receive values when these functions return a result. This difference is reflected in the syntax of programs in that a functional language typically has a syntactic category for expessions but, unlike WHILE, none for commands.

9.1.1 The language F

The language F is a simple first order Lisp-like functional language whose programs have *one recursively defined function* of *one variable*. It resembles language I of section 4.2 in that data is built by cons from the single atom nil.

Definition 9.1.1 Let F-*data* = $\mathbb{D}$. We use the conventions $d, e, f, \ldots \in \mathbb{D}$. Let X be a variable. The informal syntax of programs is given in by the following grammar:

```
Program      ∋ P       ::=  E whererec f(X) = B
Expression   ∋ E,F,B   ::=  X
                        |    nil
                        |    hd E
                        |    tl E
                        |    cons E1 E2
                        |    if E then E1 else E2
                        |    f E
```

The semantics of E whererec f(X)=B is given by the partial functions:

$$\mathcal{P} : \text{Program} \to (\mathbb{D} \to \mathbb{D}_\perp)$$

$$\mathcal{E} : \text{Expression} \to \text{Expression} \to (\mathbb{D} \to \mathbb{D}_\perp)$$

defined in Figure 9.1.   □

$$
\begin{array}{lll}
\mathcal{E}[\![\mathtt{X}]\!]\mathrm{B}v & = & v \\
\mathcal{E}[\![\mathtt{nil}]\!]\mathrm{B}v & = & \mathtt{nil} \\
\mathcal{E}[\![\mathtt{cons\ E1\ E2}]\!]\mathrm{B}v & = & (d_1.d_2) \quad \text{if } \mathcal{E}[\![\mathtt{E1}]\!]\mathrm{B}v = d_1, \mathcal{E}[\![\mathtt{E2}]\!]\mathrm{B}v = d_2 \\
\mathcal{E}[\![\mathtt{hd\ E}]\!]\mathrm{B}v & = & d_1 \quad \text{if } \mathcal{E}[\![\mathtt{E}]\!]\mathrm{B}v = (d_1.d_2) \\
\mathcal{E}[\![\mathtt{hd\ E}]\!]\mathrm{B}v & = & \mathtt{nil} \quad \text{if } \mathcal{E}[\![\mathtt{E}]\!]\mathrm{B}v \in A \\
\mathcal{E}[\![\mathtt{tl\ E}]\!]\mathrm{B}v & = & d_2 \quad \text{if } \mathcal{E}[\![\mathtt{E}]\!]\mathrm{B}v = (d_1.d_2) \\
\mathcal{E}[\![\mathtt{tl\ E}]\!]\mathrm{B}v & = & \mathtt{nil} \quad \text{if } \mathcal{E}[\![\mathtt{E}]\!]\mathrm{B}v \in A \\
\mathcal{E}[\![\mathtt{if\ E\ then\ E1\ else\ E2}]\!]\mathrm{B}v & = & d \quad \text{if } \mathcal{E}[\![\mathtt{E}]\!]\mathrm{B}v \neq \bot \text{ or } \mathtt{nil}, \mathcal{E}[\![\mathtt{E1}]\!]\mathrm{B}v = d \\
\mathcal{E}[\![\mathtt{if\ E\ then\ E1\ else\ E2}]\!]\mathrm{B}v & = & d \quad \text{if } \mathcal{E}[\![\mathtt{E}]\!]\mathrm{B}v = \mathtt{nil}, \mathcal{E}[\![\mathtt{E2}]\!]\mathrm{B}v = d \\
\mathcal{E}[\![\mathtt{f(E)}]\!]\mathrm{B}v & = & w \quad \text{if } \mathcal{E}[\![\mathtt{E}]\!]\mathrm{B}v = u, \mathcal{E}[\![\mathtt{B}]\!]u = w \\
\\
\mathcal{P}[\![\mathtt{E0\ whererec\ f(X)\ =\ B}]\!]v & = & \mathcal{E}[\![\mathtt{E0}]\!]\mathrm{B}v
\end{array}
$$

Figure 9.1: Meanings of F-programs

The function $\mathcal{E}[\![\mathrm{E}]\!]$ B v gives the result of evaluating expression E, assuming variable X has value v, and that E occurs within a recursive program of form E `whererec` `f(X)` = B. If the expression never terminates on the given value v (due to a never-ending recursion), then $\mathcal{E}[\![\mathrm{E}]\!]$ Bv will not be defined.

Example 9.1.2 The expression `append (cons (a1...am) (b1...bm))` returns the list `(a1...am b1...bm)`.

```
append Z whererec append(Z) =
    if (hd Z) then cons (hd hd Z) (append (tl hd Z) (tl Z))
            else (tl Z)
```
                                                                                                      □

Example 9.1.3 The following is a "tail recursive" version of the `reverse` program in F, esentially the imperative program of Example 2.1.4, written in functional style. The expression `reverse (cons X nil)` returns the list X reversed. The program does so by keeping the two variables X and Y from the corresponding WHILE program in packed together in the single F variable, here called Z. An update of a variable in WHILE is simulated by a function call in F.

```
rev (cons Z nil) whererec rev(Z) =
  if (hd Z)
  then reverse (cons (tl (hd Z)) (cons (hd (hd Z)) (tl Z))
  else (tl Z)
```

□

9.1.2 The language F+

An F+ program has programs with several multi-parameter functions defined by nutual recursion:

```
E whererec f1(X1...Xk)=E1, ..., fn(Y1,...,Ym)=En
```

The task of Exercise 9.1 is to define its semantics in a manner resmbling that above for F. The purpose of Exercise 9.2 is to show that this richer version of the F language is no more powerful than the simple seen above.

9.2 Interpretation of I by F and vice versa

In this section we are concerned with the problem of writing interpreters for F in WHILE or I, and vice versa. One half of this will be left to the Exercises:

Proposition 9.2.1 There exists an interpreter intIF for I written in F.

Proof. See Exercise 9.3.   □

Proposition 9.2.2 There exists an interpreter intFI for F written in I.

Proof. First we need to give a concrete syntax to F programs. This is done in Figure 9.2, where var', quote',...,doif' should be understood as distinct elements of $\mathbb{D}$.
An interpreter intFWHILE for F written in WHILE can be obtained by modifying the expression evaluation part of WHILE's universal program from section 4.1, partly by adding new variable B that is used as in the semantic equations defining F. The resulting interpreter appears in Figure 9.3.

The STEP command is similar to the one in the WHILE^{1var} interpreter written in WHILE with two exceptions: the rules pertaining to commands have been removed, and three new transitions have been added to deal with function calls.
How they work: the call assigns to X the call's argument. After the argument has been evaluated and placed on the computation stack (variable w), operation docall' saves

```
E whererec f(X)=B  =  (E.B)

X                  =  (var')
d                  =  (quote' d)
cons E F           =  (cons' E F)
hd E               =  (hd' E)
tl E               =  (tl' E)
if E F G           =  (if' E F G)
f(E)               =  (call' E)
```

Figure 9.2: Concrete syntax of F programs

the current value v of X by pushing it on the code stack. The new code stack top becomes the body B of the enclosing program, thus setting the recursive call in action. Once this is finished with its result u on top of the computation stack, operation `return'` restores X to its previous value.

Although interpreter `intFWHILE` only uses the atom `nil`, it has several variables. These may be compressed into one as in section 3.7.2, yielding the desired interpreter `intFI`.   □

9.3   A higher-order functional language LAMBDA

A commonly used model of computation is the lambda calculus [23], [7]. It is, however, seldom used in complexity texts as the notion of a computation cost is unclear. This is both because the number of reduction steps depends heavily on the reduction strategy used and because the basic reduction step in the lambda calculus – β-reduction – is considered too complex to be an atomic computation step. We will not investigate these issues here, as our prime objective is to show that the lambda calculus has the same computation power as the I language, and hence the same as WHILE.

Expressions in the lambda calculus are either variables, lambda-abstractions or applications:

$$\Lambda \ ::= \ x_1 \mid x_2 \mid \cdots$$
$$\mid \ \lambda x_i.\Lambda$$
$$\mid \ \Lambda\,\Lambda$$

```
    read X;          (* X will be ((E.B).D) where D input *)
     Cd := hd hd X;  (* Expression to be evaluated          *)
     B  := tl hd X;  (* Body of function definition         *)
     Vl := tl X;     (* Initial value of simulated X        *)
     St := nil;      (* Computation stack                   *)
     while Cd do STEP;
    write X
```

where STEP is:

```
case Cd, St of
     (quote' D).Cd,    St          ⇒  St := cons D St;
     (var' X).Cd,      St          ⇒  St := cons Vl St;
     (hd' E).Cd,       St          ⇒  Cd := list E dohd' Cd;
     dohd'.Cd,         T.St        ⇒  St := cons (hd T) St;
     (tl' E).Cd,       St          ⇒  Cd := list E dotl' Cd;
     dotl'.Cd,         T.St        ⇒  St := cons (tl T) St;
     (cons' E1 E2).Cd, St          ⇒  Cd := list E1 E2 docons' Cd;
     docon's.Cd,       U.(T.St)    ⇒  St := cons (cons U T) St;
     (call' E).Cd,     St          ⇒  Cd := list E docall' Cd;
     docall'.Cd,       W.St        ⇒  Cd := list B return' Cd;
                                       St := cons Vl St; Vl := W;
     return'.Cd,       U.V.St      ⇒  St :=cons U St; Vl:= V;
     (if' E F G).Cd,   St          ⇒  Cd := list E doif' F G Cd;
     doif'.F.G.Cd,     nil.St      ⇒  Cd := cons G Cd;
     doif'.F.G.Cd,     D.St        ⇒  Cd := cons F Cd
```

Figure 9.3: Interpretation of F by WHILE

We will, for readability, often use (possibly subscripted) single-letter names for the x_i. In the expression $\lambda x.E$, the variable x is bound by the λ and has scope in the expression E. We use the usual abbreviations:

$$\lambda ab\ldots c.A \;=\; \lambda a.\lambda b.\cdots \lambda c.A$$
$$AB\ldots C \;=\; ((AB)\ldots C)$$

where a, b, c are arbitrary variables and A, B, C are arbitrary lambda expressions. We call a lambda expression *closed* if it has no free (unbound) variables.

The intuitive meaning of an abstraction $\lambda x.E$ is a function that takes a value for the variable x and computes the value of the expression E (which may contain x) given that value. Application $F\,B$ corresponds to applying a function F to a value B. This is modeled by the basic computation step in the lambda calculus, *β-reduction*:

Definition 9.3.1 A β-redex (or just redex) is an expression of the form $(\lambda x. A)\, B$. The operation of β-reduction is done by the following rule:

$$(\lambda x. A)\, B \;\to_\beta\; A[x := B]$$

where the substitution $A[x := B]$ replaces free occurences of x with B and renames bound variables i A to avoid clash with free variables in B:

$$
\begin{aligned}
x[x := A] &= A \\
y[x := A] &= y \qquad && \text{if } x \neq y \\
(B\,C)[x := A] &= (B[x := A])\,(C[x := A]) \\
(\lambda y.\, B)[x := A] &= \lambda z.((B[y := z])[x := A]) \qquad && \text{where } z \text{ is a fresh variable}
\end{aligned}
$$

β-reduction can be performed anywhere in a lambda expression, and we lift the notation $A \to_\beta B$ to mean that A reduces to B by applying a single β-reduction anywhere in the term A (leaving the rest unchanged). A term is said to be in (full) normal form if it contains no β-redexes. A normal form of a lambda calculus term A is a normal form term B that can be obtained from A by repeated β-reductions. Not all terms have normal forms. □

The Church-Rosser theorem [7] shows that the order of reductions in a certain sense doesn't matter: if, starting with the same lambda expression, two sequences of reductions lead to normal forms (lambda expressions where no β-reductions can be performed), then the same normal form will be reached by both reduction sequences. Hence, it makes sense to talk about *the* normal form of a term, if any such exist.

The theorem is actually a bit broader than this, but this is what we need here. Note, however, that the order of reduction can have significant impact on the number of reductions required to reach the normal form, and indeed even on whether the normal form is reached.

Various notions of what is considered a *value* in lambda calculus have been used. As we want to represent arbitrary tree-structures, we have chosen to let values be normal form lambda expressions. For a discussion on other choices, including weak head normal forms and head normal forms and on the mathematical models of computation these imply, see [7]. This also discusses properties of different strategies for the order of reduction.

We define the language LAMBDA as having closed lambda calculus expressions as programs. Values in input and output are lambda calculus expressions in normal form. Running a program P with inputs $X_1, \ldots, X_n$ is done by building the application $P\,X_1\,\ldots\,X_n$ and reducing this to normal form. The output of the program is the normal form obtained this way.

9.4   Equivalence of LAMBDA and the other models

We will first show that LAMBDA is as powerful as I by writing an interpreter for I in LAMBDA. Then we will write an interpreter for LAMBDA in an extended version of the simple functional language F. Since the equipotency of F and I has already been established in section 9.1, this concludes our argument.

9.4.1   Implementing I in the lambda calculus

We will now write an interpreter for I in LAMBDA. To do so we must first decide how to represent syntax of I programs and values in the domain $\mathcal{D}$. Both values and lambda expressions will be represented in the form of normal form λ-expressions.

Values can be represented in many ways in the lambda calculus. We have chosen the representation strategies used in [126] and [125]. Values in $\mathcal{D}$ are represented by a representation function $\lceil\ \rceil^{\mathcal{D}} : \mathcal{D} \to \Lambda$, defined as follows:

$$\begin{aligned} \lceil \texttt{nil} \rceil^{\mathcal{D}} &= \lambda ab\,.\,a \\ \lceil (v.w) \rceil^{\mathcal{D}} &= \lambda ab\,.\,b\, \lceil v \rceil^{\mathcal{D}}\, \lceil w \rceil^{\mathcal{D}} \end{aligned}$$

We can do case analysis on a $\mathcal{D}$-value v by applying it (or rather, its representation) to two LAMBDA expressions N and P. If v is $\texttt{nil}$, $\lceil v \rceil^{\mathcal{D}}$ N P reduces to N. If v is a pair (a,b), $\lceil v \rceil^{\mathcal{D}}$ N P reduces to P $\lceil a \rceil^{\mathcal{D}}$ $\lceil b \rceil^{\mathcal{D}}$. Hence, by letting P $= \lambda ht\,.\,h$, we can take the head of v and by letting P $= \lambda ht\,.\,t$, we can take the tail.

We recall the syntax of I:

```
Program     ∋  P    ::=  read X; C; write X
Command     ∋  C,D  ::=  X := E
                     |   C ; D
                     |   while E do C
Expression  ∋  E,F  ::=  X
                     |   nil
                     |   cons E F
                     |   hd E
                     |   tl E
```

First we want to represent expressions. We use a somewhat different representation strategy than for values. We let the representation of an expression E, $\lceil E \rceil^{\mathcal{E}}$ be $\lambda xcht\,.\,\overline{\text{E}}^{\mathcal{E}}$, where $\overline{\mathrm{E}}^{\mathcal{E}}$ is defined by

$$
\begin{aligned}
\overline{\mathrm{X}}^{\mathcal{E}} &= x \\
\overline{\mathrm{nil}}^{\mathcal{E}} &= \lceil \mathrm{nil} \rceil^{\mathcal{D}} \\
\overline{\mathrm{cons\ E\ F}}^{\mathcal{E}} &= c\ \overline{\mathrm{E}}^{\mathcal{E}}\ \overline{\mathrm{F}}^{\mathcal{E}} \\
\overline{\mathrm{hd\ E}}^{\mathcal{E}} &= h\ \overline{\mathrm{E}}^{\mathcal{E}} \\
\overline{\mathrm{tl\ E}}^{\mathcal{E}} &= t\ \overline{\mathrm{E}}^{\mathcal{E}}
\end{aligned}
$$

Note that $\overline{\mathrm{E}}^{\mathcal{E}}$ uses the variables bound by the λ in $\lambda xcht.\overline{\mathrm{E}}^{\mathcal{E}}$. The variables "tag" expressions with their kinds. Note that nil has no tag. We represent commands in a similar way: $\lceil \mathrm{C} \rceil^{\mathcal{C}} = \lambda xsw.\overline{\mathrm{C}}^{\mathcal{C}}$, where $\overline{\mathrm{C}}^{\mathcal{C}}$ is defined by

$$
\begin{aligned}
\overline{\mathrm{X\ :=\ E}}^{\mathcal{C}} &= x\ \lceil \mathrm{E} \rceil^{\mathcal{E}} \\
\overline{\mathrm{C\ ;\ D}}^{\mathcal{C}} &= s\ \overline{\mathrm{C}}^{\mathcal{C}}\ \overline{\mathrm{D}}^{\mathcal{C}} \\
\overline{\mathrm{while\ E\ do\ C}}^{\mathcal{C}} &= w\ \lceil \mathrm{E} \rceil^{\mathcal{E}}\ \overline{\mathrm{C}}^{\mathcal{C}}
\end{aligned}
$$

And finally we represent programs by

$$
\lceil \mathrm{read\ X;\ C;\ write\ X} \rceil^{\mathcal{P}} = \lceil \mathrm{C} \rceil^{\mathcal{C}}
$$

That is, we represent a program by the command it contains. Figure 9.4 shows an I program and its encoding as a LAMBDA term.

9.4.2   Implementing the semantics of I

We will first construct a LAMBDA expression eval, which will take the representation of an expression and the value of X and return the value of the expression. Using this, we will construct a LAMBDA expression do, which will take the representation of a command and the value of X and return the value of X after the command has been executed. This will be our interpreter of I in LAMBDA.

Running an I program P on input v is done by running the LAMBDA program do on inputs $\lceil \mathrm{P} \rceil^{\mathcal{P}}$ and $\lceil \mathrm{v} \rceil^{\mathcal{D}}$. This will yield a normal form $\lceil \mathrm{w} \rceil^{\mathcal{D}}$ if and only if P given the input v yields an output w.

```
read X;
X := cons X nil;
while hd X do
    X := cons (tl (hd X)) (cons (hd (hd X)) (tl X));
X := tl X;
write X
```

An I program for reversing a list.

$\lambda xsw.$
$s\ (x\ (\lambda xcht.c\ x\ (\lambda ab.a)))$
$(s\ (w\ (\lambda xcht.h\ x)$
$\quad (x\ (\lambda xcht.c\ (t\ (h\ x))\ (c\ (h\ (h\ x))\ (t\ x)))))$
$x\ (\lambda xcht.t\ x))$

The encoding of the reverse program. The layout of the encoding (including line breaks) reflects the layout of the I program.

Figure 9.4: An I program and its encoding

Evaluation of expressions   We now define the LAMBDA expression `eval` for evaluating expressions:

$\text{eval} = \lambda \text{E}x.\text{E}\ x$
$\qquad\qquad (\lambda htab.b\ h\ t)$
$\qquad\qquad (\lambda d.d\ d\ (\lambda ht.h))$
$\qquad\qquad (\lambda d.d\ d\ (\lambda ht.t))$

The idea is that when evaluating an expression every occurrence of the 'tag' (variable) x in the representation of an expression will be replaced by the current value of X, every 'tag' c by a function $\lambda htab.b\ h\ t$ that can `cons` two arguments, every h by a function that takes the head of a pair (and returns `nil` if given `nil` as argument) and every t by a similar function returning the tail of a pair. Note that since constants are untagged in the representation of expressions, these are returned unchanged by `eval`.

Execution of commands   We use a similar idea for the do function. The recursive nature of the `while` command is a bit complex, though. We first present do, then explain the details

```
do = λC.C eval
          (λcdx.d (c x))
          (λEc.W W)
```

where

$$W = \lambda wx.\text{eval E } x\, (\lambda w.x)\, (\lambda htw.w\, w\, (c\, x))\, w$$

Occurences of eval in do and W and occurences of W in do represent that the entire expressions these represent should be inserted in place of the names. This is just substitution of macros. This means that the free variables E and c in W get bound by the λ in the last line of the definition of do (the line that uses W).

Similar to before, interpretation of a command C will replace occurrences of the tagging variables x, s and w in the representation of C by functions that 'do the right thing' with the commands. For the assignment command X := E, this is eval, which evaluates E and returns its value, which becomes the new value of X. For composite commands C; C, the function $\lambda cdx.d\, (c\, x)$ will first execute C (by its execution function c) and pass the new value of X to the execution function d of D, which then produces the final value of X.

Execution of the while statement is more tricky. The function $\lambda Ec.W$ W takes the condition expression E of the while command while E do C and the execution function c of the body C and then self-applies W. This yields

$$\lambda x.\text{eval E } x\, (\lambda w.x)\, (\lambda htw.w\, w\, (c\, x))\, W$$

When this is given a value x_0 of X, eval E x_0 evaluates E with respect to this value. If the result of the evaluation is nil, the situation becomes

$$(\lambda ab.a)\, (\lambda w.x_0)\, (\lambda htw.w\, w\, (c\, x_0))\, W$$

since $\lceil \text{nil} \rceil^{\mathcal{D}} = \lambda ab.a)$. This reduces to

$$(\lambda w.x_0)\, W$$

and finally to x_0. This is correct, as a nil condition terminates the while loop and returns the value of X unchanged. If instead the condition evaluates to a pair (p.q), we get

$$(\lambda ab.b\, \lceil p \rceil^{\mathcal{D}}\, \lceil q \rceil^{\mathcal{D}})\, (\lambda w.x_0)\, (\lambda htw.w\, w\, (c\, x_0))\, W$$

since $\lceil (\mathtt{p}.\mathtt{q}) \rceil^{\mathcal{D}} = \lambda ab.b \, \lceil \mathtt{p} \rceil^{\mathcal{D}} \, \lceil \mathtt{q} \rceil^{\mathcal{D}}$. This reduces to

$$(\lambda htw.w \, w \, (c \, x_0)) \, \lceil \mathtt{p} \rceil^{\mathcal{D}} \, \lceil \mathtt{q} \rceil^{\mathcal{D}}) \, \mathtt{W}$$

and then to

$$\mathtt{W} \; \mathtt{W} \, (c \, x_0)$$

and finally (recalling the definition of W) to

$$(\lambda x.\mathtt{eval} \, \mathtt{E} \, x \, (\lambda w.x) \, (\lambda htw.w \, w \, (c \, x)) \, \mathtt{W}) \, (c \, x_0)$$

which is the same as before we started executing the `while` loop, except that the value x_0 of X has been modified by the execution function c the body C of the loop. Hence, the entire `while` command is redone using the new value of X.

Termination and time complexity Readers familiar with the lambda calculus might wonder why we haven't used a fixed-point operator to model the `while` loop. The reason is that the present method is more robust under changes in reduction order: If an I program P terminates on some input v, then (do $\lceil P \rceil^{\mathcal{P}} \, \lceil v \rceil^{\mathcal{D}}$) terminates regardless of the order of reduction used to reduce lambda expressions. For certain reduction strategies (including call-by-value), the number of β-reductions required to reach the normal form is proportional to the number of primitive operations performed by running P (as an I program).

9.4.3 Interpreting the lambda calculus in F+

In our interpretation of the lambda calculus we are interested in reduction to normal form. This means that we can't use the usual simple abstract machines for reducing lambda-terms to weak head normal form (WHNF). Instead we will develop an abstract machine that does a one-step parallel reduction (reduces all redexes, even under lambdas) and iterate this until no redexes are left. Parallel reduction with renaming of bound variables can be expressed by the function $R[\![\ ]\!] : \Lambda \to Env \to I\!N \to \Lambda$, where $\rho \in Env : Var \to \Lambda$ is a mapping from variables to LAMBDA terms. The number $n \in I\!N$ is used for renaming variables. To obtain a normal form, $R[\![\ ]\!]$ must be applied repeatedly until its output equals its input.

$$
\begin{aligned}
R[\![x]\!]\rho n &= \rho\, x \\
R[\![(\lambda x.e_1)\, e_2]\!]\rho n &= R[\![e_1]\!]\rho[x := R[\![e_2]\!]\rho n]n \\
R[\![e_1\, e_2]\!]\rho n &= (R[\![e_1]\!]\rho n)\,(R[\![e_2]\!]\rho n) \qquad \text{if } e_1 \neq \lambda x.e' \\
R[\![\lambda x.e]\!]\rho n &= \lambda x_n.(R[\![e]\!]\rho[x := x_n](n+1))
\end{aligned}
$$

The notation $(R[\![e_1]\!]\rho n)\,(R[\![e_2]\!]\rho n)$ indicates syntax construction: that an application expression is built from the values of the components $R[\![e_1]\!]\rho n$ and $R[\![e_2]\!]\rho n$. Likewise, $\lambda x_n.(R[\![e]\!]\rho[x := x_n](n+1))$ indicates building of an abstraction expression. These should *not* be confused with semantic application and abstraction as used in denotational semantics.

With a suitable representation of syntax, numbers and environments, we can implement $R[\![\ ]\!]$ in a language F+, which is the functional language F extended with multiple functions and multiple parameters as suggested in Exercise 9.2 and with a case expression similar to the one used for the WHILE language. The extensions do not add power to the language, which can be shown by providing a translation from F+ to F. We will not do so here, though.

We will represent numbers as described in section 2.1.6, hence 0 = nil, 1 = (nil.nil), 2 = (nil.(nil.nil)) etc. We represent the variable x_i by the number i. We represent terms by pairs of tags (numbers) and the components of the term:

$$
\begin{aligned}
\lfloor x_i \rfloor^E &= (0.i) \\
\lfloor E\ F \rfloor^E &= (1.(\lfloor E \rfloor^E.\lfloor F \rfloor^E)) \\
\lfloor \lambda x_i.E \rfloor^E &= (2.(i.\lfloor E \rfloor^E))
\end{aligned}
$$

Environments (ρ) are represented as lists of (name . value) pairs. We are now ready to write the LAMBDA interpreter, shown in Figure 9.5.

The functions normalize and normalize2 make up the 'main loop' of the interpreter, which call r until no change is observed. r implements the $R[\![\ ]\!]$ function. The four cases in the case expression correspond to the four equations of $R[\![\ ]\!]$. equal implements equality over $\mathcal{D}$ and lookup fetches the value of a variable in an environment.

Time complexity   While this interpreter is guaranteed to find (the representation of) the normal form of a LAMBDA expression if one exists, we cannot say much about the complexity of this: An arbitrary amount of work can be done between each β-reduction,

```
normalize P whererec

  normalize(P) =
    normalize2(P,r(P,nil,0))

  normalize2(P,Q) =
    if equal(P,Q) then P else normalize(Q)

  r(E,R,N) =
    case E of
      (0.X)              => lookup(X,R)
      (1.((2.(X.E1)).E2))=> r(E1,cons (cons X r(E2,R,N)) R,N)
      (1.(E1.E2))        => cons 1 (cons r(E1,R,N) r(E2,R,N))
      (2.(X.E1))         => cons 2 (cons N r(E1,
                                       cons (cons X N) R,
                                       cons nil N))
  equal(X,Y) =
    if X then
      if Y then
        if equal(hd X,hd Y) then equal(tl X, tl Y) else nil
      else nil
    else if Y then nil else cons nil nil

  lookup(X,R) =
    if equal(X,hd (hd R)) then tl (hd R) else lookup(X,tl R)
```

Figure 9.5: The LAMBDA interpreter

partly because a β-reduction can require work proportional to the size of the function that is applied and partly due to the need to compare terms for equality in `normalize2`. We can not reasonably expect an interpreter to have running time which is a simple function of the number of β-reductions performed. Cost measures for the lambda calculus not based on the number of β-reductions are discussed in [98].

Exercises

9.1 Define a version F+ of the language F where programs contain several functions each of which have several arguments. That is, the syntax of programs should be E `whererec f1(X1...Xk)=E1, ..., fn(Y1,...,Ym)=En`. Program is to function f k, so there are k arguments. Note that any function may call any other function, or itself. Give a semantics similar to Figure 9.1. □

9.2 Prove that the language of Exercise 9.1 is no more powerful than F by showing that any F+ program can be translated into an equivalent F program. □

9.3 * Prove Proposition 9.2.1. Hint: the pattern used in section 4.2 will make this easier: first, construct the needed interpreter using as many functions, variables and atoms as is convenient. Then reduce the number of atoms to one; and then use the result of Exercise 9.2. □

References

The language F was introduced in [80]. It is very similar to first-order LISP or Scheme, for example see [39]. The lambda calculus has long been investigated as a branch of pure mathematics, and is now enjoying a renaissance due to its many applications within functional programming. Important works on this include those by Barendregt [7], Church [23], and Turing [162].

10 Some Natural Unsolvable Problems

We have seen earlier that there are problems that cannot be solved by programs in WHILE or any other of the computation models we have considered. By the Church-Turing thesis, these problems cannot be solved by *any* notion of effective procedures at all.

Until now, the unsolvable problems we have considered all concern properties of programs: the first examples were the Busy Beaver and halting problems, and this was subsequently extended to *all non-trivial extensional* program properties in Rice's theorem.

In this chapter we give some examples of other kinds of problems that are unsolvable: Post's correspondence problem, and several problems concerning context-free grammars: emptiness of interesction, ambiguity, and exhaustiveness. After an introduction, the remaining sections are each devoted to one of these problems.

10.1 Do there exist natural unsolvable problems?

We have argued, we hope convincingly, for two points, one formal and one informal:

1. That the halting problem for WHILE programs is not decidable by any WHILE program.
2. That decidability of membership in a set A by *any* intuitively effective computing device is exactly equivalent to decidability of membership in A by WHILE programs.

Point 1 is analogous to the classical impossibility proofs e.g., that the circle cannot be squared using tools consisting of a ruler and a compass. It asserts that one particular problem, the halting problem, cannot be solved be means of any of a powerful class of tools: WHILE programs.

Point 2 is a version of the Church-Turing thesis. It cannot be proven, as it equates an intuitive concept with a formal one. On the other hand it is widely believed, and we have given evidence for it by showing a variety of different computing engines to be equivalent.

Assuming the validity of point 2 causes point 1 to carry much more significance. In particular the halting problem for WHILE programs is not decidable by *any intuitively effective computing device whatsoever*.

The arguments used to prove point 1 use only accepted mathematical reasoning methods (even though by a subtle argument). Nonetheless, the result is still unsatisfactory. The reason is that the decision problem of point 1 is *unnatural*: One cannot imagine a daily mathematical context in which one would want to solve the halting problem for WHILE programs, unless one were specifically studying computability theory.

They are not completely unnatural in computer science, however, as an operating system designer could have a lively interest in knowing whether the programs to be executed will run the risk of nontermination. Such knowledge about program behavior in general is, alas, doomed to failure by the undecidability of the halting problem, and Rice's Theorem (see Theorem 5.4.2 and Exercise 5.5.)

This discussion motivates the desire to see whether there also exist natural problems that are undecidable. In this chapter we will present some simple problems that on the surface seem to have nothing to do with Turing machines or WHILE programs, but which are undecidable since *if they were decidable, then one could also decide the halting problem*. More generally, this technique is called *reduction*; a common definition in terms of set membership problems is seen below.

In part III we present yet another undecidable problem, concerning diophantine equations (whether a polynomial equation possesses integer roots), which was among Hilbert's list of problems, posed in 1900. It was finally shown to be undecidable, but only in 1970 after years of effort by many mathematicians.

Definition 10.1.1 Suppose one is given $A \subseteq X$ and $B \subseteq Y$. Define A to be *reducible*[1] to B if there is a total computable function $f : X \to Y$ such that for all $x \in X$, we have $x \in A$ if and only if $f(x) \in B$.

Symbolically, we write this relation as $A \underset{rec}{\leq} B$. □

Theorem 10.1.2 If $A \underset{rec}{\leq} B$ and B is decidable, then A is also decidable. Contrapositively, if $A \underset{rec}{\leq} B$ and A is undecidable, then B is also undecidable.

Proof is immediate, as one can answer any question "$x \in A$?" indirectly, by constructing $f(x)$ and then testing whether $f(x) \in B$. Since f is a total computable function and B is

---

[1]More specifically: reducible by a *many-one recursive reduction* of A to B (other problem reductions exist, e.g., the polynomial-time ones used in later chapters.)

decidable, this describes an effective terminating process. □

10.2 An undecidable problem in string rewriting

10.2.1 String rewriting by semi-Thue systems

A *string rewriting* (or *semi-Thue*[2]) system over an alphabet Σ is a finite subset of $\Sigma^* \times \Sigma^*$, i.e., a finite set $R = \{(u_1, v_1), \ldots, (u_m, v_m)\}$ of pairs of strings where each $u_i, v_i \in \Sigma^*$. A pair $(u, v) \in R$ is called a *rewrite rule* or *production*. We often write $u ::= v$ instead of $(u, v) \in R$. An example with $\Sigma = \{A, \mathsf{a}, \mathsf{b}, \mathsf{c}\}$ is:

$$R = \{(A, \mathsf{a}\,A\,\mathsf{a}), (A, \mathsf{b}\,A\,\mathsf{b}), (A, \mathsf{c}), (A, \mathsf{aca})\}$$

For a string rewriting system R over Σ, the *one-step rewrite relation* $\Rightarrow$ between strings in Σ^* is defined by:

$$rus \Rightarrow rvs \quad \text{iff} \quad u ::= v \in R \text{ and } r, s \in \Sigma^*$$

In our example, for instance,

$$
\begin{aligned}
A &\Rightarrow \mathsf{a}\,A\,\mathsf{a} \\
\mathsf{a}\,A\,\mathsf{a} &\Rightarrow \mathsf{aa}\,A\,\mathsf{aa} \\
\mathsf{aa}\,A\,\mathsf{aa} &\Rightarrow \mathsf{aacaa}
\end{aligned}
$$

The *multi-step rewrite relation* or *derivation relation* $\Rightarrow^*$ is the transitive, reflexive closure of $\Rightarrow$, defined for all $r, g, h \in \Sigma^*$ by:

1. If $g \Rightarrow h$ then $g \Rightarrow^* h$.
2. $g \Rightarrow^* g$.
3. If $g \Rightarrow^* r$ and $r \Rightarrow^* h$ then $g \Rightarrow^* h$.

In our example, for instance,

$$
\begin{aligned}
A &\Rightarrow^* A \\
A &\Rightarrow^* \mathsf{a}\,A\,\mathsf{a} \\
A &\Rightarrow^* \mathsf{aacaa}
\end{aligned}
$$

---

[2]Named after the Norwegian mathematicial Axel Thue.

10.2.2   String rewriting: undecidability of derivability

Theorem 10.2.1 The following problem DERIV is undecidable: given a string rewriting (or semi-Thue) system R over alphabet Σ and two strings $r, s \in \Sigma^*$, to decide whether or not $r \Rightarrow^* s$.

Proof. This is shown by reduction from the the halting problem for two-counter machines: $HALT\text{-}2CM \underset{rec}{\leq} DERIV$. Recall that the instructions of a two-counter machine program must lie within the set

$$\{X := X+1, X := X-1, Y := Y+1, Y := Y-1,$$
$$\text{if } X=0 \text{ goto } \ell \text{ else } \ell', \text{ if } Y=0 \text{ goto } \ell \text{ else } \ell'\}$$

Explicit instruction labels are written for notational convenience. As running example we use program p that doubles its input x, with F as "end-of-execution" label:

Production			Form of instruction L_ℓ	Case
L_ℓ	::=	$1L_{\ell+1}$	$L_\ell = $ X:=X+1	
$\#L_\ell$	::=	$\#L_{\ell+1}$	$L_\ell = $ X:=X-1	X $=0$
$1L_\ell$	::=	$L_{\ell+1}$	$L_\ell = $ X:=X-1	X $\neq 0$
$\#L_\ell$	::=	$1L_{\ell'}$	$L_\ell = $ if X=0 goto ℓ' else ℓ''	X $=0$
$1L_\ell$	::=	$1L_{\ell''}$	$L_\ell = $ if X=0 goto ℓ' else ℓ''	X $\neq 0$
L_ℓ	::=	$L_{\ell+1}1$	$L_\ell = $ Y:=Y+1	
$L\#_\ell$	::=	$L\#_{\ell+1}$	$L_\ell = $ Y:=Y-1	Y $=0$
$L_\ell 1$	::=	$L_{\ell+1}$	$L_\ell = $ Y:=Y-1	Y $\neq 0$
$L\#_\ell$	::=	$L\#_{\ell'}$	$L_\ell = $ if Y=0 goto ℓ' else ℓ''	Y $=0$
$L_\ell 1$	::=	$L_{\ell''}1$	$L_\ell = $ if Y=0 goto ℓ' else ℓ''	Y $\neq 0$
			Common rewrite rules	
S	::=	$\#1^x L_1\#$	x is program input, L_1 is first instruction.	
$\#L_{m+1}\#$	::=	ε	L_m is the last instruction and ε the empty string	
$1L_{m+1}$	::=	L_{m+1}		
$L_{m+1}1$	::=	L_{m+1}		

Figure 10.1: Construction of string rewrite system to simulate a two-counter program.

Common rules:			Rules for instructions:					
S	::=	#11A	1A	::=	1B	C	::=	D1
F1	::=	F	#F#	::=	ε	D	::=	E1
1F	::=	F	#A	::=	#F	1E	::=	1B
#F#	::=	ε	1B	::=	C	#E	::=	#F
#B	::=	#C						

Figure 10.2: Example of rewriting rules simulating a two-counter program.

```
A: if X=0 goto F else B;
B: X := X-1;
C: Y := Y+1;
D: Y := Y+1;
E: if X=0 goto F else B
```

We use reduction, showing that if the derivability problem were decidable, then the halting problem for two-counter machines would also be decidable. Suppose we are given a two-counter program $p = L_1: I_1 \cdots L_m: I_m$ with variables X (for input) and Y (initially zero), and natural number x as input. Begin by constructing from program p and input x the string rewriting system R of Figure 10.1, over alphabet

$$\Sigma = \{\#, 1\} \cup \{ L_\ell \mid I_\ell \text{ is an instruction}\}$$

Notation: a store (ℓ, u, v) containing control point L_ℓ and values u, v of variables X, Y will be represented by a *configuration string* of form $C = 1^u L_\ell 1^v$ in Σ^*.

The following is shown by an easy induction. *Assertion*: for any m, there is a computation $p \vdash C_1 \to \ldots \to C_m$ if and only if

$$\#1^x C_1\# \quad \Rightarrow^m \quad \#C_m\#$$

Consequently $S \Rightarrow^* \#1^u L_{m+1} 1^v\#$ for some u, v if and only if p terminates on input x. This implies $S \Rightarrow^* \varepsilon$ if and only if p terminates on input x, so if the derivability problem could be solved, one could also solve the halting problem, which we know to be unsolvable.
□

Figure 10.2 shows the effect in the running example, with input $x = 2$.

10.3   Post's correspondence problem

Definition 10.3.1 *Post's correspondence problem* PCP is defined as follows. Given a sequence of pairs $P = (u_1, v_1), (u_2, v_2), \ldots, (u_n, v_n)$ of nonempty strings over a finite alphabet Σ, the problem is to determine whether or not there exists an index sequence $i_1, \ldots, i_m$ such that

$$u_{i_1} u_{i_2} \ldots, u_{i_m} = v_{i_1} v_{i_2} \ldots, v_{i_m}$$

For instance, the pair sequence $(a, ab), (b, ca), (ca, a), (abc, c)$ has solution sequence $1, 2, 3, 1, 4$, with both sides above yielding

$$
\begin{aligned}
u_1 u_2 u_3 u_1 u_4 &= \text{(a)(b)(ca)(a)(abc)} \\
&= \text{(ab)(ca)(a)(ab)(c)} = \text{abcaaabc} = v_1 v_2 v_3 v_1 v_4
\end{aligned}
$$

On the other hand, one can verify that the sequence given by (a, ab), (b, ca), (ca, a), (ab, c) has no solution sequence at all.

A notational convenience: we will write $\vec{i}$ in place of index sequence $i_1, \ldots, i_m$, and $u_{\vec{i}}$ and $v_{\vec{i}}$ for (respectively) $u_{i_1} u_{i_2} \ldots, u_{i_m}$ and $v_{i_1} v_{i_2} \ldots, v_{i_m}$. Given this the PCP can be restated simply as: does $u_{\vec{i}} = v_{\vec{i}}$ for some $\vec{i}$?

If $u_{\vec{i}} z = v_{\vec{i}}$, then we call z the *remainder* of $v_{\vec{i}}$ over $u_{\vec{i}}$.

Theorem 10.3.2 The Post correspondence problem is undecidable. $\qquad\qquad$ □

We begin by reducing the derivability problem $r \Rightarrow^* s$ for string rewriting system R to a restricted version RPCP of the PCP. Thus DERIV $\underset{rec}{\leq}$ RPCP, so the RPCP is undecidable. Afterwards, we show that DERIV $\underset{rec}{\leq}$ PCP, and so the general PCP is also undecidable.

Although the constructions involved are simple, careful reasoning is needed to prove that they behave as desired.

Lemma 10.3.3 The *rooted Post correspondence problem* RPCP is undecidable: given $P = (u_1, v_1), (u_2, v_2), \ldots, (u_n, v_n) \in \Sigma^*$, does there exist an index sequence $i_1, \ldots, i_m$ such that $i_1 = 1$ and $u_{i_1} u_{i_2} \ldots, u_{i_m} = v_{i_1} v_{i_2} \ldots, v_{i_m}$? $\qquad\qquad$ □

Construction for Lemma 10.3.3 to establish DERIV $\underset{rec}{\leq}$ RPCP.

Suppose we are given a string rewriting system $R = \{(u, v), (u', v'), \ldots\}$ of pairs of strings where each $u, v \in \Sigma^*$, and strings r, s in Σ^*. Its derivability problem is to decide whether $r \Rightarrow^* s$.

Index i	u_i	v_i
1	#	#A#
2	abcba##	#
3	A	aAa
4	A	bAb
5	A	c

Index i	u_i	v_i
6	A	A
7	a	a
8	b	b
9	c	c
10	#	#

Figure 10.3: Example RPCP simulating a string rewrite system.

Construct the following RPCP problem P over alphabet $\Sigma \cup \{\#\}$ where # is a new symbol not in Σ; and $(u_1, v_1) = (\#, \#r\#)$, and $(u_2, v_2) = (s\#\#, \#)$:

$$P = \underbrace{\{(\#, \#r\#)}_{i=1}, \underbrace{(s\#\#, \#)\}}_{i=2} \cup R \cup \{(a, a) \mid a \in \Sigma \text{ or } a = \#\}$$

To distinguish the two sets of pairs R and P, we will use production notation $u ::= v$ for R instead of writing $(u, v) \in R$. Figure 10.3 shows the result of applying this construction to the rewriting system with $\Sigma = \{A, a, b, c\}$, $r = A$, and $s = \text{abcba}$, and rewrite rule set

$$R = \{A ::= a\,A\,a,\ A ::= b\,A\,b,\ A ::= c\}$$

The derivation $A \Rightarrow aAa \Rightarrow abAba \Rightarrow abcba$ is modelled in Figure 10.3 by the sequence of pairs $1, 3, 10, 7, 4, 7, 10, 7, 8, 5, 8, 7, 10, 2$ with

$$
\begin{array}{ccccccccccccccc}
\multicolumn{14}{c}{u_1 u_3 u_{10} u_7 u_4 u_7 u_{10} u_7 u_8 u_5 u_8 u_7 u_{10} u_2} & = \\
\# & A & \# & a & A & a & \# & a & b & A & b & a & \# & \text{abcba\#\#} & = \\
\#A\# & aAa & \# & a & bAb & a & \# & a & b & c & b & a & \# & \# & = \\
\multicolumn{14}{c}{v_1 v_3 v_{10} v_7 v_4 v_7 v_{10} v_7 v_8 v_5 v_8 v_7 v_{10} v_2} &
\end{array}
$$

$\square$

Henceforth an index sequence $\vec{\imath}$ not containing 1 or 2 will be called *internal*.

Lemma 10.3.4 The following are equivalent for any $t \in \Sigma^*$.

I.	$r \Rightarrow^* t$	by the string rewrite system R
II.	$u_{1\vec{\imath}} t\# = v_{1\vec{\imath}}$	for some internal $\vec{\imath}$
III.	$u_{1\vec{\imath}} t_2 \# t_1 = v_{1\vec{\imath}}$	for some t_1, t_2 with $t = t_1 t_2$, and for some internal $\vec{\imath}$

$\square$

Proof.

I implies II. We show by induction on m that $r \Rightarrow^m t$ implies $u_{1\vec{\imath}}t\# = v_{1\vec{\imath}}$ for some internal $\vec{\imath}$. The base case with $m = 0$ is $r \Rightarrow^* r$, immediate with $\vec{\imath} = \varepsilon$ since $(u_1, v_1) = (\#, \#r\#)$.

Now assume $r \Rightarrow^{m+1} t$, so $r \Rightarrow^m xgy$ and $xgy \Rightarrow xhy = t$ for some $g ::= h \in R$. By induction, $u_{1\vec{\imath}}x\,g\,y\# = v_{1\vec{\imath}}$ for some internal $\vec{\imath}$. Let $x = a_1 \ldots a_d, y = b_1 \ldots b_e$ where each $a_j, b_k \in \Sigma$.

The u-remainder of $v_{1\vec{\imath}}$ over $u_{1\vec{\imath}}$ is $xgy\#$; so to extend this partial solution, at least enough pairs (u,v) from P must be added to extend $u_{1\vec{\imath}}$ by xgy. It is easy to see that

$$u_{1\vec{\jmath}}xhy\# = u_{1\vec{\imath}}x\,g\,y\#xh\,y\# = v_{1\vec{\imath}}xh\,y\# = v_{1\vec{\jmath}}$$

by an appropriate index sequence extending the u and v strings:

$$\vec{\jmath} = \vec{\imath}j_1 \ldots j_d\, p\, k_1 \ldots k_e\, q$$

where indices $j_1 \ldots j_d$ add pairs (a,a) that in effect copy x, index p of (g,h) adds g to the u string and h to the v string, indices $k_1 \ldots k_q$ copy y by adding pairs (b,b), and index q of pair $(\#,\#)$ adds the final $\#$ to both.

II implies III. This is immediate, with $t_2 = t$ and $t_1 = \varepsilon$.

III implies I   is proven by induction, with inductive hypothesis $IH(\vec{\imath})$: for any $t_1, t_2 \in \Sigma^*$, if $u_{1\vec{\imath}}t_2\#t_1 = v_{1\vec{\imath}}$ then $r \Rightarrow^* t_1t_2$. Clearly this and $t = t_1t_2$ imply I. The base case is $\vec{\imath} = \varepsilon$, so we must show $u_1 t_2\#t_1 = v_1$ implies $r \Rightarrow^* t_1t_2$. But

$$\#t_2\#t_1 = u_1 t_2\#t_1 = v_1 = \#r\#$$

can only hold if $t_2 = r$ and $t_1 = \varepsilon$. Thus $t = t_1t_2 = r$, so $r \Rightarrow^* t$ is trivially true.

Inductively, suppose $IH(\vec{\imath})$ holds. Consider internal index sequence $\vec{\imath}j$. We analyse by cases over the pairs $(u_j, v_j) \in P$.

Case 1: $(u_j, v_j) = (f, g)$ where $f ::= g \in R$. Then

$$u_{1\vec{\imath}j}t_2\#t_1 = u_{1\vec{\imath}}ft_2\#t_1 = v_{1\vec{\imath}j} = v_{1\vec{\imath}}g$$

Now $g \in \Sigma^*$, so $t_1 = wg$ for some w, implying $u_{1\vec{\imath}}ft_2\#wg = v_{1\vec{\imath}}g$. Removing g from both sides: $u_{1\vec{\imath}}ft_2\#w = v_{1\vec{\imath}}$.

By $IH(\vec{\imath})$ (with w and ft_2 in place of t_1 and t_2) we obtain $r \Rightarrow^* wft_2$. Thus

$$r \Rightarrow^* wft_2 \Rightarrow wgt_2 = t_1t_2$$

as desired.

Case 2: $(u_j, v_j) = (c, c)$ where $c \in \Sigma$. Then

$$u_{1\vec{\imath}j} t_2 \# t_1 = u_{1\vec{\imath}} c t_2 \# t_1 = v_{1\vec{\imath}j} = v_{1\vec{\imath}} c$$

Now $c \in \Sigma$, so $t_1 = wc$ for some w, implying $u_{1\vec{\imath}} c t_2 \# wc = v_{1\vec{\imath}} c$, and so $u_{1\vec{\imath}} c t_2 \# w = v_{1\vec{\imath}}$. By $IH(\vec{\imath})$ with w and ct_2 in place t_1 and t_2, we obtain $r \Rightarrow^* wct_2 = t_1 t_2$ as desired.

Case 3: $(u_j, v_j) = (\#, \#)$. Then

$$u_{1\vec{\imath}j} t_2 \# t_1 = u_{1\vec{\imath}} \# t_2 \# t_1 = v_{1\vec{\imath}j} = v_{1\vec{\imath}} \#$$

This can only hold if $t_1 = \varepsilon$, and so implies $u_{1\vec{\imath}} \# t_2 = v_{1\vec{\imath}}$. By induction this implies $r \Rightarrow^* t_2 = t_1 t_2 = t$, as required. □

Proof of Lemma 10.3.3. Let RPCP be constructed as above, given a string rewriting system R with derivability problem: to decide whether or not $r \Rightarrow^* s$. By Lemma 10.3.4, $r \Rightarrow^* s$ if and only if $u_{1\vec{\imath}} s \# = v_{1\vec{\imath}}$ for some internal $\vec{\imath}$. Clearly if $r \Rightarrow^* s$ the RPCP has a solution $1 \vec{\imath} 2$ since $(u_2, v_2) = (s\#\#, \#)$ and so

$$u_{1\vec{\imath}2} = u_{1\vec{\imath}} s \#\# = v_{1\vec{\imath}} \# = v_{1\vec{\imath}2}$$

Conversely, suppose the RPCP P has a solution, and consider a shortest[3] one, $\vec{\imath}$, among these. The first index must be 1 (since it is a RPCP.) Further, for every proper prefix $\vec{k}$ of $\vec{\imath}$ not containing 2, there is exactly one more occurrence of symbol $\#$ in $v_{\vec{k}}$ than in $u_{\vec{k}}$, so $\vec{\imath}$ must contain 2. Let $\vec{\imath} = \vec{k} 2 \vec{\jmath}\#$. Then

$$u_{\vec{\imath}} = u_{\vec{k}} s \#\# u_{\vec{\jmath}} = v_{\vec{k}} \# v_{\vec{\jmath}} = v_{\vec{\imath}}$$

implies $u_{\vec{k}} s \#\# = v_{\vec{k}} \#$ (and $u_{\vec{\jmath}} = v_{\vec{\jmath}}$). Thus $u_{\vec{k}} s \# = v_{\vec{k}}$, which by Lemma 10.3.4 implies $r \Rightarrow^* s$. □

Proof of Theorem 10.3.2. We actually show DERIV $\leq_{rec}$ PCP, by modifying the construction of Lemma 10.3.3. Suppose we are given a string rewriting system R over alphabet Σ, and $r, s \in \Sigma^*$.

Let new $\bullet, [,]$ be new "padding" and "grouping" characters not in Σ. For any $x = a_1 a_2 \ldots a_n$ with each $a_i \in \Sigma$, define

$$x^{\rightarrow} = a_1 \bullet a_2 \bullet \ldots a_n \bullet \quad \text{and} \quad {}^{\leftarrow}x = \bullet a_1 \bullet a_2 \ldots \bullet a_n$$

---

[3] If an RPCP (or PCP, for that matter) has one solution, then it has infinitely many, obtainable by concatenating as many shorter solutions as wished.

Index i	u_i	v_i
1	[•#	[•#•A•#•
2	a•b•c• b•a•#•#•]	#•]
3	•A	a•A•a•
4	•A	b•A•b•
5	•A	c•
6	•A	A•
7	•a	a•
8	•b	b•
9	•c	c•
10	•#	#•

Figure 10.4: Example PCP simulating a string rewrite system.

Construct the PCP P' as follows, similar to P constructed for Lemma 10.3.3.

$$P' = \{ ([\bullet \#, [\,{}^{\leftarrow}r \bullet) \} \cup \{ ([s^{\rightarrow} \# \bullet \# \bullet], \# \bullet]) \} \cup$$
$$\{ ({}^{\leftarrow}f, g^{\rightarrow}) \mid (f,g) \in R \}$$

The effect on the example of Figure 10.3 is seen in Figure 10.4. Proof that in general P has a rooted PCP solution if and only if P' has an unrestricted PCP solution is left to the exercises. □

10.4   Some problems concerning context-free grammars

Theorem 10.4.1 The following problem is undecidable: given two context-free grammars $G_i = (N_i, T_i, P_i, S_i)$ for $i = 1, 2$, to decide whether or not $L(G_1) \cap L(G_2) = \emptyset$.

Proof. This is shown by reduction from the PCP. Assume given pair set (u_1, v_1), $(u_2, v_2), \ldots, (u_n, v_n)$ over alphabet Σ. Assuming disjointness of all the involved symbols and alphabets[4], we construct from this the two grammars, with $N_1 = \{S_1, E\}$, $N_2 = \{S_2, F\}, T_1 = T_2 = \Sigma \cup \{1, 2, \ldots, n, \Delta\}$ and production sets

$$P_1 = \{ S_1 ::= iEu_i, E ::= \Delta \mid iEu_i \text{ for } i = 1, 2, \ldots, n \}$$

---

[4]This can be ensured by renaming if necessary.

$$P_2 = \{S_2 ::= iS_2v_i, F ::= \Delta \mid iFv_i \text{ for } i = 1,2,\ldots,n\}$$

Clearly S_1 generates all strings of form $i_m \ldots i_2 i_1 \Delta u_{i_1} u_{i_2} \ldots, u_{i_m}$, and S_2 generates all of form $i_m \ldots i_2 i_1 \Delta v_{i_1} v_{i_2} \ldots, v_{i_m}$. Thus $L(G_1) \cap L(G_2) \neq \emptyset$ if and only if there there exists an index sequence $i_1, \ldots, i_m$ such that $u_{i_1} u_{i_2} \ldots, u_{i_m} = v_{i_1} v_{i_2} \ldots, v_{i_m}$. If it were possible to decide emptiness of $L(G_1) \cap L(G_2)$ we could also decide the PCP, and so the halting problem for two-counter machines. But this, as we know, is undecidable.   □

Theorem 10.4.2 The following problem CFAMB is undecidable: given a context-free grammar $G = (N, T, P, S)$, to decide whether or not G is ambiguous[5].

Proof. This is shown by reduction from the PCP. Given a set of correspondence pairs $(u_1, v_1), \ldots, (u_n, v_n)$ over alphabet Σ, construct from this the grammar $G = (N, \Sigma, P, S)$, with $N = \{S, S_1, E, S_2, F\}$ and production set P as follows

$$
\begin{aligned}
S &::= S_1 \mid S_2 \\
S_1 &::= iEu_i \\
E &::= \Delta \mid iEu_i \text{ for } i = 1,2,\ldots,n \\
S_2 &::= iFu_i \\
F &::= \Delta \mid iFu_i \text{ for } i = 1,2,\ldots,n
\end{aligned}
$$

Clearly S_1, S_2 derive just the same strings they did in G_1 and G_2. Thus $L(G_1) \cap L(G_2) \neq \emptyset$ if and only if the same string can be derived from both S_1 and S_2. But this is true if and only if G is ambiguous (all derivations are necessarily left-most since at most one nonterminal is involved). As a consequence, decidability of ambiguity would imply decidability of context-free interesection, in conflict with the preceding theorem.   □

Lemma 10.4.3 Given a sequence of strings $U = (u_1, u_2, \ldots, u_n)$ over alphabet Σ, the following set is generated by some context-free grammar $G_U = (N_U, T, P_U, S_U)$ where $T = \{1, 2, \ldots, n, \Delta\} \cup \Sigma$:

$$\{i_m \ldots i_2 i_1 \Delta u \mid u \neq u_{i_1} u_{i_2} \ldots u_{i_m}\}$$

Theorem 10.4.4 The following problem CFALL is undecidable: given a context-free grammar $G = (N, T, P, S)$, to decide whether $L(G) = T^*$.

Proof. Again we begin with the PCP. Given a sequence of pairs $(u_1, v_1), \ldots, (u_n, v_n)$ over alphabet Σ, construct from this three context-free grammars

---

[5]See Appendix A for the definition if unfamiliar.

1. G_U as by the preceding lemma with $U = (u_1, u_2, \ldots, u_n)$
2. G_V as by the preceding lemma with $V = (v_1, v_2, \ldots, v_n)$.
3. G_0 with $L(G_0) = \{x \in T^* \mid x$ is not of the form $i_m \ldots i_2 i_1 \Delta u_{j_1} u_{j_2} \ldots u_{j_k}\}$

It is easy (and an exercise) to see that G_0 exists, and in fact can be a regular grammar. It is also easy to construct from these a single context-free grammar $G = (N, T, P, S)$ with $L(G) = L(G_U) \cup L(G_V) \cup L(G_0)$.

Claim: $L(G) \neq T^*$ if and only if the PCP has a solution. To see this, suppose $x \in T^*$ but $x \notin L(G) = L(G_U) \cup L(G_V) \cup L(G_0)$. Then $x \in T^* \setminus L(G_0)$ implies x has the form $x = i_m \ldots i_2 i_1 \Delta u_{j_1} u_{j_2} \ldots u_{j_k}$. Further, $x \in T^* \setminus L(G_U)$ implies $x = i_m \ldots i_2 i_1 \Delta u_{i_1} u_{i_2} \ldots u_{i_m}$, and $x \in T^* \setminus L(G_V)$ implies $x = i_m \ldots i_2 i_1 \Delta v_{i_1} v_{i_2} \ldots v_{i_m}$. Thus $u_{i_1} u_{i_2} = v_{i_1} v_{i_2} \ldots v_{i_m}$, so the PCP has a solution. Similarly, if the PCP has an index sequence $i_1, \ldots, i_m$ as solution, then

$$x = i_m \ldots i_2 i_1 \Delta v_{i_1} v_{i_2} \ldots v_{i_m} \notin L(G)$$

Thus $L(G) \neq T^*$ if and only if the PCP has a solution, which is undecidable. □

Exercises

10.1 Prove the "assertion" of Theorem 10.2.1. □

10.2 Does the PCP with pairs $(10, 101), (10, 011), (011, 11), (101, 011)$ have a solution? □

10.3 Prove that the following problem is *decidable*: given a sequence of pairs (u_1, v_1), $(u_2, v_2), \ldots, (u_n, v_n)$ of nonempty strings over a finite alphabet Σ, the problem is to determine whether or not there exist two index sequences $i_1, \ldots, i_m$ and $j_1, \ldots, j_n$ such that

$$u_{i_1} u_{i_2} \ldots, u_{i_m} = v_{j_1} v_{j_2} \ldots, v_{j_n}$$

Hint: the sets of left and right sides can be described by regular expressions. □

10.4 * Complete the proof of Theorem 10.3.2 by showing that P has a rooted solution if and only if P' has an unrestricted solution. Prove both the "if" and the "only if" parts. □

10.5 Prove Lemma 10.4.3: construct the required context-free grammar G_U. □

10.6 Complete the proof of Theorem 10.4.4 (for example by showing that the set involved is recognizable by a finite automaton). □

10.7 Prove that it is undecidable, given two context-free grammars G, G', to determine whether $L(G) \subseteq L(G')$. □

References

Post's correspondence problem was first formulated and shown unsolvable in [136]. Context-free ambiguity and some related problems were proven undecidable in [6]. The book by Lewis and Papadimitriou, and the one by Rozenberg and Salomaa, contain a broad selection of natural undecidable problems [103, 148].

Part III

Other Aspects of Computability Theory

11   Hilbert's Tenth Problem

(by M. H. Sørensen)

11.1   Introduction

In the introduction to this book we mentioned Hilbert's famous list of open problems at the International Congress of Mathematicians in 1900. The tenth problem is stated as follows:

> Given a Diophantine equation with any number of unknown quantities and with rational integral numerical coefficients: to devise a process according to which it can be determined by a finite number of operations whether the equation is solvable in rational integers.

In modern terms, the problem is to give an algorithm which for a polynomial equation with integer coefficients can decide whether or not it has a solution in integers. An equation of this form is called *Diophantine*, after the Greek mathematician Diophantus from the third century, who was interested in such equations.

Hilbert's tenth problem is an example of a problem which is of independent interest in another field than computability theory, namely number theory. For instance, Fermat's famous "Last Theorem" states that the equation

$$(p+1)^{n+3} + (q+1)^{n+3} = (r+1)^{n+3}$$

has no solution in natural numbers for p, q, r, n. Whether this is true has long been one of the most famous open problems in number theory.[1] For each fixed n, Fermat's last theorem is an instance of Hilbert's tenth problem, provided we restrict solutions to the natural numbers—this restriction is not essential as we shall see shortly. Thus, an algorithm deciding for a Diophantine equation whether any solution exists in the natural numbers would prove or disprove Fermat's last theorem for each fixed n. Conversely, it has later been realized that unsolvability of Hilbert's tenth problem would imply unsolvability of many other decision problems in number theory and analysis.

---

[1] Wiles has recently given a proof of Fermat's last theorem which seems to be widely accepted, see Annals of Mathematics, May 1995.

From the proof of Gödel's famous theorem [51] it follows that every recursively enumerable set A can be defined by a Diophantine equation preceded by a finite number of existential and bounded universal quantifiers. In his doctoral dissertation, Davis [30, 31] showed that all but one of the bounded quantifiers could be eliminated. Hence, any recursively enumerable set A can be defined by a Diophantine equation $E(x, y, z, x_1, \ldots, x_n,)$ as follows:

$$x \in A \Leftrightarrow \exists y, \forall z \leq y, \exists x_1, \ldots, \exists x_n : E(x, y, z, x_1, \ldots, x_n)$$

This form of definition was subsequently called *Davis Normal Form*.

To prove that Hilbert's tenth problem is unsolvable it remains to eliminate the single bounded universal quantifier; that is, to show that any recursively enumerable set A can be defined by a Diophantine equation $E(x, x_1, \ldots, x_n)$ thus:

$$x \in A \Leftrightarrow \exists x_1, \ldots, \exists x_n : E(x, x_1, \ldots, x_n)$$

Indeed, if A is any recursively enumerable, non-recursive set, then an algorithm deciding for any x whether $E(x, x_1, \ldots, x_n)$ has a solution, i.e., whether there are $x_1, \ldots, x_n$ such that $E(x, x_1, \ldots, x_n)$ holds, would also yield a method to test membership in A, which is impossible.

While Davis showed how to simplify the form of equations necessary for defining all recursively enumerable sets, Robinson [145] attacked the problem from the other side. She showed that several sets could be defined by Diophantine equations. She also studied so-called exponential Diophantine equations, which allow unknowns in the exponents, and in particular showed, under what is now known as the *Julia Robinson hypothesis*, that any set definable by an exponential Diophantine equation is also definable by a Diophantine equation.

Davis and Putnam finally managed to eliminate the last bounded quantifier from the Davis Normal Form using the Chinese remainder theorem and Robinson's exponential Diophantine equations. The result, sometimes called the "Bounded Quantifier Theorem", states in its original form that, if there are arbitrarily long arithmetic progressions consisting entirely of primes, then every recursively enumerable set can be defined by an exponential Diophantine equation. Robinson subsequently managed to eliminate the assumption regarding primes (which is still open) and simplify the proof. The resulting joint paper by Davis, Putnam, and Robinson [35] stating that every recursively enumerable set can be defined by an exponential Diophantine equation is now a classic.

It follows from Robinson's earlier result that to prove the unsolvability of Hilbert's tenth problem, it is sufficient to prove that the Julia Robinson hypothesis is true. This remained an open problem, believed by many to be false, until it was proved ten years later in 1970 by the young Russian mathematician Matiyasevich [111].

In this chapter we give an account of the unsolvability of Hilbert's tenth problem, leaving out the details of Matiyasevich's result. The first section introduces exponential Diophantine equations. The second section develops certain tools that are used in the third section to prove the Davis-Putnam-Robinson theorem. The fourth section considers Hilbert's tenth problem.

11.2   Exponential Diophantine equations and sets

We begin by making the notions of the introduction precise. As is customary we shall be concerned with solutions in natural numbers rather than in integers. We also show that this is an inessential modification.

Definition 11.2.1

1. A function $f : \mathbb{N}^n \to \mathbb{N}$ is *exponential polynomial* if it can be written

$$f(x_1, \ldots, x_n) = t$$

   where t is defined by the following grammar with $1 \le i \le n$ and $N \in \mathbb{N}$:[2]

$$t ::= x_i \mid N \mid t_1 \cdot t_2 \mid t_1 + t_2 \mid t_1 - t_2 \mid t_1^{t_2}$$

2. An equation $f(x_1, \ldots, x_n) = 0$ is *exponential Diophantine* if f is exponential polynomial. A *solution* is a tuple $(a_1, \ldots, a_n) \in \mathbb{N}^n$ with $f(a_1, \ldots, a_n) = 0$.

3. A set $A \subseteq \mathbb{N}^n$ is *exponential Diophantine* if there exists an exponential polynomial $f : \mathbb{N}^{m+n} \to \mathbb{N}$ such that

$$(a_1, \ldots, a_n) \in A \Leftrightarrow \exists x_1, \ldots, \exists x_m : f(a_1, \ldots, a_n, x_1, \ldots, x_m) = 0$$

4. An exponential polynomial not using the last clause for t is a *polynomial*. *Diophantine equations* and *sets* are defined by polynomials, like exponential Diophantine equations and sets are defined by exponential polynomials. □

A few examples illustrating the definition may be useful.

---

[2]The construction $t_1^{t_2}$ may lead outside the integers, e.g., x^{1-y} with $x = 2$ and $y = 2$. Such situations will be tacitly avoided in what follows.

Example 11.2.2

1. The function

$$f(x,y,z) = 3x + 5xy - 71z^5$$

   is a polynomial, where we write z^5 instead of $z \cdot z \cdot z \cdot z \cdot z$. Therefore,

$$3x + 5xy - 71z^5 = 0$$

   is a Diophantine equation, and the set of all natural numbers x such that there exists y,z with $3x + 5xy - 71z^5 = 0$ is a Diophantine set.

2. The function

$$f(x,y) = x - 2y$$

   is a polynomial, so

$$x - 2y = 0$$

   is a Diophantine equation. Therefore the set of all even numbers is Diophantine; indeed, it is the set of all natural numbers x such that there exists a y with $x - 2y = 0$, i.e., $x = 2y$.

3. The function

$$f(p,q,r,n) = (p+1)^{n+3} + (q+1)^{n+3} - (r+1)^{n+3}$$

   is an exponential polynomial. Hence,

$$(p+1)^{n+3} + (q+1)^{n+3} - (r+1)^{n+3} = 0$$

   is an exponential Diophantine equation. Therefore the set of all $x,y,z > 0$ such that for some $k \geq 3$, $x^k + y^k = z^k$, is exponential Diophantine.   □

In the introduction Diophantine equations had *integer* solutions, but in the preceding definition their solutions were *natural numbers*. However, the problem of deciding whether an arbitrary (exponential) Diophantine equation has solution in integers is equivalent to the problem of deciding whether an arbitrary (exponential) Diophantine equation has solution in natural numbers.

To reduce the former problem to the latter, note that there is a solution in integers to the equation

$$f(x_1, \ldots, x_n) = 0$$

if and only if there is a solution in natural numbers to the equation

$$f(p_1 - q_1, \ldots, p_n - q_n) = 0$$

For the opposite reduction, recall that any natural number can be written as the sum of four squares (see, e.g., the appendix to [117]). Hence, there is a solution in natural numbers to the equation

$$f(x_1, \ldots, x_n) = 0$$

if and only if there is a solution in integers to the equation

$$f(p_1^2 + q_1^2 + r_1^2 + s_1^2, \ldots, p_n^2 + q_n^2 + r_n^2 + s_n^2) = 0$$

In conclusion, we have simplified the problem inessentially by considering only natural number solutions.

In a similar vein, we may allow equations of form

$$f(x_1, \ldots, x_n) = g(y_1, \ldots, y_m)$$

where $g(y_1, \ldots, y_m)$ is not simply 0, since this is equivalent to

$$f(x_1, \ldots, x_n) - g(y_1, \ldots, y_m) = 0$$

We may allow conjunctions of equations

$$f(x_1, \ldots, x_n) = 0 \wedge g(y_1, \ldots, y_m) = 0$$

since this conjunction of equations has a solution if and only if there is a solution to the ordinary equation

$$f(x_1, \ldots, x_n) \cdot f(x_1, \ldots, x_n) + g(y_1, \ldots, y_m) \cdot g(y_1, \ldots, y_m) = 0$$

Similarly we may allow disjunctions of equations

$$f(x_1, \ldots, x_n) = 0 \vee g(y_1, \ldots, y_m) = 0$$

since this disjunction of equations has a solution if and only if there is a solution to the ordinary equation

$$f(x_1, \ldots, x_n) \cdot g(y_1, \ldots, y_m) = 0$$

11.3   Encoding of finite sequences

We shall give a proof of the Davis-Putnam-Robinson theorem using encodings of counter machine computation executions. The idea will be clearer in the next section. Here it suffices to note that for this purpose it will be necessary to have available a means of expressing facts about objects in a sequence of finite, but unknown, length.

There are several such techniques available. The best known, first employed by Gödel [51], uses the Chinese Remainder theorem. In the present setting this technique has the disadvantage that it makes it rather hard to express certain necessary operations as exponential Diophantine equations. Therefore another technique was invented by Matiyasevich [113], which we present in this section.

Definition 11.3.1 For $a, b \in \mathbb{N}$, let

$$a = \sum_{i=0}^{n} a_i 2^i \ (0 \le a_i \le 1), \qquad b = \sum_{i=0}^{n} b_i 2^i \ (0 \le b_i \le 1)$$

The *bitwise less-than* relation $a \preceq b$ is defined by:

$$a \preceq b \Leftrightarrow \forall i \in \{0, \ldots, n\} : a_i \le b_i \qquad \square$$

The rest of this section is devoted to showing that $a \preceq b$ is an exponential Diophantine relation, i.e., that

$$\{(a, b) \in \mathbb{N} \times \mathbb{N} \mid a \preceq b\}$$

is a Diophantine set according to Definition 11.2.1. We prove this using two lemmas.

The first lemma is due to Robinson [145], and the proof is a modification of Robinson's proof due to Matiyasevich [114].

Lemma 11.3.2 Define for $k \le n$,

$$\binom{n}{k} = \frac{n!}{(n-k)!k!}$$

and let $\binom{n}{k} = 0$ when $k > n$. The relation $m = \binom{n}{k}$ is exponential Diophantine.

Proof. First, the less-than relation is exponential Diophantine, since

$$a < b \Leftrightarrow \exists x : a + x + 1 = b$$

Second, let $[N]_k^B$ be the k'th digit of N written in base B. For instance, since 5 in base 2 is 101 and we count from the right starting from 0, we have

$$[5]_2^2 = [5]_0^2 = 1$$

and

$$[5]_3^2 = [5]_1^2 = 0$$

The relation $d = [N]_k^B$ is exponential Diophantine since

$$d = [N]_k^B \Leftrightarrow \exists c, e : N = cB^{k+1} + dB^k + e \wedge d < B \wedge e < B^k$$

Finally, by the binomial theorem

$$(B+1)^n = \sum_{k=0}^{n} \binom{n}{k} B^k$$

Note that $\binom{n}{k}$ is the k'th digit of $(B+1)^n$ written in base B, provided $\binom{n}{k} < B$ for all k. This, in turn, holds if $B > 2^n$ (see the exercises). Hence, $m = \binom{n}{k}$ is exponential Diophantine:

$$m = \binom{n}{k} \Leftrightarrow \exists B : B = 2^n + 1 \wedge m = [(B+1)^n]_k^B \qquad \Box$$

The second lemma necessary to prove that the bitwise less-than relation is exponential Diophantine involves a bit of elementary number theory, which has been banished to the exercises.

Lemma 11.3.3 $n \preceq k \Leftrightarrow \binom{n}{k}$ is odd

Proof. See the exercises. $\qquad \Box$

Proposition 11.3.4 The bitwise less-than relation is exponential Diophantine.

Proof. The relation $m = \binom{n}{k}$ is exponential Diophantine by Lemma 11.3.2. The relation "m is odd" is also exponential Diophantine:

$$m \text{ is odd } \Leftrightarrow \exists x : m = 2x + 1$$

Hence, the proposition follows by Lemma 11.3.3. $\qquad \Box$

If $a \preceq b$ then a is also digitwise less than b using any other base B, provided the base is a power of 2. The converse does not generally hold; it may be that B is a power of 2, a is digitwise less than b in base B, and yet $a \not\preceq b$. However, if B is a power of 2, a is digitwise less than b in base B, and all the digits of b in B are 0 or 1, then also $a \preceq b$. All this is perhaps best explained with an example.

Example 11.3.5 For instance, $34 \preceq 43$, as can be seen from the first two rows in Figure 11.1. Moreover, 34 is also digitwise less than 43 with base 4, as can be seen from the last two rows in the figure. The reason is that every group of two coefficients $x \cdot 2^{i+1} + y \cdot 2^i$ in the base 2 representation is packed into a single coefficient $x \cdot 2 + y$ in the base 4 representation. If, in the base 2 representation, all bits in a number are less than or equal to those in another number, then the same holds in the base 4 representation; that is, if $x_1 \leq x_2$ and $y_1 \leq y_2$ then $x_1 \cdot 2 + y_1 \leq x_2 \cdot 2 + y_2$.

$$43 = 1 \cdot 2^5 + 0 \cdot 2^4 \quad + \quad 1 \cdot 2^3 + 0 \cdot 2^2 \quad + \quad 1 \cdot 2^1 + 1 \cdot 2^0$$
$$34 = 1 \cdot 2^5 + 0 \cdot 2^4 \quad + \quad 0 \cdot 2^3 + 0 \cdot 2^2 \quad + \quad 1 \cdot 2^1 + 0 \cdot 2^0$$

$$43 = 2 \cdot 4^2 \quad + \quad 2 \cdot 4^1 \quad + \quad 3 \cdot 4^0$$
$$34 = 2 \cdot 4^2 \quad + \quad 0 \cdot 4^1 \quad + \quad 2 \cdot 4^0$$

Figure 11.1: *Digitwise comparisons in base 2 and 4.*

$$43 = 1 \cdot 2^5 + 0 \cdot 2^4 \quad + \quad 1 \cdot 2^3 + 0 \cdot 2^2 \quad + \quad 1 \cdot 2^1 + 1 \cdot 2^0$$
$$18 = 0 \cdot 2^5 + 1 \cdot 2^4 \quad + \quad 0 \cdot 2^3 + 0 \cdot 2^2 \quad + \quad 1 \cdot 2^1 + 0 \cdot 2^0$$

$$43 = 2 \cdot 4^2 \quad + \quad 2 \cdot 4^1 \quad + \quad 3 \cdot 4^0$$
$$18 = 1 \cdot 4^2 \quad + \quad 0 \cdot 4^1 \quad + \quad 2 \cdot 4^0$$

Figure 11.2: *More digitwise comparisons in base 2 and 4.*

On the other hand, 18 is digitwise less than 43 in base 4, but $18 \not\preceq 43$, as can be seen from Figure 11.2. The reason is that a group of two coefficients $x_1 \cdot 2^{i+1} + y_1 \cdot 2^i$ in the base 2 representation of a may fail to be digitwise less than the corresponding two coefficients $x_2 \cdot 2^{i+1} + y_2 \cdot 2^i$ in the base 2 representation of b, even if it holds that $x_1 \cdot 2 + y_1 \le x_2 \cdot 2 + y_2$. For instance, this happens if $x_1 < x_2$ and $y_1 > y_2$.

However, if all the coefficients in the base 4 representation are 0 or 1, i.e., x_1 and x_2 are 0, then this cannot happen. □

11.4   The Davis-Putnam-Robinson theorem

In this section we show that any recursively enumerable set A is exponential Diophantine. As mentioned in section 11.1, the result is due to Davis, Putnam, and Robinson [35]. The present proof is due to Jones and Matiyasevich [70], and is somewhat more in the spirit of this book than the original recursion-theoretic proof.

Any recursively enumerable set A can be represented by a counter machine p in the sense that that $x \in A$ iff $[\![p]\!](x)$ terminates. This follows from the fact that counter machines can express all partial recursive functions. The idea, then, is to formalize the execution of any counter machine p by an exponential Diophantine equation $f(x, z_1, \ldots, z_k) = 0$ such that $[\![p]\!](x)$ terminates iff $f(x, z_1, \ldots, z_k) = 0$ has a solution.

Before proceeding with the general construction it will be useful to review an example, taken from [148], which illustrates how this is done.

Example 11.4.1 Consider the following counter machine p:

$$I_1: \quad \text{if X1=0 goto 4;}$$
$$I_2: \quad \text{X1:=X1-1;}$$
$$I_3: \quad \text{if X2=0 goto 1;}$$
$$I_4: \quad \text{stop}$$

We assume that every subtraction command I_l: X:=X-1 is preceded by a command I_{l-1}:if X=0 goto k. We also assume that for every conditional I_l:if X=0 goto k, I_k is not a subtraction command. This implies that a counter will never be decremented below 0. We write a stop command at the end of the program, and assume that all counters have value 0, when the program terminates. These assumptions present no loss of generality.

Recall that the input is stored in counter X_1. If the input to p is 2, then the computation has length 7, (we count a single-step computation to have length 0), and the following commands are executed in order:

$$1,2,3,1,2,3,1,4$$

The whole execution, including information about values of counters and the current program point, can be represented by the matrix in Figure 11.3.

7	6	5	4	3	2	1	0	=	t
0	0	0	1	1	1	2	2	=	$x_{1,t}$
0	0	0	0	0	0	0	0	=	$x_{2,t}$
0	1	0	0	1	0	0	1	=	$i_{1,t}$
0	0	0	1	0	0	1	0	=	$i_{2,t}$
0	0	1	0	0	1	0	0	=	$i_{3,t}$
1	0	0	0	0	0	0	0	=	$i_{4,t}$

Figure 11.3: Representation of execution of counter machine.

The two x-rows represent the values of the two counters before step t, counting the first step as step 0. For instance, X_1 has value 2 before step 0 and 1, so $x_{1,0}$ and $x_{1,1}$ are both 2. X_1 has value 1 before step 2, 3, and 4, so $x_{1,2}$, $x_{1,3}$, and $x_{1,4}$ are all 1. The i-rows express which command is executed in step t. For instance, in step 0, command 1 is executed, so $i_{1,0}$ is 1, and in step 2 command 3 is executed, and therefore $i_{3,2}$ is 1.

Instead of representing the values of, say X_1, by a *row* of numbers, we can pack the information into a single number

$$\sum_{t=0}^{y} x_{i,t} b^t$$

where $y = 7$ is the length of the computation and b is a number larger than all the numbers in the matrix. With this idea the whole matrix becomes the system of equations in Figure 11.4.

$0 \cdot b^7 +$	$0 \cdot b^6 +$	$0 \cdot b^5 +$	$1 \cdot b^4 +$	$1 \cdot b^3 +$	$1 \cdot b^2 +$	$2 \cdot b^1 +$	$2 \cdot b^0$	$=$	x_1
$0 \cdot b^7 +$	$0 \cdot b^6 +$	$0 \cdot b^5 +$	$0 \cdot b^4 +$	$0 \cdot b^3 +$	$0 \cdot b^2 +$	$0 \cdot b^1 +$	$0 \cdot b^0$	$=$	x_2
$0 \cdot b^7 +$	$1 \cdot b^6 +$	$0 \cdot b^5 +$	$0 \cdot b^4 +$	$1 \cdot b^3 +$	$0 \cdot b^2 +$	$0 \cdot b^1 +$	$1 \cdot b^0$	$=$	i_1
$0 \cdot b^7 +$	$0 \cdot b^6 +$	$0 \cdot b^5 +$	$1 \cdot b^4 +$	$0 \cdot b^3 +$	$0 \cdot b^2 +$	$1 \cdot b^1 +$	$0 \cdot b^0$	$=$	i_2
$0 \cdot b^7 +$	$0 \cdot b^6 +$	$1 \cdot b^5 +$	$0 \cdot b^4 +$	$0 \cdot b^3 +$	$1 \cdot b^2 +$	$0 \cdot b^1 +$	$0 \cdot b^0$	$=$	i_3
$1 \cdot b^7 +$	$0 \cdot b^6 +$	$0 \cdot b^5 +$	$0 \cdot b^4 +$	$0 \cdot b^3 +$	$0 \cdot b^2 +$	$0 \cdot b^1 +$	$0 \cdot b^0$	$=$	i_4

Figure 11.4: Numeric representation of execution of counter machine.

Thus every computation of p on some input x can be represented by certain values of $x, x_1, x_2, i_1, \ldots, i_4, y, b$. These values satisfy certain properties corresponding to the details of the computation. For instance, in all executions of p command 2 is followed by execution of command 3. Thus in Figure 11.4 whenever b^j has coefficient 1 in i_2, b^{j+1} has coeffient 1 in i_3. This is a purely numerical relationship between the values of i_2 and i_3. These relationships can be expressed as a set of equations such that every computation of p on some input gives a solution to the equations, and every solution to the equations correspond to a computation of p. □

The idea, in general, is now to translate any counter machine p into an exponential Diophantine equation such that if $[\![p]\!](x)$ terminates, then the details of the computation— the number of steps, the values of the counters, etc.— give a solution to the equation, and conversely, for every solution of the equation, there is a corresponding terminating computation.

Theorem 11.4.2 Every recursively enumerable set A is exponential Diophantine.

Proof. Let A be any recursively enumerable set and p be a counter machine such that $x \in A$ iff $[\![p]\!](x)$ terminates. Suppose p has form

$$p = I_1 \ldots I_n \ \text{(with counters } X_1, \ldots, X_m) \tag{11.1}$$

We now derive an exponential Diophantine equation

$$f(x, x_1, \ldots, x_m, i_1, \ldots, i_n, y, b, U) = 0 \tag{11.2}$$

such that

$$[\![p]\!](x) \text{ terminates} \ \Leftrightarrow \ (11.2) \text{ has a solution} \tag{11.3}$$

More precisely we derive 12 equation schemes which can be combined into a single conjunction using the technique in section 11.2.

1. First of all, we need a base b for the representation in Figure 11.4. Recall that b must be larger than all the coefficients in order for the representation to be correct. Since the initial value of counter X_1 is x and the other counters are initialized to 0, no counter value can exceed $x + y$ where y is the number of steps of the computation. Therefore,

$$b = 2^{x+y+n} \tag{1}$$

is large enough. We shall need later two additional facts about b, both satisfied by the above choice: that b is a power of 2 and that $b > n$.

2. It will be convenient to have a number whose representation in base b is a string of length y consisting entirely of 1's. This is the number $b^{y-1} + \cdots + b + 1$. This number satisfies the equation

$$1 + bU = U + b^y \tag{2}$$

and it is the only number satisfying the equation; indeed, if $U = (b^y - 1)/(b - 1)$ then $U = b^{y-1} + \cdots + b + 1$.

3. It will be necessary later that the coefficients in Figure 11.4 are all strictly smaller than $b/2$. This is enforced by the following equations.

$$x_j \preceq (b/2 - 1)U \quad (j = 1, \ldots, m) \tag{3}$$

Indeed, if x_j is less than $(b/2 - 1)U$ bitwise, then the same thing holds digitwise in base b, since b is a power of 2 (see Example 11.3.5). But the digits in $(b/2 - 1)U$ in base b are exactly $b/2 - 1$.

4,5. In each computation step of p, exactly one command is executed. This is expressed by the following equations.

$$i_l \preceq U \quad (l = 1, \ldots, n) \tag{4}$$

$$U = \sum_{l=1}^{n} i_l \tag{5}$$

The first equation states that in the binary representation of the two numbers, all the coefficients of i_l are smaller or equal than those of U. Since b is a power of 2, and all the coefficients of U are 1, this is the same as requiring that in base b, all the coefficients of i_l are smaller or equal than those of U, i.e., are 0 or 1 (see Example 11.3.5). That is, in terms of Figure 11.4, all coefficients in i_l are 0 or 1.

The second equation similarly expresses the fact that in every i_l-column in Figure 11.4 there be exactly one coefficient which is 1. For this it is necessary that no carry occur in the summation, and this is guaranteed by the fact that $b > n$.

6,7. In any computation with p, the first and last step are to execute command I_1 and I_n, respectively. This is expressed as follows.

$$1 \preceq i_1 \tag{6}$$

$$i_n = b^{y-1} \tag{7}$$

The first equation expresses that the rightmost coefficient of i_1 in Figure 11.4 is 1. The second states that the leftmost coefficient in i_n is 1.

8. After executing a command I_l which is either a subtraction or an addition, the next instruction should be I_{l+1}. This is expressed as follows.

$$bi_l \preceq i_k + i_{l+1} \quad \text{(for all } l \text{ with } I_l\text{: X:=X-1 or X:=X-1)} \tag{8}$$

The equation states that in Figure 11.4, if the coefficient of b^j in i_l is 1, then the coefficient of b^{j+1} should be 1 in i_{l+1}. Note how the multiplication with b represents a move to the left in Figure 11.4.

9. After executing a conditional I_l:if X_j=0 goto k the next instruction should be either I_k or I_{l+1}. This is expressed as follows.

$$bi_l \preceq i_k + i_{l+1} \quad \text{(for all } l \text{ with } I_l\text{:if X}_j\text{=0 goto k)} \tag{9}$$

The equation states that in Figure 11.4, if the coefficient of b^j in i_l is 1, and I_l is the command if X_j=0 goto k, then the coefficient of b^{j+1} should be 1 in i_{l+1} or i_k (where $k \neq l+1$ by assumption).

10. Whenever executing a command I_l:if X_j=0 goto k, the next command should be I_k if X_j is 0, and I_{l+1} otherwise. This is expressed as follows.

$$bi_l \preceq i_{l+1} + U - 2x_j \quad \text{(for all } l \text{ with } I_l\text{:if X}_j\text{=0 goto k)} \tag{10}$$

To see this, suppose that $X_j = 0$ before, and hence also after, step k, i.e.,

$$x_j = \ldots + 0 \cdot b^{k+1} + 0 \cdot b^k + \ldots$$

Then

$$2x_j = \ldots + 0 \cdot b^{k+1} + 0 \cdot b^k + \ldots$$

Here we made use of the fact that all coefficients are smaller than $b/2$, so that no bit of the coefficient of b^{k-1} is shifted into the coefficient of b^k by the multiplication with 2. Hence, the subtraction $U - 2x_j$ looks as in Figure 11.5.

U	$=$	$1 \cdot b^{y-1}$	$+$	$\cdots$	$+$	$1 \cdot b^{k+1}$	$+$	$1 \cdot b^k$	$+$	$\cdots$
$2x_j$	$=$			$\cdots$	$+$	$0 \cdot b^{k+1}$	$+$	$0 \cdot b^k$	$+$	$\cdots$
$U - 2x_j$	$=$			$\cdots$	$+$	$1 \cdot b^{k+1}$	$+$		$\cdots$	

Figure 11.5: $U - 2x_j$ when $X_j = 0$.

The subtraction may require borrowing from the coefficient 1 of b^k in U, but not from the coefficient 1 of b^{k+1} in U since the coefficent of b^k in $2x_j$ is 0. Now, since

$$bi_l = \ldots + 1 \cdot b^{k+1} + \ldots$$

(10) holds iff the rightmost bit in the coefficient to b^{k+1} in i_{l+1} is 0, i.e., iff

$$i_{l+1} = \ldots + 0 \cdot b^{k+1} + \ldots$$

i.e., iff the next command is not I_{l+1}. By (9) the next command must then be I_k, as required. This covers the case $X_j = 0$.

If, on the other hand, $X_j > 0$ before and hence also after step k, i.e.,

$$x_j = \ldots + n \cdot b^{k+1} + n \cdot b^k + \ldots$$

Then

$$2x_j = \ldots + 2n \cdot b^{k+1} + 2n \cdot b^k + \ldots$$

Then the subtraction $U - 2x_j$ looks as in Figure 11.6.

Again we made use of the fact that $n < b/2$ so that no bit is shifted from one coefficient to another by the multiplication with 2. Here the subtraction of the coefficients to b^{k-1} may or may not require borrowing, but the coefficients to b^k and b^{k+1} definitely do need borrowing. Now the coefficient $b - 2n$ to b^{k+1} in $U - 2x_j$ is even, whereas

$$bi_l = \ldots + 1 \cdot b^{k+1} + \ldots$$

						b		b	
U	$= 1 \cdot b^{y-1}$	$+$	$\cdots$	$+$	$\gamma \cdot b^{k+2}$	$+$	$\gamma \cdot b^{k+1}$	$+$	$1 \cdot b^{k}$	$+ \cdots$
$2x_j$	$=$			$\cdots$		$+$	$2n \cdot b^{k+1}$	$+$	$2n \cdot b^{k}$	$+ \cdots$
$U - 2x_j =$				$\cdots$		$+$	$(b-2n) \cdot b^{k+1}$	$+$	$\cdots$

Figure 11.6: $U - 2x_j$ when $X_j > 0$.

so (10) holds iff the rightmost bit in the coefficient to b^{k+1} in i_{l+1} is 1, i.e., iff

$$i_{l+1} = \ldots + 1 \cdot b^{k+1} + \ldots$$

i.e., iff the next command is I_{l+1}, as required.

11,12. It remains to express the fact that addition and subtraction instructions should modify the contents of the counters appropriately. Let $A(j)$ and $S(j)$ be the set of labels l such that the command I_l is $X_j := X_j + 1$ and $X_j := X_j - 1$, respectively. This is done by the following equations.

$$x_1 = x + b(x_1 + \sum_{l \in A(1)} i_l - \sum_{l \in S(1)} i_l) \tag{11}$$

$$x_j = b(x_j + \sum_{l \in A(j)} i_l - \sum_{l \in S(j)} i_l) \quad (j = 2, \ldots, m) \tag{12}$$

Indeed, consider (11). The sum $\sum_{l \in A(1)} i_l$ is a number whose base b representation has 1 for every coefficient k where the k'th step in the execution of p is $X_1 := X_1 + 1$. Similarly with the other sum. (11) now states that if X_1 is n before the k'the step, and the instruction executed in the k'th step is an addition, then X_1 is $n+1$ before the $k+1$'th step. For example, consider Figure 11.7.

In this example there is only a single addition to X_1 during the whole execution, namely in step 1, and a single subtraction in step 4. Before step 1, X_1 has value x, hence after it has value $x+1$. Similarly with subtractions. This can be expressed by requiring that if we add x_1 to the sums $\sum_{l \in A(1)} i_l$ and $- \sum_{l \in S(1)} i_l$ and shift the result one position to the left, then the coefficients should match those in x_1. Note that multiplication with b does not lead to overflow since it is assumed that all counters are 0 at the end.

Equation (12) is identical to Equation (11) except that the initial contents of x_j is 0 rather than x, for $j = 2, \ldots, m$. The whole set of equations is collected in Figure 11.8. It is now a routine matter to verify that the claim (11.3) is indeed true. $\square$

6	5	4	3	2	1	0	step	
x	x	$x+1$	$x+1$	$\underline{x+1}$	$\underline{x}$	x	$=$	x_1
0	0	0	0	0	$\underline{1}$	0	$=$	$\sum_{l \in A(1)} i_l$
0	0	1	0	0	0	0	$=$	$\sum_{l \in S(1)} i_l$
x	x	x	$x+1$	$x+1$	$\underline{x+1}$	x	$=$	$x_1 + \sum_{l \in A(1)} i_l - \sum_{l \in S(1)} i_l$
x	x	$x+1$	$x+1$	$\underline{x+1}$	x	x	$=$	$x + b(x_1 + \sum_{l \in A(1)} i_l - \sum_{l \in S(1)} i_l)$

Figure 11.7: Representing additions and subtractions.

(1)	$b = 2^{x+y+n}$	
(2)	$1 + bU = U + b^y$	
(3)	$x_j \preceq (b/2 - 1)U$	$(j = 1, \ldots, m)$
(4)	$i_l \preceq U$	$(l = 1, \ldots, n)$
(5)	$U = \sum_{l=1}^{n} i_l$	
(6)	$1 \preceq i_1$	
(7)	$i_n = b^{y-1}$	
(8)	$bi_l \preceq i_{l+1}$	$(\mathrm{I}_l : \mathrm{X}_j = \mathrm{X}_j - 1, \mathrm{I}_l : \mathrm{X}_j = \mathrm{X}_j + 1)$
(9)	$bi_l \preceq i_{l+1} + U - 2x_j$	$(\mathrm{I}_l : \text{if } \mathrm{X}_j = 0 \text{ goto } k)$
(10)	$bi_l \preceq i_k + i_{l+1}$	$(\mathrm{I}_l : \text{if } \mathrm{X}_j = 0 \text{ goto } k)$
(11)	$x_1 = x + b(x_1 + \sum_{l \in A(1)} i_l - \sum_{l \in S(1)} i_l)$	
(12)	$x_j = b(x_j + \sum_{l \in A(j)} i_l - \sum_{l \in S(j)} i_l)$	$(j = 2, \ldots, m)$

Figure 11.8: Representation of execution of counter machine.

Corollary 11.4.3 There is no algorithm that can decide for an exponential Diophantine equation whether or not is has a solution in natural numbers.

Proof. Let $A \subseteq \mathbb{N}$ be a recursive enumerable, non-recursive set (recall that such sets do exist). By the Davis-Putnam-Robinson theorem there is an exponential Diophantine equation $f(x, z_1, \ldots, z_n) = 0$ such that

$$x \in A \Leftrightarrow f(x, z_1, \ldots, z_n) = 0 \text{ has a solution}$$

Since we can construct effectively the equation $f(x, z_1, \ldots, z_n) = 0$ given x it follows that an algorithm to decide for each x whether $f(x, z_1, \ldots z_n)$ has a solution would imply a decision procedure for A, which is impossible since A is non-recursive. $\square$

11.5   Matiyasevich's theorem and Hilbert's tenth problem

In this section we briefly show that Hilbert's tenth problem is unsolvable, leaving out almost all details. As mentioned, the following theorem, due to Matiyasevich [111], was the final step in solving Hilbert's tenth problem.

Theorem 11.5.1 The relation $u = v^w$ is Diophantine.

Proof. See, e.g., [117]. □

Corollary 11.5.2 Every recursively enumerable set is Diophantine.

Proof. By the Davis-Putnam-Robinson theorem, there exists for every recursively enumerable set A an exponential Diophantine equation $f(x, z_1, \ldots, z_n) = 0$ such that

$$x \in A \Leftrightarrow \exists z_1, \ldots, \exists z_n : f(x, z_1, \ldots, z_n) = 0$$

By Matiyasevich's theorem there is a Diophantine equation $e(u, v, w, y_1, \ldots, y_m) = 0$ such that

$$u = v^w \Leftrightarrow \exists y_1, \ldots, \exists y_m : e(u, v, w, y_1, \ldots, y_m) = 0$$

Therefore every occurrence in $f(x, z_1, \ldots, z_n)$ of $t_1^{t_2}$ can be replaced by a variable u. We must then add to the original equation $f(x, z_1, \ldots, z_n) = 0$ the new equations $v = t_1$, $w = t_2$, and $e(u, v, w, y_1, \ldots, y_m) = 0$. These can all be combined into a single Diophantine equation using the technique in section 11.2. □

The following corollary then shows that Hilbert's tenth problem is unsolvable.

Corollary 11.5.3 There is no algorithm that can decide for a Diophantine equation whether or not is has a solution in natural numbers.

Proof. Similar to the proof of Corollary 11.4.3 using the preceding corollary. □

Exercises

11.1 Show that the non-strict less-than relation $a \leq b$ is Diophantine.   □

11.2 Show that the set of numbers that are not powers of 2 is Diophantine.   □

11.3 Show that the set of numbers that are not prime is Diophantine.   □

11.4 * Prove that for all $n \in \mathbb{N}$ and all $k \in \{0,\dots,n\}$

$$\binom{n}{k} \leq 2^n$$

Hint: For a real number r let $\lceil r \rceil$ denote the smallest integer larger than r, and let $\lfloor r \rfloor$ denote the largest integer smaller than r. For instance, $\lfloor 7/2 \rfloor = \lfloor 6/2 \rfloor = 3$ and $\lceil 7/2 \rceil = \lceil 8/2 \rceil = 4$. Then proceed by induction on n splitting into the cases:

1. $k = n$;
2. $0 \leq k \leq \lfloor n/2 \rfloor$;
3. $\lfloor n/2 \rfloor < k < n$.

In the last case use the fact that

$$\binom{n}{k} = \binom{n}{n-k}$$

The following rules may also be helpful:

$$n/\lceil n \rceil \leq 2$$
$$\lceil n \rceil - 1 \leq \lfloor n \rfloor$$

$\square$

The following is adopted from [148]. For a different proof of Lemma 11.3.3, see [70].

11.5 * Prove that

$$k \preceq n \Leftrightarrow \binom{n}{k} \text{ is odd}$$

Hint: Prove the assertion for the cases $k > n$, $k = n$, and $k < n$. In the last case proceed in the following steps.

1. Let $m = \sum_{i=0}^{l} m_i 2^i$ (the right hand side is the binary representation of m), and define

    $$\text{ONE}(m) = \text{the number of 1s among } m_0,\dots,m_l$$
    $$\text{EXP}(m) = \text{the exponent of the highest power of 2 dividing } m$$

    $\text{EXP}(m)$ is the same as the index in $\{0,\dots,l\}$ of the rightmost 1 among $m_0,\dots,m_l$. For example, since 76 in binary is 1001100, $\text{ONE}(76) = 3$, $\text{EXP}(76) = 2$.

2. Prove that m is odd iff $\text{EXP}(m) = 0$.

3. Prove that $\text{EXP}(m!) = m - \text{ONE}(m)$ by induction on m.
    In the induction step consider the cases: m is even, and m is odd, and use in the latter case the fact that $\text{EXP}(m+1) = \text{ONE}(m) - \text{ONE}(m+1) + 1$.

4. Prove that

$$\text{EXP}\binom{n}{k} = \text{ONE}(k) + \text{ONE}(n-k) - \text{ONE}(b)$$

5. Now let $n = \sum_{i=0}^{l} n_i 2^i$ and $k = \sum_{i=0}^{l} k_i 2^i$. Prove that $\forall i : k_i \leq n_i$ implies

$$\text{EXP}\binom{n}{k} = 0$$

and hence the left-to-right direction in the overall assertion follows.

6. For the right-to-left direction prove that if $\exists i : k_i > n_i$ then

$$\text{EXP}\binom{n}{k} > 0$$

as follows. Let i be the smallest index such that $0 = n_i < k_i = 1$. Let $N_j = k_j - [b-a]_j^2$. Prove that

$$
\begin{array}{rcll}
n_j & = & N_j & \text{for all } j < i \\
n_i(=0) & < & (2=)N_i & \\
\sum_{j+1}^{l} n_j & \leq & 1 + \sum_{j+1}^{l} N_j &
\end{array}
$$

and conclude that

$$\text{ONE}(k) + \text{ONE}(n-k) = \text{ONE}(n) = \sum_{j=0}^{l} N_j - n_j > 0$$

which gives the right-to-left direction. □

References

As mentioned, Hilbert's tenth Problem was presented at the International Congress of Mathematicians in 1900. While it was not actually stated during his lecture, it appeared in the published version, see Reid's biography [142].

Several papers by Davis, Putnam, and Robinson were mentioned in section 11.1. Another classic recursion-theoretic presentation of the unsolvability of Hilbert's tenth problem, with a historical appendix and more references, is due to Davis [33].

In Section 11.1 we also mentioned several papers by Matiyasevich. For more references and much more information about all aspects of Hilbert's tenth problem, consult Matiyasevich's book [117]. The book discusses many applications; it infers from unsolvability of Hilbert's tenth problem the unsolvability of several other problems in number theory and analysis. Its sections with commentaries at the end of each chapter give many historical details.

In several places we have adopted technical and stylistic improvements from the recent books by Floyd and Beigel [45] and Rozenberg and Salomaa [148].

12 Inference Systems and Gödel's Incompleteness Theorem

Inference systems have proven themselves very powerful for defining logical systems, in programming languages for defining operational semantics and type systems, and in many other applications as well. The main purpose of this chapter is to understand exactly what the limits are to their expressivity.

In *Computer Science*, an important application is to define a programming language's semantics: a systematic way to assign a meaning to every program in the language, thus specifying precisely the possible effects that can be realized by any program[1].

Inference systems originated in *Mathematical Logic*, for the purpose of making a precise formulation of mathematical reasoning, for example proofs in geometry from Euclid's axioms. A concrete "formal system" is often presented by beginning with definitions of some syntactic categories and then by presenting inference systems for reasoning about them. Examples of syntactic categories might be Terms T, Formulas F, Assumptions Γ, and Judgments $\Gamma \vdash F$. Such a judgment usually has an intuitive reading, for instance "F is true, provided the assumptions listed in Γ hold." An example of an inference rule is the ancient *modus ponens* rule:

$$\text{If } \Gamma \vdash F \Rightarrow G \text{ and } \Gamma \vdash F, \text{ then } \Gamma \vdash G$$

Logicians have tried to relate the question of which statements are *true* in a logical framework, e.g., geometry, to the question of which statements are *provable* according to a given formal logical system, e.g., Euclid's axioms. The truth of a statement in a mathematical system concerns its meaning in an "intended interpretation," e.g., an assertion about figures in two-dimensional Euclidean space; whereas its provability concerns whether its truth can be established by a certain system of formal proof procedures. The fact that the two may be different first became clear with the discovery of non-Riemannian geometries.

In the last analysis, formal proof procedures work by symbol manipulation, and are often presented in the form of inference systems.

---

[1] A "possible effect" might be transforming an input to an output, but in general need not be deterministic, e.g., search processes or interactive communications are other possibilities.

Overview: section 12.1 begins this chapter with some informal examples of the use of inference systems to define programming language semantics.

section 12.2 introduces a generalization of the concept of set: an *n-ary predicate*, which is much used in logic, and implicit in the informal examples. After this, section 12.3 establishes several properties cocerning recursive and recursively enumerable predicates, extending those of sets as in chapter 5.

section 12.4 contains a *general* formalization of inference systems as used to define predicates over $\mathbb{D}$, and it is proven in section 12.4.3 that every predicate definable by an inference system is a recursively enumerable subset of $\mathbb{D}$.

This framework gives enough background to state and prove, in section 12.5, a version of *Gödel's incompleteness theorem*: that no inference system can prove all and only the true statements of even a particularly simple formal language DL concerning values in $\mathbb{D}$.

12.1   Examples of operational semantics by inference systems

Language semantics can be defined in (at least) two ways. One way is by Plotkin's *structural operational semantics* [132] or Kahn's similar *natural semantics* [86]; both are used by many researchers. By this approach, a language semantics is given by a collection of inference rules that define how commands are excuted, how expressions are evaluated, etc.

In an operational semantics a language definition is a set of *inference rules* and *axioms* sufficient to execute programs. An inference rule consists of a set of *premises* which, if true, allow one to conclude or deduce a *conclusion*. An axiom is a special case of an inference rule — one with an empty set of premises. We give some examples now, and a more general framework later in section 12.4.

The I semantics defined in section 2.2 is in essence (though not in apperance) an operational semantics. For example, the definition of $C \vdash \sigma \to \sigma'$ is easy to re-express using inference rules as in the next section (Exercise 12.2). According to such rules the meaning of a recursive construction such as a while loop or a recursively defined function is typically obtained by "syntactic unfolding"; an example will be seen below.

Another way to define semantics is by *denotational semantics*, first developed by Scott [154]. (See Schmidt [150] for a gentle introduction.) By this approach, every syntactic construction in the language is assigned a meaning in some *domain*: a set plus a partial order on its elements, ordered according to their "information content." For example, the set $\mathbb{N} \to \mathbb{N}_\perp$ is a domain, ordered by $f \sqsubseteq g$ iff for all $x \in \mathbb{N}$, either $f(x) = g(x)$ or $f(x) = \perp$ (see section 14.1 for a sketch of this approach). The meaning of a recursive construction such as a `while` loop or a recursively defined function is obtained by applying the "least fixed-point operator" to a certain higher-order function.

12.1.1   Expression evaluation by inference rules

We now investigate how expressions in a programming language can be evaluated, relating the *syntactic* world of expressions as written to their *semantics*, i.e., the mathematical values which they denote.

Suppose e is an expression, such as x+y, which contains occurrences of the variables x and y. Then the value of e can be determined only under some *value assumptions* about the values of x and y. Such assumptions can be represented by a finite function $\sigma = [x \mapsto v, \ldots]$ which for instance maps x to its value, so $\sigma(x) = v$. Function σ is usually called a *store* in an imperative programming language, or an *environment* in a functional programming language.

The assertion that "if x = 5 and y = 6, then x+y = 11" is written as follows:

$$[x \mapsto 5, y \mapsto 6] \vdash x + y \Rightarrow 11$$

More generally, the notation $\sigma \vdash e \Rightarrow v$ is an example of what is called a *judgment*.

This one means that "given store (or environment) σ, expression e can be evaluated to yield result v." Here expression e is a *syntactic* object, value v is a semantic object, and store σ connects syntactic objects (variable names) with semantic objects (their current values).

Expression evaluation is often based on a set of *inference rules*, one for each form of expression in the language. For an expression which is a variable occurrence, we have the assertion:

$$\sigma \vdash x \Rightarrow \sigma(x)$$

This is an axiom: an inference rule that is true without prerequisite assumptions, assuming the value of variable x is defined by σ.

Now consider an expression `succ` e whose value is 1 more than the value of its subexpression e. If subexpression e evaluates to v, then the entire expression evaluates to $v + 1$. This is expressed by the inference rule, where the part above the line is called the *premise*:

$$\frac{\sigma \vdash e \Rightarrow v}{\sigma \vdash \texttt{succ}\ e \Rightarrow plus(v,1)}$$

For an expression $\texttt{e1}\ +\ \texttt{e2}$, if the subexpressions respectively have values u, v, then the entire expression has value $u + v$. This is expressed by a two-premise inference rule:

$$\frac{\sigma \vdash \texttt{e1} \Rightarrow u \quad \sigma \vdash \texttt{e2} \Rightarrow v}{\sigma \vdash \texttt{e1}\ +\ \texttt{e2} \Rightarrow plus(u,v)}$$

This may look "content-free" but in fact is not, since it defines the meaning of the syntactic symbol "+" appearing to the left of the $\Rightarrow$ in terms of the already well-understood mathematical operation of addition (the *plus* appearing to the right).

For another example consider boolean-valued expression $\texttt{e1}\ =\ \texttt{e2}$, which tests two values for equality. This is easily described by two rules, one for each case:

$$\frac{\sigma \vdash \texttt{e1} \Rightarrow u \quad \sigma \vdash \texttt{e2} \Rightarrow u}{\sigma \vdash \texttt{e1}\ =\ \texttt{e2} \Rightarrow true}$$

$$\frac{\sigma \vdash \texttt{e1} \Rightarrow u \quad \sigma \vdash \texttt{e2} \Rightarrow v \quad u \neq v}{\sigma \vdash \texttt{e1}\ =\ \texttt{e2} \Rightarrow false}$$

The meaning of a conditional expression $\texttt{if}\ e\ \texttt{then}\ \texttt{e1}\ \texttt{else}\ \texttt{e2}$ can also be given by two rules, the first applying when condition $\texttt{e2}$ is *true* and the other applying when it is *false*:

$$\frac{\sigma \vdash e \Rightarrow true \quad \sigma \vdash \texttt{e1} \Rightarrow v}{\sigma \vdash \texttt{if}\ e\ \texttt{then}\ \texttt{e1}\ \texttt{else}\ \texttt{e2} \Rightarrow v}$$

$$\frac{\sigma \vdash e \Rightarrow false \quad \sigma \vdash \texttt{e2} \Rightarrow v}{\sigma \vdash \texttt{if}\ e\ \texttt{then}\ \texttt{e1}\ \texttt{else}\ \texttt{e2} \Rightarrow v}$$

Using these inference rules, the value of a complex expression can be inferred from the value assumptions held in the store σ. For instance, when $\sigma = [\texttt{m} \mapsto 5, \texttt{n} \mapsto 3]$, then the inference

$$\frac{\dfrac{\sigma \vdash \texttt{m} \Rightarrow 5 \quad \sigma \vdash \texttt{n} \Rightarrow 3}{\sigma \vdash \texttt{m+n} \Rightarrow 8} \quad \dfrac{\sigma \vdash \texttt{m} \Rightarrow 5 \quad \sigma \vdash 1 \Rightarrow 1}{\sigma \vdash \texttt{m-1} \Rightarrow 4}}{\sigma \vdash \texttt{(m+n)*(m-1)} \Rightarrow 32}$$

shows that (m+n)*(m-1) has value 32, using unstated but obvious inference rules for evaluating constants, subtraction and multiplication.

12.1.2 Recursion by syntactic unfolding

For another example, consider a programming construction for minimization "min x such that e = 0." Its intended semantics is that e is to be evaluated repeatedly with $x = 0,1,2,\dots$ This is repeated until e first evaluates to 0, and the value that x has at that time is returned. (The expression's value will be undefined if e evaluates to nonzero values for all x.)

The following inference rules define this new construction's semantics. A new judgment is used, of form $\sigma[x \mapsto u] \vdash^{min} e \Rightarrow w$. It signifies "$w$ is the smallest value of x not less than u for which e evaluates to 0," where σ is an environment defining the current values of variables in e other than x.

$$\frac{\sigma[x \mapsto 0] \vdash^{min} e \Rightarrow w}{\sigma \vdash \text{min } x \text{ such that } e=0 \Rightarrow w}$$

$$\frac{\sigma[x \mapsto u] \vdash e \Rightarrow 0}{\sigma[x \mapsto u] \vdash^{min} e \Rightarrow u}$$

$$\frac{\sigma[x \mapsto u] \vdash e \Rightarrow v, \ v \neq 0, \text{ and } \sigma[x \mapsto u+1] \vdash^{min} e \Rightarrow w}{\sigma[x \mapsto u] \vdash^{min} e \Rightarrow w}$$

The following illustrates computation of min x such that 1-x = 0:

$$\frac{\dfrac{[x \mapsto 0] \vdash 1 \Rightarrow 1, \ [x \mapsto 0] \vdash x \Rightarrow 0}{[x \mapsto 0] \vdash 1\text{-}x \Rightarrow 1} \quad 1 \neq 0 \quad \dfrac{\dfrac{[x \mapsto 1] \vdash 1 \Rightarrow 1, \ [x \mapsto 1] \vdash x \Rightarrow 1}{[x \mapsto 1] \vdash 1\text{-}x \Rightarrow 0}}{[x \mapsto 1] \vdash^{min} 1\text{-}x \Rightarrow 1}}{\dfrac{[x \mapsto 0] \vdash^{min} 1\text{-}x \Rightarrow 1}{[] \vdash (\text{min } x \text{ such that } 1\text{-}x=0) \Rightarrow 1}}$$

Intuitive explanation: computation begins at the bottom of the tree with given environment σ and expression e, and the goal is to find v such that $\sigma \vdash e \Rightarrow v$.

In this case σ is an empty environment [], and the goal is to evaluate "min x such that 1-x = 0" with no defined variables, and an as yet unknown value w. The only inference rule applicable to yield the bottom tree node requires the node above, in effect initializing x to 0 and asking for the value of a $\vdash^{min}$ judgment. Both inference rules for $\vdash^{min}$ cause 1-x to be evaluated, yielding 1 in this case. This is nonzero so the only applicable $\vdash^{min}$ rule is the last one, which in effect asks for another $\vdash^{min}$ judgment, after incrementing x from 0 to 1. Again, 1-x has to be evaluated, now yielding 0. Now only the first $\vdash^{min}$ rule can be used, leading to the conclusion that [x ↦ 1] $\vdash^{min}$ 1-x ⇒ 1 and so that $w = 1$.

12.2   Predicates

The net effect of an inference system is to define a predicate, i.e., a relation among values (for example, between expressions and their values in a given store). This section introduces some terminology concerning predicates, and establishes some of their basic properties.

The extensional view: predicates are sets

In this book a *predicate* over a set S is just a subset of S. It is common in logic to express the fact that $v \in S$ as "$S(v)$ is true," or sometimes even just to assert the statement "$S(v)$."

If $S = S_1 \times \cdots \times S_n$ then P is called an *n-ary* predicate (0-ary or nullary, unary, binary, ternary, etc. for $n = 0,1,2,3,\ldots$). Examples of predicates over $\mathbb{N}$:

1. binary: $<$ is the set $\{(m,n) \in \mathbb{N} \times \mathbb{N} \mid m$ is smaller than $n\}$.
2. binary: $=$ is the set $\{(m,m) \in \mathbb{N} \times \mathbb{N} \mid m \in \mathbb{N}\}$.
3. unary: the set of prime numbers.

Operations on predicates

Suppose P and Q are *n-ary* predicates over S. Then the following are also *n-ary* predicates:

1. *conjunction*, or "and": $P \wedge Q = P \cap Q$. For $s \in S^n$, s is in $P \wedge Q$ iff s is in both P and Q.
2. *disjunction*, or "or": $P \vee Q = P \cup Q$. For $s \in S^n$, s is in $P \cup Q$ iff s is in P or Q or both.
3. *implication*, or "if-then" : $P \Rightarrow Q = \{s \in S^n \mid$ if s is in P then s is also in $Q\}$.
4. *negation*, or "not": $\neg P = S^n \backslash P$. For $s \in S^n$, s is in $\neg P$ iff s is not in P.

Some examples:

1. If P is the set of prime numbers and O is the set of odd numbers, then $P \wedge O$ is the set of odd prime numbers.
2. If O is the set of odd numbers and E is the set of even numbers then $E \vee O = \mathbb{N}$.

Recall that, although functions are just certain sets, we allow shorthand notations like $f(n,m) = n+m$. Similarly we allow short hand notations for predicates, like "$P(x,y)$ is the predicate $x = y + 1$" with the understanding that what we really mean is that $P(x,y)$ is the set $\{(1,0),(2,1),\ldots\}$.

Suppose that $P \subseteq S_1 \times \cdots \times S_n$ is an n-ary predicate. Then the following are $(n-1)$-ary predicates:

1. *Universal quantifier,* or "for all":
$$\forall x_i P = \{(x_1,\ldots,x_{i-1},x_{i+1},\ldots,x_n) \in S_1 \times S_{i-1} \times S_{i+1} \times \cdots \times S_n \mid$$
$$\text{for all } x_i \text{ in } S_i, (x_1,\ldots x_n) \text{ is in } S_1 \times \cdots \times S_n\}$$

2. *Existential quantifier,* or "there exists":
$$\exists x_i P = \{(x_1,\ldots,x_{i-1},x_{i+1},\ldots,x_n) \in S_1 \times S_{i-1} \times S_{i+1} \times \cdots \times S_n \mid$$
$$\text{there is an } x_i \text{ in } S_i \text{ such that } (x_1,\ldots x_n) \text{ is in } S_1 \times \cdots \times S_n\}$$

Examples:

1. If $P(x,y)$ is the predicate $\leq$ over $\mathbb{N} \times \mathbb{N}$ then $\forall y P(x,y)$ is the predicate over $\mathbb{N}$ which only contains 0. (0 is smaller than all other numbers.)
2. Further, $\forall x P(x,y)$ is the predicate over $\mathbb{N}$ which contains no elements at all. (There is no largest number).
3. If $P(x,y)$ is the predicate $x = y + 1$ over $\mathbb{N} \times O$ where O is the set of odd numbers then $\exists x P(x,y)$ is the predicate over $\mathbb{N}$ containing exactly the even positive numbers.

n-ary predicates over $\mathbb{D}$ as subsets of $\mathbb{D}$

Since set $\mathbb{D}$ is closed under pairing, we can represent an *n-ary* predicate P over $\mathbb{D}$ as the set of list values:

$$\{(d_1 \ldots d_n) = (d_1 . (d_2 . \ldots . (d_n . \texttt{nil}) \ldots) \mid d_1,\ldots,d_n \in P\}$$

Thus we may take over the terms "recursive" (decidable) and "r.e." or "recursively enumerable" (semidecidable) for predicates over $\mathbb{D}$, without change from those concerning sets. We will henceforth restrict our attention in some definitions and theorems to unary predicates over $\mathbb{D}$, but use the freer n-ary notation where convenient.

12.3   Predicates and program descriptions

Theorem 12.3.1 If P and Q are recursive predicates then so are $P \vee Q$, $P \wedge Q$, and $\neg P$.

Proof. By Theorem 5.5.1 $\neg P$ is decidable if P is decidable. Let p = read X1,...,Xn; Cp; write Rp and q = read Y1,...,Yn; Cq; write Rq be programs deciding P and Q, respectively. Without loss of generality they have no variables in common. The following program clearly decides $P \wedge Q$:

```
read Xp;
Y1 := X1;...; Yn := Xn;
Cp; Cq;
Result := Rp and Rq;
write Result
```

Further, $P \vee Q \equiv \neg(\neg P \wedge \neg Q)$, so by Theorem 5.5.1 $P \vee Q$ is decidable.   □

Theorem 12.3.2 If P and Q are recursively enumerable predicates then so are $P \vee Q$, $P \wedge Q$, and $\exists x.\, P(x, y_1, \ldots, y_n)$.

Proof. By Theorem 5.7.2 there are programs p, q respectively, such that $P(x_1, \ldots, x_n)$ is true iff $[\![p]\!]$ terminates on input $(x_1, \ldots, x_n)$ and similarly for Q and q. Then the program just given also semidecides $P \wedge Q$.

Unfortunately this simple approach does not work for $P \vee Q$, since if the program for P loops then the program above does too — even though the Q program might terminate, making $P \vee Q$ true. One way to prove termination is to run p and q alternately, as was done in the proof of Theorem 5.5.1, part 4.

For a more elegant solution, recall that a predicate is a set of tuples, so $P \vee Q$ is the union of two sets. If either $P = \emptyset$ or $Q = \emptyset$, then $P \vee Q$ is trivially recursively enumerable. If neither is empty, then $P = \mathrm{rng}(f)$ and $Q = \mathrm{rng}(g)$ where $f, g : \mathbb{D} \to \mathbb{D}$ are recursive total functions. Define function h by

$$h(x) = \text{if } hd(x) = \texttt{nil then } f(tl(x)) \text{ else } g(tl(x))$$

Clearly h is total recursive, and $\mathrm{rng}(h) = \mathrm{rng}(f) \cup \mathrm{rng}(g)$ as needed.

Finally, assume $P(x, y_1, \ldots, y_n)$ is r.e. If $P = \emptyset$ then $\exists x.\, P(x, y_1, \ldots, y_n) = \emptyset$ and so is trivially recursively enumerable. Assume $P = \mathrm{rng}(f)$ for a recursive total function f (recall that $\mathbb{D}$ contains tuples). Define $g(\mathrm{d}) = f(tl(\mathrm{d}))$, clearly total recursive. It is easy to see that

$$(y_1, \ldots, y_n) \in \mathrm{rng}(g) \Leftrightarrow \exists x.\, P(x, y_1, \ldots, y_n)$$

which completes the proof. (Reasoning: given $y_1, \ldots, y_n \in \mathbb{D}$, if $\exists x . P(x, y_1, \ldots, y_n)$ is true then $f(\mathrm{d}) = (x, y_1, \ldots, y_n)$ for some $\mathrm{d}, x \in \mathbb{D}$. Thus $g(\mathrm{d}) = (y_1, \ldots, y_n)$ so $(y_1, \ldots, y_n) \in \mathrm{rng}(g)$; and conversely.) $\qquad \square$

Theorem 12.3.3 There are recursively enumerable predicates P, Q such that neither the predicate $\neg Q$ nor $\forall x . P(x, y_1, \ldots, y_n)$ is recursively enumerable.

Proof. By Theorem 5.7.2, since Theorems 5.3.1 and 5.6.1 prove that *HALT* predicate is semidecidable but undecidable. For the second part, *any* nonempty r.e. set is of the form $A = \mathrm{rng}(f)$ where f is total and recursive. Thus for any $\mathrm{d} \in \mathbb{D}$

$$\mathrm{d} \in A \text{ iff } \exists \mathrm{x} \in \mathbb{D} . \mathrm{d} = f(\mathrm{x})$$

Predicate $\mathrm{d} \neq f(\mathrm{x})$ is decidable since f is total recursive, so $\exists \mathrm{x} \in \mathbb{D} . \mathrm{d} = f(\mathrm{x})$ is recursively enumerable. Finally, its negation is $\forall x . \mathrm{d} \neq f(\mathrm{x})$. This cannot be r.e., as this would imply that $\mathbb{D} \setminus A$ is also r.e., with *HALT* as a special case. $\qquad \square$

12.4 The predicates defined by an inference system

We now simplify and generalize the examples of section 12.1. The result is a framework able to express the previous examples, and most logical proof systems as well. An inference system $\mathcal{I}$ is a collection of inference rules which, acting together, define a collection of provable judgments. The idea is to think of the set of values for which each judgment is true as a predicate over $\mathbb{D}$. The system proves assertions of form $P(\mathrm{d})$ where P is a predicate name and $\mathrm{d} \in \mathbb{D}$.

12.4.1 A formalization of inference systems

Definition 12.4.1 An *inference system* $\mathcal{I}$ consists of

1. Two finite sets, one of *predicate names* $P, Q, \ldots, Z$ and another of *inference rules* $R_1, R_2, \ldots, R_m$.
2. For each inference rule R_r, a corresponding *type*: $R_r = P_1 \times \ldots \times P_k \to P$ where $P, P_1, \ldots, P_k$ are predicate names.
3. Each inference rule R_r with type $P_1 \times \ldots \times P_k \to P$ is a decidable *inference relation*: $R_r \subseteq \mathbb{D}^k \times \mathbb{D}$. $\qquad \square$

Definition 12.4.2 An inference system $\mathcal{I}$ defines the set $Thms^{\mathcal{I}}$ of all judgments (theorems) provable from $\mathcal{I}$. By definition:

1. Suppose R_r has type $P_1 \times \cdots \times P_k \to P$ and $P_1(\mathsf{d}_1), \ldots, P_k(\mathsf{d}_k) \in Thms^{\mathcal{I}}$. If $((\mathsf{d}_1, \ldots, \mathsf{d}_k), \mathsf{d}) \in R_r$, then $P(\mathsf{d}) \in Thms^{\mathcal{I}}$.

2. No set $Thms^{\mathcal{I}}$ contains any element of $\mathbb{D}$ unless it can be shown so by some finite number of applications of the preceding clause.

The *premises* of this application of rule R_r are $P_1(\mathsf{d}_1), \ldots, P_k(\mathsf{d}_k)$, and $P(\mathsf{d})$ is called its *conclusion*. A special case: if $k = 0$, the rule is called an *axiom*. The effect of an axiom is to place elements into set $Thms^{\mathcal{I}}$ with no need for premises. $\qquad\square$

12.4.2 Examples of inference systems

Operational semantics. In previous sections we saw a definition of expression evaluation by two ternary (3-ary) predicates: $\sigma \vdash$ `expression` $\Rightarrow$ *value* for normal evaluation, and an auxiliary predicate $\sigma \vdash^{min}$ `expression` $\Rightarrow$ *value* used for the minimization operator.

Horn clause deduction. section 26.3 will describe the deduction of boolean variables (also called propositional variables) from a set $\mathcal{H}$ of *Horn clauses* of form $A_1 \wedge A_2 \wedge \ldots \wedge A_k \Rightarrow A_0$. This is an archetypical example of an infernce system. In this context all judgments have form $\vdash A$ where A is a propositional variable, and one inference rule for each Horn clause $A_1 \wedge A_2 \wedge \ldots \wedge A_k \Rightarrow A_0 \in \mathcal{H}$:

$$\frac{\vdash A_1 \quad \vdash A_2 \quad \ldots \vdash A_k}{\vdash A_0}$$

Propositional logic. This system is at a higher meta-level, not being restricted to one fixed set $\mathcal{H}$ of propositional (boolean) formulas. It has only a single predicate of form $\vdash P$ where P is a boolean formula (Appendix section A.1), possibly containing boolean-valued variables. The following axioms and inference rule are from [95]. They can be used to deduce $\vdash P$ for *all and only* those boolean formulas P which are true for every assignment of truth values to their propositional variables.

It is thus an example of a *complete and consistent* logical system: one which can prove all and only the true statements in its domain of discourse (in this case, propositional logic). As we will see from Gödel's theorem, this is an unusual property: in most logical systems of a certain strength any consistent system must necessarily be incomplete, that is there must be *true* statements which are not *provable*.

$$\overline{\vdash P \Rightarrow (Q \Rightarrow P)} \quad \overline{\vdash (R \Rightarrow S) \Rightarrow [(R \Rightarrow (S \Rightarrow T)) \Rightarrow (R \Rightarrow T)]}$$

$$\overline{\vdash P \Rightarrow (Q \Rightarrow P \wedge Q)} \quad \overline{\vdash P \wedge Q \Rightarrow P} \quad \overline{\vdash P \wedge Q \Rightarrow Q}$$

$$\overline{\vdash (P \Rightarrow R) \Rightarrow [(Q \Rightarrow R) \Rightarrow (P \vee Q \Rightarrow R)]} \quad \overline{\vdash P \Rightarrow P \vee Q} \quad \overline{\vdash Q \Rightarrow P \vee Q}$$

$$\overline{\vdash (P \Rightarrow Q) \Rightarrow [(P \Rightarrow \neg Q) \Rightarrow \neg P]} \quad \overline{\vdash \neg\neg P \Rightarrow P}$$

$$\frac{\vdash P \qquad \vdash P \Rightarrow Q}{\vdash Q}$$

Following is an example of its use is to prove that $I \Rightarrow I$ for any propositional variable I (symbol $\vdash$ omitted for compactness):

$$\frac{\overline{I \Rightarrow ((I \Rightarrow I) \Rightarrow I)} \quad \dfrac{\overline{I \Rightarrow (I \Rightarrow I)} \quad \overline{[I \Rightarrow (I \Rightarrow I)] \Rightarrow \{[I \Rightarrow ((I \Rightarrow I) \Rightarrow I)] \Rightarrow (I \Rightarrow I)\}}}{[I \Rightarrow ((I \Rightarrow I) \Rightarrow I)] \Rightarrow (I \Rightarrow I)}}{I \Rightarrow I}$$

12.4.3 Recursive enumerability of sets defined by inference systems

Theorem 12.4.3 If $\mathcal{I}$ is an inference system, then $Thms^{\mathcal{I}}$ is a recursively enumerable set.

Proof. Given $\mathcal{I}$ with predicate names $P, Q, \ldots, Z$ and rules $R_1, R_2, \ldots, R_m$, define the syntax of *proof tree forms* to be all elements of $\mathbb{D}$ generated by the grammar with nonterminal symbols S and D, start symbol S, and productions:

S ::= (nil^r D S^k) for every k-premise rule $R_r, r = 1, 2, \ldots, m$
D ::= nil | (D . D)

Define a *proof tree* t to be a proof tree form such that every subtree

(nil^r d (nil$_1^r$ d$_1$...)...(nil$_k^r$ d$_k$...))

of t where $R_r \subseteq \mathbb{D}^k \times \mathbb{D}$ satisfies:

$$((d_1, \ldots, d_k), d) \in R_r$$

Further, t is a *proof tree for predicate P* if t = (nil^r ...) is a proof tree, and R_r has type $P_1 \times \ldots \times P_k \to P$. It is immediate from Definition 12.4.2 that $P(d) \in Thms^{\mathcal{I}}$ if and only if there exists a proof tree for P.

It is straightforward to show from Definition 12.4.2 that the property "t is a *proof tree for predicate P*" is decidable (Exercise 12.3). Let program checkP decide this property. Consider the program

```
read T;
if checkP T then X := hd tl T else X := false;
write X
```

If input is a proof tree T = (nil^r d ...) for P, then the program outputs d. Thus by Theorem 5.5.1 rng([[checkP]]) is recursively enumerable. Further,

$$\text{rng}([[\texttt{checkP}]]) = \{d \mid P(d) \in Thms^{\mathcal{I}}\}$$

so $Thms^{\mathcal{I}}$ is a finite union of recursively enumerable sets, and so recursively enumerable by Theorem 12.3.2.   □

12.5   A version of Gödel's incompleteness theorem

Gödel's original proof involved statements concerning arithmetic on the natural numbers. Its pathbreaking achievement was to reveal a fundamental limitation in the power of mathematical proof systems: that beyond a certain complexity level, there can be no hope to have a proof system which is simultaneously complete and consistent.

As might be expected, we will instead manipulate values in $\mathbb{D}$. This gives a substantially simpler construction, both displaying the power of our framework, and stimulating thought about the powers of logical systems in practice, for instance for reasoning about program behavior.

12.5.1   The logical language DL for $\mathbb{D}$

We now introduce a tiny logical language in which one can make statements about values in $\mathbb{D}$. Each such statement has an immediately natural reading or "truth value." We will then prove that no inference system as defined above can generate all true statements in DL.

As is traditional in logic, we first give the syntax of DL expressions. For the sake of preciseness, we will define exactly what it means for a DL statement to be true, leaving it to the reader to check that this captures his or her intuitions about statements involving values from $\mathbb{D}$.

An abstract syntax of DL   This is given by a grammar defining *terms*, which stand for values in $\mathbb{D}$, and *statements*, which are assertions about relationships among terms.

Terms: T $::=$ nil $\mid$ (T.T) $\mid$ x_0 $\mid$ x_1 $\mid$ ...
Statements: S $::=$ T=T++T $\mid$ ¬ S $\mid$ S ∧ S $\mid$ $\exists x_i$ S

The symbol ++ stands for the "append" operation on list values. Logical operators $\vee, \Rightarrow$, $\forall$, etc. can be defined from $\neg, \wedge, \exists$ above as usual, and equality $T = T'$ can be regarded as syntactic sugar for $T = T'$++ nil. Statements are intuitively interpreted in the natural way, for example the relation "x is a sublist of y" could be represented by the following statement $S(x,y)$:

$$\exists u \exists v \exists w (y = w\text{++}v \wedge w = u\text{++}x)$$

We now proceed to define "true statement" more formally and precisely.

First, a *free occurrence* of a variable x in statement S is any occurrence which does not lie within any substatement $\exists x$ T of S. The set *Freevars(S)* of *free variables* in statement S is the set of all x which have at least one free occurrence in S. Finally, S is said to be *closed* if *FreeVars(S)* $= \{\}$. We will sometimes write $S(x, y, \ldots, z)$ instead of S alone, to indicate that its free variables are $x, y, \ldots, z$.

The operation of *substitution* is done by a function $Subst(F, x, \mathrm{d})$ where $\mathrm{d} \in \mathbb{D}$ which yields the result of replacing by d every free occurrence of variable x within $S(x)$. This may also be applied to several variables, written $Subst(F, (x_1, \ldots, x_n), (\mathrm{d}_1 \ldots \mathrm{d}_n))$.

Definition 12.5.1 Let size(S) be the number of occurrences of operations ++, ¬, ∧, ∃ in S. The set $\mathcal{T}_i$ of *true closed statements of size i or less* is given inductively by

1. $\mathcal{T}_1 = \{(\mathrm{d}_1 \ldots \mathrm{d}_m\, \mathrm{e}_1 \ldots \mathrm{e}_n) = (\mathrm{d}_1 \ldots \mathrm{d}_m)\text{++}(\mathrm{e}_1 \ldots \mathrm{e}_n) \mid$
$$m, n \geq 0 \text{ and each } \mathrm{d}_i, \mathrm{e}_j \in \mathbb{D}\}$$

2. For $i \geq 1$:

$$
\begin{aligned}
\mathcal{T}_{i+1} = \mathcal{T}_i \ \cup \ &\{ \quad \neg\, \mathsf{S} \quad | \ \mathsf{S} \text{ is closed and } \mathsf{S} \notin \mathcal{T}_i \} \\
\cup \ &\{ \quad \mathsf{F1} \wedge \mathsf{F2} \ \ | \ \mathsf{F1} \in \mathcal{T}_i \text{ and } \mathsf{F2} \in \mathcal{T}_i \} \\
\cup \ &\{ \quad \exists x \mathsf{S} \quad | \ Subst(\mathsf{S}, x, \mathsf{d}) \in \mathcal{T}_i \text{ for some } \mathsf{d} \in \mathbb{D} \}
\end{aligned}
$$

The set of *true closed statements* of DL is by definition $\mathcal{T} = \mathcal{T}_1 \cup \mathcal{T}_2 \cup \cdots$ □

A concrete syntax of DL   This is simply a representation of DL-terms and statements as values within $\mathbb{D}$. Choose some pairwise distinct values $\underline{\mathtt{nil}}$, $\underline{\cdot}$, $\underline{\texttt{++}}$, $\underline{\neg}$, $\underline{\wedge}$, $\underline{\exists}$, all in $\mathbb{D}$, which are pairwise distinct from each other, and from $\mathtt{nil}^i$ for $i = 0, 1, 2, \ldots$

The concrete syntax is defined by

Terms : $CT ::= \underline{\mathtt{nil}} \mid (\underline{\cdot}\ CT\ CT) \mid \mathtt{nil}^0 \mid \mathtt{nil}^1 \mid \ldots$

Statements : $CS ::= (\underline{\texttt{++}}\ CT\ CT\ CT) \mid (\underline{\neg}\ CS) \mid (\underline{\wedge}\ CS\ CS) \mid (\underline{\exists}\mathtt{nil}^i\ CS)$

Finally, the set $\mathcal{T}_{\mathbb{D}}$ is by definition the set of concrete syntactic encodings, as just described, of statements in $\mathcal{T}$.

12.5.2   Representation of predicates in DL

Definition 12.5.2 A predicate $P \subseteq \mathbb{D}^n$ is *representable in* DL if there is a statement $\mathsf{S}(x_1, \ldots, x_n)$ such that

$$
P = \{ (\mathsf{d}_1 \ \ldots \ \mathsf{d}_n) \mid Subst(\mathsf{S}, (x_1, \ldots, x_n), (\mathsf{d}_1 \ \ldots \ \mathsf{d}_n)) \in \mathcal{T} \}
$$

Lemma 12.5.3 If set $A \subseteq \mathbb{D}$ is representable in DL, then so is $\overline{A} = \mathbb{D} \setminus A$.

Proof. Suppose statement $\mathsf{S}(x)$ represents A as above. Then

$$
\overline{A} = \{ \mathsf{d} \mid Subst(\mathsf{S}, x, \mathsf{d}) \notin \mathcal{T} \} = \{ \mathsf{d} \mid Subst(\neg\mathsf{S}, x, \mathsf{d}) \in \mathcal{T} \}
$$

□

Theorem 12.5.4 For any I-program p, the set $\mathrm{dom}(\llbracket \mathsf{p} \rrbracket)$ is representable in DL

Proof. Recall the semantics of section 2.2. We only consider the sublanguage I of WHILE, so the store σ used there can be replaced by the current value d of the single variable X.

We will show that for each I expression E and command C, there exist DL-statements $\mathsf{F_E}(d, d')$ and $\mathsf{G_C}(d, d')$ that represent the binary predicates $\mathcal{E}\llbracket \mathsf{E} \rrbracket d = d'$ and $\mathsf{C} \vdash \mathsf{d} \to \mathsf{d}'$. This suffices since if p is `read X; C; write X`, then $\mathrm{dom}(\llbracket \mathsf{p} \rrbracket)$ is represented by statement $\exists d' \mathsf{G_C}(d, d')$.

Expressions.   This is by an easy induction on syntax:

$$\text{F}_{\texttt{nil}}(d,d') \quad\quad \equiv \quad d' = \texttt{nil}$$
$$\text{F}_{\texttt{X}}(d,d') \quad\quad \equiv \quad d' = d$$
$$\text{F}_{(\texttt{E1.E2})}(d,d') \quad \equiv \quad \exists r \exists s\, \text{F}_{\texttt{E1}}(d,r) \wedge \text{F}_{\texttt{E2}}(d,s) \wedge d' = (r.s)$$

Commands.   This is also by induction on syntax. We give the definition and then explain.

$$\text{G}_{\texttt{X:=E}}(d,d') \quad\quad \equiv \text{F}_{\texttt{E}}(d,d')$$

$$\text{G}_{\texttt{C1;C2}}(d,d') \quad\quad \equiv \exists d''(\text{G}_{\texttt{C1}}(d,d'') \wedge \text{G}_{\texttt{C2}}(d'',d'))$$

$$\text{G}_{\texttt{while E do C}}(d,d') \equiv (\text{F}_{\texttt{E}}(d,nil) \wedge d = d') \vee$$
$$\exists trace\, \exists fst\, \exists lst\, (trace = (d.lst) \wedge trace = fst{+}{+}(d'.nil) \wedge \text{F}_{\texttt{E}}(d',nil) \wedge$$
$$\forall h \forall u \forall v \forall t\, (trace = h{+}{+}(u.(v.t)) \Rightarrow$$
$$\text{G}_{\texttt{C}}(u,v) \wedge \exists e \exists f\, (\text{F}_{\texttt{E}}(u,(e.f)))))$$

$$\square$$

Assignment is straightforward, and sequencing $\texttt{C1;C2} \vdash \texttt{d} \to \texttt{d}'$ is represented naturally by an intermediate state $\texttt{d}''$.

Representation of command $\texttt{while E do C}$ is a bit trickier, since its execution may take an unbounded number of steps. The idea is to represent $\texttt{while E do C} \vdash \texttt{d} \to \texttt{d}'$ by a *computation trace*. This will be a sequence $(\texttt{d}_1 \ldots \texttt{d}_n)$ where $\texttt{d} = \texttt{d}_1$, $\texttt{d}' = \texttt{d}_n$, and $\texttt{C} \vdash \texttt{d}_i \to \texttt{d}_{i+1}$ for $i = 1, 2, \ldots, n-1$.

The construction above uses this idea. The two parts concerning *fst* and *lst* ensure that the trace properly begins with $d = \texttt{d}_1$ and ends with $d' = \texttt{d}_n$. The remaining part (beginning $\text{F}_{\texttt{E}}(d',nil)$) checks to see that E evaluates to $\texttt{false}$ at the loop's end ($\texttt{d}' = \texttt{d}_n$), and that $\texttt{while E do C} \vdash \texttt{d}_i \to \texttt{d}_{i+1}$ holds for every pair $\texttt{d}_i, \texttt{d}_{i+1}$ in the trace.

12.5.3   Proof of a version of Gödel's incompleteness theorem

We now show that the set $\mathcal{T}$ of true DL statements is not recursively enumerable. On the other hand, the set of all statements deducible in any inference *is* recursively enumerable by Theorem 12.4.3. As a consequence, any inference system that only deduces true DL statements cannot deduce all of them, i.e., there must be at least one statement which is true but not provable.

Stated another way: any inference system whatever must either be inconsistent: it deduces some statements that are not true, i.e., in $\mathcal{T}$; or it must be incomplete, i.e., it cannot deduce all true statements.

Theorem 12.5.5 (Gödel's incompleteness theorem.) $\mathcal{T}_{\mathbb{D}}$ is not recursively enumerable.

Proof. Consider the set

$$HALT = \{\,(\texttt{p.d}) \mid \texttt{p} \in \texttt{WHILE}-\textit{programs}, \texttt{d} \in \texttt{WHILE}-\textit{data}, \text{and } [\![\texttt{p}]\!](\texttt{d}){\downarrow}\}$$

Now $HALT = \text{dom}([\![\texttt{u}]\!])$ where u is the universal program (self-interpreter) for $\texttt{I}$ programs, and so by Theorem 12.5.4 is representable in DL. By Corollary 5.6.2, its complement $\overline{HALT} = \mathbb{D}\backslash HALT$ is not recursively enumerable. By Lemma 12.5.3, $\overline{HALT}$ is representable by some statement $F(x)$, so

$$\overline{HALT} = \{\,(\texttt{p.d}) \mid Subst(F, x, (\texttt{p.d})) \in \mathcal{T}\}$$

Suppose $\mathcal{T}_{\mathbb{D}}$ were recursively enumerable. By Theorem 5.7.2 there must exist a program q such that $\mathcal{T}_{\mathbb{D}} = \text{dom}([\![\texttt{q}]\!])$. Then for any $\texttt{I}$-program p and input d, we have

$$(\texttt{p.d}) \in \overline{HALT} \text{ iff } [\![\texttt{q}]\!](Subst(F, x, (\texttt{p.d}))){\downarrow}$$

But this would imply that $\overline{HALT}$ is recursively enumerable, which is false. $\square$

Corollary 12.5.6 For any inference system $\mathcal{I}$ and predicate name P:

$$\text{If } \{\texttt{d} \mid P(\texttt{d}) \in Thms^{\mathcal{I}}\} \subseteq \mathcal{T}_{\mathbb{D}} \text{ then } \{\texttt{d} \mid P(\texttt{d}) \in Thms^{\mathcal{I}}\} \subsetneqq \mathcal{T}_{\mathbb{D}}$$

In effect this says that if any inference system proves only true DL statements, then it cannot prove all of them. In other words there is and always will be a difference between *truth* and *provability* by inference systems (at least for DL). This captures one essential aspect of Gödel's incompleteness theorem. In comparison with the original proof, and others seen in the literature, this one uses surprisingly little technical machinery (though it admittedly builds on the nontrivial difference between decidable and recursively enumerable problems).

Differences: first, this presentation does not involve Peano arithmetic at all, as Gödel's original work did. Our use of $\mathbb{D}$ instead gave simplified constructions, but it could well be argued that the result is different since it concerns a different logical system (although one which seems no more complex than Peano arithmetic). We believe that some form of equivalence between Peano arithmetic and DL should not be difficult to establish.

Second, Gödel's theorem is often presented as "any logical system of a certain minimal complexity must be either incomplete or inconsistent." We have avoided the problem of dealing with "logical system" as studied in mathematical logic by substituting a proper generalization: "inference system." The assumption above that $\{d \mid P(d) \in \mathit{Thms}^{\mathcal{I}}\} \subseteq \mathcal{T}_{\mathbb{D}}$ says in effect that $\mathcal{I}$ is consistent, and the proper inclusion we conclude expresses incompleteness. On the other hand, the formulation above says nothing about minimal complexity of $\mathcal{I}$, just that "the full truth" of DL statements cannot be ascertained by means of axioms and rules of logical deduction.

Third, Gödel's theorem begins with a logical system containing Peano arithmetic, and works by diagonalization to construct a witness: an example of a statement S which is true, but which cannot be provable. Gödel's original witness is (intuitively) true since it in effect asserts "there is no proof in this system of S" — so if the system were able to prove S, it would be inconsistent!

Our version indeed uses diagonalization, but on I programs instead, and to prove that the problem $\overline{HALT}$ is not recursively enumerable.

Exercises

12.1 Express the first example of section 12.1.1 as an inference system $\mathcal{I}$ in the style of Definition 12.4.1. □

12.2 Construct an inference system which defines the semantics of WHILE programs. Hint: rewrite the definitions of $\mathcal{E}$ and $C \vdash \sigma \to \sigma'$. □

12.3 Prove that the property "t is a *proof tree for predicate P*" is decidable. It suffices to sketch an algorithm. □

References

Gödel's incompleteness theorem appeared in 1931 [51], and overviews can be found in [32, 36, 130]. The original proof was expressed in terms of provability and consistency, rather than in terms of truth and the difference between recursive and r.e. sets, as we have done. Post observed in [135] that this difference is the essence of Gödel incompleteness. It may be relevant that computability theory and the Church-Turing thesis had not been developed in 1931; an interesting historical account may be found in [34].

The articles [86, 132] by Kahn and Plotkin stimulated the use of inference systems in Computer Science. They have been used widely since then, for example to define both the static and dynamic semantics of the programming language ML [122].

13   Computability Theory Based on Numbers

The partial recursive functions have been studied extensively, using a framework very similar to our own but with function arguments, results, and program descriptions drawn from the natural numbers $\mathbb{N} = \{0, 1, 2, ...\}$. This deeply studied field is known as *recursive function* or computability theory, and has been developed by Kleene, Rogers, Church, Turing, and others [95, 147, 22, 162] since the 1930s.

A wide variety of formalizations proposed in the 1930s as candidates to define the class of all computable partial functions on natural numbers have all turned out to be equivalent. The candidates included the Turing machine; the lambda calculus (Church); primitive recursive function definitions plus minimization (Gödel, Kleene); systems of recursion equations (Gödel); and systems of string or term rewrite rules (Post, Markov).

This confluence of ideas [48] led to the famous *Church-Turing-Kleene thesis*: that a partial function $f : \mathbb{N} \to \mathbb{N}_\perp$ is effectively computable *if and only if* it is computable by some Turing machine (and hence within any of the other formalisms).

Two cornerstones of recursive function theory are the existence of a universal function, and of a program specialization function (the latter under the name of the *s-m-n property*), both partial recursive. Both concepts are very natural in Computer Science, as we have seen.

Gödel numbers versus programs as data objects   Our approach differs from the classical one in that programs *are* data values in our framework, and so need not be encoded in the form of natural numbers. For the sake of perspective we briefly outline the beginning assumptions of classical recursive function theory; being entirely based on natural numbers, it is necessary to encode programs and nonnumeric data structures (e.g., *n*-tuples) as natural numbers.

A straightforward analogy can be made between $\mathbb{N}$ and $\mathbb{D}$, the set of Lisp data structures. In our framework programs *are* elements of $\mathbb{D}$, so the need to enumerate programs by assigning each one a numerical index by an often complex Gödel numbering scheme is completely circumvented.

13.1   The class of partial recursive functions

An important early formalization of the concept of computability was the class of *partial recursive* functions or *μ-recursive* functions, defined and systematically investigated largely by Kleene, but already implicit in Gödel's earlier pathbreaking work [51, 93, 95]. This is a purely mathematical characterization, with few computational aspects: The partial recursive functions are defined to be the smallest class of functions containing certain initial functions and closed under several operations on functions. For the sake of completeness and links with other work in computability theory, we prove this class equivalent to functions computable by counter machines

The lambda notation used in this chapter is defined in Appendix A.3.8. An abbreviation: we write $\overline{x}^n$ to stand for the tuple $x_1, \ldots, x_n$ or $(x_1, \ldots, x_n)$.

13.2   The μ-recursive functions

This class is defined in stages, beginning with a simpler class of functions, all of which are total.

13.2.1   Primitive recursive functions

Definition 13.2.1 A function g is obtained from f by *explicit transformation* if there are $e_1, \ldots, e_n$, each either a constant in $\mathbb{N}$ or a variable x_i, such that for all $\overline{x}^m \in \mathbb{N}$

$$g(x_1, \ldots, x_m) = f(e_1, \ldots, e_n)$$

Definition 13.2.2 If $f : \mathbb{N}^k \to \mathbb{N}_\perp, g_i : \mathbb{N}^n \to \mathbb{N}_\perp$ for $i = 1, \ldots, k$ then $h : \mathbb{N}^k \to \mathbb{N}_\perp$ is defined from $f, g_1, \ldots, g_k$ by *composition* iff for all $\overline{x}^n \in \mathbb{N}$

$$h(\overline{x}^n) = \begin{cases} f(g_1(\overline{x}^n), \ldots, g_k(\overline{x}^n)) & \text{if each } g_i(\overline{x}^n) \neq \perp \\ \perp & \text{if some } g_i(\overline{x}^n) = \perp \end{cases}$$

Definition 13.2.3 Function $h : \mathbb{N}^{n+1} \to \mathbb{N}_\perp$ is defined from $f : \mathbb{N}^n \to \mathbb{N}_\perp, g : \mathbb{N}^{n+2} \to \mathbb{N}_\perp$ by *primitive recursion* iff for all $\overline{x}^n, t \in \mathbb{N}$

$$
\begin{aligned}
h(0, \overline{x}^n) &= f(\overline{x}^n) \\
h(t+1, \overline{x}^n) &= g(t, h(t, \overline{x}^n), \overline{x}^n) & \text{if } h(t, \overline{x}^n) \neq \perp \\
h(t+1, \overline{x}^n) &= \perp & \text{otherwise}
\end{aligned}
$$

Definition 13.2.4 Function f is *primitive recursive* if it is obtainable from base functions $\lambda x.0$ and $\lambda x.x+1$ by some finite number of applications of explicit transformation, composition, and primitive recursion.

An easy induction shows that every primitive recursive function is total. The operations of primitive recursion and explicit transformation may, however, be applied both to total and to partial functions.

13.2.2 Primitive recursiveness and CM-computability

Recall Definition 8.6.1.

Theorem 13.2.5

1. The functions: $\lambda x.0$ and $\lambda x.x+1$ are CM-computable.

2. If f is CM-computable, then so is any function g obtained from f by explicit transformation.

3. If $f, g_1, \ldots, g_k$ are CM-computable functions, then so is their composition.

4. If f, g are CM-computable functions and function h is defined from them by primitive recursion, then h is also CM-computable .

Therefore any primitive recursive function is CM-computable.   □

Proof. Part 1: Function $\lambda x.0$ is computable by the program whose only command is X0 := 0, and $\lambda x.x+1$ is computable by the command X0 := X1 + 1.
Part 2: given program q that computes f, prefix its command part by straightforward code to transform store $[1 \mapsto x_1, \ldots, n \mapsto x_n]$ into store $[1 \mapsto e_1, \ldots, m \mapsto e_m]$.

Part 3: easy. Given programs to compute $f, g_1, \ldots, g_k$, concatenate the code to compute and store $g_1(\overline{x}^n)$ in X1, code to compute and store $g_2(\overline{x}^n)$ in X2, ..., with the code to compute and store $g_k(\overline{x}^n)$ in Xk, followed by the code to compute $f(\overline{x}^k)$. Some variable renaming and copying may be needed so internal variables of the g and f programs do not conflict with each other or X1, ..., Xk.

Part 4 is left as Exercise 13.1.   □

13.2.3 Definition of μ-recursiveness

In the following expression $\mu y(f(y)=0)$ operator μ, pronounced "minimum," specifies a search to find a value of argument value y such that $f(y)=0$, making zero the value of a given function f.

Definition 13.2.6 Function $h : \mathbb{N}^n \to \mathbb{N}_\perp$ is defined from $g : \mathbb{N}^{n+1} \to \mathbb{N}$ by *minimization* iff for all $\bar{x}^n \in \mathbb{N}$

$$h(\bar{x}^n) = t \quad \text{if } t \in \mathbb{N} \text{ is the smallest number such that } g(t, \bar{x}^n) = 0$$
$$h(\bar{x}^n) = \perp \quad \text{otherwise}$$

Notation: we write function h in short form as: $\mu t (g(t, \bar{x}^n) = 0)$, or even $\mu t . g$.

Definition 13.2.7 Function f is μ-*recursive* if it is obtainable from base functions $\lambda x . 0$ and $\lambda x . x + 1$ by some finite number of applications of explicit transformation, composition, primitive recursion, and minimization applied to *total* functions.

A μ-recursive function need not be total. Note that Definition 13.2.7 applies minimization only to total functions g. By Rice's Theorem (section 5.4), this property is undecidable from a program defining g, so Definition 13.2.7 does not naturally define a programming language (see also Exercises 13.2, 13.4).

13.3   Equivalence of μ-recursiveness and CM-computability

Lemma 13.3.1 If $g : \mathbb{N}^{n+1} \to \mathbb{N}$ is a CM-computable and total function, then $\mu t (g(t, \bar{x}^n) = 0)$ is a CM-computable function.

Proof. Given program p to compute $g(t, \bar{x}^n)$, the following program will compute $\mu t (g(t, \bar{x}^n) = 0)$:

```
read X1, ..., Xn;
   T := 0;
   R := p T X1 ... Xn;   (* Apply p to 0,1,2... until it yields 0 *)
while R do
   { T := T + 1; R := p T X1 ... Xn };
   write T                (* Write T when (if) that first happens *)
```
$\qquad\qquad\qquad\qquad\qquad\qquad\qquad\qquad\qquad\qquad\qquad\qquad\qquad\qquad\qquad\qquad$ □

Corollary 13.3.2 Every μ-recursive function $f : \mathbb{N}^n \to \mathbb{N}_\perp$ is CM-computable.

Theorem 13.3.3 A function $f : \mathbb{N}^n \to \mathbb{N}_\perp$ is μ-recursive iff it is CM-computable.

Proof. "Only if" is Corollary 13.3.2. We give only a sketch for "if," as this is technically rather complex, and beside the main point of this book: that using a structured data set such as $\mathbb{D}$ significantly simplifies many constructions in both computability and complexity theory. In outline, the "if" part is proven as follows.

The starting point is a CM-program p that computes f. Let $p = I_1 \ldots I_m$, and suppose it has variables X0,...,Xk where $n \leq k$. We assume input is via variables X1,...,Xn, and output is the final value of X0.

1. A CM-state $s = (\ell, \sigma)$ where $\sigma = [0 \mapsto v_0, 1 \mapsto v_0, \ldots, k \mapsto v_k]$ is represented by the number

$$\bar{s} = 2^\ell \cdot 3^{v_0} \cdot 5^{v_1} \cdot \ldots \cdot p_{k+2}^{v_k}$$

   where p_i is the i-th prime number (for any $i > 0$).

2. Prove the function $init(\bar{x}^n) = 2^1 \cdot 3^0 \cdot 5^{x_1} \cdot \ldots \cdot p_{n+2}^{x_n}$ to be primitive recursive.

3. For $\ell = 1, \ldots, m$ prove the following one-instruction *store transformation function* to be primitive recursive:

$$ins_\ell(\bar{s}) = \bar{s'} \text{ iff } I_\ell : s \to s'$$

4. Prove the following state transition function to be primitive recursive:

$$nxt(s) = \begin{cases} ins_\ell(s) & \text{if } s = 2^\ell \cdot 3^{v_0} \cdot \ldots \text{ and } \ell \leq m \\ 0 & \text{if } \ell > m \end{cases}$$

5. Prove the t-step state transition function $stp(t, s) = nxt^t(s)$ (that is, stp composed with itself t times) to be primitive recursive.

6. Clearly the function $g(x) = \mu t (stp(t, s) = 0)$ is μ-recursive.

7. Finally, it is immediate that

$$f(x) = y \text{ where } stp(g(x) - 1, s) = 2^\ell \cdot 3^y \cdot \ldots \cdot p_{k+2}^{v_k}$$

   This is μ-recursive, since it is a composition of primitive recursive functions with the primitive recursive stp.

Details of this sort of construction may be found in [32, 36].   □

13.4   Kleene's normal form theorem for the `WHILE` language

A parallel development to that of section 13.2 may be carried out using data set $\mathbb{D}$ and for the `WHILE` language, using a standard enumeration $d_0, d_1, \ldots$ of $\mathbb{D}$, for example as in Lemma 5.7.1. We omit the details as they are exact analogues of the above for the `CM` language.

Definition 13.4.1 Let $f : \mathbb{D}^{n+1} \to \mathbb{N}$ be a `WHILE`-computable total function. The partial function $\mu t(f(t, \overline{x}^n) = \texttt{true}) : \mathbb{D}^n \to \mathbb{D}_\perp$ is defined by

$$\mu t(f(t, \overline{x}^n) = \texttt{true}) = \begin{cases} d_i & \text{if } i \text{ is the least index such that } f(t, \overline{x}^n) = \texttt{true} \\ \perp & \text{otherwise} \end{cases}$$

Lemma 13.4.2 If $f : \mathbb{D}^{n+1} \to \mathbb{N}$ is `WHILE`-computable and total, then $\mu t(f(t, \overline{x}^n) = \texttt{true})$ is a `WHILE`-computable partial function.

Proof. Given program p to compute f, and `start`, `next`, `New` as in Lemma 5.7.1, the following program will compute $\mu t(f(t, \overline{x}^n) = \texttt{true})$:

```
read X1, ..., Xn; start;
R := p New X1 ... Xn;
while not R do
  { next; R := p New X1 ... Xn };
write Y
```
□

The following is interesting because it shows that *all* recursive functions can be represented in a uniform way. Intuitively, it says that selection of a function f to compute amounts to selecting the constant p below. Further, performing the computation on input d amounts to searching for the unique c that makes function $T(\texttt{p}, \texttt{d}, \texttt{c})$ the value `true`; and reading out the result is done by applying a very simple function U.

This is essentially Kleene's normal form theorem as in [95], but the result is somewhat stronger due to our use of structured data.

Theorem 13.4.3 There is a total function $U : \mathbb{D} \to \mathbb{D}$ and a total `WHILE`-computable function $T(\texttt{p}, \texttt{d}, \texttt{c})$ such that

1. For all $\texttt{p}, \texttt{d} \in \mathbb{D}$ there is at most one $\texttt{c} \in \mathbb{D}$ such that $T(\texttt{p}, \texttt{d}, \texttt{c}) = \texttt{true}$.

2. A partial function $f : \mathbb{D} \to \mathbb{D}_\perp$ is recursive *if and only if* there is a $p \in \mathbb{D}$ such that for all $d \in \mathbb{D}$

$$f(\mathrm{d}) = U(\mu\mathrm{c}(T(\mathrm{p},\mathrm{d},\mathrm{c}) = \mathtt{true})$$

Further, U is WHILE-computable in constant time and T is WHILE-computable in linear time.

Proof. Supposing T, U are recursive, the "if" of part 2 follows from WHILE-versions of Theorems 13.2.5 and 13.3.3.

For "only if," we must find T, U as described. Suppose $f = [\![p]\!]$ for some program p (assuming only one argument $x = x_1$ for notational simplicity.) Without loss of generality p has only one variable X (by section 3.7.2).

Recall the universal program u1var seen earlier for one-variable WHILE-programs. Build from it a program which we call q, and define $T(\mathrm{p}, \mathrm{d}, \mathrm{c}) = [\![q]\!](\mathrm{p.d.c})$. The idea is that q will simulate $[\![p]\!](\mathrm{d})$'s computation just as u1var does, but meanwhile it will check that argument c is a correct "trace" of its computation.

More concretely, consider the universal program u1var terminates within r iterations. Let Val_i be the values of u1var variables Val, Stk, Cd just before the ith iteration of u1var's while loop, and define u1var's *reversed trace* on input d to be c = (Val_r ... Val_1 Val_0).

Now, program q:

```
read PDC;                       (* Input is (program.data.c)    *)
Cd    := cons (hd PDC) nil;     (* Control stack = (program.nil) *)
Val   := hd (tl PDC);           (* The value of X               *)
Stk   := nil;                   (* Computation stack empty       *)
Flag  := true;                  (* Trace is OK so far            *)
Trace := reverse (tl (tl PDC)); (* Computation trace            *)
while Trace ≠ nil do
{ if hd Trace ≠ Val then Flag := false;       (* Trace mismatch *)
   Trace := tl Trace;
   STEP };
if Cd ≠ nil then Flag := false;
write Flag
```

To begin with, program q terminates since the while loop decreases Trace, so T is a WHILE-recursive function.

Program q on input (p.d.c) first stores c's reverse (Val_0 Val_1 ... Val_r) into variable Trace. It then simulates p a step at a time, checking along the way to see that Trace agrees with the values ulvar assigns to X. If p terminates on input d then ulvar terminates on (p.d), so q's while loop will terminate with Cd = nil on input (p.d.(Val$_r$...Val$_1$ Val$_0$)). Thus $[\![q]\!]$(p.d.c) = true and

$$(\mu c(T(\mathsf{p},\mathsf{d},\mathsf{c}) = \mathtt{true}) = (\mathsf{Val}_r \dots \mathsf{Val}_1\ \mathsf{Val}_0)$$

Further, if $[\![\mathsf{p}]\!](\mathsf{d}) = \perp$ then $T(\mathsf{p},\mathsf{d},\mathsf{c}) = \mathtt{false}$ for all c. Clearly $[\![\mathsf{p}]\!](\mathsf{d}) \neq \perp$ if and only if $T(\mathsf{p},\mathsf{d},\mathsf{c}) = \mathtt{true}$ where c is p's trace on input d.

Finally, the theorem follows if we set $U(c) = hd(c)$, to return the final value that p assigns to its variable X. Clearly this is computable in constant time; and the time to compute T is proportional to the length of the computation trace c.   □

Exercises

13.1 Prove that the class of CM-computable functions is closed under primitive recursion.   □

13.2 Explain why the construction used to prove Theorem 13.3.3 or Lemma 13.4.2 does not necessarily show that partial function $\mu y.f$ is recursive when f is a *partial* computable function.   □

13.3 Extend μ to functions on $\mathbb{D}$ in the natural way using the enumeration $\mathsf{d}_0, \mathsf{d}_1, \dots$ of Lemma 5.7.1. Then prove that $\mu t.f(t,p,d) = \mathtt{nil}$ may be uncomputable when f is a partial WHILE-computable function. Hint: let $f(t,p,d) = \mathtt{true}$ if $t = \mathtt{true}$, or if both $t \neq \mathtt{true}$ and $[\![\mathsf{p}]\!](\mathsf{d})\!\downarrow$, else undefined.   □

13.4 * Use the previous exercise to prove that $\mu t.f(t,x) = 0$ may be uncomputable when f is a partial CM-computable function.   □

13.5 (Hilbert's choice function.)* Define $g \approx \varepsilon y.f(x,y)$ to hold if for all x, whenever there exists some y such that $f(x,y) = 0$, then $f(x,g(x)) = 0$. In other words, $g(x)$ produces *some* witness to the truth of $\exists y.f(x,y) = 0$, but not necessarily the least one as was the case for $\mu y(f(x,y) = 0)$.

Prove that if f is partial computable, there exists a partial computable partial function g with $g \approx \varepsilon y.P(x,y)$. Hint: use dovetailing as in Theorem 5.5.1.   □

References

Classic books on recursive function are the ones by Kleene, Davis, and Rogers [95, 31, 147]. More recent ones include a newer one by Davis et.al. [36] and one by Sommerhalder and van Westrhenen [156], which has a scope similar to that of this book.

14 More Abstract Approaches to Computability

One could object to the previous treatment of recursion on the grounds that it explains recursive language constructions by means of recursion, for example in section 2.2 or Figure 9.1 (or section 12.1.2). One nonrecursive way to deal with recursion has already been given by example: "syntactic unfolding" in section 12.1.2.

This chapter begins with two additional, and different, nonrecursive ways to deal with recursion. The first is by means of fixpoints of functionals, in which a recursive definition is viewed as defining a mapping from certain partial functions to others. The second is by means of "reflexive programs": the "Second Recursion theorem" due to Kleene.

Relations: it can be proven that syntactic unfolding gives the same semantics as least fixpoints of functionals; and that its effect can be achieved by reflexive programs. Proofs may be found in [109, 147], but are beyond the scope of this book.

The final parts of the chapter concern model-independent approaches to computability. Since the robustness results of chapter 8 suggest that all computation models are equivalent, this is a popular modern starting point. Indeed, one result appearing at the chapter end is Rogers' Isomorphism theorem: Given any two programming languages L and M (with data $\mathbb{N}$) there exists a computable isomorphism (a one-to-one onto mapping) from L-programs to M-programs that does not change the computed functions.

14.1 Recursion by semantics: fixpoints of functionals

In this section we describe one approach to defining the meaning of recursively defined functions, by so-called "fixpoint semantics."

First an example: consider the recursive definition

$$f(n) = (\text{if } n = 0 \text{ then } 1 \text{ else } n * f(n-1)) \tag{14.1}$$

This is intended to define a function $f : \mathbb{N} \to \mathbb{N}_\perp$. A Pascal program corresponding to the definition is:

```
function f(n:integer):integer;
begin
   if n = 0 then f := 1 else f := n * f(n - 1)
end
```

The question naturally arises: what mathematical function $f : \mathbb{N} \to \mathbb{N}_\perp$ is defined by a recursive equation such as (14.1)?

This question amounts to "how does one interpret a recursive definition?" This is a decidedly nontrivial question since recursive functions are defined in terms of themselves, and problems of self-reference are notorious for creating philosophical problems.

An answer: the function defined by a recursive equation such as (14.1) is often taken to be the *least fixpoint* of the *functional* $\mathcal{F}$ defined by the equation. We now define and clarify these terms.

Uniqueness of functions defined by recursive equations

The factorial function is the only function satisfying (14.1). It can happen, however, that an equation has more than one solution. For example, consider equation

$$g(n) = (\text{if } n = 0 \text{ then } 0 \text{ else if } n = 1 \text{ then } g(1) \text{ else } g(n-2)+2) \qquad (14.2)$$

where $f : \mathbb{N} \to \mathbb{N}_\perp$. It is satisfied by $g(n) = n$. On the other hand, it is also satisfied by many other functions, for instance $g(n) = \text{if } n$ even then n else $n + 100$. The reason: there is no constraint on the value of $g(1)$.

Which among the range of all possible functions that satisfy a recursive equation should we select as its "meaning," i.e., the unique function defined by that recursive definition? It is desirable that

- the "meaning" always exists;
- it is unambiguous; and
- it is a computable function (though perhaps partial), provided the operations in the equation are themselves computable.

First, we define the meaning of the statement: "Function $g : \mathbb{N} \to \mathbb{N}_\perp$ satisfies equation (14.2)."

Definition 14.1.1 Function g satisfies (14.2) provided[1] $g \simeq g'$, where g' is defined by

$$g'(n) = (\text{if } n = 0 \text{ then } 0 \text{ else if } n = 1 \text{ then } g(1) \text{ else } g(n-2)+2) \qquad (14.3)$$

---

[1]Recall that $g \simeq g'$ if and only if for all $n \in \mathbb{N}$, either $g(n)$ and $g'(n)$ are both undefined ($\perp$), or are both in $\mathbb{N}$ and equal.

Note that this definition is nonrecursive, since g' is defined in terms of g and not in terms of itself. Equation (14.3) defines a transformation from g to g'. Function transformers are often called *functionals*, and one may write for example $g' = \mathcal{F}(g)$ where $\mathcal{F}$ is the functional defined by (14.3). In this case $\mathcal{F}$ has type $(\mathbb{N} \to \mathbb{N}_\perp) \to (\mathbb{N} \to \mathbb{N}_\perp)$, and is defined by

$\mathcal{F}(g) = g'$, where
$g'(n) = ($if $n = 0$ then 0 else if $n = 1$ then $g(1)$ else $g(n-2)+2)$

For an example, $\mathcal{F}$ transforms function $g_3(n) = n^2$ into

$\mathcal{F}(g_3) = g_3'$, where
$g_3'(n) = ($if $n = 0$ then 0 else if $n = 1$ then 1^2 else $(n-2)^2+2)$

Satisfying equation (14.2) thus amounts to asserting $g = \mathcal{F}(g)$. Such a function is called a *fixpoint* of $\mathcal{F}$. Our goal is therefore to select as standard interpretation a unique computable function g satisfying $g = \mathcal{F}(g)$.

Some examples (where we write $\stackrel{\text{def}}{=}$ for "equal by the definition of g"):

1. Claim: g_1 satisfies (14.2) where $g_1(n) \stackrel{\text{def}}{=} n$. We show this by considering cases $n = 0$, $n = 1$, and $n > 1$. First, $g_1(0) \stackrel{\text{def}}{=} 0 = ($if $0 = 0$ then 0 else $\ldots)$. Now suppose $n = 1$. Then

$$g_1(1) \stackrel{\text{def}}{=} 1 = (\text{if } 1 = 0 \text{ then } 0 \text{ else if } 1 = 1 \text{ then } g_1(1) \text{ else} \ldots)$$

trivially. Finally, suppose $n > 1$. Then

$$g_1(n) \stackrel{\text{def}}{=} n = n-2+2 \stackrel{\text{def}}{=} g_1(n-2)+2 =$$
$$(\text{if } n = 0 \text{ then } 0 \text{ else if } n = 1 \text{ then } g_1(1) \text{ else } g_1(n-2)+2)$$

2. (14.2) is also satisfied by $g_2(n) \stackrel{\text{def}}{=} ($if n even then n else $\perp)$. Arguing again by cases, equation (14.2) is trivially true for $n \leq 1$. If $n > 1$ is even then

$$g_2(n) \stackrel{\text{def}}{=} n = n-2+2 \stackrel{\text{def}}{=} g_2(n-2)+2 =$$
$$(\text{if } n = 0 \text{ then } 0 \text{ else if } n = 1 \text{ then } g_2(1) \text{ else } g_2(n-2)+2)$$

and if $n > 1$ is odd then

$$g_2(n) \stackrel{\text{def}}{=} \perp = \perp+2 \stackrel{\text{def}}{=} g_2(n-2)+2 =$$
$$(\text{if } n = 0 \text{ then } 0 \text{ else if } n = 1 \text{ then } g_2(1) \text{ else } g_2(n-2)+2)$$

3. (14.2) is not satisfied by $g_3(n) \stackrel{\text{def}}{=} n^2$ since $4 = g_3(2) \neq 2 = g_3'(2)$.

Fixpoints of functionals.   Among all possible fixpoints, there will always be one which is *least defined* — the one such that $g \simeq \mathcal{F}(g)$ but $g(n) = \perp$ for as many values of n as possible. This is naturally called the *least fixpoint* of $\mathcal{F}$.

   At last our standard interpretation: the effect of recursive equation $f = \mathcal{F}(f)$ is to define f to be the *least fixpoint* of $\mathcal{F}$.

Example.   The least fixpoint of equation (14.1) is its only fixpoint: $f(n) = n!$ The least fixpoint of the equation for g is the function:

   $g(n) = $ if n is odd then $\perp$ else n

The natural Pascal programs corresponding to the recursion equations for f and g have just these solutions. So a traditional Pascal implementation is correct inasmuch as it computes the least fixpoint of these equations. How can the least fixpoint be computed? We begin with an analogy from numerical analysis.

Fixpoints of first order equations.   Consider an equation of the form $x = h(x)$ where x varies over the real numbers, for example

   $$x = 0.5 - x^2$$

where $h(x) = 0.5 - x^2$. Such an equation can often be solved by *fixpoint iteration*: a solution is the limit (if it exists) of the sequence $x_0, h(x_0), h(h(x_0)), \ldots$, where x_0 is an initial approximation to x. If $x_0 = 0$, we obtain

   $$x_0 = 0, \ x_1 = h(x_0) = .5 - x_0^2, \ x_2 = h(x_1) = .5 - x_1^2, \ \ldots$$

Evaluating, we obtain

   $$x_0 = 0, x_1 = .5, x_2 = .25, x_3 = .4375, x_3 = .3086, \ldots$$

which has as limit the solution $x = 0.366\ldots = (-1 + \sqrt{3})/2$.

   Simple conditions on h guarantee convergence, i.e., that the limit of the sequence $x_0, h(x_0), h(h(x_0)), \ldots$ exists. This method of *fixpoint iteration* is widely used in numerical analysis, for instance to solve matrix equations.

Computing the least fixpoint of a functional

Similarly, the least fixpoint may be obtained as the limit of an infinite series of functions $f_0, f_1, f_2, \ldots = f_0, \mathcal{F}(f_0), \mathcal{F}(\mathcal{F}(f_0)), \ldots$ where

$$f_0(n) = \bot \text{ for all } n = 0, 1, 2, \ldots$$

Using this scheme we can verify that the least fixpoint of the equation

$$f(n) = (\text{if } n = 0 \text{ then } 1 \text{ else } n * f(n-1))$$

is $f(n) = n!$ Its computation is seen in the table below. The scheme is constructed a row at a time, with f_0 as given above. The line for f_{i+1} is constructed from the previous line by

$$f_{i+1}(n) = \mathcal{F}(f_i) = (\text{if } n = 0 \text{ then } 1 \text{ else } n * f_i(n-1))$$

i	f_i	$n=0$	$n=1$	$n=2$	$n=3$	$n=4$	$n=5,\ldots$
0	f_0	$\bot$	$\bot$	$\bot$	$\bot$	$\bot$	$\bot,\ldots$
1	f_1	1	$\bot$	$\bot$	$\bot$	$\bot$	$\bot,\ldots$
2	f_2	1	1	$\bot$	$\bot$	$\bot$	$\bot,\ldots$
3	f_3	1	1	2	$\bot$	$\bot$	$\bot,\ldots$
4	f_4	1	1	2	6	$\bot$	$\bot,\ldots$
$\vdots$							
∞	f	1	1	2	6	24	$120,\ldots$

Remarks

1. Function f_0 is an initial (and very poor) approximation to the least fixpoint of $\mathcal{F}$, and $f_1, f_2, \ldots$ are successively better approximations.

2. The individual functions f_i will most likely *not* be fixpoints (and the ones in the table are not). But the limit of $f_0, f_1, f_2, \ldots$ will always exist, and will always be $\mathcal{F}$'s least fixpoint.

3. More precisely $f_i \sqsubseteq f_{i+1}$ for all i, where $f \sqsubseteq g$ iff for all $x \in \mathbb{N}$ either $f(x) = \bot$ or $f(x) = g(x) \in \mathbb{N}$. The limit is the smallest function (with respect to partial order $\sqsubseteq$) f such that $f_i \sqsubseteq f$ for all i.

4. This scheme works in principle and as a definition, but for practical implementation a more efficient way to compute the same values would be used. For instance one would only compute those values of $f(x)$ that are needed for the final answer.

Theoretical basis.   Putting this informal discussion on solid foundations requires some mathematical "machinery," for example as presented in [109, 150]. There it is shown that the least fixpoint always exists and that the sequence $f_0, f_1, f_2, \ldots$ above always converges toward it, provided functional $\mathcal{F}$ is "continuous" (in a sense different from that of analysis). Fortunately, any recursive function definition one can write using variables, constants, tests, function calls and continuous base functions (such as $+$, $*$, and "if-then-else") defines a continuous functional.

Mutual recursion.   It is easy to generalize this approach to assign meaning to a collection of functions defined by mutual recursion, by computing the least fixpoint of a functional on a cartesian product of sets of partial functions. (In Scott's domain theory this is extended to a variety of other "domain constructors," see [150].) For an example,

$$
\begin{aligned}
f(n) &= (\text{if } n = 0 \text{ then } \textit{true} \text{ else } g(n-1)) \\
g(n) &= (\text{if } n = 0 \text{ then } \textit{false} \text{ else } f(n-1))
\end{aligned}
$$

defines functions $f, g : \mathbb{N} \to \mathbb{B}$ such that $f(n) = \textit{true}$ for even n and $\textit{false}$ for odd n, and $g(n) = \textit{false}$ for even n and $\textit{true}$ for odd n.

14.2   Recursion by syntax: Kleene's and Rogers' recursion theorems

14.2.1   The theorems and some applications

Kleene's *second recursion theorem* [95] in essence guarantees the computability of functions defined by self-referential or "reflexive" algorithms. Given this ability, it is possible to simulate recursion as a special case, without having it as a built-in language construct. The theorem thus gives an alternate way to assign meaning to recursive language constructs. The recursion theorem has many applications in recursive function theory, machine-independent computational complexity, and learning theory [13, 18]. It is valid for any programming language computing all partial recursive functions, such that the s-m-n Theorem holds and a universal program exists. Such a language is called an "acceptable enumeration" (Rogers [147]) of the partial recursive functions, and will be discussed later in this chapter.

We will first prove the recursion theorem to hold for an extension of the I language. The proof is straighforward, and yields much more efficient programs than those given by traditional constructions [95, 147]. In section 14.3 it will be shown to hold for all acceptable enumerations, thus all reasonable programming languages.

First, some motivating discussion.

The theorem and applications

Kleene's version of the recursion theorem may be stated as follows, for a language L not yet specified. Proofs will given later, at which time we will also discuss the efficiency of the programs whose existence is proven.

Theorem 14.2.1 (Kleene's second recursion theorem.) For any L-program p, there is an L-program q satisfying, for all inputs $d \in L\text{-}data$,

$$[\![q]\!](d) = [\![p]\!](q \cdot d)$$

Typically p's first input is a program, which p may apply to various arguments, transform, time, or otherwise process as it sees fit. The theorem in effect says that p may regard q as *its own text*, thus allowing self-referential programs.

Rogers has an alternative version of this theorem, which gives another viewpoint that is more convenient for some applications. It in essence says that every computable total program transformation has a "syntactic fixpoint": a program p whose meaning is unchanged by the transformation.

Theorem 14.2.2 (Rogers' recursion theorem.) For any total computable function $f : L\text{-}data \rightarrow L\text{-}data$, there is a program q such that for all inputs $\in L\text{-}data$,

$$[\![q]\!] \simeq [\![f(q)]\!]$$

A first application is to prove the existence of a program q which yields its own text as output, regardless of its input — a favorite (and nontrivial) beginning programming exercise.

Example 1: *A self-reproducing program, using Kleene's theorem.* Let program p satisfy $[\![p]\!](r.d) = r$ for all r, d. Letting q be the program given by Theorem 14.2.1, we have

$$[\![q]\!](d) = [\![p]\!](q.d) = q$$

Example 2: *A self-reproducing program, using Rogers' version.* Let the obviously computable function f be defined (informally) by

$f(p)$ = the program   "read X; Y := p; write Y"

Clearly $[\![q]\!] \simeq [\![f(q)]\!]$ implies $[\![q]\!](d) = [\![f(q)]\!](d) = q$ as desired.

Example 3: *Elimination of recursion, using Kleene's version.* Let L = I. Consider the total computable function $[\![p]\!]: \mathbb{D} \to \mathbb{D}$ defined by

```
[p](q.x) = [if x = 0 then 1 else x * [q](tl x)]
```

where x is assumed to be a numeral $\mathtt{nil}^n$, as in section 2.1.6. The call to q can be programmed as the call $[\![i]\!]((q.(\mathtt{tl}\ x)))$, where i is the universal program for I-programs. By Theorem 14.2.1, there is a "fixed-point" program e with the property

```
[e](x) =  [p](e.x) = [if x = 0 then 1 else x · [i]((e.(x-1)))] =
                     [if x = 0 then 1 else x · [e](x-1)]
```

Thus e, which was found without explicit use of recursion, is the factorial function. More generally, Kleene's theorem implies that any acceptable programming system is "closed under recursion."

Other examples, including the Blum Speedup Theorem involve computing time and appear in chapter 20.

14.2.2   Proof for a reflexive extension of I

Our first proofs of the Recursion theorems are indirect, applying only to a "reflexive" programming language extending I.

Let $I^{\uparrow}$ be an extension of language I, with syntax as in Figure 14.1. This is an abstract syntax; a concrete one is obtained as in section 4.2 by encoding * and univ as trees built from nil.

Informal semantics: the value of expression * is the text of the program currently being executed. The value of expression univ(E, F) is the value of $[\![e]\!](f)$, where e is

```
Expressions  ∋  E, F  ::=  X
                       |   nil | cons E F | hd E | tl E
                       |   *
                       |   univ(E1, E2)
Commands     ∋  C, D  ::=  X := E | C ; D | while E do C
Programs     ∋  P     ::=  read X; C; write X
```

Figure 14.1: Abstract syntax of the $I^\uparrow$ language.

the value of E and f is the value of F. In words: evaluation of E is expected to result in a program text. This program is then run with the value of F as input, and the result of this run is the value of univ(E, F). Somewhat more formally:

Definition 14.2.3 The $I^\uparrow$ language has $I^\uparrow$-*programs* $\subset \mathbb{D}$ and $I^\uparrow$-*programs* the result of encoding the programs generated by the grammar of Figure 14.1 uniquely as elements of $\mathbb{D}$. Its semantic function is defined by:

$$[\![p]\!]^\uparrow(v) = [\![i^\uparrow]\!]^I(p.v)$$

where $i^\uparrow$ is the self-interpreter for I from section 4.2, modified so that the STEP macro is replaced by the extension in Figure 14.2.

Note that $i^\uparrow$ is an I program; hence any $i^\uparrow$ program can be efficiently compiled into I.

How interpreter $i^\uparrow$ works: the program being interpreted is always available in i-variable P during interpretation. Its value is the value computed for *, as seen in the first new part of the case statement. For the rest, recall the expression evaluation and command execution invariants of section 4.1.1.

Expression univ(E1, E2) is handled by first saving the current value V1 of variable X, and then evaluating E1 and E2. This is done by the case part that pushes E1, E2, and douniv onto the control stack Cd. Once their values V1, V2 are obtained (in reverse order on the computation stack St), the case for which douniv starts Cd applies. This replaces V1 by V2, and pushes V1 onto Cd. By the command execution invariant of section 4.1.1 this will effect execution of program V1 on input V2. Once this is completed, the result of the program run is stored into variable V1. The case for which clean starts Cd re-establishes the expression invariant by: pushing V1 onto St; resetting V1 to its former value (saved on Cd); and continuing with the rest of the program.

```
   case Cd, St of
...
((hd E).Cd),      St                ⇒  Cd:= cons* E dohd Cd;
(dohd.Cd),        (T.St)            ⇒  St:= cons (hd T) St;
...
((*).Cd),         St                ⇒  St:= cons P St;
((univ E1 E2).Cd),St                ⇒  Cd:= cons* E1 E2 douniv Cd;
(douniv.Cd),      (V2.(V1.St))     ⇒  Cd:= cons* V1 clean V1 Cd; V1:= V2;
(clean.Old.Cd),   St                ⇒  St:= cons V1 St; V1:= Old;
...
((; C1 C2).Cd),   St                ⇒  Cd:= cons* C1 C2 Cd;
...
```

Figure 14.2: Reflexive extension of the STEP Macro.

Remark: running interpreter $i^\uparrow$ on an I program will be slower than running the same I program directly. However the cost is only the overhead of one extra interpretation layer — not prohibitive, even for programs using * and univ. The point is that invoking univ does not cause a new layer of interpretation, but just continues to use the current interpreter's facilities by simulating a recursive call using the stacks. Thus the multiplication of interpretive overhead mentioned in section 6.2 is avoided.

We now program the two examples above directly in $I^\uparrow$.

Example 1: a self-reproducing program. Let q be the following program, in abstract syntax form:

```
read X;
X := *;
write X
```

Running this program on any input will yield q as output.

Example 2: recursive computation in a nonrecursive imperative language. The factorial function is computed by the following $I^\uparrow$ program:

```
read x;
if x = 0
then Answer := 1
else { Temp := x - 1; Answer := x · univ(*, Temp) };
write Answer
```

Theorem 14.2.4 Kleene's and Rogers' recursion theorems hold for $L = I^\uparrow$.

Proof. Kleene's theorem: For an arbitrary $I^\uparrow$ program $\mathtt{p} = \mathtt{read\ X;\ C;\ write\ Y}$, let $\mathtt{q}$ be the following $I^\uparrow$ program:

```
read D;
X := cons * D;
C;
write Y
```

For any $\mathtt{d} \in \mathbb{D}$, $\mathtt{q}$ first assigns $(\mathtt{q.d})$ to $\mathtt{X}$, and then writes $[\![\mathtt{p}]\!]^\uparrow(\mathtt{q.d}) = [\![\mathtt{q}]\!]^\uparrow(\mathtt{d})$.

Rogers' theorem: Given $I^\uparrow$ program $\mathtt{p}$ with $f = [\![\mathtt{p}]\!]^\uparrow$, let $\mathtt{q}$ be the $I^\uparrow$ program:

```
read D;
Tem := p *;
Y := univ(Tem, D);
write Y
```

For any $\mathtt{d} \in \mathbb{D}$, $[\![\mathtt{q}]\!]^\uparrow(\mathtt{d}) = [\![\mathtt{r}]\!]^\uparrow(\mathtt{d})$ where $\mathtt{r} = [\![\mathtt{p}]\!]^\uparrow(\mathtt{q}) = f(\mathtt{q})$. Thus $[\![\mathtt{q}]\!]^\uparrow = [\![f(\mathtt{q})]\!]^\uparrow$

$\square$

14.3   A model-independent approach to computability

Turing machine computability is often expressed mathematically by beginning with a standard enumeration $\mathtt{p}_0, \mathtt{p}_1, \mathtt{p}_2, \ldots$ of all Turing machines. Letting $\mathtt{p}_i$ be the ith Turing machine in the list, for each $i \geq 0$ one may define $\varphi_i : \mathbb{N} \to \mathbb{N}_\perp$ to be the partial function that $\mathtt{p}_i$ computes.

A similarity with this book's framework is immediate, if we identify the ith Turing machine with its numerical index i (i is often called the *Gödel number* of the Turing machine "program"). Then the enumeration defines a programming language with data domain $\mathbb{N}$ and semantic function $[\![\_]\!]^{\mathrm{TM}} : \mathbb{N} \to (\mathbb{N} \to \mathbb{N}_\perp)$ where $[\![i]\!]^{\mathrm{TM}}\mathtt{d} = \varphi_i(\mathtt{d})$. This is extended to multi-argument functions by defining the partial n-ary function $\varphi_i^n : \mathbb{N}^n \to \mathbb{N}_\perp$ to be

$$\varphi_i^n(x_1, \ldots, x_n) = \varphi_i(\langle x_1, \ldots x_n\rangle)$$

where $\langle \_, \ldots, \_\rangle$ is a total computable one-to-one "tupling function" that assigns a unique natural number to each n-tuple of natural numbers. The superscript of φ_i^n is dropped when the number of arguments is clear from context.

An example 2-tupling or pairing function is $\langle x, y \rangle = 2^x \cdot 3^y$ already seen in Figure 8.4. Actually, pairing is enough since tuples can be formed by repeated pairing: define $\langle x_1, x_2, \ldots, x_n \rangle$ to be $\langle x_1, \langle x_2, \ldots, \langle x_{n-1}, x_n \rangle \ldots \rangle\rangle$.

More recent recursive function theory, e.g., as formulated by Rogers [147], begins even more abstractly: instead of an enumeration $p_0, p_1, p_2, \ldots$ of programs, one simply assumes that for each $i \geq 0$ there is given a partial function $\varphi_i : \mathbb{N} \to \mathbb{N}_\perp$. The starting point is thus an enumeration $\varphi_0, \varphi_1, \varphi_2, \ldots$ of one-argument partial recursive functions that are required to satisfy certain natural conditions. The definition given below captures properties sufficient for a development of computability theory which is entirely independent of any particular model of computation.

The underlying theme is to avoid explicit construction of programs wherever possible, so there is no formal definition of program at all; a program is merely an *index* in this standard enumeration. Informal algorithm sketches, with liberal appeals to the Church-Turing thesis, are used to establish computability.

The approach emphasizes *extensional properties* expressed in terms of numbers and mathematical functions, rather than *intensional* properties of programs, for example their appearance, time efficiency, or storage consumption.

Our goals are somewhat different, though, partly because we start from Computer Science, in which the exact nature of programs and their intensional properties is of major concern. We are more interested in efficient problem solving by programs than in exploring the outer regions of uncomputability. Nonetheless the interplay between these two viewpoints is fascinating and well worth study, since the extensional viewpoint focuses on *what* the problems are that are to be solved (computing functions, deciding membership in sets, etc.), whereas the intensional viewpoint focuses on *how* they are to be solved, by concrete programs running with measurable time and storage usage. Another way to describe this is as a distinction between problem *specification* and problem *solution* by means of programs.

14.3.1   Acceptable enumerations of recursive functions

In the following definitions, an n-argument function $f : \mathbb{N}^n \to \mathbb{N}_\perp$ is considered effectively computable iff for some total effectively computable tupling function $\langle x_1, x_2, \ldots, x_n \rangle$ there is a one-argument effectively computable $g : \mathbb{N} \to \mathbb{N}_\perp$ such that for any $x_1, \ldots, x_n \in \mathbb{N}$

$$f(x_1, \ldots, x_n) = g(\langle x_1, x_2, \ldots, x_n \rangle)$$

For conciseness we will also write $x \cdot y$ instead of $<x, y>$. Henceforth we will write a value ranging over $\mathbb{N}$ in teletype font, e.g., p, when it clearly denotes an index used as a program, otherwise in mathematical style, e.g., p.

Definition 14.3.1 A sequence $\varphi_0, \varphi_1, \varphi_2, \ldots$ of partial recursive functions is defined to be an *acceptable enumeration* [147] if it satisfies the following conditions:

1. *Turing completeness*: for any effectively computable partial function $f : \mathbb{N} \to \mathbb{N}_\perp$ there exists an index $p \in \mathbb{N}$ such that $\varphi_p = f$.

2. *Universal function property*: the *universal function* $univ : \mathbb{N} \times \mathbb{N} \to \mathbb{N}_\perp$ is computable, where $univ(p, x) = \varphi_p(x)$ for any $p, x \in \mathbb{N}$.

3. *s-m-n function property*: for any natural numbers m, n there exists a computable total function $s_n^m : \mathbb{N}^{m+1} \to \mathbb{N}$ such that for any index $p \in \mathbb{N}$ and any inputs $(x_1, \ldots, x_m, y_1, \ldots, y_n) \in \mathbb{N}^{m+n}$

$$\varphi_p^{m+n}(x_1, \ldots, x_m, y_1, \ldots, y_n) = \varphi_{s_n^m(p, x_1, \ldots, x_m)}^n(y_1, \ldots, y_n)$$

These properties correspond to quite familiar programming concepts. Completeness says that the language is "Turing powerful" and so by the Church-Turing thesis at least as strong as any other computing formalism.

By the completeness property, there must be an index $up \in \mathbb{N}$ such that $[\![up]\!](p \cdot x) = univ(p, x)$ for any $p, x \in \mathbb{N}$. By universal function property, program up is a *universal program* such that $\varphi_{up}(p, x) = univ(p, x) = \varphi_p(x)$ for all $x \in \mathbb{N}$ for any index $p \in \mathbb{N}$. But this can be re-expressed as $[\![up]\!](p \cdot x) = [\![p]\!](x)$, so up is a self-interpreter as in Definition 3.4.1.

Finally, the s-m-n function property asserts the possibility of program specialization, also known as partial evaluation. To see this, let $m = n = 1$. Since s_1^1 is computable, by property 1 there must be a program spec that computes it, so $s_1^1 = [\![spec]\!]$. The last equation above becomes, after omitting some sub- and superscripts:

$$\varphi_p(x, y) = \varphi_{\varphi_{spec}(p, x)}(y)$$

which can be re-expressed as $[\![p]\!](x \cdot y) = [\![[\![spec]\!](p \cdot x)]\!](y)$, the same as Definition 3.6.1. Further, an $m + n$-argument function may be specialized to its first m arguments by a series of one-argument specializations, using the pairing function.

Clearly any of the languages we have studied so far can be used to define an acceptable function enumeration, by appropriately numbering its programs.

Theorem 14.3.2 Language I defines an acceptable enumeration.

Proof. Let $d_0, d_1, \ldots$ enumerate $\mathbb{D}$ as in Lemma 5.7.1, and define $\varphi_i : \mathbb{N} \to \mathbb{N}_\perp$ by

$$\varphi_i(n) = m \text{ if } [\![d_i]\!]^{\mathrm{I}}(\texttt{nil}^n) = \texttt{nil}^m, \text{ else } \perp$$

Functions taking i to d_i and back are clearly computable by the Church-Turing thesis. □

A simple result using this approach is that *symbolic function composition* is possible in any language defining an accepable enumeration. This generalizes the result of Theorem 13.2.5, that symbolic function composition can be done for CM programs.

Theorem 14.3.3 Given any acceptable enumeration φ, there is a total recursive function *compose* : $\mathbb{N}^2 \to \mathbb{N}$ such that for any indices p, q and $x \in \mathbb{N}$

$$\varphi_{compose(\mathrm{p},\mathrm{q})}(x) = \varphi_\mathrm{p}(\varphi_\mathrm{q}(x))$$

Proof. By the Church-Turing thesis, the function $\varphi_i(\varphi_j(x))$ is computable; our task is to find an index for it by a *uniform* method. First, define f by

$$f(\mathrm{p},\mathrm{q},x) = \varphi_\mathrm{p}(\varphi_\mathrm{q}(x)) = univ(\mathrm{p}, univ(\mathrm{q}, x))$$

(equality holds by universality). By the Church-Turing thesis, this 3-argument function is computable, and so by Turing completeness has some index r. The needed function is then *compose* $= \varphi_{\texttt{compose}}$ where $\texttt{compose} = s_1^2(\mathrm{r},\mathrm{p},\mathrm{q})$. Alternatively this can be done using only one-argument specialization, by: $\texttt{compose} = s_1^1(s_1^1(\mathrm{r},\mathrm{p}),\mathrm{q})$. □

Remarks

Even though very natural from a computing viewpoint, these conditions are not guaranteed to be satisfied for *any arbitrary* sequence $\varphi_0, \varphi_1, \varphi_2, \ldots$ of partial recursive functions. For example, suppose the indices i correspond to positions in a listing of all finite automata, and $\varphi_i(x)$ is the result of applying finite automaton number i to input x expressed as a bit string. This fails Turing completeness since it is well known that finite automata cannot compute all computable functions. Similarly, there exist enumerations possessing a partial recursive universal function but not a partial recursive s-m-n function, or vice versa, or neither [108], [147].

14.3.2 Kleene's and Rogers' theorems revisited

Theorem 14.3.4 Kleene's recursion theorem holds for all acceptable enumerations φ:
For any program $p \in \mathbb{N}$ there is a program $e \in \mathbb{N}$ such that $\varphi_e(x) = \varphi_p(e, x)$. We call such
an e a *Kleene fixed-point* for p.

Proof. By the s-m-n property there is an effectively computable function $spec : \mathbb{N} \to \mathbb{N}$
such that $\varphi_p(y, x) = \varphi_{spec(p,y)}(x)$ holds for any program $p \in \mathbb{N}$. It is evidently possible to
construct a program $q \in \mathbb{N}$ such that for any x, y:

$$\varphi_q(y, x) = \varphi_p(spec(y, y), x)$$

Let e be the program $spec(q, q)$. Then we have

$$\varphi_p(e, x) = \varphi_p(spec(q, q), x) = \varphi_q(q, x) = \varphi_{spec(q,q)}(x) = \varphi_e(x)$$

$\square$

Remark: This proof was devised by Kleene as a realization in his framework of "reduction by the Y combinator" from the lambda calculus. Close examination reveals a
similarity, except for the use of the universal and s-m-n functions which is needed here.

Theorem 14.3.5 (The second recursion theorem, Rogers' version (1967)) For any computable function, f, taking programs as input (a *program transformation*) there is a fixed-
point program, that is an $n \in \mathbb{N}$ such that

$$\varphi_n(x) = \varphi_{f(n)}(x)$$

whenever $f(n)$ is defined. For a program p with $\varphi_p = f$, this n is called a *Rogers fixed-
point* for p.

Informally, this says that any computable program transformer has a "syntactic fixpoint," i.e., a program n whose meaning is unchanged by the transformation. Possibly
relevant applications include cryptography.

The direct proof of Rogers' version of the recursion theorem is a bit more involved
than that of Kleene's, see [147]. Due to the following propositions, the two apparently
different theorems are of equal power in the sense that given the ability to find Kleene
fixed-points Rogers fixed-points can be found as well and vice versa.

Lemma 14.3.6 *Rogers implies Kleene*: Theorem 14.3.5 and the s-m-n property implies
Theorem 14.3.4.

Lemma 14.3.7 *Kleene implies Rogers*: Theorem 14.3.4 together with the universal function property implies Theorem 14.3.5.

Proof. Lemma 14.3.6: Given p, let $f(\text{n}) = spec(\text{p}, \text{n})$ (we use the s-m-n theorem). Then by Theorem 14.3.5 we have, as required for all x:

$$\varphi_{\text{n}}(x) = \varphi_{f(\text{n})}(x) = \varphi_{spec(\text{p},\text{n})}(x) = \varphi_{\text{p}}(\text{n}, x)$$

Lemma 14.3.7: Let f be any computable program transformation. By the Church-Turing thesis applied to to the universal function and f there exists a program gp such that $\varphi_{gp}(\text{q}, x) = \varphi_{f(\text{q})}(x)$ when $\text{q} \in \mathbb{N}$ and $f(\text{q})$ is defined. By Theorem 14.3.4 the program gp has a fixed-point, that is, there is an e with $\varphi_{\text{e}}(x) = \varphi_{gp}(\text{e}, x) = \varphi_{f(\text{e})}(x)$. Thus e is a Rogers fixed-point program for the transformation f.   □

In the proofs of Theorem 14.3.4 and Proposition 14.3.7 fixed-points are obtained in a uniform manner. The second recursion theorem can therefore be generalized a bit:

Proposition 14.3.8 There exist total computable functions, kfix, rfix : $\mathbb{N} \to \mathbb{N}$, such that for any program $p \in \mathbb{N}$, kfix(p), rfix(p) are Kleene, respectively Rogers, fixed-points for p.

14.3.3   Relation to the fixpoint theorems for $\mathrm{I}^{\uparrow}$

A strength of the results just proven, in relation to that of Theorem 14.2.4, is that they hold for *any* programming language defining an acceptable enumeration. In particular they hold for I as well as for $\mathrm{I}^{\uparrow}$, and even for Turing machines.

A weakness, however, is that all nontrivial uses of either fixpoint theorem seem to require the universal program. If the constructions seen above for Theorems 14.3.4 and 14.3.5 are carried out in practice, the resulting programs e or n turn out to be unacceptably inefficient. For example, [59] reports several experiments to compute the factorial $n!$ Every program built, by either the Kleene or the Rogers method, had running time greater than exponential in n. The reason is that carrying out the constructions above literally leads to the use of n interpretation levels, each consisting of one universal program interpreting the next, in order to compute $n!$

The "reflective" construction of Theorem 14.2.4, however, only takes approximately time linear in n to compute $n!$, since only one interpretation level is ever involved. More details on experiments and efficiency of fixpoint algorithms may be found in [80, 59].

14.4   Rogers' isomorphism theorem

Rogers' remarkable theorem is that there exists a *compiling bijection* between *any two* programming languages L, M defining acceptable enumerations of the partial recursive functions on $\mathbb{N}$: compiling functions which are total, computable, meaning-preserving, one-to-one, and onto. The proof involves several steps:

1. An easy proof that there exists a meaning-preserving computable total function from L-programs into M-programs (and thus vice versa). Step 2 strengthens this by adding "one-to-one," step 4 shows the compiler can be strictly increasing, and step 5 finishes the proof.

2. A specializer is constructed which is one-to-one in its second argument. Consequence: the compiler of step 1 may be can be made one-to-one.

3. A "padding lemma" is proven: every program can be transformed into an equivalent one which is as large as desired.

4. Consequences of step 3 are proven:

   (a) There is a strictly monotonic compiler $g :$ L-*programs* $\rightarrow$ M-*programs*, meaning $g(p) < g(p+1)$ for any L-program p.

   (b) There is a strictly monotonic compiler $h :$ M-*programs* $\rightarrow$ L-*programs*.

5. g and h are merged to yield the desired one-to-one compiler, using a method drawn from a proof of the Cantor-Bernstein[2] theorem.

Notational conventions. To reduce notational overhead we henceforth assume that L, M and the anonymous φ are acceptable enumerations of the partial recursive functions, so natural numbers serve as both programs and data for each language, each is Turing complete, and each has its own universal function and one-argument specialization functions. For L, call these functions respectively $univ_L$ and $spec_L$, and the L-programs to compute them: $univ_L$ and $\texttt{spec}_L$; if we wish to emphasize the programming language viewpoint we may write $[\![p]\!]^L(d)$ instead of $univ_L(p, d)$. Language M is treated analogously; and enumeration φ has functions $univ$ or $[\![\_]\!](\_)$, $spec$, and programs: $\texttt{univ}$ and $\texttt{spec}$.

Even though all the program and data sets equal $\mathbb{N}$ we sometimes write, for example, "L-program p" to help the reader keep clear which language is being discussed.

---

[2]This theorem states that if there exist two one-to-one functions $f : A \rightarrow B, g : B \rightarrow A$, then there exists an isomorphism (a one-to-one and onto function) between A and B.

Proposition 14.4.1 There is a total computable function $r : $ L-*programs* $\to$ M-*programs* such that $[\![p]\!]^L = [\![r(p)]\!]^M$ for any $p \in$ L-*programs*.

Proof. Function $univ_L$ is partial recursive, so by Turing completeness there is an M-program $\texttt{ulm}$ with $[\![\texttt{ulm}]\!]^M = univ_L$. Consider function $r(p) = spec_M(\texttt{ulm.p})$. This is certainly total and computable. Further, it is an L-to-M compiler since

$$[\![p]\!]^L(d) = univ_L(p.d) = [\![\texttt{ulm}]\!]^M(p.d) = [\![spec_M(\texttt{ulm.p})]\!]^M(d)$$

$\square$

Solving equations with programs as unknowns by the recursion theorems

Both form of the recursion theorem amount to computable *equation solving*, in which the "unknowns" are programs. For the Kleene version: given a program p, we wish to find a q such that for all data d the equation $[\![p]\!](q.d) = [\![q]\!](d)$ holds. For the Rogers version: given a computable function f, we wish to find a q such that equation $[\![q]\!] = [\![f(q)]\!]$ holds (equality of two input-output functions).

This idea underlies the following construction.

Theorem 14.4.2 Let h be a total recursive function, and *spec* an s-1-1 function. There is an i such that $[\![h(x)]\!] = [\![spec(i,x)]\!]$ for all x, and such that $spec(i,x)$ is one-to-one as a function of x.

Proof. Call i a "1-1 specialization index" if $spec(i,x)$ is one-to-one as a function of x. We formulate an equation with free variable i such that any solution i is a 1-1 specialization index, and satisfies $[\![h(x)]\!] = [\![spec(i,x)]\!]$ for all x. The equation:

$$[\![i]\!](j,y) = \begin{cases} 0 & \text{if } spec(i,j) = spec(i,k) \text{ for some } k < j \\ 1 & \text{if } spec(i,j) \neq spec(i,k) \text{ for all } k < j \text{ and} \\ & \quad spec(i,j) = spec(i,k) \text{ for some } k \text{ with } j < k \leq y \\ [\![h(j)]\!](y) & \text{otherwise} \end{cases}$$

This is recursively defined, since program i is used on both sides. Still, the right side is clearly a computable function of i, j, y (Church-Turing!), so there is a program r such that $[\![r]\!](i, j, y)$ equals the right side's value. Define $f(i) = spec(r,i)$. Then certainly $[\![i]\!] = [\![f(i)]\!]$ is another way to express the equation.

By Rogers' version of the recursion theorem (since f is clearly total computable), $[\![i]\!] = [\![f(i)]\!]$ has a solution i. We now show that i is a 1-1 specialization index and $[\![h(x)]\!]$

$= [\![spec(i,x)]\!]$ for all x. First, suppose for the sake of contradiction that i is *not* a 1-1 specialization index. Consider the smallest k such that $spec(i,j') = spec(i,k)$ for some $j' > k$, and let j be the smallest such j' for this k. Then for any y we have

$$[\![spec(i,j)]\!](y) = [\![i]\!](j,y) = 0$$

and for all $y \geq j$ we have

$$[\![spec(i,k)]\!](y) = [\![i]\!](k,y) = 1$$

This contradicts $spec(i,j) = spec(i,k)$. Consequently i must be a 1-1 *spec*ialization index so $spec(i,x)$ is one-to-one as a function of x. But this implies that the first two cases of the equation (yielding 0 and 1) can never apply, and so that $[\![spec(i,x)]\!](y) = [\![i]\!](x,y) = [\![h(x)]\!](y)$ for all y, as required. $\qquad\square$

Computational remarks on this theorem: the first two parts of the equation serve only to detect possible violations of the one-to-one property of $spec(i,x)$, but *every* solution i must be one-to-one (in argument x), as just argued. It seems somehow paradoxical that the first two cases above can never apply for any j, y; but the cases *must* be present, else the recursion theorem would not yield a program i with the desired property.

It would be interesting to investigate the relative efficiency of the two programs $h(x)$ and $spec(i,x)$. Without the first two parts of the equation, one could compute $[\![i]\!](j,y) = univ(h(j),y)$, not too expensive. It appears, though, that the extra overhead imposed by the search over k values could be substantial.

Proposition 14.4.3 There is a one-to-one total computable $r :$ L-*programs* $\to$ M-*programs* such that $[\![p]\!]^L = [\![r(p)]\!]^M$ for any $p \in$ L-*programs*.

Proof. Let h be a total recursive compilation function as given by Proposition 14.4.1. Given this h, let i be the index from Theorem 14.4.2. Then $r(p) = spec(i,p)$ is a one-to-one compiling function as required, since $[\![h(p)]\!] = [\![spec(i,p)]\!]$. $\qquad\square$

Program padding

It is intuitively clear that one can, by adding useless instructions, transform any program into another which is arbitrarily larger but equivalent. This is the essence of the following. Remark: the condition "arbitrarily larger but equivalent" is neatly and abstractly expressed by the fact that function π is one-to-one and for all d we have $[\![p]\!]^{CM} = [\![\pi(p,d)]\!]^{CM}$ (reflect a bit on this).

Lemma 14.4.4 *The Padding Lemma.* For any language L defining an acceptable enumeration there is a one-to-one total computable function $\pi : \mathbb{N} \times \mathbb{N} \to \mathbb{N}$ such that $[\![p]\!]^L = [\![\pi(p,d)]\!]^L$ for every p, d $\in \mathbb{N}$.

Proof. Consider the pairing function $pr(x,y) = \langle x,y \rangle$ from section 14.3, and let pr_1 be its (computable) left inverse, so $x = pr_1(\langle x,y \rangle)$ for any $x, y \in \mathbb{N}$. Choosing $h = pr_1$ in Theorem 14.4.2 (and omitting superscripts), we obtain a program index i such that $[\![pr_1(z)]\!] = [\![spec(i,z)]\!]$ for all z. By definition of *spec* this implies for any p, d that

$$[\![p]\!] = [\![pr_1(\langle p,d \rangle)]\!] = [\![spec(i, \langle p,d \rangle)]\!]$$

By Theorem 14.4.2 the function $\pi(p,d) = spec(i, \langle p,d \rangle)$ is total computable, and one-to-one in $\langle p,d \rangle$.   □

Using padding, we can now strengthen Proposition 14.4.3 to make the compiling functions strictly monotonic.

Proposition 14.4.5 There is a total computable $g : $ L-*programs* $\to$ M-*programs* such that $[\![p]\!]^L = [\![g(p)]\!]^M$ for p $\in$ L-*programs*, and $0 < g(p) < g(p+1)$ for all p.

Proof. Let r be the one-to-one function from Proposition 14.4.3, and π a padding function as just constructed. Define g as follows:

$$
\begin{aligned}
g(0) \quad &= \quad \pi(r(0), \quad \min\{y \mid \pi(r(0),y) > 0\}) \\
g(p+1) \quad &= \quad \pi(r(p+1), \quad \min\{y \mid \pi(r(p+1),y) > g(p)\})
\end{aligned}
$$

Function g simply takes a program compiled from L into M by r, and "pads" it sufficiently to exceed all of its own values on smaller arguments. It is clearly computable.   □

Finally, the crux of our development:

Theorem 14.4.6 There is a one-to-one, onto, total computable function $f : $ L-*programs* $\to$ M-*programs* such that $[\![p]\!]^L = [\![f(p)]\!]^M$ for p $\in$ L-*programs*.

Proof. Let $g : $ L-*programs* $\to$ M-*programs* and $h : $ M-*programs* $\to$ L-*programs* be compiling functions from Proposition 14.4.5 such that $[\![p]\!]^L = [\![g(p)]\!]^M$, $[\![q]\!]^M = [\![h(q)]\!]^L$, and $0 < g(p) < g(p+1)$ and $0 < h(q) < h(q+1)$ for all p, q.

Both functions are one-to-one and p $< g(p)$ and q $< h(q)$; these will be key properties in the following construction. The one-to-one property ensures that g^{-1} and h^{-1} are partial functions; the monotonicity of both implies that their inverses are also computable.

Define functions zig : L-*programs* $\to$ {true,false}, zag : M-*programs* $\to$ {true, false}, and f as follows:

$$
\begin{aligned}
zig(\text{p}) &= \text{if } \exists\, \text{q} \,.\, h(\text{q}) = \text{p} \quad \text{then } zag(\text{q}) \text{ else true} \\
zag(\text{q}) &= \text{if } \exists\, \text{p} \,.\, g(\text{p}) = \text{q} \quad \text{then } zig(\text{p}) \text{ else false} \\
f(\text{p}) &= \text{if } zig(\text{p}) \text{ then } g(\text{p}) \text{ else } h^{-1}(\text{p})
\end{aligned}
$$

If zig's argument (which is always an L-program) is not in the range of h, then true is returned. If it is in the range of h, zig traces its argument backward one step, and applies zag. Symmetrically, zag returns false if its M-program argument is not in the range of g, else it traces backward with the aid of zig.

Figure 14.3 shows how they work. Given L-program p, the chain of its immediate ancestors by g, h is traced backwards until a program is found which is outside the range of h if the chain starts in L, or outside the range of g if the chain starts in M. (Being outside

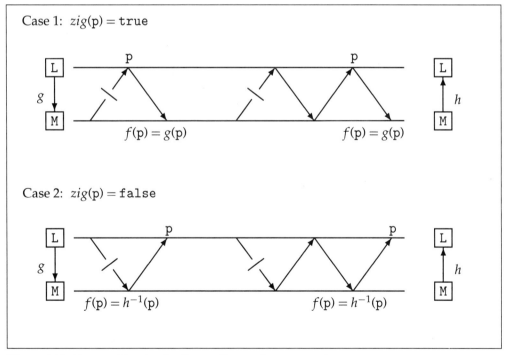

Figure 14.3: Isomorphism by the Cantor-Bernstein construction.

is marked by a crossbar over an arrow in the diagram.) In the first case $f(p) = g(p)$ and in the second, $f(p) = h^{-1}(p)$.

Note that zig, zag are both total since g, h decrease. Further, $f(p)$ is always uniquely defined. This is evident if $zig(p) = \texttt{true}$, as $f(p) = g(p)$. The other case is $zig(p) = \texttt{false}$, which can (by inspection of zig's definition) only occur if p is in the range of h, in which case $f(p)$ is the unique value of $h^{-1}(p)$.

We must now show that f is a total computable isomorphism. From the remarks above it should be clear that f is total and recursive.

Onto.　Let $q \in$ M-programs. Value $zag(q)$ is either $\texttt{true}$ or $\texttt{false}$. If $\texttt{true}$ then $q = g(p)$ for some $q \in$ L-programs for which $zig(p) = \texttt{true}$. This implies $f(p) = q$. If $zag(q)$ is $\texttt{false}$ then $zig(h(q)) = zag(q) = \texttt{false}$, which implies implies $f(h(q)) = h^{-1}(h(q)) = q$. Thus all M programs are in the range of f.

One-to-one.　Suppose $f(p) = f(p')$. As f is defined, there are two possibilities for each (the "then" or the "else" branch above), giving four combinations. First: if $f(p) = g(p)$ and $f(p') = g(p')$ then $g(p) = g(p')$ which implies $p = p'$ since g is one-to-one. Second: if $f(p) = h^{-1}(q)$ and $f(p') = h^{-1}(q')$ then $h^{-1}(q) = h^{-1}(q')$ which implies $q = q'$ since h is a single-valued function.

Third possiblity: $f(p) = g(p)$ and $f(p') = h^{-1}(p')$, which by definition of f can only happen if $zig(p) = \texttt{true}$ and $zig(p') = \texttt{false}$. But this is impossible since $p' = h(f(p')) = h(f(p)) = h(g(p))$, which implies $zig(p) = zig(p')$. The fourth possibility is the same, just with the roles of p and p' reversed. □

Exercises

14.1 Construct a self-reproducing WHILE-program directly, so $[\![p]\!](d) = p$ for all d.　□

References

Manna's book [109] has a lucid and elementary treatment of the fixpoint treatment of recursion, a subject treated from a more abstract viewpoint in denotational semantics [154, 150]. The recursion theorem is originally due to Kleene [95], and Rogers gave an alternate form involving program transformation in [147]. The isomorphism theorem is from [146]; our proof is adapted from [108].

Part IV

Introduction to Complexity

15 Overview of Complexity Theory

15.1 Where have we been?

Parts I, II and III of this book concerned understanding the nature of computability, and delineating the boundary between problems that are effectively solvable (computable) and those that are not. The problems studied involved computing partial functions and deciding memberships in sets[1].

Following Turing's analysis of computation in general, we chose at first the WHILE language as computing formalism, and proved several fundamental results using it in chapter 5. In particular Kleene's *s-m-n* theorem established the possibility of program specialization, the halting problem was shown undecidable, and Rice's theorem established the undecidability of all nontrivial extensional program properties. A universal WHILE-program, able to simulate any WHILE-program at all, was constructed.

The boundary between those sets whose membership problems are decidable, semidecidable, and undecidable was explored, as were the relations among semidecidability of set membership, effective enumerability, and the computability of possibly partial functions.

After that rather abstract chapter, relations to daily computing concepts were discussed informally in chapter 6: compilers, interpreters, partial evaluation, compiler bootstrapping, and related computational time aspects. Time was, however, only treated in a quite informal way.

The remainder of Part II very significantly broadened the scope, relevance, and applicability of the previous formal results, by showing that they hold not only for the WHILE language, but also for several other computing formalisms: both flow chart and functional analogues of the WHILE language; Turing machines; counter machines; random access machines; and classically defined "recursive functions." This was done by showing all these formalisms to be mutually simulable, or by compilations. In particular, chapter 8 on "robustness" introduced models CM, 2CM, RAM, SRAM, TM and proved their equivalences (see Figure 8.1 for an overview.) The main result was: computability, without regard to resource bounds, is equivalent for all of: F, WHILE, GOTO, CM, 2CM, RAM, and TM. A corollary: the halting problem is undecidable for any language L in this

---

[1] All over countably infinite value domains.

list.

Finally, some relatively natural and simple problems (at least in appearance!) were shown to be impossible to solve by any effective computational process. These included Post's Correspondence Problem and Context-free Ambiguity.

Part III concerned several more advanced aspects of computability, including Rogers' Isomorphism Theorem and Gödel's Incompleteness Theorem.

15.2   Where are we now going?

Parts I through III concerned only *what* was computable, and paid no attention at all (aside from the informal chapter 6) to how much time or space was required to carry out a computation. In the real computing world, however, computational resource usage is of primary importance, as it can determine whether or not a problem is solvable at all in practice.

In the remainder of the book we thus investigate computability in a world of limited resources such as running time or memory space. We will develop a hierarchy of robust subclasses within the class of all decidable sets. In some cases we will prove *proper containments*: that a sufficient resource increase will *properly increase* the classes of problems that can be solved. In other cases, questions concerning proper containments are still unsolved, and have been for many years.

In lieu of definitive answers, we will characterize certain problems as *complete* for the class of all problems solvable within given resource bounds. A complete problem is both solvable within the given bounds and, in a precise technical sense, "hardest" among all problems so solvable. Many familiar problems will be seen to be complete for various of these complexity classes.

15.2.1   How complexity differs from computability

Characteristics of complexity theory include the following. First, complexity theory is *intensional*: it concerns properties of programs and their computations, as well as what is computed. (This is in contrast to "extensional" as in Definition 5.4.1.) As a consequence, it is vital that we have "fair" resource measures with respect to actual implementations. As was the case for computability, we will not consider finite problems[2]; instead, we

---

[2]The difficult field of *Kolmogorov complexity* [105] concerns efficiency of computations on purely finite problems.

study the *asymptotic complexity* of a program solving a program: how rapidly its resource usage grows, as the size of its input data grows to infinity.

Complexity theory has as yet a great many unsolved open questions, but has evolved a substantial understanding of just what the intrinsic complexity is of many interesting general and practically motivated problems. This is reflected by a well-developed classification system for "how decidable" a problem is. Computability theory has similar classification systems, for "how undecidable" a problem is [95], [147], but this subject is beyond the scope of this book.

15.2.2   Robustness of PTIME and PSPACE

The concepts we attempt to capture all involve computational resources, the central ones being time, space, and nondeterminism (the ability to "guess").

We begin by defining what it means to decide a problem within a given *time bound*. Next, we define decidability of a problem within a given space (or memory or storage) bound. Programs running in polynomial space may, however, take too much running time to be regarded as tractable. The third "resource," nondeterminacy, will also be introduced and discussed.

These definitions will require some discussion since not entirely straightforward, partly due to our several machine models, and partly to some near-philosophical questions about "what is a fair time or space cost?" when input size grows toward infinity. After carefully investigating "fair" resource measures, we will establish that:

1. Computability, *up to linear differences in running time*, is equivalent for F, WHILE, and GOTO.

2. Computability, *up to polynomial differences in running time*, is equivalent for all of: F, WHILE, GOTO, SRAM, and TM.

3. Computability, *up to polynomial differences in memory usage*, is equivalent for all of: F, WHILE, GOTO, SRAM, and TM.

Invariance of polynomial-time computability

Conclusion 2 supports (or will, once proven) a strong "robustness" result: that there exists a class PTIME of problems solvable in time polynomially bounded in the size of its input; and that this class is essentially independent of the computation model being used[3].

The assertion that PTIME[L] is the same class of problems for all reasonable sequential (that is, nonparallel) computational models L could well be called *Cook's thesis*, after Stephen C. Cook, a pathbreaking researcher in computational complexity. A stronger version, analogous to the Church-Turing thesis but most likely too strong, is to identify PTIME with the class of *all tractable, or feasible* problems.

The *complexity equivalences* in points 2 and 3 above do not concern either the counter machine or the unrestricted RAM. Informal reasons: counter machines have so limited an instruction set that solving even trivial problems can take nonpolynomial computation time. The full RAM model has the opposite problem: it can solve some problems faster than is realistic on actual computers (details later).

Point 2 (resp. 3) will be shown by following the arcs in the chain SRAM, TM, GOTO, and SRAM: showing for each pair L, M in the chain how to construct, for an arbitrary L-program p, an equivalent M-program q whose running time is polynomially bounded in the running time (resp. space usage) of p.

15.3   Computational resources and problems

We deal with such questions as: what is the most efficient way to solve a given problem? Such a question is quite difficult to answer because it quantifies over *all possible* correct algorithms for the problem. Nevertheless we will establish *lower bounds* on needed resources (time or space) for some problems: proofs that that *any* algorithm solving the problem within a certain programming language must use at least at certain amount of computing resources.

Establishing that problem A *cannot* be solved in time $f(n)$ amounts to proving that *no matter how any program* p *is written*, if p solves A then it must take more than $f(n)$ amount of time on some inputs. Such results can only be proven in precisely defined contexts, and even then are not at all easy to obtain.

On the other hand, there exist some problems that *have no best algorithm*: the famous Blum speedup theorem (chapter 20) says that there are problems such that for any program p whatever that solves the problem, there is another program q also solving the problem which is *much faster* than p on all but finitely many inputs.

---

[3]Conclusion 1 is not as strong since it involves fewer machine types, and it seems likely that the property of linear time solvability in fact depends on the machine model used.

In this book part we are primarily concerned with the following question. When do added computational resources provably increase problem-solving ability? For instance, is there a problem P solvable by no algorithm whatsoever that runs in time n^2 (where n is the size of the input data), but which can be solved by at least one algorithm that runs in time n^3? We will see that the answer is "yes."

A similar question: given time resource bound function f, are there problems solvable in time $b \cdot f(n)$, but not in time $a \cdot f(n)$ for some constants $a < b$? (Here, again, n is the size of the input data.) In other words, do *constant time factors matter* for problems solvable in time $O(f(n))$? We will see that the answer is "yes" for a natural programming language I.

As a special case, we prove that *constant time factors are indeed important*, even within linear-time solvable problems; thus confirming in theory what one tends to think from practical experience. Practice can, however, only establish *positive* results such as: problem A *can* be solved in time $f(n)$. Negative results are much harder, as it is clearly inadequate to say "I tried to solve this problem in this way ..., but failed."

What problems are solvable in bounded time or space?

Our goal is to investigate the relative computing power of the above mentioned models for solving problems, given bounds on programs' running times or space usage. This leads first to asking the question: "what is a problem?"

If a problem is to compute a function $f(x)$ there is a risk of a trivial answer: given more time, more problems can be solved simply because larger results $f(x)$ can be written out when more time is available(!). Such answers give little real insight into the relation between available resources and problem-solving power, so we restrict ourselves to *decision problems*: determining membership in subsets of L-*data* for various languages L.

In the remainder of the book for simplicity of exposition we will, unless explictly stated otherwise, assume L is an imperative language, with programs of form: p = $I_1 \ldots I_k$. Thus a computation is a linear sequence of states $p \vdash s_1 \rightarrow s_2 \rightarrow \ldots \rightarrow s_t$, which naturally describes computations by all the languages seen so far except the functional language F.

Nondeterminism

Many practically interesting but apparently intractable problems lie is the class NPTIME, a superset of PTIME including, loosely speaking, programs that can "guess" (a precise definition will appear later.) Such programs can solve many challenging search or optimization problems by a simple-minded technique of *guessing* a possible solution and then *verifying*, within polynomial time, whether or not the guessed solution is in fact a correct solution.

The ability to guess is formally called "nondeterminism" (hence the N in NPTIME) and will be discussed in a later chapter. The concept involves a so-called *angelic* interpretation. By this view a membership decision problem is nondeterministically solvable if for each "yes" instance there exists one or more correct guess sequences leading to acceptance of the input, and for each "no" instance, no guess sequence at all can possibly lead to answering "yes."

For practical purposes it is not at all clear *how, or whether*, nondeterministic polynomial-time algorithms can be realized by deterministic polynomial-time computation. This well-studied problem "PTIME = NPTIME?," often expressed as "P = NP?," has been open for many years. In practice, all solutions to such problems seem to take at least exponential time in worst-case situations. It is particularly frustrating that no one has been able to prove no subexponential worst-case solutions exist.

15.4   PTIME and tractability

An extension of Cook's thesis would be to argue that the class of all *computationally tractable* problems comprises exactly those that lie in PTIME. This is a useful working assumption in many circumstances, but should not be taken too literally.

Identification of PTIME with the computationally tractable problems is less solidly founded than the Church-Turing thesis, which concerns computability in a world of unlimited resources. Reasons for a certain skepticism include two facts:

- An algorithm running in time $|x|^{100}$ can hardly be regarded as computationally tractable for inputs with $|x| > 2$;

- There exist algorithms that run in a superpolynomial time bounds in the worst case, but which work quite well in practice and with small constant factors. Examples:

  - The Simplex method for linear programming can take exponential time in the worst case, but works very well in practice for finding optimal solutions to systems of linear inequalities. In this interesting case, there exist alternative algorithms that are truly polynomially time-bounded (e.g., the "ellipsoid method"), but all seem to have unacceptably large constant time factors for practical use.

- Type inference in the programming language SML [122] has been proven to take exponential time in the worst case, *regardless of the algorithm used*, but again works well in practice.

There are, as well, a number of arguments in favour of identifying PTIME with tractability. While admittedly not a perfect fit, this class has good closure properties, so few reasonable operations on problems in PTIME or programs running in polynomial time take us outside the class. Further, the class has many alternative characterizations and theorems, making it mathematically appealing to work with.

15.5   A proper hierarchy based on constant time factors

The *constant speedup theorem*, well known from Turing machine based complexity theory, in essence states that any program running in superlinear time can be rewritten so as to run faster – by *any preassigned constant factor*. This counterintuitive result will be proven false for a natural imperative programming language I that manipulates tree-structured data[4]. This relieves a long-standing tension between general programming practice, where linear factors are essential, and complexity theory, where linear time changes are traditionally regarded as trivial.

Specifically, there is a constant b such that for any $a \geq 1$ there is a set X recognizable in time $a \cdot b \cdot n$ but not in time $a \cdot n$ (where n is the size of the input.) Thus the collection of all sets recognizable in linear time by deterministic I-programs, contains an infinite hierarchy ordered by constant coefficients. Constant hierarchies also exist for larger increases from time bounds $T(n)$ to $T'(n)$, provided the bounds are time-constructible in a natural sense.

15.6   A backbone hierarchy of set membership problems

Various combinations of these resources lead to a widely encompassing "backbone" hierarchy:

---

[4]I is just the WHILE language, restricted to programs with one variable and manipulating data only containing the atom nil.

$$\text{RDONLY} \subseteq \text{NRDONLY} \subseteq \text{PTIME} \subseteq \text{NPTIME} \subseteq \text{PSPACE} = \text{NPSPACE} \subset \text{REC} \subset \text{RE}$$

where RDONLY denotes those problems decidable by "read-only" algorithms[5] (i.e., without rewritable storage), and PTIME and PSPACE denote those problems solvable in time and space, respectively, bounded by polynomial functions of the problem's input size. Classes NRDONLY, NPTIME, NPSPACE denote the problems decidable within the same bounds, but by nondeterministic algorithms that are allowed to or "guess"; and REC, RE are the *recursive* and *recursively enumerable* classes of decision problems already studied in chapter 5.

Invariance of with respect to problem representation

The significance of this hierarchy is that a great number of practically interesting problems (e.g., maze searching, graph coloring, timetabling, regular expression manipulation, context-free grammar properties) can be precisely located at one or another stage in this progression.

Its significance is notably enhanced by the fact that the placement of a problem within the hierarchy is in general quite *independent of the way the problem is described*, for example whether graphs are represented by connection matrices or by adjacency lists. (There are a few exceptions to this rule involving degenerate problem instances, for example extremely sparse graphs, but such exceptions only seem to confirm that the rule holds in general.)

A collection of open problems

A long-standing open problem is whether every "backbone" inclusion is proper. Many researchers think that every inclusion is proper, but proofs have remained elusive. All that is known for sure is that NRDONLY $\subset$ PSPACE, a very weak statement.

15.7   Complete problems for (most of) the problem classes

In spite of the many unresolved questions concerning proper containments in the "backbone," a great many problems have been proven to be *complete* for the various classes.

---

[5]This problem class will be seen to be identical to the Turing-machine-defined class LOGSPACE.

If such a problem P is complete for class C, then it is "hardest" in the sense that if it lay within the next smaller class (call it B with B $\subseteq$ C), then *every* problem in class C would also be in class B, i.e., the hierarchy would "collapse" there, giving B = C. Complete problems are known to exist and will be constructed for every class in the "backbone" except for RDONLY (since no smaller class is present) and REC (for more subtle reasons.)

15.8   Intrinsic characterizations of LOGSPACE and PTIME

The classes LOGSPACE and PTIME have been traditionally defined by imposing space, respectively time, bounds on Turing machines. We will give two "intrinsic" characterizations, free of any externally imposed bounds. In particular, we will see that LOGSPACE is identical to the class RDONLY of problems solvable by WHILE-programs that do not use the cons operation; and that PTIME is identical to the class RDONLY^{rec} of problems solvable by the same programming language, extended by recursion. We anticipate the first result briefly as follows.

Read-only computation models   A one-tape Turing machine with input length n can run for time $2^{O(n)}$, i.e., exponential time, without ever moving its read/write head beyond the boundaries of its input string d. This time bound is "intractable," i.e., well beyond the running times of practically usable algorithms. This problem thus motivates a study of space bounds that are small enough to give running times closer to practical interest: smaller than $n = |d|$, the length of the input.

A solution is to use "read-only" models that allow only *read-only* access to the input value d and, when measuring program space consumption, to count only the "workspace" that is used beyond the input length. (This is intuitively reasonable, since read-only input will remain unchanged during the entire computation.) We will see that the following all define the same class of decidable problems:

- Read-only Turing machine programs for which the work space is bounded by $k \log(|d|)$ for some k and all d

- Read-only counter programs in which each counter is bounded by $|d|$, or a polynomial in $|d|$

- GOTO programs without "cons," i.e., which use no additional space at all, beyond the input d

Further, all problems in this class will be seen to lie in PTIME (though whether the class is a *proper* subset of PTIME is still an open question).

References

More information about the scope and historical development of complexity theory may be found in the surveys [14, 16, 27, 60, 139]. Broadly encompassing surveys of complete problems may be found in the books by Garey and Johnson, and by Greenlaw, Hoover, and Ruzzo [49, 53]. The approach taken in this book stems from article [80], and [83] contains a preview of some of its results on complexity.

16   Measuring Time Usage

Parts I-III concerned only the limits of computability and completely ignored questions of running time and space, except for the very informal treatment of time in chapter 6.

In the remainder of the book we will need to be much more precise about running time and space: partly to be able to prove theorems concerning what can or cannot be done within various resource bounds; and partly to justify that these results reflect facts about real-world computations (at least in contexts where resource bounds may be expanded whenever needed).

16.1   Time usage in imperative languages

Functional languages as well as imperative ones can be classified by time and space usage, but require more subtle definitions because of properly timing function calls and returns, and accounting for implicit space consumption caused by recursion. For simplicity we ignore them, except in some special circumstances.

In an imperative language, a computation is a sequence of state transitions $p \vdash s_1 \to s_2 \to \ldots \to s_t$. Two tree-manipulating imperative languages will be the main focus: the language GOTO already seen, but restricted to data with only the atom nil; and the language I of section 4.2.

16.1.1   Some simplifications

For technical convenience we make some small changes in the machine or programming models seen earlier, and precisely define program running times in the revised computation models. The main changes are the following. None affect the class of problems that can be solved, though some problem's representations may be encoded. Their aim is to provide better descriptions of computations within limited time or space resources (with fairer cost assignments, or technically more manageable.)

- In WHILE, GOTO and F, the only atom used is nil.
- A *fixed input set*, namely $\{0,1\}^*$ or a subset $\mathbb{D}_{01}$ of $\mathbb{D}$ isomorphic to it will consistently be used. The motivation is to make it easier to compare various models without having continually to invoke data coding and decoding functions.

16.1.2   The unit-cost time measure

Recall Definition 6.1.1 of a *timed programming language* L. The simplest time measure is the *unit cost* time measure, quite commonly used in complexity theory:

Definition 16.1.1 For an imperative language L, the function $time^L$: L$-programs$ $\rightarrow$ (L$-data \rightarrow \mathbb{N}_\perp$) is defined as follows, for any p $\in$ L$-programs$, d $\in$ L$-data$:

$$time^L_p(d) = \begin{cases} t & \text{if } p \vdash s_1 \rightarrow s_2 \rightarrow \ldots \rightarrow s_t, \text{ and } s_1 = (1, Readin(d)), \text{ and } s_t \text{ is final} \\ \perp & \text{otherwise} \end{cases}$$

This associates with any completed computation $p \vdash s_1 \rightarrow s_2 \rightarrow \ldots \rightarrow s_t$ the number of transition steps t it takes. This seems reasonably faithful to daily computational practice, but some special cases can be questioned: the cost of `cons` and `=?` in the `GOTO` language, and the cost of RAM operations in case register contents or memory sizes become extremely large. These will be discussed carefully below in sections 17.1 and 16.5.

A "non-unit-cost" measure will account for differences in time that executing individual instructions may take. The idea is to assign a cost to each instruction as it is executed (perhaps depending on the current store σ), and to let the cost of a computation be the sum of the costs of its individual steps.

16.2   Relating binary trees and bit strings

Before continuing, there is a difference in data sets that must be reconciled: Turing machines read bit strings, and counter machines read numbers, whereas our `WHILE`, `GOTO` and other languages read binary trees. Function c_N of section 8.3.2 provides an isomorphism between numbers and bit strings, so all we need is a way to represent a bit string in $\{0, 1\}^*$ as a binary tree in $\mathbb{D}$, and vice versa.

Isomorphism of $\{0, 1\}^*$ and a subset of $\mathbb{D}$

We regard 0, 1 as standing for standard encodings in $\mathbb{D}$ of `nil` and `(nil.nil)`, respectively. Clearly any $\mathbb{D}$-value in the set $\mathbb{D}_{01}$ generated by the following grammar

```
D01  ::=  nil  |  (nil . D01)  |  ((nil.nil) . D01)
```

can be regarded as a string from $\{0,1\}^*$. Further, string $a_1 a_2 \ldots a_k \in \{0,1\}^*$ with $a_i \in \{0,1\}$ can be regarded as an element of $\mathbb{D}_{01}$ by the coding $c : \{0,1\}^* \to \mathbb{D}_{01}$ defined by

$$c(a_1 a_2 \ldots a_k) = (a_k a_{k-1} \ldots a_1) \in \mathbb{D}_{01}$$

using Lisp list notation. (The order reversal is inessential, only a technical convenience for use in later constructions.)

Treating all of $\mathbb{D}$

Our restriction to the subset $\mathbb{D}_{01}$ of $\mathbb{D}$ makes things simpler, but is by no means essential. A coding of arbitrary $\mathbb{D}$ elements is easy to define and work with, with for example $c_{\mathbb{D}} : \mathbb{D} \to \{0,1\}^*$ representing $d \in \mathbb{D}$ by its "Polish prefix form" in $\{0,1\}^*$. This is obtained by traversing its tree structure in preorder, writing 0 every time `nil` is seen, and 1 every time an internal "cons" node is seen.

The constructions seen below could be carried out using the full $\mathbb{D}$ (or even with $\mathbb{D}_A$ for a fixed atom alphabet A), at the expense of some complications (see Exercise 16.3).

16.3 Comparing times between computation models

We now refine the definition of "simulation," as formulated by Definition 3.1.2, to include time factors. For complexity purposes it will often be necessary to compare the efficiency of source and target programs of some simulation.

The following is expressed assuming two timed languages, L and M with L-*data* = M-*data*; but it is easily generalized with respect to simulations with respect to a 1-1 data coding function $c : $ L-*data* $\to$ M-*data*.

16.3.1 Comparing languages

Definition 16.3.1 Suppose one is given two timed programming languages, L and M with L-*data* = M-*data*. Then by definition[1]

---

[1] To avoid trivial exceptions, the requirements only apply to programs **p** and languages **S** such that $|d| \le time_p^s(d)$ for all data **d**. This is not unreasonable, since a program running in time less than this would be unable to examine all of its input data value.

1. L $\preceq^{ptime}$ M if every for L-program   p   there exists an L-program q such that $[\![p]\!]^L$ = $[\![q]\!]^M$ and there is a polynomial $f(n)$ such that for all d $\in$ L$-data$

   $$time_q^M(d) \leq f(time_p^L(d))$$

   In words: M can simulate L up to a polynomial time difference.

2. L $\preceq^{lintime}$ M if every for L-program p there exists a constant $a_p \geq 0$ and an L-program q such that $[\![p]\!]^L$ = $[\![q]\!]^M$ and for all d $\in$ L$-data$

   $$time_q^M(d) \leq a_p \cdot time_p^L(d)$$

   In words: M can simulate L up to a linear time difference. Here a_p is called the *overhead factor*. It can be either less than 1 (*speedup*) or greater than one (*slowdown*).

3. L $\equiv^{ptime}$ M iff L $\preceq^{ptime}$ M and M $\preceq^{ptime}$ L. In words: L and M are *polynomially equivalent*.

4. L $\equiv^{lintime}$ M iff L $\preceq^{lintime}$ M and M $\preceq^{lintime}$ L. In words: L and M are *linearly equivalent*.

Lemma 16.3.2 Let xxx be either *ptime* or *lintime*. If L $\preceq^{xxx}$ M and M $\preceq^{xxx}$ N, then L $\preceq^{xxx}$ N. Consequently L $\preceq^{xxx}$ M $\preceq^{xxx}$ L implies L $\equiv^{xxx}$ M.

Proof. The composition of two polynomials, or of two linear functions, is also polynomial or linear.   □

16.3.2   Program-dependent or -independent overhead

We now define a more refined version $\equiv^{lintime-pg-ind}$ of linear-time simulation. This subtle difference will turn out to be important in chapter 19 where it will be proven that constant factors make a difference in the problems that can be solved in linear time, for the languages I and F. Therefore we describe this simulation more explicitly.

Definition 16.3.3 Suppose one is given two timed programming languages, L and M with L-*data* = M-*data*. Then by definition

1. L $\preceq^{lintime-pg-ind}$ M if there is a constant $a \geq 0$ such that for every L-program p there exists an L-program q such that $[\![p]\!]^L$ = $[\![q]\!]^M$ and for all d $\in$ L$-data$

   $$time_q^M(d) \leq a \cdot time_p^L(d)$$

   In words: M can simulate L up to a program-independent linear time difference (or overhead factor) a.

2. $L \equiv^{lintime-pg-ind} M$ iff $L \preceq^{lintime-pg-ind} M$ and $M \preceq^{lintime-pg-ind} L$. In words: L and M are *strongly linearly equivalent*.

The only difference between program-independent and program-dependent linear overhead as in Definition 16.3.1 is in the *order of the quantifiers*. The program-independent version is stricter since the same constant a has to suffice *for all programs* p.

Lemma 16.3.4 If $L \preceq^{lintime-pg-ind} M$ and $M \preceq^{lintime-pg-ind} N$, then $L \preceq^{lintime-pg-ind} N$. Consequently $L \preceq^{lintime-pg-ind} M \preceq^{lintime-pg-ind} L$ implies $L \equiv^{lintime-pg-ind} M$.

Proof. The composition of two program-independent linear functions is also a program-independent linear function.   □

16.4   Tree-manipulating programs

16.4.1   Henceforth: only atomic comparisons

In section 2.4 it was shown that any program using tree comparison operator =? could be replaced by an equivalent one using only comparison of atoms `atom=?`. Consequently in the remainder of this book we assume that tree-manipulating programs only compare values only against the atom `nil`, and that such a comparison has unit time cost. Remark: this avoids any need to have either of the operations =? and `atom=?`, since their effects can be achieved using `if` and `while`.

16.4.2   `GOTO` revisited

The language `GOTO` will henceforth have the following syntax (slightly restricted) and semantics, and running times:

Definition 16.4.1 Let program $p = I_1 \ldots I_m$, and let `Vars` be a countable set of variables. We use the conventions $d, e \in \mathbb{D}$ and $X, Y, Z \in \texttt{Vars}$. The informal syntax of `GOTO` is given by the following grammar for instruction forms where $d \in \mathbb{D}$:

```
I  ::=  X := nil | X := Y | X := hd Y | X := tl Y
     |   X := cons Y Z  |  if X goto ℓ else ℓ'
```

Labels ℓ in if statements must be between 1 and $m+1$. Program semantics $[\![p]\!]^{\text{GOTO}}(d)$ is as in Definition 7.2.2. Program running time $time_p^{\text{GOTO}}(d)$ is given by the unit-cost measure of section 16.1.2.   □

16.4.3   Running times of WHILE programs

Conceptually, this is very simple: one counts one time unit for each operation or test performed on data during execution. Technically, we use parts of the definitions of $\mathcal{E}$ etc. from section 2.2.

Definition 16.4.2 Given a store σ containing the values of the variables in an expression E, the function $\mathcal{T}$ maps E and σ into the time $\mathcal{T}[\![E]\!]\sigma \in \mathbb{N}$ taken to evaluate E. Function $\mathcal{T} : \text{Expression} \to (\text{Store}^p \to \mathbb{N})$ is defined by:

$$
\begin{aligned}
\mathcal{T}[\![\text{X}]\!]\sigma &= 1 \\
\mathcal{T}[\![\text{nil}]\!]\sigma &= 1 \\
\mathcal{T}[\![\text{hd E}]\!]\sigma &= 1 + \mathcal{T}[\![\text{E}]\!]\sigma \\
\mathcal{T}[\![\text{tl E}]\!]\sigma &= 1 + \mathcal{T}[\![\text{E}]\!]\sigma \\
\mathcal{T}[\![\text{cons E F}]\!]\sigma &= 1 + \mathcal{T}[\![\text{E}]\!]\sigma + \mathcal{T}[\![\text{F}]\!]\sigma
\end{aligned}
$$

□

Given a store σ, the relation $\text{C} \vdash^{time} \sigma \Rightarrow t$ expresses the fact that t time units are expended while executing the command C, beginning with store σ. (If command C does not terminate in the given store σ, then there will be no t such that $\text{C} \vdash^{time} \sigma \Rightarrow t$.) By definition $\text{C} \vdash^{time} \sigma \Rightarrow t$ is the smallest relation satisfying:

$$
\begin{aligned}
&\text{X := E} &&\vdash^{time} \sigma \Rightarrow t+1 &&\text{if } \mathcal{T}[\![\text{E}]\!]\sigma = t \\
&\text{C; D} &&\vdash^{time} \sigma \Rightarrow t+t' &&\text{if } \text{C} \vdash^{time} \sigma \Rightarrow t, \text{C} \vdash \sigma \to \sigma', \\
& && && \qquad\qquad \text{and } \text{D} \vdash^{time} \sigma' \Rightarrow t' \\
&\text{while E do C} \vdash^{time} \sigma \Rightarrow t+1 &&&&\text{if } \mathcal{E}[\![\text{E}]\!]\sigma = \text{nil and } \mathcal{T}[\![\text{E}]\!]\sigma = t \\
&\text{while E do C} \vdash^{time} \sigma \Rightarrow t+t'+1 &&&&\text{if } \mathcal{E}[\![\text{E}]\!]\sigma \neq \text{nil}, \mathcal{T}[\![\text{E}]\!]\sigma = t, \\
& && && \text{C} \vdash \sigma \to \sigma', \text{ and while E do C} \vdash^{time} \sigma' \Rightarrow t'
\end{aligned}
$$

□

16.5   Fair time complexity measures

Since all our programs are imperative, the only natural cost to assign to a computation is the sum of the costs of its individual steps. The "unit cost per operation" model will consistently be used unless other measures are specified. Thus Turing machines and the GOTO language use unit cost, whereas I uses time as specified by Definition 16.4.2.

One-step instruction times for random access machines can be defined in more than one way, and some are closer to daily computational practice than others. Even though the exact choice of instruction set is unimportant for computability in the limit, it becomes important when talking about computing within limited resources.

Time measures on the counter machine CM do not give much insight. The problem is that the CM instructions are too weak to solve interesting problems within reasonable time, since in any one instruction, a counter may change in value by at most 1. We will see, however, that a reasonable measure of computation *space* can be defined for a counter machine.

The full RAM model has somehat the opposite problem under the unit-cost model, if memory cells are unlimited in value: its instruction set is typically too strong to yield a reasonable time measure. The problem is one of data value size: if instructions such as X:=Y+Z are allowed, executing X:=X+X k times will multiply X's value by 2^k; and an instruction X:=X*X (allowed on many RAM models) can, if repeated, construct extremely large values within short time.

A symptom of this problem is that some problems known to be "NP-complete" (presented later in this book) can be solved in polynomially many steps on the unlimited RAM model [151]. One solution to this problem is to use a nonuniform cost measure, in effect "charging" instructions according to how large the values are that they manipulate. This leads to the *logarithmic cost* model discussed below.

Another solution, which we will use, is to limit the RAM model to be a "successor RAM" or SRAM, with indirect addressing to load and store data, but only with data computation instructions X:=Y+1 or X:=Y-1. We will see that this yields the same class PTIME under unit time costing as Turing machines and other models. Further, it is essentially equivalent to "impure Lisp," meaning Lisp with instructions to change already existing cells via operations such as SETCAR! or RPLACA. Another equivalent formulation is Schönhages *storage modification machine* [152].

16.5.1   Random access machine instruction times

There is some controversy about what a "fair charge" should be for instruction times on a RAM, for at least two reasons. First, the model is close enough to actual machine hardware instruction sets to relate its computation times to those we deal with in practice (unlike, for example, the counter machine). Second, the model allows *arbitrarily large natural numbers* to be stored in its registers or memory cells — a feature in conflict with the first.

It is not easy to get around allowing arbitrarily large values in memory cells, since if one assumes all cells are finite then the machine becomes a kind of *finite automaton*. While interesting in themselves and useful for many purposes (e.g., lexical analysis in a compiler), finite automata are *not Turing complete*, and daily Computer Science algorithms become quite unnatural when truncated to fit within finitely bounded word sizes.

We here have a paradoxical situation: that the most natural model of daily computing on computers, which we know to be finite, is by an infinite (i.e., potentially unbounded) computation model. This question can be discussed at great length, which we will not do here. One element in such a discussion, though, would surely be the fact that we carefully *design and build our computers* to provide a faithful model of a mathematical world, e.g., great attention is paid to ensure that an ADD instruction behaves as closely as possible to the idealized *mathematical* addition function.

Consequently it would seem unnatural *not* to model our descriptions of computer capacities on mathematical idealizations, at least until one exceeds limits due to word size, run time cost, or memory capacity. It is also relevant that today's computers are extremely fast and have very large memories, so such limitations are not encountered as often as in the earlier days of our field.

Back to the point of assigning fair costs to the RAM model: factors relevant to "fair costing" can include:

1. Should the size of the data being manipulated be considered?

   One view: one data item fits into one machine word, which takes a constant time to fetch or store.

   Another view: very large data values take longer to manipulate, and this should be accounted for in the instruction cost.

2. Should program-dependent factors be included?

   A basic example is the address (index) of an explicitly named program variable. Some other examples follow.

3. Should the time to locate the current instruction be included?

4. What effect does instruction pipelining have on times? Should a linear sequence of instructions be charged less time than code with control transfers?

5. What about page faults, or data or instruction cache misses? These involve distinctions between data in local memory, e.g., on the chip with the CPU, and memory in a global store.

6. Computer circuits exist in three-dimensional space, so time $O(n^{1/3})$ is surely a lower bound in the limit for the time to access data at address n. (Actually time $O(n^{1/2})$ could well be argued, due to the essentially two-dimensional nature of today's layered circuit technology.)

   These are much larger than the logarithmic cost assumed in many "realistic" models (see below.)

Points 4 and 5 make "only constant differences," but constant factors that are sometimes large enough to be critical. Following are the two most popular RAM cost models.

16.5.2   Two time cost models for the RAM

The unit-cost measure.   As for Turing machines, this charges 1 step for any current instruction $I\ell$.

The logarithmic-cost measure.   This charges to each operation a time proportional to the number of bits occupied by its operands. The reasoning is that data are traditionally stored in binary form, and it takes more time to manipulate longer data values. Further, the same reasoning is applied to addresses or register numbers involved in indirect fetch and store operations.

   Some literature accounts for point 1 above, some accounts for point 2, and most of the literature ignores the remaining points. Accounting for 1 and 2 gives the following instruction time charge (ignoring constants). The idea is to "charge" time proportional to the number of bits manipulated by each instruction when executed.

Instruction form	Execution time, given store σ
`Xi := Xi+1`	$\log i + \log \sigma(i)$
`Xi := Xi-1`	$\log i + \log \sigma(i)$
`Xi := 0`	$\log i$
`if Xi=0 goto `ℓ` else `ℓ'	$\log i + \log \sigma(i)$
`Xi := Xj`	$\log i + \log j + \log \sigma(j)$
`Xi := <Xj>`	$\log i + \log j + \log \sigma(j) + \log \sigma(\sigma(j))$
`<Xi> := Xj`	$\log i + \log j + \log \sigma(i) + \log \sigma(j)$

Which time measure is more realistic?   We will see that, when discussing polynomial time bounds and the class PTIME, it makes little difference which time measure is chosen. However, these factors become highly relevant if we discuss either or both of *linear time computability*, or the effect of *increasing both data and storage size toward infinity*.

The assumption that both data and storage size tend toward infinity implies a computing model where more and more hardware or circuitry is needed. It thus models one aspect of *distributed computing*, e.g., situations involving very large data bases, but not daily practice within a single stored-program computer.

In spite of the argument that one should "charge" time proportional to the address length for access to a memory cell, or a dag or graph node, this is not the way people think or count time when they program. Memories are now quite large and quite cheap per byte, so most programmers need to take little account of the time to access memory in external data storage.

Further, computer memories are carefully designed to make pointer access *essentially a constant time operation*, so users rarely need to be conscious of address length in order to make a program run fast enough. In practice computer hardware is fixed: word sizes or memory capacities cannot practically be increased on demand.

An analogy is with arithmetic: even though the computer certainly *cannot* deal with arbitrary integers, it is carefully designed to model operations on them faithfully as long as they do not exceed, say, 32 bits. Given this fact, programmers have the freedom to assume that the computer faithfully realizes the world of arithmetical calculations, thinking of his or her problem and ignoring the computer's actual architecture unless boundary cases arise.

Our choice of SRAM timing

We are especially interested in problems that can be solved within small resource usage, for example linear time algorithms and those using limited storage (e.g., logarithmic space). Such programs simply do not run long enough to fill astronomically many memory cells, or to create long addresses or values. Thus for the purpose of this book we feel that the unit-cost SRAM model is more faithful to daily programming, and so take it as our model. This view is biased toward problems with reasonable memory requirements, where time is the limiting factor of greatest interest.

Fortunately, the SRAMro model above is so restricted that this cannot happen, but if, for example, multiplication were allowed as a primitive operation, extremely large values could be constructed in a short time, bringing the fairness of the unit-cost time measure into question.

Exercises

16.1 Find a program-independent bound on the slowdown of the translation in Proposition 3.7.9.   □

16.2 Find a program-dependent bound on the slowdown of the translation in Proposition 3.7.7 as a function of p.   □

16.3 The purpose of this exercise is to show how to modify the coding between bit strings in $\{0,1\}^*$ and binary trees $d \in \mathbb{D}_{01}$ of section 16.2 to include all of $\mathbb{D}$. Coding $c_{\mathbb{D}}$ represents $d \in \mathbb{D}$ by its "Polish prefix form." This is obtained by doing a preorder traversal of its tree structure, writing 0 every time nil is seen, and 1 every time an internal "cons" node is seen.

Formally it is defined by $c_{\mathbb{D}}(\text{nil}) = 0, c_{\mathbb{D}}(\text{d1}.\text{d2}) = 1c_{\mathbb{D}}(\text{d1})c_{\mathbb{D}}(\text{d2})$. Figure 16.1 shows an example.

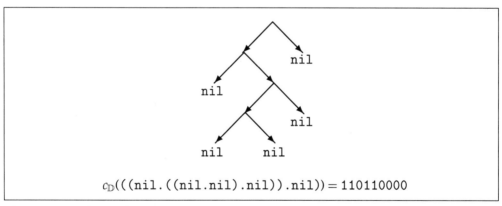

$$c_{\mathbb{D}}(((\text{nil}.((\text{nil}.\text{nil}).\text{nil})).\text{nil})) = 110110000$$

Figure 16.1: Polish prefix code for a binary tree.

The exercise is to prove the following:

1. $|c_{\mathbb{D}}(d)| = |d|$ for all $d \in \mathbb{D}$.
2. $c_{\mathbb{D}}$ is one-to-one.

3. Let the *balance bal*(x) of $x = a_1 \ldots a_n \in \{0, 1\}^*$ be the number of 1's in x minus the number of 0's in x. Then $x = c_{\mathbb{D}}(d)$ for some $d \in \mathbb{D}$ if and only if $bal(x) = -1$, and $bal(y) \geq 0$ for every prefix $y = a_1 \ldots a_i$ of x with $i < n$.

The lemma gives a simple algorithm to determine whether a bit string corresponds to a tree: initialize a counter to 1, and scan the bit string from the left. Add 1 every time a 1 is seen and subtract 1 whenever a 0 is seen. The string represents a tree if and only if the counter equals 0 when the scan is finished, and never becomes negative.

Hint: Part 3 can be used for part 2.   □

References

The random access machine was introduced by Shepherdson and Sturgis in 1963 [155]. Discussions of the delicate issue of what is a fair time cost measure are found the the book by Aho, Hopcroft and Ullman [2], and in articles by Schönhage and by Jones [151, 80].

17 Time Usage of Tree-manipulating Programs

17.1 A DAG semantics for GOTO

To deserve its name, complexity theory must concern realistic models of program behaviour. In this (admittedly low-level) chapter we examine several basic assumptions, hoping that the discussion will give greater faith that our complexity models faithfully capture intuitive complexity concepts.

As in the preceding chapter, nil will be the only atom used in any construction or definition henceforth — even though for the sake of readability we may use other atomic abbreviations in examples, for instance 0 and 1 as alternate ways to write nil and (nil.nil). Extension to multiple atoms is straightforward but more complex.

17.1.1 Justification of unit cost timing for GOTO programs

We have assumed every elementary operation cons, hd, etc. as well as every conditional to take one time unit in GOTO, and similar costs appear in WHILE. These costs may seem illogical and even unreasonable since, for example, the command X := cons Y Y binds to X a tree with more than twice as many nodes as that bound to Y.

In fact, it *is* reasonable to assign constant time to a cons operation and the others using the *data-sharing implementation techniques* common to Lisp and newer functional languages. In this section we give such a semantics for GOTO.

The first subsection introduces a certain form of graphs. The second subsection reveals the connection between these graphs and elements of $\mathbb{D}$. The third subsection uses the graphs to state the new semantics and the fourth subsection proves the correctness of the new GOTO semantics with respect to the standard GOTO-semantics. The last subsection sketches a Pascal-like implementation of the semantics, which will be used in later chapters.

Definition 17.1.1

1. A *DAG* is a directed acyclic graph.

2. A *data-storage graph* (*DSG* for short) is a DAG with the following properties:

   (a) Every node has either no out-edges or two out-edges. The first is called an *atom-node*, and the second is called a *cons-node*.

   (b) For every cons-node, one out-edge has label *l* and the other has label *r*. The node pointed to by the edge with label *l* is called the *left child* of the cons-node, and the node pointed to by the edge with label *r* is called its *right child*.

   (c) There is only one atom-node, named *node 0*, to represent atom nil.

3. A *rooted DSG* is a DSG together with a designated node chosen as the root. A DSG may have nodes that are unreachable from its root.

4. Suppose δ is a DSG with two nodes n_1, n_2, and let n be a fresh node not already in δ. Then $add(\delta, n_1, n_2, n)$ is the DSG obtained by adding the node n to δ, and adding an edge from n to n_1 labelled *l*, and a node from n to n_2 labelled *r*. For instance, the DSG in the right of Figure 17.1 could arise from the one to its left by an $add(\delta, n_1, n_2, n)$ operation. $\qquad\qquad\Box$

Figure 17.1 shows two example DSGs; consider the leftmost one. (It represents ((nil.nil).(nil.nil)), which can also be written as (1 0) or even (1.1).) For simplicity, the labels *l* and *r* have not been written; instead the same information is represented by the physical horizontal relationship between the edges on paper. There is in reality only one node labeled nil, but we have duplicated it to make it easier to read the diagrams.

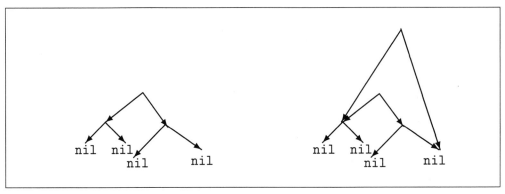

Figure 17.1: Two example DSGs

17.1.2   From $\mathbb{D}$ to DSGs and back

In connection with the DAG semantics we shall view elements of $\mathbb{D}$ as DSGs, and conversely. To view a DSG δ as an element of $\mathbb{D}$ we *unfold* it from a given node n to give

$unf(\delta, n) \in \mathbb{D}$, see below.

Definition 17.1.2 Given a $d \in \mathbb{D}$ define a DSG $\delta = dag(d, n)$ with root node n as follows.

1. if d is the atom `nil` then δ consists of the dag with one node named 0.
2. if $d = (d_1.d_2)$ then δ has a root n, which has edges to n_1 and n_2 where n_1 and n_2 are the roots of the DSGs for d_1 and d_2, respectively.

Definition 17.1.3 Given a DSG δ and a node n in δ define $d = unf(\delta, n) \in \mathbb{D}$ as follows.

$$
unf(\delta, n) = \begin{cases} 0 & \text{where 0 is the atom-node for } \texttt{nil} \\ (d_1.d_2) & \text{Where } unf(n_1, \delta) = d_1 \text{ and } unf(n_2, \delta) = d_2 \text{ and} \\ & n \text{ is a cons-node with left child } n_1 \text{ and right child } n_2 \end{cases}
$$

For example, let δ be the leftmost DSG in Figure 17.1, and n its topmost node. Then $unf(\delta, n) = ((\texttt{nil.nil}).(\texttt{nil.nil})) = (\texttt{1 0})$.

The idea in the DAG semantics is that during execution in GOTO a DSG δ is built, and rather than binding every variable to a $d \in \mathbb{D}$ we bind the variable to a node in the DSG by an environment $\rho : \texttt{Vars(p)} \rightarrow \texttt{DagNodes}$. Where a variable before was bound to atom `nil` it will now be bound to atom-node 0, and where it was bound earlier to a pair $(d_1.d_2)$ it is now bound to a cons-node. An example: the `reverse` program seen in section 7.2.

```
0: read X;
1: Y:= nil;
2: if X then goto 4;
3: goto 8;
4: Z := hd X;
5: Y := cons Z Y;
6: X := tl X;
7: goto 2;
8: write Y
```

Consider this program, applied to input (`1 0`). The left part of Figure 17.2 illustrates the DSG at the start: X is bound to DAG structure for (`1 0`) = ((`nil.nil`) `nil`), while Y and Z point to `nil`. At the end of execution two more nodes have been allocated and Y points to the node denoting the result (`0 1`), the reverse of input (`1 0`).

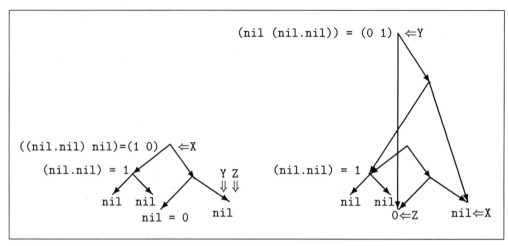

Figure 17.2: First and last DSG in execution of `reverse`

DAG semantics

In general the DAG semantics is as follows.

Definition 17.1.4 (DAG semantics for GOTO). Let program $p = 1:I_1; \ldots; m:I_m$ with both input and output via variable X, and let $\text{Vars}(p)=\{X,Z1\ldots,Zn\}$ be the set of all variables in p.

1. A *store* for p is a pair (δ,ρ) where δ is a DSG and ρ is a mapping from $\text{Vars}(p)$ to nodes of δ. A *state* for p is a pair (ℓ,σ) where $1 \leq \ell \leq m+1$ and σ is a store for p.

2. The *initial store* $\sigma_0^p(d)$ for p with input d is (δ_0,ρ_0) where $\delta_0 = dag(d,l)$ and

$$\rho_0 = [X \mapsto l, Z1 \mapsto 0, \ldots, Zn \mapsto 0]$$

3. The rules for the DAG semantics of GOTO appear in Figure 17.3. We define

$$[\![p]\!]^{\text{DAG}}(d) = e \text{ iff } (1,(\delta_0,\rho_0)) \to \ldots \to (m+1,(\delta,\rho)) \text{ and } \mathit{unf}(\delta,\rho(Y)) = e$$

4. We define the running time of p on input d by:

$$\mathit{time}_p^{\text{DAG}}(d) = t \text{ iff } \underbrace{(1,(\delta_0,\rho_0)) \to \ldots \to (m+1,(\delta,\rho))}_{t+1 \text{ states}}$$

$$
\begin{array}{lll}
s(\delta,\rho,\mathtt{a}) & = & (\delta,0) \qquad\qquad\qquad\quad \text{wWhere } 0 \text{ is } \delta\text{'s } \mathtt{nil} \text{ node.} \\
s(\delta,\rho,\mathtt{Y}) & = & (\delta,\rho(\mathtt{Y}))
\end{array}
$$

$$
s(\delta,\rho,\mathtt{cons\,Z\,Y}) \;=\; (add(\delta,\rho(\mathtt{Z}),\rho(\mathtt{Y}),n),n) \quad \text{Where } n \text{ is fresh.}
$$

$$
s(\delta,\rho,\mathtt{hd\,Y}) \;=\;
\begin{cases}
(\delta,n) & \text{If } \rho(\mathtt{Y}) \text{ is a cons-node} \\
& \quad \text{with left child } n, \text{ else} \\
(\delta,0) & \text{Where } 0 \text{ is } \delta\text{'s } \mathtt{nil} \text{ node.}
\end{cases}
$$

$$
s(\delta,\rho,\mathtt{tl\,Y}) \;=\;
\begin{cases}
(\delta,n) & \text{If } \rho(\mathtt{Y}) \text{ is a cons-node} \\
& \quad \text{with right child } n, \text{ else} \\
(\delta,0) & \text{Where } 0 \text{ is } \delta\text{'s } \mathtt{nil} \text{ node}
\end{cases}
$$

$$
\begin{array}{ll}
(\ell,\sigma)\rightarrow(\ell+1,(\delta',\rho[\mathtt{X}\mapsto n])) & \text{If } I\ell=\mathtt{X\!:=\!E},\ \sigma=(\delta,\rho),\ s(\delta,\rho,\mathtt{E})=(\delta',n) \\
(\ell,\sigma)\rightarrow(\ell',\sigma) & \text{If } I\ell=\mathtt{if\ X\ goto}\,\ell'\ \mathtt{else}\ \ell''\ \text{and}\ \rho(\mathtt{X})\neq 0 \\
(\ell,\sigma)\rightarrow(\ell'',\sigma) & \text{If } I\ell=\mathtt{if\ X\ goto}\ \ell'\,\mathtt{else}\ \ell''\ \text{and}\ \rho(\mathtt{X})= 0
\end{array}
$$

Figure 17.3: DAG Semantics of GOTO-programs, where $\sigma = (\rho,\delta)$.

17.1.3   Correctness of the DAG semantics

Informally a DSG store (δ,ρ) corresponds to a GOTO store $\sigma : \mathtt{Vars}(\mathtt{p}) \rightarrow \mathbb{D}$ if ρ and σ bind the same variables, and unfolding the node bound to Z by ρ gives the value bound to Z by σ.

Definition 17.1.5 Correspondence $(\delta,\rho) \sim \sigma$ between a DSG store (δ,ρ) and a GOTO store σ is defined as follows.

$$(\delta,\rho) \sim \sigma \text{ iff } \mathrm{dom}(\rho) = \mathrm{dom}(\sigma) \text{ and } \mathit{unf}(\delta,\rho(\mathtt{Z})) = \sigma(\mathtt{Z}) \text{ for all } \mathtt{Z} \in \mathrm{dom}(\rho)$$

Theorem 17.1.6 For any program p, $[\![\mathtt{p}]\!]^{\mathrm{DAG}}(\mathtt{d}) = [\![\mathtt{p}]\!]^{\mathrm{GOTO}}(\mathtt{d})$, that is the standard and DAG semantics are equivalent.

Proof. First prove that $(\delta_0,\rho_0) \sim \sigma_0$ for the initial stores in the DAG and standard semantics (use the property that $\mathit{unf}(dag(\mathtt{d},n),n) = \mathtt{d}$). Then prove that $(\delta,\rho) \sim \sigma$ implies

$$(\ell,\sigma) \rightarrow (\ell',\sigma') \text{ for some } \sigma'$$

iff

$$(\ell,(\delta,\rho)) \rightarrow (\ell',(\delta',\rho')) \text{ for some } (\delta',\rho')$$

and that if these two reductions hold then $(\delta', \rho') \sim \sigma'$. It follows that given a program $p = 1 : I_1; \; \ldots; \; m : I_m$ and some input d, either

1. Neither the standard nor the DAG semantics ever arrive at label $m + 1$;

2. Both the standard and the DAG semantics arrive at label $m + 1$ in t steps, and the final states $(m + 1, (\delta, \rho))$ and $(m + 1, \sigma)$ satisfy $(\delta, \rho) \sim \sigma$. If so, then $unf(\delta, \rho(Y)) = \sigma(Y)$, so the final result in the two semantics are the same.   □

17.2   A Pascal-like implementation of GOTO

We now give a Pascal-like implementation using arrays of the DAG semantics of flow chart language GOTO. This will be used for several purposes:

- To justify the unit-cost timing used for GOTO programs, or that assigned in section 16.4.3 to WHILE programs.

- To prove that the problems solvable by functional F programs without cons are exactly those solvable in polynomial time, in section 24.2.

- To prove that boolean program nontriviality and Horn clause satisfiability are "complete for PTIME," meaning that they are in a sense "most difficult" among all problems solvable in polynomial time (chapter 26).

17.2.1   Simulating input-free programs

The first is now the main goal: to make it evident that each operation takes time bounded by a constant. As usual we assume there is only one atom, nil (the technique is easily extendible to any fixed finite set of atoms). The implementation technique is easier to explain for an input-free program, so we begin assuming no input, and then explain how to account for initialization for input data.

Given a GOTO program $p = 1 : I_1; \; \ldots; \; m : I_m$. Let $\{X, Z1 \ldots, Zk\}$ be the set of variables in p with output through variable X. Construct a Pascal-like simulating program as follows:

```
type Index = 1..infinity;
     Node  = 0..infinity;          (* 0 encodes nil *)
var  X, Y, Z1, ..., Zk : Node;
     Hd, Tl : array Index of Node;
         Time : Index;             (* The current step number    *)
Hd[0] := 0; Tl[0] := 0;           (* So Hd and Tl of nil give nil *)
X := 0; Z1 := 0; ...; Zn := 0;    (* Initialize all vars to nil  *)
Time := 1;                        (* Step number initially 1     *)
1    : I̅₁;            (* Code simulating p's instructions  *)
2    : I̅₂;
...
m    : I̅ₘ;
m+1  : writeout;
```

The idea is that the two parallel arrays Hd, Tl hold all pointers to hd and tl substructures. Variables assume *only* node pointers as values in this implementation. A variable has value 0 if it is bound to nil, and otherwise points to a position in the arrays Hd and Tl arrays which contains pointers to its first and second components.

For simplicity we handle allocation by using variable Time to find an unused index in these arrays[1]. Command $\overline{I_\ell}$, which simulates command I_ℓ for $1 \le \ell \le m+1$, is defined in Figure 17.4. Note that each of the simulation sequences above takes constant time, under the usual assumptions about Pascal program execution.

Instruction I	Simulating instruction $\overline{I}$
Z := nil	Z := 0; Time := Time + 1
Z := V	Z := V; Time := Time + 1
Z := hd V	Z := Hd[V]; Time := Time + 1
Z := tl V	Z := Tl[V]; Time := Time + 1
Z := cons V W	Hd[Time] := V; Tl[Time] := W;
	Z := Time; Time := Time + 1;
if Z = nil goto r else s	if Z = 0 then goto r else s

Figure 17.4: Pascal-like implementation of GOTO.

We leave the actual programming of the writeout procedure as an exercise for the reader (Exercise 17.1).

---

[1] A more realistic implementation could maintain a "free list" of unused memory cells.

17.2.2   Data initialization

Suppose now that program p has input $d = (d_1\, d_2 \ldots d_n) \in \mathbb{D}$. This data has to be stored into the Pascal data structures Hd, Tl. One way to describe this is to assume that variable X has been initialized by the following sequence of instructions, inserted at the start of p, where Zero indicates the always-present cell 0:

```
One := cons Zero Zero; X := Zero; Init₁;...Initₙ;
```

where for $1 \le i \le n$ Init_i is:

```
X := cons Zero X
```

if $a_i = 0$, else

```
X := cons One X
```

This adds $n + 2$ instructions and so has the effect of incrementing every instruction label in p by $n + 3$, so the simulation should now implement GOTO code if Z = nil goto r else s in p by Pascal-like code if Z = 0 then goto r+n+3 else s+n+3.

The following indicates the initial DAG built this way for input $d = (1\ 0)$, coded as ((nil.nil) nil).

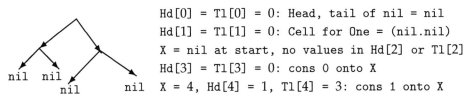

```
Hd[0] = Tl[0] = 0: Head, tail of nil = nil
Hd[1] = Tl[1] = 0: Cell for One = (nil.nil)
X = nil at start, no values in Hd[2] or Tl[2]
Hd[3] = Tl[3] = 0: cons 0 onto X
X = 4, Hd[4] = 1, Tl[4] = 3: cons 1 onto X
```

An alternative approach. Some readers may object to the approach of building the input into the Pascal-like simulating program. While we will find this convenient later, there is a simple alternative: Just replace the line

```
X := Zero; Z1 := 0;... Zn := 0;   (* Initialize all vars to nil *)
```

above by

```
readin; Z1 := 0;... Zn := 0;   (* Initialize X to d, others to nil *)
```

where procedure readin reads $d = (d_1\, d_2 \ldots d_n)$ and initializes Hd, Tl and sets Time to n+3 (all just as the initialization sequence above would do). This is Exercise 17.2.

Trace of an example simulation. Consider the `reverse` program seen before, and assume that it is given input X = (1 0), coded as ((nil.nil) nil), which is represented in the Hd, Tl table positions 0 through 4. This would give rise to the sequence of memory images in Figure 17.5, where

$\mathtt{Instr}_t$ = the instruction about to be executed at time t

$\mathtt{U}_t$ = the DAG cell variable U is bound to at time t

$\mathtt{Hd}_t, \mathtt{Tl}_t$ = the final values of Hd[t], Tl[t], respectively

This models the right part of Figure 17.1, except that all of nil, a and b are represented by cell number 0.

Time t	$\mathtt{Instr}_t$	$\mathtt{Hd}_t$	$\mathtt{Tl}_t$	$\mathtt{X}_t$	$\mathtt{Y}_t$	$\mathtt{Z}_t$
0		0	0		0	0
1	Initialize data at	0	0		0	0
2	times	-	-		0	0
3	$t = 1, \ldots, n+2$	0	0	3	0	0
4		1	3	4	0	0
5	1: Y := nil	-	-	4	0	0
6	2: if X goto 4	-	-	4	0	0
7	4: Z := hd X	-	-	4	0	1
8	5: Y := cons Z Y	0	0	4	8	1
9	6: X := tl X	-	-	3	8	1
10	7: goto 2	-	-	3	8	1
11	2: if X goto 4	-	-	3	8	1
12	4: Z := hd X	-	-	3	8	0
13	5: Y := cons Z Y	0	8	3	13	0
14	6: X := tl X	-	-	0	13	0
15	7: goto 2	-	-	0	13	0
16	2: if X goto 4	-	-	0	13	0
17	3: goto 8	-	-	0	13	0
18	8: write Y	-	-	0	13	0

Figure 17.5: Some values.

Memory reuse

Practical implementations of programs manipulating tree-structured data *re-use memory cells*, in contrast to the method above which allocates a new cell every time the clock ticks. This is often done by organizing all free cells into a single linked list called the *freelist*. A `cons` operation can be implemented by detaching a cell from the freelist, and assigning its two fields. When memory is exhausted (assuming it is finite, unlike in the model above), a *garbage collection* phase ensues, in which cells that have no pointers to them are located and collected together into a new freelist (assuming there are any unused cells, else execution aborts). Describing such methods in more detail is beyond the scope of this book.

Exercises

17.1 Write a Pascal-like program "`writeout(index)`". Its effect should be to print out the value in $\mathbb{D}$ denoted by position `index` in the Hd and Tl arrays.   □

17.2 Write a Pascal-like program "`readin`." Its input should be a list $(a_1 \ldots a_n) \in \mathbb{D}_{01}$. Its effect should be to initialise the Hd and Tl arrays so that cell $n+2$ denotes the value $(a_1 \ldots a_n)$.   □

References

The implementation ideas sketched in this chapter stem from McCarthy's original work on Lisp [118]. A more pedagogical treatment can be found in Henderson's book [64]. Relevant ideas are also discussed in [80, 151].

18 Robustness of Time-bounded Computation

In chapter 8 the term "robust" had a precise meaning: that the classes of problems decidable by a wide range of computation models are essentially invariant, aside from inessential data encodings. Computing in a resource-limited context leads to a new aspect of robustness. Ideally, resource-bounded problem solvability should be:

1. invariant with respect to choice of machine model;
2. invariant with respect to size and kind of resource bound (e.g., quadratic time, polynomial space, etc.); and
3. invariant with respect to problem representation (e.g., does the choice to represent a directed graph by an incidence matrix or by adjacency lists make a complexity difference).

In this chapter we will affirm the first two points for polynomial time bounds, and leave the last to chapter 25. As before we are only interested in decision problems expressible by a "yes-no" answer, and not in computation of functions.

18.1 Classifying programs by their running times

We begin by defining a complexity class to be a *set of programs* that run within a certain resource bound[1]. Next, we define the sets of *problems* solvable by programs running within these classes; for instance the well-known class PTIME is defined below to be exactly the set of problems solvable by programs in $\mathtt{WHILE}^{ptime}$.

Consequent to the discussion of section 16.2, we assume L-*data*= $\{0,1\}^*$ for every language L. Recall that $|d|$ is the *size* of a data value d: the number of symbols in it if d is a string in $\{0,1\}^*$, and the number of nodes if d is a tree in $\mathbb{D}$.

Definition 18.1.1 Given programming language L and a total function $f : \mathbb{N} \to \mathbb{N}$, we define three *sets of time-bounded programs*:

$$\mathrm{L}^{time(f(n))} = \{\mathrm{p} \in \mathrm{L}\text{-}program \mid time_{\mathrm{p}}^{\mathrm{L}}(\mathrm{d}) \leq f(|\mathrm{d}|) \text{ for all } \mathrm{d} \in \mathrm{L}\text{-}data\}$$

---

[1]This is somewhat more concrete than is customary; the literature mostly defines a complexity class to be a set of *problems*. One reason to differ is that the number of programs in a given language is countably infinite, whereas the number of problems, e.g., subsets of $\{0,1\}^*$, is *uncountably* infinite.

$$L^{ptime} = \bigcup_{p \text{ a polynomial}} L^{time(\lambda n . p(n))}$$

$$L^{lintime} = \bigcup_{k=0}^{\infty} L^{time(\lambda n . kn)}$$

The corresponding classes of *decision problems* solvable within limited time are easy to define.

Definition 18.1.2 Given programming language L and a total function $f : \mathbb{N} \to \mathbb{N}$

1. The class of *problems L-decidable in time f* is:

$$\text{TIME}^L(f) = \{A \subseteq \{0,1\}^* \mid A \text{ is decided by some } p \in L^{time(f(n))}\}$$

2. The class of *problems L-decidable in polynomial time* is:

$$\text{PTIME}^L = \{A \subseteq \{0,1\}^* \mid A \text{ is decided by some } p \in L^{ptime)}\}$$

3. The class of *problems L-decidable in linear time* LINTIME is:

$$\text{LINTIME}^L = \{A \subseteq \{0,1\}^* \mid A \text{ is decided by some } p \in L^{lintime}\}$$

Lemma 18.1.3 $L \preceq^{lintime} M$ implies $\text{LINTIME}^L \subseteq \text{LINTIME}^M$, and so $L \equiv^{lintime} M$ implies $\text{LINTIME}^L = \text{LINTIME}^M$ and $\text{PTIME}^L = \text{PTIME}^M$.

Proof. Let $A \in \text{LINTIME}^L$. Then A is decided by some L-program p such that $time_p^L(d) \leq a \cdot |d|$ for some a and all d. By Definition 16.3.1, $L \preceq^{lintime} M$ implies there exists an M-program q such that $[\![p]\!]^L = [\![q]\!]^M$, and $time_q^M(d) \leq b \cdot time_p^L(d)$ for some b and all data d. Combining these two we get

$$time_q^M(d) \leq b \cdot time_p^L(d) \leq b \cdot a \cdot |d|$$

Consequently $A \in \text{LINTIME}^M$. The rest of the proof is very similar. $\qquad \square$

18.2 Robustness of polynomial time

Recall the several simulations and constructions from chapter 8. We now do time analyses of some of them, and give another construction. Recall from Definition 16.3.1 that notation $\preceq^{lintime-pg-ind}$ is used for linear-time simulation overhead with a program-independent constant factor a.

Theorem 18.2.1 TM $\preceq^{lintime-pg-ind}$ GOTO

Proof. Let program $p = I_1 \ldots I_m$ be a Turing machine program using alphabet $\{0,1,B\}$. By the construction of section 8.5, each Turing machine instruction is mapped into a nonlooping sequence of GOTO instructions. Thus the total GOTO program run time is slower than the Turing machine by at most a constant factor. This factor is independent of program p, giving a *lintime-pg-ind* simulation. □

18.2.1 Efficiently compiling GOTO to SRAM

chapter 8 showed how one could compile a GOTO program to an equivalent CM program. That construction will not do for time analyses, though, for several reasons. First, the CM is too limited for polynomial time to be meaningful. Second, the translation of chapter 8 took no account of data sharing (as used in the DAG semantics), so the time to simulate X:=cons X X, for instance, would be unrealistically high, even if the first problem were somehow overcome.

Instead, we will show how to compile an GOTO-program p into an equivalent SRAM-program. The idea is simply to implement the DAG semantics of section 17.1 on the SRAM model.

Theorem 18.2.2 GOTO $\preceq^{lintime-pg-ind}$ SRAM

Proof. section 17.2 sketched a Pascal-like implementation of a GOTO program. The implementation assumed data to be stored in registers representing the tree structures of GOTO programs by means of graph structures: The SRAM memory represents a DAG, which in turn represents a memory state of the GOTO program being simulated. The simulation sketched in section 17.2 preserves these representations after simulating any one GOTO instruction.

The running time of the Pascal-like program from the construction of Figure 17.4 is clearly at most linearly slower (by a program-independent constant factor) than the

GOTO program from which it was obtained. The construction can be refined to yield an equivalent SRAM program, as in Exercise 18.6.

Given these representations, each GOTO operation is conceptually realized by a simple operation on the DAG, and in practice is realized by a bounded sequence of SRAM operations. Further, the running time of the SRAM program is shown in Exercise 18.6 to be slower than the GOTO program from which it was obtained by at most a program-independent linear factor.   □

18.2.2   Compiling SRAM to TM

Theorem 18.2.3 Under the unit-cost measure, SRAM $\preceq^{ptime}$ TM

Proof. Assume the construction of section 8.4 is applied to an SRAM-program $p = \bar{I}_1 ; \bar{I}_2 ; \ldots \bar{I}_m$, yielding a 5-tape TM-program q with $[\![p]\!]^{SRAM} = [\![q]\!]^{TM}$.

Suppose that program p, after executing t steps on an input d of length n, has store

$$[0 \mapsto v_0, 1 \mapsto v_1, \ldots, k \mapsto v_k, \ldots]$$

Since an SRAM-program can at most increase any cell Xi by 1 in one step, none of the values v_i can exceed t in value (since the initial value of every cell Xi is 0.) Further, *at most t of the values $v_0, v_1, \ldots$ can be nonzero,* since initially all are zero except for X0.

This has as consequence that in the Turing machine simulation of section 8.4, the Address and Contents tapes can have length at most $O(t \log t)$ bits. The same length bound applies to the accumulator and scratch tapes.

Now, a time analysis: one instruction of SRAM-program p is simulated on the Turing machine by at most five scans and copyings of the various tapes. Thus *one* step of p is simulated by at most $O(t \log t)$ Turing machine steps. Consequently no step takes time more than $time_q^{TM}(d) \leq a \cdot u \log u$ to simulate, where $u = time_p^{SRAM}(d)$. Definition 16.3.1 assumes all of d is read, so $n = |d| \leq time_p^{SRAM}(d) = u$. Thus one simulation step takes time at most $O(u \log u)$ steps. As a result the entire u-step simulation takes time at most $O(u^2 \log u)$ Turing machine steps. This yields $time_q^{TM}(d) = O(u^2 \log u)$ where $u = time_p^{SRAM}(d)$. This is polynomially bounded, as required.   □

18.2.3   The polynomial-time robustness theorem

Theorem 18.2.4 PTIME^{TM} = PTIME^{GOTO} = PTIME^{SRAM}

Proof. By the constructions just given,

$$\text{TM} \preceq^{lintime-pg-ind} \text{GOTO} \preceq^{lintime-pg-ind} \text{SRAM} \preceq^{ptime} \text{TM}$$

Now $\text{L} \preceq^{lintime-pg-ind} \text{M}$ or $\text{L} \preceq^{lintime} \text{M}$ implies $\text{L} \preceq^{ptime} \text{M}$, so by Lemma 16.3.2 $\text{TM} \equiv^{ptime}$ $\text{GOTO} \equiv^{ptime} \text{SRAM}$. By Lemma 18.1.3 this implies $\text{PTIME}^{\text{TM}} = \text{PTIME}^{\text{GOTO}} = \text{PTIME}^{\text{SRAM}}$. $\square$

This theorem justifies writing only PTIME, since the class of problems so defined s independent of (any reasonable) computing model used to define it. *Remark*: using the logarithmic cost measure, the general RAM is polynomially equivalent to the models above; see Exercise 18.7.

18.3   Linear time

Some of the following results concern programs in the functional language F, leading to the need to define its time usage function $time_\text{p}^\text{F}(\text{d})$.

18.3.1   Running times of F programs

Consider program $p = \text{E0 whererec f(X) = B}$. The following uses the F semantic function $\mathcal{E} : \text{Expression} \to \text{Expression} \to \mathbb{D} \to \mathbb{D}_\perp$ as defined in Figure 9.1. Given a value v of the variable X in an expression E, the function $\mathcal{T}$ maps E and v into the time $\mathcal{T}[\![\text{E}]\!]\text{v} \in \mathbb{N}$ taken to evaluate E. Further, function $\mathcal{P}$ maps p and d into the time $\mathcal{P}[\![\text{p}]\!]\text{d} \in \mathbb{N}$ taken to run p on d, i.e. $\mathcal{P}[\![\text{p}]\!]\text{d} = time_\text{p}^\text{F}(\text{d})$.

Definition 18.3.1 The functions $\mathcal{T} : \text{Expression} \to \text{Expression} \to \mathbb{D} \to \mathbb{N}_\perp$ and $\mathcal{P} : F\text{-}program \to \mathbb{D} \to \mathbb{N}_\perp$ are defined by:

$$
\begin{aligned}
\mathcal{P}[\![\text{E0 whererec f(x) = B}]\!]\text{d} &= \mathcal{T}[\![\text{E0}]\!]\text{B d} \\
\mathcal{T}[\![\text{X}]\!]\text{B v} &= 1 \\
\mathcal{T}[\![\text{d}]\!]\text{B v} &= 1 \\
\mathcal{T}[\![\text{hd E}]\!]\text{B v} &= 1 + \mathcal{T}[\![\text{E}]\!]\text{B v} \\
\mathcal{T}[\![\text{tl E}]\!]\text{B v} &= 1 + \mathcal{T}[\![\text{E}]\!]\text{B v} \\
\mathcal{T}[\![\text{cons E F}]\!]\text{B v} &= 1 + \mathcal{T}[\![\text{E}]\!]\text{B v} + \mathcal{T}[\![\text{F}]\!]\text{B v} \\
\mathcal{T}[\![\text{if E then E1 else E2}]\!]\text{B v} &= 1 + \mathcal{T}[\![\text{E}]\!]\text{B v} + \mathcal{T}[\![\text{E1}]\!]\text{B v}, \text{ if } \mathcal{E}[\![\text{E}]\!]\text{B v} \neq \text{nil} \\
\mathcal{T}[\![\text{if E then E1 else E2}]\!]\text{B v} &= 1 + \mathcal{T}[\![\text{E}]\!]\text{B v} + \mathcal{T}[\![\text{E2}]\!]\text{B v}, \text{ if } \mathcal{E}[\![\text{E}]\!]\text{B v} = \text{nil} \\
\mathcal{T}[\![\text{f(E)}]\!]\text{B v} &= 1 + \mathcal{T}[\![\text{E}]\!]\text{B v} + \mathcal{T}[\![\text{B}]\!]\text{B} (\mathcal{E}[\![\text{E}]\!]\text{B})
\end{aligned}
$$

$\square$

18.3.2   Linear-time equivalence of GOTO, WHILE, I, and F

Lemma 18.3.2 There exist two programs intIF and intFI and constants c, d such that for any $\mathrm{p} \in \mathrm{I}-programs, \mathrm{q} \in \mathrm{F}-programs$ and $\mathrm{d} \in \mathbb{D}$:

$$[\![\,\mathtt{int\,IF}\,]\!]^{\mathrm{F}}(\mathrm{p}.\mathrm{d}) = [\![\mathrm{p}]\!]^{\mathrm{I}}(\mathrm{d}) \text{ and } time^{\mathrm{F}}_{\mathtt{int\,IF}}(\mathrm{p}.\mathrm{d}) \leq c \cdot time^{\mathrm{I}}_{\mathrm{p}}(\mathrm{d})$$

$$[\![\,\mathtt{int\,FI}\,]\!]^{\mathrm{I}}(\mathrm{q}.\mathrm{d}) = [\![\mathrm{q}]\!]^{\mathrm{F}}(\mathrm{d}) \text{ and } time^{\mathrm{I}}_{\mathtt{int\,FI}}(\mathrm{q}.\mathrm{d}) \leq d \cdot time^{\mathrm{F}}_{\mathrm{q}}(\mathrm{d})$$

Proof. The result follows from an easy time analysis of the constructions in Propositions 9.2.1 and 9.2.2. Program independence holds because I and F programs have only one variable. □

Theorem 18.3.3 GOTO $\equiv^{lintime}$ WHILE $\equiv^{lintime}$ I $\equiv^{lintime}$ F, so

$$\mathrm{LINTIME}^{\mathtt{GOTO}} = \mathrm{LINTIME}^{\mathtt{WHILE}} = \mathrm{LINTIME}^{\mathrm{I}} = \mathrm{LINTIME}^{\mathrm{F}}$$

Therefore a fortiori L $\equiv^{ptime}$ M for any two of the languages just listed

Proof. This follows partly from the compilations of Propositions 8.2.1 and 8.2.2. In each case, the translated program q runs slower than the original p by a constant factor. For example in going from WHILE to GOTO by Proposition 8.2.1, $time^{\mathtt{GOTO}}_{\mathrm{q}}(\mathrm{d}) \leq a \cdot time^{\mathtt{WHILE}}_{\mathrm{p}}(\mathrm{d})$ for some a and all d.

   The remainder follows from Lemma 18.3.2.

□

Theorem 18.3.3 states a form of robustness within linear-time decidable problems: for the cluster we have studied until now of programming languages L manipulating trees in $\mathbb{D}$, the class $\mathrm{LINTIME}^{\mathrm{L}}$ is stable.

Robustness of the concept of linear time

The question "just which problems can be solved in linear time" has aroused some controversy and many differences of opinion, as it depends critically on the exact commputation model used (i.e., it is not "robust"). One might hope that Theorem 18.3.3 could be extended, for example to

$$\mathrm{LINTIME}^{\mathrm{TM}} = \mathrm{PTIME}^{\mathrm{TM}} = \mathrm{LINTIME}^{\mathtt{GOTO}} = \mathrm{LINTIME}^{\mathrm{SRAM}}$$

but this seems false: the class of problems solvable in linear time is nonrobust since it appears to be different for various models. In particular, the multitape Turing machine model is unnatural for linear time, and seems unable to solve as many problems in linear time as the SRAM.

18.4   Linear time factors don't matter for Turing machines

In the classical Turing machine model (described in section 7.6), one-step transitions are defined to cost one time unit each. The definition is unrealistic, as it ignores two important program-dependent parameters: the *number of tapes k*, and the *size of the tape alphabet Σ*. The assumption that these can be chosen arbitrarily large is also questionable in view of Alan Turing's analysis of computation, cf. Exercise 1.1.

In this section we show that not accounting for these factors[2] implies the well-known *Turing machine constant speedup theorem*. It in essence asserts that for any classical Turing machine running in superlinear time, there is an equivalent one that runs faster *by any desired constant factor*. The central idea in the proof is to replace the tape alphabet Σ by another alphabet $Σ^m$ for a possibly large constant m.

There is some controversy as to the interpretation of the speed-up theorem and its proof. Papadimitriou [130] claims that "advances in hardware make constants meaningless," since the proof shows that increasing the word size of the computer decreases the running-time by a constant-factor. Saying that a program runs in $2 \cdot n^2$ time does not make sense, because while this may be true of today's computer, the program may run in n^2 time on the computer of tomorrow. Instead, one should simply say that the program runs in $O(n^2)$ time, thus abstracting from the constant factor.

This however, does not account for the fact that constant-factors may make a difference when considering programs that run *on the same computer*, i.e., when the word size is fixed. Indeed, claiming that every superlinear program's running time can be cut in half clearly contradicts daily programming experience. Moreover, a sign of a mismatch of theory with practice is seen in its proof which, in practical terms, amounts to increasing the word size. Intuitively speaking, the speedup is obtained by *a change of hardware* — unrealistic from a programming perspective. In any case, the physical realizability of this trick is dubious.

Further, it is not at all clear that the technique could be adapted to more familiar machine architectures, even if one assumed that hardware could be increased in size upon

---

[2]Together with the one-dimensional nature of the storage tapes.

demand. The constant speedup theorem is in fact false for the I and F languages: Theorem 19.3.1 shows that increased constant factors give a provable increase in decision power for linear time bounds, and Theorem 19.5.3 does the same for a broad class of so-called constructible time bounds. A consequence is that the classical Turing machine computation model is provably different from I and F for problems solvable in linear and many other time bounds. One view of this is that I and F are more faithful models of computational practice than classical Turing machines.

Before proving the main result it may be useful to review a simple example illustrating the essential idea in the speed-up theorem.

Example 18.4.1 The following Turing machine M decides the set of even unary numbers.

1. $\Sigma = \{0, 1, B\}$;
2. $Q = \{\ell_0, \ldots, \ell_3\}$;
3. $\ell_{init} = \ell_0$;
4. $\ell_{fin} = \ell_3$;
5. $T = \{(\ell_0, B, B, \rightarrow, \ell_1), (\ell_1, 1, B, \rightarrow, \ell_2), (\ell_1, B, 1, \leftarrow, \ell_3), (\ell_2, 1, B, \rightarrow, \ell_1), (\ell_2, B, 0, \leftarrow, \ell_3)\}$

The machine first moves to the right of the initial blank and then reads past 1's. It is in state ℓ_1 whenever it has read an even number of 1's, and in state ℓ_2 whenever it has read an odd number of 1's. Therefore, if the blank following the input is arrived at in ℓ_1, the input is even and the output hence is 1. The machine requires around $|x|$ steps to compute its result, where x is the input, and $|x|$ its length.

We will now consider an equivalent machine M' which, apart from an initial setup phase, runs in half the time. The idea is to use an alphabet which allows us to express two consecutive occurrences of 1 in a single symbol 11. This allows us to read past two 1's in a single transition, and therefore the new machine will run twice as fast.

However, M' receives its input in the same form as M and must therefore first transform it into the compressed format. We will use an extra tape to carry the compressed form of the input. Here is M':[3]

1. $\Sigma = \{0, 1, B, 11, 1B\}$;
2. $Q = \{\ell_0, \ldots, \ell_5\}$;
3. $\ell_{init} = \ell_0$;
4. $\ell_{fin} = \ell_5$;

---

[3]Remember that *nop* is short for $(B, B, \downarrow)$.

5. $T = \{(\ell_0, (B, B, \rightarrow), nop, \ell_1),$

$(\ell_1, (1, B, \rightarrow), nop, \ell_2), (\ell_2, (1, B, \rightarrow), (B, 11, \rightarrow), \ell_1),$

$(\ell_1, (B, B, \downarrow), (B, B, \leftarrow), \ell_3), (\ell_2, (B, B, \downarrow), (B, 1B, \leftarrow), \ell_3),$

$(\ell_3, nop, (11, 11, \leftarrow), \ell_3), (\ell_3, nop, (B, B, \rightarrow), \ell_4),$

$(\ell_4, nop, (11, B, \rightarrow), \ell_4), (\ell_4, (B, 0, \leftarrow), (1B, B, \downarrow), \ell_5), (\ell_4, (B, 1, \leftarrow), (B, B, \downarrow), \ell_5)\}$

As usual the first transition just skips the initial blank. The next group of transitions move the input to the second tape in compressed form. If the input does not have even length, then it is necessary to pad an extra blank to the last 1, since we collect pairs of symbols into single symbols. The symbol 1B is used for this. The third group of transitions move to the start of the compressed input on the second tape (alternatively we could have processed the input backwards). Finally, the last group of transitions process the compressed input.

The last phase takes around $\lceil |x|/2 \rceil$ steps so we have roughly reduced the running-time by half. The price to be paid is that we need to compress the input and go back to the start, and this takes around $|x| + \lceil |x|/2 \rceil$ steps.   □

In this example, the total cost has been increased. However, this is just because M has linear running time. If M runs in superlinear time then the added linear time to compress the input may be outweighed by the halfing of the superlinear running time, as the next theorem shows.

Theorem 18.4.2 Let M be a classical Turing machine deciding a set L in time f. For any $\varepsilon > 0$ there is a Turing machine deciding L in time g where $g(n) = \varepsilon \cdot f(n) + 2n + 4$.

Proof. We shall prove that if

$$M = (\Sigma, Q, \ell_{init}, \ell_{fin})$$

is a 1-tape Turing machine running in time f and $\varepsilon > 0$, then there is a 2-tape machine

$$M' = (\Sigma', Q', \ell'_{init}, \ell'_{fin})$$

running in time $\lambda n. \varepsilon \cdot f(n) + 2n + 4$. It is easy to modify the proof to show that if M is a k-tape machine, for $k > 1$, then M' also is a k-tape machine.

The essential idea of the proof is similar to that of the example above. Each symbol of M' encodes several symbols of M. As a consequence, several successive transitions in M can be encoded by a single transition of M'.

More specifically, we shall encode $m = \lceil 6/\varepsilon \rceil$ symbols of M into a single symbol of M' (the choice of m will be clear at the end of the proof). Thus Σ' contains all m-tuples of symbols from M. Since M' must be able do deal with the input to M, Σ' must also include the alphabet of M. Hence:

$$\Sigma' = \Sigma \cup \Sigma^m$$

The transitions of M' are divided into three phases: a compression phase, a simulation phase, and a decompression phase.

In the *compression phase* M' reads the input x from tape 1 and stores it in compressed form of length $\lceil |x|/m \rceil$ on the auxiliary tape, erasing tape 1 at the same time.[4] Whenever m symbols $\sigma_1, \ldots, \sigma_m \in \Sigma$ have been read from tape 1, the single symbol $(\sigma_1, \ldots, \sigma_m) \in \Sigma^m$ is written to the auxiliary tape. This can be done by recalling in the state the symbols that are read.

More specifically, we include in M' states

$$Q' = \Sigma^0 \cup \Sigma^1 \cup \ldots \cup \Sigma^{m-1}$$

with the following meaning:

state	in	has meaning
()	Σ^0	no symbols read from tape 1 yet
(σ)	Σ^1	σ read from tape 1
(σ_1, σ_2)	Σ^2	σ_1, σ_2 read from tape 1
$\vdots$	$\vdots$	$\vdots$
$(\sigma_1, \ldots, \sigma_{m-1})$	Σ^{m-1}	$\sigma_1, \ldots, \sigma_{m-1}$ read from tape 1

The transitions to do the compression appear in Figure 18.1, to which the following numbers refer. As long as less than m symbols have been read from tape 1, another symbol is read and recorded in the state (1). When m symbols have been read from tape 1, the compressed symbol is written to tape 2, and control returns to the initial state (2). If the whole input has been read, the compression phase ends (3). In case the input ends in the middle of an m-tuple, additional blanks are padded (4). When the compression phase ends, the read/write head on tape 2, moves to the beginning of the input (5). All this takes $2 + |x| + \lceil |x|/m \rceil$ steps.

We are then ready to the *simulation phase* in which all operations take place on the second tape. In the simulation phase M' repeatedly simulates m transitions of M by at most 6 transitions. Such a simulation of m steps is called a *stage*. At every stage M' moves one square to the left, two to the right, and one to the left again. Recalling the

---

[4]Note that in the general case where M is a k-tape machine, $k > 1$, such an auxiliary tape is available already in M' which is also given k tapes.

Compression phase. For all $(\vec{\tau}) \in \Sigma^m, \sigma_i \in \Sigma$:

(1) $((\sigma_1,\ldots,\sigma_l),(\sigma,B,\rightarrow),nop,(\sigma_1,\ldots,\sigma_l,\sigma))$ $0 \le l \le m-1$

(2) $((\sigma_1,\ldots,\sigma_{m-1}),(\sigma,B,\rightarrow),((\sigma_1,\ldots,\sigma_{m-1},\sigma),B,\rightarrow),())$

(3) $((),(B,B,\downarrow),(B,B,\leftarrow),\ell_{eos})$

(4) $((\sigma_1,\ldots,\sigma_l),(B,B,\downarrow),((\sigma_1,\ldots,\sigma_l,B,\ldots,B),B,\leftarrow),\ell_{eos})$ $1 \le l \le m-1$

(5) $(\ell_{eos},nop,(\vec{\tau},\vec{\tau},\leftarrow),\ell_{eos})$

Simulation phase I. For all $(\vec{\sigma}),(\vec{\tau}),(\vec{\rho}) \in \Sigma^m \cup \{B\}, q \in Q, j \in \{1,\ldots,m\}$:

(6) $(\ell_{eos},nop,(B,B,\downarrow),(\ell_{init},m))$

(7) $((q,j),nop,(\vec{\tau},\vec{\tau},\leftarrow),(q,j,\vec{\tau}))$

(8) $((q,j,,\vec{\tau}),nop,(\vec{\sigma},\vec{\sigma},\rightarrow),(q,j,\vec{\sigma},\vec{\tau}))$

(9) $((q,j,,\vec{\sigma},\vec{\tau}),nop,(\vec{\tau},\vec{\tau},\rightarrow),(q_*,j,\vec{\sigma},\vec{\tau}))$

(10) $((q_*,j,\vec{\sigma},\vec{\tau}),nop,(\vec{\rho},\vec{\rho},\leftarrow),(q,j,\vec{\sigma},\vec{\tau},\vec{\rho}))$

Simulation phase II. For $(\vec{\sigma}),(\vec{\tau}),(\vec{\rho}) \in \Sigma^m \cup \{B\}, q \in Q, j \in \{1,\ldots,m\}$ with
$(q,(L\vec{\sigma}\tau_1\ldots\tau_{j-1},\tau_j,\tau_{j+1}\ldots\tau_m,\vec{\rho}R)) \rightsquigarrow (q',(L\pi_1\ldots\pi_{l-1},\pi_l,\pi_{l+1}\ldots\pi_{3m}R))$

where $t = m$, or $t < m$ and $q' = \ell_{fin}$

and $\vec{\pi}_1 = \pi_1,\ldots,\pi_m,\ \vec{\pi}_2 = \pi_{m+1},\ldots,\pi_{2m},\ \vec{\pi}_3 = \pi_{2m+1},\ldots,\pi_{3m}$:

(11) $\begin{array}{l}((q,j,(\vec{\sigma},\vec{\tau},\vec{\rho})),nop,((\vec{\tau}),(\vec{\pi}_2),\leftarrow),(q_*,j,(\vec{\sigma},\vec{\tau},\vec{\rho})))\\((q_*,j,(\vec{\sigma},\vec{\tau},\vec{\rho})),nop,((\vec{\sigma}),(\vec{\pi}_1),\downarrow),(q',l))\end{array}$ if $1 \le l-1 \le m$

(12) $\begin{array}{l}((q,j,(\vec{\sigma},\vec{\tau},\vec{\rho})),nop,((\vec{\tau}),(\vec{\pi}_2),\rightarrow),(q_*,j,(\vec{\sigma},\vec{\tau},\vec{\rho})))\\((q_*,j,(\vec{\sigma},\vec{\tau},\vec{\rho})),nop,((\vec{\sigma}),(\vec{\pi}_3),\downarrow),(q',l))\end{array}$ if $2m+1 \le l-1 \le 3m$

(13) $\begin{array}{l}((q,j,(\vec{\sigma},\vec{\tau},\vec{\rho})),nop,((\vec{\tau}),(\vec{\pi}_2),\leftarrow),(q_*,j,(\vec{\sigma},\vec{\tau},\vec{\rho})))\\((q_*,j,(\vec{\sigma},\vec{\tau},\vec{\rho})),nop,((\vec{\sigma}),(\vec{\pi}_3),\rightarrow),(q',l))\end{array}$ if $m+1 \le l-1 \le 2m$ and $\vec{\pi}_1 \ne \vec{\sigma}$

(14) $\begin{array}{l}((q,j,(\vec{\sigma},\vec{\tau},\vec{\rho})),nop,((\vec{\tau}),(\vec{\pi}_2),\rightarrow),(q_*,j,(\vec{\sigma},\vec{\tau},\vec{\rho})))\\((q_*,j,(\vec{\sigma},\vec{\tau},\vec{\rho})),nop,((\vec{\sigma}),(\vec{\pi}_3),\leftarrow),(q',l))\end{array}$ if $m+1 \le l-1 \le 2m$ and $\vec{\pi}_3 \ne \vec{\rho}$

(15) $((q,j,(\vec{\sigma},\vec{\tau},\vec{\rho})),nop,((\vec{\tau}),(\vec{\pi}_2),\downarrow),(q',l))$ if $m+1 \le l-1 \le 2m$ and $\vec{\pi}_1 = \vec{\sigma},\vec{\pi}_3 = \vec{\rho}$

Decompression phase. For all $(\vec{\sigma}) \in \Sigma^m \cup \{B\}, j \in \{1,\ldots,m\}$:

(16) $((\ell_{fin},j),(B,\sigma_{j+1},\leftarrow),(\vec{\sigma},\vec{\sigma},\downarrow),\ell_\infty)$

Figure 18.1: Transitions in the sped-up machine.

scanned tuples in the state, M' now has sufficient information to predict the next m steps of M. These m steps can affect at most m successive squares, spanning over at most two consecutive m-tuples, and so M' can implement the next m transitions of M by at most two transitions.

More specifically, at each stage, M' begins in a state (q, j), where q represents the state of M and j is the position of M's read/write head within the m-tuple that M' currently scans. This requires the addition to Q':

$$Q' = \ldots \cup Q \times \{1, \ldots, m\}$$

At the very first stage, control must be passed from the compression phase to the simulation phase (6). M' now moves one square to the left (7), then two to the right (8-9), and one to the left again (10), recalling the scanned m-tuples in the state. This requires the addition to Q':

$$
\begin{aligned}
Q' \quad = \quad & \ldots \\
& \cup\, Q \times \{1, \ldots, m\} \times \Sigma^m \\
& \cup\, Q \times \{1, \ldots, m\} \times \Sigma^{2m} \\
& \cup\, Q \times \{1, \ldots, m\} \times \Sigma^{3m}
\end{aligned}
$$

After these move operations, M' is in a state[5]

$$(q, j, \vec{\sigma}, \vec{\tau}, \vec{\rho})$$

representing the information that at this point M is in state q, τ_j is its scanned symbol, and to the left on the tape it has $\vec{\sigma}, \tau_1, \ldots, \tau_{j-1}$, and to the right it has $\tau_{j+1}, \ldots, \tau_n, \vec{\rho}$. Now suppose that M has the following computation in m steps (all such m-step computations can be computed from just the definition of M, without knowing the input).[6]

$$(q, (\mathrm{L}\vec{\sigma}\tau_1 \ldots \tau_{j-1}, \tau_j, \tau_{j+1} \ldots \tau_m, \vec{\rho}\mathrm{R})) \rightsquigarrow^m (q', (\mathrm{L}\pi_1 \ldots \pi_{l-1}, \pi_l, \pi_{l+1} \ldots \pi_{3m}\mathrm{R}))$$

Then M' simulates that in two steps, splitting into cases according to whether changes are made in $\vec{\sigma}$, $\vec{\tau}$, and $\vec{\rho}$ (11)-(15). If the computation happens in fewer than m steps, but ends ℓ_{fin}, similar transitions are made by M'. Thus the simulation phase comprises a total of at most $6\lceil f(|x|)/m\rceil + 1$ steps.

The *decompression phase* begins, if M ever terminates, and simply consists in decompressing the output.

---

[5]From now on it will be convenient to use the vector notation $\vec{\sigma} = \sigma_1, \ldots, \sigma_m$. We shall bit a bit sloppy and write, e.g., $\vec{\sigma} \in \Sigma^m$ instead of the more correct $(\vec{\sigma}) \in \Sigma^m$.

[6]Some of the σ_i, τ_j, ρ_l could be blanks; m-tuples of blanks are treated as a single blank.

More specifically, if M terminates, the initial configuration of M leads to

$$(\ell_{fin}, (\mathrm{L}\tau_1 \cdots \tau_{j-1}, \tau_j, \tau_{j+1} \cdots \tau_m \mathrm{R}))$$

where τ_{j+1} is either 1 or 0. Correspondingly, M' terminates in a configuration,

$$(((\ell_{fin}, j), (\mathrm{L}', \vec{\sigma}, \mathrm{R}'), (\mathrm{L}, \vec{\tau}, \mathrm{R}))$$

Therefore, τ_j is written on tape 1, and M' ends in its final state ℓ_∞ (17). This adds just one to the running time.

The total running time, then, of the simulation is

$$(2 + |x| + \lceil |x|/m \rceil) + (6 \lceil f(|x|)/m \rceil + 1) + 1 \le \varepsilon f(|x|) + 4 + 2|x|$$

as requried.   □

The reader should not be surprised to see analogs of the preceding theorem with the term $2n + 4$ replaced by some other term. The term is sensitive to small changes in the definition of Turing machines. For instance, some models only allow a machine to write a symbol or move one square, but not both, in a single step, and this makes a difference.

Exercises

18.1 Show that that the interpreter `int` of F by `WHILE` of Proposition 9.2.2 induces at most a constant slowdown: given any F-program `p` and input `d`, $time_{\mathrm{int}}^{\mathrm{WHILE}}(\mathtt{p.d}) \le b \cdot time_{\mathrm{p}}^{\mathrm{F}}(\mathtt{d})$.   □

18.2 Complete Lemma 18.3.2 part 1 by showing that the interpreter `int` of Exercise 18.1 can be replaced by an `I` program.   □

18.3 Show that the interpreter `int` of I by F of Proposition 9.2.2 induces at most constant slowdown: for any `I` program `p` and input `d`, $time_{\mathrm{int}}^{\mathrm{F}}(\mathtt{p.d}) \le b \cdot time_{\mathrm{p}}^{\mathrm{I}}(\mathtt{d})$. This finishes Lemma 18.3.2.   □

18.4 Why can the proof method of Theorem 18.4.2 not be applied to `WHILE` or `GOTO`?   □

18.5 Show that multiple arrays can be simulated in `RAM`   □

18.6 * The Pascal-like implementation of `GOTO` was not quite a `SRAM` program because it had several arrays, and records as well. Prove that this is equivalent to an `SRAM` program running at most linearly more slowly. Consequence: any `GOTO` program `p` can be implemented by a `SRAM` program `q` which runs in time linear in `p`'s running time.

Does the constant coefficient depend on program `p`?   □

18.7 Argue informally that the RAM $\preceq^{ptime}$ TM under the logarithmic time cost measure for RAM computations. Show that this implies PTIME = PTIME^{RAM}.   □

References

The random access machine was introduced by Shepherdson and Sturgis in 1963 [155]. The book by Aho, Hopcroft and Ullman contains a good discussion of robustness of polynomial time [2]. This insight arose in work by several authors including Cobham, Edmonds, Cook, and Karp. [24, 40, 25, 90]

19 Linear and Other Time Hierarchies for WHILE Programs

An interesting question is: for a given programing language L, does $a < b$ imply

$$\text{TIME}^{\text{L}}(\lambda n.a \cdot n) \subsetneq \text{TIME}^{\text{L}}(\lambda n.b \cdot n)$$

In other words: does increased linear-bounded computing time give strictly increased problem-solving power for our various programming languages? In this chapter we prove that increasing the time available for problem-solving can properly increase the class of solvable problems.

The first result concerns an extremely simple language version of the WHILE language called I, in which programs are limited to one atom and one variable. We prove that *constant time factors do matter* for both I and F (the functional language of section 9.1), for linear time bounds. This result, in agreement with daily experience, is in contrast to the situation for Turing machines as seen by Theorem 18.4.2.

A key to the proof is the existence of an "efficient" self-interpreter for I. This is used in a time-bounded version of the diagonalization argument used earlier to show the existence of uncomputable functions.

This is first shown for I, then results are extended to the functional language F, and to superlinear time bounds: proper increases can occur when one time bound function dominates another in the limit. Finally, some limits to the construction of hierarchies are referenced; proofs of those results will appear in a later chapter.

For I, we show specifically that there is a constant b such that for any $a \geq 1$ there is a decision problem which cannot be solved by any program that runs in time bounded by $a \cdot n$, *regardless of how clever one is* at programming, or at problem analysis, or both. On the other hand, the problem *can* be solved by an I-program in time $a \cdot b \cdot n$ on inputs of size n. In other words, sufficiently more linear time provably gives more problem-solving power.

Essentially the same construction has been carried out in detail on the computer by Hesselund and Dahl. By carefully examining the constant factors in their construction, they establish in [29] that $\text{TIME}^{\text{I}}(201 \cdot a \cdot n + 48)$ properly includes $\text{TIME}^{\text{I}}(a \cdot n)$, so the result holds for the value $b = 201 + 48 = 249$.

19.1   An efficient universal program for I

Running times of I programs are just as in section 16.4.3 (reasonable, since I is a subset of WHILE).

   We show that the universal program for I developed in section 4.1.1 is "efficient," a term we use with a definite technical meaning. An "efficient" interpreter is one that introduces *program-independent linear overhead*, as in section 16.3.2. Note that constant a below is quantified *before* p, so the overhead caused by an efficient interpreter is independent of p.

Definition 19.1.1 An S-interpreter int written in L is *efficient* if there is a constant a such that for all $p \in S-programs$ and $d \in S-data$:

$$time^{L}_{int}(p.d) \leq a \cdot time^{S}_{p}(d)$$

Time analyses of some earlier constructions

The following are easy to verify:

1. The compiling function from WHILE to WHILE^{1var} of Proposition 3.7.7 gives program-dependent linear overhead.

2. The compiling function from WHILE to WHILE^{1atom} relative to the coding c of Proposition 3.7.9 introduces program-independent linear overhead.
   This translation involves an amount of extra time overhead which depends on the (fixed) number of atoms in $\mathbb{D}_A$, but not on the program to which the translation is applied.

Constructing the efficient interpreter

Recall the interpreter i1var for one-variable WHILE programs constructed in section 4.1.1. It had form:

```
read PD;              (* Input (p.d)                          *)
  P  := hd PD;        (* P = ((var 1) c (var 1))              *)
  C  := hd (tl P)     (* C = c          program code is c     *)
  Cd := cons C nil;   (* Cd = (c.nil), Code to execute is c   *)
  St := nil;          (* St = nil,     Stack empty            *)
  Vl := tl PD;        (* Vl = d        Initial value of var.  *)
  while Cd do STEP;   (* do while there is code to execute    *)
write Vl;
```

where STEP is the large `case` command in section 4.1.1. This program `i1var` is easily seen to be efficient in the sense above:

Proposition 19.1.2 There exists a such that for all p and d

$$time_{\mathtt{i1var}}^{\mathtt{WHILE}}(\mathtt{p.d}) \leq a \cdot time_{\mathtt{p}}^{\mathtt{WHILE}^{1var}}(\mathtt{d})$$

Proof. Note that the entire STEP command is a fixed piece of noniterative code, so it only takes constant time (independent of p and d) to perform the commands to find the appropriate case in Figure 4.1 and to realize its effect. The appropriate case is the one matching the top of the control stack Cd and, in some cases, the form of the top of the computation stack St.

Any single step of the interpreted program is realized by applying at most two iterations of STEP. For example, the decision of whether while E do C should perform C the first time takes one step in p (in addition to the time to evaluate E). It is realized interpretively by two iterations: one to set up the code stack before evaluating the expression E and one done afterwards, to check E's value to see whether to enter C or escape from the while loop.

In this way a uniform and program-independent upper bound on the interpretation/execution time ratio may be obtained for *all* computations.

Variable access in the simulated program p is simulated by actions in `i1var`. Since p has at most one variable, their execution times are independent of p. They *are* dependent on the interpreter `i1var`, but are independent of program p.

However it is not clear that a program-independent upper bound can exist if p is allowed to be an arbitrary WHILE program — if interpreted programs have multiple variables, the actions to simulate variable access will typically take time depending on p. □

Remark: `i1var` satisfies another natural inequality, in the opposite direction: there exists a constant b such that for all p and d

$$time_{\mathtt{p}}^{\mathtt{WHILE}^{1var}}(\mathtt{d}) \leq b \cdot time_{\mathtt{i1var}}^{\mathtt{WHILE}}(\mathtt{p.d})$$

Such a bound is quite natural, because every single step of the interpreted program p is simulated by several actions (always more than one) of `i1var`.

Although natural, such a constant b does not exist for *all* universal programs, since there are infinite classes of programs that can be simulated faster than they run, for example by remembering whether a certain subcomputation has been performed before and, if so, fetching its result from memory rather that by repeating the computation. An example is by using Cook's construction involving stack programs [28, 5].

An efficient self-interpreter for I

Program i1var is not, however, a self-interpreter, since it itself uses more than one variable (such as Cd and St) and more than one atom. However it can be translated into one, as in section 3.7.2.

Theorem 19.1.3 The self-interpreter i of Theorem 4.2.4 is efficient.

Proof. A correctness proof resembles that of Exercise 4.1. Each operation hdrep, tlrep, or consrep is realized by a program-independent constant number of operations.   □

19.2   An efficient timed universal program for I

Definition 19.2.1 An I-program tu is a *timed universal program* if for all $p \in$ I-*programs*, $d \in \mathbb{D}$ and $n \geq 1$:

1. If $time_p(d) \leq n$ then $[\![tu]\!](p \,.\, d \,.\, nil^n) = ([\![p]\!](d).nil)$, and
2. If $time_p(d) > n$ then $[\![tu]\!](p \,.\, d \,.\, nil^n) = nil$.

The effect of $[\![tu]\!](p.d.nil^n)$ is to simulate p for $min(n, time_p(d))$ steps. If $time_p(d) \leq n$, i.e., p terminates within n steps, then tu produces a non-nil value containing p's result. If not, the value nil is yielded, indicating "time limit exceeded."

Similar to the terminology for interpreters, we say:

Definition 19.2.2 A timed universal I-program tu is *efficient* if there is a constant k such that for all $p, d \in \mathbb{D}$ and $n \geq 1$:

$$[\![tu]\!](p.d.nil^n) \leq k \cdot min(n, [\![p]\!](d))$$

We will now construct an efficient timed universal program tu for I.

Construction 19.2.3 Recall the universal program i for I in section 19.1 by translating a certain WHILE^{latom} program i1var with the STEP command into I. The idea in constructing tu is to take i1var and add some extra code and an extra input, a *time bound* of the form nil^n stored in a variable Cntr, so obtaining a program tt. Every time the simulation of one operation of program input p on data input d is completed, the time bound is decreased by 1. Translating tt into I gives the desired program tu.

Here is tt:

```
read X;                   (* X = (p . d . nil") *)
Cd := cons (hd X) nil;    (* Code to be executed *)
Vl := hd (tl X);          (* Initial value of simulated X *)
Cntr := tl (tl X);        (* Time bound *)
St := nil;                (* Computation stack *)
while Cd do
  if Cntr
  then { if hd (hd Cd) ∈ {quote,var,do_hd,do_tl,
                              do_cons,do_asgn,do_while}
             then Cntr := tl Cntr;
             STEP; X := cons Vl nil;}
    else { Cd := nil; X := nil};
write X
```

where we have used a shorthand notation for the membership test. This is easily turned into actual I commands. Let tu be the result of translating tt from WHILE^{latom} to I as in Theorem 19.1.3.

Lemma 19.2.4 tu is an efficient timed universal I-program.

Proof. To prove tu efficient, we must find a k such that for all $p \in I-programs, d \in \mathbb{D}$, and n we have both of:

$$[\![tu]\!](p.d.nil^n) \leq k \cdot [\![p]\!](d)$$
$$[\![tu]\!](p.d.nil^n) \leq k \cdot n$$

The proof of the first inequality is similar to Proposition 19.1.2. The second is immediate from the form of tu, since Cntr decreases with each iteration. If k_1, k_2 respectively satisfy the first and second, then $\max(k_1, k_2)$ satisfies both.   □

19.3   A linear-time hierarchy for I: constant time factors *do* matter

Theorem 19.3.1 There is a constant b such that for all $a \geq 1$, there is a set A in $\text{TIME}^{I}(a \cdot b \cdot n)$ that is not in $\text{TIME}^{I}(a \cdot n)$.

Proof. First define program diag informally:

```
read X;
Timebound := nil^(a·|X|);
Arg := cons X (cons X Timebound);
X := tu Arg;                (* Run X on X for up to a·|X| steps *)
if hd X then X := false else X := true;
write X
```

Claim: the set $A = \{d \mid [\![\text{diag}]\!]^{L}(d) = \text{true}\}$ is in $\text{TIME}^{I}(a \cdot b \cdot n)$ for an appropriate b, but is not in $\text{TIME}^{I}(a \cdot n)$. Further, b will be seen to be independent of a.

We now analyze the running time of program diag on input p. Since a is fixed, $\text{nil}^{a \cdot |d|}$ can be computed in time $c \cdot a \cdot |d|$ for some c and any d. We implicitly assume that command "Timebound := $\text{nil}^{a \cdot |X|}$" has been replaced by code to do this computation.

From Definition 19.2.2, there exists k such that the timed universal program tu of Theorem 19.2.4 runs in time $time_{\text{tu}}((\text{p.d.nil}^{n})) \leq k \cdot min(n, time_{\text{p}}(d))$. Thus the command "X := tu Arg" takes time at most

$$k \cdot min(a \cdot |p|, time_{\text{p}}(p)) \leq k \cdot a \cdot |p|$$

so on input p, program diag runs in time at most

$$c \cdot a \cdot |p| + k \cdot a \cdot |p| + e$$

where c is the constant factor used to compute $a \cdot |X|$, k is from the timed universal program, and e accounts for the time beyond computing Timebound and running tu. Now $|p| \geq 1$ so

$$c \cdot a \cdot |p| + k \cdot a \cdot |p| + e \leq a \cdot (c + k + e) \cdot |p|$$

which implies that $A \in \text{TIME}^{I}(a \cdot b \cdot n)$ with $b = c + k + e$.

Now suppose for the sake of contradiction that $A \in \text{TIME}^I(a \cdot n)$. Then there exists a program p which also decides membership in A, and does it quickly, satisfying $time_p(\text{d}) \leq a \cdot |\text{d}|$ for all $\text{d} \in \mathbb{D}$. Consider cases of $[\![\text{p}]\!](\text{p})$ (yet another diagonal argument). Then $time_p(\text{p}) \leq a \cdot |\text{p}|$ implies that tu has sufficient time to simulate p to completion on input p. By Definition 19.2.2, this implies

$$[\![\text{tu}]\!](\text{p.p.nil}^{a \cdot |\text{p}|}) = ([\![\text{p}]\!](\text{p}).\text{nil})$$

If $[\![\text{p}]\!](\text{p})$ is false, then $[\![\text{diag}]\!](\text{p}) = \text{true}$ by construction of diag. If $[\![\text{p}]\!](\text{p})$ is true, then $[\![\text{diag}]\!](\text{p}) = \text{false}$. Both cases contradict the assumption that p and diag both decide membership in A. The only unjustified assumption was that $A \in \text{TIME}^I(a \cdot n)$, so this must be false. □

Two open problems

1. Theorem 19.3.1 holds for the value $b = 201 + 48 = 249$. Can b be reduced still farther, perhaps even to $1 + \varepsilon$ for any $\varepsilon > 0$?
2. Does Theorem 19.3.1 hold for languages WHILE or GOTO?

The theorem's proof technique can be extended to the SRAM, although somewhat more complex programming is involved.

Theorem 19.3.2 For either the unit-cost or the logarithmic cost measure, there is a constant b such that for all $a \geq 1$, there is a decision problem A in $\text{TIME}^{\text{SRAM}}(a \cdot b \cdot n)$ that is not in $\text{TIME}^{\text{SRAM}}(a \cdot n)$.

Proof. Exercises 19.3 and 19.4.

19.4 A linear-time hierarchy for F

Theorem 19.4.1 The result of Theorem 19.3.1 holds for the one-variable, one-atom functional language F.

Proof. By Theorem 19.3.1 $\text{TIME}^I(a \cdot n) \subsetneq \text{TIME}^I(ab \cdot n)$ for all a. Using this and Lemma 18.3.2 we obtain a chain of inequalities:

$$\text{TIME}^F(a \cdot n) \subseteq \text{TIME}^I(ad \cdot n) \subsetneq \text{TIME}^I(abd \cdot n) \subseteq \text{TIME}^F(abcd \cdot n)$$

so the result holds with bcd in place of the b of Theorem 19.3.1. □

19.5   Hierarchy results for superlinear times

We showed earlier for languages I and F that within *linear* time bounds, increased time gives provably greater decision power. The proof technique involved diagonalization. In this section we carry the theme further, showing analogous results for other computation models, and for other time bounds. In particular we will look at *asymptotic complexity*, showing that when one functional time bound grows faster than another in the limit, there are problems solvable in the larger time bound but not in the smaller.

First, a slight generalization of the construction seen earlier.

Construction 19.5.1 Given an I-program b, define program diag as follows, where tu is the timed universal program of Lemma 19.2.4:

```
read X;
Timebound := b X;              (* Insert body of b here *)
Arg := cons X (cons X Timebound);
X := [[tu]](Arg);              (* run X on input X until it stops, *)
if X                  (* or until Timebound is reduced to nil *)
then X := false else X := true;
write X
```

Behavior   Suppose $[\![b]\!](d)$ always yields values of the form nil^m (as it always will in our applications). Then for any input $p \in \mathbb{D}$:

$$[\![\text{diag}]\!](p) = \begin{cases} \text{true} & \text{if } time_p(p) > |[\![b]\!](p)| \\ \text{false} & \text{if } time_p(p) \leq |[\![b]\!](p)| \text{ and } [\![p]\!](p) \neq \text{false} \\ \text{true} & \text{if } time_p(p) \leq |[\![b]\!](p)| \text{ and } [\![p]\!](p) = \text{false} \end{cases}$$

Time analysis   Let k be the interpretation and counting overhead incurred by the timed universal program tu, and e the time to perform the final test above. Then for any $p \in \mathbb{D}$

$$\begin{aligned} time_{\text{diag}}(p) &\leq \min(time_b(p) + k \cdot |[\![b]\!](p)| + e, time_p(p)) \\ &\leq time_b(p) + k \cdot |[\![b]\!](p)| + e \end{aligned}$$

For a time bound function $f(n)$ to be usable, it must be possible when given an input of size n to find out how much time $f(n)$ is available *by a computation not taking more than the order of $f(n)$ steps*. This is the intuitive content of the following restriction.

Definition 19.5.2 Function $f : \mathbb{N} \to \mathbb{N}$ is *time constructible* if there is a program b and a $c > 0$ such that for all $n \geq 0$

$$[\![b]\!](\texttt{nil}^n) = \texttt{nil}^{f(n)} \text{ and } time_b(d) \leq c \cdot f(n)$$

Many familiar monotone functions are time-constructible, e.g., all linear functions, all polynomials, and $f + g, f * g, f^g$ whenever f, g are time-constructible (Exercise19.8).

A more liberal definition is to let $[\![b]\!](\texttt{nil}^n)$ be the *binary* representation of $f(n)$. All the following works with this broader formulation; only small changes are necessary.

Theorem 19.5.3 If f is time-constructible and no $f(x) = 0$, then there exists $b > 0$ such that

$$\text{TIME}^{\text{I}}(bf) \backslash \text{TIME}^{\text{I}}(f) \neq \emptyset.$$

Proof. Suppose b and c are as in the definition of time-constructible, and let program diag be as in Construction 19.5.1. Then

$$time_{\texttt{diag}}(\texttt{p}) \leq c \cdot f(|\texttt{p}|) + k \cdot f(|\texttt{p}|) + e \leq (c + k + e) \cdot f(|\texttt{p}|)$$

so the set A decided by diag lies in $\text{TIME}((c + k + e)f)$.

Now suppose $A \in \text{TIME}(f)$. Then $[\![\texttt{diag}]\!] = [\![\texttt{p}]\!]$ for some program p satisfying $time_p(\texttt{d}) \leq f(|\texttt{d}|)$ for all $\texttt{d} \in \mathbb{D}$. Looking at diag's behaviour on input p, we see that Timebound is set to $\texttt{nil}^{f(|\texttt{p}|)}$, so the timed universal program tu has enough time to simulate p on p to completion. Consequently

$$[\![\texttt{p}]\!](\texttt{p}) = [\![\texttt{diag}]\!](\texttt{p}) = \begin{cases} \texttt{false} & \text{if } [\![\texttt{p}]\!](\texttt{p}) \neq \texttt{false} \\ \texttt{true} & \text{if } [\![\texttt{p}]\!](\texttt{p}) = \texttt{false} \end{cases}$$

This is a contradiction, which suffices to prove the theorem. □

Some traditional theorems

The following theorem generalizes Theorem 19.5.3, since the upper and lower time bounds f, g may be two quite different functions. Its proof uses the following small but central result, which is easy to prove for GOTO and holds for any other natural programming language.

Theorem 19.5.4 If functions f, g are time constructible, $f(n) \geq n, g(n) \geq n$ for all n, and $\lim_{n \to \infty} g(n)/f(n) = 0$, then $\text{TIME}^{\text{I}}(f) \backslash \text{TIME}^{\text{I}}(g) \neq \emptyset$.

Proof. This is very similar to the proof of Theorem 19.5.3, but needs the "padding lemma" 14.4.4.   □

Corollary 19.5.5 For any $\varepsilon > 0$ and integer $k > 0$, $\text{TIME}^{\text{I}}(\lambda n. n^{k+\varepsilon}) \backslash \text{TIME}^{\text{I}}(\lambda n. n^k) \neq \emptyset$.

The following can be proven directly by diagonal constructions similar to that of Theorem 19.5.3, though more complex since self-interpreters are less easy to write for languages TM or RAM than for GOTO. Alternatively, somewhat weaker versions may be proven using Theorem 19.5.4.

Theorem 19.5.6 If functions f, g are time constructible, $f(n) \geq n, g(n) \geq n$ for all n, and $\lim_{n \to \infty} f(n)/(g(n) \log g(n)) = \infty$ then $\text{TIME}^{\text{TM}}(f) \backslash \text{TIME}^{\text{TM}}(g) \neq \emptyset$.

Theorem 19.5.7 If functions f, g are time constructible, $f(n) \geq n, g(n) \geq n$ for all n, and $\lim_{n \to \infty} f(n)/g(n) = \infty$ then $\text{TIME}^{\text{SRAM}}(f) \backslash \text{TIME}^{\text{SRAM}}(g) \neq \emptyset$.

Exercises

19.1 Why can the proof method of Theorem 19.3.1 not be applied to WHILE or GOTO?   □

19.2 Prove that there are problems solvable by WHILE programs in time n^3 but not in time n^2.   □

19.3 Sketch the construction of a universal program for SRAM programs. This can store the program to be interpreted in odd memory locations, and can represent program memory cell *loc* in the interpreter's memory cell $2 \cdot loc$. Discuss its running time in relation to that of the interpreted program, under the unit-cost asumption.   □

19.4 For the interpreter of the previous exercise, consider a logarithmic cost which also accounts for the cost of instruction access. Thus all times are as in the table given before for SRAM instruction times, but with factor $\log \ell$ added to execute instruction in location ℓ.

Show that under this cost, the total interpretation time will be bounded by a program-independent constant times the interpreted program's running time.   □

19.5 Prove the unit-cost version of Theorem 19.3.2 from Exercise 19.3: that linear time SRAM-decidable sets possess an infinite hierarchy ordered by constant coefficients, as in Theorem 19.3.1.   □

19.6 Prove the logarithmic cost version of Theorem 19.3.2 from Exercise 19.4.   □

19.7 Prove that the following functions are time constructible:

1. $f(n) = an + b$, for non-negative integer constants a and b.
2. $f + g$, assuming that f, g are time constructible.
3. $f * g$, assuming that f, g are time constructible.
4. f^g, assuming that f, g are time constructible.   □

19.8 We say that a numeric function $f : \mathbb{N} \to \mathbb{N}$ is WHILE-computable if there is a WHILE program that computes $\text{nil}^{f(n)}$ given nil^n. Prove, that if f is WHILE computable then there is a function h such that $h(n) \geq f(n)$ for all n, and h is time constructible.   □

References

The earliest work on time-bounded hierarchies is from 1965, due to Hartmanis, Lewis and Stearns [61, 62]. The hierarchy result for linear time in the I language appeared in 1993 in [80]. Papers by Gurevich and Shelah, and by Schönhage contain related work [57, 151].

20 The Existence of Optimal Algorithms

(by A. M. Ben-Amram)

The previous chapter's hierarchy theorems (19.3.1, 19.4.1, 19.5.3) show that there exist programs whose running time cannot be improved beyond a constant multiplicative factor. We call such programs *optimal*[1].

These theorems construct, from *a given time bound* $T(n)$, a problem which is solvable by an optimal program with running time $cT(n)$ for some c and all n. In practice, however, we are typically given a *problem* that we wish to solve by computer, rather than a time bound. We attempt to write a program that will solve it as fast as possible. But how fast can a given problem be solved?

The branches of Computer Science that deal with such questions are *the design of efficient algorithms* and, on the negative side, *lower-bound theory*. (This book deals mainly with the hierarchy and completeness results underlying lower-bound theory.) In this chapter we consider what may be the most essential question to begin with: given a problem, does there necessarily exist a "fastest" algorithm to solve it? In other words, is the *goal* of algorithm design always well defined?

One of the major results in complexity theory, Blum's speedup theorem, shows that there exist problems for which this goal cannot be achieved. For every algorithm to solve such a problem, there is another one that is *significantly* faster. These problems are, however, artificially constructed to prove the theorem. It is therefore edifying to discover that for an important class of problems that occur in practice an optimal algorithm *does* exist: one whose time cannot be improved by more than a constant multiplicative factor. This result is known as Levin's theorem. In this chapter we formulate and prove, first Levin's theorem, and then Blum's theorem. We conclude with a theorem of a somewhat different flavour, known as the gap theorem. This theorem shows that the results of the hierarchy theorems depend on the time bound T being a "nice" (that is, time constructible) function: there exist functions t such that no program can be designed to have running time inside some large zone lying just above t.

Remarks: Levin's theorem exploits the existence of an efficient interpreter. All of these theorems can be proven in a general form that applies not only to running time but to

---

[1] Actually, "optimal up to a constant factor" would be a more precise description.

other reasonable computing resources, e.g., space. We do not go into details of this generalization here.

20.1   Levin's theorem

For $R \subseteq \mathbb{D} \times \mathbb{D}$ the *first projection* of R is the set

$$\pi_1 R = \{x \in \mathbb{D} \mid (\exists y \in \mathbb{D})(x,y) \in R\}$$

Definition 20.1.1 Let $R \subseteq \mathbb{D} \times \mathbb{D}$ be a semi-decidable predicate. A function $f : \mathbb{D} \to \mathbb{D}_\perp$ is called a *witness function for* R if $x \in \pi_1 R$ implies $(x, f(x)) \in R$.

For example, let SAT be the set of satisfiable propositional formulae; recall from section A.1.1 that $\mathrm{eval}\,\theta\mathcal{F}$ evaluates formula $\mathcal{F}$ for truth assignment θ. Let $R_{\mathrm{SAT}} = \{(\mathcal{F}, \theta) \mid \mathcal{F} \in \mathrm{SAT}, \mathrm{eval}\,\theta\mathcal{F} = true\}$. Then a witness function for R_{SAT} would be any function f that produces a satisfying assignment for a formula that has one, and produces any answer whatsoever (or loops) for an unsatisfiable one.

The reason that such an f is called a witness function is that problems like SAT are often considered as decision problems; for instance, in chapter 27 we will consider the problem of deciding membership in SAT. In this situation, the role of f is to witness that a formula is satisfiable. In practice, however, computing f will often be our actual goal, since we would not be content just with knowing that a solution (e.g. a satisfying assignment, a clique in the graph, etc.) exists.

Remark: if $[\![r]\!](d) = \perp$ we define $time_r(d) = \infty$.

Theorem 20.1.2 *Levin's theorem.*

Let $R \subseteq \mathbb{D} \times \mathbb{D}$ be a semi-decidable binary predicate, so $R = \mathrm{dom}([\![r]\!])$ for some program r. Then there is a WHILE program opt such that $[\![opt]\!]$ is a witness function for R, and for every program q that computes a witness function f for R, we have

$$time_{\mathrm{opt}}(x) \leq a_q(time_q(x) + time_r(x \cdot f(x)))$$

for all x, where a_q is a constant that depends on q but not on x. Further, the program opt can be effectively obtained from r.   □

Proof will be given later, after discussion of motivations and consequences.

A *brute-force search* program for finding a witness immediately comes to mind. Given $x \in \mathbb{D}$ we just enumerate elements $y \in \mathbb{D}$, checking one after the other until a witness pair

$(x, y) \in R$ has been found[2]. It is quite obvious that this strategy can yield an extremely inefficient program, since it may waste a lot of time on wrong candidates until it finds a witness. Levin's theorem states a surprising fact: for many interesting problems there is another brute-force search strategy that not only is efficient, but *optimal* up to constant factors. The difference is that Levin's strategy generates and tests not *solutions*, but *programs*.

Problems with easy witness checking.   A common situation with many problems is that verifying membership of a pair (x, y) in R (*checking a witness*) is relatively straight-forward, not withstanding that *producing* a witness might be difficult. For example, verifying membership in R_{SAT} amounts to evaluating $\theta(\mathcal{F})$; this can be done in linear time. On the other hand, finding a witness for $\mathcal{F}$ is at least as hard as just deciding whether the witness exists, a problem complete for NPTIME.

This situation holds for a great many problems. For example it has been open for many years whether SAT has any solution algorithm at all that runs in subexponential time. The beauty of Levin's theorem is that, even though no-one knows how fast (say) satisfiability can be decided, the construction nonethelss gives an algorithm for it that is *asymptotically optimal* (up to constant factors).

For Levin's theorem to be of interest, it suffices that we be able to check witnesses *efficiently enough* so that having the complexity of checking as a lower bound for witness-searching is acceptable. However, in many cases, it can actually be proved that searching for a witness cannot be done asymptotically faster than checking; for instance, this is obvious when checking takes linear time (as in the SAT example).

This is a quite general phenomenon, which led to formulation of the class NPTIME, also called NP (to be discussed at length in chapters 25 and 27). By definition, all problems in NPTIME can be soved by "guess-and-verify" algorithms, where both guessing and verification can be done in polynomial time. The *only* cause of superpolynomial time is that the number of possible guesses is typically exponential in the problem input size, and thus too large to enumerate.

A more sophisticated result that is relevant: by the version we saw of Kleene's normal form (Theorem 13.4.3), for any program p there is a predicate R, decidable in linear time, such that $R(x, y)$ is true if and only if y is the computation of p on input x. In this

---

[2]If R is decidable, this is straightforward by testing $(x, y) \in R$ for all finite binary trees y, using a loop as in Lemma 5.7.1 to enumerate them. If R is semi-decidable but not decidable, then one could use a "dovetailing" of computations as in Theorem 5.5.1 to test $(x, d_0) \in R?, (x, d_1) \in R?, \ldots$ in parallel.

case, finding a witness for x is exactly equivalent to running p on x, and so can have arbitrarily high complexity.

Ease of witness checking is captured in the following definition. (section A.3.11 explains the $o(\ )$ notation.)

Definition 20.1.3 We call a semi-decidable binary predicate R *easy to check* if there is a program r such that $R = \text{dom}([\![r]\!])$, and no witness function f can be computed (on input x) in $o(time_r(x.f(x)))$.   □

Suppose R is easy to check, and that program r satisfies Definition 20.1.3. Then program opt of Theorem 20.1.2 is asymptotically fastest (that is, up to a constant factor) among all programs that compute witnesses for R.

Proof of Levin's theorem

Proof. We make a simple, non-restrictive assumption on the program r: when run with input (x.y), if $(x,y) \in R$ it gives y as output. Otherwise, it loops forever.

Recall that the concrete syntax for I programs uses only the atom nil. Enumerate $\mathbb{D} = \{d_0, d_1, \ldots\}$ as in Lemma 5.7.1 by programs start and next. We build program opt from these parts (a concrete program will be given shortly):

1. A "main loop" to generate all finite trees. At each iteration one new tree is added to list $L = (d_n \ldots d_1 d_0)$. Tree d_n for $n = 0,1,2,\ldots$ will be treated as the command part of the n-th I program p_n.

2. Iteration n will process programs p_k for $k = n, n-1, \ldots, 1, 0$ as follows:

   (a) Run p_k on input x for a "time budget" of at most $b_k(n) = 2^{n-k}$ steps.

   (b) If p_k stops on x with output y, then run r on input (x.y), so p_k and r together have been executed for at most $b_k(n)$ steps.

   (c) If p_k or r failed to stop, then replace k by $k-1$, double the time budget to $b_{k-1}(n) = 2^{n-k+1}$ steps, and reiterate.

3. If running p_k followed by r terminates within time budget $b_k(n)$, then output $[\![\text{opt}]\!](x) = y$ and stop; else continue with iteration $n+1$.

Thus the programs are being interpreted concurrently, every one receiving some "interpretation effort." We stop once any one of these programs has both *solved our problem and been checked,* within its given time bounds. Note that opt will loop in case no witness is found.

The keys to "optimality" of opt are the efficiency of STEP, plus a policy of allocating time to the concurrent simulations so that the total time will not exceed, by more than a constant factor, the time of the program that finishes first. The following table showing the time budgets of the various runs may aid the reader in following the flow of the construction and correctness argument.

Time budget	p_0	p_1	p_2	p_3	p_4	p_5	...
$n = 0$	1	-	-	-	-	-	...
$n = 1$	2	1	-	-	-	-	...
$n = 2$	4	2	1	-	-	-	...
$n = 3$	8	4	2	1	-	-	...
$n = 4$	16	8	4	2	1	-	...
$n = 5$	32	16	8	4	2	1	...
$n = 6$	64	32	16	8	4	2	...
...	...						

We first argue that the abstract algorithm just given is correct, then give it in concrete program form, and finally analyze its time usage.

Correctness of the algorithm. Proving correctness of opt has two parts: showing that opt produces *only* witnesses, and that it produces a witness for *every* $x \in \pi_1 R$. First, if $[\![\text{opt}]\!](x) = y$ then $[\![r]\!](x . y)$ terminates, so $(x, y) \in R$. Thus every output of opt is a witness for its input.

Second, suppose $x \in \pi_1 R$. *Claim:* there is a pair (n, k) with $k \leq n$ such that

1. $\text{time}_{p_k}(x) \leq 2^{n-k}$; and
2. $\text{time}_{p_k}(x) + \text{time}_r(x . y) \leq 2^{n-k}$ where $y = [\![p_k]\!](x)$.

Proof of claim: since $x \in \pi_1 R$ there exists a pair $(x, y) \in R$. For this y, clearly $[\![r]\!](x . y)$ terminates. Choose any program p_k such that $y = [\![p_k]\!](x)$, and choose a value n large enough so that 1 and 2 hold.

The computation of $[\![\text{opt}]\!](x)$ stops at iteration n or before. This implies $[\![\text{opt}]\!](x) = [\![r]\!](x . y) = y$ and $(x, y) \in R$, so opt has a witness as output for every input $x \in \pi_1 R$.

```
read X; start;      (* Start enumeration of the d's         *)
Go := true;         (* Set up main loop (1)                  *)
while Go do         (* Iterate until (if) witness found      *)
{
  L1 := L;          (* Copy list  L = (dₙ ... d₁ d₀)         *)
  T := (nil);       (* Budget: time t = 2^(n−k) = 1 for k=n  *)

  while L1 do       (* Loop (2): set up to run pₖ on x       *)
  {
    Cd := hd L1; St := nil; Vl := X;
    T1 := T;        (* Copy time bound t                     *)

    while T1 do     (* 2(a): Run pₖ on x for t steps         *)
      {STEP; T1 := tl T1;}

    if Cd = nil     (* 2(b): If pₖ stopped on x in <= t steps *)
    then            (*       Prepare to run r on (x.y)       *)
      {Y := Vl;     (*       Save y := final variable value  *)
      Cd := r; St := nil; Vl := cons X Y;}

      while T1 and Cd do    (*     Run r on (x.y)            *)
        {STEP; T1 := tl T1;} (* for remaining steps          *)

      if Cd = nil (*       If r stopped on x in time left    *)
      then {L1 := nil; Go := false;}    (*     then stop!    *)

    if Go then      (* (2c): If pₖ or r failed to stop       *)
      {L1 := tl L1;(*       k := k-1                          *)
      T1 := T;      (*       Double time budget t := 2^(n−k) *)
      while T1 do
        {T1 := tl T1; T := cons nil T;}
      }                (* End of if Go                       *)
    next; L1 := cons New L1;
  }                 (* End of 2(a-b-c)                       *)
}                   (* End of loop (1); try n := n+1         *)
write Y
```

Figure 20.1: Program opt.

A program for opt. Let STEP be the WHILE macro used in Lemma 4.2.3 to execute an arbitrary I program. This uses variables Cd, St and Vl to contain the control stack, computation stack, and current value of the (unique) variable, respectively. By the proof of Proposition 4.1.1, any single step of the interpreted program is simulated by at most two applications of STEP.

Program opt is built from STEP and start, next of Lemma 5.7.1, and can be seen in Figure 20.1. The list of all elements of $\mathbb{D}$ considered to date is maintained in variable L, with a local copy L1. The time budget is maintained in variable T, with a local copy T1.

The main loop of the program is (1). During its n-th iteration, the inner loop (2) first applies STEP to simulate each program p_k on L1 on input x for 2^{n-k} steps.

Program opt stops once one of the programs yields an output y (loop (2a)), provided that value has been verified using r without overrunning the time budget (loop (2c)). Faithfulness to the informal algorithm above should be clear.

Time analysis of opt.   The following are easy to establish for $n > 0$. The phrase "simulation of p_k" includes running both p_k and subsequently r (Steps 2(a) and 2(b) above).

(1) The time for each iteration of the main loop, *outside* the code to simulate p_k by STEP or to double t, is bounded by $c_0 n$ where c_0 is a constant and n is the iteration number (cf. Exercises 5.11, 5.12).
(2) In iteration n, STEP is applied to $n + 1$ programs: $p_n, \ldots, p_1, p_0$.
(3) In iteration n, program p_k is simulated for a number of interpretation steps, no larger than 2^{n-k}.
(4) The total time to maintain time counter t is of the order of $1 + 2 + \ldots + 2^{n-k} = 2^{n-k+1} - 1$, thus $O(2^n)$.
(5) The total time for iteration n is bounded by the sum of the times for the p_k:

$$c_0 n + \sum_{k=0}^{n} c_1 2^{n-k} + c_2 2^n \leq c_3 2^n$$

for constants $c_0, \ldots, c_3$ and all n.
(6) The total time up to and including iteration n is bounded by $c_3 2^{n+1}$.

Another important fact has already been demonstrated in section 19.2 on "timed interpreters": if program q, followed by program r, terminates within time t, then $2t$ invocations of STEP are enough to bring the interpretation to completion.

Now let x be the input to opt, and suppose that a program q computes a witness y for x. Thus, running q followed by r will yield the output y in time

$$t_{q;r}(x) = time_q(x) + time_r(x \cdot y)$$

Sure enough, q appears somewhere in the enumeration of all I programs; say $q = p_k$. Choose n so that

$$2^{n-k} \leq 2t_{q;r}(x) < 2^{n+1-k}$$

If program opt reaches iteration n and simulates $q = p_k$ on x, it will have enough time to simulate both q and r to completion. The effect is that opt will yield its result within time

$$time_{opt}(x) \leq c_3 2^{n+1} \leq c_3 2^{k+1} 2^{n-k} \leq c_3 2^{k+2} t_{q;r}(x)$$

The other possibility is that program opt has already stopped earlier and so does not reach iteration $n+1$ to simulate $q = p_k$ on x because another simulated program was successfully completed and checked. In this case $time_{opt}(x)$ is even smaller.

We conclude that $time_{opt}(x) \leq c_3 2^{k+2} t_{q;r}(x)$. Since 2^{k+2} is a constant that depends only on q, the proof is complete.   □

Final remarks.   Levin's theorem shows, that for a large class of important problems, we can obtain an "optimal" program with only the effort of devising a solution checker. This is obviously a tremendous reduction of the effort in developing programs for many practical problems. However, this is also an example of how important it is to observe that a constant factor is program-dependent. Program opt is slower than program p_k by the factor $c_3 2^{k+2}$. Note that k is the number in the enumeration of the program p_k. If our problem is indeed complicated, we can expect even the smallest program that solves it to be quite large; if it appears at, say, position p_{1000}, then opt will be slower by $c_3 \cdot 2^{1002}$. Conclusions:

- Assuming that checking a solution is indeed easy (as often happens), the only achievement that can be claimed by the hard-working algorithm developer is a saving on the constant factor!
- "there is no free lunch": since the constant factor is enormous, there is still point in spending energy on devising programs to solve problems directly.

20.2   Functions arbitrarily hard to compute

Blum's speedup theorem involves two techniques: a diagonalization argument more subtle than that seen before in Theorem 5.3.1; and a search process executing programs under a time budget, similar to that used in proving Levin's theorem. Before proving Blum's result, we establish a simpler result that uses the same sort of diagonalization.

We define the following simplifying framework for the proof, only considering input of the form $\texttt{nil}^n$. A program accepts a set of integers, in the sense that it program accepts n if it outputs a non-$\texttt{nil}$ value for input $\texttt{nil}^n$. The time complexity of program p, then, can be expressed as a function on $\mathbb{N}$, namely $t_\mathrm{p}(n) = time_\mathrm{p}(\texttt{nil}^n)$.

On diagonalization.   In chapter 19 we used diagonalization to prove the hierarchy theorem. In this chapter we use diagonalization in a slightly more involved manner, so it may be useful to present first a general form of the diagonalization argument.

Let Q be a set of programs. We wish to construct a program p and ensure that $\mathrm{p} \notin Q$. We construct p so $[\![\mathrm{p}]\!] \neq [\![\mathrm{q}]\!]$ for all $\mathrm{q} \in Q$. More explicitly, p will be built so for every $\mathrm{q} \in Q$ there is at least one input d such that $[\![\mathrm{p}]\!](\mathrm{d})$ differs from $[\![\mathrm{q}]\!](\mathrm{d})$.

Such a q will be said to have been "killed." We construct p so every $\mathrm{q} \in Q$ will be "killed" at some stage during p's computations, thus making $\mathrm{p} \in Q$ impossible. This is done by inverting q's output for some input d, so $[\![\mathrm{p}]\!](\mathrm{d}) = \texttt{true}$ if $[\![\mathrm{q}]\!](\mathrm{d}) = \texttt{false}$ and $\texttt{false}$ otherwise.

The following shows that there exist problems arbitrarily hard to solve, no matter what algorithm is used. The result is stronger than Theorem 19.3.1 since the lower bound on run time applies to all but finitely many inputs.

Theorem 20.2.1 For every total recursive function $g : \mathbb{N} \to \mathbb{N}$ there exists a total recursive $f : \mathbb{N} \to \{\texttt{true}, \texttt{false}\}$ such that if $f = [\![\mathrm{p}]\!]$ for any program p, then $t_\mathrm{p}(n) > g(n)$ for all but finitely many $n \in \mathbb{N}$.   □

Proof.   The proof uses some ideas from the proof of Levin's theorem 20.1.2. We assume that the reader is familiar with this, and now just give a sketch. Let p_0, $\mathrm{p}_1, \mathrm{p}_2, \ldots$ enumerate all I-programs. Program p_k can be generated by code $\texttt{start}$; $\texttt{next}; \ldots;$ $\texttt{next}$ with k occurrences of $\texttt{next}$ (as in the proof of Levin's theorem).

Call program p "quick on m" if $t_\mathrm{p}(m) \leq g(m)$. Our goal is to find a function f such that $f = \mathrm{p}$ implies $\mathrm{p} \notin Q$, where Q is the set of programs that are quick on infinitely many inputs. This is done progressively. The value of any $f(n)$ is computed in stages: for each $m = 0, 1, 2, \ldots, n$ we construct two sets

$$
\begin{aligned}
\texttt{Dead}_m \quad &= \quad \text{Those programs } \mathrm{p}_k \text{ that have been "killed" so far} \\
\texttt{Quick}_m \quad &= \quad \text{All programs } \mathrm{p}_k \text{ with } k \leq m \text{ that are not in } \texttt{Dead}_{m-1} \\
&\qquad \text{and are "quick" on } m
\end{aligned}
$$

```
    read n;
    Dead  := ∅;                (* Programs that have been killed    *)
    for m := 0 to n do         (* Compute f(0),...,f(n)             *)
       Quick := ∅;             (* Programs that run with time <= g  *)
       for k := 0 to m do      (* Iterate on different inputs       *)
         if k ∉ Dead and t_{p_k}(m) ≤ g(m)   (* Collect unkilled pgms   *)
         then Quick := Quick ∪ {k};          (* quick on input m        *)
       if Quick ≠ ∅                          (* Now compute f(m)        *)
       then k := the smallest index in Quick;
              Dead  := Dead ∪ {k};
              Quick := Quick \ {k};
              Answer := ¬[[p_k]](m)           (* The value of f(m)       *)
       else Answer := true;
    (* End of all the loops *)

    write Answer
```

Figure 20.2: A function that is hard to compute.

The set sequences will be monotone: $r \leq s$ implies $\text{Dead}_r \subseteq \text{Dead}_s$ and $\text{Dead}_r \cup \text{Quick}_r \subseteq \text{Dead}_s \cup \text{Quick}_s$.

The value of $f(n)$ will be made different from $p_k(n)$ where k is the smallest index in Quick_n, assuming this set is nonempty. Function f is (by definition) computed by the program of Figure 20.2. This program reads n, then computes $\text{Dead}_i, \text{Quick}_i, f(i)$ in turn for $i = 0, 1, \ldots, n$, and finally writes $f(n)$. It is evident that f is total.

In the program (which omits the subscripts on Quick and Dead) any index k such that $t_{p_k}(m) \leq g(m)$ for some value $k \leq m \leq n$ will be entered into Quick, unless already in Dead.

For each n, the value of $f(n)$ is defined so as to make $f \neq [[p_k]]$ for a new p_k in Quick. (This happens provided Quick is nonempty, which will occur infinitely often.) When program p_k has been killed, it is removed from the set Quick and placed in set Dead.

Suppose now that $f = p_r$. By construction $[[p_k]] \neq f$ for every element k put into Dead, so r is not in any set Dead_m. Suppose further that program p_r is fast on infinitely many inputs. Then it is also fast on infinitely many inputs $n_0, n_1, \ldots$ larger than r (see Figure 20.3 for a pictorial representation). For every one of these of these, r will be entered into Quick_{n_i} (since r is not in Dead_{n_i}). Eventually r will be the smallest index in some Quick_{n_i}, at which point it will be added to Dead_{n_i}. A contradiction arises because of the

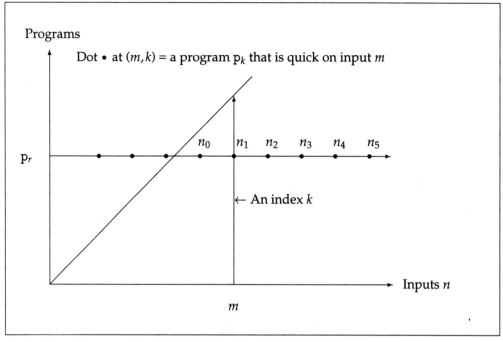

Figure 20.3: Program p_r is quick infinitely often.

assumption that $f = [\![p_r]\!]$:

$$f(n_i) = \texttt{Answer} = \neg[\![p_r]\!](n_i) = \neg f(n_i)$$

$\square$

20.3 Blum's speedup theorem

Theorem 20.3.1 For any total recursive function h there exists a total recursive function f such that for any program p computing f, there is another program p' such that $f = [\![p]\!] = [\![p']\!]$, and for all but finitely many $d \in \mathbb{D}$

$$time_p(d) \geq h(time_{p'}(d))$$

To appreciate the significance of this theorem, let h be a "fast growing" function such as 2^n. The theorem says that there is a function f such that, for every program p_0 you choose for computing f, there is an infinite sequence of programs $p_1, p_2, \ldots$ which all compute f, and such that *every* p_{i+1} is exponentially faster than p_i for all but finitely many inputs. Interestingly, the proof shows the *existence* of these programs, but it can also be shown that there is no algorithm which can construct a p_{i+1} from p_i.

Proof. The proof of Blum's theorem uses some ideas from the proof of Levin's theorem 20.1.2 and some from Theorem 20.2.1. We assume that the reader is familiar with them, and now just give a sketch.

We further assume the "speedup" function h to be time-constructible. This is no loss of generality, since a time-constructible function always exists "above" h (see Exercise 19.8). Further, we assume that $h(n) \geq 2n$ for all n, and h is monotone. We let $h^{(k)}(x) = h(h(\ldots h(x) \ldots))$ with k applications (and $h^{(0)}(x) = x$).

We now describe a "diagonalizing" program blum and define $f = [\![\texttt{blum}]\!]$. In the construction below, we use the STEP macro to simulate programs concurrently in the manner of section 20.1, with two modifications.

First, the checking phase using the program r is irrelevant to the current construction. Secondly, we modify the computation of the *number of steps t*. In the proof of Theorem 20.1.2, t began at 1 and was doubled after every round of simulation, so that on iteration n, we performed 2^{n-k} interpretation steps on behalf of p_k. In the current construction, t will be replaced at the end of each round by $h(t)$, so p_k is interpreted for $h^{(n-k)}$ steps.

On input n, the main task of program blum is to compute a set $\text{Dead}_n \subseteq \{0, 1, 2, \ldots, n\}$. By computing a set we mean, creating a list of its elements (in $\texttt{nil}^i$ notation). Note that checking whether k is in the set, using this representation, takes $O(n^2)$ time.

Computation of Dead_n. If $n = 0$, Dead_n is empty. For $n > 0$ compute Dead_{n-1} first. Next, perform precisely n iterations of the following generate-and-simulate loop. During the loop, we maintain a list Quick_n of programs to be "killed". Initially Quick_n is empty. Iteration m will process programs p_k for $k = m, m-1, \ldots, 1, 0$ as follows:

1. Run p_k on input m for a "time budget" of at most $t = h^{(m-k)}(1)$ steps.
2. If $k \notin \text{Dead}_{n-1}$ and p_k stops on m with output y, then add k to Quick_n.
3. Replace k by $k - 1$, and change the time budget to $t := h(t) = h^{(m-(k-1))}(1)$ steps.

Once n iterations have been completed, we define Dead_n as follows: if list Quick_n is empty, $\text{Dead}_n = \text{Dead}_{n-1}$. If it is not, Dead_n is Dead_{n-1} plus the lowest index that appears on Quick_n (note that it is necessarily not in Dead_{n-1}).

```
read n;
Dead   := ∅;               (* Programs that have been killed      *)
for m := 0 to n do         (* Compute f(0),...,f(n)               *)
   Quick := ∅;             (* Programs to be killed               *)
   T := 1;                 (* Time budget t = h^(m-k)(1) for k = m *)
   for k := m, m-1,...,0 do       (* Iterate on different inputs *)
      if k ∉ Dead and t_{p_k}(m) ≤ T   (* Collect unkilled pgms     *)
      then Quick := Quick ∪ {k};    (* that stopped in time       *)
      T := h(T);           (* Increase time budget and decrease k *)
   if Quick ≠ ∅            (* Now compute f(m)                    *)
   then k := the smallest index in Quick;
        Answer := ¬⟦p_k⟧(m); (* The value of f(m)                 *)
        Dead   := Dead ∪ {k};
        Quick  := Quick \ {k}
   else Answer := true;
(* End of all the loops *)

write Answer
```

Figure 20.4: A program to compute Blum's function.

Completion of the program.   The program is completed by removing from Quick_n the smallest index k, and "killing" program p_k by setting the output of blum to true if p_k on input n yields false, and false otherwise. Figure 20.4 contains this algorithm in program form.

Time analysis.   Clearly $h^{(k)}(1) \geq 2^k$. Thus the "budget" for p_k in iteration n is $b_k(n) = h^{(n-k)}(1)$.

Claim 1: Let p be *any* I program such that $\llbracket p \rrbracket = \llbracket \text{blum} \rrbracket$. Then $(\exists k)\, t_p(n) > b_k(n)$ for all but finitely many n.

Proof: Since the enumeration p_i includes all I programs, there is a k so that $p = p_k$. Assume to the contrary that $t_p(n) \leq b_k(n)$ for infinitely many values of n. In particular, infinitely many such values are larger than k. For each such value, the generate-and-simulate loop will generate p and find that it terminates within its budget of $b_k(n)$ steps. Hence it will put it on Quick (unless it has been killed already). Since for every n, the lowest index on Quick is killed, k will eventually be killed. This contradicts the hypothesis that $\llbracket p \rrbracket = \llbracket \text{blum} \rrbracket$.

Claim 2: The running time of the iteration that computes Dead_n from Dead_{n-1} is bounded by $c_2 h^{(n+1)}(1)$ where c_2 is a constant.

Proof: This is rather similar to the analysis for Levin's theorem. It is straightforward from the estimations already performed, since we used the generate-and-simulate loop, and only added the effort of lookup in Dead for programs that terminate; this effort takes at most $O(n^3)$ time, which (due to the growth rate of h) is bounded by $c_1 h^{(n+1)}(1)$ for an appropriate constant c_1.

Claim 3: For every $k \geq 0$ there is a program blum_k such that $[\![\text{blum}_k]\!] = [\![\text{blum}]\!]$ and $t_{\text{blum}_k}(n) \leq h^{(n-k-1)}(1)$, for all but finitely many n.

Proof: Let $k_0 = k + \lceil \log c_2 \rceil + 3$. Let n_0 be a value of n such that no program among $\text{p}_0, \text{p}_1, \text{p}_2, \ldots, \text{p}_{k_0}$ is killed for $n > n_0$ (observe that such an n_0 always exists). Program blum_k is a "shortcut" version of program blum, that skips the computation of $\text{Dead}_0, \text{Dead}_1, \ldots, \text{Dead}_{n_0}$. Instead, it has Dead_{n_0} initialized as a quoted constant. This actually only helps if the input n is larger than n_0; for $n \leq n_0$ the program does the same as blum. However for larger n the time of computing Dead_{n_0} is saved.

Also, in the generate-and-simulate loops for $n_0 + 1, n_0 + 2, \ldots, n$ it is not necessary to simulate p_j for any $j \leq k_0$ (this follows from the definition of n_0). We next compute the running time of blum_k for $n > n_0$.

A simple modification of Claim 2 above shows that the iteration that computes Dead_n from Dead_{n-1} now runs in time $c_2 h^{(n+1-k_0)}(1)$. Summing over the iterations for $\text{Dead}_{n_0+1}, \text{Dead}_{n_0+2}, \ldots, \text{Dead}_n$ we obtain the bound:

$$
\begin{aligned}
c_2 \sum_{i=n_0+1}^{n} h^{(n+1-k_0)}(1) \ &\leq \ c_2 h^{(n+2-k_0)}(1) \\
&\leq \ 2^{k_0-k-3} h^{(n+2-k_0)}(1) \\
&\leq \ h^{(k_0-k-3)}\left(h^{(n+2-k_0)}(1)\right) \leq h^{(n-k-1)}(1)
\end{aligned}
$$

This completes the proof of the claim.

We are ready to complete the proof of Theorem 20.3.1 (modulo the simplifying framework). Let $\text{p} = \text{p}_k$ be an arbitrary program such that $[\![\text{p}]\!] = [\![\text{blum}]\!]$. Using Claim 3 we obtain a program blum_k such that $[\![\text{blum}_k]\!] = [\![\text{p}]\!]$, and for all but finitely many values of n,

$$
t_{\text{blum}_k}(n) \leq h^{(n-k-1)}(1)
$$

On the other hand, by Claim 1,

$$
t_{\text{p}}(n) > b_k(n) = h^{(n-k)}(1)
$$

Combining the last two inequalities and using monotonicity of h, we get

$$t_{\mathtt{p}}(n) > h(t_{\mathtt{blum}_k}(n))$$

and the proof is complete. □

20.4   The gap theorem

The gap theorem shows that for an arbitrarily chosen computable increase in time bounds, there exist functions such that applying the increase to the bound does not enlarge the class of decidable problems (in sharp contrast to the hierarchy results of the last chapter). The theorem provides such a function that satisfies a pair of conditions, one an arbitrarily chosen computable lower time bound g and another, h, that defines the amount of increase to be applied.

Theorem 20.4.1 *the gap theorem.* For any (arbitrarily large) total recursive functions $g : \mathbb{D} \to \mathbb{N}$ and $h : \mathbb{N} \to \mathbb{N}$ such that $(\forall n)\, h(n) \geq n$, there is a total recursive function $t : \mathbb{D} \to \mathbb{N}$ such that $(\forall \mathtt{d})\, t(\mathtt{d}) \geq g(\mathtt{d})$ and for every I program p we have

$$time_{\mathtt{p}}(\mathtt{d}) \leq h(t(\mathtt{d})) \Longrightarrow time_{\mathtt{p}}(\mathtt{d}) \leq t(\mathtt{d})$$

for all but finitely many values d.

Thus, time bound $h \circ t$ is not "stronger" than t when infinitely many inputs are considered. Note that by the assumption on h, we have $h \circ t \geq t$, so the statement is significant. We say that there is a *complexity gap* between t and $h \circ t$.

Proof. First define a macro TEST that accepts as input a tree variable X and an integer-valued variable N, and gives a Boolean result. Macro TEST generates I programs $\mathtt{p}_1, \mathtt{p}_2, \ldots, \mathtt{p}_j$ until $\mathtt{p}_j = \mathtt{X}$ (this will happen because our enumeration process generates all trees). Using the timed interpreter from the previous chapter, TEST runs each generated program for at most $h(N)$ steps on X. If any of these programs terminates within s steps where $N < s \leq h(N)$ the result of TEST is $\mathtt{false}$. Otherwise it's $\mathtt{true}$.

We now use the macro TEST to write a program that computes a function $t : \mathbb{D} \to \mathbb{N}$. On input X, the program computes $n = g(\mathtt{X})$, then repeatedly applies TEST to X and $N = n, n+1, n+2, \ldots$ until $\mathtt{true}$ is obtained. The result, $t(\mathtt{X})$, is the last value of N. We claim that function t is total, and satisfies the theorem.

Proving that t is total amounts to showing that the loop in the program will always terminate, i.e., that TEST eventually yields $\mathtt{true}$. To this end, note that all the calls to

TEST run the same set of programs on the same input, X. Among these programs, some may terminate on input X, while others do not. Let τ be the largest number of steps that a program that does terminate takes to do so. Then unless the loop stops for some $N \leq \tau$, it will surely stop for $N = \tau + 1$ (the reader may care to verify this).

To prove that t satisfies the theorem, suppose that for some program p, $time_p(\mathrm{d}) \leq h(t(\mathrm{d}))$. Suppose that $\mathrm{p} = \mathrm{d}$ or appears before d in the enumeration of trees; then p is among the programs enumerated by TEST in computing $t(\mathrm{d})$. Note that $t(\mathrm{d})$ is defined as a value of N for which TEST yields `true`. This means, that $time_p(\mathrm{d}) \leq t(\mathrm{d})$, for otherwise TEST would have yielded `false`.

We conclude, that $time_p(\mathrm{d}) \leq h(t(\mathrm{d})) \implies time_p(\mathrm{d}) \leq t(\mathrm{d})$, except possibly if p appears later than d in the enumeration of trees. But this case applies to finitely many d. □
The statement of the gap theorem would not be very surprising if, when we relate the time bound $t(\mathrm{d})$ to the size of d, we find that t does not grow monotonically with $|\mathrm{d}|$ but keeps oscillating up and down. For then $h \circ t$ would also be such an oscillating function, and why would any program have a running time that is "sandwiched" between such strange bounds? Actually the gap feature is not restricted to such functions. Exercise 20.8 shows, that the theorem can be modified to guarantee that t is monotone increasing in $|\mathrm{d}|$.

Another natural question to ask is, where do we find these strange time bounds? For instance, could they be polynomial? Versions of the gap theorem that describe the growth rate of the function t have been proven, but are beyond the scope of our book. However, exercise 20.9 gives an illustration of the fact, that these functions would in general be very fast-growing.

Exercises

20.1 The proof of Levin's theorem assumes program q to be coded in language I, while opt is a WHILE program. Explain why this discrepancy does not affect the result. □

20.2 * What is the space complexity of opt? In particular, how does it relate to the space consumption of a given program q for the problem in question? □

20.3 Suppose we change every "semi-decidable" in Levin's theorem to "decidable," and require r to halt on every input, with some appropriate convention to signal whether the checking was successful or not. Would then opt halt always? □

20.4 Prove a version of Levin's theorem for space complexity (it suffices to explain the differences from the given proof). □

20.5 Give an upper bound on the time required to compute function f in Theorem 20.2.1. □

20.6 * Extend the proof of Blum's theorem to cover arbitrary inputs. □

20.7 section 20.3 claimed that Blum's theorem establishes the existence of a faster program p′, but there is no algorithm to construct it, given p. However, from the proof of the theorem we know that $\texttt{blum}_{k+1}$ is that faster program. Why doesn't the proof imply an algorithm to obtain the faster program? In other words, why is the construction of $\texttt{blum}_{k+1}$ not effective? □

20.8 Modify the proof of Theorem 20.4.1 to ensure that function t will increase when $|\mathsf{d}|$ is increased. □

20.9 * Let us restrict attention to time bounds which only depend on the size of the input, $t(\mathsf{d}) = f(|\mathsf{d}|)$. Demonstrate that for some constant $a > 0$, it is not possible to find such a time bound t such that there is a "gap" between t and at, and $0 < f(n) \leq n^2$. *Hint*: Design a program p_1 such that for every odd n and $0 < i \leq n$

$$(\exists \mathsf{d})\, i < time_{\mathsf{p}_1}(\mathsf{d}) \leq ai$$

for an appropriate constant a. Design another program p_2 whose time similarly lies between in and ain. Show, that for t, f as above, and for infinitely many inputs, one of these programs will have its running time inside the intended "gap." *Remark*: It is actually possible to generalize this result to any polynomial function of n (instead of n^2). □

References

Levin's theorem has been presented in a form quite similar to the above in an article by Gurevich [56]. This is rather different from (and simpler than) the original Russian article [102, 100].

Blum's speedup theorem is from [13]. The gap theorem is attributed to two independent works, [15] and [159]. Both theorems can be found, together with an assortment of related results, in [165].

The fields of designing efficient algorithms and of proving lower bounds for computational problems have been the issue of extensive literature, for example [2, 96] and numerous more recent publications.

21 Space-bounded Computations

We have hitherto emphasized computation *time*. There is a similar but somewhat different way to classify problems according to how much *memory space* is required to solve them. For simplicity of exposition we limit ourselves to imperative languages in which a computation is a linear sequence of states, i.e., all the languages seen so far except the functional language F^1.

For the computation models of chapter 7 the input is contained in the initial store, which *always* has length at least $|d|$, i.e., space linear in the size of the input. In other words, there are no problems solvable in sublinear space in the models given earlier.

In general (see Theorem 21.5.2), linear space decidable sets can take exponential time to decide; and no better bound is known. This time bound is intractable, i.e., well beyond that of practically usable algorithms, and thus motivates a study of space bounds that are small enough to give running times closer to practical interest, and so smaller than $|d|$, the length of the input.

A solution to this problem is to use "offline" models that allow only *read-only* access to an input value d and, when measuring program space consumption, to count only the "workspace" that is used beyond the input length. (This is intuitively reasonable, since read-only input will remain unchanged during the entire computation.) For the moment we are only interested in decision problems expressible by a yes-no answer, and not in computation of functions.

In order to study space-bounded computations, we will equip Turing, counter, or random access machines with a *read-only input*, instead of the earlier device of incorporating the program input value into its initial state. A motivation is that it will become possible to analyse computations in *sublinear space*, i.e., using space smaller than the size of the program input, thus bringing space-limited computation nearer practically interesting problems than before.

The models will later be extended to allow output as well. This will be *write-only*, symmetric with the read-only restriction on input, in order to maintain the separation of work storage from storage used for input-ouput data. Classes of functions computable in limited space analogous to the above time-bounded decidable classes will turn out to be quite useful for investigating *complete*, i.e., hardest problems for the various com-

---

[1]Functional languages can also be classified spacewise, but require more subtle definitions because of implicit space usage caused by recursion.

plexity classes. Of special use will be those computable in *logarithmic space*.

21.1 Space-bounded computation models

21.1.1 Space measures for imperative machine models

The following is to be regarded as a generic definition, parametrized by the definition of state space or size used for the various machine types. Precise definitions of these will be given shortly.

Definition 21.1.1 Let $p = 1 : I_1 \ldots m : I_m$ be any imperative program in some language L, and let $p \vdash s_1 \to s_2 \to \ldots \to s_t$ be a terminating computation with $s_1 = (1, Readin(d))$ for some input value $d \in L-values$. Then by definition (parametrized on the length $|s|$ of a state s):

$$space_p^L(d) = \max\{|s_1|, |s_2|, \ldots, |s_t|\}$$

Turing machine space usage is the standard used to define space-bounded computation. First, we define this for the multitape Turing machines seen earlier in section 7.3.

Definition 21.1.2 Let p be a k-tape Turing machine program. We define the *length of a state* $s = (\ell, \sigma)$, where ℓ is the instruction counter and $\sigma = (L_1 \underline{S}_1 R_1, \ldots, L_k \underline{S}_k R_k)$ is a k-tuple of tapes, to be

$$|s| = \max(|L_1 \underline{S}_1 R_1|, |L_2 \underline{S}_2 R_2|, \ldots, |L_k \underline{S}_k R_k|)$$

$\square$

21.1.2 Some read-only machine models and their space or size usage

The read-only Turing machine variant has *read-only* access to its input d. Further, only the "workspace" that is used beyond the input data will be counted. (This is intuitively reasonable, since read-only input will remain unchanged during the entire computation.)

Definition 21.1.3 A *read-only Turing machine* TMro is a two-tape Turing machine whose input is a string d in $\{0,1\}^*$. Its instructions are as follows, where subscript $u = 1$ indicates that the two-way read-only *input tape* 1 is involved; or $u = 2$ indicates that the two-way read-write *work tape* 2 is involved. Instruction syntax is as follows:

Tape 1: $I ::= $ $\text{right}_1 \mid \text{left}_1 \mid \text{if}_1$ S goto ℓ else ℓ'

Tape 2: $I ::= $ $\text{right}_2 \mid \text{left}_2 \mid \text{if}_2$ S goto ℓ else $\ell' \mid \text{write}_2$ S

Symbols: $S ::= $ $0 \mid 1 \mid B$

A tape together with its scanning position will be written as $\ldots BL_1\underline{S}_1R_1B\ldots$, where the underline indicates the scanned position. We assume the program never attempts to move right or left beyond the blanks that delimit the input, unless a nonblank symbol has first been written[2].

We define the *length of a read-only TMro state* $s = (\ell, \sigma)$, where ℓ is the instruction counter and $\sigma = (\ldots BL_1\underline{S}_1R_1B\ldots, \ldots BL_2\underline{S}_2R_2B\ldots)$, to be $|s| = |L_2S_2R_2|$, formally expressing that only the symbols on "work" tape 2 are counted, and not those on tape 1.

$\square$

Definition 21.1.4 A *read-only* counter machine CMro is a register machine whose input is a string d in $\{0,1\}^*$. Input access is by instruction if $\text{In}_{Ci} = 0$ goto ℓ else ℓ', which tests symbol a_k in input $d = a_1 a_2 \ldots a_n$ indirectly: index k is the value of counter Ci. Data initialization sets counter C0 to n, giving the program a way to "know" how long its input is.

$$I \quad ::= \quad Ci := Ci + 1 \mid Ci := Ci \doteq 1 \mid Ci := Cj$$
$$\mid \quad \text{if } Ci = 0 \text{ goto } \ell \text{ else } \ell' \mid \text{if } \text{In}_{Ci} = 0 \text{ goto } \ell \text{ else } \ell'$$

Storage has form CMro-*store* $= (d, \sigma) \in \{0,1\}^* \times \{\, \sigma \mid \sigma : \mathbb{N} \to \mathbb{N}\}$ where d is the input data and $\sigma(i)$ is the current contents of counter Ci for any $i \in \mathbb{N}$. The counter values σ are initialized to zero except for C0: initially,

$$\sigma = [0 \mapsto |d|, 1 \mapsto 0, 2 \mapsto 0, \ldots]$$

A state has form $s = (\ell, (d, \sigma)) = a_1 a_2 \ldots a_n$, where ℓ is the instruction counter. The effect of instruction execution is as expected from the syntax, plus definition of the effect of instruction if $\text{In}_{Ci} = 0$ goto ℓ else ℓ'. Informally: if $1 \leq i \leq n$ and $a_{\sigma(i)} = 0$ then control is transferred to $I_{\ell'}$, else to $I_{\ell''}$.

We define the *space of a read-only* CMro state $s = (\ell, (d, \sigma))$ to be

$$|s| = \sum_{\sigma(i) \neq 0} \log(\sigma(i))$$

---

[2]This condition simplifies constructions, and causes no loss of generality in computational power, or in time beyond a constant factor.

where $\log v$ is the number of bits required to represent v. This formally expresses that only the space usage of nonempty registers (measured in bits) is counted.   □

Remark: this differs slightly from the counter machines seen earlier in section 7.4, in that input is a bit string instead of a number. The difference is easily reconciled by using the isomorphism c_N between numbers and trees in $\mathbb{D}$ as defined in section 8.3.2.

21.1.3   Comparing ordinary and read-only machines

The following easily proven propositions assert that, as far as space usage is concerned, multiple tapes are only essential when considering computations that use space less than the length of the input.

Proposition 21.1.5 For any k-tape Turing machine p such that $space_p^{TM}(d) \geq |d|$ for any input d, there exists a 1-tape Turing machine q with $[\![p]\!]^{TM} = [\![q]\!]^{TM}$ and a constant a such that $space_q^{TM}(d) \leq a \cdot space_p^{TM}(d)$ for any input d.

Corollary 21.1.6 If p is a read-only Turing machine such that $space_p^{TMro}(d) \geq |d|$ for all inputs d, there is a 1-tape Turing machine q with $[\![p]\!]^{TMro} = [\![q]\!]^{TM}$, and a constant a such that $space_q^{TM}(d) \leq a \cdot space_p^{TMro}(d)$ for any input $d \in \{0,1\}^*$.

Proof. Exercises 21.1 and 21.2.   □

Essentially the same results hold for counter machines, except that we must take account of the isomorphism $c_N : \mathbb{N} \rightarrow \{0,1\}^*$. Hints for the straightfoward proofs are give in Exercises 21.3, 21.4.

Proposition 21.1.7 For any counter machine p as in section 7.4 there exists a read-only counter machine q and a constant a such that for any input $v \in \mathbb{N}$:

$$[\![q]\!]^{CMro}(c_N(v)) = c_N([\![p]\!]^{CM}(v)) \text{ and } space_q^{CMro}(c_N(v)) \leq a \cdot space_p^{CM}(v)$$

Proposition 21.1.8 For any read-only counter machine p such that $space_p^{CMro}(d) \geq |d|$ for any input d, there exists a counter machine q as in section 7.4 and a constant a such that for any input $v \in \mathbb{N}$:

$$c_N([\![q]\!]^{CM}(v)) = [\![p]\!]^{CMro}(c_N(v)) \text{ and } space_q^{CM}(v) \leq a \cdot space_p^{CMro}(c_N(v))$$

21.1.4   Space-bounded classes of programs and problems

Definition 21.1.9 Given programming language L and a total function $f : \mathbb{N} \to \mathbb{N}$, we define classes of *space-bounded programs* by

1. $L^{space(f)} = \{p \in L\text{-}program \mid space^L_p(d) \leq f(|d|) \text{ for all } d \in L\text{-}data\}$

2. $L^{logspace} = \bigcup_{k=0}^{\infty} L^{space(\lambda n . k \log n)}$

3. $L^{pspace} = \bigcup_{f \text{ a polynomial}} L^{space(f)}$

The corresponding classes of *problems* solvable within limited space are easy to define:

Definition 21.1.10 Given programming language L and a total function $f : \mathbb{N} \to \mathbb{N}$

1. The class of problems L-*decidable in space f* is:

$$\text{SPACE}^L(f) = \{A \subseteq L\text{-}data \mid A \text{ is decided by some } p \in L^{space(f(n))}\}$$

2. The class of problems L-*decidable in logarithmic space* is:

$$\text{LOGSPACE}^L = \{A \subseteq L\text{-}data \mid A \text{ is decided by some } p \in L^{logspace}\}$$

3. The class of problems L-*decidable in polynomial space* is:

$$\text{PSPACE}^L = \{A \subseteq L\text{-}data \mid A \text{ is decided by some } p \in L^{pspace}\}$$

21.2   Comparing space usage of Turing and counter machines

Theorem 21.2.1 For any f with $f(n) \geq \max(\log n, 1)$

$$\bigcup_c \text{SPACE}^{\text{TMro}}(cf) = \bigcup_d \text{SPACE}^{\text{CMro}}(df)$$

Corollary 21.2.2 For any f with $f(n) \geq n$

$$\bigcup_c \text{SPACE}^{\text{TM}}(cf) = \bigcup_d \text{SPACE}^{\text{CM}}(df)$$

Proof. The corollary is immediate from Theorem 21.2.1 and the preceding propositions. Two constructions follow to prove Theorem 21.2.1, one building from an f-space-bounded Turing machine program a corresponding counter machine operating in the desired size bound, and another construction in the opposite direction. We leave it to the reader to verify that the constructed programs decide the same sets as their sources, that is that the simulations are faithful. This should not be surprising, as each program simulates the operations of the other in exactly the same order, so it is only important to verify that the desired space bounds are preserved, and that the two programs' states continue to correspond properly.   □

Construction 21.2.3 $A \in \text{SPACE}^{\text{TMro}}(cf)$ implies $A \in \bigcup_d \text{SPACE}^{\text{CMro}}(df))$.

Representation of TMro storage in a CMro program.   A TMro total state is

$$s = (\ell, \dots \text{BL}_1 \underline{S_1} R_1 B \dots, \dots \text{BL}_2 \underline{S_2} R_2 B \dots)$$

where ℓ is the instruction counter.   Assume $A \in \text{SPACE}^{\text{TMro}}(cf)$.   Clearly the *scanning positions* on both tapes can be represented by counters, each no larger than $2 + \max(n, cf(n)) \leq 2^{2cf(n)}$. The idea of the simulation is to represent the *work tape contents* by two counters, each no larger than $2^{2cf(n)}$, and to simulate operations on both tapes by corresponding counter operations.

A work tape containing $b_1 \dots \underline{b_i} \dots b_m$ where $m \leq cf(n)$ can be represented by a pair of numbers l, r, where

- l is the value of $b_1 \dots b_i$ as a base 3 number (counting B as digit 0, 0 as digit 1, and 1 as digit 2), and
- r is the value of $b_m b_{m-1} \dots b_{i+1}$, also as a base 3 number.

The work tapes are initially all blank, so $l = r = 0$ at the simulated computation's start. Since $m \leq cf(n)$, we have

$$l, r \leq 3^{cf(n)} \leq 4^{cf(n)} = 2^{2cf(n)}$$

Putting these together, we have two counters to represent the input and work tape scanning position, and two counters to represent the work tape contents.

The effect of moving a work tape head right one position is to replace l by $3 \cdot l + (r \bmod 3)$, and to divide r by 3, and similarly for moving left. It is easy to see that these operations can be done by counters. Testing the scanned square's contents amounts to a test on $l \bmod 3$, also easily done.

These counters are all bounded in size by $2^{2cf(n)}$ and so by $2cf(n)$ bits; and collectively represent the Turing machine's total state. Each Turing machine operation can be faithfully simulated by operations on counters, concluding the construction. ☐

Construction 21.2.4 $A \in \text{SPACE}^{\text{CMro}}(df)$ implies $A \in \bigcup_c \text{SPACE}^{\text{TMro}}(cf)$:

Representation of CMro storage in a TMro program. Suppose p is a CMro program, and $d = a_1 a_2 \ldots a_n$ is an input. The CMro input $a_1 a_2 \ldots a_n$ will be present on tape 1 of the TMro.

The TMro code to simulate p will represent each variable Ci by a block of bits on the work tape containing the binary representation of value j of Ci. Some TM data initialization is needed, as the initial value of counter C0 is n. It is easy to write TM code to accomplish this; the main task is to construct the binary representation of value n (which occupies $\log n$ bits, whence the lower bound on f).

Each CMro counter C1,..., Ck is assumed to have length at most $df(n)$ bits. One may think of having as a new symbol the marker 2, so the work tape form would be

$$\ldots \text{B B Block}_1 \text{ 2 Block}_2 \text{ 2}\ldots\text{2 Block}_k \text{ B B}\ldots$$

The same effect can be achieved without the extra symbol 2 by a simple data encoding into 0, 1, at most doubling the tape space. Since there is a fixed number k of CMro variables, the total amount of work tape storage, including markers to separate the blocks, is at most a constant times $f(n)$ bits, as required.

Each CMro operation is straightforwardly simulable by the Turing machine. For example, command if In_{Ci}=0 goto ℓ else ℓ' can be realized by steps:

- Locate the block containing the value j of Ci, and copy it into another block for use as a counter c.
- If $1 \le c \le n$ then continue, else goto the code simulating ℓ.
- Move to the left end of input tape 1 containing $a_1 a_2 \ldots a_n$.
- If $c = 1$, the input symbol a_j has been found and may be tested for zero.
- If $c > 1$ then decrement it by 1, scan forward one symbol on the input tape, and repeat from the previous step. ☐

21.3 Relation of LOGSPACE to counter machines and PTIME

Corollary 21.3.1 $\text{LOGSPACE}^{\text{TM}} = \text{LOGSPACE}^{\text{CM}}$

Proof. Immediate from Theorem 21.2.1. □

Corollary 21.3.2 $\text{LOGSPACE} \subseteq \text{PTIME}$

Proof. Suppose $A \in \text{LOGSPACE}$ is decided by some Turing machine p with m instructions in space $k \log n$ for some k and all inputs of length n. Then p cannot run for more than $m \cdot (n+2) \cdot 3^{k \log n}$ steps, else it would have repeated a state

$$(\ell, \ldots B_1 \underline{S_1} R_1 B \ldots, \ldots BL_2 \underline{S_2} R_2 B \ldots)$$

and so be in an infinite loop. The expression above is certainly polynomial-bounded, since $a^{\log n} = n^{\log a}$ for any $a, n > 0$, and so $3^{k \log n} = n^{k \log 3}$. □

21.4 Robustness of PSPACE

Theorem 21.2.1 gives a pleasingly tight connection between the space used by Turing machine computations and the sizes of counters used by counter machines solving the same problems. Further, any counter machine is also a RAM, so we now briefly consider the translation compiling RAM to TM from a memory usage perspective.

The amount of Turing machine tape used by a translated program can be assumed to be bounded by the sum of the lengths and addresses of the nonzero RAM memory cells[3]. Now every nonconstant address must have first appeared in a register; so if the RAM program uses at most space $f(\text{d})$ bits of storage on input d, then the simulating Turing machine uses at most linearly more space.

From this (informal) argument we can conclude $\text{PSPACE}^{\text{TM}} = \text{PSPACE}^{\text{CM}} = \text{PSPACE}^{\text{RAM}}$. Therefore we henceforth often write PSPACE rather than $\text{PSPACE}^{\text{TM}}$.

---

[3]Using the construction of chapter 8 , this could only fail if the RAM repeatedly stored first a nonzero value, and then 0, in a great many cells. This would create many useless but space-consuming blocks on the Turing machine's tape. The problem is easy to circumvent; each time a register-changing RAM instruction is performed, the simulating Turing machine checks to see whether the new value is zero. If so, the address and value are removed from address and contents tapes, thus "compacting" the tape storage. This yields the desired space bound.

Extending this result to GOTO programs has some complications that require a more subtle implementation; the complications and an alternate implementation are sketched below.

Storage usage in GOTO programs

The original tree-based semantics gives unrealistically high space measures for two reasons. First, the tree model did not account for sharing, whereas an assignment such as X:=cons X X should clearly not double the memory assigned to X.

A second problem is that even if the more realistic DAG model of section 17.1.1 is used, it often happens that nodes become inaccessible. For example, consider the translation compiling a Turing machine program to an equivalent GOTO seen in section 18.2. Without accounting for unreachable nodes, this would require space roughly proportional to the simulated Turing machine's *running time*, since every tape head motion is simulated by a cons. This is far in excess of what seems reasonable. The following seems to be a fairer definition:

Definition 21.4.1 *A space measure for the flow chart language GOTO:* Consider the semantics of section 17.1.1 in which the store σ is a DAG (δ, ρ) where ρ maps Vars(p) to nodes, and δ is a DSG that specifies the structure of the DAG. By definition, the size $|\sigma|$ of such a store is the number of nodes in the dag that can be reached from some node variable, that is the number of nodes reachable via δ from the entry nodes in the range of ρ.

Storage in the TM to GOTO to RAM translations

In the translation compiling TM to GOTO, the number of DAG nodes accessible from variables can be seen to be proportional to the sum of the lengths of the tapes of the Turing machine being simulated. Consequently $\text{PSPACE}^{\text{TM}} \subseteq \text{PSPACE}^{\text{GOTO}}$.

In the translation compiling GOTO to SRAM, the number of *accessible* SRAM memory cells is proportional to the DAG size since the implementation simply realizes the DAG as described. On the other hand, the implementation as sketched does not perform garbage collection. Revising the implementation to do this would give $\text{PSPACE}^{\text{GOTO}} \subseteq \text{PSPACE}^{\text{RAM}}$ and thus

$$\text{PSPACE}^{\text{GOTO}} = \text{PSPACE}^{\text{RAM}} = \text{PSPACE}^{\text{TM}} = \text{PSPACE}^{\text{CM}}$$

21.5   Relations between space and time

Proposition 21.5.1 TIME$^{\text{TM}}(f) \subseteq$ SPACE$^{\text{TM}}(f)$ for any f. Consequently PTIME $\subseteq$ PSPACE .

Proof. TIME$^{\text{TM}}(f) \subseteq$ SPACE$^{\text{TM}}(f)$ is obvious, since a TM-program p that runs in time bounded by $f(|\mathsf{d}|)$ cannot write on more than $f(|\mathsf{d}|)$ tape cells. Thus $space_\mathsf{p}^{\text{TM}}(\mathsf{d}) \leq f(|\mathsf{d}|)$ by Definition 21.4.1 so

$$\text{PSPACE}^{\text{TM}} \supseteq \text{PTIME}^{\text{TM}} = \text{PTIME}^{\text{SRAM}} = \text{PTIME}^{\text{GOTO}}.$$

$\square$

Theorem 21.5.2 If $f(n) \geq n$ for all n then

$$\text{SPACE}^{\text{TM}}(f) \subseteq \bigcup_c \text{TIME}^{\text{TM}}(c^f)$$

Proof. We show that if a one-tape Turing machine program p runs in space f and terminates on its inputs, then it also runs in time c^f for appropriate c.

Clearly p cannot repeat any computational state $s = (\ell, \ldots \mathsf{B}\,\mathsf{L}\,\underline{\mathsf{S}}\,\mathsf{R}\,\mathsf{B}\,\ldots)$ in the computation on input d, since if this happened, p would loop infinitely on d. So to prove our result it suffices to show that a terminating program running in space f has at most $c^{f(|\mathsf{d}|)}$ different states for some c.

Consider any computational state s reachable on input d. By the assumption on p, $|\mathsf{L}\,\underline{\mathsf{S}}\,\mathsf{R}| \leq f(|\mathsf{d}|)$. The total number of possible values of the nonblank tape contents LSR with this space bound is bounded by $3^{f(|\mathsf{d}|)}$, since each symbol in LSR must be 0, 1, or B. Further, the scanning position where S is located has at most $f(|\mathsf{d}|)$ possibilities.

Combining these bounds, the total number of different possible values of the tape, including both tape scanning position and contents, is bounded by

$$f(|\mathsf{d}|) \cdot 3^{f(|\mathsf{d}|)}$$

Now $n \leq 2^n$ for all $n \geq 1$, so by the assumption that $f(n) \geq n$ we have

$$f(|\mathsf{d}|) \cdot 3^{f(|\mathsf{d}|)} \leq 2^{f(|\mathsf{d}|)} \cdot 3^{f(|\mathsf{d}|)} = 6^{f(|\mathsf{d}|)}$$

Finally, a total configuration of program p includes the control point and the state of its tape. The number of these is bounded by $(|\mathsf{p}| + 1) \cdot 6^{f(|\mathsf{d}|)} \leq c^{f(|\mathsf{d}|)}$ for all d where, for example, $c = 12|\mathsf{p}|$ will do since

$$(|\mathsf{p}| + 1) \cdot 6^{f(|\mathsf{d}|)} \leq (2|\mathsf{p}|)^{f(|\mathsf{d}|)} \cdot 6^{f(|\mathsf{d}|)} = (12|\mathsf{p}|)^{f(|\mathsf{d}|)}$$

Since no state in $\mathsf{p} \vdash s_0 \to s_1 \to \ldots s_t \to s_{t+1} \ldots$ can be repeated, the running time of p is bounded by $c^{f(|\mathsf{d}|)}$. Thus A lies in $\text{TIME}(c^{f(|\mathsf{d}|)})$. □

21.6   Functions computable in logarithmic space

For later usage in chapter 26 (and for the sake of curiosity), we show that a number of familiar functions can be computed in logarithmic space. The read-only Turing machine has binary integers as inputs (multiple entries are separated by blanks), and is now assumed equipped with a one-way write-only output tape to write function values.

Proposition 21.6.1 The following functions $f : \{0,1\}^* \to \{0,1\}^*$ are Turing computable in space $\log n$:

1. $\lambda(x,y).x + y, \lambda(x,y).x \cdot y, \lambda(x,y).x \le y$
2. $\lambda(x,y).x \cdot y$
3. $f(x_1, x_2, \ldots x_n) = $ the same sequence sorted into nondecreasing order

Proof. Exercises 21.5, 21.6, 21.7.

Lemma 21.6.2 The following statements about a function $f : \{0,1\}^* \to \{0,1\}^*$ are equivalent, provided $|f(\mathsf{d})|$ is bounded by some polynomial $p(|\mathsf{d}|)$ for all d:

1. f is Turing computable in space $k \log n$ for some k.
2. The following function is computable in space $k' \log |\mathsf{d}|$:

   $\lambda(\mathtt{i},\mathsf{d}).$the $\mathtt{i}$-th bit of $f(\mathsf{d})$

Proof. To show 1 implies 2, suppose f is Turing computable by program p in space $k \log n$ with input $\mathtt{X}$, and that it produces its output by executing a series of instructions of form `write Z`. The idea is simply to produce the bits of $f(\mathsf{d}) = [\![\mathsf{p}]\!](\mathsf{d})$, one at a time, but to ignore them until the $\mathtt{i}$-th bit has been produced, at which time that bit is written.

Add to p an extra input variable $\mathtt{I}$ and a counter variable $\mathtt{C}$, and prefix p's code by the following:

```
if I >  p(|X|) then stop; Otherwise:
read I;    (* from input tape (I.X) into memory *)
C := 0;    (* initialize bit counter *)
```

(nil is written for a nonexistent bit.) Because of the polynomial bound on $|f(d)|$, variable I, if stored, will not require more than $O(\log p(|d|))$ bits. This is bounded by a constant times $\log |d|$. To complete the construction, replace every instruction write Z in p by the following:

```
C := C + 1;
if C = I then write Z and stop;
```

To show 2 implies 1, let program p compute $\lambda(i,d)$.the i-th bit of $f(d)$. Embed it in a program q of form:

```
for C := 1 to p(|d|) do
{ B := p C Input;
    if B = 0 or B = 1 then write B }
```

The idea is to write the bits of $f(d) = [\![p]\!](d)$, one bit at a time in order, by computing the i-th bit of $f(d)$ for $i = 1, 2, \ldots, p(|d|))$ and printing its results.

The expression p C Input above is realized by running p, modified to take the Input part of its argument from the read-only tape, and the C part from the work tape.

□

Theorem 21.6.3 If f, g are both computable in space $\log n$ then so is $f \circ g$.

Proof. One cannot simply compute $g(x)$ and then apply f to this result, as $g(x)$ may occupy more that $k \log n$ bits (e.g., if g is the identity function). On the other hand, a logspace f program does not look at its input all at once, but rather one symbol at a time. Our strategy is thus not to store $g(x)$ explicitly but rather virtually, using the result of Lemma 21.6.2. Let TM-program p_f compute f, and assume program p_g computes

$$\lambda(i, x).\text{the } i\text{th bit of } g(x)$$

as in Lemma 21.6.2. We sketch the construction of a 6-tape Turing program r to compute $f(g(x))$.

Storage representation   r's tape contents are as shown in Figure 21.1.
Initialization is trivial, as programs p_f and p_g for functions f and g both begin scanning the blank to the left of their respective inputs $g(x)$ and x. Thus the only initialization action is to set $i = 0$ by writing 0 on tape 3, as all other tapes are initially blank.

Tape number	Tape contents
1 (read-only input)	$x = a_1 \ldots a_n$
2	Program p_f's work tape
3	i = scan position on program p_f's input tape
4	b = program p_f's scanned input symbol from $g(x)$
5	Program p_g's work tape
6 (write-only output)	Program p_f's output tape

Figure 21.1: Tape contents for 6-tape Turing program r.

Instruction simulation. First, any instructions in program p_f of forms right_2, left_2, goto ℓ and if_2 S goto ℓ can be performed without change; and write_2 S is of course simulated by write_6 S. Instruction if_1 S goto ℓ can be performed by testing the contents b of tape 4.

The remaining p_f instruction forms are right_1 and left_1; we only describe the first, as the other is nearly identical. Instruction right_1 is simulated by code to effectuate:

```
i := i + 1; b := p_g x i;   (* i = scan position from tape 3    *)
```

Finally, it must be seen that this code can be programmed on a Turing machine, and that the resulting machine r works in logarithmically bounded space.

As to programming, command b := p_g x i can be realized by modifying p_g's program to use tape 5 as its work tape, and to take its input from tape 1 as long as it is scanning the x part of its two-part input xBi, and to shift over to reading from tape 3 when reading from the i part.

As to r's space consumption, let $n = |x|$. Tape 4 is of constant size, and tape 5 is p_g's work tape on x and so is logarithmically bounded in n. The value of $g(x)$, which is p_f's simulated input, must be bounded by some polynomial $\pi(n)$ by the running time argument of Corollary 21.3.2. Thus $0 \leq i \leq 1 + \pi(n)$, so tape 3 is logarithmically bounded (assuming i to be represented in binary notation). Finally, tape 2 has length at most $k' \log |g(x)| \leq k' \log(\pi(n)) = O(\log n)$.

Tape 1 is not counted, and all 4 work tapes are logarithmically bounded. They can all be combined into one work tape, also logarithmically bounded, which completes the argument. $\square$

21.7   Hierarchies of problems solvable in bounded space

Very similar results to those seen earlier for time bounds can also be proven for space bounds. The following is analogous to Definition 19.5.2.

Definition 21.7.1 Function $f : \mathbb{N} \to \mathbb{N}$ is *space-constructible* if there is a TM program f and a constant $c > 0$ such that for all $n \geq 0$

$$[\![f]\!]^{TM}(0^n) = c_{\mathbb{N}}(f(n)) \text{ and } space_f^{TM}(0^n) \leq c \cdot f(n)$$

Many familiar monotone functions are space-constructible, e.g., all linear functions, all polynomials, and $f + g, f * g, f^g$ whenever f, g are time-constructible (Exercise21.8).

Theorem 21.7.2 For one-tape Turing machines: If f is space-constructible there exists $b > 0$ such that $\text{PSPACE}^{TM}(bf) \backslash \text{PSPACE}^{TM}(f) \neq \emptyset$.

Proof. The proof is very similar to that of Theorem 19.5.3 and so is just sketched here. The technique used is again diagonalization to construct a program diag defining a set A in $\text{PSPACE}^{TM}(bf) \backslash \text{PSPACE}^{TM}(f)$ for suitable b.

There are, however, some differences. To begin with, we must assume that one-tape Turing machine programs are encoded as strings over $\{0,1\}^*$. The next step is to construct a self-interpreter that uses such a description of a program by a string. This is technically rather messy, and has been done in numerous books and articles, so we omit the details.

The diagonalizing program diag is then a modification of the self-interpreter, just as in section 19.5.3. Program diag is constructed so that for any input $p \in \{0,1\}^*$:

$$[\![diag]\!](p) = \begin{cases} 1 & \text{if } space_p(p) > f(|p|) \\ & \quad \text{or } [\![p]\!](p) \text{ does not terminate within } limit(p) \text{ steps} \\ 0 & \text{if } space_p(p) \leq f(|p|) \text{ and } [\![p]\!](p) \neq 0 \\ 1 & \text{if } space_p(p) \leq f(|p|) \text{ and } [\![p]\!](p) = 0 \end{cases}$$

It is of course essential that the diagonalizing program diag terminate on all inputs, and that it does not use more than $bf(|p|)$ space on input p. Termination can be achieved by observing that the simulated Turing program p on input d may not run for more than

$$limit(d) = (|p| + 1) \cdot 3^{f(|d|)} \cdot f(|d|)$$

steps without entering an infinite loop, since exceeding this limit would imply it had repeated a total state and so was in an infinite loop. If $[\![p]\!](p)$ has not terminated within this number of steps, it will never terminate. Thus this value may be used for a variable Timebound, playing the same role as in Theorem 19.5.3. The code `Timebound := tl Timebound` from section 19.5.3 must thus be replaced by code to perform the binary number operation `Timebound := Timebound - 1`.

Space analysis   It must be guaranteed that `diag` runs in space $bf(|d|)$ for some b. First, note that $O(f(|p|))$ space is enough to store `Timebound` as a binary number. Second, the space condition above can be checked by monitoring the space usage of p, rejecting it if it uses more than $f(|p|)$ memory, or more than *limit*(p) time. If `diag` is itself written in a space-economical way as just described, it will not use more than linearly more space than $f(|p|)$.

Finally, assuming the set decided by `diag` can be decided by another program in space not exceeding $f(|d|)$ leads to a contradiction, just as in section 19.5.3; this proves the theorem.   □

Theorem 21.7.3 If functions f, g are space constructible, $f(n) \geq n, g(n) \geq n$ for all n, and $\lim_{n \to \infty} g(n)/f(n) = 0$, then $\text{SPACE}^{\text{TM}}(f) \backslash \text{SPACE}^{\text{TM}}(g) \neq \emptyset$.

Proof. This is very similar in concept to the proof of Theorems 19.5.3 and 21.7.2.   □

Exercises

21.1 Prove Proposition 21.1.5.   □

21.2 Prove Proposition 21.1.6.   □

21.3 Prove Proposition 21.1.7. This can be done by filling in the details of the following sketch.

Given CM program p, its code can be modified as follows: First, CMro program q scans the symbols of its input $a_1 \ldots a_n = c_N(v)$, and computes $v = c_N^{-1}(a_1 \ldots a_n)$, which it stores into a counter. It then executes the code of p without modification. A straightforward size analysis of the values involved shows that this can be done in the required space.   □

21.4 Prove Proposition 21.1.8. This can be done by filling in the details of the following sketch.

Given CMro program p, its code can be modified as follows: First, q copies input v into a counter Cv not used by p, and then determines its length n and puts it into counter C0. This is straightforward using the definition of c_N: divide $v+1$ by 2 repeatedly and discard the remainder until 0 is obtained; the number of times halving is done is $n+1$.

Second, p can be simulated stepwise, all instructions that q executes being identical to those of p with a single exception: In$_{Ci}$=0 goto ℓ else ℓ'. The value of the needed bit from $c_N(v)$ can be found by repeatedly halving $v+1$ a number of times equal to the value of Ci. If the result is positive and even then the bit is 0, else if positive and odd then 1, else Ci exceeds n. A straightforward size analysis of the values involved shows that this can be done in the required space.   □

21.5 Prove Proposition 21.6.1, part 1. An informal construction, for instance a sketch of a Turing machine, will do; just make it clear that the algorithm works, and that all values involved are logarithmically bounded.   □

21.6 Prove Proposition 21.6.1, part 2.   □

21.7 Prove Proposition 21.6.1, part 3.   □

21.8 Prove that the following functions are space-constructible:

  1. $f(n) = an + b$, for non-negative integer constants a and b.
  2. $f + g$, assuming that f, g are space constructible.
  3. $f * g$, assuming that f, g are space constructible.
  4. f^g, assuming that f, g are space constructible.   □

References

The earliest work on space-bounded hierarchies is from 1965, due to Hartmanis, Lewis and Stearns [61, 62]. Early results on sublinear space are found in papers by Savitch, Meyer, Jones, and Jones, Lien and Laaser [149, 120, 79, 71, 75].

22   Nondeterministic Computations

A *nondeterministic program* is one that may "guess," i.e., one whose next-state transition relation is multivalued rather than a partial function, as has been the case hitherto. This capacity may be added to any of the imperative computation models already seen by adding a single instruction form $\ell:$ goto ℓ' or ℓ''. Its semantics is to enlarge the state transition relation of Figure 7.1 to also allow transitions

$$(\ell, \sigma) \to (\ell', \sigma) \text{ and as well: } (\ell, \sigma) \to (\ell'', \sigma)$$

Correspondingly, one makes a while program nondeterministic by adding a "choice command," for example

```
C  ::=  choose C1 or C2
```

with the natural semantics: Either command C1 or command C2 may be executed.

Note that nondeterministic programs are not functional: the same input may give rise to many different computations, some of which may fail to terminate, and some which may terminate with different outputs.

22.1   Definition of nondeterministic acceptance

Definition 22.1.1 A computation $p \vdash s_1 \to s_2 \to \dots s_t$ is *accepting* if it terminates and writes the output true. An input $d \in L$-*data* is *accepted* by nondeterministic program p if p has at least one accepting computation $p \vdash s_1 \to s_2 \to \dots s_t$ with $s_1 = (1, Readin(d))$. The *set* $Acc(p) \subseteq D$ *accepted by* p is by definition

$$Acc(p) = \{d \in \Sigma^* \mid p \text{ accepts } d\}$$

This is sometimes called "angelic nondeterminism": in essence d is accepted if there exists at least one sequence of "guesses" leading to output true, but does not specify how such a sequence can be obtained. One can think of acceptance as the result of a search through the tree of all possible comptations on the given input, a search which succeeded in finding a branch ending in "accept."

22.2   A simple example: path finding

The problem is, given a directed graph $G = (V, E, s, t)$ with edges $E = \{(u_1, v_1),$ $(u_2, v_2), \ldots\}$ and a source and target nodes s, t, to decide whether there exists a path from s to t. The following nondeterministic WHILE program sketch assumes inputs s, t, and that the graph G is given as a list $((u_1.v_1) \ (u_2.v_2) \ \ldots (u_n.v_n))$ in $\mathbb{D}$.

```
read S, T, G;
W := S;

while W ≠ T do          (* Repeat until (if ever) T is reached    *)
   Copy := G;
   while Copy do         (* This chooses an edge at random:        *)
      choose
         Copy := tl Copy  (* Either omit the first edge of G's copy *)
      or { Edge := hd Copy; Copy := nil };          (* or keep it *)

   if    W = hd Edge     (* If W = source of chosen edge then      *)
   then  W := tl Edge;   (*    continue from target of chosen edge *)

write true               (* If it gets here, a path was found      *)
```

This straightforward nondeterministic program just "guesses" a path from s to t.

22.3   Resource-bounded nondeterministic algorithms

Time and space usage are also interpreted angelically, taking the least possible values over all accepting computations:

Definition 22.3.1 Given a computation $C = \mathsf{p} \vdash s_1 \to s_2 \to \ldots s_t$, its *running time* is t (its number of states). The *space usage* of C is by definition $|C| = \max\{|s_0|, |s_1|, \ldots, |s_t|\}$. The *time usage (space usage) function* of program p on input d is the shortest length (minimum space) of any accepting computation:

$time_{\mathsf{p}}(\mathsf{d}) = \min\{t \mid \mathsf{p} \vdash s_1 \to \cdots \to s_t$ is an accepting computation on input d$\}$
$space_{\mathsf{p}}(\mathsf{d}) = \min\{|C| \mid C = \mathsf{p} \vdash s_1 \to \cdots \to s_t$ is an accepting computation on input d$\}$

Definition 22.3.2 In the following, L- program p may be nondeterministic.

$$\begin{aligned}
\text{NPTIME}^{\text{L}} &= \{Acc(\text{p}) \mid time_{\text{p}}^{\text{L}}(\text{d}) \leq \text{a polynomial } p \text{ in } |\text{d}|\} \\
\text{NPSPACE}^{\text{L}} &= \{Acc(\text{p}) \mid space_{\text{p}}^{\text{L}}(\text{d}) \leq \text{a polynomial } p \text{ in } |\text{d}|\} \\
\text{NLOGSPACE}^{\text{L}} &= \{Acc(\text{p}) \mid space_{\text{p}}^{\text{L}}(\text{d}) \leq k \log |\text{d}| \text{ for some } k\}
\end{aligned}$$

The symbol N in the classes above indicates nondeterminism. Note that, by definition and in contrast to deterministic computation as defined before, if p fails to accept an input d then it may enter an infinite loop (though it is not required to do so).

Proposition 22.3.3

PTIME^{L} $\subseteq$NPTIME^{L}, PSPACE^{L} $\subseteq$NPSPACE^{L}, and LOGSPACE^{L} $\subseteq$NLOGSPACE^{L}.

Proof. Immediate since every deterministic program is also nondeterministic, and uses no more time nor space under the nondeterministic measure than under the deterministic one. $\square$

Theorem 22.3.4 Aside from data encoding,

- NPTIME^{TM} $=$NPTIME^{SRAM} $=$NPTIME^{GOTO}
- NPSPACE^{TM} $=$NPSPACE^{SRAM} $=$NPSPACE^{GOTO}$=$NPSPACE^{CM}
- NLOGSPACE^{TM} $=$NLOGSPACE^{CM}

Proof. The constructions seen earlier for deterministic programs can without modification be applied to the nondeterministic ones. $\square$

Exercises

22.1 Prove that a set $A \subseteq \{0,1\}^*$ is accepted by a nondeterministic Turing machine if and only if it is recursively enumerable. $\square$

References

The earliest work on nondeterministic space-bounded computation is by Kuroda from 1964 [97], soon followed by Hartmanis, Lewis and Stearns [61, 62]. Edmonds explored nondeterministic algorithms from a more practical viewpoint [40].

23   A Structure for Classifying the Complexity of Various Problems

This chapter introduces a wide-ranging sequence of problem classes, and proves them to be a hierarchy. Many familiar and important computational problems can be located precisely in this hierarchy, hence the chapter's title.

It is not yet known, however, which or how many of the inclusions below are proper ones, for instance whether there exists at least one problem solvable in polynomial time but not in logarithmic space. The containments we will establish are:

$$\text{LOGSPACE} \subseteq \text{NLOGSPACE} \subseteq \text{PTIME} \subseteq \text{NPTIME} \subseteq \text{PSPACE} = \text{NPSPACE}$$

Computation models henceforth

We will henceforth refer to LOGSPACE, PTIME, etc. without naming the computation model involved. When time bounds are being discussed, a *one-tape* Turing machine will generally be used because of its simplicity, and "work tape" will refer to its only tape. When possibly sublinear space bounds are involved, the model will be the *read-only* version with read-only input and an additional work tape.

Input format

Turing machine inputs will in principle always be strings in $\Sigma^* = \{0,1\}^*$. It will, however, sometimes be convenient to represent inputs as strings over an alphabet $\Sigma \supset \{0,1\}$, for example with markers or parentheses for the sake of readability. Clearly any Turing machine with such an extended input tape alphabet can be simulated by one with just $\{0,1\}$ with only a constant slowdown, and space multiplied by a constant.

23.1   Some convenient normalizations

In this and following chapters many constructions start with a Turing machine program p, deterministic or nodeterministic, that accepts a set $A \subseteq \{0,1\}^*$. These constructions become technically more convenient if we can assume without loss of generality that program p has been normalized so that acceptance of an input only occurs in a fixed way, less general than as defined before, and so easier to recognize in our constructions. This is the content of

Proposition 23.1.1 For any Turing machine program p there is a program q = $I_1 \ldots I_m$ such that for any d $\in \{0,1\}^*$

1. p has a computation that accepts d if and only if q has a computation

   $$Readin(d) = (0, \sigma_0) \to \ldots \to (m, \sigma_m) \to (m, \sigma_m) \to \ldots$$

   where the work tape of σ_m contains $\underline{1}$BB . . . .

2. p has a computation that does not accept d if and only if q has a computation

   $$Readin(d) = (0, \sigma_0) \to \ldots \to (m-1, \sigma_{m-1}) \to (m-1, \sigma_{m-1}) \to \ldots$$

   where the work tape of σ_{m-1} contains $\underline{0}$BB . . . .

3. In the computations above, q first reaches configurations with label m or $m - 1$ after using the same space as p on the same input, and time at most a constant factor larger than that used by p on the same input.

Proof. First, add instructions at the end of p to "clean up" by erasing its work tape except for the answer (0 or 1), and moving to scan the answer. Given this normalization, q can be constructed by adding instructions

```
m-1: if 0 goto m-1;
m:   if 1 goto m
```

at the end of p, so it loops infinitely at fixed control points on the answer.

Clearly the cleanup code costs no extra space, and uses time at most the length of the nonblank part of p's work tape, which is of course bounded by p's run time. The final code only adds a constant amount to time usage.   □

23.2   Program state transition graphs

Definition 23.2.1 *A concrete syntax for graphs.* Graph $G = (V, E, v_0, v_{end})$ can be represented by listing its vertices, edges, and source and target as the following string over the alphabet $\Sigma = \{0, 1, [,], (,), ,\}$, where each vertex v_i is represented by i as a binary number:

$$[v_1, \ldots, v_r],\ [(u, u'), (v, v'), \ldots, (w, w')],\ v_0,\ v_{end}$$

Definition 23.2.2 We assume given a deterministic or nondeterministic read-only Turing machine program p with m instructions, normalized as in Proposition 23.1.1; an input $d = a_1 a_2 \ldots a_n \in \{0,1\}^*$ of length n; and a function $f : \mathbb{N} \to \mathbb{N}$, which will be used to bound p's work tape size.

An *f-bounded configuration* of p for input d is by definition a tuple $C = (\ell, i, j, W)$, where

- $1 \leq \ell \leq m$ is a control point in p;
- $W = b_1 b_2 \ldots b_w \in \{0,1,B\}^*$ is the contents of its work tape, satisfying $|\ell| + |r| \leq f(n)$; and
- i, j satisfying $0 \leq i \leq n+1, 0 \leq j \leq f(n)+1$ are the scan positions on its input and work tapes, respectively, so symbol a_i and b_j are scanned (blank if at one end of either tape).

The *state transition graph* $G_p(d)$ of p for input d is a directed graph $G_p(d) = (V, E, v_0, v_{end})$ with identified initial and final vertices v_0, v_{end}, where

1. Vertex set $V = V_p(d)$ equals the set of all f-bounded configurations $C = (\ell, i, j, W)$ of p;
2. Edge set $E = E_p(d)$ equals the set of all configuration pairs (C, C') (or more suggestively: $C \to C'$) such that program p takes configuration C to C' in one computation step;
3. The initial vertex of $G_p(d)$ is $v_0 = (1, 0, 0, B)$, i.e., the empty work tape; and
4. The final vertex of $G_p(d)$ is $v_{end} = (m, 0, 0, 1)$, where m is the number of instructions in p.

When the work space is bounded, a program p may only enter finitely many different configurations. Since the graph vertex set V is a *set* of configurations, the graph for any program that runs in space f is *always finite*, even though p may have infinitely long computations.

The state transition graph can certainly be defined without any restriction of the program's work space, in which it may sometimes be infinite.

Lemma 23.2.3 Suppose $A \subseteq \{0,1\}^*$ is accepted in space f by program p, where $f(n) \geq \log n$ for all n. Let transition graph $G_p(d)$ of p for input d be as above. Then

- $d \in A$ if and only if $G_p(d)$ has a path from v_0 to v_{end}; and
- Any vertex of $G_p(d)$ can be represented in $O(f(|d|))$ space.

The first part is immediate. As to the second, in any configuration $C = (\ell, i, j, W)$ we have $0 \leq i \leq n+1$ and $0 \leq j \leq f(n)+1$. Thus in binary notation, i takes at most $1 + \log n = O(f(n))$ bits, and j takes at most $\log(f(n)+1) = O(f(n))$ bits. The number of control points ℓ is independent of n, and $|W| \leq f(n)$ by definition.

23.3   Algorithms for graph searching

The following apparently rather specialized problem will turn out to play a central role in establishing several parts of the space-time complexity hierarchy.

Decision problem GAP (graph accessibility):

Input: a directed graph $G = (V, E, v_0, v_{end})$ as in the concrete syntax of Definition 23.2.1.
Output: `true` if G has a path $v_0 \rightarrow^* v_{end}$, else `false`.

We present no less than four algorithms for the problem. The first two are nondeterministic and use logarithmic space: one gives positive answers and the other, negative answers. The others are deterministic. The third uses polynomial time, and polynomial space as well; and the last runs in space $O(\log^2 n)$. Each is expressed by giving an informal procedure, after which its time or space usage on a Turing machine is analysed.

23.3.1   Graph accessibility in nondeterministic logarithmic space

Theorem 23.3.1 The GAP problem is in the class NLOGSPACE^{TM}.

Proof. Let $G = (V, E, v_0, v_{end})$ be a graph with designated start and finish vertices v_0, v_{end} and vertex set $V = \{v_1, \ldots, v_r\}$. Note that $r \leq size(G)$. Consider the program sketch (assuming graph G is given as read-only data):

```
w := v_0;
while w ≠ v_end do
    choose an arbitrary node x with w → x ∈ E;
    w := x
write true
```

This straightforward nondeterministic program just "guesses" a path from v_0 to v_{end}. Its storage is two vertices. Given r vertices in V, this takes at most $O(\log r)$ bits, which is at most $O(\log size(G))$. □

23.3.2   Graph *inaccessibility* in nondeterministic logarithmic space

Surprisingly, the negation of this problem can also be solved within logarithmic space using nondeterminism.

Theorem 23.3.2 The following set is in the class NLOGSPACE[TM]:

$$\overline{\text{GAP}} = \{\ G = (V, E, v_0, v_{end})\ |\ \text{graph } G \text{ has no path from vertex } v_0 \text{ to } v_{end}\ \}$$

Proof. Let G be a graph be as above. Let

$$n_i = |\{u\,|\,v_0 \to^{\le i} u\}|$$

be the number of nodes that can be reached from node v_0 by a path of length at most i. We will soon show how each n_i can be computed. First, though, we show a nondeterministic algorithm which, assuming n_{r-1} to be given in advance, can answer "Nopath = true" iff $G \in \overline{\text{GAP}}$. Consider the program sketch of Figure 23.1.

```
Nopath := true;   (* Attempt to scan all and only the nodes *)
Count := 0;        (* reachable from v0                      *)
for z := 1 to r do
    choose        (* Guess whether node z is reachable or not *)
       skip       (* negative guess                           *)
    or            (* positive guess                           *)
       if ∃ path  v0 →*z
       then  Count := Count + 1;    (* One more node reached *)
                if z = v_end then Nopath := false
       else abort;                  (* e.g. loop infinitely *)
if Count ≠ n_(r-1)
then abort;
write Nopath
```

Figure 23.1: Nondeterministic graph inaccessibility algorithm.

Assume that n_{r-1} is given correctly. This program, for every node z, can either ignore it, or "guess" that there exists a path from v_0 to z. After this, it checks to see whether its guess was correct, and aborts if the verification attempt fails[1]. The number of such verified guesses is counted. If it equals n_{r-1} then *every* accessible node has been examined.

---

[1]This can be done by a random walk exactly as in section 23.3.1.

In this case, the final value of Nopath is true if and only if there exists no path from v_0 to v_{end}. In all other cases the program fails to terminate, so only correct answers are ever produced.

The algorithm above uses several variables, each either of value bounded by either a constant or $\log r$, and so runs in logarithmic space (assuming n_{r-1} given in advance).

What remains is to verify that n_{r-1} can be computed in logarithmic space; this is done by the following algorithm, also nondeterministic. First, note that $n_0 = 1$ since there is exactly one path $v_0 \to^0 v_0$ of length 0 from v_0.

The rest of the algorithm is based on the fact that $v_0 \to^i u$ for $i \geq 1$ iff $v_0 \to^{i-1} w$ and $w \to u$ is a G edge for some node w. The algorithm determines for every node u whether or not there is an edge from at least one node w with $v_0 \to^{i-1} w$. Assuming inductively that the count n_{i-1} is known, this can be done as in the algorithm above: nondeterministically choose *some* nodes w with $v_0 \to^{i-1} w$, and use the count n_{i-1} to verify that *all* such nodes have been examined. If so, $v_0 \to^i u$ iff there is an edge $w \to u$ where w is one of the nodes that was examined.

The program of Figure 23.2 embodies these ideas. □

The algorithm above uses several variables, each either of value bounded by either a constant or $\log r$, and so runs in logarithmic space.

23.3.3   Graph accessibility in polynomial time

Lemma 23.3.3 GAP is in PTIME.

Proof is omitted; it is just the correctness of the well-known "depth-first search" algorithm of Figure 23.3. Time analysis, at first abstractly: the loop to initialize Seenbefore takes time $O(|V|)$. Procedure Probe can call itself recursively at most r times. No edge is probed more than once, so the total time used in Probe is $O(\max(|V|, |E|))$. Combining these, the algorithm's total run time is $O(\max(|V|, |E|))$.

Now a more concrete analysis, of Turing machine computation time. Suppose graph G is represented by listing its vertices and edges as in Definition 23.2.1.

The algorithm can be implemented on a Turing machine, storing array Seenbefore and the recursion stack on its tape. Extra time is required, however, to scan up and down its tape to find edges in E and to test Seenbefore[v]. A straightforward analysis shows the total run time to be bounded by a small polynomial in $\max(|V|, |E|)$, and thus in the size of the representation of G, since $\max(|V|, |E|) \leq (|V| + |E|) \leq size(G)$.

```
n := 1; i := 0;
repeat                          (* Invariant here: n = n_i  *)
  i := i + 1;
  n := 0;         (* Search for all and only nodes u reachable  *)
  for u := 1 to r do                 (* from v_0 in ≤i steps  *)
    Counter := n_i;  (* Find all nodes reachable in <i steps *)
    Foundu := false;
    for w := 1 to r do               (* Examine EVERY node w *)
      choose                 (* Guess w unreachable in <i steps  *)
        skip
      or                     (* Guess w reachable in <i steps    *)
        if ∃ path v_0 →^{<i} w
        then Counter := Counter-1; (* w reached in <i steps  *)
             if w → u then Foundu := true;  (* If reachable *)
        else abort;
    if Counter ≠ 0
      then abort   (* Missed nodes reachable in <i steps      *)
    if Foundu
      then n := n + 1;  (* Another u reachable in ≤i steps     *)
until i = r-1;
  (* End of outermost loop *)
write n
```

Figure 23.2: Nondeterministic algorithm to compute n_r.

23.3.4   Graph accessibility in $\log^2 n$ space

Lemma 23.3.4 GAP is in $\bigcup_k \text{SPACE}^{\text{TM}}(k(\log n)^2)$.

Proof. Correctness of the following algorithm is based on the observation that $x \to^k y$ iff one of three cases holds: $k = 0$ and $x = y$; or $k = 1$ and $(x,y) \in E$; or $k > 1$ and for some $z \in V$, both of $x \to^{\lceil \frac{k}{2} \rceil} z$ and $z \to^{\lfloor \frac{k}{2} \rfloor} y$ are true.   □

Algorithm   Divide-and-conquer search.

This algorithm (Figure 23.4) uses recursion to decide whether there exists a path from vertex i to vertex j of length at most ℓ. Termination is ensured by dividing ℓ by two at each recursive call. Space bound $\log^2 r$ is understood to mean $(\log r)^2$.   □

Space analysis: procedure Path can call itself recursively to a depth of at most $O(\log r)$, as this is the number of times r can be halved before reaching 1. The "call stack" of

```
procedure Main: Graph -> Boolean;
begin
   read V, E, v₀, v_end;
   forall v in V do Seenbefore[v] := false;
   Probe(v₀);
   write Seenbefore[v_end];
end (* Main program *);

procedure Probe(v);   (* Side effect on Seenbefore *)
begin
   if not Seenbefore[v] then {
      Seenbefore[v] := true;
      for every edge v -> v' in E do Probe(v') }
end
```

Figure 23.3: Depth-first Graph Search.

```
procedure Main: Graph -> Boolean;
begin
   read V, E, v₀, v_end ;
   r := Number of vertices in V;
   write Path(v₀, v_end, r);
end (* Main program *);

procedure Path(i,j,ℓ);
begin          (* Gives true if ∃ path i→*j no longer than ℓ *)
   if ℓ = 0 then {return truth of 'is i = j?'};
   if ℓ = 1 then {return truth of 'is i -> j in E?'};
   for k := 1 to n do {
      ℓ' := ℓ div 2;        (* Integer division *)
      if Path(i, k, ℓ') and Path(k, j, ℓ - ℓ')
      then return true };
   return false
end
```

Figure 23.4: Divide-and-conquer search.

traditional implementations thus has at most $O(\log r)$ stack frames, each containing 3
numbers between 0 and r (and a return address of constant size). Each number can be
represented in $O(\log r)$ bits, so the total storage requirement is at most $O(\log^2 r)$ bits.
This bound is easily achieved on a Turing machine, by storing the call stack on its tape.

23.3.5   Time and space to generate a state transition graph

Assume given program p with m instructions, an input d of length n, and a work space size bound function $f : \mathbb{N} \to \mathbb{N}$. Let $G_p(d) = (V, E, v_0, v_{end})$ be the state transition graph from Definition 23.2.2.

Lemma 23.3.5 If f is space constructible and $f(n) \geq \log n$ for all n, then for a fixed program p there is a c such that for all d, graph $G_p(d)$ can be constructed in time at most $c^{f(|d|)}$.

Construction 23.3.6 The abstract algorithm of Figure 23.5 will write $G_p(d)$.   □

```
    read d;
    n := length(d); (* Input size *)
    z := f(n);      (* Work tape space bound *)
    V := {};        (* No vertices initially *)
    E := {};        (*  No edges initially *)

    for ℓ := 1 to m+1 do    (* Compute the set of all vertices *)
    for i := 0 to n+1 do
    for j := 0 to z+1 do
    forall strings w ∈ {0,1,B}* with |w| ≤ z do
        V := V ∪ {(ℓ,i,j,w)};

    forall c1 ∈ V do forall c2 ∈ V do (* Compute all edges *)
        if c1 → c2 by program p
        then E := E ∪ {c1 → c2};

    v₀:=(1,0,0,B); v_end:=(m,0,1,1); (* Initial and final *)
    write V;
    write E;
    write v₀, v_end;
```

Figure 23.5: Build state transition graph.

Proof. First, the number of configurations $C = (\ell, i, j, W)$ is at most $(m+1)(n+2)(f(n) + 2)3^{f(n)}$, which is $O(g^{f(n)})$ for appropriate g.

Since f is space constructible, step $z := f(n)$; can be performed in space $f(n)$ and so in time $h^{f(n)}$ for appropriate h.

The first nest of four loops takes time proportional to the number of configurations. The second nest of two loops takes time at most quadratic in the number of configurations, which only serves to increase the base of the exponent. The test "if c1 → c2" can be done in time $O(|\text{c1}| + |\text{c2}|)$.

Implementation of the above on a Turing machine is straightforward, the only effect of slow access to data stored on its tapes being to increase the value of c. This completes the proof.   □

Lemma 23.3.7 If f is space constructible and $f(n) \geq \log n$ for all n, then for a fixed program p there is a c such that for all d, graph $G_p(d)$ can be constructed using work space at most $cf(|d|)$.

Proof. A slight modification of Construction 23.3.6 can be used. The change is that instead of storing the vertices and edges of $G_p(d)$ in memory, they are written on a write-only output tape as they are constructed.

First, note that a single configuration $C = (\ell, i, j, \text{w})$ takes space at most

$$O(\max(\log(m+1), \log(n+1), \log(f(n)), f(n))$$

which is of size $O(f(n))$ by the assumption that $f(n) \geq \log n$ (recall that m is fixed). The first nest of loops require storing values of ℓ, i, j and w, which together occupy the space of one configuration. Instead of storing the result, the algorithm is modified to write configurations on the output tape as soon as computed.

The second nest of loops require storing the two configurations c1 and c2 at once. Listing all values of $\text{c1} \in V$ can be done by the same four nested loops just mentioned, and the values of $\text{c2} \in V$ can be generated by four more. Again, edges are written out as soon as generated.

The total storage usage of the algorithm just sketched is clearly $O(f(n))$, as required.   □

23.4   Some inclusions between deterministic and nondeterministic classes

We have now done most of the work needed for the following result, which strengthens that of Theorem 21.5.2.

Theorem 23.4.1 NSPACE$(f) \subseteq$ TIME(c^f) for some constant c, if f is space constructible and $f(n) \geq \log n$ for all n.

Proof. Given p that runs in space f, Construction 23.3.6 yields its state transition graph $G_p(d) = (V, E, v_0, v_{end})$ in time $O(g^{f(n)})$ for appropriate g, where $n = |d|$. We have shown that p accepts d if and only if $G_p(d)$ has a path from v_0 to v_{end}. This can be tested by the depth-first graph searching algorithm of section 23.3 in time polynomial in $g^{f(n)}$, which is again exponential in $f(n)$ (for example $(g^{f(n)})^k = (g^{kf(n)})$). $\qquad\square$

Corollary 23.4.2 NLOGSPACE $\subseteq$ PTIME

Proof. $c^{k\log n} = n^{k\log c}$, so NPSPACE$(k\log n) \subseteq$ TIME$(c^{k\log n}) =$ TIME$(n^{k\log c})$. $\qquad\square$

Theorem 23.4.3 NSPACE$(f) \subseteq$ SPACE(f^2), if f is space constructible and $f(n) \geq \log n$ for all n.

Proof. Suppose $A \in$ NSPACE(f) is accepted by program q. Let program p be as in Proposition 23.1.1, and let $G_p(d)$ be p's state transition graph. As observed before, $d \in A$ iff q accepts d, so $d \in A$ iff $G_p(d)$ has a path from v_0 to v_{end}. It thus suffices to show that this path test can be done in space $(f(n)^2)$, where $n = |d|$.

By Lemma 23.3.7 there is a c such that the function $g(d) = G_p(d)$ can be constructed using work space at most $cf(|d|)$, and graph $G_p(d)$ has at most $r = c^{f(n)}$ nodes. By the result of section 23.3.4, this graph can be tested to see whether a path from v_0 to v_{end} exists in space $O((\log r)^2)$. Finally

$$(\log r)^2 = (\log(c^{f(n)}))^2 = (f(n)\log c)^2 = (\log c)^2 f(n)^2$$

Consequently the test for existence of a path from v_0 to v_{end} can be carried out in space at most $O(f(n)^2)$. $\qquad\square$

Corollary 23.4.4 PSPACE $=$ NPSPACE

Proof. Left-to-right containment is immediate by definition. The opposite containment follows from Theorem 23.4.3, since the square of any polynomial is also a polynomial. $\qquad\square$

23.5   An enigmatic hierarchy

Theorem 23.5.1 LOGSPACE $\subseteq$ NLOGSPACE $\subseteq$ PTIME $\subseteq$ NPTIME $\subseteq$ PSPACE = NPSPACE, and NLOGSPACE $\neq$ PSPACE.

Proof. The set inclusions are immediate consequences of the definitions of the various complexity classes, plus Theorem 23.4.2 and 23.4.3. Further, Theorem 23.4.3 establishes

$$\text{NLOGSPACE} \subseteq \bigcup_{k \geq 1} \text{SPACE}(k \log^2 n)$$

For any $k \geq 1$ we have $\lim_{n \to \infty} k \log^2 n / n = 0$, so by the hierarchy theorem for space constructible bounds (Theorem 21.7.2), there exist problems in SPACE(n) but not in SPACE($k \log^2 n$) for any k, and so a fortiori not in NLOGSPACE. Since n is certainly polynomially bounded, there are problems in PSPACE but not in NLOGSPACE.   □

An interesting but unpleasant fact is that, even after many years' research, it is still not known which of the inclusions above are proper inclusions. The undoubtedly best-known of these several open questions is whether PTIME = NPTIME, also known as the P=NP? question.

Frustratingly, the result that NLOGSPACE $\subsetneq$ PSPACE implies that *at least one* among the inclusions

$$\text{LOGSPACE} \subseteq \text{NLOGSPACE} \subseteq \text{PTIME} \subseteq \text{NPTIME} \subseteq \text{PSPACE}$$

must be a proper inequality (in fact, one among the last three, since equality of all three would violate NLOGSPACE $\subsetneq$ PSPACE); but it is not known *which* ones are proper.

The gap in computational resources between, say, LOGSPACE and NPTIME seems to be enormous. On the one hand, NPTIME allows both polynomially much time, and as much space as can be consumed during this time, and as well the ability to guess. On the other hand, LOGSPACE allows only deterministic program that move a fixed number of pointers about, without changing their data at all. (This claim will be substantiated in section 24.1.)

Nonetheless, no one has been able either to prove that LOGSPACE = PTIME, nor to find a problem solvable in the larger class that is provably unsolvable in the smaller. Many candidates exist that are plausible in a very strong sense, as will be seen in a later chapter on "complete problems," but the problems of proper inclusion remain open.

Theorem 23.5.2 If $A \in$ NSPACE(f) and $f(n) \geq \log n$ is space-constructible, then $\overline{A} \in$ NSPACE($c \cdot f$) for some $c > 0$, where $\overline{A}$ is the complement of A.

Proof. Suppose nondeterministic Turing machine program p accepts A in space f. Then an arbitrary input d is in A iff there is a path in the transition graph $G_p(d)$ of p for input d from v_0 to v_{end}. In other words, $d \in A$ iff $G_p(d) \in$ GAP. But this implies $d \in \overline{A}$ iff $G_p(d) \in \overline{\text{GAP}}$.

By Lemma 23.3.7 there is a c such that for all d, graph $G_p(d)$ can be constructed using work space at most $cf(|d|)$. Combining the construction of $G_p(d)$ with the algorithm of Theorem 23.3.2, we obtain a nondeterministic algorithm to test membership in $\overline{A}$.

Its space usage is at most $\log size(G_p(d))$, and $size(G_p(d))$ is at most $b^{f(|d|)}$ for some b and all inputs d. Consequently the algorithm uses at most $\log b^{f(|d|)} = O(f(|d|))$ space, as required. □

Exercises

23.1 Estimate the running time of the graph searching algorithm of section 23.3.4. □

23.2 Estimate the running time of the state transition graph-building algorithm of section 23.2. □

23.3 Prove carefully that GAP ∈ NLOGSPACE. □

23.4 Estimate the running time of the algorithm of Theorem 23.3.2 for deciding membership in GAP in LOGSPACE. □

References

The "backbone hierarchy" presented here is the result of work by many researchers. These include the first works on space- and time-bounded computation by Hartmanis, Lewis and Stearns [61, 62]; the role of nondeterminism as seen in theory and practice by Kuroda and Edmonds [97, 40]; Savitch's pathbreaking works on logspace computation and reduction plus later results by Meyer, Stockmeyer, Jones and others [149, 120, 79, 71, 75]; and Immerman and Szelepcsenyi's answers in 1987 to Kuroda's question of 23 years before [158, 67].

24   Characterizations of LOGSPACE and PTIME by GOTO Programs

24.1   Characterizing LOGSPACE by cons-free GOTO programs

A tree-manipulating program is *read-only* if it never constructs new values, but instead just scans its input. While limited in their computational power, such programs are by no means trivial. For example (if equipped with a write-only output string) the "append" function is easy to program, and arithmetic operations are not difficult (see the Exercises.) The following defines this and two other restrictions more precisely:

Definition 24.1.1 The restricted languages below have exactly the same semantics as before, except that their sets of programs are limited in various ways.

1. WHro, GOTOro, and F+ro will henceforth denote the read-only versions of the languages WHILE, GOTO and F, respectively, meaning: the same programs and semantics, except that programs restricted not to contain cons. An F program will, however, be allowed to have any fixed number of variables.

2. A $CM^{\backslash C:=C+1}$ program is a CM program without any operations to increase a counter. It is allowed, however, to have instructions Ci := Cj to copy one counter into another.

3. A $CM^{value(n)}$ program is a CM program that, if given input of length n, computes so that no counter ever exceeds n in value.

4. An F+-program is *tail-recursive* if no function call is nested inside another operation or function call (nesting inside the then or else branch of an if expression is allowed, though). F+tr will henceforth denote F restricted to tail-recursive programs, and F+rotr will henceforth denote F restricted to cons-free tail-recursive programs. □

First, an easy result:

Proposition 24.1.2 WHro $\equiv^{lintime}$ GOTOro $\equiv^{lintime}$ F+rotr

Proof. WHro $\equiv^{lintime}$ GOTOro is immediate from the proof of Theorem 18.3.3, as the operation cons was not used in Propositions 8.2.1 or 8.2.2. The point of Exercise 24.1 is to prove GOTOro $\equiv^{lintime}$ F+rotr (straightforward).   □

Looking ahead, we will eventually prove that, when applied to inputs from $\{0,1\}^*$

1. WHro, GOTOro, and F+rotr decide exactly the problems in LOGSPACE.
2. F+ro decides exactly the problems in PTIME (even though F+ro programs may run for exponentially many steps!).

Read-only tail-recursive programs are just those output by Wadler's treeless transformer [164] when applied to (possibly nonlinear) input programs of type $\{0,1\}^* \rightarrow \{0,1\}$. This is interesting since the concept of treelessness was introduced for the "deforestation" program optimization without thought of complexity; and the result above characterizes the computations performable by programs that can be deforested.

24.1.1   Some central simulation lemmas

To establish the first point above, we show that the following all define the same decidable problems (on inputs from $\mathbb{D}_{01}$ for GOTOro programs):

- Turing machine programs that run in space $k \log(|d|)$ for some k.
- Read-only counter programs in which each counter is bounded in value by $|d|$, or a polynomial in $|d|$, or even restricted so that no counter may be incremented.
- GOTOro programs.
- Frotr programs.

Proofs are by a series of lemmas progressing from GOTOro programs to the logspace counter-length bounded machines of Corollary 21.3.1.

Lemma 24.1.3 $A \subseteq \{0,1\}^*$ is decidable by a $\text{CM}^{\backslash \text{C:=C+1}}$ program iff A is decidable by a GOTOro program.

Lemma 24.1.4 If $A \subseteq \{0,1\}^*$ is decidable by a $\text{CM}^{value(n)}$ program then A is decidable by a $\text{CM}^{\backslash \text{C:=C+1}}$ program.

Lemma 24.1.5 If $A \subseteq \{0,1\}^*$ is decidable by a $\text{CM}^{logspace}$ program then A is decidable by a $\text{CM}^{value(n)}$ program.

Together these lemmas imply the following:

Corollary 24.1.6 $A \subseteq \{0,1\}^*$ is decidable by a $\text{CM}^{logspace}$ program iff A is decidable by a $\text{CM}^{\backslash C:=C+1}$ program.

Proof. Corollary 24.1.6: "If" is immediate since $\text{CM}^{\backslash C:=C+1} \subseteq \text{CM}^{value(n)} \subseteq \text{CM}^{logspace}$. "Only if" follows from from Lemmas 24.1.5 and 24.1.4. □

Theorem 24.1.7 $A \subseteq \{0,1\}^*$ is in LOGSPACE^{TM} iff A is decidable by a GOTOro program iff A is decidable by a F+rotr program. □

The theorem is immediate from Corollary 21.3.1, Corollary 24.1.6, and Proposition 24.1.2.

24.1.2 Constructions to prove the simulation lemmas

We must now prove the three Lemmas. The following is an easy result on very limited counter machines:

Proof. Lemma 24.1.3: we must show that any $\text{CM}^{\backslash C:=C+1}$ program p is equivalent to some GOTOro program program, and conversely. Input to a CM-program is a string $a_1 a_2 \ldots a_n$, corresponding to input list

$$(a_n a_{n-1} \ldots a_k \ldots a_1) \in \mathbb{D}_{01}$$

(using Lisp list notation) for a GOTOro-program. Each a_i is nil or (nil.nil).

Suppose we are given a $\text{CM}^{\backslash C:=C+1}$ program p. Its counters Ci can only assume values between 0 and n. Thus any Ci with value k can be represented by a GOTOro program variable Xi which points to sublist $(a_k \ldots a_1)$ (and to the nil at the end of the input list, in case $k = 0$).

Counter command Ci := Cj can obviously be simulated by Xi := Xj. Command Ci := Ci$\dot{-}$1 can be simulated by Xi := tl Xi (recall that $tl(\text{nil}) = \text{nil}$). Command if Ci = 0 goto ℓ else ℓ' can be simulated by if Xi goto ℓ' else ℓ (the test is reversed since counter value 0 corresponds to the end of the list, which has list value nil = false). Command if in$_{\text{Ci}}$ = 0 goto ℓ else ℓ' can be simulated by if hd Xi goto ℓ' else ℓ (the test is again reversed since symbol 0 is coded as nil = false).

Conversely, suppose that we are given a GOTOro-program p and the input list $(a_n a_{n-1} \ldots a_k \ldots a_1) \in \mathbb{D}_{01}$. We assume $n > 0$; a special case can be added to give the correct answer if $n = 0$.

The variables X of p can only point to: one of three things: 1) a position $(a_i...a_k...a_1)$ within the list with $i \geq 1$; or 2) the root of (nil.nil), encoding some $a_i = 1$; or 3) the atom nil.

Thus variable X may be represented by two counter variables X1, X2. In case 1) X1 has $i \geq 1$ as value. In case 2) X1 has value 0 and X2 has value n. In case 3) both variables have value 0.

Counter code to maintain these representation invariants is straighforward to construct, by enumerating the possible forms of GOTOro commands.   □

Proof. Lemma 24.1.4: we must show that any $CM^{value(n)}$ program p is equivalent to some program q without C := C+1. All counters are by assumption bounded by n, so we need not account for "overflow." Recall that counter C0 is initialized to the length n of the input.

We can simulate C := C+1 (without addition!) by using an auxiliary variable Tem and exploiting the instruction Tem := C0 which assigns input length n to Tem. Let the initial value of C be i.

The following works in two phases: first, variable Tem is initialized to n, and then C and Tem are synchronously decremented by 1 until C = 0. Thus Tem ends at $n - i$, at which point it is decremented once again, to $n - i - 1$. For the second pass C is reset to n, and Tem and C are again synchronously counted down until Tem = 0. Once this happens, C is $i + 1 = n - (n - i - 1)$, as required. Note that if C = n, the effect is to leave C unchanged.

```
Tem := C0;                        (* Tem := n *)
while C ≠ 0 do                    (* Tem := n − i and C := 0 *)
   {C := C-1; Tem := Tem-1};
Tem := Tem - 1;                   (* Tem := n − i − 1 *)
C := C0;                          (* C := n *)
while Tem ≠ 0 do                  (* C := i + 1 by decreasing Tem to 0 *)
   {C := C - 1; Tem := Tem - 1};
```
    □

Proof. Corollary 24.1.5: We must show that any $CM^{logspace}$ program p is equivalent to some $CM^{value(n)}$ program q. We do this in two stages.

Representation of an n^2-bounded CM counter by a fixed number of $2n$-bounded counters. Consider the traditional enumeration of pairs of natural numbers:

$$\{(0,0),(0,1),(1,0),(2,0),(1,1),(0,2),(0,3),\ldots\}$$

as described in Appendix A.7. We represent any one counter Cz with value z by two counters Cx, Cy with values x, y such that z is the position of the pair (x, y) in this enumeration. Note that

$$z = (x+y)(x+y+1)/2 + y = (x^2 + 2xy + y^2 + x + 3y)/2$$

so $0 \leq x^2, y^2 \leq 2z$. Thus $x, y \leq 2n$ if $z \leq n^2$.

Each CM operation on Cz is simulable by operation on Cx, Cy as in Figure 24.1. For example, Cz:=Cz+1 involves moving Northwest one position along a diagonal unless $x = 0$, in which case one moves to the start of the next diagonal.

We showed earlier that without loss of generality one may assume that test if $In_C = 0$ goto ℓ else ℓ' is only performed when the value i of C satifies $i \leq n$. This is harder, as it involves reconstructing i from the representation Cx, Cy of C. First, Cx and Cy are copied into Dx, Dy, giving representation of a variable we could call D. By manipulating Dx and Dy the loop decrements D until it reaches 0 or n decrements have occurred, meanwhile counting variable R up by 1 at each iteration. The net result is to set R to $i = \min(i, n)$, and that input position is then tested.

This reduces the counter bound from n^2 to $2n$; the technique below can be used to reduce this further to n. □

The development above supports the intuition that LOGSPACE is precisely the class of all problems solvable by read-only programs, which may move any fixed number of markers around their input, but cannot use any other form of storage. The characterization by GOTO programs is particularly elegant, although one has a suspicion that such programs will take extra time due to the complexity of "backing up" to inspect an already-seen input.

Representation of one $2n$-bounded CM counter C by several n-bounded counters. We represent C containing x by counters Under and Over, where Under contains $\min(x, n)$, and Over contains 0 if $x \leq n$ and $x - n$ otherwise. Each CM operation on C is simulable as in Figure 24.2. Variable N is counter CO, initialized to the input length n (again assumed to be posititve).

24.1.3   Relation to functional and Wadler's treeless programs

Wadler's "treeless transformer," when applied to any of a quite useful class of first-order programs, will automatically yield a linear-time equivalent program which *builds*

operation on C	Simulation on C1, C2
Cz := Cz+1	if Cx ≠ 0 then {Cx := Cx-1; Cy := Cy+1} else {Cx := Cy+1; Cy := 0}
Cz := Cz-1	if Cy ≠ 0 then {Cx := Cx+1; Cy := Cy-1} else {Cy := Cx-1; Cx := 0}
if Cz ≠ 0 goto ℓ	if C1 ≠ 0 or C2 ≠ 0 then goto ℓ
if In$_C$ ≠ 0 goto ℓ	R := 0; S := C0; Dx := Cx; Dy := Cy; while S ≠ 0 and not(Cz1 = Cz2 = 0) do {R := R+1; Code for D := D-1} if In$_R$ ≠ 0 goto ℓ

Figure 24.1: Simulating an n^2-bounded counter by two $2n$-bounded counters.

Operation on C	Simulation
C := C+1	if Under = n then Over := Over+1 else Under := Under+1
C := C-1	if Over = 0 then Under := Under-1 else Over := Over-1
if C ≠ 0 goto ℓ	if Over ≠ 0 or Under ≠ 0 then goto ℓ
if In$_C$ ≠ 0 goto ℓ	if In$_{Under}$ ≠ 0 goto ℓ

Figure 24.2: Simulating a $2n$-bounded counter by n-bounded counters.

no intermediate tree structures [164]. Here cons operations may appear (and other constructors too, henceforth ignored); but their only function is to construct output values, not to produce data in one program part that will be consumed in another (the functional world's equivalent of "storage").

Relaxing Wadler's requirement that right sides must be linear (not contain two references to the same variable), we obtain a language identical to F+rotr. Consider a treeless program that yields only constant values as output. Even though it may use cons internally, the program output by his transformation then contains no "cons" operations at all. Again relaxing the linearity requirement on right sides, we obtain a language essentially identical with F+rotr.

Theorem 24.1.8 Without the right side linearity requirement, treeless programs with input in $\{0,1\}^*$ and output in $\{0,1\}$ decide exactly the problems in LOGSPACE.

24.2 Characterizing PTIME by cons-free programs with recursion

We now prove that PTIME is identical to the set of problems solvable by cons-free programs with recursion. This is analogous to the intrinsic characterization of LOGSPACE, without reference to time or storage bounds.

24.2.1 The recursive extension of a programming language

Definition 24.2.1 Suppose L is a programming language in which each program has form

    1:I1 2:I2 ... k:Ik

The *recursive extension* L^{+rec} is defined so L^{+rec}-*programs* consists of all programs with syntax as in Figure 24.3. where each instruction In, Jn or Kn can be either:

- "call Pr" where $1 \leq r \leq m$; or

- Any L-instruction (unlimited, except that in each procedure Pi, any referenced variable X must satisfy $X \in \{U1, \ldots, Uu, Pi1, Pi2, \ldots\}$, i.e. it must be either local or global).

Semantics is what you expect and so only briefly described. A *total state* is a sequence $(10, \sigma_0, 11, \sigma_1, \ldots, 1n, \sigma_n, \text{exit})$.

Storage: σ_n contains the global variable bindings, σ_0 contains the variable bindings of the most recently called procedure, and $\sigma_1, \ldots, \sigma_{n-1}$ contain bindings of earlier procedures that have been called but not yet returned from. Variable fetches and assignments are done using only σ_n and σ_0.

Control: 10 is the current control point, $11, \ldots, 1n$ are return addresses, and exit· indicates program termination. The *initial state* is $(1, [U1 \mapsto input], \text{exit})$. Instruction "1:call Pi" causes $10, \sigma_0$ to be replaced by

$$1, \sigma_{new}, 10+1, \sigma_0$$

Here 1 is the new procedure's initial control point, and σ_{new} assigns default values to all of Pi's local variables. Thus label 10+1 plays the role of "return address" (or exit for the initial call.) When a procedure's last instruction has been executed, the leftmost

```
globalvariables U1,...,Uu;

procedure P1; localvariables P11,...,P1v;
    1:I1 2:I2 ... i:Ii

procedure P2; localvariables P21,...,P2w;
    1:J1 2:J2 ... j:Jj
    .....
procedure Pm; localvariables Pm1,...,Pmx;
    1:K1 2:K2 ... k:Kk

read U1; 1:call P1; 2: write U1
```

Figure 24.3: Recursive program syntax.

label and store $10, \sigma_0$ are popped off, and control is transferred to the instruction whose label is on the stack top.

24.2.2   Simulating PTIME without cons

As a first step we use the flow chart implementation of GOTO using arrays, as in section 17.2 of chapter 17. An example appears in Figure 17.5.

Lemma 24.2.2 Given a GOTO-program $p = 1:I_1 \ 2:I_2 \ \dots m:I_m$ and an input $d \in \mathbb{D}_{01}$. Let $(\ell_1, \sigma_1) \to \dots (\ell_t, \sigma_t) \to \dots$ be the (finite or infinite) computation of p on d, where $\ell_1 = 1$ and σ_1 is the initial DAG for input d. Then for any $t \geq 0$ and variable X the equations in Figure 24.4 hold.

Proof. A simple induction on t, using the definitions from Figure 17.4.   □

Theorem 24.2.3 If $V \subseteq \mathbb{D}_{01}$ is decidable by a (recursive or nonrecursive) WHILE-program p in polynomial time, then V is decidable by a $CM^{logspace+rec}$-program.

Proof. Suppose one is given a WHILE-program p that runs in time $f(n)$ where f is a polynomial, and an input d. The various functions $\text{Instr}_t, \text{Hd}_t, \text{Tl}_t, \text{X}_t$ are computable by mutual recursion, at least down to $t = n + 3$ (the time used to build the initial DAG as in section 17.2.2). Further, the values of Hd_t, Tl_t for $t = 0, 1, \dots, n + 2$ are determined solely by the program input d, and easily computed.

$$\text{Instr}_{t+1} = \begin{cases} 1' : I_{1'} & \text{if } \text{Instr}_t = 1\text{: goto } 1' \\ 1' : I_{1'} & \text{if } \text{Instr}_t = 1\text{: if X goto } 1' \text{ else } 1'' \text{ and } X_t \neq 0 \\ 1'' : I_{1''} & \text{if } \text{Instr}_t = 1\text{: if X goto } 1' \text{ else } 1'' \text{ and } X_t = 0 \\ 1{+}1 : I_{1+1} & \text{otherwise} \end{cases}$$

$$\text{Hd}_{t+1} = \begin{cases} Y_t & \text{if } \text{Instr}_t = 1\text{: X := cons Y Z} \\ 0 & \text{otherwise} \end{cases}$$

$$\text{Tl}_{t+1} = \begin{cases} Z_t & \text{if } \text{Instr}_t = 1\text{: X := cons Y Z} \\ 0 & \text{otherwise} \end{cases}$$

$$X_{t+1} = \begin{cases} Y_t & \text{if } \text{Instr}_t = 1\text{: X := Y} \\ \text{Hd}_{(Y_t)} & \text{if } \text{Instr}_t = 1\text{: X := hd Y} \\ \text{Tl}_{(Y_t)} & \text{if } \text{Instr}_t = 1\text{: X := tl Y} \\ t+1 & \text{if } \text{Instr}_t = 1\text{: X := cons Y Z} \\ X_t & \text{otherwise} \end{cases}$$

Figure 24.4: Relations among the values of Hd, Tl, X in general.

Regard each equation in Figure 24.4 as a definition of a function of one variable t. This is always an integer, between 0 and $f(n) + n + 3$ where $n = |d|$.

The calls all terminate, since in each call the value of argument t decreases. Now t is bounded by the running time, which is a polynomial in the size of d, hence p can be simulated by a recursive counter machine with polynomial size bounds on its counters.

The value of output variable X is thus available, e.g., to a "print" function, through $X_{f(n)+n+3}$. □

Corollary 24.2.4 If A is decidable in polynomial time, then it is decidable by an F+ro program.

Proof. By the means seen seen earlier in section 24.1, the $\text{CM}^{logspace+rec}$-program can be simulated by a $|d|$-bounded counter machine with recursion (the addition of recursion requires no changes to the constructions), and this in turn can be simulated by a cons-free F+-program. □

Remark.   Time analysis of this procedure reveals that it takes exponential time, due to recomputing values many times (for example, Instr_t is recomputed again and again). Thus even though a polynomial-time problem is being solved, the solver is running in superpolynomial time. Fortunately, the following result gives a converse.

Theorem 24.2.5 If $V \subseteq \mathbb{D}_{01}$ is decidable by an F+ro program, then V is decidable in polynomial time.

Proof. (Sketch.) This is done by tabulation. Suppose we are given an F+ro program p, and an input $\text{d}_0 = (\text{a}_1 \dots \text{a}_n) \in \mathbb{D}$.

The idea is to collect a set MFG^1 of triples of forms $(\text{f}, \sigma, \bullet)$ or $(\text{f}, \sigma, \text{d})$, where f is the name of a function defined in p, σ is a tuple of arguments to f, and $\text{d} \in \mathbb{D}$. These signify the following.

1. $(\text{f}, \sigma, \bullet) \in MFG$: function f appearing in program p has been called, with argument tuple σ. Computation of the value of $\text{f}(\sigma)$ is not yet finished.

2. $(\text{f}, \sigma, \text{d}) \in MFG$: function f appearing in program p has been called, with argument tuple σ, and the value $\text{f}(\sigma) = \text{d}$ has been computed.

Since p is cons-free, the value that σ assigns to any variable X must be a pointer to some part of d_0. There are at most n of these, and so there exist at most $2m \cdot n^{k+1}$ possible triples in MFG, where m is the number of functions defined in p.

The simulation algorithm:

1. $MFG := \{(\text{f}1, [\text{X}1 \mapsto (\text{d}_0)], \bullet)\}$, where the first function in p is f1 and has argument X1.

2. Repeat steps 3 through 9 until MFG cannot be changed.

3. Pick a triple $(\text{f}, \sigma, \bullet) \in MFG$, and find the definition f(X1, ..., Xn) = Exp in program p.

4. Attempt to evaluate Exp with X1, ..., Xn bound to the values in σ.

5. If the value of a call g(Exp1, ..., Expm) is needed in order to evaluate Exp, try to evaluate the arguments Exp1, ..., Expm to yield a tuple σ'.

6. If argument evaluation fails, then abandon the current attempt to evaluate Exp.

7. If argument evaluation succeeds and MFG contains a triple $(\text{g}, \sigma', \text{d}')$, then continue to evaluate Exp with d' as the value of the call g(Exp1, ..., Expm).

---

[1]MFG stands for "minimal function graph." as in [78].

8. If argument evaluation succeeds but MFG contains no triple (g, σ', d') with $d' \in \mathbb{D}$, then perform $MFG := MFG \cup \{(g, \sigma', \bullet)\}$, and abandon the current attempt to evaluate Exp.

9. If evaluation of Exp with X1 , . . . , Xn bound to the values in σ succeeds with result value d, then replace $(f, \sigma, \bullet) \in MFG$ by $(f, \sigma, d) \in MFG$.

10. If $(f, [X1 \mapsto (d_0)], d) \in MFG$, then $[\![p]\!](d_0) = d$, else $[\![p]\!](d_0) = \bot$.

MFG is used for two purposes while simulating program p. The first is as an "oracle," from which to fetch values of already computed function applications, rather than re-computing them. The second is as a "repository" in which the triple (f, σ, d) is placed every time a new fact $f(\sigma) = d$ has been established. If this happens, the triple $(f, \sigma, \bullet)$ (which must already be in MFG) is replaced by the new (f, σ, d).

This process is repeated until MFG cannot be increased. If one ever adds a triple $(f1, [X1 \mapsto d_0], d)$, then we know that $[\![p]\!](d_0) = d$, and the computation stops. The entire algorithm can be made terminating, since there exists only a polynomially bounded number of possible triples to put in MFG.

Interestingly, the same technique also works if p is nondeterministic, and the method applies as well if the functions are replaced by relations. □

Further developments. Cook [28] proved similar results in the framework of "auxiliary push-down automata." Further developments involving efficient memoization led to the result that any 2DPDA (*two-way deterministic pushdown automaton*) can be simulated in linear time on a RAM ([26, 72, 5]). This in turn led to efficient pattern-matching algorithms, in particular the Knuth-Morris-Pratt string matcher – an interesting case where investigations in "pure theory" led to a practically significant algorithm.

An interesting open problem. The results above can be interpreted as saying that, in the absence of "cons," functional programs are capable of simulating imperative ones; but at a formidable cost in computing time, since results computed earlier cannot be stored but must be recomputed. In essence, the "heap" can be replaced by the "stack," but at a high time cost.

It is not known, however, *whether this cost is necessary*. Proving that it is necessary (as seems likely) would require proving that there exist problems which can be solved in small time with general storage, but which require large time when computed function-ally. A simple but typical example would be to establish a nonlinear lower bound on the time that a one-tape, no-memory *two-way pushdown automaton* [28] requires to solve some decision problem. One instance would be to prove that string matching must take superlinear time. We conjecture that such results can be obtained.

Exercises

24.1 Prove the missing part of Theorem 24.1.2. (Note that two inclusions need to be established.)   □

24.2 Prove that it is possible to construct from any GOTOro program an equivalent WHro program, and vice versa. (You may appeal to constructions seen earlier.)   □

24.3 Prove that it is possible to construct from any GOTO program an equivalent Fro program.   □

24.4 Try to show how to construct from any Fro program an equivalent GOTOro or WHro program. Reflect on the results of your attempt.   □

24.5 Assume that WHro programs are allowed a command "`write X`" whose effect is to extend a write-only output string by 0 in case the value of X is `nil`, and to extend it by 1 otherwise. The output string is initially empty.

Denote by $\bar{x}$ the binary representation of number x, as a list of bits written in reverse order, i.e., least significant bit first. Write a WHro program which, when given input $(\bar{x}\ \bar{y})$, will write out $\overline{x+y}$.   □

24.6 Assume WHro programs have outputs as described in the previous exercise. Write a WHro program which, when given input $(a_1 a_2 \ldots a_n)$ where each $a_i \in \{0, 1\}$, will write out its reversal $(a_n a_{n-1} \ldots a_1)$.   □

References

Both of the main results of this chapter have been seen before in other forms.

It has long been a "folklore theorem" that LOGSPACE consists of exactly to the sets decidable by a multihead, two-way read-only Turing machine. The result of Theorem 24.1.7 implies this, since such a Turing machine is essentially identical to a $CM^{value(n)}$ program. Our result is a bit stronger since Theorem 24.1.7 can be read as saying that the Turing machine could be restricted only to move its heads right, or to reset them back to the start of the input tape.

More than 25 years ago Cook [26] used a somewhat different framework, "auxiliary push-down automata," to characterize PTIME. In essence this is very close to our proof that PTIME equals the sets decidable by `Frotr`-programs, the main difference being that our recursive programs have an implicit call stack in place of Cook's nonrecursive automata with an explicit single stack.

In comparison to these classical results, our program-oriented version seems more natural from a programming viewpoint (both appear in [83], which sums up the results of this chapter). In particular, the results are still of considerable interest as regards relationships between time and space, or the power of "cons" in a functional language.

Part V

Complete Problems

25 Completeness and Reduction of One Problem to Another

An old slogan: "If you can't solve problems, then at least you can classify them."

25.1 Introduction

The unsolved problems of Theorem 23.5.1 concerning proper containments within

$$\text{LOGSPACE} \subseteq \text{NLOGSPACE} \subseteq \text{PTIME} \subseteq \text{NPTIME} \subseteq \text{PSPACE} = \text{NPSPACE}$$

are apparently quite difficult, since they have remained open since the 1970s in spite of many reseachers' best efforts to solve them. This has led to an alternative approach: to define *complexity comparison* relations $\leq$ between decision problems (different relations will be appropriate for different complexity classes).

The statement $A \leq B$ can be interpreted as "problem A is no more difficult to solve than problem B," or even better: "given a good way to solve B, a good way to solve A can be found." Further, we can use this idea to break a problem class such as NPTIME into *equivalence subclasses* by defining A and B to be of equivalent complexity if $A \leq B$ and $B \leq A$.

Complexity comparison is almost always via *reduction* of one problem to another: $A \leq B$ means that one can efficiently transform an algorithm that solves B within given resource bounds into an algorithm that solves A within similar resource bounds[1]. Two interesting facts lie at the core of modern complexity theory, and will be proven in the following chapters:

1. Each of the several complexity classes $\mathcal{C}$ already studied possesses *complete problems*. Such a problem (call it H) lies in class $\mathcal{C}$, and is "hardest" for it in the sense that $A \leq H$ for each problem A in $\mathcal{C}$. Class $\mathcal{C}$ may have many hard problems.

2. A complete problem H for class $\mathcal{D}$ has the property that if $H \in \mathcal{C}$ for a lower class $\mathcal{C}$ in the hierarchy of Theorem 23.5.1, then $\mathcal{C} = \mathcal{D}$: the two classes are identical. Informally said, the hierarchy *collapses* at that point.

---

[1]Examples have already been seen in chapter 10 including Definition 10.1.1. There several problems were proven undecidable by reducing the halting problem to them. Intuitively: if *HALT* is thought of as having infinite complexity, proving $HALT \leq B$ shows that B also has infinite complexity.

3. Even more interesting: Many *natural and practically motivated* problems have been proven to be complete for one or another complexity class $\mathcal{C}$.

25.1.1 Forms of reduction

The idea of *reduction* of one problem to another has been studied for many years, for example quite early in Mathematical Logic as a tool for comparing the complexity of two different unsolvable problems or undecidable sets. Many ways have been devised to reduce one problem to another since Emil Post's pathbreaking work in 1944 [135].

A reduction $A \le B$ where (say) $A, B \subseteq \mathbb{D}$ can be defined in several ways. First, the reduction may be *many-one*: one shows that $A \le B$ by exhibiting a total computable function such that for any $\mathrm{d} \in \mathbb{D}$ we have $\mathrm{d} \in A$ if and only if $f(\mathrm{d}) \in B$. Clearly, an algorithm for deciding membership in B can be used to decide membership in A. (A concrete example will be given shortly.) A stronger version is *one-one*, in which f is required to be injective.

An alternative is *truth-table reducibility*, where one answers a question $x \in A$? by asking several questions $y_1 \in B, \ldots, y_k \in B$?, and then combining the truth values of their answers in some preassigned way. Yet another variant is *Turing reducibility*, where question $x \in A$? gives rise to a dialogue: a whole series of questions about membership in B. The first question depends only on x. The second question (if any) can depend both on x and the response (positive or negative) to the first question; and so forth. The chief requirement on such a reduction is that the series is required to terminate for every x and answer sequence.

If computability is being studied, the only essential requirement is that the reduction be effective. Complexity classifications are naturally involve bounds on the complexity of the questions that can be asked, for example of the function f used for many-one reducibility. In order to study, say, the class NPTIME using many-one reducibility, it is natural to limit one's self to questions that can be computed by deterministic algorithms in time polynomial in $|x|$.

25.1.2 Three example problems

Appendix section A.1 describes graphs, and boolean expressions and their evaluation. We use the term CNF to stand for *conjunctive normal form*.

Definition 25.1.1

1. A k-clique in undirected graph G is a set of k vertices such that G has an edge between every pair in the set. Figure 25.1 shows a graph G containing two 3-cliques: one with vertices $1, 2, 5$ and another with vertices $1, 4, 5$.

2. A boolean expression $\mathcal{F}$ is said to be *closed* if it has no variables. If closed, $\mathcal{F}$ can be *evaluated* by the familiar rules such as $true \wedge false = false$.

3. A *truth assignment* for $\mathcal{F}$ is a function θ mapping variables to truth values such that $\theta(\mathcal{F})$ is a closed boolean expression. $\mathcal{F}$ is *satisfiable* if it evaluates to *true* for some truth assignment θ.

4. By definition

$$\text{SAT} = \{\mathcal{F} \mid \mathcal{F} \text{ is a satisfiable boolean CNF expression}\}$$

For an example of the satisfiability problem, the CNF expression

$$(A \vee \neg B) \wedge (B \vee C) \wedge (\neg A \vee \neg C)$$

is satisfied by truth assignment $\theta = [A \mapsto false, B \mapsto false, C \mapsto true]$. □

Three combinatorial decision problems. Following are three typical and interesting problems which will serve to illustrate several points. In particular, each will be seen to be complete, i.e., hardest, problems among all those solvable in a nondeterministic time or space class. The problems:

$$\text{GAP} \quad = \quad \{\, G \quad \mid \quad \text{directed graph } G = (V, E, v_0, v_{end}) \text{ has a path}$$
$$\text{from vertex } v_0 \text{ to } v_{end} \,\}$$

$$\text{CLIQUE} \quad = \quad \{\, (G, k) \quad \mid \quad \text{undirected graph } G \text{ has a } k\text{-clique} \,\}$$

$$\text{SAT} \quad = \quad \{\, \mathcal{F} \quad \mid \quad \mathcal{F} \text{ is a satisfiable boolean CNF expression} \,\}$$

25.1.3 Complete problems by reduction to programs with only boolean variables

In this and the following chapters, we prove problems complete for various classes using a novel approach. Supose we are given a decision problem H that we wish to show complete for complexity class $\mathcal{C}$. The most intricate part is usually to show that H is

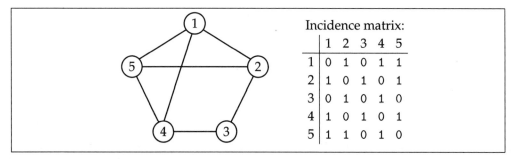

Figure 25.1: *An undirected graph, and its incidence matrix.*

"hard" for C: to show that $A \leq H$ for any arbitrary problem $A \in C$, using an appropriate reduction notion $\leq$ for classifying problems[2] in C.

To say we are given an arbitrary problem $A \in C$ usually means we are given an L-program p (for some language L) that decides membership in A within the time, space, or other resource bounds defining problem class C. Reduction usually establishes hardness by showing how, given a resource-bounded program p $\in$ L-*prog* that solves A, to construct a *reduction function f*.

Such a function maps problems in C into problems in C, and has the property that for any input d $\in$ L-*data*, the answer to the question "does p accept d?" is "yes" if and only if $f(\text{d}) \in H$. Our approach usually proves a problem H hard for C in two steps:

1. Reduce the question "is d $\in A$" to a question involving a very simple class SBP of programs involving only boolean variables.

2. Then we further reduce the question about programs in SBP to a question involving problem H. Typically H is a simple mathematical, logical, or combinatorial problem defined without any reference to programs at all.

25.2 Invariance of problem representations

Before comparing problem complexities, we have to address a question: can *the way a problem is presented* significantly affect the complexity of its solution? For one example, a number n can be presented either in binary notation, or in the much longer unary notation, such as the list form nil^n used before. Another example is that a directed or

---

[2]Showing that $H \in C$ is usually much more straightforward.

undirected graph $G = (V, E)$ with $V = \{v_1, v_2, \ldots, v_n\}$ can be presented in any of several forms:

1. An n by n incidence matrix M with $M_{i,j}$ equal to 1 if $(v_i, v_j) \in E$ and 0 otherwise. Figure 25.1 contains an example.

2. An adjacency list $(u, u', u'', \ldots)$ for each $v \in V$, containing all vertices u for which $(v, u) \in E$. An example is

   $[1 \mapsto (2, 4, 5), 2 \mapsto (1, 3, 5), 3 \mapsto (2, 4), 4 \mapsto (1, 3, 5), 5 \mapsto (1, 2, 4)]$.

3. A list of all the vertices $v \in V$ and edges $(v_i, v_j) \in E$, in some order. Example:

   $[1, 2, 3, 4, 5], \ [(1, 2), (2, 3), (3, 4), (4, 5), (5, 1), (1, 4), (2, 5)]$; or

4. In a compressed format, in case the graph is known to be sparse, i.e., have few edges between vertices.

Loosely speaking, unary notation for numbers seems unnatural given that we measure complexity as a function of input length, since unary notation is exponentially more space-consuming than binary notation.

There are also differences in the graph representations, though less dramatic. For example, the incidence matrix is guaranteed to use n^2 bits, but a sparse matrix could be stored in much less space; and even the apparently economical adjacency list form is less than optimal for dense graphs, as adjacency lists can take as many as $O(n^2 \log n)$ bits, assuming vertex indices to be given in binary.

Problem equivalence modulo encodings

One may circumvent many of these problems by considering problems "modulo encodings," i.e., to consider two problem representations P1 and P2 to be equivalent if there exist computable functions to convert instances of P1 problems into instances of P2 problems with corresponding solutions, and vice versa. Ideally such conversion functions should be simple, and efficiently computable, so a good solution immediately gives rise to a good solution to P2 and vice versa.

It is not known whether the CLIQUE problem is in PTIME or not — all known algorithms take exponential time in the worst case. However a little thought shows that the choice of representation will not affect its status, since one can convert back and forth among the representations above in polynomial time; so existence of a polynomial time

CLIQUE algorithm for one representation would immediately imply the same for any of the other representations.

From this viewpoint the most "sensible" problem representations are all equivalent, at least up to polynomial-time computable changes in representation. The question of representation becomes trickier when one moves to lower complexity classes, and especially so for linear time computation.

Recent work by Paige on the "reading problem" [129] shows that data formed from finite sets by forming tuples, sets, relations, and multisets can be put into a canonical and easily manipulable storage form in linear time on an SRAM[3]. This ensures the independence of many standard combinatorial algorithms from the exact form of problem presentation.

25.3   Reduction for complexity comparisons

Reducing SAT to CLIQUE in polynomial time

Many superficially quite different problems turn out to be "sisters under the skin," in the sense that each can be efficiently reduced to the other. We show by informal example that SAT $\leq_{ptime}$ CLIQUE. This means that there is a polynomial time computable function f which, when given any CNF boolean expression $\mathcal{F}$, will yield a pair $f(\mathcal{F}) = (G, k)$ such that graph G has a k-clique if and only if $\mathcal{F}$ is a satisfiable expression.

This implies that CLIQUE is at least as hard to solve as SAT in polynomial time: given a polynomial time algorithm p to solve CLIQUE, one could answer the question "is $\mathcal{F}$ satisfiable?" by first computing $f(\mathcal{F})$ and then running p on the result.

Construction 25.3.1 Given a conjunctive normal form boolean expression $\mathcal{F} = C_1 \wedge \ldots \wedge C_k$, construct a graph $f(\mathcal{F}) = (G, k)$ where graph $G = (V, E)$ and

1. V = the set of occurrences of literals in $\mathcal{F}$
2. $E = \{(a, b) \mid a$ and b are not in the same conjunct of $\mathcal{F}$, and neither is the negation of the other$\}$

For an instance, the expression

$$(A \vee \neg B) \wedge (B \vee C) \wedge (\neg A \vee \neg C)$$

---

[3]The term "pointer machine" is sometimes used but imprecise, as argued in [9]. By most definitions, the programs obtained by compiling GOTO programs into SRAM code are all pointer programs.

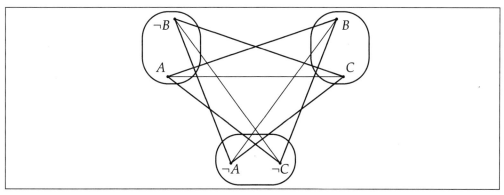

Figure 25.2: The graph $f((A \vee \neg B) \wedge (B \vee C) \wedge (\neg A \vee \neg C))$.

would give graph $f(\mathcal{F})$ as in Figure 25.2. The expression $\mathcal{F}$ is satisfied by truth assignment $[A \mapsto false, B \mapsto false, C \mapsto true]$, which corresponds to the 3-clique $\{\neg A, \neg B, C\}$. More generally, if $\mathcal{F}$ has n conjuncts, there will be one n-clique in $f(\mathcal{F})$ for every truth assignment that satisfies $\mathcal{F}$, and these will be the only n-cliques in $f(\mathcal{F})$.

It is also possible to show that $\text{CLIQUE} \underset{ptime}{\leq} \text{SAT}$, but by a less straightforward construction. We now proceed to define these concepts more formally.

25.3.1 A general definition of problem reduction

Recall that a *problem* is identified with deciding membership in a set of strings $A \subseteq \Sigma^*$ where $\Sigma = \{0,1\}$.

Definition 25.3.2 Let $\leq$ be a binary relation between decision problems over $\Sigma = \{0,1\}$. Let $\mathcal{C}, \mathcal{D} \subseteq \mathcal{P}(\Sigma^*)$ be two sets of problems[4] with $\mathcal{C} \subseteq \mathcal{D}$. Relation $\leq$ is called a $\mathcal{C}, \mathcal{D}$-*classifier* if for all $A, B, C \subseteq \Sigma^*$

1.	$A \leq A$	Reduction is reflexive
2.	$A \leq B$ and $B \leq C$ implies $A \leq C$	Reduction is transitive
3.	$A \leq B$ and $B \in \mathcal{C}$ implies $A \in \mathcal{C}$	$\mathcal{C}$ is downwards closed under reduction
4.	$A \leq B$ and $B \in \mathcal{D}$ implies $A \in \mathcal{D}$	$\mathcal{D}$ is downwards closed under reduction

---

[4]For example we could have $\mathcal{C} = \text{PTIME}$ and $\mathcal{D} = \text{NPTIME}$. Generally, $\mathcal{C}$ and $\mathcal{D}$ will be two classes for which we know that $\mathcal{C} \subseteq \mathcal{D}$, but we do not know whether the inclusion is proper.

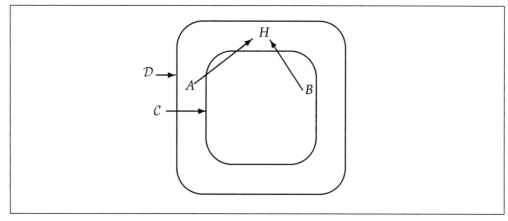

Figure 25.3: A complete problem H for D.

Definition 25.3.3 Given a C, D-classifier $\leq$ and sets $A, B, H \subseteq \Sigma^*$

- A, B are $\leq$-*equivalent* if $A \leq B$ and $B \leq A$.
- H is $\leq$-*hard for* D if $A \leq H$ for all $A \in D$.
- H is $\leq$-*complete for* D if $H \in D$, and H is $\leq$-hard for D.

Figure 25.3 illustrates the idea that problem H is complete; it lies within set D, and every problem in D or its subset C is reducible to H. The following shows the utility of these ideas: if a problem complete for a larger class is contained in a smaller class (with an appropriate reduction), then the two classes are identical.

Proposition 25.3.4 If $\leq$ is a C, D-classifier, and $C \subseteq D$, and H is $\leq$-complete for D, then $H \in C$ if and only if $C = D$.

Proof. "If" is trivial. For "only if," suppose $H \in C$, and let $A \in D$ be arbitrary. By completeness $A \leq H$, and by the definition of a classifier, $A \in C$. Thus $D \subseteq C$ and so $D = C$.   □

Proposition 25.3.5 If A is $\leq$-complete for D, and $A \leq B$, and $B \in D$, then B is also complete for D.

Proof. Let $D \in D$ be arbitrary. By completeness $D \leq A$, and by the definition of a classifier, $A \leq B$ implies $D \leq B$. Thus B is D-hard, so $B \in D$ implies it is D-complete.   □

The following shows thatthe complement of a complete problem is also complete, provided the class it is in is closed under complementation.

Theorem 25.3.6 Suppose that $\mathcal{D}$ is closed under complementation, meaning $A \in \mathcal{D}$ implies $\Sigma^* \setminus A \in \mathcal{D}$. If $\leq$ is a $\mathcal{C}, \mathcal{D}$-classifier and problem H is $\leq$-complete for $\mathcal{D}$, then so is $\Sigma^* \setminus H$.

Proof. Since H is $\leq$-complete for $\mathcal{D}$ it is in $\mathcal{D}$, which implies $\Sigma^* \setminus H$ is also in $\mathcal{D}$. Note that by completeness of H we have $\Sigma^* \setminus H \leq H$. Further, it is immediate that $A \leq B$ if and only if $\Sigma^* \setminus A \leq \Sigma^* \setminus B$ for any A, B. This implies $H \leq \Sigma^* \setminus H$.

To show hardness, consider an arbitrary problem $A \in \mathcal{D}$. Then $A \leq H$ by hardness of H and so $A \leq \Sigma^* \setminus H$ by transitivity of reduction. Thus $\Sigma^* \setminus H$ is $\leq$-complete for $\mathcal{D}$. □

Many-one reductions

A common classification technique is by so-called many-one *reduction functions*. A function f that reduces A to B has the property that $x \in A$ iff $f(x) \in B$ for all x. Thus the question "is $x \in A$?" can be answered by first computing $f(x)$, and then asking "is $f(x) \in B$?" Provided f is essentially simpler to compute than the problem of deciding membership in A, this shows a way that answering one problem can help to answer another.

Definition 25.3.7 Given a class *Fns* of total functions $f : \Sigma^* \to \Sigma^*$, define

$$A \underset{Fns}{\leq} B \text{ if and only if } \exists f \in \mathit{Fns}(\forall x \in \Sigma^* . x \in A \text{ if and only if } f(x) \in B)$$

The general idea is that *Fns* is a class of "easy" *reduction functions*, that can be used to classify complex problems by reducing one to another. An example would be the function f used to reduce SAT to CLIQUE in the example seen earlier.

Lemma 25.3.8 $\underset{Fns}{\leq}$ is a $\mathcal{C}, \mathcal{D}$-classifier, provided

1. Class *Fns* contains the identity function $id : \Sigma^* \to \Sigma^*$,
2. *Fns* is closed under composition (so $f, g \in \mathit{Fns}$ implies $f \circ g \in \mathit{Fns}$),
3. $f : \Sigma^* \to \Sigma^* \in \mathit{Fns}$ and $B \in \mathcal{C}$ implies $\{x \mid f(x) \in B\} \in \mathcal{C}$, and
4. $f : \Sigma^* \to \Sigma^* \in \mathit{Fns}$ and $B \in \mathcal{D}$ implies $\{x \mid f(x) \in B\} \in \mathcal{D}$.

Proof. Condition 1 implies $A \underset{Fns}{\leq} A$ for any A. If $A \underset{Fns}{\leq} B$ by function f in *Fns* and $B \underset{Fns}{\leq} C$ by function g in *Fns*, then $A \underset{Fns}{\leq} C$ by function $g \circ f$ in *Fns*, by Condition 2. Finally, by Conditions 3 and 4 $A \leq B, B \in \mathcal{C}$ imply $A \in \mathcal{C}$, and $A \leq B, B \in \mathcal{D}$ imply $A \in \mathcal{D}$. □

Definition 25.3.9 Some special cases of many-one classifiers:

$$\underset{rec}{\leq} \quad : \quad Fns = \{\text{total recursive functions } f : \Sigma^* \to \Sigma^*\}$$

$$\underset{ptime}{\leq} \quad : \quad Fns = \{\text{polynomial time computable functions } f : \Sigma^* \to \Sigma^*\}$$

$$\underset{logs}{\leq} \quad : \quad Fns = \{\text{logarithmic space computable functions } f : \Sigma^* \to \Sigma^*\}$$

Theorem 25.3.10 Consider the list of problem classes LOGSPACE, NLOGSPACE, PTIME, NPTIME, PSPACE, REC, RE.

1. $\underset{rec}{\leq}$ is a REC, RE-classifier

2. $\underset{ptime}{\leq}$ is a PTIME, $\mathcal{D}$-classifier for any $\mathcal{D}$ appearing later in the list than PTIME.

3. $\underset{logs}{\leq}$ is a LOGSPACE, $\mathcal{D}$-classifier for any $\mathcal{D}$ appearing later in the list than LOGSPACE.

Proof. Straightforward verification of the conditions of Lemma 25.3.8. □

25.3.2 Sources of complete problems

It may seem surprising that complete problems exist at all for our various complexity classes. Interestingly, most of the classes mentioned before (excepting linear time) have *natural and interesting* complete problems. The following chapters will discuss several in detail

Existence of complete problems

Given a class $\mathcal{D}$ and an appropriate notion of problem reduction $\leq$, a first question to ask is whether or not $\mathcal{D}$ has at least one $\leq$-complete problem, say, H. This can be technically difficult since it involves showing that *any* problem A in $\mathcal{D}$ can be reduced to H, i.e., that H is "hard" for $\mathcal{D}$. The other part, showing that $H \in \mathcal{D}$, is often (though not always) fairly straightforward.

The usual way to show H to be $\leq$-hard for $\mathcal{D}$ is to begin with an arbitrary Turing machine (or other) program p that decides a problem A within the resource limits that define $\mathcal{D}$, and to show how, given an arbitrary p-input d, to construct a value $f(\mathsf{d})$ such that $\mathsf{d} \in A \Leftrightarrow f(\mathsf{d}) \in H$. If f defines a $\leq$-reduction, the task is completed since one has shown $A \leq H$ for any $A \in \mathcal{D}$.

A powerful and general way to prove the existence of such problems is to make variants of the set accepted by the universal programs seen before (for instance we will see that the halting problem *HALT* is complete for the recursively enumerable sets). While this proves the existence of complete problems, the problems obtained this way are often, however, somewhat unnatural and unintuitive. An example will be seen below for nondeterministic linear time in section 25.6.

Showing other problems complete

Once the existence of one $\leq$-complete problem for $\mathcal{D}$ has been established, other problems can be shown complete by Proposition 25.3.5: If H is $\leq$-complete for $\mathcal{D}$, and $H \leq B$, and $B \in \mathcal{D}$, then B is also complete for $\mathcal{D}$. This is usually much simpler since it does not involve reasoning about arbitrary programs in a computation model. The technique has been used extensively since Cook's pathbreaking work proving the existence of problems $\leq_{ptime}$-complete for NPTIME. Several hundred problems have been shown complete for NPTIME and for PTIME. Relevant books include [49] and [53].

However for this approach to be useful it is necessary that problem H be well-chosen: simply stated, and such that many interesting problems can easily be reduced to it. It is for this reason that the problems SAT and GAP have taken prominent roles within the classes NPTIME and NLOGSPACE, respectively. We will see similarly archetypical problems for both PTIME and PSPACE.

We begin with two examples: one obtained by a universal construction, and one obtained from the state transition graphs used earlier.

25.4 Complete problems for RE by recursive reductions

Theorem 25.4.1 The following set is $\leq_{rec}$-complete for the class RE:

$$HALT = \{(\mathtt{p.d}) \mid \mathtt{p} \text{ is a GOTO-program and } [\![\mathtt{p}]\!](\mathtt{d}) \neq \bot\}$$

Proof. $HALT \in$ RE by Theorem 5.6.1. We now need to show that $A \leq_{rec} HALT$ for any $A \in$ RE. By Theorem 5.7.2, $A \in$ RE implies that there exists a GOTO-program p such that $A = dom([\![\mathtt{p}]\!])$. Thus for any $\mathtt{d} \in \Sigma^*$

$\mathtt{d} \in A$ if and only if $[\![\mathtt{p}]\!](\mathtt{d}) \neq \bot$ if and only if $(\mathtt{p.d}) \in HALT$

Thus $A \underset{rec}{\leq} HALT$ by the (obviously recursive) reduction function $f(\mathtt{d}) = (\mathtt{p.d})$. □

We conclude that *HALT* is a "hardest" problem among all recursively enumerable problems. Further, for each problem X shown undecidable in chapter 10, either X or its complement is $\underset{rec}{\leq}$-complete for RE:

Theorem 25.4.2 The following sets are $\underset{rec}{\leq}$-complete for the class RE:

1. *HALT-2CM* = {(p.d) | p is a 2CM-program and $[\![p]\!](\mathtt{d}) \neq \perp$}.
2. The string rewriting problem DERIV.
3. Post's correspondence problem PCP.
4. {$(G_1, G_2) | G_1, G_2$ are context-free grammars and $L(G_1) \cap L(G_2) \neq \emptyset$}.
5. CFAMB = {$G | G$ is an ambiguous context-free grammar}.
6. CFNOTALL = {$G | L(G) \neq T^*$ where T is CF grammar G's terminal alphabet}.

Proof. chapter 8 showed that $HALT \underset{rec}{\leq} HALT\text{-}2CM$, and chapter 10 had proofs that $HALT \underset{rec}{\leq} X$ for each remaining set X in this list. By Theorem 25.4.1, $A \underset{rec}{\leq} HALT$ for any $A \in$ RE, so by Theorem 25.3.10, $HALT \underset{rec}{\leq} X$ implies $A \underset{rec}{\leq} X$ for any $A \in$ RE. Thus each of the sets X above is hard for RE.

Further, it is quite easy to see that each of the sets X above lies in RE, concluding the proof. □

By the Friedberg-Muchnik theorem (see [147] for a proof) there exist incomparable recursively enumerable problems, that is to say, there are problems A, B such that neither $A \underset{rec}{\leq} B$ nor $B \underset{rec}{\leq} A$ holds.

25.5 Complete problems for NLOGSPACE by logspace reductions

Theorem 25.5.1 The following set is $\underset{logs}{\leq}$-complete for the class NLOGSPACE:

$$GAP = \{ G = (V, E, v_0, v_{end}) \mid \text{graph } G \text{ has a path from vertex } v_0 \text{ to } v_{end} \}$$

Proof. Let $G = (V, E, v_0, v_{end})$ be a given graph with designated start and finish vertices v_0, v_{end} and vertex set $V = \{v_1, \ldots, v_r\}$. Note that $r \leq size(G)$ for any natural representation.

First, GAP $\in$ NLOGSPACE by Theorem 23.3.1. We now need to show that if $A \in$ NLOGSPACE then $A \underset{logs}{\leq}$ GAP. Let $A = Acc(\mathrm{p})$ where p is a nondeterministic TMro-program running in logarithmic space.

Section 23.2 showed how to build the state transition graph $G_\mathrm{p}(\mathrm{d})$ from d for a given TMro-program p. Further, the proof of Lemma 23.3.7 showed that the vertices and edges of $G_\mathrm{p}(\mathrm{d})$ could be listed using at most $k \log n$ space, where $n = |\mathrm{d}|$. In other words, function $f(\mathrm{d}) = G_\mathrm{p}(\mathrm{d})$ is computable in logarithmic space.

Clearly $\mathrm{d} \in A$ if and only if p accepts d, which in turn holds if and only if $f(\mathrm{d}) = G_\mathrm{p}(\mathrm{d}) \in$ GAP. Consequently $A \underset{logs}{\leq}$ GAP, so GAP is NLOGSPACE-hard. It is also in NLOGSPACE, so it is $\underset{logs}{\leq}$-complete for NLOGSPACE. $\qquad\square$

Thus GAP is a "hardest" problem among all problems in NLOGSPACE:

Corollary 25.5.2 GAP is in LOGSPACE if and only if LOGSPACE = NLOGSPACE.

Theorem 25.5.3 The nonemptiness problem for regular grammars is $\underset{logs}{\leq}$-complete for NLOGSPACE. $\qquad\square$

Proof. First, it is in NLOGSPACE: Given regular grammar $G = (N, T, P, S)$, build a graph with edge from A to B whenever there is a production $A ::= xB$. Then $L(G) \neq \emptyset$ iff there is a path from S to some C where $C ::= x$ with $x \in T^*$ is a production in P. In section 23.3 we saw that graph searching could be done by a nondeterministic algorithm in logarithmic space. The graph built has size no larger than that of the grammar, so this shows that the nonemptiness problem for regular grammars is in NLOGSPACE.

Conversely, since the graph accessibility problem GAP is complete for NLOGSPACE it suffices by Proposition 25.3.5 to reduce GAP to the regular nonemptiness problem. Given a graph accessibility problem instance (G, v_0, v_{end}), construct a grammar with start symbol v_0, productions $A ::= B$ for all edges $A \to B$ of G, and a single terminal production $v_{end} ::= \varepsilon$. This regular grammar will generate the set $\{\varepsilon\}$ if G has a path from v_0 to v_{end}, and $\emptyset$ if there is no such path. $\qquad\square$

The following are immediate from Theorem 25.3.6.

Corollary 25.5.4 The following set is $\leq_{logs}$-complete for the class NLOGSPACE:

$$\overline{\text{GAP}} = \{ \, G = (V, E, v_0, v_{end}) \mid \text{graph } G \text{ has no path from } v_0 \text{ to } v_{end} \}$$

Corollary 25.5.5 The emptiness problem for regular grammars is $\leq_{logs}$-complete for NLOGSPACE.

25.6   A problem complete for NLINTIME

We now show that NLINTIME has a "hardest" problem with respect to linear-time reductions. This problem is a variant of the set accepted by the universal program u; one of the complete problem sources mentioned in section 25.3.2.

A nondeterministic universal program

By definition $A \in$ NLINTIME iff A is accepted by a nondeterministic program p which runs in time bounded by $a \cdot |\text{d}|$ for some a and all $\text{d} \in \mathbb{D}$.

Recall the universal program u of chapter 4. Construct a universal program nu for nondeterministic programs by extending the STEP macro by adding two rules to interpret the instruction choose C1 or C2, as follows. These can be implemented simply by using a choose instruction in the interpreter itself.

Code	Comp. stack	Value	⇒	Code	Comp. stack	Value
(choose C1 C2).Cd	St	Vl	⇒	C1.Cd	St	Vl
(choose C1 C2).Cd	St	Vl	⇒	C2.Cd	St	Vl

It is easy to see that nu is efficient as we have defined the term, and that (p.d) is accepted iff p accepts d.

Definition 25.6.1 $f : \mathbb{D} \to \mathbb{D}$ is *linear time and size computable* if there are a, b, p such that $f = [\![\text{p}]\!]$, and $t_\text{p}(\text{d}) \leq a \cdot |\text{d}|$, and $|f(\text{d})| \leq b \cdot |\text{d}|$ for all $\text{d} \in \mathbb{D}$.

Definition 25.6.2 Let $L, M \subseteq \mathbb{D}$. Then L is *reducible* to M (written $L \leq_{ltime} M$) iff there is a linear time and size computable function f such that $\text{d} \in L$ iff $f(\text{d}) \in M$ for all d in $\mathbb{D}$.

Further, $P \subseteq \mathbb{D}$ is *complete* for NLINTIME iff $P \in$ NLINTIME and $L \leq_{ltime} P$ for all $L \in$ NLINTIME.

Lemma 25.6.3 $\underset{ltime}{\leq}$ is a reflexive and transitive relation.

Proof. This is essentially the same as for Lemma 25.3.8. It is immediate that the identity function is linear time computable. Further, the composition of any two linear time computable functions is also linear time computable. Note that the size condition $|f(\mathrm{d})| \leq b \cdot |\mathrm{d}|$ for some b and all $\mathrm{d} \in \mathbb{D}$ is needed for this: Functions computable within linear time without a size limit are not closed under composition since they can build values exponentially larger than their argument, for example by repeatedly executing X := cons X X.   □

Lemma 25.6.4 $L \underset{ltime}{\leq} M$ and $M \in$ LINTIME implies $L \in$ LINTIME.

Corollary 25.6.5 If H is complete for NLINTIME, then $H \in$ LINTIME if and only if NLINTIME = LINTIME.

Theorem 25.6.6 *WFA* (while-free acceptance) is complete for NLINTIME, where

$$WFA = \{\,(\mathrm{p.d}) \mid \mathrm{p} \text{ is while-free and p accepts d}\,\}$$

Proof. To show *WFA* $\in$ NLINTIME, modify the nondeterministic universal program nu as follows. First, check that input p is an encoded while-free program, and then run nu. The checking can be done in time linear in $|\mathrm{p}|$, and while-freeness implies that $t_\mathrm{p}(\mathrm{d}) \underset{ltime}{\leq} |\mathrm{p}|$ regardless of d. Thus recognition of *WFA* takes time at most linear in $|(\mathrm{p.d})|$ for all p, d in $\mathbb{D}$.

Now suppose problem A is accepted by p in time $a \cdot |\mathrm{d}|$. Given d, define $f(\mathrm{d}) = (\mathrm{q.d})$ where q is the following program, and STEP$^{a \cdot |\mathrm{d}|}$ stands for $a \cdot |\mathrm{d}|$ copies of the code for the STEP macro of section 4.1.1:

```
read X;            (* Input is d                         *)
Cd := cons p nil;  (* Control stack = (p.nil)            *)
Vl := X;           (* The value of X = d                 *)
Stk := nil;        (* Computation stack is initially empty *)
STEP^{a·|d|};      (* a·|d| = time bound                 *)
write Vl;          (* Final answer is value of X         *)
```

Clearly f is linear time computable. Program q is while-free, and it works by simulating p on d for $a \cdot |\mathrm{d}|$ steps. This is sufficiently long to produce p's output[5], so $\mathrm{d} \in A$ if and only if $f(\mathrm{d}) \in WFA$.   □

---

[5]It also works if p stops in fewer than $a \cdot |\mathrm{d}|$ steps, since the STEP macro makes no changes to Vl if Cd is nil.

Exercises

25.1 Prove that SAT $\underset{logs}{\leq}$ CLIQUE, i.e. that the reduction described before can be done in logarithmic space.   □

25.2 Prove that GAP $\underset{logs}{\leq}$ GAP1, where GAP1 is the set of all *acyclic* graphs with a path from v_0 to v_{end}. Show that GAP1 is also $\underset{logs}{\leq}$ -complete for the class NLOGSPACE.   □

25.3 Prove that CLIQUE $\underset{ptime}{\leq}$ VERTEXCOVER, where VERTEXCOVER is the set of all of all triples (G, S, k) such that S is a subset containing k of G's nodes, such that every edge of G includes a node from S as an endpoint. Hint: consider the complement graph $\overline{G}$, with the same vertices but with all and only the edges that are *not* edges of G.   □

25.4 Prove two parts of Theorem 25.3.10.   □

References

The approach used in chapters 25 through 28, of reducing arbitrary computations to computations of programs using only boolean variables, was first used (to our knowledge) in [52], and was an organizing theme of two papers by Jones and Muchnick [76, 77].

The concepts of many-one reduction (and several other reductions) stem from recursive function theory. They are very clearly explained in Post's 1944 paper [135], which also shows in essence that $HALT$ is $\underset{rec}{\leq}$ -complete for RE.

The use of reductions in complexity theory began in a burst of activity in several locations in the early 1970s, pioneered by work of Stephen Cook and his student Walter Savitch. The breakthrough was Cook's 1971 paper [25], in which the SAT problem was first proven $\underset{ptime}{\leq}$ -complete for NPTIME. Interestingly, Levin proved a very similar result independently in 1972 [101, 99], but this was unrecognized for several years due to its terseness and inaccessibility. Cook's and Levin's results were not widely remarked until Karp showed that a great many familiar combinatorial problems are also complete for NPTIME [90], at which time wide interest was aroused.

Somewhat earlier in 1970, Savitch had in essence shown that the GAP problem is $\leq_{logs}$ -complete for NLOGSPACE in [149]; and in 1971 Cook had proved the "path problem" to be $\leq_{logs}$ -complete for PTIME [25]. In 1972 Meyer and Stockmeyer proved some problems concerning regular expressions complete for PSPACE [120].

This author's 1973-77 papers [79, 71, 75, 74] defined the idea of logspace reduction[6], defined the terms "complete for NLOGSPACE" and "complete for PTIME," and proved a fairly large set of problems complete for NLOGSPACE or PTIME. The NLINTIME-complete problem of Theorem 25.6.6 comes from [80].

Since the the 1970s, the field has grown enormously. Wide-ranging surveys of complete problems for NPTIME and PTIME, respectively, may be found in the books by Garey and Johnson, and by Greenlaw, Hoover, and Ruzzo [49, 53].

---

[6]This was done independently by Cook, and by Meyer and Stockmeyer too, at around the same time.

26 Complete Problems for PTIME

26.1 PTIME reduced to goto-free boolean programs

Definition 26.1.1 (The language BOOLE) A *boolean program* is an input-free program $q = I_1 \ldots I_m$ where each instruction I and expression E is of form given by:

$$
\begin{aligned}
\text{I} \ &::= \ \text{X} := \text{E} \mid I_1; \ I_2 \mid \text{goto } \ell \mid \text{if E then } I_1 \text{ else } I_2 \\
\text{E} \ &::= \ \text{X} \mid \text{true} \mid \text{false} \mid E_1 \lor E_2 \mid E_1 \land E_2 \mid \neg \text{ E} \mid E_1 \Rightarrow E_2 \mid E_1 \Leftrightarrow E_2 \\
\text{X} \ &::= \ \text{X0} \mid \text{X1} \mid \ldots
\end{aligned}
$$

Program q is

- *goto-free* if it has no goto instructions; and
- *single-assignment* if no variable appears on the left sides of two different assignment statements

Program semantics is as one would expect, where unassigned variables are initialized to false. Since there is no input, rather than the form $[\![q]\!](d)$ used until now we instead write $[\![q]\!]{\downarrow}$ and $[\![q]\!]{\uparrow}$ to indicate that the computation by q does or does not terminate; and notation $[\![q]\!]$ to denote the value computed by q: the value stored by the last assignment done by program q, assuming $[\![q]\!]{\downarrow}$.

A BOOLE program $q = I_1 \ldots I_m$ is sometimes called a *monotone circuit* if its instruction and expression forms are given as follows (monotone in the sense that the output value is a monotone function of the imitial variable values):

$$
\begin{aligned}
\text{I} \ &::= \ \text{X} := \text{E} \\
\text{E} \ &::= \ \text{X} \mid \text{true} \mid E_1 \lor E_2 \mid E_1 \land E_2 \\
\text{X} \ &::= \ \text{X0} \mid \text{X1} \mid \ldots
\end{aligned}
$$

$\square$

Taking larger steps than before, we omit formally defining an explicit concrete syntax, instead defining program length below as though this had been done. The effect of the following is to assume that variable Xi is represented by a tag (such as the var used earlier) together with the value of i in binary notation.

Definition 26.1.2 The *length* |q| of a BOOLE program is the number obtained by counting one for every operator :=, ;,..., ⇔ appearing in q, and adding $1 + \lceil \log i \rceil$ for each occurrence of a variable Xi in q.

Lemma 26.1.3 Goto-free BOOLE programs always terminate, and can be executed in polynomial time (as a function of their length).

Proof. Immediate by a simple algorithm slightly extending that of section 3.4.2.   □

The following result in essence says that if goto-free programs can be executed in logarithmic space, then PTIME = LOGSPACE. The proof is in stages, and relies heavily on ideas from the Pascal-like implementation of GOTO described in section 17.2. This is perhaps worth reviewing before reading further, in particular Figure 17.5.

Theorem 26.1.4 The following set[1] is $\underset{logs}{\leq}$ -complete for PTIME:

Bacc$^{\backslash \text{GOTO}}$ = {p | p is a goto-free BOOLE program whose last assignment yields true}

Proof. By Lemma 26.1.3 Bacc$^{\backslash \text{GOTO}}$ is in PTIME. The following Lemma proves that Bacc$^{\backslash \text{GOTO}}$ is $\underset{logs}{\leq}$ -hard for PTIME.   □

Lemma 26.1.5 Let p be an arbitrary GOTO program running in polynomial time, and d be an input. There exists a goto-free BOOLE program q such that $[\![q]\!]$ = true if and only if $[\![p]\!](d)$ = true. Further, q can be constructed from p and d in space $O(\log |d|)$.

Proof. Let p run in polynomial time $g(\_)$, and let $d = (a_1\ a_2\ \ldots a_n)$. Using the ideas from section 17.2, we show how to construct from p, d an input-free GOTO program $p^d = I_1 \ldots I_m$ and a polynomial $\pi(\_)$ such that

1. $[\![p^d]\!]$ terminates if and only if $[\![p]\!](d)$ = true; and
2. if $[\![p^d]\!]$ terminates then it does so in time at most $\pi(|d|)$.

The construction of section 17.2 added $|d| + 3$ instructions at the start of p to initialize X to d. Let the resulting program have $m - 1$ instructions (this defines m). The addition of one more GOTO instruction:

```
m : if X goto m+1 else m
```

---

[1]Bacc$^{\backslash \text{GOTO}}$ stands for "the goto-free boolean program acceptance" problem.

at the end (to test the output variable X) gives the desired termination property. This program's running time is bounded by the polynomial $\pi(n) = g(n) + n + 4$. Now consider the p^d computation

$$(\ell_1, \delta_1, \rho_1) \to (\ell_2, \delta_2, \rho_2) \to \ldots \to (\ell_t, \delta_t, \rho_t) \to \ldots$$

where in general at time t, ℓ_t is the current control point in p, δ_t is the current DAG, and ρ_t is the current environment mapping variables to DAG nodes. Recall from section 17.2 that the initial state $(\ell_1, \delta_1, \rho_1)$ has $\ell_1 = 1$ (execution starts at the first instruction of p^d), $\delta_1 =$ the DAG containing only 0 (the `nil` node), and $\rho_1(X) = 0$ for all variables of p^d.

Variables of the BOOLE **program.**   Let $r + 1 = \lceil \log \pi(n) \rceil$. This is large enough so any number between 0 and $\pi(n)$ can be represented as a sequence $b_r \ldots b_1 b_0$ of $r + 1$ bits. Note that $r = O(\log n)$ because $\pi(n)$ is a polynomial.

The program we will construct manipulates the following boolean variables[2]: L_ℓ, X^i, H^i_c, T^i_c, where $c, \in [0, \pi(n)]$, $\ell \in [1, m+1]$, $i \in [0, r]$, and X stands for any variable of p^d. Their intended interpretation at any time t is:

$$
\begin{aligned}
L_\ell &= \text{true iff } \ell \text{ is the currently active instruction \textbf{L}abel at time } t, \text{ i.e., } \ell = \ell_t \\
X^i &= \text{true iff } 1 \text{ is the } i\text{th bit of the binary representation of } c = \rho_t(X), \\
&\qquad \text{where } p^d \text{ variable X refers to DAG node } c \text{ at time } t \\
H^i_c &= \text{true iff } i \text{ is the } i\text{th bit of the \textbf{H}ead child of DAG node } c, \text{ i.e.,} \\
&\qquad \text{the } i\text{th bit of the left child of node } \delta(c) \\
T^i_c &= \text{true iff } i \text{ is the } i\text{th bit of the \textbf{T}ail child of DAG node } c, \text{ i.e.,} \\
&\qquad \text{the } i\text{th bit of the right child of node } \delta(c)
\end{aligned}
$$

Note the analogy to Figure 24.4. Variables H^i_c and T^i_c have no time index t, and are defined in terms of an unindexed DAG δ. The reason for this is that the DAGs $\delta_0, \delta_1, \delta_2, \ldots$ are increasing, so later DAGS have all the nodes and edges of earlier ones; so δ represents the "limit" of the δ_i. Since no node c ever gets changed, we record in H^i_c and T^i_c the information about the unique left and right δ-children of c (if any, else zero).

---

[2]We use a traditional notation from analysis, where $[a, b]$ denotes the closed interval $\{c \mid a \leq c \leq b\}$; (a, b) denotes the open interval $\{c \mid a < c < b\}$; and similarly for the "half-open" intervals $(a, b]$ and $[a, b)$.

GOTO Instruction I_ℓ	$\textbf{Bacc}^{\backslash \texttt{GOTO}}$ instructions $\overline{I}_\ell^t$ for $t \in [0, \pi(n)]$
goto ℓ'	L_ℓ := false; $L_{\ell'}$:= true
if X goto ℓ' else ℓ''	L_ℓ := false; if $X^0 \vee \ldots \vee X^r$ then $L_{\ell'}$:= true else $L_{\ell''}$:= true
X := nil	X^0 := false;...; X^r := false; L_ℓ := false; $L_{\ell+1}$:= true
X := Y	X^0 := Y^0;...; X^r := Y^r; L_ℓ := false; $L_{\ell+1}$:= true
X := cons Y Z	H_t^0:=Y^0;...; H_t^r:=Y^r; T_t^0:=Z^0;...T_t^r:=Z^r; $\vec{X}$:= $bin(t)$; L_ℓ := false; $L_{\ell+1}$:= true
X := hd Y	$\mathcal{H}_0(Y^r,\ldots,Y^0)$; L_ℓ := false; $L_{\ell+1}$:= true
X := tl Y	$\mathcal{T}_0(Y^r,\ldots,Y^0)$; L_ℓ := false; $L_{\ell+1}$:= true

Figure 26.1: BOOLE instructions to simulate a GOTO program.

The BOOLE program.   We will construct from p^d a BOOLE program

$$q = \quad L_1 := \texttt{true}; \ \overline{I}^1; \ldots; \overline{I}^{\pi(n)}; \ \texttt{Answer} := L_{m+1}$$

All boolean variables are by default `false` when q begins, so the first instruction properly simulates the initial state of p^d. Intended behavior: $[\![q]\!]$ will simulate the computation of $[\![p^d]\!]$, so after $\overline{I}^1; \ldots; \overline{I}^{\pi(n)}$ have been executed, boolean variable `Answer` is assigned `true` if and only if the p^d computation terminated, which holds if and only if p answers `true` on input d.

Simulation of computational steps.   The BOOLE instructions $\overline{I}^t$ simulating I at time t first perform a switch to determine which of p^d's instructions is to be realized. Thus

$$\overline{I}^t = \quad \text{if } L_1 \text{ then } \overline{I}_1^t \text{ else if } L_2 \text{ then } \overline{I}_2^t \text{ else } \ldots \text{ else}$$
$$\text{if } L_m \text{ then } \overline{I}_m^t \text{ else } L_{m+1} := \texttt{true}$$

Finally, the code $\overline{I}_\ell^t$ to simulate individual instructions is found in Figure 26.1. Notation: the syntax $bin(t)$ stands for the r-bit vector of the binary expansion of t, where $t \in [0, \pi(n)]$. Command $\vec{X} := bin(u)$ stands for a sequence of $r+1$ assignment statements X^i:=true or X^i:=false for $i = 0, 1, \ldots, r$, each according as to whether the ith bit of u is a 1 or a 0. (The value of u will be known, not a variable, so no computation is needed.)

Explanation of Figure 26.1: The entry for goto ℓ' just updates L_ℓ and $L_{\ell'}$ to preserve their intended meanings. The code for if X goto ℓ' else ℓ'' tests the bits of X's value. If any is nonzero (so X's value is not `nil`), control is in effect transferred to $L_{\ell'}$, else to $L_{\ell''}$. The entries for X:=nil and X:=Y just set the bits X^i for $i = 0, \ldots, r$ and update the control point appropriately.

The entry for X := cons Y Z sets the bits X^i for $i = 0, \ldots, r$ to bits in the address of a free DAG cell. For this we use the current "time of day" or execution step t. In addition, the bits of Y and Z are copied into the boolean variables H^i_t, T^i_t representing the head and tail component of the new DAG cell t.

Finally, the entry for X := hd Y (the one for X := tl Y is similar so explanation is omitted) has a more complex task: first to locate the DAG cell c to which Y is bound, and then to copy the bits from that cell's head component over into those of X. This is done by the following code, called $\mathcal{H}$ for hd; code $\mathcal{T}$ for tl is also included:

$$
\begin{aligned}
\mathcal{H}_c(\varepsilon) &= \quad X^0 := H^0_c; \; \ldots; \; X^r := H^r_c \\
\mathcal{H}_c(W^s, \ldots, W^1, W^0) &= \quad \text{if } W^0 \text{ then } \mathcal{H}_{2c+1}(W^s, \ldots, W^1) \text{ else } \mathcal{H}_{2c}(W^s, \ldots, W^1)
\end{aligned}
$$

$$
\begin{aligned}
\mathcal{T}_c(\varepsilon) &= \quad X^0 := T^0_c; \; \ldots; \; X^r := T^r_c \\
\mathcal{T}_c(W^s, \ldots, W^1, W^0) &= \quad \text{if } W^0 \text{ then } \mathcal{T}_{2c+1}(W^s, \ldots, W^1) \text{ else } \mathcal{T}_{2c}(W^s, \ldots, W^1)
\end{aligned}
$$

Remarks: the code $\mathcal{H}_0(Y^r, \ldots, Y^0)$ in effect traverses a search tree to find the head component of the leaf whose number is the binary value of bit string $Y^r, \ldots, Y^0$. Its execution time is $O(\log n)$, but the code size of $\mathcal{H}_0(Y^r, \ldots, Y^0)$ is $O(\pi(n) \log n)$. Analogous remarks apply to $\mathcal{T}$.

Program q as just constructed exactly simulates the computation by p on d. Equivalence can be established by proving that the boolean variables $L_\ell, X^i, H^i_c, T^i_c$ each preserve their "intended interpretations." Doing this formally would involve two proofs by induction on computation lengths, one by p and the other by q.

Constructibility in logarithmic space. The translation above involves a number of counters for t, i, etc., all bounded in value by $\pi(n)$ and thus representable within $O(\log n)$ bits. Construction is quite straightforward except for $\mathcal{H}$ and $\mathcal{T}$. These can also be handled, once one observes that it is only necessary to keep track of the current subscript of $\mathcal{H}$ or $\mathcal{T}$ (a number bounded by $\pi(n)$), and the length s of the current argument sequence $W^s, \ldots, W^0$; this is always a prefix of $Y^r, \ldots, Y^0$. $\qquad\square$

26.2   The monotone circuit value problem

Some BOOLE programs are so simple they can be regarded as circuits. We now show that these too yield a decision problem complete for PTIME. The key is to show that goto-free BOOLE programs can be reduced still further, by eliminating if and ¬.

The following proves this, plus another result we will use later (in Theorem 26.3.3): that no variable is assigned in two different commands.

Lemma 26.2.1 There is a logspace computable translation from any goto-free BOOLE program p to another q such that $[\![p]\!] = [\![q]\!]$ and q has each of the following properties:

1. The right sides of assignments in q are all of form X, true, X ∧ Y, X ∨ Y, or ¬X, where X, Y are variables; and the if instruction tests only variables.

2. Property 1 plus: q has no if instructions, so it is just a sequence of assignments.

3. Properties 1 and 2 plus: no right side of any assignment in q contains ¬.

4. Properties 1, 2 and 3 plus: q has the single-assignment property.

Proof. We prove these accumulatively, in order. Item 1 is quite straightforward by adding extra assignments to simplify complex expressions (using methods seen before), and expressing the operators ⇒ and ⇔ in terms of ∨ and ¬. Any occurrence of false can be replaced by an ininitialized variable.

Items 2 and 3 are less trivial. For item 2, suppose $p = I_1 \dots I_m$ is a goto-free BOOLE program. We define an if-free translation $\underline{I}$ of each instruction I, and set program q to be:

```
Go := true; I₁...Iₘ
```

The translation $\underline{I}$ is given below. Variable S below is to be chosen as a new variable for each occurrence of if in I, but the same Go is used for all of q. We have used expressions with more than one right-side operator for readability, but they can obviously be eliminated.

```
if U then I else J  =  S:=Go; Go:=S∧U; I; Go:=S∧¬U; J; Go:=S
I; J                =  I; J
X := E              =  X := (E ∧ Go) ∨ (X ∧ ¬Go)
```

Remark: this translation is to be proven correct in Exercise 26.3. It definitely has deleterious effects on run time: Instead of choosing to execute *either* instruction I or J in if

U then I else J, the translated program executes them *both*, but in such a way that only one of them has any effect (so the other is in effect a "no-operation").

Correctness is based on the following claim: For any simple or compound instruction I, its translation I̲

- has exactly the same effect as I on variables assigned in I, provided Go is true when its execution begins, and
- has no effect at all on variables assigned in I, provided Go is false when its execution begins.

First, it is easy to see that the translation of X:=E will make no change to X if variable Go is false, and that it will effectuate the assignment X:=E if variable Go is true. Second, if Go is false when execution of instruction if U then I else J or instruction I; J begins, then it will remain false until its end, so I̲ has no effect.

Third, assuming Go is initially true, the translation of if U then I else J will execute the translations of both branches I̲ and J̲, and in that order; and it will also set Go to true in the branch to be executed, and to false in the other branch.

For item 3: first, a reference to the constant false can be eliminated by replacing it by an unused variable, since these are all assumed initialized to false. This allows reducing the instruction forms to those cited plus X := ¬Y.

This too can be eliminated by a straightforward program transformation. The device is to represent every p variable X by two complementary variables, X' and X'', in its translation p'. The idea is that each will always be the negation of the other, and the value of X in p is the value of X'. This property is ensured at the start by prefixing the code of p' by instructions X'' := true for every X occurring in p (since all are initially false). The last step is to show how each of p's instructions can be simulated while perserving this invariant representation property. This is easy, as seen in the following table.

Instruction in p	**Translation in** p'	
X := true	X' := true;	X'' := Freshvariable
X := Y	X' := Y';	X'' := Y''
X := Y ∧ Z	X' := Y' ∧ Z';	X'' := Y'' ∨ Z''
X := Y ∨ Z	X' := Y' ∨ Z';	X'' := Y'' ∧ Z''
X := ¬Y	Tem := Y';	X' := Y''; X'' := Tem

Variable Tem is used in the last line so an assignment X := ¬ X will not go wrong.

Finally, for item 4 we must make p single-assignment. A logspace algorithm to do this will be described shortly,

Logspace computability. This is straightforward; since logspace computable functions are closed under composition we need only argue that each individual transformation can be done in logarithmic space.

Item 1 is not difficult; the only trick is to use counters to keep track of expressions' nesting level (a fully parenthesized concrete syntax should be used). Item 2 is also straightforward — one must just assign unique S variables, which can be done by indexing them 1,2, etc. Item 3 can be done in two passes. Pass one finds all variables X in p, and to generate X'':=true for each to prefix the translation. Pass two translates each instruction as described above.

Finally, item 4 (variable renaming): each instruction I_i in a given $p = I_1 \ldots I_m$ is an assignment; denote it by X_i:=E_i. There may, however, be several assignments with the same left side $X_i = X_j$ even though $i \neq j$. Transformation: replace every I_i by X^i:=E^i where $X^1, \ldots, X^m$ are new variables, and E^i is identical to E_i except that reference to any Y in E_i is replaced as follows:

- Trace backward from I_i until you first find an instruction $I_j = Y := \ldots$, or the program start.
- If $I_j = Y := \ldots$ is found then replace Y by X^i, else leave Y unchanged.

This can be done using three pointers: one for the current I_i, one for tracing backward, and one used to compare variables for equality.   □

Theorem 26.2.2 The *monotone circuit value problem* is $\leq_{logs}$-complete for PTIME:

$$\text{MCV} = \{p \mid p \text{ is a monotone circuit and } [\![p]\!] = \texttt{true}\}$$

Proof. Lemma 26.1.3 implies that the MCV problem is in PTIME (all that is needed is an extra program syntax check). By the construction of Theorem 26.1.4, $A \leq_{logs} \text{Bacc}^{\backslash \texttt{GOTO}}$ for any problem $A \in$ PTIME. The construction just given implies $\text{Bacc}^{\backslash \texttt{GOTO}} \leq_{logs} \text{MCV}$, which implies $A \leq_{logs} \text{MCV}$ as required.   □

26.3 Provability by Horn clauses

Definition 26.3.1 A *Horn clause* is a boolean expression

$$A_1 \wedge A_2 \wedge \ldots \wedge A_k \Rightarrow A_0$$

where each A_i is a boolean variable and $k \geq 0$. An *axiom* is a Horn clause with $k = 0$. Given a conjunction $\mathcal{H}$ of Horn clauses, we define variable A to be *provable* from $\mathcal{H}$, written $\mathcal{H} \vdash A$, as follows:

1. Any axiom in $\mathcal{H}$ is provable from $\mathcal{H}$.
2. If $A_1, A_2 \wedge \ldots \wedge A_k \Rightarrow A_0 \in \mathcal{H}$ and $\mathcal{H} \vdash A_i$ for $i = 1, 2, \ldots k$, then $\mathcal{H} \vdash A_0$.
3. No other variables are provable from $\mathcal{H}$.

(The second case includes the first as the case $k = 0$.) It is natural to read $A_1 \wedge A_2 \wedge \ldots \wedge A_k \Rightarrow A_0$ as "A_0 is true if $A_1, \ldots, A_k$ are all true." The *Horn clause provability problem* is defined to be

$$\text{HORN} = \{(\mathcal{H}, A) \mid \mathcal{H} \vdash A\}$$

Remark: the *disjunctive form* of a Horn clause $\mathcal{F} = A_1 \wedge A_2 \wedge \ldots \wedge A_k \Rightarrow A_0$ is

$$\mathcal{F}' = \neg A_1 \vee \neg A_2 \vee \ldots \vee \neg A_k \vee A_0$$

This is a *logically equivalent* expression, meaning that expressions $\mathcal{F}$ and $\mathcal{F}'$ have the same value under any truth assignment. Thus a conjunction of Horn clauses $\mathcal{H}$ is logically equivalent to an expression in conjunctive normal form.

Such an expression $\mathcal{H}$ can be trivially satisfied, by assigning *true* to every variable. A link fully characterising the *syntactically* defined notion of provability $\mathcal{H} \vdash A$ in terms of the *semantic* notion of satisfibility is the following (Exercise 26.4):

Proposition 26.3.2 $\mathcal{H} \vdash A$ holds if and only if $\mathcal{H} \wedge \neg A$ is unsatisfiable.

The HORN problem has been studied under several names including "attribute closure" and is essentially equivalent to deciding whether a context-free grammar generates a nonempty set of strings. The following result in essence says that if propositional Prolog programs can be executed in logarithmic space, then PTIME = LOGSPACE.

Theorem 26.3.3 HORN is $\leq_{logs}$ -complete for PTIME.

Proof. *HORN is in* PTIME: Consider the following simple marking algorithm. It is easy to verify that it runs in polynomial (quadratic) time. The HORN problem can, in fact, be solved in linear time on a pointer machine [38, 9].

Algorithm. Given $(\mathcal{H}, A)$, begin with every boolean variable being unmarked. Then for each Horn clause $A_1 \wedge A_2 \wedge \ldots \wedge A_k \Rightarrow A_0 \in \mathcal{H}$ with unmarked A_0, mark A_0 if all of $A_1 \wedge A_2, \ldots, A_k$ are marked; and repeat until no more variables can be marked.

Clearly the algorithm works in time at most the square of the size of $\mathcal{H}$. *Correctness* is the assertion that $\mathcal{H} \vdash A$ iff A has been marked when the algorithm terminates (it is clear that it *does* terminate since no variable is marked more than once). For "if," we use induction on the number of times the algorithm above performs "for each Horn clause..."

Note that all axioms will be marked first, and these are trivially provable from $\mathcal{H}$. Now consider $A_1 \wedge A_2 \wedge \ldots \wedge A_k \Rightarrow A_0$ in $\mathcal{H}$, and suppose a mark has just been placed on A_0. By the inductive assumption each left side variable is provable, so the right side will also be provable (by Definition 26.3.1). In this way every provable variable will eventually be marked, so if A has been marked when the algorithm terminates, then $\mathcal{H} \vdash A$.

Similar reasoning applies in the other direction ("only if"), using induction on the number of steps in a proof. The base case where A is an axiom is immediate. Assume $\mathcal{H} \vdash A$ by a proof of $n+1$ steps whose last step uses Horn clause $A_1, A_2 \wedge \ldots \wedge A_k \Rightarrow A_0 \in \mathcal{H}$. By induction all of $A_1, A_2 \ldots, A_k$ have been marked, so A_0 will be marked if not already so. Thus every variable that is provable from $\mathcal{H}$ will get marked.

HORN is hard for PTIME: Suppose $A \in$ PTIME is decided by GOTO program p. For a given input d, consider the single-assignment straightline monotone BOOLE program q constructed from p, d in the proof of Theorem 26.2.2. It had the property that $d \in A$ iff $[\![q]\!] = \text{true}$.

Construct from this a Horn problem $\mathcal{H}$ which has

1. An axiom $\Rightarrow$ X for every assignment X := true in q.
2. A clause Y $\Rightarrow$ X for every assignment X := Y in q.
3. A clause Y $\wedge$ Z $\Rightarrow$ X for every assignment X := Y $\wedge$ Z in q.
4. Clauses Y $\Rightarrow$ X and Z $\Rightarrow$ X for every assignment X := Y $\vee$ Z in q.

Exercise 26.5 is to show that this construction can be done in logarithmic space. Letting A be the last variable assigned in q, the following Lemma 26.3.4 shows $(\mathcal{H}, A)$ has a solution if and only if $[\![q]\!] = \text{true}$.   □

Remark: the single-assignment property is essential for this, since there is no concept of order in the application of Horn clauses to deduce new boolean variables. If applied to an *arbitrary* monotone straightline BOOLE program, $\mathcal{H}$ can deduce as true every X that the program makes true, but it could possibly also deduce more than just these, since it need not follow q's order of executing instructions.

Lemma 26.3.4 Let $q = 1 : X_1 := E_1 \ldots m : X_m := E_m$, and let

$$q \vdash (1, \sigma_0) \to \ldots \to (m+1, \sigma_m)$$

be q's computation where $\sigma_0(X) = \mathtt{false}$ for every q variable X. Then for every $i \in [0, n]$ we have $\mathcal{H} \vdash X_i$ if and only if $\sigma_{i+1}(X_i) = \mathtt{true}$.

Proof. This is by induction on i. Assume the statement holds for all k with $0 \le k < i \le m$, and consider the form of the ith instruction $X_i := E_i$. If it is $X_i := \mathtt{true}$ then $\sigma_{i+1}(X_i) = \mathtt{true}$ and $\mathcal{H} \vdash X_i$ since $\Rightarrow X_i$ is an axiom. Suppose the ith instruction is $X_i := X_j$; then $j < i$ by the single-assignment property as established in Lemma 26.2.1. By induction $\sigma_{j+1}(X_j) = \mathtt{true}$ iff $\mathcal{H} \vdash X_j$.

One direction: suppose $\sigma_{i+1}(X_i) = \mathtt{true}$. This implies $\sigma_i(X_j) = \sigma_{j+1}(X_j) = \mathtt{true}$. Then by induction $\mathcal{H} \vdash X_j$, which implies $\mathcal{H} \vdash X_i$ by clause $X_j \Rightarrow X_i$. The other direction: suppose $\mathcal{H} \vdash X_i$. This can *only* be deduced from clause $X_j \Rightarrow X_i$ because of q's single-assignment property, so $\mathcal{H} \vdash X_j$ holds, and $\sigma_{j+1}(X_j) = \mathtt{true}$ by induction. Again by q's single-assignment property, this implies $\sigma_i(X_j) = \mathtt{true} = \sigma_{i+1}(X_i)$.

The other two cases are very similar and so omitted. $\square$

26.4 Context-free emptiness and other problems complete for PTIME

Corollary 26.4.1 The following set is $\underset{logs}{\le}$-complete for PTIME:

$$\mathrm{CF}^{\ne \emptyset} = \{\text{context-free grammar } G \mid L(G) \ne \emptyset\}$$

Proof. Given G it is easy to decide whether it generates at least one terminal string by a marking algorithm like the one above: first mark all productions whose right sides consist exclusively of terminal symbols, then all productions whose right sides contain only marked symbols, and repeat until no more marks can be added. Then $G \in \mathrm{CF}^{\ne \emptyset}$ if and only if its start nonterminal has been marked. Thus the problem "is $G \in CF^{\neq \emptyset}$?" is in PTIME.

By Theorem 26.3.3, $A \in$ PTIME implies $A \underset{logs}{\leq}$ Horn for any A. Thus it suffices to prove that Horn $\underset{logs}{\leq} CF^{\neq \emptyset}$, since $\underset{logs}{\leq}$-reduction is transitive. This is easy: Given a pair $(\mathcal{H}, B)$, construct a context-free grammar G whose nonterminals are the boolean variables appearing in $\mathcal{H}$, with start symbol B, and which has productions:

```
A ::= ε (the empty string)   if → A is an axiom in H
A ::= A₁A₂...Aₖ              if A₁A₂...Aₖ → A ∈ H
```

It is easy to see that $L(G) = \{\varepsilon\}$ if $\mathcal{H} \vdash B$, and $L(G) = \emptyset$ if $\mathcal{H} \vdash B$ does not hold, so $(\mathcal{H}, B) \in$ HORN iff $G \in CF^{\neq \emptyset}$. $\square$

The following is immediate from Theorem 25.3.6.

Corollary 26.4.2 The complementary set $CF^{\emptyset}$ is $\underset{logs}{\leq}$-complete for PTIME.

GAME is complete for PTIME

Definition 26.4.3 A *two-player game* is a quadruple $G = (P_1, P_2, M, W)$ where P_1, P_2, M, W are finite sets such that $P_1 \cap P_2 = \emptyset, W \subseteq P_1 \cup P_2, M \subseteq (P_1 \times P_2) \cup (P_2 \times P_1)$. The set of *positions for player 1* (respectively 2) is P_1 (respectively P_2), the set of *moves* is M, and the set of *won positions* is W.

The set of *winning positions* is defined inductively by: any won position in $p \in W$ is winning (for player 1 if $p \in P_1$, else for player 2). Further, position $p \in P_1$ is winning for player 1 if *there is* a move $(p, q) \in M$ such that q is winning for player 1; and position $p \in P_2$ is winning for player 1 if *for every* move $(p, q) \in M$, position q is winning for player 1. Winning positions for player 2 are defined analogously.

Theorem 26.4.4 The following problem GAME is complete for PTIME: *given a two-player game (P_1, P_2, M, W) and a start position s, to decide* whether s is a winning position for player 1.

Proof. First, GAME is in PTIME by a simple marking algorithm: mark each position in $W \cap P_1$; and then add marks to each position that is winning for player 1 by the above definition, until no new marks can be added. Anwer "yes" if start position s gets marked.

Second, we will prove that a HORN problem $(\mathcal{H}, A)$ can be reduced to GAME. Construct

$$G = (Vars, \mathcal{H}, M, Axioms) = (P_1, P_2, M, W)$$

where *Vars* is the set of boolean variables appearing in $(\mathcal{H}, A)$, and *Axioms* is the set of clauses of form $\Rightarrow B$ in $\mathcal{H}$, and

$$
\begin{aligned}
M \;=\; & \{(A_0,\ A_1 \wedge \ldots \wedge A_k \Rightarrow A_0) \mid A_1 \wedge \ldots \wedge A_k \Rightarrow A_0 \in \mathcal{H}\} \\
\cup\; & \{(A_1 \wedge \ldots \wedge A_k \Rightarrow A_0,\ A_i) \mid 1 \le i \le k\}
\end{aligned}
$$

In words: a position for player 1 is a variable, and a position for player 2 is clause in $\mathcal{H}$. A move for player 1 from position A is to choose a clause implying A, and a move for player 2 from $A_1 \wedge \ldots \wedge A_k \Rightarrow A_0$ is to choose a premise A_i to prove.

It is easy to verify (Exercise 26.6) that position A is winning for player 1 if and only if A is deducible from $\mathcal{H}$, i.e., $G = (Vars, \mathcal{H}, M, Axioms) \in$ GAME iff $(\mathcal{H}, A) \in$ HORN. Further, it is easily seen that G is constructible from $\mathcal{H}$ in logarithmic space.   □

26.5 Parallel computation and problems complete for PTIME

There seems to be a clear gap between those problems that are easy to solve using parallelism, and problems that are complete for PTIME. A sketch follows, although parallelism is outside the scope of this book.

The class NC (standing for "Nick's Class") is the set of all problems that can be solved on inputs of size n in time $O(\log^k n)$ (very fast), provided one is given a number of processors that is polynomial in n, and that these can communicate instantaneously (a rather liberal assumption). Analogous to identifying PTIME with the class of all feasibly solvable problems, many researchers identify NC with the class of all problems that have efficient parallel solutions. While the identification is not perfect, it gives a starting point, and has been used in many investigations.

The classes LOGSPACE and NLOGSPAGE are easily seen to lie within NC, which certainly lies within PTIME. On the other hand, if any problem that is $\le_{logs}$-complete for PTIME lies in NC, then PTIME = NC, that is *all polynomial-time solvable problems have fast parallel solutions*. This would be a remarkable result, comparable in its significance to showing that PTIME = NPTIME.

Thus to show that certain problems are hard to parallelize, it suffices to show that they are complete for PTIME. This property is often used in the literature, and is a major motivation of the book [53]. More details can be found in that book, or in the one by Papadimitriou [130].

Exercises

26.1 Prove correctness of the translation of Lemma 26.1.5, using inductions on computation length.   □

26.2 Prove that the translation of Lemma 26.1.5 can all be carried out in space $O(\log|p|)$.   □

26.3 Prove correctness of the translation of Lemma 26.2.1, using induction on program length.   □

26.4 Prove Proposition 26.3.2.   □

26.5 Complete the proof of Theorem 26.3.3 by showing that function f is computable in logarithmic space.   □   □

26.6 Fill in the missing details of the proof of Proposition 26.4.4.   □

26.7 A two-player game as in Definition 26.4.3 is played on a finite directed graph $(P_1 \cup P_2, M)$. In general, this graph may contain cycles. Prove that GAME is complete for PTIME even if restricted to DAGs, i.e., acyclic directed graphs.   □

26.8 Prove that GAME is in LOGSPACE when restricted to graphs that are trees. Hint (by Ben-Amram): the problem is essentially one of tree traversal. Choose a data representation of the game tree that makes this convenient.   □

References

The first problem shown $\leq_{\textit{logs}}$-complete for PTIME was Cook's "path problem," described in [25]. The circuit value problem was proven complete for PTIME by Goldschlager in 1977 [52]. The remaining problems in this chapter were proven complete by Jones [74]. The book by Greenlaw, Hoover, and Ruzzo [53] has a very large collection of problems complete for PTIME, with particular emphasis on parallel computation.

27 Complete Problems for NPTIME

In chapter 26 we showed the Horn clause deducibility problem to be complete for PTIME. Hardness was proven by steps whose net effect is to reduce acceptance of an input by a deterministic polynomial time program to provability of a goal by a set of Horn clauses. A variation on this construction is used to prove the central result of this chapter: that SAT is $\leq_{logs}$-complete for NPTIME.

A recapitulation. Much of chapter 26 can be re-used for NPTIME, so we recapitulate its two-phase development. Phase 1:

1. Begin with a deterministic GOTO program p running in polynomial time, and an input d.
2. Build input-free GOTO program p^d such that $[\![p]\!](d) = $ true iff $[\![p^d]\!]= $ true.
3. Build from p^d a goto-free BOOLE program q so $[\![p]\!](d) = $ true iff $[\![q]\!]^{BOOLE} = $ true.

Conclusion: Problem Bacc$^{\backslash GOTO}$ is $\leq_{logs}$-complete for PTIME. Completeness of Horn clause deducibility was proven by carrying this development further as follows:

1. Eliminate if's from q to obtain an equivalent goto-free BOOLE program q' whose instructions are all of form: X:=true, X:=Y, X:=Y∨Z, or X:=Y∧Z.
2. Build from q' an equivalent single-assignment goto-free BOOLE program q''.
3. Build from q'' a Horn problem $\mathcal{H}, A$ such that $[\![q'']\!] = $ true iff $\mathcal{H} \vdash A$.

The development for NPTIME is quite analogous. The essential difference from PTIME is that a nondeterministic program p (recall chapter 22) can "guess" from time to time by executing an instruction of form: goto ℓ' or ℓ''. Phase 1 is almost as above:

1. Begin with a *nondeterministic* GOTO program p running in polynomial time, and an input d.
2. Build input-free nondeterministic GOTO program p^d such that $[\![p]\!](d)$ can yield true iff $[\![p^d]\!]$ can yield true.
3. Build from p^d a *deterministic* goto-free BOOLE program q such that $[\![p]\!](d)$ can yield true iff $[\![Init;q]\!] = $ true for some sequence of assignments Init.

First conclusion: the problem "Nontrivial" is complete for NPTIME: is a given a goto-free boolean program, does there exist an initialization of its variables causing it to produce output `true`?

Phase two also involves constructing a boolean expression $\mathcal{F}$ from program p and input d, but asking a different question than in chapter 26: is expression $\mathcal{F}$ *satisfiable*, i.e., is it possible to assign truth values to its variables to make $\mathcal{F}$ evaluate to *true*? By Proposition 26.3.2, Horn clause deducibility is a special case of *non*satisfiability, and so Horn clause *nondeducibility* is a special case of satisfiability. By Theorem 25.3.6 Horn clause nondeducibility is also complete for PTIME, so phase two's result naturally extends that for PTIME.

The construction proceeds as follows:

1. Build from q an equivalent goto-free BOOLE program q_1 without conditional instructions.

2. Build from q_1 an equivalent single-assignment no-if, no-goto BOOLE program q_2.

3. Build from q_2 a boolean expression $\mathcal{F}$ such that $\mathcal{F}$ is satisfiable iff $[\![\texttt{Init};q]\!]=$ $[\![\texttt{Init};q_2]\!]= \texttt{true}$ for some assignment sequence `Init`.

27.1   Boolean program nontriviality is complete for NPTIME

A very simple problem complete for NPTIME is the following:

Theorem 27.1.1 The following problem NonTrivial is $\underset{logs}{\leq}$ -complete for NPTIME:

Given: a deterministic goto-free BOOLE program p.
To decide: is there a sequence of assignments $X_1:=b_i;\dots X_k:=b_k$ with $b_i \in \{\texttt{true},\texttt{false}\}$ such that

$$[\![X_1:=b_i;\dots X_k:=b_k;\ p]\!] = \texttt{true}$$

Proof. NonTrivial is in NPTIME by a simple "guess and verify" algorithm: choose values b_i nondeterministically, set up an initial store binding the variables to them, and then evaluate p.

The following Lemma 27.1.2 shows that NonTrivial is $\underset{logs}{\leq}$ -hard for NPTIME, and so complete. $\square$

Assume A is accepted by nondeterministic GOTO program[1] p. To show: A can be reduced to goto-free boolean program nontriviality in logarithmic space.

Lemma 27.1.2 Let p be a nondeterministic GOTO program running in time $g(|d|)$ for any input $d \in \mathbb{D}$ where $g(n)$ is a polynomial. Then for any input d there exists a deterministic goto-free boolean program q such that $[\![\texttt{Init};\texttt{q}]\!]^{BOOLE} = \texttt{true}$ for some assignment sequence Init iff p can accept d. Further, q can be constructed from p and d in space $O(\log|d|)$.

Proof. We mostly follow the pattern of the proof of Lemma 26.1.5.

Step A.   Given p and d with $n = |d|$, construct a nondeterministic input-free GOTO program $p^d = I_1 \ldots I_m$ and a polynomial π such that

1. p^d has a terminating computation if and only if p accepts d; and
2. if p^d has a terminating computation then it has one that terminates in time at most $\pi(n)$.

This is done exactly as in Lemma 26.1.5. The only difference is that p^d may contain nondeterministic instructions goto ℓ' or ℓ'' copied over from those in p.

Step B.   The next step is, as in Lemma 26.1.5, to construct from $p^d = I_1 \ldots I_m$ a goto-free BOOLE program

$$\texttt{q}' = \texttt{L}_1 := \texttt{true}; \ \overline{\texttt{I}}^1; \ldots; \overline{\texttt{I}}^{\pi(n)}; \ \texttt{Answer} := \texttt{L}_{m+1}$$

Exactly the same construction from Figure 26.1 can be used, plus the following translation of the nondeterministic choice instruction:

GOTO **Instruction** $\texttt{I}_\ell$	**SqBacc instructions** $\overline{\texttt{I}}_\ell^t$ for $t \in [0, \pi(n)]$
goto ℓ' or ℓ''	$\texttt{L}_\ell :=\texttt{false};$ if $\texttt{O}_t$ then $\texttt{L}_{\ell'} :=\texttt{true}$ else $\texttt{L}_{\ell''} :=\texttt{true}$

This is clearly a deterministic program. Construct q from q' by prefixing it with instructions X:=false for every variable in q, *except* the oracle variables $\texttt{O}_t$. Clearly $\{O_0, O_1, \ldots, O_{\pi(n)}\}$ includes all variables not assigned in q.

---

[1]From chapter 22: a GOTO program which may also have instructions of form goto ℓ' or ℓ''.

Now q has the property that GOTO program p^d has a terminating computation if and only if $[\![\,\mathtt{Init;q}\,]\!] = \mathtt{true}$ for some initialization assignment sequence Init. (This was not true for q' since its construction relied on the falsity of unassigned variables.) An example initialization sequence:

$$\mathtt{Init} \quad = \quad \mathtt{0_0:=true; \ ; \ 0_1:=false; \ldots 0_{\pi(n)}:=true;}$$

Correctness of q. First, if $[\![\,\mathtt{Init;q}\,]\!] = \mathtt{true}$ for some initialization sequence Init, then the accepting computation by Init;q clearly corresponds to an accepting computation by p^d. Now consider any computation (there may be many) by p^d:

$$p^d \vdash (1,\ell_0) \rightarrow^* (\ell_{t_1},\sigma_{t_1}) \rightarrow (\ell'_{t_1},\sigma'_{t_1}) \rightarrow^* \ldots (\ell_{t_r},\sigma_{t_r}) \rightarrow (\ell'_{t_r},\sigma'_{t_1}) \rightarrow^* \ldots$$

where $(\ell_{t_1},\sigma_{t_1}),(\ell_{t_2},\sigma_{t_2}),\ldots$ is a list of all states (ℓ_t,σ_t) such that I_{ℓ_t} has form goto ℓ' or ℓ''. For each such t_i, let Init contain assignment $\mathtt{0_{t_i}:=}$ true if branch ℓ'_{t_i} is taken in this computation, else assignment $\mathtt{0_{t_i}:=}$ false if branch ℓ''_{t_i} is taken. Then Init;q will, when it encounters its t_i-th instruction

$$\mathtt{L_\ell \ := \ false; \ if \ 0_{t_i} \ then \ L_{\ell'} \ := \ true \ else \ L_{\ell''} \ := \ true}$$

take the branch that p^d takes. Consequently Init;q will have a computation that is parallel to the one by p^d, yielding result $[\![\,\mathtt{Init;q}\,]\!] = \mathtt{true}$.

It should be evident that this construction can be done in logarithmic space because it is so similar to that of Lemma 26.1.5.   □

27.2   Satisfiability is complete for NPTIME

Expression $\mathcal{F}$, to be built from p and d, will have the same boolean variables as in the previous section, plus new boolean "oracle" variables 0_t, one for each point in time, i.e., polynomially many new variables.

A "choice" by p to transfer control to ℓ' at time t will amount to setting $0_t = \mathit{true}$ in $\mathcal{F}$, and a transfer to ℓ'' will amount to setting $0_t = \mathit{false}$ in $\mathcal{F}$. Each 0_t is called an *oracle variable*, since the choice of a satisfying truth assignment (Definition 25.1.1) for $\mathcal{F}$, in effect, predetermines the sequence of choices to be taken by program p, just as the initialization sequence Init of the preceding section. The values of variables 0_t will *not* be uniquely determined: Since p may have many different computations on the same input d, some accepting and others not, there may be many satisfying truth assignments.

$\mathcal{F}$ will be constructed from q very similarly to the way $\mathcal{H}$ was built, but a few additional clauses will be needed to be certain that $\mathcal{F}$ can be satisfied *only* in ways that correspond to correct computations.

Theorem 27.2.1 SAT is $\leq_{logs}$-complete for NPTIME.

Proof. First, SAT $\in$ NPTIME by a simple "guess and verify" algorithm. Given a boolean expression $\mathcal{F}$, a nondeterministic program can first select a truth assignment θ, using the instruction goto ℓ or ℓ' to choose between assigning true or false to each variable. Then evaluate $\theta(\mathcal{F})$ (in polynomial time by Lemma 26.1.3. If true, accept the input, else don't. All this can certainly be done by a nondeterministic polynomial time computation.

The next task is to show that $A \leq_{logs}$ SAT for any set $A \subseteq \mathbb{D}_{01}$ in NPTIME^{GOTO}. This is done by modifying the construction of a Horn clause program from a GOTO program seen before; details appear in the following section. After that, correctness and space usage of the construction will be established. □

27.2.1 Construction of a 3CNF expression from a program and its input

Lemma 27.2.2 Let p be a nondeterministic GOTO program running in time $g(|d|)$ for any input $d \in \mathbb{D}$ where $g(n)$ is a polynomial. Then for any input d there exists a 3CNF boolean expression[2]

$$\mathcal{F} = C_1 \wedge C_2 \wedge \ldots \wedge C_t$$

which is satisfiable iff p can accept d. Further, $\mathcal{F}$ can be constructed from p and d in space $O(\log|d|)$.

Proof. Begin with goto-free BOOLE program q from Lemma 27.1.2. Apply a construction in Lemma 26.2.1 to q to construct an equivalent goto-free BOOLE program q_1 without conditional. Its instructions can only have forms X:=true, X:=false, X:=Y, X:=¬Y, X:=Y∨Z, or X:=Y∧Z.

---

[2]Meaning of 3CNF: each C_i is a disjunction of at most three literals. See Appendix section A.1 for terminology if unfamiliar.

Next, apply another construction from Lemma 26.2.1 to q_1 to construct an equivalent single-assignment no-if, no-goto BOOLE program $q_2 = I_1 I_2 \ldots I_m$. Finally, construct boolean expression

$$\mathcal{F} = \overline{I_1} \wedge \ldots \wedge \overline{I_m}$$

where each $\overline{I}$ is defined as follows:

BOOLE Instruction I	Clauses $\overline{I}$	3CNF equivalent
X := true	X	X
X := false	¬X	¬X
X := Y	Y ⇒ X	¬Y∨X
X := ¬Y	¬Y ⇒ X	Y∨X
X := Y∨Z	(Y ⇒ X) ∧ (Z ⇒ X)	(¬Y∨X) ∧ (¬Z∨Y)
X := Y∧Z	Y∧Z ⇒ X	(¬Y∨¬Z∨X)

Expression $\mathcal{F}$ does not have the form of a set of Horn clauses because the negation operator appears in two places. Further, we are asking a different question, satisfiability, rather than Horn clause deducibility.

Correctness. First, note that expression $\mathcal{F}$ has exactly the same variables as q_2. Second, the only unassigned variables in q_2 are the oracle variables O_i. If $[\![\mathtt{Init} ; q_2]\!]^{\mathrm{BOOLE}} = \mathtt{true}$ for some initialization Init of the oracle variables, it is clear that the truth assignment

$$\theta(\mathtt{X}) = \text{ the value Init assigns to X}$$

causes $\theta(\mathcal{F})$ to evaluate to *true*.

Conversely, suppose $\theta(\mathcal{F})$ evaluates to *true* for some truth assignment θ, and let Init contain X:=true for each X with $\theta(\mathtt{X}) = true$ and X:=false for each X with $\theta(\mathtt{X}) = false$. Since q_2 is single-assignment, a simple induction on computation length very like the proof of Lemma 26.3.4 shows that for each assignment X:=... performed by Init;q_2, truth assignment θ must map variable X to the (unique) value that Init;q_2 stores into X.

Thus $\mathcal{F}$ is satisfiable if and only if $[\![\mathtt{Init} ; q_2]\!] = \mathtt{true}$ for some truth assignment θ. We have already seen that this holds if and only if $[\![\theta(q_1)]\!] = \mathtt{true}$ for some truth assignment θ, and that this holds iff $[\![p^d]\!] = \mathtt{true}$, which holds iff $[\![p]\!](d) = \mathtt{true}$.

Thus $\mathcal{F}$ is satisfiable if and only if p accepts d. Exercise 27.2 is to show that this construction can be done in logarithmic space. □

27.3   Other problems complete for NPTIME

Thousands of problems have been shown complete for NPTIME. For a large selection, see [49]. Many of the first problems shown complete for NPTIME concern graphs, as indicated by the following selection. However there is a wide variety in nearly all areas where combinatorial explosions can arise. For historical reasons we now sometimes write "vertex" where "node" has been used other places in the book; but the meaning is exactly the same.

Corollary 27.3.1 The CLIQUE problem is $\leq_{logs}$-complete for NPTIME.

Proof. First, CLIQUE $\in$ NPTIME by a simple algorithm. Given graph G and number k, just guess a subset of k of G's vertices and check to see whether every pair is joined by an edge of G. This takes at most quadratic time.

Second, we saw in Construction 25.3.1 how the SAT problem can be reduced to CLIQUE. It is easy to see that the construction can be done in logarithmic space, so SAT $\leq_{logs}$ CLIQUE. By Proposition 25.3.5, CLIQUE is also $\leq_{logs}$-complete for NPTIME. $\square$

Theorem 27.3.2 The VertexCover problem is $\leq_{logs}$-complete for NPTIME:

Given: an undirected graph $G = (V, E)$ and a number k.

To decide: is there a subset $S \subseteq V$ with size k such that every edge in E has an endpoint in S?

Proof. It is clear that VertexCover is in NPTIME by a simple guess-and-verify algorithm. Second, we show CLIQUE $\leq_{logs}$ VertexCover which by the previous result and Proposition 25.3.5 implies SetCover is also $\leq_{logs}$-complete for NPTIME.

The reduction is as follows, given a CLIQUE problem instance (G, k) (does $G = (V, E)$ have k mutually adjacent vertices?). Construct the "complement" graph $\overline{G} = (V, E')$ where $E' = \{(v, w) \mid (v, w \in V, v \neq w, (v, w) \notin E\}$, and let n be the number of vertices in V.

Claim: C is a k-element clique of G if and only if $S = V \setminus C$ is a $n - k$-element vertex cover of $\overline{G}$. Assume C is a k-clique. An arbitrary edge (v, w) of $\overline{G}$ connects two distinct vertices and is *not* in E. Thus at least one of v or w must not be in C, and so must be in $S \setminus C$. Thus every edge has an endpoint in S, so S is an $n - k$-element vertex cover of $\overline{G}$.

Now assume S is an $n - k$-element vertex cover of $\overline{G}$ and v, w are any two distinct vertices of C. If (v, w) were an edge in E' then one would be in $S = V \setminus C$. Thus (v, w) is an edge in E, so C is a clique.

Thus $(G,k) \in$ CLIQUE iff $(\overline{G}, n - k) \in$ VertexCover. Further, $(\overline{G}, n - k)$ can be constructed from (G,k) in logarithmic space, so CLIQUE $\underset{logs}{\leq}$ VertexCover.   □

Theorem 27.3.3 The SetCover problem is $\underset{logs}{\leq}$-complete for NPTIME:

Given: a number k and a collection of sets[3] $S_1, \ldots, S_n$.

To decide: is there a subcollection $S_{i_1}, \ldots, S_{i_k}$ of at most k of these whose union covers all elements in any S_i:

$$\bigcup_{j=1}^{j=n} S_i = \bigcup_{j=1}^{j=k} S_{i_j}$$

Proof. It is again clear that SetCover is in NPTIME by a simple guess-and-verify algorithm. Second, we show VertexCover $\underset{logs}{\leq}$ SetCover which by the previous result and Proposition 25.3.5 implies SetCover is also $\underset{logs}{\leq}$-complete for NPTIME.

The reduction is as follows, given a VertexCover problem instance (G,k) (does $G = (V,E)$ have a set of k vertices that contact every edge?). Construct the collection of sets S_v, one for each vertex $v \in V$, such that

$$S_v = \{(u,w) \in V \mid v = u \lor v = w\}$$

Clearly, $S_{i_1}, \ldots, S_{i_k}$ is a set cover of $V = \bigcup_{v \in V} S_v$ if and only if $\{v_{i_1}, \ldots, v_{i_k}\}$ is a vertex cover of E. Constructibility in logarithmic space is simple.   □

Exercises

27.1 Prove Theorem 27.1.1. Hint: for hardness, show that SAT $\underset{logs}{\leq}$ NonTrivial.   □

27.2 Complete the proof of Theorem 27.2.1 by showing that function f is computable in logarithmic space.   □

27.3 Verify the equivalence stated in Theorem 27.3.3.   □

---

[3]For example, by listing each as a string $\{v_1, \ldots, v_m\}$, using binary integers to denote the various elements v_i.

27.4 Prove that the FeedbackVertexSet problem is $\leq_{logs}$-complete for NPTIME:

Given: a directed graph $G = (V, E)$ and a number k.

To decide: is there a k-element subset $S \subset V$ such that every cycle of G contains at least one vertex in E? Hint: reduce VertexCover to FeedbackVertexSet.   □

References

Many thousands of combinatorial and other problems have been proven complete for NPTIME. A wide-ranging survey may be found in the book by Garey and Johnson [49].

28 Complete Problems for PSPACE

First, we will prove the following:

Theorem 28.0.4 The following set is $\underset{logs}{\leq}$-complete for PSPACE:

$$\text{Bacc} = \{p \mid p \text{ is a BOOLE program such that } [\![p]\!] = \text{true}\}$$

In light of Theorem 26.1.4, this says that the difference between simulating programs with or without goto corresponds to the difference between PSPACE and PTIME (if any). Using this as a basis, we will proceed to show the following problems complete for PSPACE:

$$
\begin{array}{lcl}
\text{REGALL} & = & \{R \mid R \text{ is a regular expression over } \Sigma \text{ and } L(R) = \Sigma^*\} \\
\text{QBT} & = & \{\mathcal{F} \mid \mathcal{F} \text{ is a true quantified boolean expression}\}
\end{array}
$$

28.1 Acceptance by boolean programs with goto

Lemma 28.1.1 Boolean programs can be executed in space at most a polynomial function of their length. Further, execution can be guaranteed to terminate.

Proof. A simple interpreter slightly extending that of section 3.4.2 can execute an arbitrary BOOLE program. It uses space for the current control point and the current values of all program variables. Each of these is bounded by the length of the program being interpreted.

This naive interpreter will of course loop infinitely if the interpreted program does so. It can be modified always to terminate as follows. Let the interpreted program p have m labels and k boolean variables. Then it can enter at most $m \cdot 2^k$ configurations without repeating one and so looping.

Modify the interpreter to maintain a binary counter c consisting of $r = k\lceil \log m \rceil$ boolean values (initially all false), and increase this counter by 1 every time an instruction of p is simulated. If c becomes $2^r - 1$ (all true's) then the interpreter stops simulation and signals that p has entered an infinite loop. This is sufficient since $2^r \geq m \cdot 2^k$.

Clearly the modified interpreter uses space at most polynomial in the length of p. □

Theorem 28.0.4 in essence says that if boolean programs can be executed in polynomial time, then PTIME = PSPACE. To show that Bacc is hard for PSPACE we reduce computations by an arbitrary polynomially space-bounded counter machine to Bacc.

Lemma 28.1.2 Let p be a CM program running in polynomial space $f(n)$, and let d = a_1 $a_2 \ldots a_n \in \{0,1\}^*$ be an input of length n. Then there exists a boolean program q such that $[\![q]\!]^{\text{BOOLE}} = \texttt{true}$ if and only if $[\![p]\!](d) = \texttt{true}$. Further, q can be constructed from p and d in space $O(\log n)$.

Proof. We follow a pattern seen for Theorems 26.1.4 and 27.2.1, with one boolean variable for each bit of each of p's counters.

Step A.   There is a polynomial π such that for any d, an input-free CM program p^d = $I_1 \ldots I_m$ with counters $C1, \ldots, Ck$ can be built in space $O(\log |d|)$ such that

1. p^d terminates if and only if $[\![p]\!](d) = \texttt{true}$; and

2. if p^d terminates, its counter values are bounded by $\pi(n)$.

This is done in a way close to that of Lemma 26.1.5. The only essential difference is that p^d must initialize its input counter C0 to the number $c_N(d)$. This can easily be computed, as sketched in Exercise 21.3.

Step B.   The next step is, as in Lemma 26.1.5, to construct from p^d = $I_1 \ldots I_m$ a BOOLE program q such that $[\![q]\!]^{\text{BOOLE}} = \texttt{true}$ if and only if p terminates on input d. It has form:

```
q =  1 : I̲₁; ...; m : I̲ₘ; m+1 : Answer := true
```

BOOLE program q has boolean variables C_i^j for $i \in [1,k], j \in [0, \pi(n)]$. The intended interpretation: variable C_i^j will be `true` if and only if the j-th bit of the current value of counter Ci is a 1. Instructions $\underline{I}_\ell$ to simulate instruction I_ℓ of p^d are now easily defined as follows:

CM Instruction I_ℓ	Bacc instructions $\underline{I}_\ell$
`Ci := Ci + 1`	if $\neg C_i^0$ then $C_i^0 :=$ true else $\{C_i^0 :=$ false; if $\neg C_i^1$ then $C_i^1 :=$ true else $\{C_i^1 :=$ false; ...else $\{C_i^{\pi(n)-1} :=$ false; $C_i^{\pi(n)} :=$ true;$\}...\}\}$
`Ci := Ci - 1`	if C_i^0 then $C_i^0 :=$ false else $\{C_i^0 :=$true; if C_i^1 then $C_i^1 :=$false else $\{C_i^1 :=$true;...else if $C_i^{\pi(n)}$ then $C_i^{\pi(n)} :=$false;$\}...\}\}$
`if Ci=0 goto` ℓ' `else` ℓ''	if $C_i^0 \vee ... \vee C_i^{\pi(n)}$ goto ℓ' else ℓ''

Program q can easily be constructed within logarithmic space. □

Proof. Theorem 28.0.4: By Lemma 28.1.1, Bacc is in PSPACE. If A is in PSPACE then by Theorem 21.2.1 it is decidable by some polynomially space-bounded counter machine program p. The preceding Lemma shows how to reduce A to Bacc, so Bacc is $\underset{logs}{\leq}$-hard for PSPACE. □

The following variant is a bit simpler, and so will be used in some later reductions to prove problems hard for PSPACE.

Corollary 28.1.3 The following set is $\underset{logs}{\leq}$-complete for PSPACE:

Bterm = $\{$p $|$ p is a BOOLE program which terminates$\}$

28.2 Quantified boolean algebra

Definition 28.2.1 A *quantified boolean expression* is an expression E of form given by:

E ::= X | true | false | $E_1 \vee E_2$ | $E_1 \wedge E_2$ | $\neg$ E | $E_1 \Rightarrow E_2$ | $E_1 \Leftrightarrow E_2$
    | $\forall$X . E | $\exists$X . E
X ::= X0 | X1 | ...

It is *closed* if every variable X is bound, i.e., lies within the scope of some quantifier $\forall$X . E or $\exists$X . E. The *value* of a closed quantified boolean expression E is either *true* or *false*.

An expression of form $\forall$X . E has value *true* if both E+ and E− have value *true*, where E+, E− are obtained from E by replacing every unbound occurrence of X in E by true, respectively false. Expression ∃X.E has value *true* if E+ or E- have value *true* (or both), and expressions $E_1 \lor E_2$, etc. are evaluated by combining the values of their components in the usual way for boolean expressions. □

Theorem 28.2.2 The set QBT of true quantified boolean expressione is $\leq_{logs}$-complete for PSPACE.

Proof. First, it should be clear that truth of a quantified boolean expression can be established in linear space, by an algorithm that enumerates all combinations of values *true, false* of its quantified variables, and combines the results of subexpressions according to the logical operators and quantifiers in E. This requires one bit per variable.

We next show Bterm $\leq_{logs}$ QBT, so QBT is $\leq_{logs}$-complete for PSPACE by Theorems 28.0.4 and 25.3.5.

Consider BOOLE program $p = I_1 \ldots I_m$ with variables X1,...,Xk. Without loss of generality we may assume every instruction in p is of the form X := true, X := false, or if X goto ℓ else ℓ', where the allter abbreviates if X then goto ℓ else goto ℓ'. The reason is that the boolean operators and assignments may all be transformed into code to "test and jump" with at most linear increase in program size (a transformation obviously computable in logspace).

For example, the assignment X := Y could be realized by

```
1: X := true;
2: if Y goto 4 else to 3
3: X := false
```

and similarly for the other forms.

One-step simulation   We start out by constructing a quantified boolean expression $Nx(\vec{X}, \vec{L}, \vec{X}', \vec{L}')$ where $\vec{X}$ stands for the sequence $X_1, \ldots, X_k$, $\vec{L}$ stands for $L_1, \ldots, L_{m+1}$, and similarly for their primed versions. The expression will be such that

$$p \vdash (\ell, [1 \mapsto v_1, \ldots, k \mapsto v_k]) \to (\ell', [1 \mapsto v'_1, \ldots, k \mapsto v'_k])$$

if and only if

$$Nx(v_1, \ldots, v_k, false, \ldots, true, \ldots, false, \ v'_1, \ldots, v'_k, false, \ldots, true, \ldots, false)$$

evaluates to *true*, where the first sequence of truth values has *true* in position ℓ only, and the second has *true* in position ℓ' only. Intention: $L_\ell = true$ ($L'_\ell = true$) if the current control point (next control point) is instruction I_ℓ.

Some auxiliary notation: if vectors $\vec{U}, \vec{V}$ have the same length s, then $\vec{U} \Leftrightarrow \vec{V}$ stands for $(U_1 \Leftrightarrow U_1) \wedge \ldots \wedge (U_s \Leftrightarrow U_s)$. Similarly, if $I \subseteq \{1, 2, \ldots, s\}$, then $\vec{U} \Leftrightarrow_I \vec{V}$ stands for $\bigwedge_{i \in I} (U_i \Leftrightarrow U_i)$. Finally, two more abbreviations:

Lab(ℓ) stands for $\quad L_\ell \wedge \bigwedge_{i \in [1, \ell) \cup (\ell, k]} \neg L_i$

Lab$'(\ell)$ stands for $\quad L'_\ell \wedge \bigwedge_{i \in [1, \ell) \cup (\ell, k]} \neg L'_i$

Given this machinery, define

$$\text{Nx}(\vec{X_k}, \vec{L}_{m+1}, \vec{X}'_k, \vec{L}'_{m+1}) \equiv (\text{Lab}(1) \wedge E_1) \vee \ldots \vee (\text{Lab}(m) \wedge E_m) \vee \text{Lab}(m+1)$$

where the E_ℓ are defined by the table

BOOLE Instruction I_ℓ	Quantified boolean expression E_ℓ
`goto` ℓ'	Lab$'(\ell') \wedge \vec{X} \Leftrightarrow \vec{X}'$
`Xi := true`	Lab$'(\ell+1) \wedge \vec{X} \Leftrightarrow_{[1,i)} \vec{X}' \wedge X'_i \wedge \vec{X} \Leftrightarrow_{(i,k]} \vec{X}'$
`Xi := false`	Lab$'(\ell+1) \wedge \vec{X} \Leftrightarrow_{[1,i)} \vec{X}' \wedge \neg X'_i \wedge \vec{X} \Leftrightarrow_{(i,k]} \vec{X}'$
`if Xi goto` ℓ' `else` ℓ''	$(X_i \wedge \text{Lab}'(\ell')) \vee (\neg X_i \wedge \text{Lab}'(\ell'')) \wedge \vec{X} \Leftrightarrow \vec{X}'$

The size of this expression is clearly polynomial in $m + k$, and it is also evident that it is logspace computable with the aid of a few counters bounded by k or m.

Multi-step simulation For this we will construct quantified boolean expressions $\text{Nx}^{2^i}(\vec{X}, \vec{L}', \vec{X}', \vec{L}')$ for $i = 0, 1, 2, \ldots$, which evaluate to true if program p can go from state represented by $(\vec{X}, \vec{L})$ to the state represented by $(\vec{X}', \vec{L}')$ by a 2^i-step sequence of transitions.

This can be defined inductively as follows. To illustrate the technique without unduly long argument lists, we consider only a binary predicate $P^{2^i}(a, b)$ rather than the $2(m+k)$-ary boolean predicate $\text{Nx}^{2^i}(\ldots)$.

$$P^1(a, b) \quad \equiv \quad P(a, b)$$
$$P^{2t}(a, b) \quad \equiv \quad \exists c \, \forall u \, \forall v \, \{[(u = a \wedge v = c) \vee (u = c \wedge v = b)] \Rightarrow P^t(u, v)\}$$

Claims: first, expression $P^{2^i}(a, b)$ will be true if and only if there exists a sequence $a_1, a_2, \ldots, a_{2^i}$ such that $P^{2^{i-1}}(a_i, a_{i+1})$ holds for every $i \in [1, 2^i)$. Second, the size of the expression $P^{2^i}(a,b)$ is $O(i+s)$ where s is the size of expression $P(a,b)$, since each doubling of the exponent only adds a constant number of symbols to the previous expression.

Now let $r = \lceil k \cdot \log(m+1) \rceil$, so $2^r \geq (m+1)2^k$ (the number of configurations p can enter without looping). Consider quantified boolean expression $\text{Nx}^{2^r}(\vec{X},\vec{L'},\vec{X'},\vec{L'})$. Value 2^r is large enough so that if program p can go from state represented by $(\vec{X},\vec{L})$ to the state represented by $(\vec{X'},\vec{L'})$ by any sequence of transitions, then it can do so in at most 2^r transitions.

Consequently p terminates iff its start transition can reach one with control point $m+1$ within 2^r steps. Thus $[\![p]\!] = \texttt{true}$ iff the following quantified boolean expression is true (the part $[\dots]$ describes p's initial state):

$$\exists\vec{X}\exists\vec{L} \,.\, [\vec{X} \Leftrightarrow \overrightarrow{\texttt{false}} \wedge L_1 \wedge \vec{L} \Leftrightarrow_{(1,m+1]} \overrightarrow{\texttt{false}}] \wedge \text{Nx}^{2^r}(\vec{X},\vec{L},\vec{X'},\vec{L'}) \wedge L'_{m+1}$$

Finally, a size analysis: by the argument above about $P(a,b)$, the size of boolean expression $\text{Nx}^{2^r}(\dots)$ is of the order of r times the size of $\text{Nx}(\vec{X},\vec{L'},\vec{X'},\vec{L'})$. The latter has been argued to be polynomial in the size of program p, so the total is polynomially bounded. The final step, logspace computability of the reduction, is Exercise 28.4.   □

28.3   Regular expression totality

Theorem 28.3.1 The totality problem REGALL for regular expressions (is $L(R) = \Sigma^*$?) is $\underset{logs}{\leq}$ -complete for PSPACE.

Proof. We actually show the complementary problem REGNOTALL = $\{R \mid L(R) \neq \Sigma^*\}$ to be $\underset{logs}{\leq}$ -complete for PSPACE. This suffices by Theorems 25.3.6 and 23.5.2.

REGNOTALL is in PSPACE.   Given regular expression R over alphabet Σ, the property $L(R) \neq \Sigma^*$ can be decided in linear space as follows. First, construct an NFA $M = (Q, \Sigma, m, q_0, F)$ (nondeterministic finite automaton, see the appendix) such that $L(M) = L(R)$. This can be done so the size of M is linear in the size of R [3].

Then apply the usual "subset construction" [3] to define a DFA (deterministic finite automaton) M_D accepting the same set $L(R) = L(M) = L(M_D)$. Note that M_D may have a number of states exponential in the size of M, since each state is a subset of the states of M.

The property $L(M_D) \neq \Sigma^*$ holds if and only if there is some path from the automaton's initial state $\{q_0\}$ to a nonaccepting state. As seen before, this can be done by a nondeterministic search through M_D's transition graph, storing at most one graph node at a time (it is not necessary to build all of M_D first). The natural way to represent a state of automaton M_D is by storing one bit for each M state, that is as a bit vector of size $O(|R|)$. Thus the nondeterministic search can be done in at most linear space.

This shows the problem $L(R) \neq \Sigma^*$ is in NSPACE(n), and so in PSPACE by Theorem 23.4.3.

REGNOTALL is hard for PSPACE. We prove Bterm $\underset{logs}{\leq}$ REGNOTALL.

Suppose we are given a BOOLE program $p = I_1 \ldots I_m$ with variables $X1, \ldots, Xk$. Without loss of generality we may assume every instruction in p is of the form X := true, X := false, or if X goto ℓ else ℓ'. We will show how to construct a regular expression R_p over $\Sigma = \{\#, 0, 1, t, f\}$ which generates all sequences that are *not terminating computations* by p. Thus $L(R_p) = \Sigma^*$ iff p does not terminate (which implies *every* string in Σ^* is a noncomputation), so $p \in$ Bterm iff R_p is in REGNOTALL.

Represent a configuration $C = (\ell, [1 \mapsto b_1, \ldots, k \mapsto b_k])$ by the following string over alphabet Σ of length $m + 1 + k$:

$$\overline{C} = 0^{\ell-1} 1 0^{m+1-\ell} b_1 \ldots b_k$$

where $b_i = t$ if $b_i = true$ and $b_i = f$ if $b_i = false$ for $i = 1, \ldots, k$. A *computation trace* will be a string over alphabet Σ:

$$
\begin{aligned}
Traces_p = \quad &\{\#\overline{C_1}\# \ldots \#\overline{C_t}\# \mid p \vdash C_1 \to \ldots \to C_t \text{ and} \\
&\quad C_1 = (1, [1 \mapsto false, \ldots, k \mapsto false]) \text{ and } C_t = (m+1, [\ldots])\}
\end{aligned}
$$

Claim: for each BOOLE program p there is a regular expression R_p such that

1. $L(R_p) = \Sigma^* \setminus Traces_p$
2. R_p is constructible in space $O(|p|)$
3. $R_p = R_1 \mid R_2 \mid R_3 \mid R_4$ where the R_i behave as follows:

$$
\begin{aligned}
L(R_1) = \quad & \Sigma^* \setminus \#[(0|1)^{m+1}(t|f)^k\#]^* \quad && \text{Wrong format} \\
L(R_2) = \quad & \Sigma^* \setminus \#10^m\#f^k\Sigma^* \quad && \text{Wrong start} \\
L(R_3) = \quad & \Sigma^* \setminus \Sigma^*\#0^m1(t|f)^k\# \quad && \text{Wrong finish} \\
L(R_4) = \quad & \Sigma^*\#(E_1|E_2|\ldots|E_m)\#\Sigma^* \quad && \text{Some } C_i \not\to C_{i+1}
\end{aligned}
$$

Exercise 28.2 is to show that R_1, R_2, R_3 can be defined without using $\backslash$.

Regular expressions E_ℓ for each instruction label ℓ define the set of strings $\overline{C} \# \overline{C'}$ such that $p \not\vdash C \to C'$. In order to define them, we use abbreviation $\Sigma \backslash a$ for the obvious finite union, and $\bigvee_{i \in I} X_i$ for the union ($|$) of X_i for each $i \in I$.

Strings having symbol a at position i are generated by $Y_i^a = \Sigma^{i-1} a \Sigma^*$.
Strings not having symbol a at position i:

$$N_i^a = \Sigma^* \backslash Y_i^a = \varepsilon \mid \Sigma \mid \ldots \mid \Sigma^{i-1} \mid \Sigma^{i-1}(\Sigma \backslash a)\Sigma^*$$

Strings including $\overline{C} \# \overline{C'}$ with $a, b \in \{t, f\}$ at positions i of $\overline{C}$ and $\overline{C'}$ (respectively):

$$B_i^{ab} = (0|1)^{m+1}(t|f)^{i-1} a \, (t|f)^{k-i} \# Y_{i+m+1}^b$$

Strings including $\overline{C} \# \overline{C'}$ with $a, b \in \{t, f\}$ at some position i of $\overline{C}$ and $\overline{C'}$ (resp.):

$$B^{ab} = B_1^{ab} \mid \ldots \mid B_k^{ab}$$

Strings with a at position i of $\overline{C}$ such that ℓ is not the control point in $\overline{C'}$:

$$C_i^{a\ell} = (0|1)^{m+1}(t|f)^{i-1} a (t|f)^{k-i} \# N_\ell^1$$

Given these, definition of the E_ℓ is straightforward:

BOOLE Instruction I_ℓ	Regular expression E_ℓ
goto ℓ'	$N_\ell^1 \mid \Sigma^{m+1+k} N_{\ell'}^1 \mid B^{ft} \mid B^{tf}$
Xi := true	$N_\ell^1 \mid \Sigma^{m+1+k} N_{\ell'}^1 \mid B_i^{ff} \mid B_i^{tf} \mid \bigvee_{j \in [1,i] \cup (i,k]}(B^{ft}|B^{tf})$
Xi := false	$N_\ell^1 \mid \Sigma^{m+1+k} N_{\ell'}^1 \mid B_i^{ft} \mid B_i^{tt} \mid \bigvee_{j \in [1,i] \cup (i,k]}(B^{ft}|B^{tf})$
if Xi goto ℓ' else ℓ''	$N_\ell^1 \mid B^{ft} \mid B^{tf} \mid C_i^{t\ell'} \mid C_i^{f\ell''}$

Verification of this construction's correctness is straightforward but tedious.   □

A generalization: regular expressions with squaring. Suppose the class of regular expressions is enriched by adding the operator R^2, where by definition $L(R^2) = L(R) \cdot L(R)$. The totality problem for this class (naturally called REG^{2}ALL) can by essentially similar methods be shown complete for $\bigcup_c \text{SPACE}(2^{cn})$.

The ability to square makes it possible, by means of an extended regular expression of size $O(n)$, to generate all noncomputations of an exponentially space-bounded counter machine. Intuitively, the point is that an expression $(\ldots (\Sigma^2)^2 \ldots)^2$ of size n generates all strings in Σ^* of length 2^n, so the "yardstick" $m + k + 1$ used above can be made exponentially long by an extended regular expression of length $O(n)$. This allows generation of all noncomputations by an exponential space counter or Turing machine by a linear-length regular expression with squaring.

28.4 Game complexity

Board games. We showed a simple one-token game to be complete for PTIME in Theorem 26.4.4. A natural question is what the complexity is for many-token games such as $n \times n$-board size chess, Hex, or Go. It might be expected that their complexity is higher, since the number of possible configurations is exponential in the board size. This is indeed the case; constructions and references may be found in [156], [165], [49]-

Blindfold games. Games such as Battleship, Kriegspiel (blindfold chess), and even card games are based on *imperfect information*: no player is fully aware of the total game state. Again, it might be expected that their complexity is higher. It is shown in [73] that the one-token game shown complete for PTIME in Theorem 26.4.4 becomes complete for PSPACE in its natural blindfold version. The technique used is a simple reduction from REGALL.

Exercises

28.1 Prove Corollary 28.1.3. □

28.2 Construct regular expressions for R_1, R_2, R_3 without using set complement $\setminus$. Give bounds on their lengths in relation to the size of program p. □

28.3 Prove that the membership problem for context-sensitive grammars is complete for PSPACE. □

28.4 Prove that the quantified boolean expression of the proof of Theorem 28.2.2 can be built in logarithmic space. □

References

The technique of reducing computations by arbitrary programs to ones using only boolean variables was used extensively by Jones and Muchnick in [76, 77]. Completeness for PSPACE of the REGALL and QBT problems is due to Meyer and to Stockmeyer [120, 157].

Part VI

Appendix

A Mathematical Terminology and Concepts

This appendix introduces a number of mathematical concepts that are used throughout the book. Readers with little or no mathematical background may read the appendix from one end to the other and do the exercises. Readers familiar with the notions introduced may consult the appendix if the need arises. The index should make this easy.

Section A.1 gives a short introduction to the manipulation of logical expressions. Section A.2 introduces sets and operations on sets, and Section A.3 is concerned with functions. Section A.4 introduces graphs. Section A.5 describes grammars, regular expressions, and finite automata. Section A.6 introduces definition and proof by induction. Section A.7 describes pairing functions.

Section A.7 contains a number of exercises; in general the reader is encouraged to try all the exercises. Section A.7 gives references for further reading.

A.1 Boolean algebra

Boolean algebra is the manipulation of logical expressions or *propositional formulas*. In boolean algebra we work with two *truth values*, *true* and *false*. We use $p, q, r, \ldots$ to denote *boolean variables*.

A *boolean expression* or *formula*, is formed by combining truth values, variables and smaller boolean expressions with the *boolean operators* shown in the following table:

operator	pronounced	arity	precedence	associativity
$\neg$	not	unary	5	—
$\wedge$	and	binary	4	left
$\vee$	or	binary	3	left
$\Rightarrow$	implies	binary	2	left
$\Leftrightarrow$	if and only if	binary	1	left

"If and only if" is usually abbreviated to "iff," and $p \wedge q$ is called the *conjunction* of p and q. Likewise, $p \vee q$ is called the *disjunction* of p and q, and $\neg p$ the *negation* of p. The $\neg$-operator has the tightest binding strength, so $p \vee q \vee \neg q \wedge true \Leftrightarrow r \Rightarrow \neg false$ is a boolean expression equivalent to $((p \vee q) \vee ((\neg q) \wedge true)) \Leftrightarrow ((\neg false) \Rightarrow r)$. A *literal* is either a boolean variable or its negation, making p and $\neg q$ literals, whereas $\neg\neg p$, $(p \wedge q)$ and *true* are not.

It is interesting to note that by using the following equations:

$$\neg(p \wedge q) \equiv \neg p \vee \neg q \qquad \neg(p \vee q) \equiv \neg p \wedge \neg q \quad \text{(de Morgan's laws)}$$

$$\left.\begin{array}{l} (p \wedge q) \vee r \equiv (p \vee r) \wedge (q \vee r) \quad (p \vee q) \wedge r \equiv (p \wedge r) \vee (q \wedge r) \\ p \wedge (q \vee r) \equiv (p \wedge q) \vee (p \wedge r) \quad p \vee (q \wedge r) \equiv (p \vee q) \wedge (p \vee r) \end{array}\right\} \text{(distributivity)}$$

$$\neg(p \Rightarrow q) \equiv p \wedge \neg q \qquad \neg(p \Leftrightarrow q) \equiv (\neg p \vee \neg q) \wedge (p \vee q)$$

$$\neg\neg p \equiv p \qquad true \equiv p \vee \neg p \qquad false \equiv p \wedge \neg p$$

it is possible to convert *any* boolean formula into *conjunctive normal form* (CNF), that is a finite conjunction of finite disjunctions of literals: $(A_{11} \vee \cdots \vee A_{1n_1}) \wedge \cdots \wedge (A_{m1} \vee \cdots \vee A_{mn_m})$. A concrete example of a boolean formula in CNF is $(p \vee \neg q) \wedge \neg q \wedge (\neg p \vee p \vee q)$.

A.1.1   Evaluation of boolean expressions

When we want to determine the truth value of a boolean expression, we must specify how the variables in the expression are to be interpreted. To this end we let θ be a *truth assignment* mapping boolean variables to truth values. If all the boolean variables occurring in an expression E are in the domain of (θ), then we define *the value of E under the truth assignment θ* to be the result of applying the function eval : *truth assignments* $\rightarrow$ *boolean expressions* $\rightarrow$ *truth values* given by

$$\text{eval}\,\theta\,E = \begin{cases} true, & \text{if } E \text{ is } true \\ false, & \text{if } E \text{ is } false \\ \theta(E), & \text{if } E \text{ is a variable} \\ \bar{p}\,op\,\bar{q}, & \text{if } E \text{ is } p\,op\,q \text{ and}\,\bar{p} = \text{eval}\,\theta\,p \text{ and } \bar{q} = \text{eval}\,\theta\,q \\ \neg\bar{p}, & \text{if } E \text{ is } \neg p \text{ and } \bar{p} = \text{eval}\,\theta\,p \end{cases}$$

where the truth value of $p\,op\,q$ is given by the following *truth table*:

p	q	$\neg p$	$p \wedge q$	$p \vee q$	$p \Rightarrow q$	$p \Leftrightarrow q$
true	true	false	true	true	true	true
true	false	false	false	true	false	false
false	false	true	false	false	true	true
false	true	true	false	true	true	false

A.2 Sets

A.2.1 Definition and examples

A *set* is informally defined to be a collection of objects. The only requirement a collection must satisfy to be called a set is that for any object x, either x is definitely *in* the collection, or x is definitely *not* in it. If S is a set and x is an object in S we say that x is an *element* of S (or x is *in S*, or x *belongs* to S, or x is a *member* of S, or even that x is *contained in S*) and write $x \in S$. If x is not in S we write $x \notin S$.

Well-known examples of a set inlude:

1. $\mathbb{N}$: the set of all non-negative integers (thus including zero), also called the *natural numbers*.

2. $\mathbb{R}$: the set of all real numbers, e.g., $2.1, 1/3, 400, -32, \pi, e$.

3. $\mathbb{R}^+$: the set of positive real numbers, e.g., $2.1, 1/3, 400, \pi, e$.

4. The collection of all graphs with at most five edges.

If a set contains only finitely many different objects $a_1, a_2, \ldots, a_n$ then the set is written $\{a_1, a_2, \ldots, a_n\}$. For example, the set containing the first three prime numbers (and nothing else) is written $\{2, 3, 5\}$.

An infinite set may be described similarly if there is an obvious rule for listing its elements. For instance the set of odd non-negative numbers may be written $\{1, 3, 5, 7, \ldots\}$.

Two sets T and S are *equal*, written $T = S$, if and only if they contain the same elements, i.e., if and only if every element in T is also an element in S and vice versa. Thus the sets $\{2, 5, 2, 5, 3\}$ and $\{2, 3, 5\}$ are equal. If $T = S$ we also say that T and S are one and the same set.

A set T is a *subset* of another set S, written $T \subseteq S$ if every element of T is also an element of S. If T is a subset of S and vice versa, T and S are equal by the definition of equality.

By definition of equality there is only one set without any members at all. This set is written $\emptyset$, and is called the *empty set*.

If S is some set and $P(x)$ is some condition involving x we use the notation $\{x \in S \mid P(x)\}$ to denote the set of all those members of S that satisfy the condition $P(x)$. For instance the set

$$\{x \in \mathbb{N} \mid x \geq 2 \text{ and the only divisors of } x \text{ are } 1 \text{ and } x\}$$

is the set of all prime numbers.

A.2.2   Some operations on sets

If T and S are two sets then the *union* $S \cup T$ is the set of all those objects that are elements in T or in S (or both). For example, $\{1,3\} \cup \{3,5\} = \{1,3,5\}$. The *intersection* $S \cap T$ is the set of all those objects that are elements in both T and S. For example, $\{1,3,4\} \cap \{3,4,5\} = \{3,4\}$. S and T are *disjoint* if they have no members in common, i.e., if $S \cap T = \emptyset$. Finally, the *difference* $S \setminus T$ is the set of all those objects that belong to to S but not T. Thus $\{1,2,5\} \setminus \{3,5,7\} = \{1,2\}$.

An *ordered pair* is a sequence of two (not necessarily distinct) objects in parentheses (a,b). The *first component* is a and the *second component* is b. If S and T are sets the *cartesian product* $S \times T$ is the set of all ordered pairs where the first component belongs to T and the second component belongs to S.

Similarly we speak of *triples* (a,b,c), *quadruples* (a,b,c,d), and in general *n-tuples* $(a_1, a_2, \ldots, a_n)$, and of the cartesian product of n sets $S_1, S_2, \ldots, S_n$.

$\mathcal{P}(S)$ denotes the set of all subsets of S. For instance,

$$\mathcal{P}(\{1,2,3\}) = \{\ \emptyset, \{1\}, \{2\}, \{3\}, \{1,2\}, \{1,3\}, \{2,3\}, \{1,2,3\}\ \}$$

If S is a finite set we let $\mid S \mid$ denote the number of elements in S.

A.2.3   An abbreviation

We use the *vector notation* $\vec{x}_n$ to denote the sequence $x_1, x_2, \ldots, x_n$ (also when $x_1, x_2, \ldots, x_n$ are numbers, graphs, etc.). Note that $\vec{x}_n$ does not include parentheses, so $(\vec{x}_n)$ means $(x_1, x_2, \ldots, x_n)$. Moreover, if $\vec{x}_n$ denotes $x_1, x_2, \ldots, x_n$ and $\vec{y}_m$ denotes denotes $y_1, y_2, \ldots, y_m$ then $(\vec{x}_n, \vec{y}_m)$ means $(x_1, x_2, \ldots, x_n, y_1, y_2, \ldots, y_m)$.

A.3   Functions

A.3.1   Total Functions

A *function* from a set A into a set B is a correspondence which associates to every a in A exactly one b in B. More precisely, a function from A into B is a subset f of $A \times B$ satisfying:

1. For all a in A there is *at least* one b in B such that (a,b) is in f (*definedness*).
2. For all a in A there is *at most* one b in B such that (a,b) is in f (*uniqueness*).

If f is a function from A into B, a is an element of A, and b is the unique b in B such that (a,b) is in f, we write $f(a) = b$ and call a the *argument* and b the *result*. Note that by the definition of a function there corresponds to every argument exactly one result.

The set of all functions from A into B is written $A \rightarrow B$, and the fact that f is a function from A into B is written $f : A \rightarrow B$.

Some examples:

1. The function *double* $f : \mathbb{N} \rightarrow \mathbb{N}$ associates to every n in $\mathbb{N}$ the number $n + n$. This is the set $\{(0,0),(1,2),(2,4),(3,6),\ldots\}$. For example, $f(2) = 4$.

2. The function *predecessor* $g : \mathbb{N} \rightarrow \mathbb{N}$ associates to every $n \neq 0$ the number $n - 1$ and associates 0 to 0. This is the set $\{(0,0),(1,0),(2,1),(3,2),\ldots\}$. For example, $f(3) = 2$.

3. The function *monus* $\dot{-} : \mathbb{N} \times \mathbb{N} \rightarrow \mathbb{N}$ which associates to every pair (m,n) with $m \geq n$ the difference $m - n$ and associates 0 to all other pairs. This is the set $\{((0,0),0),((0,1),0),((1,0),1),((2,0),2),((1,1),0),((0,2),0),\ldots\}$. For example $f(0,2) = 0$.

The set-theoretic definition of a function can be thought of as a table listing the arguments in one column (first component) and the result of applying the function to the arguments in the second column. For instance, *double* is:

0	0
1	2
2	4
$\vdots$	$\vdots$

A more customary way of writting the example functions is symbolically, e.g.:

1. $f(n) = n + n$.

2. $f(n) = \begin{cases} n - 1 & \text{if } n > 0 \\ 0 & \text{if } n = 0 \end{cases}$

3. $f(m,n) = \begin{cases} m - n & \text{if } m > n \\ 0 & \text{if } m \leq n \end{cases}$

We shall also employ this shorthand notation. However it is important to keep in mind that a function is just a certain set.

A function is sometimes called a *total function* to make explicit the difference from the *partial functions* introduced in the next subsection. The unqualified term *function* will always refer to a *total* function.

A.3.2   Infinite sequences

Let S be some set. An *infinite sequence* of elements from S is a total function from $\mathbb{N}$ to S. For example, the identity function $i : \mathbb{N} \to \mathbb{N}$ defined by $i(x) = x$ is a sequence, and the function $i : \mathbb{N} \to \mathbb{N} \times \mathbb{N}$ defined by $i(x) = (i, 2i)$ is a sequence.

Instead of presenting a sequence by a function definition, one often simply writes the first few values $i(0), i(1), i(2)$, etc. when it is obvious how i is then defined. For instance, the first sequence above would simply be written "$0, 1, 2, \ldots$" and the second would be written "$(0, 0), (1, 2), (2, 4), (3, 6), \ldots$"

A.3.3   Partial functions

A *partial function* from A into B is a correspondence which associates to every a in A at *most* one b in B, i.e., a subset f of $A \times B$ such that for every a in A there is at most one b in B such that $(a, b) \in f$.

This is the same as a total function except that there is no definedness condition; a partial function may not have a result in B for some argument in A. However, when a partial function has a result for some argument, then it has only one result.

If f is a partial function from A into B and $(a, b) \in f$ then we say that f is *defined* or *converges* on a, and we write $f(a)\!\downarrow$. If a is an element of A on which f is defined, and b is the unique element in B such that (a, b) is in f, we again write $f(a) = b$ and call a and b the argument and result, respectively.

If, on the other hand, for some a in A there is no b in B with (a, b) belonging to f we say that f is *undefined* or *diverges* on a and write $f(a)\!\uparrow$, or alternatively $f(a) = \perp$. In these two notations one should not think of $f(a)$ or $\perp$ as objects existing in B or some other set; the notations simply state that *there exists no $b \in B$ such that $(a, b) \in f$*. If $f(a)\!\uparrow$ and $g(a)\!\uparrow$ we will even write $f(a) = g(a)$. Again this simply means that f and g are both undefined on the value that they are applied to.

The set of all partial functions from A into B is written $A \to B_\perp$, and the fact that f is a partial function from A into B is written $f : A \to B_\perp$.

As an example of a partial function, consider $f : \mathbb{N} \times \mathbb{N} \to \mathbb{N}_\perp$, which maps any pair (m, n) to the result of rounding $\frac{m}{n}$ up to the nearest integer. For instance $f(3, 2) = 2$. This function is defined on (m, n) if and only if $n \neq 0$, e.g., $f(2, 0) = \perp$.

The cautious reader will have noticed a small error in the preceding example. Recall that $\mathbb{N} \times \mathbb{N}$ is the set of all pairs (m, n) where $m, n \in \mathbb{N}$. Thus f associates to every (m, n) with $n \neq 0$ a number k in $\mathbb{N}$. Recall also that if $a \in A$ and $g : A \to B_\perp$ and $(a, b) \in g$

we write $b = g(a)$, that is, we put parentheses around a. Thus above we should have written $f((3,2)) = 2$, rather than $f(3,2) = 2$. However it is customary to drop one set of parentheses, and we shall also do so.

For a partial function $f : A \to B_\perp$ the *domain* of f is the set

$$\text{dom}(f) = \{a \in A \mid f(a) \downarrow\}$$

In case f is total, $\text{dom}(f) = A$.

The *codomain* of a total or partial function from A into B is the set B.

The *range* of a total or partial function from A into B is the set

$$\text{rng}(f) = \{b \in B \mid \text{ there is a } a \in A \text{ such that } f(a) = b\}$$

A.3.4 Total versus partial functions

Any total function is also a partial function. For a partial function $f : A \to B_\perp$ it may happen that for all $a \in A$, $f(a)$ is defined, i.e., $\text{dom}(f) = A$. In that case f is also a total function.

There are two standard ways of obtaining a total function f' from a partial function $f : A \to B_\perp$:

1. Remove all those elements of A on which f is undefined: Define $f' : \text{dom}(f) \to B$ by $f'(a) = f(a)$ for all $a \in \text{dom}(f)$.
2. Add a new element $*$ to B and let that be the result whenever f is undefined: Define $f' : A \to (B \cup \{*\})$ by: $f'(a) = f(a)$ for all $a \in \text{dom}(f)$, and $f'(a) = *$ for $a \in A \backslash \text{dom}(f)$.

A.3.5 Equality of functions

Recall that functions are just certain sets, and that two sets are equal if and only if they contain the same elements. This implies that two total functions $f, g : A \to B$ are equal if and only if they are the same sets of pairs. Equal total functions f and g thus satisfy $f(a) = g(a)$ for all $a \in A$.

Similarly, two partial functions $f, g : A \to B_\perp$ are equal, written $f \simeq g$, iff $\text{dom}(f) = \text{dom}(g)$ and for all $a \in \text{dom}(f) : f(a) = g(a)$, i.e., iff for all $a \in A$:

1. $f(a)\uparrow$ and $g(a)\uparrow$; or

2. $f(a)\!\downarrow$ and $g(a)\!\downarrow$ and $f(a) = g(a)$.

Since we have agreed to write $f(a) = g(a)$ if both f and g are undefined on a, an equivalent definition of $f \simeq g$ would be to require that for all $a \in A : f(a) = g(a)$.

A.3.6   Some operations on partial functions

The *composition* of two partial functions $f : A \to B_\perp$ and $g : B \to C_\perp$ is the partial function $(g \circ f) : A \to B_\perp$ defined by

$$(g \circ f)(a) = \begin{cases} g(f(a)) & \text{if } a \in \text{dom}(f) \text{ and } f(a) \in \text{dom}(g) \\ \perp & \text{otherwise} \end{cases}$$

The *function updating* of two partial functions $f, g : A \to B_\perp$ is the partial function $f[g] : A \to B_\perp$ defined by

$$f[g](a) = \begin{cases} g(a) & \text{if } a \in \text{dom}(g) \\ f(a) & \text{otherwise} \end{cases}$$

Note that if both g and f are undefined on $a \in A$, then so is $f[g]$.

A function $f : A \to B_\perp$ with finite domain $\text{dom}(f) = \{a_1, a_2, \ldots, a_n\}$ is also written $[a_1 \mapsto b_1, a_2 \mapsto b_2, \ldots, a_n \mapsto b_n]$ where $f(a_1) = b_1, f(a_2) = b_2, \ldots, f(a_n) = b_n$. (This is just a slight variant of the notation $\{(a_1, b_1), (a_2, b_2), \ldots, (a_n, b_n)\}$ for f.) So (omitting a pair of square brackets)

$$f[a_1 \mapsto b_1, a_2 \mapsto b_2, \ldots, a_n \mapsto b_n]$$

is the function $h : A \to B_\perp$ such that $h(a_1) = b_1, h(a_2) = b_2, \ldots, h(a_n) = b_n$, and $h(a) = f(a)$ for $a \in A \backslash \{a_1, a_2, \ldots, a_n\}$.

Let $f, g : X \to \mathbb{R}_\perp$ for some set X. Then

1. The *sum* $f + g : X \to \mathbb{R}_\perp$ is defined by:

$$(f + g)(x) = \begin{cases} f(x) + g(x) & \text{if } f(x)\!\downarrow \text{ and } g(x)\!\downarrow \\ \perp & \text{otherwise} \end{cases}$$

2. The *product* $f \cdot g : X \to \mathbb{R}_\perp$ is defined by:

$$(f \cdot g)(x) = \begin{cases} f(x) \cdot g(x) & \text{if } f(x)\!\downarrow \text{ and } g(x)\!\downarrow \\ \perp & \text{otherwise} \end{cases}$$

3. The *difference* $f - g : X \to \mathbb{R}_\perp$ is defined by:

$$(f - g)(x) = \begin{cases} f(x) - g(x) & \text{if } f(x)\!\downarrow \text{ and } g(x)\!\downarrow \\ \perp & \text{otherwise} \end{cases}$$

4. The *quotient* $f/g : X \to \mathbb{R}_\perp$ is defined by:

$$(f/g)(x) = \begin{cases} f(x)/g(x) & \text{if } f(x){\downarrow} \text{ and } g(x){\downarrow} \text{ and } g(x) \neq 0 \\ \perp & \text{otherwise} \end{cases}$$

5. Similar notation is used with a constant $a \in X$ in place of f. For instance, $a \cdot f : X \to \mathbb{R}_\perp$ is defined by $(a \cdot f)(x) = a \cdot f(x)$.

In the special case where f, g are total functions (see section A.3.4) the operations 1-3 and 5 give as a result a total function. In 4 the result may be a partial function even when f, g are both total.

A.3.7   Higher-order functions

A *higher-order function* is a function that returns a function as its value.

One example is *twice* : $(\mathbb{N} \to \mathbb{N}) \to (\mathbb{N} \to \mathbb{N})$ where by definition for any $f : \mathbb{N} \to \mathbb{N}$ we have $twice(f) = g$ where $g(n) = f(f(n))$ for all $n \in \mathbb{N}$.

Another example is *apply* : $(\mathbb{N} \to \mathbb{N}) \times \mathbb{N} \to \mathbb{N}$ where for any $f : \mathbb{N} \to \mathbb{N}, n \in \mathbb{N}$ we have $apply(f, n) = f(n)$.

A.3.8   Lambda notation

Lambda notation is a device to define a function without giving it a name. For instance, we have previously described the successor function as

$$f : \mathbb{N} \to \mathbb{N}, f(n) = n + 1$$

Using the lambda notation this function could be written:

$$\lambda n . n + 1 : \mathbb{N} \to \mathbb{N}$$

The notation $\lambda n . n + 1$ should be read: the function that maps any n to $n + 1$.

In the usual notation we write for example $f(3) = 3 + 1$. What we do when we write $3 + 1$ on the right hand side of this equality is that we take the definition of f, $f(n) = n + 1$ and substitute 3 for n in the right hand side of the definition. In the lambda notation we do something similar by writing

$$(\lambda n . n + 1)3 = 3 + 1 = 4$$

Note the unusual bracketing in this expression.

428 Mathematical Terminology and Concepts

We write functions of several variables, e.g., addition, as:

$$(*) \qquad \lambda(m,n).m+n : \mathbb{N} \times \mathbb{N} \to \mathbb{N}$$

and for instance $(\lambda(m,n).m+n)(3,4) = 3+4 = 7$.

Another slightly different function is a higher-order verion of the same:

$$(**) \qquad \lambda m.\lambda n.m+n : \mathbb{N} \to (\mathbb{N} \to \mathbb{N})$$

Whereas the first function expects a pair (m,n) and then gives $m+n$ as result, the second function expects a number and then gives a *function* as result. For instance,

$$(\lambda m.\lambda n.m+n)3 = \lambda n.3+n$$

This function, "add 3" can itself be applied to some argument, for instance

$$(\lambda m.3+m)4 = 3+4 = 7$$

Thus

$$((\lambda m.\lambda n.m+n)3)4 = (\lambda n.3+n)4 = 3+4 = 7$$

It is clear that for any two numbers $k,l \in \mathbb{N}$

$$(\lambda(m,n).m+n)(k,l) = ((\lambda m.\lambda n.m+n)k)l$$

This suggests that one can represent functions of several variables by means of functions of just one variable. Indeed this holds in general as was discovered independently by several people. The transformation from a function like the one in $(*)$ to the one in $(**)$ is called *currying* after H. B. Curry, one of the discoverers of the idea.

From now on multiple function applications associate to the left, so $e_1 e_2 e_3$ means $(e_1 e_2) e_3$.

A.3.9 Injective, surjective, bijective, and monotonic total functions

An *injective* function is a function $f : A \to B$ such that for all $a,a' \in A$, if $a \neq a'$ then $f(a) \neq f(a')$. An injective function is also said to be *one-to-one*.

A *surjective* function is a function $f : A \to B$ such that for all $b \in B$ there is an $a \in A$ such that $f(a) = b$, i.e., if and only if $\text{rng}(f) = B$. Note that this does not follow from the fact that f is a function from A into B. A surjective function is also said to be *onto*.

A *bijective* function is a function which is both injective and surjective.

Examples:

1. $f : \mathbb{N} \to \mathbb{N}, f(n) = n+1$ is injective but not surjective.

2. $g : \mathbb{N} \times \mathbb{N} \to \mathbb{N}, g(m,n) = m + n$ is surjective but not injective.

3. $h : \mathbb{N} \to O$, where O is the set of odd non-negative numbers, defined by $h(n) = 2 \cdot n + 1$ is bijective.

A function $f : \mathbb{N} \to \mathbb{N}$ is *monotonic* if $n \leq m$ implies $f(n) \leq f(m)$, and *strictly monotonic* if $n < m$ implies $f(n) < f(m)$. If a function $f : \mathbb{N} \to \mathbb{N}$ is strictly monotonic then it is also injective, but not necessarily vice versa.

A.3.10   Some useful functions

We review some functions that are used in the remainder.

The *logarithmic function* with base 2, $\log : \mathbb{N} \to \mathbb{N}$ is defined by:

$$\log(n) = \begin{cases} 0 & \text{if } n = 0 \\ m & \text{otherwise, where } m \in \mathbb{N} \text{ is the largest number such that } 2^m \leq n \end{cases}$$

For instance, $\log(65536) = 16$ since $2^{16} = 65536$. It is convenient to assume that $\log(0) = 0$. Thus log is a total function from $\mathbb{N}$ into $\mathbb{N}$.

For a non-empty set N of natural numbers $\max(N)$ denotes the largest number in N if it exists, and ∞ otherwise. Thus max is a total function from the set of non-empty subsets of $\mathbb{N}$ into $\mathbb{N} \cup \{\infty\}$, i.e., $\max : \mathcal{P}(\mathbb{N}) \setminus \{\emptyset\} \to \mathbb{N} \cup \{\infty\}$.

For a non-empty set N of natural numbers $\min(N)$ denotes the smallest number in N. Such a number exists in every non-empty subset of $\mathbb{N}$.

A.3.11   Comparing the growth of functions

Below all functions are from $\mathbb{N}$ into $\mathbb{R}^+$. Given a total function f.

1. $O(f)$ (pronounced *big oh*) is the set of all functions g such that for some $r \in \mathbb{R}^+$, and for all but finitely many n,

$$g(n) < r \cdot f(n)$$

2. $\Omega(f)$ is the set of all functions g such that for some $r \in \mathbb{R}^+$ and for infinitely many n,

$$g(n) > r \cdot f(n)$$

3. $\Theta(f)$ is the set of all functions g such that for some $r_1, r_2 \in \mathbb{R}^+$ and for all but finitely many n,

$$r_1 \cdot f(n) \leq g(n) \leq r_2 \cdot f(n)$$

4. $o(f)$ (pronounced *little oh*) is the set of all functions g such that

$$\lim_{n\to\infty} \frac{g(n)}{f(n)} = 0$$

If $g \in O(f)$ then for some r the graph of g is below that of $r \cdot f = \lambda x . r \cdot f(x)$ for all but finitely many arguments. If $g \in o(f)$ then the graph of g is below that of $r \cdot f = \lambda x . r \cdot f(x)$ for all $r > 0$ and all but finitely many arguments.

If $g \in \Theta(f)$ then for some r_1, r_2 the graph of f stays between the graph of $r_1 \cdot f$ and $r_2 \cdot f$ for all but finitely many arguments.

The following properties are useful. Their proofs are left as exercises.

1. $g \in \Theta(f)$ iff $g \in O(f)$ and $f \in O(g)$
2. $g \in \Theta(f)$ iff $f \in \Theta(g)$

Some examples of the O-notation, whose proofs are also left as exercises:

1. $\lambda n . k \in O(\lambda n . n)$, but $\lambda n . n \notin O(\lambda n . k)$, for any $k \in \mathbb{R}^+$.
2. $\lambda n . \log n \in O(\lambda n . n)$, but $\lambda n . n \notin O(\lambda n . \log n)$.
3. $\lambda n . n^a \in O(\lambda n . b^n)$, but $\lambda n . b^n \notin O(\lambda n . n^a)$, for all $a, b \in \mathbb{R}^+$.

A common but sloppy notation is to write $f = O(g)$ instead of $f \in O(g)$. Such notation is harmless as long as one keeps in mind that the $=$ is neither symmetric nor transitive. Thus if $f = O(g)$ and $h = O(g)$ one should conclude neither $O(g) = f$ which is meaningless nor $f = h$ which may be plain wrong.

A.4   Graphs

A *graph* consists of a number of *nodes* and a number of *edges* between these nodes. For instance the following graph has three nodes and three edges. The edges have arrows in one direction, so this is a *directed* graph.

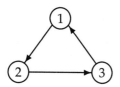

More precisely, we define a *directed graph* to be a pair (V, E) where V is called the set of *nodes* or *vertices* and $E \subseteq V \times V$ is called the set of *edges*. The graph above is $(\{1, 2, 3\}, \{(1, 2), (2, 3), (3, 1)\})$. An edge $(x, y) \in E$ may also be written as $x \to y$.

A *path* in (V, E) (from x_1 to x_n) is a finite sequence $x_1, \ldots, x_n$ where $n \geq 1$ and $x_i \to x_{i+1}$ is an edge in E for each i with $1 \leq i < n$. The *length* of the path is n. The *empty path* is the unique path of length 0. The path is a *cycle* if $n > 0$ and $x_1 = x_n$. A graph is *cyclic* if there is a cycle in it, and *acyclic* otherwise. A *DAG* is a directed acyclic graph.

We write

- $x_1 \to \ldots \to x_n$ for a path $x_1, x_2, \ldots, x_n$
- $x \to^* y$ if there is a path from x to y
- $x \to^n y$ if there is a path from x to y of length n
- $x \to^{\leq n} y$ if there is a path from x to y of length n or less.

A directed *graph with source and target nodes* is a 4-tuple $G = (V, E, v_0, v_{end})$ where $v_0, v_{end} \in V$ and (V, E) is a directed graph.

An *undirected graph* is a directed graph (V, E) such that E is symmetric: whenever edge $(x, y) \in E$ then we also have $(y, x) \in E$.

A.5 Grammars and finite automata

A.5.1 Alphabets and strings

A finite non-empty set is sometimes called an *alphabet*, in which case the members of the set are called *symbols*. If $\Sigma = \{a_1, \ldots, a_k\}$ is an alphabet, a *string* over Σ is a sequence $b_1 b_2 \ldots b_m$ where $m \geq 0$ and each $b_i \in \Sigma$. For example, if $\Sigma = \{0, 1\}$, then 11, 101, and 100011 are all strings over Σ. The *empty string* ε is the unique string with $m = 0$.

If $x = b_1 \ldots b_m$ and $y = c_1 \ldots c_n$, then x and y are equal, written $x = y$, if $m = n$ and $b_i = c_i$ for all $i \in \{1, \ldots n\}$. If $x = b_1 \ldots b_m$ and $y = c_1 \ldots c_n$, their *concatenation* is the string $xy = b_1 \ldots b_m c_1 \ldots c_n$. If $z = xy$ then we say x is a *prefix* of z, and that y is a *suffix* of z. If $z = xwy$ then we say w is a *substring* of z.

If A, B are two sets of strings over Σ, then we define

$$
\begin{aligned}
AB &= \{xy \mid x \in A, y \in B\} \\
A^* &= \{x_1 x_2 \ldots x_n \mid n \geq 0, x_1, \ldots, x_n \in A\} \\
A^+ &= \{x_1 x_2 \ldots x_n \mid n \geq 1, x_1, \ldots, x_n \in A\} \, (\text{so } A^* = A^+ \cup \{\varepsilon\})
\end{aligned}
$$

The *reverse* of string $x = b_1b_2 \ldots b_m$ is the string $\tilde{x} = b_m \ldots b_2b_1$, i.e., "$x$ written backwards."

A.5.2   Grammars

A grammar includes a rewrite system P (as defined in section 10.2.1), used as a tool to generate strings over an alphabet. We often write $\delta ::= \gamma$ instead of $(\delta, \gamma) \in P$. For instance

$$
\begin{aligned}
A &::= \ aAa \\
A &::= \ bAb \\
A &::= \ c \\
A &::= \ aca
\end{aligned}
$$

with $\Sigma = \{a, b, c\}$ is a grammar. For conciseness we often group productions with the same left side, separated by the symbol "|" (pronounced "or"). Thus the four productions above could be expressed as one:

$$A \ ::= \ aAa \mid bAb \mid c \mid aca$$

The usage of a grammar is that one starts out with the start symbol S and then replaces non-terminals A (in particular S) by the right hand sides of their productions, so the preceding grammar, beginning with A, can generate strings over $\{a, b\}$ like:

```
  aacaa
aaabcbaaa
bbaacaabb
 baacaab
```

(What is the underlying structure of all these strings?)

More formally, a *grammar* is a 4-tuple $G = (N, T, P, S)$ where

1. N is an alphabet whose members are called *nonterminals*.
2. T is an alphabet, disjoint from N, whose members are called *terminals*.
3. P is a string rewriting system over $N \cup T$ such that $(\delta, \gamma) \in P$ implies $\delta \notin T^*$.
4. S is a member of N called the *start symbol*.

In the preceding example

1. $N = \{A\}$.
2. $T = \{a, b, c\}$.

3. $P = \{(A, \mathsf{a}\,A\,\mathsf{a}), (A, \mathsf{b}\,A\,\mathsf{b}), (A, \mathsf{c}), (A, \mathsf{aca})\}$.

4. $S = A$.

The requirement on δ in part 3 of the definition of a grammar states that no production may allow a sequence of terminals to be rewritten further, hence the name "terminal symbol."

We now give precise definitions of one-step and multi-step rewriting. These are called the *one-step derivation relation* $\Rightarrow$ and the *multi-step derivation relation* $\Rightarrow^*$ and are defined as follows where $\alpha, \beta, \rho, \sigma \in (N \cup T)^*$:

1. $\alpha \delta \beta \Rightarrow \alpha \gamma \beta$ iff $\delta ::= \gamma \in P$.

2. If $\rho \Rightarrow \sigma$ then $\rho \Rightarrow^* \sigma$.

3. $\rho \Rightarrow^* \rho$.

4. If $\rho \Rightarrow^* \alpha$ and $\alpha \Rightarrow^* \sigma$ then $\rho \Rightarrow^* \sigma$.

The *set generated by a grammar* $G = (N, T, P, S)$ is:

$$L(G) = \{x \in T^* \mid S \Rightarrow^* x\}$$

The set generated by our example grammar is the set of all strings $xc\tilde{x}$ where x is a string of a's and b's, and $\tilde{x}$ is the reverse string of x.

A.5.3 Classes of grammars

Some classes of grammars are particularly interesting, and well-studied for programming language applications.

A *regular grammar* $G = (N, T, P, S)$ is a grammar in which every production is of form $A ::= x$ or $A ::= xB$ where $A, B \in N, x \in T^*$. Our example grammar above is not regular.

A *context-free grammar* $G = (N, T, P, S)$ is one such that in every production $\delta ::= \gamma \in P$, δ is a single nonterminal symbol. Our example grammar above is context-free.

Clearly every regular grammar is context-free, but not necessarily vice versa.

A *context-sensitive grammar* $G = (N, T, P, S)$ is one such that in every production $\alpha ::= \beta \in P$, the length of β is larger than or equal to that of α, or $\alpha ::= \beta$ is $S ::= \varepsilon$, and S does not appear on the right side of any production in P.

Let $G = (N, T, P, S)$ be a context-free grammar. There is a specific form of one-step and multi-step rewriting where one always rewrites the left-most non-terminal. These are called the *left-most one-step derivation relation* $\Rightarrow_l$ and the *left-most multi-step derivation relation* $\Rightarrow_l^*$ and are defined as follows where $\rho, \sigma \in (N \cup T)^*$:

1. $\alpha\delta\beta \Rightarrow_l \alpha\gamma\beta$ iff $\delta ::= \gamma \in P$ and $\alpha \in T^*, \beta \in (N \cup T)^*$.
2. If $\rho \Rightarrow_l \sigma$ then $\rho \Rightarrow_l^* \sigma$.
3. $\rho \Rightarrow_l^* \rho$.
4. If $\rho \Rightarrow_l^* \alpha$ and $\alpha \Rightarrow_l^* \sigma$ then $\rho \Rightarrow_l^* \sigma$.

Sometimes one can generate the same terminal string from a context-free grammar by two different left-most derivation sequences. For instance, in our example grammar

$$A \Rightarrow_l \text{aca}$$

by the last production, but also

$$A \Rightarrow_l \text{a} A \text{a} \Rightarrow_l \text{aca}$$

In this case the grammar is said to be *ambiguous*.

A.5.4   Decidability problems for grammars

We mention some decision problemsoncerning grammars and strings:

1. The *membership problem* for grammar $G = (N, T, P, S)$ is: given a string $x \in T^*$, to decide whether or not $x \in L(G)$.
2. The *non-emptiness problem* for G is to decide whether or not $L(G) = \emptyset$.
3. The *completeness problem* for G is to decide whether or not $L(G) = T^*$.
4. The *ambiguity problem* for context-free grammar G is to decide whether or not G is ambiguous.

Some special cases of these problems are so important that they have their own names:

1. $\text{CF}^{\neq\emptyset}$: The non-emptiness problem for context-free grammars.
2. CFALL: the completeness problem for context-free grammars.
3. CFAMB: the ambiguity problem for context-free grammars.
4. $\text{REG}^{\neq\emptyset}$: The non-emptiness problem for regular grammars.
5. REGALL: the completeness problem for regular grammars.
6. REGAMB: the ambiguity problem for regular grammars.

A.5.5   Regular expressions

One way to represent a set of strings is to find a grammar generating exactly that set. Another way is to find a *regular expression*. Let Σ be an alphabet. The set of *regular expressions over* Σ is defined as follows.

1. ε is a regular expression over Σ.
2. If $a \in \Sigma$ then a is a regular expression over Σ.
3. If r, s are regular expressions over Σ then so are $(r \mid s)$, (rs), and (r^*)

To save parentheses we adopt the conventions that

1. $*$ has the highest precedence;
2. concatenation has the second highest precedence, and associates to the left;
3. $\mid$ has the lowest precedence, and associates to the left.

For instance the regular expression $r = (((00)^*) \mid (1((11)^*)))$ can be written shorter as $(00)^* \mid 1(11)^*$.

As for grammars we define $L(r)$, the *set generated by the regular expression r*, as follows:

1. $L(\varepsilon) = \emptyset$;
2. $L(a) = \{a\}$ for every $a \in \Sigma$;
3. $L(r \mid s) = L(r) \cup L(s)$;
4. $L(rs) = L(r)L(s)$;
5. $L(r^*) = L(r)^*$

where $L(r)L(s)$ and $L(r)^*$ are defined in Subsection A.5.1. For the regular expression r above $L(r)$ is the set of all strings consisting either of an even number of 0's or an odd number of 1's.

The cautious reader may have noticed that a certain class of grammars was called the *regular grammars*. This suggests some connection to the *regular expressions*. Indeed the following property holds:

Proposition A.5.1

1. For any regular grammar G there is a regular expression r with $L(G) = L(r)$.
2. For any regular expression r there is a regular grammar G with $L(G) = L(r)$.

On the other hand there are certain sets of strings that are generated by a context-free grammar but not by any regular expression or regular grammar. For instance, this is the case with the set of strings consisting of n a's followed by n b's.

A.5.6 NFA and DFA

Grammars and regular expressions are compact representations of sets of strings. We now introduce a third kind of representation of a set of strings, namely a *non-deterministic finite automaton*, or *NFA* for short. Pictorially an NFA is a directed graph where every edge has a label, one node is depicted as the *start node*, and zero, one or more nodes are depicted as *accept nodes*. Here is an example where the start node stands out by having an arrow labelled "start" into it, and where the single accepting node has two circles rather than just one:

The idea of representing a set L of strings by this NFA is as follows. From the start node 1 we can "read" a c and then proceed to node 2. From this node we can read any number of a's without leaving the state and then read a b, jumping to node 3. Again we can read any number of a's and then a c, jumping to the accepting node. Thus altogether we have read a string of form: ca...aba...ac. The set L consists of all the strings we can read in this manner; in other words, L is the same set of string as the set generated by the regular expression ca*ba*c.

The reason why these automata are called "non-deterministic" is that there can be two different edges out of a node with the *same* label, and there can be edges labelled ε, as illustrated in the following NFA, which accepts the set of strings generated by ε | ab | ac:

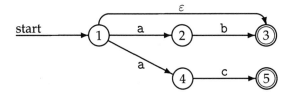

More formally an *NFA* is a 5-tuple (Q, Σ, m, q_0, F) where

- Q is a set of *states*;
- Σ is an alphabet;
- $m : Q \times (\Sigma \cup \{\varepsilon\}) \to \mathcal{P}(Q)$ is a *transition function* that maps a state and a symbol to a set of states;
- q_0 is a state, the *start state*;

- F is a set of states, the *accepting states*.

In the first example above:

- $Q = \{1, 2, 3, 4\}$;
- $\Sigma = \{\texttt{a}, \texttt{b}, \texttt{c}\}$;
- $\begin{aligned}
m(1, c) &= \{2\} \\
m(2, a) &= \{2\} \\
m(2, b) &= \{3\} \\
m(3, a) &= \{3\} \\
m(3, c) &= \{4\}
\end{aligned}$
- $q_0 = 1$;
- $F = \{4\}$.

Formally, a string $x = a_1 \ldots a_n$ with each $a_i \in \Sigma$ is *accepted* by an NFA (Q, Σ, m, q_0, F) if there is a sequence of states $q_1, \ldots q_{n+1} \in Q$ and symbols $a_1, \ldots, a_n \in \Sigma \cup \{\varepsilon\}$ such that $m(q_i, a_i) \ni q_{i+1}$ for all $i \in \{1, \ldots, n\}$, and $q_0 = q_1$. Given an NFA N, $L(N)$ denotes the set of all strings accepted by N, and this is called the *language accepted by* N.

A *deterministic finite automaton,* or *DFA* for short, is an NFA such that no edge is labelled ε and all edges out of the same node are labelled by different symbols. The first of the above NFAs is a DFA, the second is not. Formally, a DFA can be dscribed as a 5-tuple (Q, Σ, m, q_0, F) where

- Q is a set of *states*;
- Σ is an alphabet;
- $m : Q \times \Sigma \to Q$ is a *transition function* that maps a state and a symbol to a state;
- q_0 is a state, the *start state*;
- F is a set of states, the *accepting states*.

Note that m now maps from Σ (instead of $\Sigma \cup \{\varepsilon\}$) to Q (instead of $\mathcal{P}(Q)$). A string $x = a_1 \ldots a_n$ with each $a_i \in \Sigma$ is *accepted* by a DFA (Q, Σ, m, s_0, F) if there is a sequence of states $q_1, \ldots q_{n+1} \in Q$ and symbols $a_1, \ldots, a_n \in \Sigma \cup \{\varepsilon\}$ such that $m(q_i, a_i) = q_{i+1}$ for all $i \in \{1, \ldots, n\}$, and $q_0 = q_1$. $L(N)$ denotes the set of all strings accepted by the DFA N, and this is called the *language accepted by* N.

It is easy to turn the second of the above NFA's into a DFA accepting the same language. It is also easy, as we have done, to express the language accepted by the two NFA's by means of regular expressions. It is natural to wonder what the connections are in general between NFA's, DFA's, and regular expressions. This is settled in the `lowing proposition.

Proposition A.5.2 the following conditions are equivalen for any language L:

1. There is a DFA accepting L.
2. There is an NFA accepting L.
3. There is a regular expression generating L.
4. There is a regular grammar generating L.

Proofs of these properties can be found in [3].

In constructing 2 from 1, the number of states of the two automata are the same since any DFA may be converted into an equivalent NFA by a trivial change in the transition function (to yield a singleton set of states instead of one state). In constructing 1 from 2, the DFA may have as many as 2^n states where n is the number of states of the NFA. In constructing 2 from 3, the NFA has at most twice as many states as the size of the regular expression.

A.6   Induction

A.6.1   Inductive proofs

Consider the formula

$$(*) \qquad 1 + 2 + \ldots + n = \frac{n(n+1)}{2}$$

Is this equation true for all $n \in \mathbb{N}$?[1] If $n = 0$ it states that[2] $0 = (0 \cdot 1)/2$ which is true. For $n = 1$ it states $1 = (1 \cdot 2)/2$ which is true. For $n = 2, 3$ it states that $1 + 2 = (2 \cdot 3)/2$ and $1 + 2 + 3 = (3 \cdot 4)/2$, which are both true, and so on.

The formula seems to be true for all examples. However this does not constitute a proof that it really *is* true in all cases. It could be that the formula fails for some number.[3] On the other hand, if we don't know what n is, we need a general technique to prove the equation.

Suppose we could prove the following.

1. $(*)$ holds for $n = 0$.

---

[1] Recall that predicates are certain sets. In this section we often discuss whether or not something *holds* or *is true*. This always boils down to set membership, cf. section 12.2.

[2] By convention $1 + 2 + \ldots + n = 0$ when $n = 0$.

[3] Allenby [4] mentions a a striking example of this kind. Consider the following property that a number n may or may not have: n can be written as $n_1^3 + n_2^3 + n_3^3 + n_4^3 + n_5^3 + n_6^3 + n_7^3 + n_8^3$ where $n_1, \ldots, n_8 \in \mathbb{N}$. It turns out that the property holds for all natural numbers *except* 23 and 239.

2. Whenever (∗) holds for some number n it also holds for $n + 1$.

Then (∗) would hold for 0, for 1, for 2, and so on. The *principle of mathematical induction* states that if the above two properties hold then (∗) holds for *all* numbers:

> *Mathematical induction.* If for some predicate $P(n)$ on $\mathbb{N}$, $P(0)$ is true, and it holds that for all $n \in \mathbb{N}$ $P(n)$ implies $P(n + 1)$, then $P(n)$ holds for all $n \in \mathbb{N}$.

We can prove (∗) by applying this principle, using (∗) in place of $P(n)$:

Base case: If $n = 0$ then (∗) states that $0 = 0 \cdot 1/2$ which is true.

Induction Step: Suppose that (∗) holds for some n. (This is called the *induction hypothesis*). Then

$$1 + 2 + \ldots + n = \frac{n(n + 1)}{2}$$

Then

$$
\begin{aligned}
1 + 2 + \ldots + n + (n + 1) &= \tfrac{n(n+1)}{2} + (n + 1) \\
&= \tfrac{n(n+1)}{2} + \tfrac{2(n+1)}{2} \\
&= \tfrac{n(n+1) + 2(n+1)}{2} \\
&= \tfrac{(n+1)(n+2)}{2}
\end{aligned}
$$

so (∗) also holds for $n + 1$.

Hence by mathematical induction, (∗) holds for all $n \in \mathbb{N}$.

If one wants to prove for some predicate $P(n)$ that $P(n)$ holds for all $n \geq 1$ one must prove in the base case that $P(1)$ holds and prove for all $n \geq 1$ that $P(n)$ implies $P(n + 1)$.

For a predicate $P(n)$ it sometimes happens that we can prove $P(n + 1)$ more easily if we know that $P(k)$ holds not only for $k = n$ but for *all* $k \leq n$. This can be stated as the mathematically equivalent principle of *complete induction* or *course-of-values induction*:

> *Complete induction.* If for some predicate $P(n)$ on $\mathbb{N}$ $P(0)$ is true, and it holds that $P(k)$ for all $k \leq n$ implies $P(n + 1)$, then $P(n)$ holds for all $n \in \mathbb{N}$.

Again if one proves $P(1)$ in the base case, the conclusion is that $P(n)$ holds for all $n \geq 1$.

A.6.2 Inductive definitions

One can define objects *inductively* (or *recursively*). For instance, the sum $s(n) = 1 + 2 + \ldots + n$ can be defined as follows:

$$
\begin{aligned}
s(0) &= 0 \\
s(n + 1) &= (n + 1) + s(n)
\end{aligned}
$$

More generally we may use:

Definition by Recursion. If S is some set, a is an element of S, and $g : S \times \mathbb{N} \to S$ is a total function, then the function $f : \mathbb{N} \to S$

$$
\begin{aligned}
f(0) &= a \\
f(n+1) &= g(f(n), n)
\end{aligned}
$$

is well-defined.

In the preceding example S was $\mathbb{N}$, a was 0, and $g(x, n) = (n+1) + x$.
   Many variations of this principle exist. For instance:

1. $f(n+1)$ may use not only n and $f(n)$, but all the values $0, \ldots, n$ and $f(0), \ldots, f(n)$.

2. Function f may have more parameters than the single one from $\mathbb{N}$.

3. Several functions may be defined simultaneously.

As examples of the three variations:

1. The fibonacci function $f : \mathbb{N} \to \mathbb{N}$ is defined by:

$$
\begin{aligned}
f(0) &= 1 \\
f(1) &= 1 \\
f(n+2) &= f(n+1) + f(n)
\end{aligned}
$$

2. The power function $\lambda(m, n). m^n : \mathbb{N} \times \mathbb{N} \to \mathbb{N}$ is defined by:

$$
\begin{aligned}
m^0 &= 1 \\
m^{n+1} &= m \cdot m^n
\end{aligned}
$$

3. The functions even : $\mathbb{N} \to \{T, F\}$ returning T iff the argument is even, and odd : $\mathbb{N} \to \{T, F\}$ returning T iff the argument is odd can be defined by mutual recursion:

$$
\begin{aligned}
\text{even}(0) &= T \\
\text{even}(n+1) &= \text{odd}(n)
\end{aligned}
$$

$$
\begin{aligned}
\text{odd}(0) &= F \\
\text{odd}(n+1) &= \text{even}(n)
\end{aligned}
$$

A.6.3   Other structures than numbers

The set of strings generated by a grammar can be viewed as defined inductively. Here is an example:

A *parenthesis string* is a string over the alphabet $\{(,)\}$. The set of all *balanced parenthesis strings* is defined as the set of strings generated by the following grammar:

$$
\begin{aligned}
S &::= \varepsilon \\
S &::= S\,S \\
S &::= (S)
\end{aligned}
$$

Example strings generated by the grammar: () and (()()) and (()(())). Some examples, *not* generated by the grammar:)(and ()(() and ())).

There is a well-known algorithm to test whether a parenthesis string is balanced. Let $l(x)$ and $r(x)$ be the number of left and right parentheses in x, respectively. A *prefix* of x is a string y such that $x = yz$ for some z, i.e., an initial part of x. *Claim:* a parenthesis string x is balanced iff $l(x) = r(x)$ and for all prefixes y of x $l(y) \leq r(y)$.

Actually we can *prove* correctness of this claim. This has two parts. First, that any string x generated by the grammar satisfies the test; and second, that any string satisfying the test is also generated by the grammar.

For the first part, the proof is by complete induction on n, the number of steps in the derivation $S \Rightarrow^* x$, with base case $n = 1$. So $P(n)$ is: any string x in a derivation $S \Rightarrow^* x$ with n steps satisfies the test.

Base case. If $n = 1$ then the derivation must be $S \Rightarrow^* \varepsilon$ (remember that every derived string consists only of terminals). Clearly, $l(\varepsilon) = 0 = r(\varepsilon)$, and since the only prefix of ε is ε itself, $l(y) \leq r(y)$ for all prefixes y.

Induction step: Suppose all strings generated in n or fewer steps from the grammar satisfy the test, and consider some string x generated in $n+1$ steps. The rewriting must begin with either $S \Rightarrow S\,S$ or $S \Rightarrow (S)$.

We consider first the case beginning with $S \Rightarrow S\,S$. Here x has form uv where $S \Rightarrow^* u$ and $S \Rightarrow^* v$ are derivations in n or fewer steps. By induction hypothesis the test holds for both u and v. Then

$$
\begin{aligned}
l(x) &= l(uv) \\
&= l(u) + l(v) \\
&= r(u) + r(v) \\
&= r(x)
\end{aligned}
$$

Now we only need to show that $l(y) \leq r(y)$ for any prefix y of $x = uv$, so let y be some prefix of x. If y is a prefix of u then $l(y) \leq r(y)$ by induction hypothesis. If y is not a prefix of u then $y = uw$ where w is a prefix of v. Then by induction hypothesis:

$$
\begin{aligned}
l(y) &= l(uw) \\
&= l(u) + l(w) \\
&= r(u) + l(w) \\
&\leq r(u) + r(w) \\
&= r(uw) \\
&= r(x)
\end{aligned}
$$

as required.

The case where the derivation begins with $S \Rightarrow (S)$ is left as an exercise, and the proof of the *remaining part*, that any string x satisfying the test is generated by the grammar, is also an exercise.

Induction proofs occur frequently in computability and complexity theory as well as in other branches of theoretical computer science. The only way to get to master such proofs is to try and do a number of them. Therefore the reader is strongly encouraged to try out Exercises A.17 and A.18.

A.7 Pairing functions

A *pairing decomposition* of set X consists of three total functions

$$pr : X \times X \to X, hd : X \to X, tl : X \to X$$

such that for all $x, y \in X$ and all $z \in \mathrm{rng}(pr)$:

$$
\begin{aligned}
hd(pr(x, y)) &= x \\
tl(pr(x, y)) &= y
\end{aligned}
$$

In a pairing decomposition pr is called a *pairing function*.

The pairing function pr is one-to-one since $pr(x, y) = pr(x', y')$ implies that $x = hd(pr(x, y)) = hd(pr(x', y')) = x'$ and similarly for y, y'. Function pr need not be onto, although such functions do exist.

There are several pairing functions for the set $\mathbb{N}$ of natural numbers. One example is $pr_1(x, y) = 2^x \cdot 3^y$. To understand that one can find corresponding hd, tl one must know that if $2^x 3^y = 2^a 3^b$ then $x = a$ and $y = b$. This follows from the *fundamental theorem of arithmetic*: Any $n \neq 0$ can be written in exactly one way as a product $p_1^{n_1} p_2^{n_2} \ldots p_m^{n_m}$ where $p_1 < p_2 < \ldots < p_m$ are prime numbers and $n_1, n_2 \ldots, n_m$ are all numbers different from 0.

For a more economical example in which pr is onto, consider the pairing decomposition where the pairing function is $pr_3(x,y) = (x+y)(x+y+1)/2 + y = (x^2 + 2xy + y^2 + x + 3y)/2$. This pairing is surjective.

This can be illustrated by the figure:

y							
$\vdots$	$\dots$	$\dots$	$\dots$	$\dots$	$\dots$	$\dots$	
4	10	$\dots$	$\dots$	$\dots$	$\dots$	$\dots$	
3	6	11	$\dots$	$\dots$	$\dots$	$\dots$	
2	3	7	12	$\dots$	$\dots$	$\dots$	
1	1	4	8	13	$\dots$	$\dots$	
0	0	2	5	9	14	$\dots$	
	0	1	2	3	4	$\dots$	x

In both of the two last pairing decompositions the pairs in the sequence

$$\{(0,0),(0,1),(1,0),(2,0),(1,1),(0,2),(0,3),\dots\}$$

receive increasing values by the pairing function, and in the last example these values are even consecutive. Further, Polya has proven that any surjective polynomial pairing function must be identical to $pr_3(x,y)$ or its converse $pr_4(x,y) = pr_3(y,x)$.

Exercises

A.1

1. Place the implicit parentheses in the boolean expression $p \Rightarrow \neg q \Rightarrow \neg q \Leftrightarrow \neg p \Rightarrow \neg q$

2. Convert the expression to CNF and indicate which equations you use.

3. Given the truth assignment $\theta(p) = true$, $\theta(q) = false$, what is the value of the expression in question 1? What is the value of the CNF-converted expression?
   A boolean expression is called *satisfiable* iff there exists a truth assignment for the variables of the expression such that the value of the expression is *true*. It is called *valid* iff the value of the expression is *true* under all truth assignments of the variables.

4. Is the expression in question 1 satisfiable? Is it valid? □

A.2 Suppose $f : A \to B_\perp$ and $g : B \to C_\perp$ are two partial functions. What function is the set

$$h = \{(a,c) \in A \times C \mid \text{ there is a } b \in B : (a,b) \in f \text{ and } (b,c) \in g\}?$$

Give a similar explicit description of $f[g]$.　　　☐

A.3 Prove 1-3 in Subsection A.3.9.　　　☐

A.4 Prove that if $f : A \to B$ is a bijective function then there exists exactly one function $f^{-1} : B \to A$ such that: $f(a) = b$ if and only $f^{-1}(b) = a$. The function f^{-1} is called the *inverse* of f.　　　☐

A.5 Prove that if $f : A \to B$ is an injective function then there exists exactly one function $f^{-1} : \text{rng}(f) \to A$ such that: $f(a) = b$ if and only $f^{-1}(b) = a$. The function f^{-1} is again called the *inverse* of f.　　　☐

A.6 Prove that the inverse of an injective function is surjective.　　　☐

A.7 Give an example of a function which is neither injective nor surjective.　　　☐

A.8 What is the inverse of the composition of two bijective functions?　　　☐

A.9 Show that if $f \in O(g)$ and $g \in O(h)$ then $f \in O(h)$.　　　☐

A.10 Prove the five properties at the end of section A.3.11.　　　☐

A.11 Suppose $f \in O(f')$ and $g \in O(g')$. Which of the following are true?

1. $f + g \in O(f' + g')$.
2. $f \cdot g \in O(f' \cdot g')$.
3. $f/g \in O(f'/g')$.
4. Suppose that $f - g$ and $f' - g'$ are functions from $\mathbb{N}$ into $\mathbb{R}^+$. Then $f - g \in O(f' - g')$.

　　　☐

A.12 Construct NFAs accepting the following regular expressions:

1. $(a|b)^*$
2. $(a^*|b^*)^*$
3. $((\varepsilon|a)b^*)^*$

　　　☐

A.13 Convert the NFAs of the preceding exercise into DFAs.   □

A.14 Give a regular expression generating the language accepted by the following NFA:

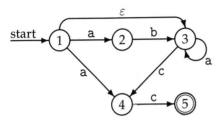

□

A.15 Convert the NFA of the preceding exercise into a DFA.   □

A.16 What is wrong with the following alledged induction proof?

A set of natural numbers is *odd* if all its members are odd.

Claim: Every finite set of natural numbers N is odd.

proof: By induction on the number of elements in N.

Base case: $n = 0$. Then trivially all elements are odd, since there are no elements [the rat is not buried here].

Induction step: We assume that all sets with n members are odd and must show that all members with $n + 1$ members are odd. Let S have $n + 1$ members. Remove one element l and let the resulting set be called L. Since L has n members the induction hypothesis guarantees that L is odd. Now put l back and take another element k out resulting in a set K. K again has n elements and so is odd. In particular l is odd, and since $S = L \cup \{l\}$ and L is odd, S is odd.   □

A.17 Prove the last case in the proof that every string generated by the grammar for balanced parenthesis strings satisfies the test for parenthesis strings (see Subsection A.6.3).   □

A.18 Prove that every parenthesis string satisfying the test in Subsection A.6.3 is also generated by the grammar in the same subsection. *Hint:* use induction on the number of symbols in the string x with base case 0. In the induction step argue that since x satisfies the test, x must have form (y) where y satisfies the test, or vw where v and w satisfy the test. Then use the induction hypothesis.   □

A.19 Give algorithms to compute *hd* and *tl* for the three pairing decompositions in section A.7.   □

References

Most of the contents of this appendix is covered by many books on discrete mathematics. For more specialized texts, an excellent introduction to sets and functions can be found in Halmos' book [58], and finite automata are covered by the classic text by Aho, Hopcroft, and Ullman [2].

Bibliography

[1] W. Ackermann. Zum Hilbertschen Aufbau der reelen Zahlen. *Mathematische Annalen*, 99, 1928.

[2] A. Aho, J.E. Hopcroft, and J.D. Ullman. *The Design and Analysis of Computer Algorithms*. Computer Science and Information Processing. Addison-Wesley, 1974.

[3] A. Aho, R. Sethi, and J.D. Ullman. *Compilers: Principles, Techniques, and Design*. Addison-Wesley, 1986.

[4] R.B.J.T. Allenby. *Rings, Fields, and Groups*. Edward Arnold, 1988.

[5] N. Andersen and N.D. Jones. Generalizing cook's transformation to imperative stack programs. In Juhani Karhumäki, Hermann Maurer, and Grzegorz Rozenberg, editors, *Results and Trends in Theoretical Computer Science*, volume 812 of *Lecture Notes in Computer Science*, pages 1–18. Springer-Verlag, 1994.

[6] Y. Bar-Hillel, M. Perles, and E. Shamir. On formal properties of simple phrase structure grammars. *Z. Phonetik, Sprachwiss. Kommunikationsforsch.*, 14:143–172, 1961.

[7] H.P. Barendregt. *The Lambda Calculus: Its Syntax and Semantics*. North-Holland, second, revised edition, 1984.

[8] L. Beckman, A. Haraldson, Ö. Oskarsson, and E. Sandewall. A partial evaluator and its use as a programming tool. *Artificial Intelligence*, 7:319–357, 1976.

[9] M. Ben-Amram. What is a "pointer machine"? *SIGACT News*, 26(2):88–95, June 1995.

[10] A. Berlin and D. Weise. Compiling scientific code using partial evaluation. *IEEE Computer*, 23:25–37, 1990.

[11] D. Bjørner, A.P. Ershov, and N.D. Jones, editors. *Partial Evaluation and Mixed Computation*. North-Holland, Amsterdam, 1988.

[12] L. Blum, M. Shub, and S. Smale. On a theory of computation over the real numbers, np-completeness, and universal machines. *Proc. IEEE Symposium on Foundations of Computer Science*, 29, 1988.

[13] M. Blum. A machine independent theory of the complexity of recursive functions. *Journal of the Association for Computing Machinery*, 14:322–336, 1967.

[14] P. van Emde Boas. Machine models and simulations. In J. val Leeuwen, editor, *Handbook of Theoretical Computer Science, vol. A*. Elsevier, 1990.

[15] A.B. Borodin. Computational complexity and the existence of complexity gaps. *Journal of the Association for Computing Machinery*, 19:158–174, 1972.

[16] A.B. Borodin. Computational complexity — theory and practice. In A.V. Aho, editor, *Currents in the Theory of Computing*, pages 35–89. Prentice-Hall, 1973.

[17] H. Bratman. An alternate form of the uncol diagram. *Communications of the ACM*, 4:3:142, 1961.

[18] J. Case and C. Smith. Comparison of identification criteria for machine inductive inference. *Theoretical Computer Science*, 25:193–220, 1983.

[19] C.-L. Chang and R.C.-T. Lee. *Symbolic Logic and Mechanical Theorem Proving*. Computer Science and Applied Mathematics. Academic Press, 1973.

[20] T. Chuang and B. Goldberg. Real-time deques, multihead turing machines, and purely functional programming. *International Conference on Functional Programming Languages and Computer Architecture*, 6:289–298, 1995.

[21] A. Church. A note on the Entscheidungsproblem. *Journal of Symbolic Logic*, 1:40–41, 1936.

[22] A. Church. An unsolvable problem of elementary number theory. *American Journal of Mathematics*, 58:345–363, 1938.

[23] A. Church and J.B. Rosser. Some properties of conversion. *Transactions of the American Mathematical Society*, 39:11–21, 1936.

[24] A. Cobham. The intrinsic computational difficulty of functions. In *Proceedings of the Congress for Logic, Mathematics, and Philosophy of Science*, pages 24–30, 1964.

[25] S.A. Cook. Path systems and language recognition. In *Proceedings of the 2nd Annual ACM Symposium on on the Theory of Computing*, pages 70–72, 1970.

[26] S.A. Cook. Characterization of pushdown machines in terms of time-bounded computers. *Journal of the Association for Computing Machinery*, 18(1):4–18, January 1971.

[27] S.A. Cook. An overview of computational complexity. *Communications of the ACM*, 26(6):401–408, 1983.

[28] Stephen A. Cook. Linear-time simulation of deterministic two-way pushdown automata. In V. Freiman C. editor, *Information Processing 71*, pages 75–80. North-Holland Publishing Company, 1972.

[29] C. Dahl and M. Hessellund. Determining the constant coefficients in a time hierarchy. Technical report, Department of Computer Science, University of Copenhagen, feb 1994.

[30] M. Davis. Arithmetical problems and recursively enumerable predicates. *Journal of Symbolic Logic*, 18:33–41, 1953.

[31] M. Davis. *Computability and Unsolvability*. McGraw-Hill, New York, 1958. Reprinted in 1982 with [33] as an appendix, by Dover Publications.

[32] M. Davis. *The Undecidable*. New York, Raven Press, 1960.

[33] M. Davis. Hilbert's tenth problem is unsolvable. *American Mathematical Monthly*, 80:233–269, 1973.

[34] M. Davis. Why Gödel didn't have Church's thesis. *Information and Control*, 54(1/2):3–24, July/August 1982.

[35] M. Davis, H. Putnam, and J. Robinson. The decision problem for exponential Diophantine equations. *Annals of Mathematics*, 74(3):425–436, 1961.

[36] M. Davis, R. Sigal, and E.J. Weyuker. *Computability, Complexity, and Languages*. Academic Press, 1994.

[37] J. Dixon. The specializer, a method of automatically writing computer programs. Technical report, Division of Computer Research and Technology, National Institute of Health, Bethesda, Maryland, 1971.

[38] W.F. Dowling and J.H. Gallier. Linear-time algorithms for testing the satisfiability of propositional horn formulae. *Journal of Logic Programming*, 3:267–284, 1984.

[39] R.K. Dybvig. *The Scheme Programming Language*. Prentice-Hall, 1987.

[40] J. Edmonds. Paths, trees and flowers. *Canadian Journal of Mathematics*, 17:449–467, 1965.

[41] A.P. Ershov. On the partial computation principle. *Information Processing Letters*, 6(2):38–41, 1977.

[42] A.P. Ershov. On the essence of compilation. In E.J. Neuhold, editor, *Formal Description of Programming Concepts*, pages 391–420. North-Holland, 1978.

[43] A.P Ershov. Mixed computation: Potential applications and problems for study. *Theoretical Computer Science*, 18:41–67, 1982.

[44] A.P. Ershov. Opening key-note speech. In Bjørner et al. [11].

[45] R. W. Floyd and R. Beigel. *The Language of Machines*. Freeman, 1994.

[46] Y. Futamura. Partial evaluation of computing process – an approach to a compiler-compiler. *Systems, Computers, Controls*, 2(5):45–50, 1971.

[47] Y. Futamura. Partial computation of programs. In E. Goto, K. Furukawa, R. Nakajima, I. Nakata, and A. Yonezawa, editors, *RIMS Symposia on Software Science and Engineering*, volume 147 of *Lecture Notes in Computer Science*, pages 1–35, Kyoto, Japan, 1983. Springer-Verlag.

[48] R. Gandy. The confluence of ideas in 1936. In R. Herken, editor, *The Universal Turing Machine. A Half-Century Survey*, pages 55–112. Oxford University Press, 1988.

[49] M. R. Garey and D. S. Johnson. *Computers and Intractability: A Guide to Theory of NP-Completeness*. Freeman, New York, 1979.

[50] R. Glück. On the generation of specializers. *Journal of Functional Programming*, 4(4):499–514, 1994.

[51] K. Gödel. Über formal unentscheidbares Sätze der Principia Mathetatica und verwandter Systeme. *Monatsheft, Math. Phys.*, 37:349–360, 1931.

[52] L.M. Goldschlager. The monotone and planar circuit value problems are logspace complete for p. *SIGACT News*, 9:25–29, 1977.

[53] R. Greenlaw, H.J. Hoover, and W.L. Ruzzo. *Limits to parallel computation*. Oxford University Press, New York, 1995.

[54] K. Grue. Arrays in pure functional programming languages. *Lisp and Symbolic Computation*, 2:105–113, 1989.

[55] A. Grzegorczyk. Some classes of recursive functions. *Rozpraqy Mathematyczny*, 4:1–45, 1953.

[56] Y. Gurevich. Kolmogorov machines and related issues: the column on logic in computer science. *Bull. of the EATCS*, 35:71–82, 1988.

[57] Y. Gurevich and S. Shelah. Nearly linear time. In *Lecture Notes in Computer Science 363*, pages 108–118. Springer Verlag, 1989.

[58] P. Halmos. *Naive Set Theory*. Springer-Verlag, undergraduate texts in mathematics, 1974 edition, 1960.

[59] T.A. Hansen, T. Nikolajsen, J. Träff, and N.D. Jones. Experiments with implementations of two theoretical constructions. In *Lecture Notes in Computer Science 363*, pages 119–133. Springer Verlag, 1989.

[60] J. Hartmanis and J.E. Hopcroft. An overview of the theory of computational complexity. *Journal of the Association for Computing Machinery*, 18(3):444–475, 1971.

[61] J. Hartmanis, P.M. Lewis II, and R.E. Stearns. Classification of computations by time and memory requirements. In *Proc. IFIO Congress 65, Spartan, N.Y.*, pages 31–35, 1965.

[62] J. Hartmanis and R.E. Stearns. On the complexity of algorithms. *Transactions of the American Mathematical Society*, 117:285–306, 1965.

[63] J. Håstad. *Computational Limitations for Small-depth Circuits (Ph.D. thesis)*. MIT Press, Cambridge, MA, 1987.

[64] P. Henderson. *Functional Programming: Application and Implementation*. PH, 1980.

[65] D. Hilbert and P. Bernays. *Grundlagen der Mathematik*, volume I. Springer, 1934.

[66] D. Hofstaedter. *Gödel, Escher, Bach: An Eternal Golden Braid*. Harvester Press, 1979.

[67] N. Immerman. Nondeterministic space is closed under complement. *SIAM Journal of Computing*, 17:935–938, 1988.

[68] K. Jensen and N. Wirth. *Pascal User Manual and Report*. Springer-Verlag, revised edition, 1985.

[69] D. S. Johnson. Approximation algorithms for combinatorial problems. *Journal of Computer and Systems Sciences*, 9:256–278, 1974.

[70] J.P. Jones and Y.V. Matiyasevich. Register machine proof of the theorem on exponential diophantine representation of enumerable sets. *Journal of Symbolic Logic*, 49(3):818–829, 1984.

[71] N. D. Jones. Space-bounded reducibility among combinatorial problems. *Journal of Computer and System Science*, 11:68–85, 1975.

[72] N. D. Jones. A note on linear time simulation of deterministic two-way pushdown automata. *IPL: Information Processing Letters*, 1977.

[73] N. D. Jones. Blindfold games are harder than games with perfect information. *Bulletin European Association for Theoretical Computer Science*, 6:4–7, 1978.

[74] N. D. Jones and W. Laaser. Complete problems for deterministic polynomial time. *Theoretical Computer Science*, 3:105–117, 1977.

[75] N. D. Jones, E. Lien, and W. Laaser. New problems complete for nondeterministic log space. *Mathematical Systems Theory*, 10:1–17, 1976.

[76] N. D. Jones and S. Muchnick. Even simple programs are hard to analyze. *Journal of the Association for Computing Machinery*, 24(2):338–350, 1977.

[77] N. D. Jones and S. Muchnick. Complexity of finite memory programs with recursion. *Journal of the Association for Computing Machinery*, 25(2):312–321, 1978.

[78] N. D. Jones and A. Mycroft. Data flow analysis of applicative programs using minimal function graphs. In *Proceedings of the Thirteenth ACM Symposium on Principles of Programming Languages*, pages 296–306, St. Petersburg, Florida, 1986.

[79] N.D. Jones. Reducibility among combinatorial problems in log n space. In *Proceedings 7th Annual Princeton Conference on Information Sciences and Systems*, pages 547–551. Springer-Verlag, 1973.

[80] N.D. Jones. Constant time factors do matter. In *ACM Symposium on Theory of Computing proceedings.*, pages 602–611. Association for Computing Machinery, 1993.

[81] N.D. Jones. Mix ten years later. In William L. Scherlis, editor, *Proceedings of PEPM '95*, pages 24–38. ACM, ACM Press, 1995.

[82] N.D. Jones. An introduction to partial evaluation. *Computing Surveys*, 1996.

[83] N.D. Jones. Computability and complexity from a programming perspective. *TCS*, 1997.

[84] N.D. Jones, C.K. Gomard, and P. Sestoft. *Partial Evaluation and Automatic Program Generation*. Prentice-Hall, 1993.

[85] N.D. Jones, P. Sestoft, and H. Søndergaard. An experiment in partial evaluation: the generation of a compiler generator. In J.-P. Jouannaud, editor, *Rewriting Techniques and Applications, Dijon, France.*, volume 202 of *Lecture Notes in Computer Science*, pages 124–140. Springer-Verlag, 1985.

[86] G. Kahn. Natural semantics. In *Proceedings of the Symposium on Theoretical Aspects of Computer Science*, Passau, Germany, February 1987. Proceedings published as Springer-Verlag Lecture Notes in Computer Science 247. The paper is also available as INRIA Report 601, February, 1987.

[87] L. Kalmar. Ein einfaches Beispiel für ein unentscheidbares arithmetisches Problem. *Mathematikai és Fizikai Lapok*, 50:1–23, 1943. In Hungarian, with German abstract.

[88] S.N. Kamin. *Programming Languages: An Interpreter-Based Approach*. Addison-Wesley, 1990.

[89] V. Kann. *On the Approximability of NP-complete Optimization Problems (Ph.D. thesis)*. Royal Institute of Technology, Stockholm, 1991.

[90] R.M. Karp. Reducibility among combinatorial problems. In R.E. Miller and J.W. Thatcher, editors, *Complexity of Computer Computations*. Plenum Press, 1972.

[91] R.M. Karp and V. Ramachandran. Parallel algorithms for shared.memory machines. In J. val Leeuwen, editor, *Handbook of Theoretical Computer Science, vol. A*. Elsevier, 1990.

[92] A.J Kfoury, R.N. Moll, and M.A. Arbib. *A Programming Approach to Computability*. Texts and monographs in Computer Science. Springer-Verlag, 1982.

[93] S.C. Kleene. General recursive functions of natural numbers. *Mathematische Annalen*, 112:727–742, 1936.

[94] S.C. Kleene. Recursive predicates and quantifiers. *Transactions of the American Mathematical Society*, 53:41–74, 1943.

[95] S.C. Kleene. *Introduction to Metamathematics*. Van Nostrand, 1952.

[96] D.E. Knuth. *The Art of Computer Programming: Fundamental Algorithms*, volume 1. Addison-Wesley, 1968.

[97] S.Y. Kuroda. Classes of languages and linear-bounded automata. *Information and Control*, 7:207–223, 1964.

[98] Julia L. Lawall and Harry G. Mairson. Optimality an inefficiency: what isn't a cost model of the lambda calculus. In *International Conference on Functional Programming 1996*. ACM, ACM Press, 1996.

[99] L.A. Levin. Universal sequential search problems. *Plenum Press Russian translations*, pages 265–266, 1973. Translation of [101].

[100] L.A. Levin. Complexity of algorithms and computations. *Ed. Kosmiadiadi, Maslov, Petri, "Mir", Moscow*, pages 174–185, 1974. In Russian.

[101] L.A. Levin. Universal sequential search problems. *In Russian; Problemy Peredachi Informatsii, Moscow*, pages 115–116, 1974.

[102] L.A. Levin. Computational complexity of functions. Technical report, Boston University report BUCS-TR-85-005, 1985. One-page translation of [100].

[103] H. Lewis and C. Papadimitriou. *Elements of the Theory of Computation*. Prentice-Hall, 1981.

[104] P.M. Lewis II, R.E. Stearns, and J. Hartmanis. Memory bounds for recognition of context-free and context-sensitive languages. In *Conf. Rec., IEEE 6th Annual Symposium on Switching Circuit Theory and Logic Design*, 1965.

[105] M. Li and P.M.B. Vitányi. Kolmogorov complexity and its applications. In Jan van Leeuwen, editor, *Handbook of Theoretical Computer Science*, volume 1. Elsevier and MIT Press, 1990.

[106] L.A. Lombardi. Incremental computation. In F. L. Alt and M. Rubinoff, editors, *Advances in Computers*, volume 8, pages 247–333. Academic Press, 1967.

[107] L.A. Lombardi and B. Raphael. Lisp as the language for an incremental computer. In E.C. Berkeley and D.G. Bobrow, editors, *The Programming Language Lisp: Its Operation and Applications*, pages 204–219, Cambridge, Massachusetts, 1964. MIT Press.

[108] M. Machtey and P. , Young. *An Introduction to the General Theory of Algorithms*. North-Holland, 1978.

[109] Z. Manna. *Mathematical Thoery of Computation*. MH, 1974.

[110] A.A. Markov. The theory of algorithms. Technical report, Israeli Program for Scientific Translations, Jerusalem, 1962. Translated from the Russian version which appeared in 1954.

[111] Y.V. Matiyasevich. Enumerable sets are diophantine. *Doklady Akedemii Nauk SSSR*, 191:279–282, 1970. English translation in [112].

[112] Y.V. Matiyasevich. Enumerable sets are diophantine. *Soviet Mathematics: Doklady*, 11:354–357, 1970.

[113] Y.V. Matiyasevich. Diofantova predstavlenie perechislimykh predikatov. *Izvestia Akdemii Nauk SSSR. Seriya Matematichekaya*, 35(1):3–30, 1971. English translation in [116].

[114] Y.V. Matiyasevich. Diophantine representation of the set of prime numbers. *Doklady Akademii Nauk SSSR*, 196:770–773, 1971. English translation in [115].

[115] Y.V. Matiyasevich. Diophantine representation of the set of prime numbers. *Soviet Mathematics: Doklady*, 12:249–254, 1971.

[116] Y.V. Matiyasevich. Diophantine representations of enumerable predicates. *Mathematics of the USSR. Izvestia*, 15(1):1–28, 1971.

[117] Y.V. Matiyasevich. *Hilbert's Tenth Problem*. MIT Press, 1993.

[118] J. McCarthy. Recursive functions of symbolic expressions and their computation by machine. *CACM*, 3(4):184–195, 1960.

[119] A. Meyer and D.M. Ritchie. The complexity of loop programs. In *Proceedings of the ACM National Meeting*, pages 465–469, 1967.

[120] A. Meyer and L. Stockmeyer. The equivalence problem for regular expressions with squaring requires exponential space. In *Proceedings of the IEEE 13th Annual Symposium on Switching and Automata Theory*, pages 125–129, 1972.

[121] R. Milner. Operational and algebraic semantics of concurrent processes. *Handbook of Theoretical Computer Science*, B:1203–1242, 1990.

[122] R. Milner, M. Tofte, and R. Harper. *The Definition of Standard ML*. MIT, Cambridge, Massachusetts, 1990.

[123] P.B. Miltersen. *Combinatorial Complexity Theory (Ph.D. thesis)*. BRICS, University of Aarhus, Denmark, 1993.

[124] M. Minsky. *Computation: Finite and Infinite Machines*. Prentice-Hall Series in Automatic Computation, 1967.

[125] T. Æ. Mogensen. Self-applicable online partial evaluation of the pure lambda calculus. In William L. Scherlis, editor, *Proceedings of PEPM '95*, pages 39–44. ACM, ACM Press, 1995.

[126] T.Æ. Mogensen. Efficient self-interpretation in lambda calculus. *Functional Programming*, 2(3):345–364, July 1992.

[127] N. Nagel and J.R. Newman. *Gödel's Proof*. New York University Press, 1958.

[128] H.R Nielson and F. Nielson. *Semantics with Applications*. John Wiley & Sons, 1991.

[129] R. Paige. Efficient translation of external input in a dynamically typed language. In B. Pehrson and I. Simon, editors, *Technology and Foundations – Information Processing 94*, volume 1 of *IFIP Transactions A-51*, pages 603–608. North-Holland, 1994.

[130] C.H. Papadimitriou. *Computational Complexity*. Addison-Wesley Publishing Company, 1994.

[131] L.C. Paulson. *ML for the Working Programmer*. Cambridge University Press, 1991.

[132] Gordon D. Plotkin. A structural approach to operational semantics. Technical Report 19, Aarhus University, 1981.

[133] E.L. Post. Finite combinatory processes—formulation I. *Journal of Symbolic Logic*, 1:103–105, 1936.

[134] E.L. Post. Formal reductions of the general combinatorial decision problem. *American Journal of Mathematics*, 65:197–215, 1943.

[135] E.L. Post. Recursively enumerable sets of positive natural numbers and their decision problem. *Bulletin of the American Mathematical Society*, 50:284–316, 1944.

[136] E.L. Post. A variant of a recursively unsolvable problem. *Bulletin of the American Mathematical Society*, 50:264–268, 1946.

[137] M.O. Rabin. Speed of computation and classification of recursive sets. In *Third Convention of the Scientific Society, Israel*, pages 1–2, 1959.

[138] M.O. Rabin. Degree of difficulty of computing a function and a partial ordering of recursive sets. Technical Report 1, O.N.R., Jerusalem, 1960.

[139] M.O. Rabin. Complexity of computations. *Communications of the ACM*, 20(9):625–633, 1977.

[140] M.O. Rabin. Probabilistic algorithm for testing primality. *Journal of Number Theory*, 12:128–138, 1980.

[141] T. Rado. On a simple source for non-computable functions. *Bell System Technical Journal*, pages 877–884, May 1962.

[142] C. Reid. *Hilbert*. Springer-Verlag, New York, 1970.

[143] H.G. Rice. Classes of recursively enumerable sets and their decision problems. *Transactions of the American Mathematical Society*, 89:25–59, 1953.

[144] J. Richard. Les principes des mathématiques et le problème des ensembles. *Acta Mathematica*, 30:295–296, 1906.

[145] J. Robinson. Existential definability in arithmetic. *Transactions of the American Mathematical Society*, 72:437–449, 1952.

[146] H. Rogers Jr. Gödel numberings of partial recursive functions. *Journal of Symbolic Logic*, 23(3):331–341, 1958.

[147] H. Rogers Jr. *Theory of Recursive Functions and Effective Computability*. McGraw-Hill, 1967.

[148] G. Rozenberg and A. Salomaa. *Cornerstones of Undecidability*. Prentice-Hall, 1993.

[149] W. Savitch. Relationship between nondeterministic and deterministic tape complexities. *Journal of Computing and Systems Sciences*, 4(2):177–192, 1970.

[150] D.A. Schmidt. *Denotational Semantics*. Boston, MA: Allyn and Bacon, 1986.

[151] A. Schönhage. On the power of random access machines. In H. A. Maurer, editor, *Proceedings of the 6th Colloquium on Automata, Languages and Programming*, pages 520–529. LNCS 71. Springer, July 1979.

[152] A. Schönhage. Storage modification machines. *SIAM Journal of Computing*, 9:490–508, 1980.

[153] D.S. Scott. Some definitional suggestions for automata theory. *Journal of Computer and System Sciences*, 1:187–212, 1967.

[154] D.S. Scott. Lectures on a mathematical theory of computation. Technical Report PRG-19, Programming Research Group, Oxford University, 1981.

[155] J.C. Shepherdson and H.E. Sturgis. Computability of recursive functions. *Journal of the Association for Computing Machinery*, 10(2):217–255, 1963.

[156] R. Sommerhalder and S.C. van Westrhenen. *The Theory of Computability: Programs, Machines, Effectiveness and Feasibility*. International Computer Science Series. Addison-Wesley, 1988.

[157] L. Stockmeyeri. The polynomial time hierarchy. *Theoretical Computer Science*, 3:1–22, 1977.

[158] R. Szelepcsenyi. The method of forcing for nondeterministic automata. *Bull. EATCS*, 33:96–100, 1987.

[159] B.A. Trakhtenbrot. *Complexity of Algorithms and Computations (lectures for students of the NGU)*. Novosibirsk, 1967. In Russian.

[160] V.F. Turchin. The language Refal, the theory of compilation and metasystem analysis. Courant Computer Science Report 20, Courant Institute of Mathematical Sciences, New York University, 1980.

[161] V.F. Turchin. The concept of a supercompiler. *Transactions on Programming Languages and Systems*, 8(3):292–325, 1986.

[162] A.M. Turing. On computable numbers with an application to the Entscheidungsproblem. *Proceedings of the London Mathematical Society*, 42(2):230–265, 1936-7.

[163] L. Valiant. General purpose parallel architectures. In J. val Leeuwen, editor, *Handbook of Theoretical Computer Science, vol. A*. Elsevier, 1990.

[164] P. Wadler. Deforestation: Transforming programs to eliminate trees. In H. Ganzinger, editor, *Proceedings of the European Symposium on Programming*, volume 300 of *Lecture Notes in Computer Science*, pages 344–358. Springer Verlag, 1988.

[165] K. Wagner and G. Wechsung. *Computational Complexity*. Reidel Publ. Comp., Dordrecht, Boston, Lancaster, Tokyo, 1986.

[166] J. Welsh and J. Elder. *Introduction to Pascal*. International series in Computer Science. Prentice-Hall, second edition, 1982.

List of Notations

$\perp$	10
$\downarrow$	10
$\uparrow$	10
$[\![p]\!]$	12, 47
$\mathbb{D}, \mathbb{D}_A$	28
$|d|$	29
$\mathcal{N}$	34
$\underline{n}$	34
$\vdash$	38
$\equiv$	48
$time_P^{\perp}(d)$	90
$p \vdash s \to s'$	112
$p \vdash s \to^* s'$	112
$\leftarrow$	121
$\downarrow$	121
$\to$	121
c_{01B}	131
c_{pr}	131
c_N	131
c_{2CM}	131
λ	141, 427
β	142
$\underset{rec}{\leq}$	152, 374
$\preceq$	172
$\Gamma \vdash F$	187
μ	205
φ	225
$\mathbb{D}_{01}$	250
$c : \{0,1\}^* \to \mathbb{D}_{01}$	251
$\underset{}{\preceq}^{ptime}$	252
$\underset{}{\preceq}^{lintime}$	252
$\underset{}{\equiv}^{ptime}$	252
$\underset{}{\equiv}^{lintime}$	252
$\underset{}{\preceq}^{lintime-pg-ind}$	252
$\underset{}{\equiv}^{lintime-pg-ind}$	253
$c_{\mathbb{D}}$	259
$L^{time(f(n))}$	272
L^{ptime}	272
$L^{lintime}$	272

$\leq$-equivalent	372
$\leq$-hard	372
$\leq$-complete	372
$\leq$	373
$\underset{Fns}{\leq}$	374
$\underset{ptime}{\leq}$	374
$\underset{logs}{\leq}$	374
$\neg$	419
$\wedge$	419
$\vee$	419
$\Rightarrow$	419
$\Leftrightarrow$	419
$\mathbb{N}$	421
$f(a)\downarrow$	424
$f(a)\uparrow$	424
$f(a) = \perp$	424
dom	425
rng	425
$\simeq$	425
$\log(n)$ $(n \in \mathbb{N})$	429
$O(f)$	429
$\Omega(f)$	429
$\Theta(f)$	429
$o(f)$	430
ε	431, 435
Σ	431
Σ^*	431
AB (for sets of strings)	431
A^*	431
A^+	431
$\tilde{x}$	432
$::=$	432
$\mid$	432, 435
$G = (N, T, P, S)$	432
$L(G)$ (G a grammar)	433
r^*	435
$L(r)$ (r a regular expression)	435

Index

2CM, 127, 135
2DPDA, 359

acceptable enumeration, 227
acceptance, *see also* decision
    by a non-deterministic program, 331
    by finite automata, 437
accepting states, 437
Ackermann's function, 97, 104
algorithm, 9
alphabet, 431
    tape, 115
annotated program, 106, 110
approximation, xv
asymptotic, 299, 300
atom?, 33
atoms (definition), 28
automata
    finite, 436

Bacc, 407
Bacc$^{\backslash \texttt{GOTO}}$, 384
binding-time engineering, 96
bit strings, related to binary trees, 250
bitwise less-than, 172
Blum's speedup theorem, 307
boolean algebra
    quantified, 409
boolean expression, 419
boolean operators, 419
boolean programs
    acceptance, *see* Bacc
    defined, 383
    nontriviality, 398
boolean variables, 419
busy beaver, 16

c, 434
cartesian product, 422
case command, 39

CF$^{\neq \emptyset}$, 393, 434
CF$^{\emptyset}$, 394
CFALL, 161, 434
CFAMB, 161, 434
CFG, *see* grammar, context free
Church-Rosser theorem, 142
Church-Turing thesis, 4, 8, 127
Church-Turing-Kleene thesis, 205
circuit complexity, xv, 9
circuit, monotone, 383, 388
CLIQUE, 367, 369, 370
CM, 111, 116, *see also* 2CM
CM$^{\backslash \texttt{C:=C+1}}$, 349
CM-computability, 127, 208
CM-computable, 134, 208
CM^{logspace}, 350, *see also* space-bounded
        programs
CM$^{logspace+rec}$, 356
CMro, 317, 319
CM$^{value(n)}$, 349
CNF, 367, 370, 420
communicating systems, xv
compilation, 50, 59
    for proving equivalence of languages,
        127
    versus interpretation, 91
    with change of data, 52, 129
compiler, 50, 53, 231
    bootstrapping, 93
    diagrams, 51, 56
    generation, 97
compiling function, 50
    w.r.t. coding, 53
complete logical system, 196, 198
complete problems, 365, 372, 374
    for NLOGSPACE, 376, 380
    for NPTIME, 397
    for NLINTIME, 378
    for PSPACE, 407

for PTIME, 383
for RE, 375
completeness, 365
complexity classes, *see also* completeness;
    complete problems
    PTIME, 272, 275
    LINTIME, 272, 276
    characterizaton without resource
        bounds, 349
    definition of, 271
    non-deterministic, 333
    relations among, 322, 324, 333, 345, 346
    robustness of, 276
    space classes
      LOGSPACE, 319
      PSPACE, 319, 322
      definition of, 319, 333
      robustness of, 322
    time classes
      PTIME, 244
      definition of, 333
      robustness of, 273, 276
composition, 206
    of (primitive) recursive functions, 206
    of compiler and interpreter diagrams,
        56
    of functions, symbolic, 228
    of general functions, 426
    of space-bounded programs, 326
computable, 75
    in linear time and size, 378
    in logarithmic space, 325
computable function, 205, *see also* CM
    computable; decidable;
    effectively computable;
    equivalence of languages;
    recursive function; WHILE
    computable
computation model
    CM, 116
    RAM, 118
    SRAM, 119
    TM, 115

machine models, *see* CM; RAM; SRAM; TM
    read-only, *see also* CMro; TMro
computation models
    comparison of times, 251, 273
    default for complexity classes, 335
    effect on complexity theory, 20, 241
    equivalence v.r.t. computability, 127
    fair time measures, 254
    introduced, 111
    read-only, 247, 316
    space measures, 316
computational completeness
    of a specializer, 102
    optimality of a specializer, 103
    turing completeness, 227
computationally tractable, 20
concrete syntax, 48, 53, 143, 336
conditionals, 32
configuration, 337
configuration string, 155
conjunction, 32, 192, 419
conjunctive normal form, *see* CNF
cons*, 35
cons-free programs, 349, 355
cons?, 33
conservative extension, 93
consistent logical system, 196, 198
constant time factor, 290
constant time factors, 243, 285, 290
constructible, 293
    space, 328
context-free grammar, *see under* grammar
context-sensitive grammar, *see under*
      grammar
convergent, 10
Cook's construction, 288, 359
Cook's thesis, 20, 242
counter machine, *see* CM
currying, 428
cycle, 431

DAG, 261, 431
DAG semantics, 264

data sharing, 261
data-storage graph, 261
Davis-Putnam-Robinson theorem, 176
decidable, 76
    in linear time, 272
    in logarithmic space, 319
    in polynomial space, 319
    in polynomial time, 272
    in space f, 319
    in time f, 272
decision problems, 243
derivation relation, 153
deterministic finite automaton, 437
DFA, 437
`diag`, 290, 328
diagonal argument, *see* diagonalization
diagonalization, 14, 290, 328
Diophantine equations, 169
directed graph, 431
disjoint, 422
disjunction, 32, 192, 419
distributed computing, 258
divergent, 10
divide-and-conquer search, 341
DL, 198
dovetailing, 81, 87, 299
DSG, 261

edges, 430
effective procedure, 3
effectively computable, 11
effectively decidable, 13
effectively enumerable, 13
effectively solvable, 4
encoding
    booleans as trees, 32
    in compilaxious with change of data,
        129
    integers as trees, 34
    many atoms using one, 63, 73
    numbers as bit strings, 131
    of bit strings in trees, 250
    of problem input, 368

    of trees in bit strings, 251
    programs in mumbers (Gödel), 205
    sequences in numbers (Matiyasevich),
        171
Entscheidungsproblem, 23
enumerable, 76
enumeration, 14
environment, 189
equation
    Diophantine, 169
    exponential Diophantine, 169
equation solving, 232
equivalence of μ-recursiveness, 208
equivalence of languages
    with respect to complexity, 252
    with respect to computability, 48
evaluation, 36
execution, 36
existential quantifier, 193
explicit transformation, 206
expression
    evaluation, 189
extensional, 226, 240

F, 137, 275, 291
`F+ro`, 349
false, 419
`false`, 32
finite automaton, 256, 436
first component, 422
fixpoint, 215, 221, 230
fixpoint iteration, 218
formula, 419
function, 422
    Ackermann's, 97, 104
    addition, 426
    argument, 423
    bijective, 428
    codomain of, 425
    composition, 426
    computable in logarithmic space, 325
    computing a, 10
    converging, 424

defined, 424
defined inductively, 439
definedness, 422
diverging, 424
division, 427
domain of, 425
double, 423
exponential polynomial, 169
injective, 428
inverse, 444
logarithmic, 429
maximum, 429
minimum, 429
monotonic, 429
monus, 423
multiplication, 426
one-to-one, 428
onto, 428
pairing, 442
partial, 424
polynomial, 169
predecessor, 423
range of, 425
recursive, 205
recursively defined, 439
result, 423
semantic, 47
strictly monotonic, 429
subtraction, 426
surjective, 428
total, 423
undefined, 424
uniqueness, 422
updating, 426
function call, 137
Futamura projections, 98

GAME, 394
game complexity, 415
GAP, 367
Gap theorem, 311
garbage collection, 270
Gödel numbers, 205

Gödel's incompleteness theorem, 198
GOTO, 111
goto-free, 383
GOTOro, 349
grammar, 432
    ambiguous, 161, 434
    context-free, 160, 433
        decision problems for, 160, 393, 434
        definition, 433
    context-sensitive, 433
        decision problems for, 415
        definition, 433
    regular, 433, 435
        decision problems for, 412, 434
        definition, 433
    set generated by, 433
graph, 430
    accessibility, 338
    acyclic, 431
    algorithm, 338, 339, 341, 342
    building, 343
    cyclic, 431
    directed, 430
    inaccessibility, 339
    searching, 338
    state transition, 337

halting problem, 77
hardware viewpoint, 9
hierarchy, 285, 291, 365
higher-order function, 427
Hilbert's choice function, 212
Hilbert's program, 23
Hilbert's tenth problem, 167
Hilbert, D., 167
Horn clause, 391

I, 72
I$^\uparrow$, 222
implements, 52
implication, 192
indirect fetch, 119
indirect store, 119

induction, 439
    complete, 439
    course-of-values, 439
    hypothesis, 439
inference relation, 195
inference rule, 189
inference system, 188, 195
infinite sequence, 424
initial store, 264
intensional, 226, 240
interpreter, 54
    efficient, 286
    overhead, 90
interpreting function, 54
invariance, 241
Invariance Thesis, 21
isomorphism theorem, 231

judgment, 189

LAMBDA, 140
lambda calculus, 8
lambda notation, 427
language
    accepted by DFA, 437
    accepted by NFA, 437
    equivalent, 48
    functional, 137
    imperative, 137
    implementation, 53, 58
    simulating one by another, 48
    source, 53, 57
    target, 57
left-most multi-step derivation relation, 433
left-most one-step derivation relation, 433
length (of a list), 33
length of a read-only TMro state, 317
length of a state, 316
linear time, 276, 291
linearly equivalent, 252
LINTIME, 272, 276
list, 33
list, 35

list representation, 33
literal, 419
logarithmic cost, 255, 257
LOGSPACE, 319, 322, 346, 351
LOGSPACE functions, 325
lookup, 55

Markov algorithms, 8
match, 40, 57
MCV, 390
minimization, 208
model-independent, 225
monotone circuit, 383
multi-step derivation relation, 433
multi-step rewrite relation, 153

natural numbers, 421
natural semantics, 188
negation, 32, 192, 419
NFA, 436
NLINTIME, 378
NLOGSPACE, 333, 345, 346
nodes, 430
non-deterministic finite automaton, 436
nondeterminism, 243, 331
nonterminals, 432
nonuniform complexity, xv
normal form, 142
normal form theorem, 210
normalizations, 335
NPSPACE, 333, 345, 346
NPTIME, 243, 333, 346
numerals, 34

O-notation, 429
o-notation, 430
omega-notation, 429
one-step derivation relation, 433
one-step rewrite relation, 153
operational semantics, 188
optimality of a specializer, 103
ordered pair, 422
overhead factor, 252

pairing, 53
pairing decomposition, 442
parallelism, xv
parallelism, PTIME, 395
partial evaluation, 65, 77, 96
    off-line, 106
    techniques, 104
partial recursive, 205
partial recursive functions, 24
Pascal-like implementation of GOTO, 266
path finding, 332
pattern, 40
PCP, 156
polynomial-time, 274
polynomially equivalent, 252
Post's correspondence problem, 156
predecessor, 34
predicate, 192, 195
prefix, 431
primitive recursion, 206
problem, 3
    ambiguity, 161, 434
    complete for NLOGSPACE, 376
    complete for NLINTIME, 378
    complete for RE, 375
    completeness, 161, 434
    membership, 434
    natural unsolvable, 151
    non-emptiness for, 434
    representation, 271
    representation of, 368
    undecidable, 154
production, 153
program
    boolean, 407
    computes a function, 38
    function computed by, 38
    looping, 38
    self-reproducing, 222
    stack, 288
    terminating, 38
    time-bounded, 271
    timed universal, 288

program padding, 233
program point specialization, 105
program property, 79
    extensional, 79
    intensional, 79
    non-trivial, 79
program specializer, 58, 227
    optimal, 103
program-dependent, 253, 256
program-independent, 253
programming language, 47
programs
    cons-free, 349, 355
proof tree, 197
propositional formulas, 419
provability, 202
PSPACE, 319, 322, 345, 346, 407
PTIME, 244, 272, 275, 322, 345, 346, 355
pushdown automaton, 359

quadruples, 422
quantified boolean algebra, 409

r.e., *see* recursively enumerable
RAM, 111
random access machine, 8, 118
read-only, 315
Readin, 113
Readout, 113
real numbers, xv, 421
    positive, 421
recursion theorem, 220, 229
recursive, 86
recursive function theory, 205
recursive extension, 355
recursive function, 8, 205
recursively enumerable, 86, 195, 197, 202
redex, 142
reducing SAT to CLIQUE, 370
reduction, 152, 365, 366
reduction function, 368
reflexive extension, 222
REG$^{\neq\emptyset}$, 434

REGALL, 434
REGAMB, 434
regular expression, 435
    set generated by, 435
    totality, 412
regular grammar, *see under* grammar
representable predicate, 200
resource bound, 271, 332
resources, 242
restriction
    to one operator, 60
    to one variable, 61
reverse, 30, 432
rewrite rule, 153
Rice's theorem, 78
robust, 147, 274, 276, 322
robustness, 241, 271
    computability, 127
Rogers, H., 226, 231
rooted DSG, 262
running time
    WHILE program, 254
running time, 275
running time function, 90
Russell's Paradox, 15

s-m-n function property, 227
SAT, 367, 370, 397
satisfiable, 443
second component, 422
self-interpreter, 72, 227
self-reproducing program, 222
semantic function, 47, 90
semi-decidable, 76
semi-Thue, 153
set, 421
    contained in, 421
    countable, 14
    deciding membership of, 10
    difference, 422
    Diophantine, 169
    element of, 421
    empty, 421

    equality, 421
    exponential Diophantine, 169
    intersection, 422
    member of, 421
    union, 422
simulation
    invariant, 135
    with data change, 129
single-assignment, 383
size (of a tree), 29
slowdown, 252
software viewpoint, 9
solvable, 4
source program, 50
space usage, 332
SPACE(f), 319
space-bounded programs, 319
space-constructible, 328
specialization, 205
specializer, 59
specializer properties
    computational completeness, 102
    optimality, 103
    totality, 102
specializing function, 59
speedup, 252
SRAM, 119
stack programs, 288, 359
start state, 436, 437
start symbol, 432
state, 112, 114, 264
    terminal, 112
state transition graph, 337, 343
states (of an DFA), 437
states (of an NFA), 436
stochastic algorithms, xv
storage modification machine, 255
store, 36, 37, 112, 114, 137, 189, 264
    initial, 37
string, 431
    accepted by DFA, 437
    accepted by NFA, 437
    bit, 250

concatenation, 431
configuration, 155
empty, 431
string matching, 359, 360
string rewriting, 153
strongly linearly equivalent, 253
structural operational semantics, 188
sublinear, 315
subset, 421
substring, 431
successor, 34
successor random access machine, 119
suffix, 431
superlinear time, 292
symbolic computation, 105
symbols, 431

tape alphabet, 115
terminals, 432
theorem, 196
    normal form, 129
theta-notation, 429
TI-diagrams, 51
time
    linear, 276
    superlinear, 292
time constructible, 293, 297
time usage, 332
$\mathrm{TIME}(f)$, 272
timed universal program, 288
timed programming language, 89
TM, 111
TMro, 316
totality of a specializer, 102
tractable, 244
transition function, 436, 437
treeless transformer, 353
triples, 422
true, 419
true, 32
truth, 202
truth assignment, 420
truth table, 420

truth values, 419
n-tuples, 422
tupling function, 225
Turing completeness, 227
Turing machine, 5, 8, 115, 316
    configuration, 122
    deterministic, 121
    enumeration, 225
    program, 225

uncomputable function, *see* undecidable
uncomputable functions, 16
undecidable, 78, 154
undirected graph, 431
unfolding, 191
unfolding function calls, 105
unit cost, 250, 257, 261
universal function, 205
universal function property, 227
universal program, 72
universal quantifier, 193
unnecessary code elimination, 86
unsolvable, 4
update, 137
update, 55

valid, 443
value assumption, 189
variable
    bound, 141
    free, 141
vector notation, 422
VERTEXCOVER, 380
vertices, 431

Wadler, P., 350, 353
WHILE, 27
WHILE-computable, 75
WHILE^{latom}, 63
WHILE^{1op}, 60
WHILE^{1var}, 61
WHILE_A, 29
WHro, 349